In the Name of Self-Defense

No Nonsense Self-Defense
http://marcmacyoung.com/
http://www.nononsenseselfdefense.com

Edited by Dianna Gordon

ISBN-13: 978-0692250211
ISBN-10: 0692250212
ISBN - epub - 978-0-692-24929-1

Cover photography Dan LaGrasso /Will Rowe
Cover Design and Interior Design Kamila Miller
Additional text RaeMarie Knowles

In the Name of Self-Defense
What It Costs and When It's Worth It

MARC MACYOUNG

NNSD
PRₑSS

Knowing what to do is not enough. What will kill you are all the things you don't know not to do.

— MM

TABLE OF CONTENTS

AUTHOR'S *WARNING* AND SUGGESTION

Muggers, robbers and rapists. If you only think of self-defense in those terms you're like a man so busy looking for a mugger he fails to see the person about to hit him over the head with a bottle—a person he actively enraged.

Here's the first news flash of this book: There are more people willing to physically assault you for angering them then there are muggers. Consequently, you're more likely to be assaulted, raped, and murdered by someone you know than you are of being mugged, robbed, or raped by a stranger. Murdered by a stranger? You're more likely to drown in a pool.

News flash number two: Contrary to what you might think, the people who are physically assaulted are *not* mousey little victim-types. They're confident, competent, and sure what they're doing is both right *and* will work. They often self-identify themselves as nice people and then proceed to do not nice things to others in either complete confidence they won't be assaulted or while acting in emotional self-righteousness. They act right up until they get attacked. From there, one of two things happen: Either their name gets written in the police report as victim (often while at the hospital) or they 'defend' themselves . . .   and are immediately arrested.

Most violence occurs between people who know each other. That makes claiming self-defense a lot more complicated. I tell people self-defense is a very small target in a big landscape of violence. It's very easy to miss, and most people do. Then they whine about getting arrested for "defending themselves." This book is going to help keep you from engaging in illegal violence—while thinking what you're doing is self-defense.

Let's keep that from happening. Are we going to cover crime too? Yes. Knowing the difference between criminal violence and other types is literally a life saver.

Violence has been my life. My career. Growing up on the streets of Los Angeles, I do *not* remember a time when I wasn't surrounded by conflict, fights, death, criminals, and violence. I spent a lot of time running to or from, training, preparing for, witnessing stopping, and living with the threat of violence, also dealing with the consequences. That's to say the cops, revenge seekers, and, of course, injuries. As I often tell people, I used to be part of the problem. If spitting blood and aching was all I had after an incident, it was a good day. (Weapons weren't just common, in certain circumstances they were the norm.) Violence has also paid my bills. Being a bouncer, bodyguard, part of event security personnel, director of a correctional institute, and other such occupations, I spent decades telling criminals and violent people no. Again, it was time spent preventing violence, waiting for it, and being at ground zero when it happened. Now I'm an author, teacher, court-recognized expert witness, and POST-certified instructor. That's decades more of researching, studying, writing, teaching and lecturing about violence. Yet, I'm amazed by how much I still *don't* know about the subject.

The complexity and variability of violence arises from one simple fact—humans are involved. Still, I have learned a thing or two. Enough to fill more than 400 pages.

Reading this book is going to be like drinking from a fire hydrant. It's a brain dump of five decades of experience and knowledge. Experience ranging from being an outlaw street fighter by the name of "Animal," to a violence professional to a grand old man in the fields of self-defense and violence dynamics. (As fair warning, I do tend to revert now and then— especially when it comes to my language and humor.) If I've learned nothing else in fifty years of dealing with it—there's more to violence than just the physical. *A lot more.* And that's what we're going to be covering here.

I'll categorically state, this book is an *introduction.* I limit it to the kinds of violence and consequences the average citizen is likely to face. I don't cover what law enforcement, military, violence professionals, or criminals deal with *or* their specialized circumstances. Like a manual, we'll cover the long process a citizen will go through regarding self-defense. But realize that's like an ocean journey. While it's a long haul from one port o' call to another, the trip doesn't cover the width and breadth of the ocean. Nor does it delve the depths, including the many topics we're passing through. This book may be a manual, but there is still lots more to learn. How far you take it is up to you.

What makes this book unique is its focus on the *nonphysical* elements of violence and claims of self-defense. It's stuff you probably don't want to hear. Elements that'll offend you. Burdens you won't want to carry. Uncomfortable perspectives on your behavior. Beliefs will be challenged. Ideals crushed by the way the legal system works, people's behavior, and why violence occurs in the first place. In short, there's a lot of stuff *that'll just piss you off.* Now the real bad news, if you're not careful, violence *will* destroy your life—as in dead, crippled, in prison or bankrupt. This book is going to help you keep that from happening.

I suggest you read it in small doses. In fact, I *strongly* encourage it. Plan to read it over weeks, if not a month. Expect some chapters to take a week. I say this because—if you try to read it in one sitting—odds are you'll be overwhelmed.

I'm not joking about the fire hydrant, brain dump. I guarantee you your eyes will cross many times, and your brain will melt. Violence is *not* simple. It contains deep complexities. Things you've never thought about. Small things connected in weird ways that become big—*very* big (like the connection between feelings and violence). Multiple levels and mixed motivations add to this complexity. Then there's the boondoggle of the legal aftermath.

What the book **won't** give you is simplistic "you just do this" answers. There are *no* easy answers. No this is always the right thing to do solutions. Most of all, when it comes to self-defense, there are *no* push this button and you're done answers. Safely getting through the minefield that is self-defense isn't fixed answers. It's more a *way of thinking*. You have to be able to do the math.

By this I mean you must be able to assess the circumstances and come up with the right answer to that *particular* situation—on the spot. When those circumstances change, you come up with a *new* answer. (The good news is you actually do this kind of thinking already—it's called driving.)

Also, don't try to memorize this book. Read for a while and put it down. Chew it over—especially the parts that make you uncomfortable or angry. There *will* be conflicts between this new information and what you 'know' or 'believe.' The good news? Mostly it's going to be a matter of adjustment and scale. There is very little self-defense information that's flat out wrong. But a lot of small, conditional truths have been sold to you as universals. Take for example what say to the police. Self-defense is more complicated than a simplistic "shut up and lawyer up." But knowing *when* to do that is important. (We'll cover that, too.)

Most of all, don't be intimidated by how easy it is to cross out of self-defense into illegal violence. Just learn how to do the math. This book isn't just a manual, it's a tutorial. There's a lot of stuff that I talk about in this book that—if you're lucky—you'll never need. But when you need it, you'll *really* need it.

The main reason this book is so big is it covers the *most* neglected, ignored, and misunderstood aspects of self-defense—assessment and articulation.

Most people in prison for violence are there because what they did *wasn't* self-defense. There's also a fair number in prison because although they acted in self-defense, they couldn't explain *why* what they did *was* self-defense. I'm not just showing you how to assess the situation and come up with the appropriate response. I'm also teaching you how to articulate that *process* and explain to others *why* it was self-defense.

Hopefully you'll never need the information in this book. But it's critical for articulation. You're going to have to be able to communicate *why* what you did *wasn't* a fight, attempted murder, or manslaughter. If you can't, you're in deep trouble. Particularly when someone throws you a curve ball question or the other guy lies.

This book was peer reviewed by many people in many fields. One question I kept on being asked was who's the audience for this? Martial artists? Shooters? Women's self-defense? Violence professionals?

The answer is simple. It's for citizens who are likely to find themselves in a self-defense situations. It's especially for anyone who has ever taken any self-defense training. (It's also very much for instructors to improve what they present as self-defense.) In essence, this book covers all the elements about violence your instructor *didn't* tell you about violence and self-defense. Usually because he or she didn't know it . . .

Marc MacYoung

They're normally called acknowledgments.
I call them, "Thank you's"

Iain Abernathy, *British Combat Association, WCA*
Jesse Alcorta
Page Alcorta
Josh Amos
Animal List
Dr. Drew Anderson
Massad Ayoob, *Ayoob Group*
Lex Bijlsma, *Sportschool 013/ Kidsafety Netherlands*
Wayne Bradbury, *KAMON Wing Chun, Bristol*
Alain Burrese, JD, *Burrese Enterprises, Inc.*
Randy Carpadus
Martin Cooper, *IPDTA*
Dr. Maude Dull
Ed Fanning
Lt. Col. (ret.) John Finch
SSgt, 'Grizzly Bear,' *U.S. Special Forces*
Lt. Col. (ret.) David Grossman
Lt. Col. (ret.) John Hannigan
Brian Hassler
Gila Hayes, *Firearms Academy of Seattle*
Marty Hayes, JD, *Armed Citizens' Legal Defense Network*
Gary Hickox
Ian Hogan, *Oppugnate Combatives, Australia*
Kathy Jackson, author, *Cornered Cat*
Lawrence Kane, author, *Martial Minute*
Officer Kasey Keckeisen, *KTC/SOCT*
Dr. Ron Kirsner
Justin Kocher
Dani Kollin, author
Dan Lagrasso, *A Feral Gentleman Productions*
Lt. Jon Lupo, *NY State Police*
Marnie McDowell, *Elite Physical Therapy*
Dr. Katherine McQueen
Jeff Meek, *Carry on Colorado*
Jenna Meek, *Carry on Colorado*
Dr. Connie Menard
Dr. Kevin Menard
Kamila Miller
Rory Miller, *Chiron Training/Conflict Communications*

Zak Mucha, LCSW
Anthony Muhlenkamp
Richard Nelson, *FBI* (ret.)
Mike Orendorf
Clint Overland
Peyton Quinn, author, *RMCAT*
Fred Ross
Dr. Floyd Rusak
Maj. (ret.) Slugg
Paul Spiegel, *Law Office of*
Dr. Lise Steenerson
Garry Smith, *Academy of Self-Defense*
Terry Trahan, *KSMA, Denver*
Dr. Alan Trimpi, author
Andrew Vachss, *The Zero*
Anna Valdisseri, *God's Bastard*
Teja Van Wicklen, *Devi Protective Offense*
Edwin Voskamp
Irene Voskamp
Adam Weitzel, *Law office of ALW*
Sam Walker
Doug Wittrock, NREMT-P
Kris Wilder, author, *Martial Minute*
Brett Zambruk, PMTTH

And most of all to my wife, editor and she who puts up with me, Dianna
Gordon MacYoung

INTRODUCTION

The difference between an amateur and a professional is, to the amateur, the event is the big deal. To the pro, it's the before and after.

—**Lawrence Kane**

Reality Break

When you claim self-defense, you are confessing to a crime.

That is one of three things you *need* to know—right up front—about self-defense (SD). We'll get back to this confessing to a crime thing in a bit, but for right now let's keep going with the other two need-to-know items.

Two is that the self-defense pool has been peed in.

After SODDI (some other dude did it) self-defense is the second most common claim of people who have committed *illegal* violence. Got it? SD pool equals needs lots of chlorine. Even hardened criminals—when confronted with evidence that it *wasn't* some other dude—will often switch and claim self-defense. This is a tactical mistake. A mistake made by professional criminals who *know* how to play the system. But where the tainted self-defense plea *is* most common is among amateurs. And usually it's emotional and aggressive amateurs who participated in illegal violence.

Young bucks out on a Friday night get in a fight. When the cops come through the door, they stop in mid-swing and chorus, "He attacked me! I was defending myself!" That's self-defense, right?

Two neighbors get in a squabble and both claim it was self-defense. Except they *both* stopped what they were doing in their own yards and walked over to confront each other. After commenting on each other's sexual practices with their mothers, it goes physical. Self-defense, right?

Participants in a screaming match over a fender bender go physical—same thing. Isn't that self-defense?

Some drunken asshole jumps on and beats the hell out of someone for something that person said. When the cops show up on his doorstep, he claims he was acting in self-defense. Uhhh . . . beating someone for hurting my feelings counts as self-defense doesn't it?

A road rage incident, he cuts you off and blocks you. You get out of your car and approach him. It goes physical. Come on, that's gotta be self-defense, right?

A tattooed mixed martial arts (MMA) guy in a bar gets in another dude's face. The second dude smashes Tap-Out Boy in the face with a mug. "What do you mean aggravated assault? I felt threatened. I was defending myself!"

Same players, different outcome. This time, MMA guy does a ground-and-pound (puts the other person on the ground and continues to assault him) and gets the aggravated assault charge—if he's lucky. If he's not, he faces manslaughter charges. "Manslaughter? But it was self-defense! Besides, I didn't mean to kill him by beating his skull on the concrete floor! I was just defending myself."

Someone threatens to kick someone's ass if he doesn't leave. Instead of leaving, the other person pulls a gun and shoots the first person. "What do you mean that *wasn't* self-defense?"

This book will help keep you from making the biggest mistake people make.

That is: ***Claiming self-defense when it wasn't.***

Strike one.

Often with these tainted self-defense claims, the motive is to wiggle out of consequences. Especially when—after the heat of the moment has passed—the person realizes he or she was *out of bounds.* Trying to justify it (and save himself) the amateur starts calling it self-defense.

Strike two.

But far more common, these aggressive amateurs believe they acted in self-defense. Not just saying it either—they *honestly* believe it. That's the position they're going to try to sell. Except to everyone else it looks like the amateur is lying. Often because witnesses saw the incident, and everyone else has seen the security video.

Strike three, you're out.

Let me give you an important safety tip: When it comes to self-defense, what you believe does *not* matter. What matters is what you *actually* did, especially if you were involved in the creation and escalation of the incident—whether you meant for violence to happen or not. Your *participation* seriously undermines your claim of self-defense.

Learn the following and never forget it: Your words and actions before, during, and after an incident *will be gone over with a microscope* as officials seek misconduct. And the raw truth is they don't usually have to look that hard. Way too many people believe they acted in self-defense when they are—in fact—fighting. And that is where most people don't just step on their dicks, but pogo stick on them. While self-defense is legally justifiable, fighting is *illegal.* So, too, is a one-sided assault. As is excessive force and other similar procedures. Those *actions*, not that they defended themselves, are what get people into trouble. After crossing certain lines what people did is *not* legal self-defense, but illegal violence. *That* is the crime they are confessing to when they claim self-defense.

I told you you'd see that confessing to a crime part again. But let's do something you'll see a lot of in this book and that's returning to a topic with more understanding than before and then adding something else. We'll start with the addition of an important adjustment to the confessing to a crime statement. This was pointed out to me by Marty Hayes from the Armed Citizen's Legal Defense Network. Even when you did act in legitimate self-defense—"What you are confessing to is performing the elements of a crime (the intentional killing or causing injury or causing someone to fear injury). This is what gives police the right to arrest. But it is only a crime when the jury says it is a crime."

Two things: One, welcome to the hair splitting that is our legal system. A system you *will* meet when you act in self-defense. In case you missed it, what Marty said is the ye olde "innocent until proven guilty" maxim. But by confessing, you've—ordinarily—made it easier to prove . . .

Two, too often those squealing loudest about being 'arrested for self-defense' have no idea what self-defense *actually* involves. Despite that, they've poured thousands of dollars into so-called self-defense training. Often all they ever focused on was the physical skills. In fact, that financial investment helps cement their absolute conviction they *know* what self-defense is. Until what they *don't know* bites them in the butt. Or to be more accurate, what they believe comes back and bites them . . .

Of course, stomping a downed opponent on the head is self-defense. "We call that a 'finishing move' in the deadly Asian warrior art I study." "Of course it's self-defense when I give him the boot that keeps him from getting up and attacking again. Besides, that's what we do in combatives." And slugging someone for threatening you is self-defense. "That's why I train in MMA—to keep from being disrespected." Of course tapping into your inner anger and going ballistic on someone is self-defense. "I learned that while being empowered in the women's self-defense course I took."And using a knife on an unarmed guy, who just hit me, is self-defense. "We have special techniques for that in my knife-fighting system." Of course, pulling a gun on a crazy guy who wants to tell me about Jesus's involvement in the Roswell cover up is self-defense. "That's why I carry a gun." And of course fighting for your rights is *always* self-defense.

Isn't it?

The ignorance about the limitations of self-defense is appalling. It's bad enough when it's yahoos on the Internet spreading the misinformation.

It's more terrifying when it's from a so-called self-defense instructor. Things like teaching a neck break from behind on a downed and helpless opponent. (When he saw my horrified expression, the Tae Kwan Do instructor explained the move was "only for self-defense.") Or teaching you to pull a knife and stab a downed opponent to finish him. And of course, always shoot him to the ground. These little excursions into manslaughter convictions are if not cavalierly then casually taught. Mere details to finish the job as it were.[1]

Unfortunately much of so-called self-defense training falls into two general categories. One is the self-help focus (empowerment, confidence building, and similar psychological benefits) Two is exclusively physical (and this includes sports, martial arts, tactical shooting, and other defensive training.) While these do have value—and I actually do mean that—this *does not* qualify them as self-defense training. Even though there *is* overlap, physical training and self-help are subjects different from self-defense.

That's because self-defense is *not* just one thing. It's a stew of different elements. Some are unique to SD. Others are complete fields unto themselves, but take on a particular flavor when added to the self-defense stew. Then there are the ones that look similar, but are different. Take for example the strategies and mindset necessary to win a mixed martial arts bout. These definitely exist. When it comes to winning sporting events, these are qualities of championship. Yet, there is little— *if any*—similarity between those and self-defense. Even though you're still talking about strategy and mindset—there is *not* automatic cross over.

Self-defense, as a *subject*, does have physical and emotional aspects. But that's not all. As a subject, self-defense includes many different factors. Let me repeat something because it's important: Many of these otherwise independent elements take on specialized manifestations within SD. For example, adrenal response and legal, psychology, and social organization. All of them are unique subjects and fields, but they take on unique flavors in the self-defense stew.

These different elements are commonly overlooked aspects of self-defense training. This is dangerous because teaching just the physical part is like giving you a high performance car without teaching you how to drive or an understanding of traffic laws. Mixing it with ideology and

---

1   I purposely split student interpretations and instructor misconduct. The truth is, it's usually a horrid blend of what the instructor actually said and the students taking it and running with it. The teacher demonstrates a finishing kick on a downed opponent, the student interprets that to mean jump up and down on the guy's chest. One is excessive force (assault) the other is attempted murder.

pop psychology is like giving people whiskey before handing them the car keys.[2]

Worse, there's an assumption that you already know and understand the issues missing from your training. First, some instructors assume you understand conflict and violence. Second, they assume you'll recognize a criminal coming at you. Third, they don't have to teach how not to misuse what they're teaching because you'd *never* do such a thing. These assumptions are flawed because that's where things *worsen* in live-fire situations. Much of this book is about the common mistakes people make while emotional and adrenalized, and how reliably those mistakes turn potential violence into physical violence.

There's an old saying common among survival trainers: What you *think* you know will kill you. In this case, or if not kill then put you into prison. I've seen too much blood spilled when people get scared, angry, self-righteous, and offended to believe it can't happen to someone, much less anyone. You are human, these are things humans do naturally when we're under stress and in conflict. That is until you learn how to take control of them. Just because we often behave a certain way doesn't mean we *always* have to.

That's why I wrote this book. While it will be instrumental in helping you stay within the boundaries of self-defense, a big part shows you how *not* to make the same mistakes as aggressive amateurs, who commit illegal violence and then try to claim self-defense.

All these abuses of the SD claim are why cops, prosecutors, judges, prison guards, and defense attorneys are cynical when they hear someone hollering, *"Self-defense."* They know who claims it and why. They've. Heard. This. Noise. Before.

And this bring us to you. Even *if* it really was self-defense (and not a fight) when you claim SD, they're going to give you the hairy eyeball. In case you missed it, it's *not* a good sign when your *own* attorney thinks you did something illegal. The sad part—as you'll soon see—is odds are good, *he's right.* There are a lot of ways to screw up self-defense.

Worse yet, there are ways a prosecutor can punish you for using force, even if it actually *was* self-defense. That's often in the form of additional minor charges. They'll grudgingly concede you may have killed someone in self-defense, but they can still try to nail you for discharging a firearm in city limits. While a good attorney can argue the lesser charges are negated by legitimate self-defense (like discharging a firearm in city limits) this *isn't* a free pass. What *will* still stick are things like unlawful

2   Certain self-defense training programs come packaged with political and social agendas (which is why they are so often a turn off to most customers). Often this results with people, who are attracted to these programs, training to empower dysfunction. Now these folks can fight for their right to be angry and have poor social skills.

possession of a weapon (e.g., carrying a concealed pistol without a permit) or carrying an illegal weapon (e.g., a blackjack). This is why it's so important to know the laws about what you can carry, as well as where and when to *behave*. These are the sort of damned-if-you-do, damned-if-you-don't problems that you'll run into with self-defense and our legal system. So be ready to pick your poison.

Everything I've just said sets up understanding for the third thing you *need* to know about violence and self-defense. That is: *Someone is going to be unhappy with your use-of-force choice.*

No matter what level of force you use, someone is going to feel you were wrong in doing so. If it fails to protect you, the unhappy person is you. If it works, the other person will be unhappy. If it really works, the family of the other person, the cops, the prosecutor, and the civil attorney for the family will all be unhappy. In fact, they'll be lining up to show you how unhappy they are with your choice.

There is *never* going to be a celestial chorus, clouds parting, beams of light, and doves fluttering down carrying a banner reading, "You done right," over a use-of-force decision.

Now while that sounds silly and hyperbolic, it's important. It brings your attention to the second biggest mistakes people make—especially those who have actually acted in self-defense. And that is: *They get angry, indignant, and hostile when the cops, court, and jury treat them like 'bad guys.'*

Why doesn't this officer believe what they say? Isn't it obvious, they're the victims here! They're the good guys in this situation. Why are they being charged? They may not be expecting a pat on the back and a hearty 'atta boy,' but they certainly *don't* expect to be treated like criminals.

Here's a news flash, Precious, the officer is going to investigate *any* violent situation as a *criminal act*. Until it is clear in his or her mind that it was self-defense, the criminal investigation *will continue*. If the patrol officer can't make a determination, the case gets handed over to a detective. That is how the system works. Knowing this in *advance* will help keep you from making mistakes that commonly hang someone who *did* act in legitimate self-defense.

Self-defense doesn't end when a body hits the floor. There *will be* an aftermath. If you lose your cool during this time, you can take the most clean, righteous self-defense act and piss all over it. You—*and nobody else*—will convince the cop that it wasn't self-defense, usually by acting like a self-righteous, outraged jackass.

This is *one* of the reasons why understanding and accepting the fact somebody won't be happy is so important. And even one reason for that discontent has many manifestations. With this realization:

- You'll be prepared for being treated with suspicion.
- You won't lose your cool when the other guy starts lying about what happened.
- You'll be able to stay calm enough to decide either to make a statement at the scene or wait until your lawyer is present. (Hint, the higher the level of force, the better idea it is to wait.)
- You'll not fall for the common tricks cops use to get confessions.
- You be better able to understand your lawyer's damage control approach of plea bargaining (especially when it wasn't clearly self-defense).
- You'll know when to tell your lawyer yes or no about damage control. (E.g., Why—when it really was self-defense—you don't want to plead guilty to a crime you didn't commit.)

See how one simple concept can have many manifestations? Get used to it. That's what makes self-defense a complex subject. While the components are simple, there are all kinds of ways they can mix and manifest. Those are the waters you must learn to navigate.

So after the first (claiming SD when it wasn't) and second (getting upset about having to deal with the aftermath) the third biggest mistake people make is: They want a painless answer.

A raw reality here, folks, if you have to act in self-defense, *life as you know it is over!* But here's the counterpoint: If you *don't* act, life—as you know it—*is still over.* Finding yourself in a self-defense situation is simple: All your options suck. You need to embrace the suck. If you act, you're going to do horrible, hurtful things to another person. If you don't, those horrible hurtful things are going to be done to you. You're damned if you do. You're damned if you don't.

But you'll be doubly damned if you *didn't* act within self-defense boundaries. And this is why we're going to spend so much time on:
1) Understanding violent situations
2) Knowing what subconscious processes get us into them
3) Staying out of these situations in the first place
4) Staying within self-defense parameters
5) Understanding and coping with the aftermath.

Believe me, it's still going to suck, but at least it won't kill you. Or put you in prison. Like I said, pick your poison. And yes, this book is an antidote. It will help you to survive choosing the self-defense poison. But just because an antidote will keep you from dying doesn't mean the process isn't going to be a rough ride. Knowing that self-defense is like drinking the least toxic poison will go a long way to keep you out of unnecessary situations.

This is especially important for people who think I'm telling you to be a wimp and not stand up for yourself. Or that knowing some fighting system (or being armed) means you can be stupid and put yourself into dangerous situations. Or thinking you have the right to do something means doing it is a good idea. When the consequences mean being poisoned then antidote or not choosing to take a swig doesn't mean you should.

Let's tie this back to the third thing you need to know about SD. Remembering unhappy people will guide your actions pre-incident. And that should start with the most important outcome of all: *Don't* get into a situation in the first place. Believe me, once you know how much of a hassle it is acting for anything less than the preservation of life and limb should make you pause—as in seriously think about it before you open that can of worms.

But let's say things still develop. This knowledge of unhappy others can work miracles for keeping you from making the same mistakes made by amateurs—especially when it comes to aggressively trying to scare away the bad guy. (This is where most people demolish their own SD claim.)

Let me tell you, it's hard enough staying calm when the other guy is lying about your actions. It seriously sucks when he's telling the truth about what *you did* that led to illegal violence. In these circumstances the more truth he tells, the more you'll realize why claiming self-defense was a bad idea.

Worse yet, if—under these circumstances—you panic and try to talk your way out of it, you'll just be digging yourself in deeper. So, let's add another important safety tip: If what you did *wasn't* self-defense, then S.H.U.T. U.P! Your lawyer already has his work cut out for him, your talking will only make it worse.

Knowing about:
a) Confessing to a crime,
b) The bias against claiming self-defense
c) Unhappy people will help you get your head in the self-defense game.

It's a suck-ass game, but it's one you buy into when you decide *not* to allow yourself to be victimized by criminals and violent people.

So now that you made that decision let's look at how to if not win at least not lose. This book is not about punching or kicking. It's not about techniques for shooting and stabbing either. What's more, it's *not legal advice*. It's about *all* the other things you need to know *not* to screw up your life.

CHAPTER 1

*When it comes to using your self-defense training, you only
have one of two problems:*
1) It doesn't work;
2) It does work.

MM

What We're Going to Cover in This Book

First and foremost, this book is about understanding violence dynamics.

That is to say: What is violence? What causes it? What behavior *will* put you into a violent confrontation? What are the different types of violence? The different goals? What will de-escalate it, and what will cause it to blow up on you? What type of violence *cannot* be de-escalated? What type of violence can only be deterred? And in what kind of violence if you engage in it are you *always* breaking the law?

We're going to do an in-depth study on violence dynamics. Why? Well, for several reasons.

First, understanding violence dynamics will usually keep you from having to use physical self-defense.

Second, a lot of people who get self-defense training assume the only time they'd ever need it would be against a mugger. They are shocked when they are arrested for getting sucked into a road-rage incident. It's bad enough when they have to defend themselves against people they know. Way worse is sitting handcuffed in the back of the police car wondering how the situation with their _____ (fill in the blank) escalated. Know the differences between violence, fighting, and self-defense *before* you even think of claiming self-defense.

Third, an observation my wife made is that martial arts and self-defense instructors operate on the premise that their students are always going to be the good guys in a scenario. Unfortunately, experience has taught me that many people who come to martial arts or self-defense training lack a certain social adroitness. Many use training as a way to build self-esteem. Often they have bad incidents in their past or are struggling with internal issues. This is not to say they are bad people. But someone who has issues, mediocre social skills, and who is trying to prove something can—and will—easily overreact to conflict.

The most common problem, however, is simple naïveté on the part of good people. People who've lived quiet lives and never really had to think about this subject. Often something major happens to such people. This could be a first-time encounter with violence or crime. But just as common are lifestyle changes (such as divorce, moving to a new city, etc.). While the dangers of crime and violence have always been there, now they are intruding on such people's consciousness.

The problem with this is those same people try to make sense of this new subject based on what they think they know or believe. Take for example, the assumption that violence is always emotional. If such people get into potentially violent situations, they tend to become scared and angry. Scared and angry people often behave aggressively. This mixed with lack of experience often causes people to cross the line out of legitimate self-defense. At the same time, such people are caught flat footed when they are attacked by someone who can commit violence without having to get worked up about it. When this happens they falsely believe that "it came out of nowhere."

Fourth with great power comes great responsibility. Yes, I just quoted Spiderman's Uncle Ben Parker. But let me quote my barrio-raised stepdad when I was nine and he found me carrying a switchblade: "Don't carry a knife if you aren't willing to pull it. Don't pull it if you aren't willing to use it. Don't use it if you're not willing kill. Don't kill unless you're willing to take the punishment."

I have spent most of my life capable of taking other people's lives. Bare handed or with a weapon, I can end someone's life in seconds. I tell you this so you'll understand my next words. That and two bucks will get me a cup of coffee. I still have to do the dishes. I still have to vacuum. I still have to obey the law. I'm still obliged to be kind to people. I'm still polite in my dealings with everyone. In short, this ability is not a power rush. It is not something that allows me to fear no man. I don't swagger down the street expecting lesser beings to scramble out of my way. It is not a carte blanche for me to go out and do stupid and dangerous things (e.g., like go into a biker bar and talk trash because nobody dares mess with me). It's not an excuse for me to vent my spleen on the world for past wrongs. The truth is the direct opposite: My ability is a *responsibility*, as well as a *restriction*.

Because I am armed with these skills, I must conduct myself to a higher standard of behavior. I cannot give in to whims, impulses, and emotional temper tantrums or engage in the selfish, negative behavior that many people exhibit. Nor can I lose my temper and self-control. Doing so will result in someone being transported to the hospital or the morgue. This is the onus I *acquired* when I chose to develop these skills. You, too, took it up when you decided to develop the skills to defend yourself. You now have the ability to injure someone, maybe take someone's life. That ability comes with a burden.

Fifth, contrary to what modern society teaches us, conflict and violence are *very much* normal human behavior. As in: *We are wired for them.* Having said that, there's a difference between drives and instincts—both are powerful internal motivations. But instincts *don't* have to be taught. (Birds don't need to be taught to fly south for the winter; wasps don't need to be taught how to build a nest.)

Drives are more complicated, more flexible, but just as *powerful*. Cats have the drive to hunt, but they must learn how to be good hunters. Working dog breeds must be trained to the tasks they were bred for. The same goes for the way human drives manifest. Because you have to learn the process, drives are strongly influenced by culture, training, and experience. The big question: Is violence a human drive or is it a mechanism by which we accomplish other drives? Are we, as humans, predisposed toward violence or is it more cultural? (Yep, nature versus nurture.) Or is it genetic?

The answer? *We don't know.* And anyone who claims they do is full of it. What we do know is it's been a big part of our species survival. And that brings us to a pothole in the road. Back in the 1950s, sex was a taboo subject resulting in massive ignorance and misconceptions about a natural human activity. While people were obviously doing it (the fact you're reading this means someone had sex back then) those raised under this taboo sucked at it (and not in a good way). Today, the taboo human behaviors are conflict and violence. And once again ignorance abounds.

We are told we can achieve all if we talk and if we just listen and try to understand. We are told that violence is bad, only the cruel, evil, bad, and stupid use it. If you want to number among the elite, the civilized, the superior, you must believe violence is wrong. This is the taboo about violence we have been raised with.

Except for one thing, conflict and violence are wired into us. They are how we achieve other goals and manifest certain drives. They are how we overcome resistance. How we enforce our boundaries and rules. And—if truth be told—they underlie the workings of our society. In a very real sense, violence is the reason why we negotiate and compromise. The cost of *not* doing so when all parties are armed is too high.

Conflict and violence allowed our species to develop, to rule this planet. We as a species are alive because of them. They are deeply embedded in our psyches. For millions of years, they have been an everyday part of human existence and consciousness. Humans knew how to conduct themselves accordingly. By making them taboo, we've lost that knowledge. We no longer learn the process. It's not only that we don't know how conflict and violence work nor is it that we don't know the rules. We don't even know there *are* rules. In our ignorance, we unwittingly break them. Then we're shocked, appalled, confused, and self-righteous when things go south.

But more than that as a society our understanding of violence is a giant gaping black hole. We fear what we don't know or understand. We don't know what to do when confronted or threatened with violence. Without understanding violence dynamics, we won't be able to tell if we can de-escalate a situation or if trying will mean our deaths. No wonder so many people lack confidence.

These are some of the reasons why understanding violence dynamics is so important. But for our purposes, that *knowledge* will keep you from making mistakes when it comes to self-defense. It might seem, sometimes, that I'm taking things to a . . .well . . . no-duh level. More often, it will seem I'm talking about stuff that has nothing to do with self-defense. Just remember that you were raised in this new and enlightened society where violence is taboo. You don't *know* what you *don't* know.[3]

There's a reason I take things to such fundamentals. Let's revisit, "What you think you know will kill you." What most people know about how crime and violence materialize conceals deep and hidden pools of ignorance. That's not necessarily saying what we know is wrong. It's more like when we have an answer that satisfies us, we stop researching. Why should we look further? We have the answer.

No. You have *an* answer, not *the* answer. That answer you have isn't necessarily wrong, but it's not the only one. In fact, it very much applies to certain types of violence. It only becomes a wrong answer if you try to apply it to *all* violence. If we look at the different types of violence like a buffet—that answer you have is only a small taste of one dish. There're lots more.

Here's an example of what we think we know: Weak and fearful body language attracts predators. It's a green light to them. You *know* this. That concept is a staple of self-defense training. It makes sense, too. Be afraid and look like a victim, and you'll be selected. So now you know how not

---

3   There's what you know. There's what you know you don't know (e.g., quantum physics). But there's also what you knew (back then) that has changed since you were there. Then there are unknown unknowns (unk unks). These are thing that you not only don't know, but don't know you don't know them. (An example is not knowing someone in your company is leaking secrets to the competition. And you won't know until things blow up.)

to be selected as a target, right? Walk with confidence. Don't look like a victim![4] Except, contrary to what you might think, *most* violence doesn't take place when you're scared. Nor is it the person acting like a victim who is overwhelmingly attacked. In fact, it's the direct opposite.

Most violence takes place when you're angry, aggressive, or confident. Things go south when people think they're handling a situation. They're sure what they do is the correct response—right up until it goes horribly wrong. If they're lucky spitting blood is the only cost. That's violence dynamics out on the sharp end. It's not the quivering mouse who is going to get robbed. Often such a person *never hesitates* to flee from a dangerous situation. It's the person who looks at a bunch of robbers—waiting in a developed trap—and decides, "They wouldn't bother me." Then walks right into the trap: Being *certain* is a greater *danger* to you than fear.

When it comes to robberies, the most common forms take place when someone is thinking, "I'm too busy" or "I can handle this." When it comes to other kinds of violence, the willingness to be offensive, but not intending to physically fight, is what will get you into trouble. News flash here, folks. It's not the person showing submission signals who is most likely to be assaulted, but the person who thinks he or she is standing up for him- or herself—right up until the moment he or she gets punched. This really shouldn't come as a surprise. You don't say things to certain people and not expect to get punched. (Oh and incidentally talking trash and then trying to go submissive just before the ass whuppin' starts qualifies as too little, too late.)

Yet if you ask folks—in their normal state of mind—about trash talking, they'd be offended for your even suggesting that they'd be that stupid. But in conflict and danger, you're *not* in your normal mind. I'll go into more into specific reasons why later in this book. But for now: Being emotional and in conflict means a *different part* of your brain activates. Read that again. Make a note. Scrawl 'different part of the brain' on the wall. Tattoo it on your forehead in reverse (so you see it in the mirror). Do whatever it takes to *never* forget that.

The problem is when this part of your brain is active, you *think* you are rational and in control. An easy way to understand the change is

---

4   The 'walk like you're going somewhere' meme is a simplistic sound bite and misunderstanding of a study. Incarcerated criminals were shown video of eight students and asked whom they would attack. Given only eight options, there was a high consensus. But there's more to target selection than just how someone moves. Moving with purpose is indeed a way to improve body continuity, but it is not by itself sufficient. For some insights, read a piece by K. Costello, and J.A. Camilleri (2013) "Psychopathy and victim selection: The use of gait as a cue to vulnerability," *Journal of Interpersonal Violence*, Feb. 19, 2013, DOI: 10.1177/0886260512475315.

it's like being drunk. When you're buzzed, you think you have things under control. Flat out though, you're *not* operating at 100 percent. More importantly when you're operating in this part of your brain—like being drunk—certain behavior seems like a really *good* idea . . . Unfortunately, a whole lot of those ideas aren't good.

Take Nicole Dufresne, the New York City actress, whose last words were, "What are you going to do now? Shoot us?" It's a sure bet if you asked her a week before her death if she'd *ever* say that to an armed man, she'd say, "No." More than that, odds are good she would be angry and offended that you'd think she'd ever be so stupid. Yet that's exactly what she said—to an armed man who had just robbed them and pistol-whipped her boyfriend. And she died for it.

This is why remembering there are different parts to your brain is so important. While calmly reading this, such things seem utterly stupid, and foolish. It's easy to convince yourself *you'd* never be that stupid. Yet when you're adrenalized and operating in those parts of your brain, it's likely. I'm *not* joking when I say—at the time—such behavior seems like the most brilliant idea you've ever had.

Understanding both violence dynamics and that another part of your brain is active in these situations *helps* keep you out of trouble. Believe me, by the time you're done with this book you'll have a whole new appreciation for keeping out of situations where you'd end up using physical force. Consciously knowing what is normally subconscious and how it affects your behavior lets you see the basis for reactions in others and yourself. That is a *huge* advantage. It allows you to remain in conscious control of your actions—instead of just reacting to what these other parts of your brain scream at you to do.

Putting it another way: Emotions and adrenaline are like a flash flood. We're often hit by them and carried away. Even if we don't drown, they move us and change our behavior. After reading this book, you'll be aware of (and know how to break free from) the flash flood, instead of just being caught in it. That's the first step in keeping *all* parts of your brain engaged not just the emotional, freaked-out part. That's the part that *will* get you into conflict in the first place.

Additionally, knowledge of violence dynamics is important so you can control yourself. When one segment of your brain is pushing you to say something, another part can veto it as a bad idea. In fact, you have stable, anchoring data about exactly how *bad* an idea that is.

So there's a little conversation going on in your head:

"I want to say _____(fill in blank) to him."

"Hmmm, how about not only no, but hell no."

But just knowing isn't enough. You have to be able to *apply* this in the heat of the moment. And that takes conscious effort and practice.

You don't have to go to the dojo or shooting range every day, but you *do* have to practice daily to engage your whole brain—especially under stress. If you cannot master these different impulses in small daily issues, I guarantee you *won't* be able to manage them in the middle of a crisis. Being emotional and freaked-out with a gun or knife available is not going to end well for you. It sucks when facing those, too. (And as you'll soon see, emotions are contagious.)

There's some not-so-good news about understanding violence dynamics. That is, you'll find lots of opportunities to practice staying out of what we call the "monkey brain." At first, it will seem people love to trigger that part of you. I'm saying it'll seem people are just going out of their way to piss you off. That's because you're now consciously seeing what was previously subconscious.

The good news about recognizing violence dynamics is that the amount of conflict and stress in your everyday life will be greatly reduced. This is technically a bigger benefit. In self-defense terms, this knowledge significantly lessens your chances of having to blow someone's brains into a fine pink mist or crush someone's throat with your elbow. If it still comes to that, knowledge of violence dynamics will help keep you out of prison.

Perhaps the most important thing knowledge of violence dynamics will do is give you time to think, to find other viable options. It introduces you to subconscious behavior, habits, and—most of all—your own self-southing actions that usually provoke violence. Self-southing is something we all do. Basically it means when we have an uncomfortable emotion, we do something to relieve the tension. In and of itself, self-southing *isn't* bad. It's how we do it that can become a problem.

Maybe you're thinking this is beginning to sound more like a pop psychology book than one on self-defense. Let me assure you that recognizing self-southing behavior in others and resisting the impulse in yourself is one of the best ways to keep things from becoming physically violent. That's because as human beings, we are *designed* to emotionally infect each other. That's another write-on-the-wall, as well as your forehead statement. Someone throws an emotionally charged signal or behavior at you, it triggers your own emotional monkey brain. (We'll go into that in Chapter 4.) Faster than conscious thought, you react and throw back another emotion-provoking signal. This spins him out more, in return you get further upset. Now you're both infected. And you're likely to keep on re-infecting each other unless you break the escalating spiral.

Remember I said many people think fear is the problem when it comes to who is targeted for violence? Here's why I say it's usually something else. A lot of people self-soothe by verbally attacking others. This is their default reaction to unacceptable emotions. They vocally lash out in response to something that caused them emotional distress. This is aimed at those near them (an attack), a specific group (hate speech) or at the world in general. Venting their spleen relieves their internal discomfort. It feels good to throw out a vicious and nasty remark; it is an internal flush of power. You showed him, wrongs are avenged, and the world order is set right again. I liken this to masturbating in public. Saying something petty and mean relieves the whacker's stress at that exact instant. But it upsets everyone else. Conflict occurs when someone else responds in kind.

But let's look at this bigger perspective. To the people involved, the conflict is intense and overwhelming. But to everyone else it's *really* embarrassing—especially if you're in a mixed-age crowd.[5] Here are two people publicly shaming themselves, displaying the fact they are socially inept and lack social intelligence, and the audience doesn't know what to do. That's why people not directly involved in the incident get stressed out over public displays of conflict. Mostly, they don't know how to react to such a vulgar, immature display of bad behavior.

Recognizing how much verbal aggression is self-southing will save you all kinds of grief. The guy said something obnoxious and offensive. So what? Now you recognize it for what it is most often—self-southing, *not* the opening gambit of a planned attack. Thinking of him publicly displaying himself will do wonders for not taking it as an insult you *have to* respond to, both for calming the feeling you *have* to react and keeping you from shaming yourself in public.

But let's look at it this a little deeper. Lashing out at an innocent because you're in a pique is bad enough (e.g., you're having a bad day and snap at someone). Many people want to believe that is the *only* time they do this. In fact, they self-certify[6] that's the only time they do it. But entirely too many people routinely give themselves permission to constantly behave this way. In fact for some, conflict is like good sex. They not only get off on it, but they bask in the afterglow. (Yes, there's an endorphin rush.)

Here is where we run into the first of many problems regarding self-defense. At a most basic level, it seems simple: When others throw shit at them, they throw it back. Then they call returning fire defending

---

5   This behavior is especially common among the young, immature, insecure, and less-than-socially adept. When these congregate in numbers, this behavior is seen as a demonstration of status and dominance. Looking around, all they see is the same. There aren't other ages and groups to be seen displaying disgust.

6   Self-certifying is a term I'll use throughout this book. Basically, it means a person tells him- or herself he or she is _____ (fill in blank) and then—despite doing the direct opposite—insists on maintaining that self-identity. For example, someone who self-certifies him- or herself as well informed, but does no research on a subject beyond watching a pundit on a preferred 'news' station.

themselves. That's *not* self-defense. They're not defending themselves, *they're evening the score.*

The problem with this is twofold. One, there might not have been an initial attack at all.

Something triggered an unacceptable emotion in someone. That person self-soothees and lashes out at someone else to relieve the stress. The trigger could be entirely *inside* that person's head. But just whipping it out and self-southing is kind of embarrassing. So the person convinces him- or herself it was a deliberate affront and attack. As such, that person believes he or she is defending him- or herself. But to everyone present, that person's self-certified counter attack came out of nowhere. It's not a counter attack. That *is* the first attack. Or at least the first real one.

Problem two, when someone is verbally and emotionally attacked, the knee-jerk reaction is to attack back. The mechanism is the same in both people. Here is where things start escalating. What triggered the first person might *not* have been an actual attack. But his (or her) self-southing verbal aggression *is* an attack that triggers the second person's monkey brain. (We call the part of the brain that handles socio-emotional issues the monkey.) The second person reacts with a counter offensive. Like I said, same mechanism for a perceived attack as a real one.

This reaction, in turn, further proves to the first person that he or she is under attack. Therefore, another counter offensive is justified. This additional attack reconfirms the second person's belief that he or she is under attack. Now you have two people convinced the other one started it. Usually, this spiral goes on until someone backs down.

I use the term counter offensive, fortunately most of the time it's just two people self-southing in public. You've probably seen this behavior thousands of times. So you do actually know the pattern, but now you consciously know the mechanism.

Not everyone is going to be content to engage in a public circle jerk, however. With some, these exchanges will result in physical action. That's a whole different set of problems. For example, making that comment about his testicles on his mother's chin might have been emotionally gratifying, but:
a) You got punched for it.
b) Now—if you do anything except bleed—the cops will look at what happened next as a *fight,* not self-defense.

Many amateurs who claim self-defense have fallen into this very trap. They get caught up in this monkey-brain game of escalato (what Rory Miller calls "the monkey dance"). While busy attacking each other, they both are convinced they are defending themselves from the unprovoked aggression of the other person. What's scary is how people go speeding down this road and then are shocked that things went physical. Really? Where did you think behaving this way was going to end up?

But the monkey *doesn't* believe that. In fact, the monkey is protecting something it considers much more important—feelings. The importance of this goal blinds it to all other considerations. An excited, out-of-control monkey protecting itself sees no problem with going to extremes. So, here is something else to write on the wall: Overwhelmingly, physical violence is *about* someone's feelings. That is a simple but profound truth. And that truth remembered in the heat of the moment *can* save your life. Not just in the sense of keeping you from getting killed or crippled, but out of prison. Violence committed over feelings is categorically illegal. If you fall into this trap, what you're doing isn't self-defense, it's a *crime*.

Understanding violence dynamics has another critical benefit. Specifically, it allows you to articulate *why* what you did was self-defense and *not* illegal violence. This is a huge factor when talking to the cops and your attorney, as well as convincing the jury you acted in self-defense. I've said it before, but I'll say it again: A big part of this book isn't just teaching you how to assess situations, but how to articulate what happens. You need to first see A, B, C, and then explain that's why you acted. I'm also going to add a new twist. That is: You explaining yourself to people who are unhappy with your use-of-force decision.

Part of the reason this book is so long and involved is that violence is not a simple subject. A bigger part is because just saying A, B, C, is not enough. A, B, C, is all you need? Oh no. These people are going to demand you explain why A means this. What is the significance of B? How did you know A and B? And why was it C and not twenty-seven? When asked, you need to be able to explain that A, B, C, are the first three letters of a bigger thing called the alphabet. In this culture, we use the twenty-six letter English alphabet—but there are others. In this type of alphabet, there are upper and lower case letters, 'A' and 'a' can both be correct given the use. There also are two types of letters, vowels and consonants. The purposes of these are . . .

Let me make something very clear. You won't be questioned, you will be *interrogated*. And you *will* have to go into this kind of detail over your use of force. *That's* what happens when you claim self-defense. Sound like a pain in the ass? It is. Now the real bad news: some of the people who demand that you explain yourself are going to be *trying* to trip you up!

Remember unhappy? They're going to be throwing you curve-ball questions. Questions you damned well better be able to answer. "Oh, so A, B, and C are part of an alphabet? How many vowels in that alphabet? How many consonants?" Do you know that off the top of your head? If not, do you know how to come up with the right answer on the fly?

This book is going to help you *deal* with these kinds of curve balls. When it's a cop or a prosecutor asking, these questions aren't ones where you can get away with a "how the hell do I know?" response. You have to be able to *answer*. If you can't—or if they can trip you up—you're going to prison. So you better know how to answer rough and tricky questions about what you did.

That's why this book is so big. I don't expect you to memorize every detail. In fact if you try, you'll get lost. Just relax and read. You may even want to finish it then reread it six months from now. (Your understanding will have changed.) The way I wrote it, I keep returning to things I've said before. The approach is one that acknowledges that you know this already, but here are some more tweaks and how they apply. I tie in new information to show you different aspects and how they apply. Basically it's not the information that's important, but that I'm helping you create a filing system from which you can *pull out* the right answers.

Let's go back to someone trying to trip you up. How many vowels in the alphabet? Let's see, A, E, I, O, U, and sometimes Y. Five or six, twenty-six letters minus (it depends). So "twenty-one normally, twenty if you include Y as a vowel" is the correct answer to that curve-ball question.

While we're talking about articulable facts, it's helpful to be able to explain all the things you tried to *keep* the *situation* from *becoming* a physical confrontation. This especially applies if there's video of the incident. "That's where I tried to . . . " "This is where I was saying . . . " These are just a few examples of the importance of knowing violence dynamics—not only to avoid conflict and violence, but in order to stay inside the parameters of self-defense. And most of all to *not* engage in self-offense. (I'll explain that in a bit.)

The second thing this book will do is introduce you to the different kinds of violence. Violence isn't homogenized. It comes in many forms and types. The purposes, goals, and behavior of people engaging in different forms of violence vary widely. Even within the same type, there are degrees and levels, as well as different strategies, tactics, and goals. These vary from situation to situation. This is why there is *no* one-size-fits-all response. That's another scrawl-it-on-the-wall note to self. Here's why: What *works* with one is a *disaster* in others.

There is a time for empty-hand techniques, there's a time for weapons. There is a time for bone-breaking combatives, and there's a time for grappling, submission, and control. There's a time for fighting, and there's a time you have to kill someone quickly and effectively. (Not only before he or she kills you, but so he or she can't take you with them.) Some violence can be resolved through words, some by use of force, and other types by running like hell.

More than that, some violence is extremely ritualized—and gods help you if you break 'scripts.'[7] Sometimes it's best to just take a hit and shut up. That's because the consequences of not doing so are much worse. Don't believe me? Live-fire story: I once had an entire bar stand up to kick my ass because I broke the rules and dropped a local too fast. In a rural roadhouse, I dropped the guy like I would have in the streets of Los Angeles. The locals took offense to my breaking the rules. This is why knowing about the different levels is important. I didn't have to win that situation. I could have taken a punch. Hell, a few punches. But not the beating fifteen or so guys would have handed me for what I did to that guy. The appropriate response is not so much about fighting style, technique, equipment, or kind of bullet as it is *level of force*.

Are you beginning to see why there is no one-size-fits-all training solution?

But here's the real problem: If you *don't* recognize what type of violence you're dealing with, your reactions are going to either be overkill (like I did with the guy in the bar) or insufficient (like trying to fight a mugger). Without the knowledge of different kinds of violence, your chances of choosing the *appropriate* level of force are slim to none . . . and Slim left town. Know this now: What you face—at that exact moment—will *determine* the right response. There's another wall scrawl, one that gets you thinking in some critical ways. How much force do you need? Do you need to act at all? These are life-changing questions. The answers *will* depend on the situation. But to make that decision, it helps to be able to tell what type of violence you are dealing with.

This ability to spot exactly what's in front of you is especially important because actual predators usually disguise their intentions behind *social behavior*.[8] That mugger asking you for directions is setting you up for a robbery. Until you know how to differentiate the real social situations from the pseudo ones, it's difficult to decide to act *before* it's too late.

Even worse if you can't spot the deception, his pseudo-social behavior will trigger an insufficient response from you *if* and *when* you try to resist. Even if you do manage to act in time, your response will be too little. This cryptic and ominous threat will make a whole lot more sense by the end of this book. But more importantly, you'll be in less danger of it happening to you. I say "even worse" because this is a specific danger

---

7   Scripts are ritualized social behaviors that help us navigate through life. They can range from complex, falling in love, or success stories to fast micro-scripts like saying, "Excuse me," as you reach past someone in the grocery store. That seems like nothing, but there is a complex set of ritualized actions and counter actions. Next time you're in that simple interaction, watch what people do. The complex predictability is astounding.

8   I say actual because there is entirely too much hyperbole surrounding anybody who does something a person disagrees with and being called a predator.

for martial artists. In a predatory situation, an insufficient response is *more* dangerous than *no* response at all. And way too many martial artists try to fight in the wrong circumstances. Conversely, overkill is very much a problem—especially when that's the only level of force you've learned. *~cough cough concealed carry cough~*

If you react with force appropriate for a predator—when the situation is not potentially fatal or damaging—then *you* will have committed aggravated assault if not manslaughter, especially if you carry a knife or a gun for self-defense.

Before you get too nervous about all this, don't worry. I'll show you how to spot when the situation is a set-up. It's actually rather obvious. This book will help keep you from making mistakes in either direction. Related to this topic, but more an idea to help you get your head in the game: Recognize that physical force is just physical force. To sound all Bruce Lee, "A punch is just a punch."

It's the context that matters. The same punch could be thrown in a sparring, against a bag, into the air, in self-defense, in a fight, or it could be used to knock an eighty-year-old woman down and kill her. The punch itself is neutral. It's the circumstances that it's thrown in that are important. This seriously calls into question training that only focuses on the physical—especially lethal force training.

A third thing this book will do is help you *stay out* of violence. Not because you have the confidence of having a black belt, know how to fight, or have assumed the responsibility that goes with carrying a gun. But because you know what creates conflict and escalates situations into violence. Although there's a lot of overlap, with knowledge of violence dynamics this third topic has far more on-the-ground tactical application, particularly when someone is in your face, barking, snarling, and growling at you.

Remember the first quote of this book? What's going to kill you is the stuff you *don't* know *not* to do. Violence actually is *extremely* predictable. There's a reliable list of do's and don'ts. The problem with learning a list of things to do about violence is you miss the equally important list of what *not* to do. Yet if you don't complete the list with things *not* to do, doing something extra will seem to make sense—at that moment at least.

There are things that someone experienced with violence will subconsciously *not* do.[9] They are so subconscious, they are usually left out of training. Because nobody tells you, there seems to be no reason not to do them, especially when you think doing them will make what you are doing work just that much better. For example, if I were to tell

---

9   And if you do see them do these things, there are very specific circumstances and dynamics.

you to say to a guy challenging you, "I don't want any trouble," that's good advice. Except, you might think that isn't strong enough. So to make it work better, you might decide to add a little zest to it. What comes out of your mouth is, "I don't want any trouble, *Asshole!*"

Did that hurt? That looked real painful. But more than that, the only person who didn't see it coming was you.

Do's and don'ts apply to more than just the incident itself. Huge parts of avoiding violence are knowing *what* causes it, *why* it happens, *where* it happens, and *who's* most likely to be involved. Then either staying out of those situations or following the rules will give you a giant head start over most people.

It's amazing how well not breaking social rules can keep you from being involved in a violent situation (especially if you think those social conventions are stupid). The same goes for not insisting on your rights (especially rights regarding breaking local rules or misbehaving). It's even more impressive how not insulting, belittling, or looking at people like they're dog turds can keep you out of conflict and violence. This *should* be a no brainer.

It's appalling how many people get emotional, prideful, self-righteous, and aggressive when someone gets in their faces. Then they find themselves wondering how it all went so wrong while sitting in the jail cell or the ER (emergency room) waiting room.

Now tracking back to the different kinds of violence point, some violence *can* be de-escalated. Some can only be *deterred.* (Man, your walls are going to be covered from top to bottom in graffiti by the time you're done with this book.) Knowing *which* type you're dealing with *is* critical for picking the right strategy to prevent it. But also notice the emphasis on the word 'can' when it comes to de-escalation. Can is a troublesome word. It's neither a guarantee nor is it a free pass.

Using words like bastard, dickhead, and son-of-a-bitch take a situation that could have been de-escalated and flushes it down the toilet. But here's the flip side of that coin. All types of violence can be *escalated* by your saying or doing the wrong thing. Sometimes, it escalates to extremes. A lot of people get all hairless about situations exploding into extreme violence. They claim it's unpredictable. It's not. In fact, even extreme violence is really predictable—*especially* if you provoke it. Let's take a look at an example. (And I actually do mean look.) Before you read farther, go to YouTube and type in "Casino bar scene" (Or "Casino pen scene"). *Casino* is a 1995 movie starring Robert Di Niro and Joe Pesci.

For those of you who didn't watch the video clip, this is what happens: Joe Pesci's character, Nicky, explodes on a guy and repeatedly stabs him in the throat with a pen the victim used as an excuse to demean Robert De Niro's character, Sam.

We're going to spend some time on this clip. (Pssssst, seriously go watch it.) Many people deem the attack was without reason and made without warning. Also, the speed and brutality is unnerving for many viewers.

First and foremost, I'm going to point out something that could save your life. The reason I wanted you to watch that clip is that's how *fast* professional violence and violent lifestyle incidents take place. They literally explode. And when it comes to explosions, there isn't much you can do when you're unexpectedly caught in one. No kung fu skill or concealed carry permit could have saved Mr. Pen-in-the-Throat.

The brutality of the attack is shocking to folks who haven't dealt with that level of violence. Yeah, yeah, big deal. Welcome to my world, a place where survival is more about seeing, hearing, or smelling the burning fuse in time. Where the lack of experience (and dare I say even ignorance) really shows is with people who claim it happened "without warning." Let's go back to the analogy of this kind of violence and explosion. The way you avoid getting killed by explosions is by:

1) Taking safety measures
2) Making preparations
3) Controlling when, where, and how they happen
4) Recognizing when the fuse has been lit
5) Most of all knowing—in the first place—when you're dealing with things that go boom.

If you know how violence dynamics work that attack was about as predictable as the sunrise. That's why we're going to dissect the scene. Not to show it didn't just come out of nowhere, but that it was *throwing flaming matches into a gas can.*

As the audience, we know De Niro's Sam is a friend of Pesci's mafioso character. But not too many recognize the significance of Pesci's being tasked by a mob boss to "look after" De Niro. De Niro was a valued asset to the mafia don. (We'll introduce you to the concept of resource protection later. Know now that it means the degree and effectiveness of violence *will* grow—both when getting and protecting resources.) The look after comment was a game changer. What a lot of people don't understand is Nicky's ass was on the line. If he failed to protect Sam, Nicky would be killed.

In fact, if Sam had so much as complained to the don about Captain Tracheotomy getting away with demeaning him there would be negative consequences for Nicky. That is how the game is played *at that* level. Excessive violence is safer than insufficient. Knowing this, the extreme violence makes more sense.

But let's forget the mobsters and look at the pen-stabbed 'victim.' This is what scares people: How a simple rude comment results in such brutality. Except it's not that simple. It wasn't just a rude comment. Nor was that guy a victim. For those of you who haven't seen the movie or watched the clip, what led to the stabbing was when De Niro tried to return an expensive pen to the owner. It's pretty simple: When someone tries to do you a solid, you thank him and go about your business. Instead, the pen owner became verbally abusive and insulting. Then he turned his back on De Niro.

We can assume two things about the soon-to-be-stabbed man. One is—because of how fast he became verbally abusive—he routinely relied on verbal intimidation to get his way. Within three seconds of him opening his mouth, you can tell he had a long-standing pattern of aggression and verbal violence. That makes him anything but innocent.

He expected his verbal abuse to cow and silence De Niro. But there's more. Not only was he aggressive and insulting, he poured on a final insult to De Niro by turning his back on him. (This is called a cut-off gesture.) Again, a practiced and studied insult. Yet because he'd turned his back, he was caught completely unaware.

Right up until it all went horribly wrong, the so-called victim thought he was successful and in complete control of the situation. Keep that in mind, it's part of the second thing we can assume. But it's running off on a side track time:

Notice the use of the term so-called when I talk about the victim. The victim narrative has become very strong in modern culture, often in the form of someone angling for a free pass for the person wearing the title (whether it's themselves or others). Along with this, come attempts to redefine the word victim to mean a person who loses a fight. I have multiple problems with this. First, victim carries the connotation of innocent. A loser of a fight *isn't*. He or she was an active participant in the creation and escalation of the conflict. It's called losing . . . get over it.

Second, if he lived Mr. Pen-in-the-Throat would have called himself a victim. His provocative behavior would be either edited out or downplayed when he told the story. By the time his friends and family all heard the tale, he'd be Little Bo Peep. This sanitized story includes his statement to the cops. And this is a big reason why cops will give you the hairy eyeball when you claim you did nothing to provoke a violent situation. Way too many people edit out their bad behavior in their stories. (We'll spend a lot of time later about articulating to the cops regarding what transpired.)

Third, entirely too many people self-certify themselves as the victim when they don't win. Of course, this sootheees the sting of losing. But it does something else, it allows them to tell themselves that they were right. If you're right, you don't need to stop the behavior that got you into the mess. It's carte blanche for bad behavior.

Fourth, it allows assignment of blame. They weren't aggressive assholes, it was the other guy who was out of control and hence the bad guy.

Fifth being a victim is very closely tied with feelings. Often these are ridden around town in a carriage of entitlement and a belief in someone's 'specialness.' I tell you this because odds are good that person who is trying to crack your skull open has a long list of wrongs *done to him or her*. Because you've added one more is why he or she is physically attacking you. Yeah, and in case you missed it that means he's attacking you while thinking he's the victim in the situation.

The sixth problem is that when you take all these charming traits and mix them together, you have the ingredients for vendetta. As day follows night, it's that predictable. The only question is how. Is he going to come back and shoot you in the back? Show up with five buddies? Sic the cops on you or sue you? One way or the other, that poor innocent victim will try to win round two.

<start world-weary, been-there-done-that sarcastic voice > Oh joy, oh fuckin' rapture . . . </voice >

I tell you this because these traits are often the toxic mix you encounter from someone, who forces you to defend yourself, and then claims to be the victim. Odds are good that's what you'll be facing. Knowing that, you can prepare to handle what is thrown at you.

Having said that, let's get back to Mr. Pen-in-the-Throat. The second thing we can safely assume is he was so wrapped up in himself that he felt it was beneath him to have to notice lesser beings. He felt he could do what he wanted with impunity. This is a situational awareness failure on multiple levels.

Okay, another jackrabbit off into left field . . . get used to them. That's how my brain works. A lot of people talk about situational awareness as if it's some kind of mystic ninja skill. It's not. It's basically breaking the habit of going through life on autopilot. Technically speaking being aware is easier than you might think. It's just that we've become comfortable with living on autopilot. Awareness isn't difficult, it's just that it's easier being off in your own private Idaho.

With that in mind, there are four major sources of failure in situational awareness. I'm going to count them down in magnitude of "fail."

One source is when you believe you're so special nobody would dare touch you—*regardless* of what you're doing. This goes beyond reliance on the social rules that make people leave you alone (failures two and four). It shades into intentionally acting like a cretin—regardless of your self-justification for it.

I have horror stories about deceased people, who believed that nobody would touch them. Believing they were untouchable and—if anyone dared—they could take care of themselves, these people engaged in what turned out to be suicidally stupid and aggressive behavior in the wrong places.[10] These aren't movie scenes. These are people who died in frenzies of blood and pain that make the *Casino* stabbing look warm and fuzzy.

Two is the assumption that whatever you are doing is so important you can ignore the rest of the world. Usually with that supposition comes the belief people will leave you alone until you're finished, and you're safe doing it. Using a real life example: Walking down the while street texting. Or worse, texting while driving. Using *Casino* as an example, Mr. Cross-Pen-Piercing was picking up on a woman to the exclusion of noticing his environment. *Not* a smart thing to do if you're in a place where wise guys are known to hang out, especially when there are two of them standing at the bar right by you.

Failure number three is thinking a situation is over when you deem you've won. This type of failure has become particularly endemic in our fast-paced world. We want it over and done with *now*, so we don't have to deal with it anymore. Putting this crudely, "Now that you've got your nut, it's over." Yeah, well, it doesn't always work that way.

Often people who have an overabundance of failures one and two get a double dose of three. Basically, they lash out and figure that's that. They've dealt with this jackass, so they turn back to whatever important business they had before this peon showed up and dared to bother them. That's what Pen Neck did.

Turning one's back is a cut-off gesture. It indicates the interaction is done (such as your walking away from the counter in a store or deli). Another meaning is you don't wish to deal with a person (turning your back to your spouse in bed). In certain circumstances, however, a cut off is an insult and sign of contempt. In a conflict or dangerous situations, it's a great way to get blindsided—just like in *Casino*.

Violent people have a habit of circling back on you—unless you've turned your back on them, then they'll just come straight at you. In their culture, it's a sign of disrespect. (We will go into how to safely extract yourself from such a situation later.) For now, learn to accept: The situation *isn't* over until everyone involved *deems* it's over. In case you missed it, I just gave you an important safety tip about survival. Certain people wait with shotguns in the shadows near your parking spot. That's

---

10   While I don't normally talk about the bad stuff in my past, I can give you an example: The 2001 murder of Cynthia Garcia in Mesa, Arizona, by members of the Hell's Angels. She'd gone to their clubhouse, gotten drunk, and became verbally abusive to the chapter president. She was beaten into unconsciousness, thrown in the trunk of the car, driven out to the desert, and murdered.

Miller brought to Conflict Communications the strategies and comfort levels of violence and conflict. It is a simple but profound model. One that will help you understand how people often win by simply escalating one step above your comfort zone.

Most people are nice. They follow the rules, they try and get along. This is a good thing. It makes the world a better place. But . . .

- Nice people fall to the manipulator.
- The manipulator crumbles under the assertive. (I know what you're doing, knock it off!)
- The assertive shrinks before the aggressive (barking, howling, drooling in your face).
- The aggressive have no plan for the assaultive (decks someone).
- The assaultive are unprepared for the homicidal.

First, familiarity with one level does not prepare you for handling the next.

Second, if someone is comfortable using a level that *doesn't* mean they can handle the same coming *back* at them. Take for example, someone who won't hesitate to hit people who are not likely to strike back. That doesn't mean he or she is a good fighter. This simple fact has strong influence on who that person targets with this behavior. Many an assaultive person has fallen before a better fighter.

Third, although people may occasionally pop up to the next level, they tend to routinely function on a lower level. This is their real comfort zone. It is the threat of taking it to the next level that gives their strategy credence. For example, an aggressive person gets by on the threat of assault. But in the same vein if you confront a manipulative person, he's going to swell up about his innocence (faux-assertive).

Fourth, while people can often pop up one level, two levels up and beyond people begin to lose knowledge, facts, and experience and replace them with mythology. (Usually, those people are monsters.) They are often unprepared to handle these kinds of strategies.

Fifth, directly quoting Miller, " . . . people comfortable with a high level of violence have learned to skip steps in the escalation."

Commenting on the fifth, I'll add,
a) that's why they're seen as unpredictable and scary;
b) they've learned to rely on this strategy;
c) once you know it, it's as predictable as normal escalation.

the other problem with engaging in violence—the consequences may not be legal.

Awareness 'fail' number four is— and this wraps back to both violence dynamics and the previous points—*do not* assume everyone does it the way you do things back home.

Certain behavior may work in certain areas, but it is not universal. Sometimes and in some places, the only way to keep from becoming a statistic is to know where you are and what the rules are. Then *follow* them. Your survival isn't based on how much of a thug you are, but how well you can keep from irritating the wrong people. This especially means expecting someone else to follow your rules about the appropriate response to your actions.

The late Richard Jeni had a comedy routine that started with the story of his getting punched "without warning" in Louisiana.[11] He then proceeded to explain New York pre-fight etiquette. First, you introduce yourself. ("Do you know who the fuck I am?") Then you ask the other person to introduce himself. ("Who the fuck are you?") He continues through street-fighting etiquette to gales of laughter. Because of this laughter, people often overlook a key point. This is when he mentions that after a half hour—of this New York ritual—no violence has occurred. There are all kinds of huffing and puffing, sturm und drang, but *no* physical violence.

This is why he was so shocked when the guy slugged him. He was from

---

11   "Crazy From the Heat," 1995

a place where verbal aggression and insults are not only the accepted norm, but are a way to deflect and deter physical violence. Whereas, the Louisianan was from a place where the rules state you don't say or do certain things unless you are ready to rock and roll. In fact, in some places saying such things is assumed to be a pre-attack indicator. As in: It's a *war cry*.

In such places, everyone knows the rules. If you weren't about to physically attack, you *wouldn't* have said it. So the other guy has no hesitation about driving your nose through the back of your skull.

Jeni didn't get punched for what he said. He got punched because he was in a New York state of mind while in Louisiana. When in Louisiana, do as the Louisianans. Or advice Jeni should have followed: When in Louisiana don't act like you're in New York—no matter how much time you spend in the Big Apple.

Tying this back to violence dynamics, when we are emotionally distressed we revert to these subconscious habits, behavior, and assumptions, as well as customary thinking. That's the other part of our brain activating (and if we're not careful taking over). We laugh at Jeni and gasp in horror at the pen-stabbing scene in *Casino*, but both are examples of the same mechanism. Someone defaulting to a certain behavior and assuming it's going to work to get the desired results.

Not only do we have expectations about what will work, but we also have another shadow set of expectations. Something we're loath to admit, yet those thoughts have a powerful influence on our decision to behave in a specific way. That is: We expect the worst that can happen when something doesn't work. That's the flip side of this behavioral coin. Looking at both Jeni and *Casino*, we assume the worst either man expected was counter verbal aggression. "Fuck me? No. Fuck you!" If the person doesn't flat-out get away with verbal aggression, the worst that usually happens is voices are raised, insults fly, and unpleasant emotions abound.

This is the *normal* cost for someone's bad behavior. And if we're being honest about it that's no cost at all. Despite the overemphasis on emotional trauma in pop psychology, yelling, posturing, and potty mouth words *are* an acceptable cost. I'm a prick to him, he's a goon right back at me. After dicks are measured, we go on our ways convinced the other guy is the sleazeball. End of story.

You're not *supposed* to pay such a high price for being a jackass. Giving oneself permission to be a jerk is supposed to be safe. That's why people get so freaked out about Mr. Pen-in-the-Throat. They know the cost of their bad behavior—it's hurt feelings. It is *not* supposed to be waking up in the hospital (or not waking up at all). Believing the only cost will be an emotional butt ache is one of those autopilot assumptions that can catapult you into a violent situation. You need to be able to recognize it in *yourself* and *others*. Someone cuts you off in traffic, and you flip them off. Next thing you know, you're involved in a road-rage incident. Yeah, but then there's that gun you have with you. So now what do you do?

I cannot stress enough how we follow these guidelines reflexively when we *fall* into that part of our brains. We act without thinking about any possible reactions other than what we expect. Both Jeni and Mr. Impromptu-Tracheotomy assumed their actions would have results—within what was normal to them—parameters. In fact, both assumed the worst that could happen would involve Jeni's etiquette about posturing. As such, both not only willfully *engaged* in the actions that provoked the attack, but were caught unprepared for the level of response.

Having pointed this out, there's more bad news. It wasn't that they weren't aware of what they were doing. They knew *exactly* what they were doing—they were going for the win. It was the fact something worse could happen that *never* entered their minds. Without this knowledge, there was no incentive for them *not* to behave the way they did. This is where most people screw the pooch when it comes to their self-defense claims. Not expecting it to go physical, they engage in all kinds of behavior that creates and escalates the situation. When this behavior is revealed, it blows their self-defense defense (yeah, that was deliberate) up and out of the ocean in miniscule fragments.

This is not just a situational awareness failure, but a crash and burn. (We'll go into it more later.) A huge part of situational awareness is being cognizant of your own internal landscape, so you can stay in control of yourself to better influence the situation and make good decisions.

Another extremely common version—especially among the young—is to go to a place where normal rules don't apply. They proceed to act as if there are no rules at all. I call this the Disneyland State of Mind.[12] It's a fast track to screwed. I've spent a lot of time out where the wild things play. As such I can guarantee you, while there might be fewer rules, they are more *savagely* enforced. I have seen some extremely brutal beatings, shootings, and stabbings result from someone deciding there are no rules

---

12   I coined the term Disneyland State of Mind (DSOM) after reading Lawrence Gonzales's *Deep Survival*. He used the term Vacation State of Mind (which is what I call "Hermit Crab Mindset"). DSOM or Hermit Crab both assume safety outside one's normal environment. The Disneyland State of Mind, however, is a pernicious variation in that it mixes that with someone's perceived right to have fun. DSOM usually crosses into illegal and dangerous behavior (e.g., drunk driving, wandering the streets while high, partying with criminals and violent people, and other such behavior). The problem with the DSOM is how often the danger is considered part of the fun. There is a rather disturbing video on YouTube called, "Set Yourself Free." It is an anti-slacking video, but also works with how things go bad with DSOM—if you were to add booze and drugs.

because they are away from home—or in party mode. And I've also encountered rapes, assaults, and deaths from this same attitude. (Partly because of how fast that state of mind can get hostile and violent when interrupted or told no.)

The good news is most violence comes with instructions on how to avoid it. *If* you let yourself hear these instructions, you will be safe. It's when all the things we've talked about get in the way of your listening that you'll get into trouble. Believe me when I tell you—from personal experience—"fuck off" is not the appropriate response to "you better shut your mouth."

Still another version of situational awareness failure is not shifting mental gears when you are traveling through different environments. It sounds a lot like what I've already been saying, but it goes a level deeper. Bad things don't happen where you spend most of your time. So in effect, you go about your business usually via a combination of autopilot and a focus on the task at hand. Stepping outside of that environment and into a different one requires a change in your mental state. This change in environment can be as small as walking into a parking lot. You're not likely to be robbed when you're shopping in the supermarket. Your task at hand is shopping (and often talking on the phone). Your focus is elsewhere. And in that environment, that's *fine*.

You're also are not likely to get robbed while driving down the road at thirty-plus miles an hour. In both cases, you don't need to waste too much attention on the possibility of a robbery. You need to be paying attention to other stuff, like driving your vehicle.

But the time—and place—it takes to transition between those two safe environments is a "fringe area." A great deal of crime occurs in fringe areas, they're close enough to where people are, but far enough away the criminal can be successful. A large number of robberies take place in parking lots for this reason. Therefore, always look at a parking lot as a fringe area.

Your mental landscape needs to reflect any change in environment. You don't have to be ultra-alert or super paranoid all the time. All you need to do is pay attention when you're in areas where violence can be effectively used against you—usually without interruption. Next time you're in a parking lot, look to see how far someone is from you and guess how long it would take him to get to where you are (distance equals time). If a mugger were to magically appear next to you, he'd have at least that long to rob you before help could arrive.

Here's the good news: If you're a regular citizen kicking into alertness in a parking lot ordinarily takes less than four seconds, *total*. Even better, it doesn't interfere with your going to or from your car. You walk out the door and look around (two seconds). As you approach your car, you look around again (two seconds). If you really want to be tacti-cool, add another two seconds in the middle to look around. Situational awareness is *not* a life-changing burden; ordinarily, it's nothing more than looking around when you enter or leave an environment. If nothing is happening, go back to what you were doing. In other situations, it's a simple assessment of the environment and not being an idiot.

Overall, situational awareness is a huge part of avoiding violence. But I'd like to introduce you to a new idea: Situational awareness as a tactical consideration. For the record, I've come to despise the overuse and abuse of the word tactical. So, when I use the word, it's significant. I specifically want to start you thinking that way before the incident occurs. This upgrades it from tactical to strategic. Your actions to prevent a situation from developing are as much tactical considerations as anything you do *in* the situation. For a boatload of reasons, they become part of a larger strategy. Not only because those measures can keep you alive and out of trouble, but they change the way your behavior can come back to bite you in the butt in the aftermath.

The next 400 pages of this book are going to be expanding on the following 'simple' statement: You do *not* want to provoke an attack through conscious behavior based on bad subconscious assumptions.

So simple, so profound, so easy to step on your dick.

Your behavior must be consistent with any actions culminating in self-defense. If you act strategically beforehand, you're going to have an easier time explaining to the cops *why* what you did really was self-defense. For example, communicating you didn't want trouble combined with a good faith effort to withdraw, but he followed you. You did everything in your power to steer clear of it, and you can truthfully articulate what you did to avoid a physical confrontation.

And a big part of being able to think and act strategically will be to monitor your emotions so you can discover your default conflict behavior and subconscious expectations *before* you find yourself in a shit storm—then learn how to better control them in your daily life. Learn how to keep from telling someone to go screw himself before your (or his) life depends on that ability. If you can't do this in day-to-day circumstances, the lack of control will blow up in your face in a self-defense situation.

I use the *Casino* example because—once you get over the brutality of the physical attack—you can see what provoked it. It *wasn't* an innocent mistake. Nicky's so-called 'victim' went out of his way to be obnoxious, intimidating, verbally violent, and disrespectful. It just didn't pan out the way he expected it to. When I point out this deliberate action, the next response is usually, "Well, yes, but he didn't deserve that."

Deserve is a word I want you to drop when it comes to self-defense. In fact, I want you to flush it down the toilet. It is not only utterly subjective, but judgmental to a fault—usually in a very biased and selfish way. Your telling yourself you (or someone else) didn't deserve something is the exact same mechanism the person is using to decide you *did* deserve it. Deserve is a root cause of entirely too much violence and conflict, as well as a fast track to running into trouble. Yet people use it both as a shield and an excuse for their own bad behavior.

We tend to selfishly define the word deserve. Mr. Pen-in-the-Throat didn't deserve the assault. But since we're tossing that term around, De Niro's character didn't deserve to be verbally abused, either. Yet that's not what the victim thought. Right up until he was being stabbed, he was sure De Niro *did* deserve abuse for daring to interrupt him.

What I am saying is people are really fast to dish out what they think others deserve and equally fast to squeal about them *not* deserving the consequences. Oh by the way, notice the subtle shift of Mr. Pen-in-the-Throat back to victim in the previous paragraph? That was an example of both how subtly deserves manifests and how easy it is to justify bad behavior. Looking at that scene again if you're okay with one behavior, but not okay with the other, you better seriously check yourself out. That's a time bomb waiting to blow the plane of your self-defense claim from the sky.

The term deserve usually comes from that same emotional part that takes over just before violence erupts. The component that thinks fighting over feelings is a good idea. If you don't learn to recognize when that element is guiding your actions in your everyday world, there's *no way* in hell you're going to be able to control it when someone is barking and drooling in your face. Restating something, you don't deserve it is *exactly* the same type of thinking people use when they decide to kick your butt for disrespecting them. Stop and think about the implications of that for a second.

They have deemed you *deserve* a butt-kicking for what you said or did. They've set themselves up as victim, judge, jury, and executioner. You hurt them, so you *deserve* to be hurt. Odds are you thought he deserved what you said or did to him. And you're saying you don't deserve what he's going to do about it. So why's it bad when he does it, but okay when you do the same thing? How can you claim to be better than that other person when you're doing the exact same thing?

People who believe they don't deserve to be physically assaulted for their words or deeds also tend to be more verbally aggressive. They're just dishing out what everyone deserves. And there are a whole lot of people who believe their emotional states are an excuse to heap verbal and emotional abuse on the world. Their feelings are paramount. And if you are their target, you deserve it. The worst are the ones who insist this is their right to do this. With this belief, they've upgraded you deserve verbal abuse to a higher power. But *no one* has the right to respond physically.[13]

This behavior is especially pronounced in 'peaceful' protestors, who not only become verbally aggressive and disobey lawful orders, but mimic pre-attack behavior when they stand out of range of any retaliation. It's when they move into attack range and exhibit the same behavior that the police react. The protestors scream they don't deserve (or the police have no right) to a physical reaction. Particularly common to these situations is the insistence that they weren't going to attack—so their actions didn't merit a physical response.

So, since you're not likely to be out protesting anytime soon, why is knowledge of this important? You will encounter this *exact attitude* when you act in self-defense. They weren't attacking you! They didn't mean to hurt you! You had no right to lay hands on them! Be prepared for it. People like this are fast on the attack, but even faster at running to the cops when they lose.

Why am I spending so much time harping on all this psychology mumbo-jumbo? Well not only does everything I've said so far apply to you, but—I can almost guarantee—it's going to be what is motivating that guy who is up in your face. The ability to recognize these behavioral patterns from *both* sides is an important starting point in the skill to keep a situation from blowing up—better known as avoiding violence.

I've said it before, but I'll say it again: Emotions *are* contagious. Like the flu, if someone has the asshat-bug, there's a good chance you're going to catch it, too. This is what scuttles most self-defense claims. A huge part of this book helps you immunize yourself.

If it still blows up, you'll know you did everything right to keep a conflict from taking place. This—as you'll soon see—is more important than you think. Here's a small taste of that. Thinking you don't deserve something creates all kinds of social issues and also affects your ability to act. People who think they don't deserve or "he wouldn't dare . . ." are often caught flat footed. It's not just a freeze. There are about ten counties over before you reach freeze. It's shock and trauma that someone would *dare* physically attack them. They literally don't know what to do.

---

13   This kind of thinking is largely based on a concept popular among philosophers and political science majors, positive and negative rights. People who have to work for a living tend to look at someone espousing the concept like he or she is on drugs. As the idea can be easily argued against, positive and negative rights are seldom specifically mentioned. But it plays a significant part in many people's self-definition of rights, which is why talking to them about rights can be so confusing.

They're at a serious loss to know what to do. But often they don't freeze. In fact, what they try is to do is more of the same thing that got them slugged in the first place. For example, it's normal for someone who has just been punched for being a jackass to jump back and become a louder, bigger jackass. This can be a form of saving face (barking as he backs away). The physical part of the incident is over. But, it can be building oneself up to attack to avenge the insult. That other person *deserves* to be attacked for attacking him.

Later, the same guy claims self-defense because the other guy hit him first. Whereas, the other guy will claim self-defense because it all started when he got hit back. (~sigh~ Sometimes I despair for my species.) Both sides are convinced they didn't deserve such treatment while the other guy did deserve it.

There's still another reason to drop the word deserve from your self-defense vocabulary. If you're thinking he deserves punishment for daring to attack you, it's entirely too easy to cross into excessive force. You just have to get that last lick in to punish. Of course, it won't be a fully formed thought; more an emotional you *son-of-a-bitch* as you pull that trigger one more time while standing over him. The prosecutors have a word for that in most states of the U.S. . . . it's manslaughter. It'll be that last kick to punish him for attacking you that crosses the line into aggravated assault.

Those are just some of the reasons to get rid of the term deserve when it comes to self-defense. But in case you missed it, the biggest one is: Thinking in terms of deserve makes it *harder* to stay out of conflict and violence. Behavior that will cause a situation to escalate is pretty predictable. In fact, it's also common sense—you already *know* the social guidelines. Things like be polite, don't be rude, and don't call a guy with a gun a mofo. But when you think you don't deserve to be treated this way, it's *easy* to make these mistakes. Hell, being tired and cranky at the aftermath of a long day, you can easily slip into being the verbal aggressor. That's because your monkey brain takes over when you're confronted, challenged, or emotional.

Until you know about the monkey, you won't be able to control it. It will sneak in, take control for just a few seconds, and make you say or do something that is not in your best interests—something that throws you out of the line of a self-defense vindication. And just so you know, the monkey's often a coward. It'll say and do trash, then dive back into your subconscious, leaving you to deal with the aftermath. But at that very moment, these impulses will seem like the absolute best things you could possibly do. Knowing about these monkey-brain impulses allows you to control them, instead of the other way around.

If you doubt me on this let me ask you, "Have you ever flipped someone off while driving?" Have you ever had a bad day and snapped at someone? Have you ever just said to hell with it and done something you knew you shouldn't? This is the same mechanism. We *all* do it.

It's when we do it with the wrong people that things become violent. The trick is to get control of this behavior before you find yourself in such a situation. It is especially important if you've decided to carry a firearm or a knife. A monkey with a knife is never a good thing.

I know it may seem like we've wandered from what this book is going to show you, but we've still been at number three: Staying out of violence. It's a lot deeper subject than people know. And this lack of knowledge shades into deliberate ignorance when people think they already know everything about it.

But let's move onto another aspect of avoiding violence that is both a paradox and a disaster waiting to happen. That is: The willingness to use force usually means you *won't* have to. It is a paradox because our modern culture conditions us to believe violence attracts violence, and violence never solves anything. To hear one of the best ways *not* to have to use force is the *willingness* to use force flies in the face of these popular anti-violence memes.

When you reach the end of this book, you'll understand why. Also how to use the willingness to act to prevent violence. This chiefly means preventing the one-sided violence that will explode if a thug thinks you're scared or incapable of fighting back. (This is a specialized type of violence and, yes, we'll cover how to spot that's what you face.) When the cost of tangling with you is blood, many people will choose easier targets.

Conversely, the willingness to use force is a disaster waiting to happen. Why? Because of the way self-defense most often crosses into illegal violence. That occurs when people fail to recognize that their would-be attacker has *changed* his mind. His commitment has wavered. Seeing the willingness in your demeanor, the aggressor *stops* the behavior that is creating the danger. Put in simple English: The circumstances have changed. You are no longer in *immediate* danger.

That also means if you still pull the trigger, you are *not* acting in self-defense. Until you train yourself to accurately observe and assess situations, your perceptions are likely to be about three seconds *behind* what is really happening. That's how you can find yourself trying to explain to cops, prosecutors, and the jury why his being shot in the back was still self-defense.

Way too many people are obsessed with not being able 'to go.' When you're trained, an even bigger problem is *not* being able to stop. No matter where you are in the process, you *need* to be able to abort action when the danger ceases. If you don't, the prosecutor is going to have you for lunch.

Slight change of emphasis: There are a lot of people out there willing to hurt you to get their way. Some are willing to kill you to get what they want. Oooooohhhh, scary. That's why people want to learn to be able to defend themselves. But here's a reality break: People who are willing to die to get their way are as scarce as turkey teeth.

Odds are good you didn't wake up in a war zone this morning. You won't be facing professional soldiers who are committed to killing you before you kill them. You're not living in squalor where shadowy organizations recruit and indoctrinate people with promises of economic support for their families, an immediate trip to heaven, and fame for themselves if they become suicide bombers. You're not dealing with someone who wants to commit suicide by cop. And if you're lucky, you're not dealing with deranged meth heads or someone in a psychotic break. These conditions are going to seriously influence the commitment of any would-be attacker. When you're willing to use force to protect yourself, it is not uncommon for someone—even someone who is flying at you—to suddenly realize, oops, bad idea. When they have this epiphany, they usually try to break off the attack.

And when they break off, *so do you*. Not only has the immediate threat passed, but if you keep going *you* have become the aggressor. I know of no easier way for a prosecutor to hang you by the balls than crossing this line. It's *that* important.

But before we worry about the prosecutor, let's look at the event itself. I can't even begin to tell you the number of times I've seen people break off an attack when it started hurting too much. The challenge *is* to let them go. It's a challenge because your monkey brain will want complete victory. But chasing him down the street takes it out of self-defense.

I've also seen on multiple occasions seemingly berserk, out-of-control chargers suddenly look like they ran into a force field when the target whipped around and turned into a werewolf on the spot. The impending attacker goes from a dead run to a wild backward leap in 0.5 seconds.

As an aside, while legitimately out-of-control does actually happen on occasion, it's usually an intimidation tactic. Granted, it's an incredibly effective tactic for dealing with people less willing to use violence than the pseudo-berserk. But when facing someone who is sincere about stopping the threat, their dangerous behavior usually disappears faster than a politician's promise. And when it stops, you stop.

Let's now look at people who break off an attack when things start going wrong. I've seen them try to turn tail and run when it starts hurting. I've seen them turn, hunch up, and stagger away. I've seen them collapse and curl up. I've seen people who have been shot and stabbed stop, turn, and walk away. And most of all, I've seen punchers jump back from a counter-puncher and start talking all kinds of trash. In *all* of these cases, the immediate danger has passed. It is here where it's really hard to *let* them go. In an adrenalized and fearful state, if he's right there and in front of you, he's still attacking, right? NO!

Way too often people keep defending themselves long after the other guy has stopped attacking. Hell, I've seen people chase someone who attacked them down the street and still try to claim self-defense. I've also seen people come at an attacker so hard, they *provoke* a self-defense response from the guy who was just threatening or attacking them. I've not only seen it happen, but (as we'll discuss in the self-defense law chapter) there's often a statute subsection that nails both parties. I cannot stress this enough: Once the immediate threat has passed, you are *no longer* acting in self-defense.

The problem is, in the heat of the moment, this change from aggressor to defense on the part of that former antagonist can be very difficult to spot—particularly if you don't know to look for it. But it *will* show up on the security camera. And the prosecutor *will* use your continued actions to send you to prison. Not for self-defense, but for assault, attempted murder, manslaughter, or on countless other felony charges. This book will help you know when to stop.

Okay, I know it seems we've been wandering around like a drunken sailor on shore leave, but we're still listing the things this book will do for you. The fifth thing this book will do is prepare you to know when it's time to act.

Here is an important point. *Some* violence is going to happen no matter what. I often tell cops around ninety percent of violent behavior can be prevented, but there still is that other ten percent. But those are professionals who deal with more crap in a month than you will in your entire lifetime. As a civilian with no duty to act (such as cops have) your numbers for "avoidable" are going to go up into the high nineties. That's why cops and prosecutors will give you such a hairy eyeball about things going sideways. Billions of people manage to get through the day without being involved in violence. Where did you mess up? What were you doing wrong that put you into conflict? Cynical as this may sound, doubtful officials are usually right. Mom was right, it takes two to fight.

This is an example of spreading the strategic umbrella to cover both before and after. It's important to be able to explain what the circumstances were and why you weren't fighting. Yet given that be able to explain why violence was not only the necessary answer, but the best one. To do that, you first have to know and recognize those specific conditions. And in doing so, you increase your chances of surviving the incident. In circumstances where it's going to happen no matter what, your safety depends on taking control of when and on what level the violence takes place.

The problem is, to the uninformed, it looks like you were the aggressor. Being able to explain your reasons becomes critical when you *have* to act, not exactly preemptively,[14] but before the high level of danger you're facing has fully manifested. The kind of danger where if you wait that long, you're dead. This also is helpful because there are certain circumstances where you will have to use force, and it will *not* be self-defense. (We'll touch on these as we go.) If you have a use of force that is necessary—but is not self-defense—don't screw it up by calling it self-defense.

Although not specific to the subject, this same information will help overcome the freeze people are so scared of. Here's a news flash: While there are times freezing will dig your grave, most of the time freezing will keep you from getting your butt kicked. Why? Because you're not tossing the wrong body language signals or saying the wrong thing. This takes it out of the my-dick-wasn't-big-enough moaning so many people do over their freezing when confronted by an aggressive person in a social situation.

"I froze!"

"Were you spitting your teeth the next morning?"

"No."

"Then what are you whining about?"

"Well he was in my face, threatening me, and I didn't do anything." "Yeah let's look at what you didn't do. You didn't end up in the ER. You didn't end up in jail. And you didn't end up pouring wood glue over your back, waiting until it dried to peel it off and pull the broken glass out after rolling around on the bar floor, fighting the guy. How's this a bad thing?"

People, no blood, no foul. What's more important than your ego is unnecessary physical violence did *not* occur. You can't be thrown in jail or sued for a fight that didn't happen. On the other hand, a fight that did happen . . .

The sixth thing this book will help you do is dealing with the legal aftermath of what you did. As I said before, this book is *not* legal advice. While I am a court-recognized expert witness, I am *not* a lawyer. Yet, it is because of my dealings with court cases, I tell you an important distinction: There is a *difference* between the law and our legal system. Add that one to your collection of graffiti and tattoos.

Laws vary from state to state, and interpretation varies from district

---

14   The legal concepts expressed here are by in large very Americentric. One of the differences between British common law and that in the U.S. is the former allows for preemptive strikes if the person reasonably believes he or she is about to be attacked. But like the right to self-defense, that's not as simple as it sounds.

to district. Things allowed in Texas will get you convicted in any other of the forty-nine states. New York technically doesn't have a self-defense law, but it does have a justifiable homicide statute. California and Massachusetts have seemingly reasonable self-defense laws, but their interpretation is often draconian. Some states have a stand-your-ground law, others enforce duty to retreat. You *must know* the rules of engagement in your state. I can't help you with that. You need to talk to an attorney *before* any incident and have him or her explain your state's self-defense laws and what they mean to you.

There's another reason to keep in mind the phrase: Law isn't the legal system. You may have acted *within* the law, but you still have to deal *with* the legal system. And that system has all kinds of policies, procedures, and agendas, as well as monetary, political, and career pressures influencing it. There are games within games going on inside it. What is to you the most horrible thing that has ever happened is just another day at the office for those in the legal system.

There is no more obvious example of this than the Trayvon Martin-George Zimmerman shooting and trial. On the night of the shooting, the Sanford Police Department contacted the office of the district attorney (DA) and asked, "Do we arrest?" They explained the evidence they had, and the DA—rightly—told them no. There wasn't enough evidence either way. Even gathering more evidence (with Zimmerman's complete cooperation) failed to produce enough proof to make a winnable case. That and *no* other reason was why he was not arrested immediately or throughout the initial investigation.[15]

Yet the media (and social activists) got hold of it, and the story went national. From there on, it was a political and media-incited circus. The case was taken away from the Sanford police and the DA. A special Florida prosecutor was appointed. Pretty much after that decision, the state *had* to prosecute. Using exactly the same evidence on which the original DA said there was not enough information to prosecute, the special prosecutor's office lost the case.

Incidentally, the Zimmerman case, while exhibiting how much politics and the media influence our legal system shows something more important—at least important to you. That is: *Why* being able to articulate what happened and *why* your use of force was justified is *so* important. While you can argue with people until you're blue in the face about whether or not Zimmerman should even have been arrested,

---

15   Once you are arrested, the clock starts ticking for the prosecution. The Sixth Amendment guarantees the right to a speedy trial. The prosecution must have the evidence to prosecute. They don't arrest until they have it. This often delays arrests while investigators compile evidence. Long delays before trial *after* someone has been arrested come from the defense filing for extension(s).

articulation and a good lawyer is what *got* him *acquitted*. Overall, I refer to our legal system as a meat grinder. What you're going to learn in this book will help keep you from getting chewed up in it.

Like I said, this isn't legal advice, but this book is the first of its kind. It's a first in that I'm showing you the connection between your pre-incident actions and the legal aftermath. I'm explaining the common mistakes people make that involve them in illegal aggression and how those errors can be turned against you. I'm giving you a way to communicate to your lawyer why he is defending someone who acted *within* the law. I'm providing critical information you can pass on to your attorney to keep you from being convicted of a crime you did not commit.

But most of all, I'm helping keep *you* from committing that crime in the first place. Another way of putting it: Despite what you will learn from this book, you will *still* be moving through the minefield that is our legal system. You can pass through a minefield using care and caution, it just takes work and a lot of patience. Refusing to invest the time and effort usually results in loud noises and wet and sticky messes.

The seventh and final thing this book will do is help you with the emotional and social aftermath. Remember I said that if you have to act in self-defense, your life as you know it is over? The individual you were before you had to pull that trigger, plunge that knife, gouge out someone's eyeball, or bite his throat out is not going to be the same person ever again.

Violence. Changes. You.

It is a doorway. Once you walk through it, you will never be the same. A different part of you awakens. A part people, who haven't been there, often fear or misunderstand. It will change how people treat you. It will change how you interact with people, how you see the world, and whom you are comfortable around. Information you never suspected will come flooding into your consciousness. Not always in a good way, either. You'll discover things about yourself you never knew. And not all of this will be fun.

You'll struggle with trying to redefine yourself. Are you still a good person after you've taken someone's life? Are you a bad person? How are those in your life going to react to those same questions? Will you hate yourself? Will you be cast out from your social group? Will you go to hell for what you did? And physically and psychologically, you also can find yourself unexpectedly sobbing or experiencing flashbacks. This is some of the turbulence you encounter after a self-defense situation. Or—and this is a possibility, too—you might feel bad for not feeling anything. Realistically, you might never feel anything. Or nothing for five years, then all of a sudden it hits you from out of nowhere.

You are your own unique and individual person; what happens with you also will be specific to you. But a large part of coping with what you did is the knowledge you actually *had* to do it—knowing that given the circumstances it was either you or him. There's a big difference between being right and self-righteous; when it comes to hurting others, it really helps to be the former not the latter.

I added social to the list because it's something many people don't consider. You can (and probably will) lose friends over such an incident—*especially* if it involves lethal force. Massad Ayoob calls this the "mark of Cain" syndrome. You have broken one of society's primary rules, you have taken a human life. Not in some far-off land, but here at home. People who know you will be uncomfortable in your presence. You'll feel distances develop in your relationships. Many people will quietly float away. Still others will have a morbid fascination about what you did. They'll want to know what it felt like. (These types can be particularly annoying.)

The stresses and strains of a self-defense aftermath are many. This takes place immediately post-incident. But there are long-term effects, as well. You must plan for these, lest acting in self-defense destroys you.

Many people find long-term comfort in helping others. These philanthropic endeavors are less about donating money to help faceless people and more about going out amongst humanity and helping people who struggle. Still others find comfort in isolation. And there are those who find the greatest comfort in family and friends. Again, it depends on who you are. But there will be long-term results.

So with all of this in mind, let me give you a different set of standards about self-defense. In order to win in a self-defense situation, you must succeed on five different levels:

1) You must be able to act in a timely manner.
2) You must be able to stop the threat.
3) You must be cleared of all criminal charges.
4) You must be cleared of all civil charges.
5) You must be able to pass through all the emotional and social changes that will arise.

If you fail in any of these, you've lost. This book is going to help you win in all five areas. But perhaps the biggest win of them all is after reading this, you'll be much better at keeping situations from escalating to where you need to physically defend yourself. Safety without the hassle of violence . . . yeah, baybeee!

CHAPTER 2

Self-defense isn't only about the physical. When I say this, many people assume I'm talking about the mindset you need during the physical act. That's still focusing on the physical. I'm talking about expanding your understanding to the connection between what happens before, during, and after an incident. This overview is critical for your survival and success. Because not all the dangers of self-defense are physical.

—**MM**

The Lines of Self-defense

Let's start by shifting how you view self-defense. Imagine it as a square marked out on the floor. Now stand inside that square. Look very closely at those lines. You have to *stay* inside those boundaries for your actions to qualify as legitimate self-defense. We'll go into what those lines are in a second. But right now, knowing about this square is an important first step. Step outside that square—*in any direction*—and what you're doing will *no longer* be considered self-defense.

(As an aside: This is also a multi-tiered model. The higher the level of force, the smaller and more restrictive the square becomes. Therefore, the easier it is to cross a line. But that's another we'll-talk-about-it-later-and-in-more-depth topic.) What you need to know now [even with the bigger, lower squares] is: *Most* people cross a line.)

The four lines people cross that take their actions out of the self-defense justification are:

1) The threat isn't physical;
2) The threat isn't immediate;
3) They cross into excessive force;
4) They participate in the creation and escalation of the situation.

It could be *this* line you cross. It could be *that* one. Or you can cross multiple lines. It could happen before it goes to a physical confrontation, afterward, or somewhere in the middle. It can be something as simple as you turning around and coming back instead of leaving. (Yes, it happens when the other person gets in that dig as you're walking away.) It could be your involvement in a conflict that goes physical. It could be as complex as how adrenal stress effects your perceptions in a crisis.

It depends on the circumstances and the people involved. There's a reason I tell people, "Self-defense is a small target in a big landscape of violence. It's easy to miss." Putting it into these terms, it's easy to step outside the square.

That's why it's important to think of self-defense as a square on the floor. Somehow or the other, most people step *outside* that square. Hell, realistically with most violence people aren't anywhere close to the square. Often they are actively fighting. That is to say—unlike self-offense—they had no delusions about not being violent. They came intending to kick some butts. Fighting is not only *way* outside the box, but—realistically—they have become part of the problem.

The same goes for being self-offensive, these people actively put themselves into a conflict. As such, they are part of the problem. Yet, they've come with neither the willingness to fight nor compromise. Unlike fighters, though, they are willfully blind to the fact their words and actions provoke violence. They're also blind—as I'll explain later—to the fact they are *being violent.*

Here's some hints about when your actions are actually self-defense:

A) Trouble comes to you;

B) It won't let you leave;

C) You're not provoking the other person.[16]

There are many people who are willing to confront you—and they are downright nasty when they do it. They are not willing, however, to physically fight. Nor are they willing to lose. Something else they are not willing to do is calmly negotiate for what they want.

They aggressively get up into other people's faces, trying to intimidate while claiming they weren't intending physical violence. (In fact, they weren't—they just wanted to win.) They're playing a game of chicken. If it works, they win. When this behavior provokes a physical response, they claim the other person "just attacked" them. Some try to assert what happened next was self-defense. Sorry, that wasn't SD. What they did qualifies as 'self-offense.' They went out of their way to create, participate in, and escalate the situation with their aggressive, confrontational, hostile, and demanding behavior. This is where the mental disconnect ensues. Because they *didn't* go there intending *physical violence,* they don't consider their behavior as contributing to it. As far as they're concerned, it's the other person's fault—even though they actively provoked the situation. Claiming self-defense is the same as their original aggression. It allows them to believe they are the aggrieved party, regardless of how obnoxious and condemning they were when they confronted you.

Common to self-offense is the adamant refusal to compromise, negotiate, or even be civil. Why should they? You're wrong. They're right. This self-righteousness is part of why they don't feel they have to be civil. As Jesse Alcorta (the man who came up with this term) says, "It's as if by their words alone you're going to have an epiphany that they're right," no matter how nasty, aggressive, and insulting they are.

The worst is when it is from strangers demanding you change your behavior to suit them. There is no established relationship or 'economy' (give and take) between the two of you. They simply walk up and demand you change your behavior to satisfy their wants. Then they are done with you. There is a willful blindness about how insulting, aggressive, and demeaning their behavior is to the target of their wrath. Or how many boundaries they have crossed in order to confront.   →

16   Alain Burrese breaks the principles of self-defense into 1) innocence, 2) imminence, 3) proportionality, 4) avoidance.

The classic example of self-offense is the person who leaves his or her property to pound on the neighbor's door because of a noisy party. That person, has left his or her own property (where there are certain legal rights) willfully traveled to confront, gone onto another's property (territory) without invitation, pounded on the door, confronted— and when told to back off—upgraded to trespassing. Refusing to leave and escalating the confrontation, the situation becomes a physical altercation.

If this person has the bad luck to win, he or she can claim self-defense all he or she wants, but it's *not* going to fly. Not to the police, not to the courts, not to anyone who isn't a friend or family member. Whether they intended it or not, their aggressive behavior and refusal to negotiate resulted in violence.

The challenge you face is *not* to fall into the trap of being self-offensive— while telling yourself you're defending yourself.

Going out to meet it? Better double check where that not-participating line is because there's a good chance it's now behind you.

For the moment, though, let's say action *started* as self-defense. But because of fear, anger, and adrenaline, it didn't end that way. It crossed a different line. What do I mean cross a line? It's *not* that final punch, last kick, finishing knife slash, concluding bullet. It's usually the last five *or* six. Welcome to the excessive force part of the evening.

Now if this was some dirtbag losing his cool and stomping someone that would be one thing. But these are ordinary people who—in the heat of the moment—*sincerely believe* that jumping up and down on the chest of some guy they've downed after he attacked them *is* self-defense.

Later they'll claim fear and (maybe) adrenaline made them do it. While it is true they were scared and adrenalized that *doesn't* mean they acted within self-defense parameters. Self-defense *stops* when the threat *stops*. That can be an easy line to cross when you're scared and adrenalized. Important safety tip: When it comes to self-defense, adrenaline is a bitch. But that *doesn't* mean you're adrenaline's bitch. That is unfortunately a popular meme in certain self-defense circles. When you're adrenalized, you're unable to function. You can only do gross movements. Adrenaline will make you forget all your training. When you're scared and adrenalized, you won't be able to (read 'shouldn't have to') think about all these things, yada, yada, yada.

Hey, you know what? First time you had sex, you were both all excited and not that good at it. But gosh, golly, gee, the more you do it, the better you get about controlling your excitement and not being such a fumbling, bumbling case (as you were the first time). Same thing with adrenaline, the more you practice your skills under the influence of adrenaline, the better you'll become at functioning while adrenalized. Duh!

This especially means you being able to think, assess, and react appropriately to stay in the SD square *while* adrenalized. Helping you learn to control yourself while adrenalized is not the intent of this book, but it is a side benefit. You should know, I'm a fan of adrenal stress training (when done correctly) and learning how to control yourself while adrenalized. Why? You should know the popular SD meme that you can't think while adrenalized is a fast track to becoming someone's prison bitch. Again, why? Because it encourages sloppiness, lack of self-control, and out-of-control aggression.

Here's a hint: The inability to *stop yourself* because you didn't train to do so will send you speeding over the excessive force line. How? Repeatedly stomping that downed guy who just attacked you will seem like a great idea to your out-of-control, adrenalized self. It's not. It's in fact extremely illegal. But that's not the only way excessive force can manifest. Like I said before, many people's *honest beliefs* spur their illegal and excessive actions. Where'd they get this idea? Well, a lot of places. Hollywood. The Internet—especially from forums. And their own imaginations. But often, it's because that's what their self-defense instructor *told them.*

People don't usually get these wild-assed ideas on their own. And yes, I have witnessed instructors teaching all kinds of murderous stuff then calling these techniques self-defense. Way more common—especially with martial arts—I've seen fighting strategies and training marketed *as* self-defense education. Where this becomes extreme is with so-called combatives and mixed martial arts.

There's a reason I tell people "most of what you think you know about this topic is advertising." These instructors aren't teaching you self-defense, they are teaching you fighting *marketed* as self-defense. This is rebranding an old product under the more socially acceptable label of self-defense—and it's a great way to get arrested if you believe it and use what you've been taught.

Why is knowing about relabeling important? Fighting is a specific form of social violence that comes chock full of subconscious rules, tactics, and limitations. These strategies, *while appropriate* for that kind of violence, can get you killed in a self-defense situation. (And yes, we'll go into that, too.) The problem is: If that's what you're trained to do, that's what you'll *try* to do.

There's a simple formula here. Empty-hand training equals training for social violence. To most people that means fighting. It also really applies to *self-offense*. (As some people look at training as a means to back up their right to behave badly.) Self-defense *isn't* about fighting over social or emotional issues. It's about protecting your body. Recognizing that is not only a game changer, but it steers you away from so many of the traps people fall into regarding use of self-defense training.

Fighting also is illegal. No cop, prosecutor, or jury is going to look at a fight as anything other than what it was—illegal violence. The only people who believe it was self-defense are the ones who pay for that training.[17] The biggest danger lies in mixed martial arts, combatives, uber-aggressive reality-based self-defense training, and Filipino and Indonesian martial arts. These systems have a high probability of injuring someone when applied out in the streets.

Not in the sense of the 'big bad streets' of macho fantasy, but hard concrete meets skull danger. The same ground-and-pound one can safely do in a padded ring can quickly turn into manslaughter on a cement floor. (And yes, I've encountered ground-and-pound actions promoted as part of a "self-defense solution.")

Knives are lethal force instruments. That means their use is limited by the *same* rules as a gun. You don't use a knife unless you are in "immediate danger of death or grievous bodily injury." This lethal force instrument designation also includes using a closed knife as a strike enhancer. (Bet your guru didn't teach you that.)

Flat-out wrong information is one thing. A far bigger problem is what their instructors *didn't* tell students about self-defense. Mostly because the instructor *didn't* know it him- or herself. That's what started this book: *By claiming self-defense, you are confessing to a crime.* Did your self-defense instructor ever mention this little detail? That's sort of important don't you think? It's illegal to strike, stab, shoot, kill, or cripple your fellow citizens. *Never* forget that—because that's *exactly* what you are doing when you act in self-defense.

Yet your right to defend yourself has been repeatedly upheld in court and under your state laws. This is where a lot people get hung up. Self-defense is a *legal paradox*. Yes, you have the legal right to defend your person, but stabbing, shooting, or beating someone is *still* illegal. A technically wrong statement, but a good way to understand this idea is: With self-defense, you're not forgiven for taking a life, you're just *not* prosecuted for it. (But there's a damned good chance, you'll be sued for it or face other consequences.) We'll go into it more later, but for now the self-defense legal defense is basically you saying you had good and necessary reason to do the horrible thing you did. This is why it's so important to stay *inside* the square. If your actions were all taken within that square, you *can* defend them. You *were* justified to act.

But, even if you stayed in that square, you're going to deal with a lot of folks who won't believe it. Some you're going to have to convince. Others will try to convince everyone else that you didn't. And don't be surprised when they go out of their way to lie (especially by omission) to sell that idea.

17   This fighting being called a self-defense approach also is a huge factor in students leaving. They came to learn self-defense. They don't know what to call what they're being taught, but they know it isn't SD.

So now that you understand the problems of coming out of the square, let's look at the square itself. The first line people cross to leave legitimate self-defense protection is when they are *not* defending their bodies. Most commonly they defend their emotions, self-esteem, and imagined social status.

I often explain this in terms of a wheelbarrow. Can you put what caused the physical violence into a wheelbarrow? With most violence, no. You cannot put your pride, your anger, your hurt feelings, or threatened self-esteem into a wheelbarrow. You can, however, physically crawl into and sit in a wheelbarrow. If your body is being endangered, you *can* act. Yet, this is the most commonly crossed line when it comes to SD. People mistake their emotions for physical danger. There is a physical *sensation* with emotions. (They're called feelings for a reason.) That sensation convinces them their bodies are in danger when something else is going on. This is a small and subtle thing, but knowing it is very important for staying inside the SD square.

Here is something else you need to know. If the threat is not to you, in most states you *cannot* use lethal or extreme force to protect property. That is because human life is given priority over property. That means— in almost every state—you can't chase someone down the street while shooting at them after they steal something from you. You cannot stab someone for attacking your car. You can't beat someone for breaking something you own. The danger must be to *you,* not your possessions.

The second line people cross is when they are *not* reacting to an immediate threat to their bodies. Is the physical danger right now? It's *not* a maybe, could be, "he might. . ." or "I felt. . ." The physical danger has to be then and there and based on something *more tangible* than your emotions.

We'll go into immediate and immanent in another chapter. Right now I'm going to take a slight side track to introduce you to an important concept. I'd like you to poke yourself with your finger. I'm serious. It's important to show you a critical distinction. When you poke yourself, you feel that poke. Feeling is a *physical sensation.*

Your emotions, however, are *not* physical. They have *no* physical existence. They are an internal, subjective state produced entirely within your own consciousness. And yes, they alter your consciousness and ability to think. But they're not something you can put in a wheelbarrow.

Here's a big problem. When most people are talking about their "feelings," they are *ascribing emotional descriptors* to an adrenaline rush. When you think you are being swept away by an emotion, you really feel it, right? No. The physical sensations you experience are because of an adrenaline dump and other physiological changes—*not* the emotion. You basically get the same sensations from adrenaline, but you ascribe good or bad to them through emotional interpretation and intensity.

This is significant because, from an internal perspective, your reality is being affected by these chemicals. Yes, adrenaline is a drug.[18] This drug influences what you perceive as real *and* true. When you have these sensations, you are not feeling the emotion—you are experiencing the physical effects of adrenaline. And one of the biggest effects of adrenaline is the sense of immediacy. This is why I call it the "Do It *NOW!*" hormone.

Here's where it gets tricky. We are designed to interpret the combination of external stimuli, internal interpretation, emotions, other parts of our brains activating, adrenaline's physical sensations, and sense of urgency as *reality*. We react to this turbo-charged combination *faster* than conscious thought. And we do it in absolute certainty that we are correct in our interpretation. Now this was a vital survival trait when lions, tigers, and bears were jumping out of the bushes and trying to eat us. In modern, civilized, rule-of-law society . . . not so much. Even though we are absolutely convinced what we feel is real, it may not be what is actually happening.

I make a distinction between reality and actuality. Reality is a person's subjective interpretation of what's happening. Actuality is what shows up on tape. I do this because when you're under adrenal stress, it's real easy to react to *your* reality, instead of what is actually happening. Remember when you're adrenalized, you're on drugs and that's your reality. Every fiber in your being will be screaming to act according to your reality. You can—and will—believe that *any* threat is an immediate danger to your body. I cannot tell you how many times I've seen people react to words like, "Well, what if I kick your ass?" as though it is already happening. Then try to claim self-defense. But what's on the video is their closing and assaulting the person who just threatened them.

This also is where people start reacting to imaginary fears, instead of what is actually happening. Often such people are running entire movies inside their heads about what the other guy intends, is doing, and will do. This can result in their going out of their way to create an incident because they are convinced this other guy is gunning for them. More often, it results in their overreacting in a small confrontation and escalating it to physical assault—because they were *sure* the other person was about to attack.

Even more common is the micro-version of this. For example, after dropping an attacker to the ground a half formed "he could get up" thought flashes through their heads. They start giving the guy the boot.

18   Well, technically what we call adrenaline is a chemical and hormonal cocktail. There's more than just epinephrine. It gets deep and scientific real fast, but a good layman's explanation is to call it a drug or cocktail.

People do this to keep him from getting up and attacking again (an imaginary future). Or that is what they believe they are doing. (They've changed a possible future into a perceived reality. He moved! He's getting up to attack again!) But in stomping a downed person, they cross into aggravated assault or attempted murder charges. Remember when you're adrenalized and emotional, it feels like the threat is physical. And it's happening *RIGHT NOW!*

This is a problem in a world full of security cameras. You swear the guy was about to attack you, and the video shows you crossing ten feet to punch the guy. He says—as he is turning away—that he's going to come back and kill you, so you draw your gun and shoot him. The video shows him walking away, and you shooting him in the back. That is what actually happened.

Even without cameras, this can be a problem. In the middle of a heated argument, someone leaves, walks into the kitchen, gets a knife, comes back, and stabs the other person—then claims self-defense. Wait, you had time to go into the kitchen and come back? And you're saying you were in immanent danger? And you couldn't go out the kitchen door, why?

We'll cover the legal aspect in another chapter, but for right now let's just say before you act, the physical danger has to be *immediate*. It can't be in the past or at some vague time in the future, especially if he's threatening now about what he'll do to you at some later time.

The third line people cross that nullifies self-defense is *not* knowing when to stop. I tie this with excessive and ineffective force. While each of these can be a stand-alone issue, in general, they tend to come bundled.

The why is easier to explain via a story. Miller once told me about a briefing he got from a park ranger. The ranger said bears tend to strike once and walk away. Moose, on the other hand, will stomp a car flat. The popular thought at the time was that predators know dead is dead. Moose, despite being big, are prey animals. Their reaction is pound on danger until it is grass (grass is non-threatening). So basically the bear stops when the danger stops; the moose freaks out and acts until it perceives the danger is gone. The two are not necessarily the same (actuality versus reality).

That brings us to how this can happen. But before we go there— there is a very real complicating factor. That is the force it takes to stop a committed, enraged, adrenalized, or drunken attacker can be very high. This level of force is much higher than most juries—much less attorneys—understand. It very well may have taken that much force to stop him, but it will appear excessive to someone who doesn't understand this.

Having said that, one of the fastest ways to go moose-berserk is if you perceive what you're doing isn't working. If you're in the middle of a situation, and you don't think your response is working, you will do more of the *same*. You'll hit more (trying to hit harder) you'll stab more, you'll shoot more.

There are three basic ways this can happen. One possibility is—especially with empty-hand defense—your movement is ineffective. Instead of efficiently delivering force into the person, you lose all kinds of power. I liken this to trying to bail out a boat with a spaghetti strainer. In these circumstances, there is a very good chance your perception is correct: *It's not working*. Still, the more you try the more excessive it seems to others.

Another possibility is—under the grip of adrenaline—you're mistaking proximity for continuation of the threat. We'll go into this more later, but often we don't see that the attacker is trying to turn away and escape when his plans go wrong. His means of attack are reduced by his turning away, but we're so freaked out about how close he is we still think we're being assailed. This is how someone can get knife wounds not only on the front of his body, but on his back. And the person who carved him still claims self-defense. In extremis—and I have seen this—the person with the knife chases the attacker while slashing his back. Because of continued proximity and a defender oriented on the threat, that person perceives him- or herself to be *still* under attack. In the meantime, the jury is watching the video of the chase and counting the slash wounds on the other person's back. Good luck selling that as self-defense.

Third, it's not working 'fast enough.' And that's a can of worms. To understand why we have to take a side trip, I say there are five levels of physical force (allowing for a lot of overlap):

1) Pain
2) Injury
3) Submission or control
4) Incapacitation
5) Lethal

Any one of these *can* stop an attack. And any one of them can be the wrong answer to the situation. The circumstances dictate the right answer. Basically, pain hurts, but it doesn't injure you. There are places on the human body where you can hit full force, and he'll stand there and merely look at you. There are other spots where, if you get poked, prodded, jerked, or gouged, you'll scream. But nothing is broken nor is there significant injury. A taser hurts like hell, but if you've ever cut yourself shaving that's about the same injury level.

Of all levels of force, pain will prove the *most* unreliable. People expecting pain to destroy someone's commitment to attack are often rudely surprised when all it does is enrage the attacker more. (This especially applies to one-time pain, like a punch or strike.) Instead of stopping the situation, pain alone is just as likely to escalate it.

The way I use the term injury means you need to go to the emergency room. We're talking stitches, blood flowing, setting broken bones, and putting joints back into place. As an aside, in my lexicon, injury also carries the connotation of deliberately trying to inflict it. (It's the difference between trying to inflict pain by punching someone versus injuring him by hitting him with a tire iron. While injury might result from the first, it's the intent behind the second.) People who are inflicting injury are hoping for incapacitation. And it might . . . or it might not . . . cause that. Again, some people can fight through the pain and injury to keep on attacking or resisting.

Submission and control is a spectrum. It can range from sitting on someone to complicated joint locks and restraints to going octopus on someone until they tire to a dog pile to coordinated CERT[19] tactics and restraints. Basically through restraint, you remove the person's ability to do injury to you, others, and self. (Notice the order, it's important.) Realistically, this kind of force is where it is the most difficult to achieve the correct balance between control and safety.

Remember intent in injury? Contrary to what you might think, very few people are deliberately injured by the police. Most injuries occur when someone resists being arrested and fights being controlled. It's the difference between me coming in and deliberately dislocating your shoulder and me trying to restrain you and you dislocating your own shoulder while trying to wrench away. If someone gets injured while you're trying to restrain them, you need to be able to articulate this.

I'm going to break the order I gave you and bring up lethal next. Lethal means the person is going to die from the injuries he receives. There are three problems with lethal force:

1) With modern triage and medicine, lethality is way less cut and dried than it used to be;

2) Lethal force can only be legally applied in very strict and narrow circumstances;

3) Lethal doesn't mean *immediate*.

I once read a statistic that 80 percent of all people who died from head injuries walked under their own power into the emergency room. Violence isn't like the movies, especially when it comes to how fast someone dies. But there is another way immediate becomes important. Not only in the sense of the death comes later (sometimes days) but the

---

19   CERT is cell extraction response team or correctional emergency response team depending on the agency

danger doesn't immediately stop. I've read reports of people with bullets in their hearts staying up and offering a viable threat to their shooter for up to two minutes. (Conversely, I've seen people shot who simply turned and walked away—so as not to get shot again.) A whole lot of people get seriously hurt because their lethal force move didn't work as fast as they thought it would.

This brings us to incapacitation—the holy grail of self-defense. It's the search for something that immediately removes someone's ability to attack. Like control, incapacitation covers a broad spectrum. It can be through pain. It can be through injury. It can be lethal. Knocking someone unconsciousness is a good way to immediately remove his or her ability to attack. So, too, is breaking someone's kneecap. A bullet in the brain is both lethal and immediately incapacitating. It can be control techniques or throwing the guy across the room (before he can physically assault you again, he has to close the distance—that takes time). Any and all of these procedures remove a person's ability to immediately attack or continue attacking.

Incapacitation has some pretty specific standards. Not necessarily as high as some submission and control moves, but it's not as simple as injury. The latter you can cause by hitting someone hard with a baseball bat. Incapacitation requires hitting someone with that bat in just the right spot.

I listed these five types of force because most people have this fantasy about self-defense working immediately[20]—whether it's a punch and the bad person stops and leaves them alone or they shoot someone and he falls down, just like in the movies. If it doesn't allow immediate incapacitation, then they want—whatever they do—to make an attacker stop and go away. In either scenario, it makes the attack stop immediately. Pay close attention to this attitude. When whatever they're doing fails to work fast enough, they go berserk and pour it on. While the technical term for lots and lots of ineffective force is fighting, this is excessive force if not outright assault. It's not going to look good to the jury.

While you are legally allowed to use the minimum amount of force necessary, adrenaline will alter your perception—and by extension—your reality about what minimum means. It's way too easy to throw an extra kick, pull the trigger again, or slash again when you don't think it's working fast enough. See why that bit about adrenaline influencing reality is important? I'll show you some tricks to keep you from being the moose. You can break the adrenal stress cycle to keep from crossing this line. But first, you have to know it's possible.

In this chapter, you were introduced to the four lines people routinely

---

20   See "Writing Violence: Getting Shot," 2014, by me.

cross that take what they did out of the realm of self-defense. But the biggest and most common line they cross is thinking what they do is self-defense—when it is, in fact, self-offense. While they legitimately did not intend for violence to take place, they *did* participate in the creation and escalation of the situation that resulted in violent behavior. That sinking feeling was your claim of self-defense going down to the bottom of the well.

CHAPTER 3

Ignorance is not a sustainable paradigm in violence professions.

—SSgt 'Grizzly Bear'[21]

What Is Self-Defense?

"Self-defense is a legal term."

Often five seconds after hearing that, I have to fight down a strong urge to slap someone. Usually because the person has responded with something like, "Sure. I know that. Now let's talk about what I can do to defend myself."

Brace yourself, this is one long, complex chapter; one of the longest in this book. Given the nature of the business, I can almost guarantee you something: If you've had self-defense training, what you *think* you know about the meaning of self-defense is *wrong*. In fact, it's likely to be one of the fastest ways I know to put you into the prison showers. That's because most training doesn't just reinforce, but actively panders to what "everybody knows" about self-defense.

There are many words, which everybody knows their meaning. A nice way to describe these terms is non-technical. A more direct way of saying it is they are invented, marketing terms designed to sell you something (e.g., hypoallergenic, martial arts). Or they can be obscure pre-existing terms picked up, *redefined,* then popularized to promote a political agenda (assault rifle, Christian, liberal, conservative). This redefinition also materializes with marketing (e.g., organic, self-defense). Other times, the words are emotional, hot-button terms that shut down rational conversation (racism, violence, rape).

Or they are specific terms that have been picked up by the public from

21   Due to his active duty status, I'm not giving his name. We had a conversation about modeling behavior for future sergeants. His contention was, "Sergeants get it done, no matter what," whereupon he casually mentioned kicking a bear in the throat. He was leading the platoon in their PT run in Alaska. A bear wandered into their path. Unfortunately for it, SSgt had told the platoon they *were* going to make time. He ran up, kicked it, and it turned and ran. The platoon made time. When I mentioned kicking a bear wasn't all that smart, the Tennessee Ridge Runner replied, "Nah, it's nothing. I've seen my grandmother chase 'em off the porch with a broom. 'Sides it was a young bear, I knew I could buffalo it. I wouldn't have tried it with a mature one." So, brave, but not stupid.

a specific field of knowledge. Often the public use is technically incorrect, but useful for conveying a popular sentiment (e.g., he has a big ego). Often, the word is used as an umbrella term. An everybody knows an umbrella term that is meaningless in its supposed field (e.g., 'insane' for psychology and medicine).

All of these examples apply to how the term 'self-defense' is used. And there are three reasons why I told you that. The *first* reason is most of what you think you know about self-defense is *marketing*—which goes beyond mere advertising. Marketing is designed to get your money and promote the system or training, instead of serving any real safety function or application. In fact, I'll say most training is more about handling fear than danger management. It won't actually help you with the dangers involved in crime and violence, but you'll feel more confident and less fearful (as long as you don't have to use it).

As long as you think you are getting something that is useful for self-defense, you'll continue paying for the training—especially advanced training.[22] *Never forget* training is a for-profit business. That strongly influences:

- What is taught;
- How it's taught;
- The time it takes to teach it.

You can spend a lot of money for specialized training in one aspect and miss the many other parts of self-defense. Not getting ripped off this way is just one of the many reasons to understand what the words self-defense mean. It helps to keep you from falling for the one-stop shopping for all your SD needs marketing.

Speaking of for-profit businesses, we also have the entertainment industry. Pretty much anything you think you know about violence is strongly influenced by movies and TV. Unfortunately, many people pride themselves on being able to tell the difference between movies and real life. There are three problems with that:

One: Have you ever seen a show or movie about something you know really well? I know doctors who loathe medical dramas. Lawyers who sneer at legal shows. Vets who despise war movies. Why? Because Hollywood gets it *wrong*—often on purpose. Insiders defend this misinformation as, "We're not educating, we're in the business of entertaining." But unless you're in that field, you won't know what is wrong with the Tinseltown version or why.

Two, remember I said adrenaline affects our reality? When you watch

---

22   Usually advanced training means going deeper into a particular aspect instead of out broader into the wider subject. When it comes to self-defense training, a lot of people are very deeply trained in the physical aspects, but woefully ignorant about the bigger picture.

an exciting movie, you get an adrenaline dump. That means you're anchoring a feeling and perception to a visual interpretation of an event. For example, I grew up believing that when someone was shot, they threw up their arms, then collapsed. (In today's movies, they fly backward.[23]) Until I actually saw a few people shot, I *didn't* know better. I honestly believed that's what would happen.

Three is a quote from Joseph Wannamaker: "I know half of my money in advertising is wasted; I just don't know which half." How do you know which half of what you *think* you know about violence is accurate and which isn't? Especially when it comes to how Hollywood has influenced you. I got news for you, it's *not* clearly divided. Truth and fiction blur together inside our brains.

Why is knowing this critical? Realistically, too many so-called self-defense instructors—in order to stay in business much less turn a profit—tailor what they teach to the *expectations* of the customers. They aren't teaching what is actually involved in self-defense, they are teaching what the customers *think* is self-defense. This results in the huge amounts of misinformation when it comes to the subject.

Knowing about Hollywood and advertising is the first step in sorting fact from fiction when it comes to self-defense. It's important because it's your life that's in danger from bad information. A good way to start filtering out incorrect information is to stop thinking of self-defense in terms of martial arts or shooting and start thinking of it in legal terms. Want to know why? Your actions—although influenced by what you think the words mean—will be judged by self-defense's legal definition. If those aren't even in the same ball park, you're in deep trouble.

So let's start looking at what things mean in a legal context. When you utter the words self-defense, you use an affirmative defense defense (and no I did not just stutter). An affirmative defense is basically you saying, "Yep! I did it. I know it's a crime to use force on another person (the confession). But I had good reason to do it. So may I please be excused from punishment?"

Before the police, district attorney (DA), and jury give you a pass, they *will* want to know your good reasons. And those reasons had damned well better be excellent. While we're at it, you better have lots of them. We'll talk about what to expect and how to deal with the cops and courts later. Right now, you need to know: They're going to crawl up your butt with a microscope to disprove your assertion that what you did was in self-defense.

---

23   It's impossible for a handheld weapon to do this. Newton's Third Law of Physics (paraphrased): For every action there is an equal and opposite reaction. Anything capable of blowing a one-hundred-eighty-pound man back would do the same to anyone shooting him. But it looks great on film—that's why they do it.

Bear this mind that with an affirmative defense, they don't have to refute SODDI (some other dude did it). You've already admitted you did it. All they have to do is *undermine* your claim of self-defense. Knowing this creates a different mindset. It's not quite a siege mentality, but it helps to prepare for such. The prosecutor or plaintiff's attorney will try to urinate all over your self-defense claim. It is in that attorney's self-interest (winning) to sell the idea it wasn't self-defense. That's why you need *excellent* reasons and *many* of them.

Another rehash with a new layer added. Remember I explained self-defense as a square on the floor? Same idea, but now you're standing on a table. If you get close to an edge and reach over, they can easily grab you and pull you off. Even if you stay safely in the middle, they will *try* to cut off one of the table's legs. You have to stay inside the boundaries of self-defense, so you can't be pulled over the edge or your claim undercut.

Pulling you over is less work for the prosecutor since you've admitted to a crime. So what do you say to stay away from the edges? Your pre-incident behavior is vital. Those actions if appropriate to the situation put you more firmly in the middle of the table. You or someone else being able to articulate *why* what you did was necessary? That's a big part of making those table legs harder to saw through.

It varies from state to state, but general guidelines about self-defense include:

Texas Penal Code 9.31 Self-defense:

```
. . . a person is justified in using force against
another when and to the degree he reasonably believes
the force is immediately necessary to protect himself
against the other's use or attempted use of unlawful
force.
```

Colorado Revised Statues 18-1-704. Use of physical force in defense of a person

```
. . . a person is justified in using physical force
upon another person in order to defend himself or a
third person from what he reasonably believes to be
the use or imminent use of unlawful physical force by
that other person, and he may use a degree of force
which he reasonably believes to be necessary for that
purpose.
```

I'm stealing an idea from Miller, who does a word-by-word break down of the significance of this law in his Logic of Violence: Thugs and Ambushes courses (which I seriously recommend you attend or at least read his books). The following information is not legal advice, but acquaints you with concepts you *must* know. It also encourages you to learn *more*. And this includes talking with a lawyer *before* anything happens.

There's a difference between the examples I provided and the one Miller uses. These say "justified in using;" the phrase he quotes is "may use." Both concepts are important. Notice that both states allow you to act in the defense of others. We often think in terms of learning self-defense to protect family. Well, okay, the law allows you to act in defense of a third party. You also can play white knight and gallop in to save a maiden fair.

The key word in that last sentence is *can*. You *don't* have to! You can see someone attacked, and you don't have to try and stop it. Call the cops? Go for it. But you *don't* have to jump in the middle of it. Police on the other hand have a duty to act if they see someone assailed. They *have* to try to stop it. If they are there . . . [24] That brings us to using force to protect yourself. Believe it or not, you *don't* have an obligation to act if you are the one assaulted. You can just curl up and take it. That might seem insane, but it's important to understand the context in which your actions will be viewed.

May use is important; it means you *have* a choice. With that choice come responsibilities. The significance of 'may' is that if you use force— even in self-defense—you *consciously* choose to do so. By acting, you're sailing close to the wind. Accept that responsibility as the price for choosing to defend yourself.

Justified is the other word they use. Going to 'Lectric Law Library, we are given this as the definition of justification: *The act by which a party accused shows and maintains a good and legal reason, in court, why he did the thing he is called upon to answer.*

Here's a hitch. Most people's definition of justified goes no further than answering to themselves. They feel justified in what they did. They felt it was necessary; that's why they did it. And while we're on the subject, who the hell are you to question them? It doesn't take much imagination to see how a douche bag could twist this self-reinforcing definition to his or her advantage. Removing the douche factor, you also can see how someone—who has only focused on justifying something to himself— will have a hard time explaining his actions to others. This articulation is where most people screw the pooch with legitimate self-defense.

What I am about to say will have attorneys twitching and drooling (it's technically wrong) but laymen understand it. *When you claim self-*

---

24   And by the way, we'll go into the Second Amendment argument that the police have no obligation to protect you later. That's a sound bite misunderstanding of two court cases: *Castle Rock vs. Gonzales* (545 US 748 (2005) and *Warren vs. District of Columbia* (444 A.2d. 1, D.C. Ct. of Ap. 1981)

defense, the burden of proof shifts to you.[25] You can't just say self-defense and expect everything to be hunky dory. *You* have to *prove* it was self-defense. By claiming self-defense, proving your actions were justified is now *your* responsibility. And that requires a boatload of evidence to confirm your actions were truly in defense of self. That's why knowing the significance of the rest of the law is important. Knowing *answering to others* is part of the legal meaning of justified gets you into the mindset that you also must prove it to others. If you can't—even if it was legitimate self-defense—you're going to prison.

"Reasonably believes" . . . . ohhhh that's a booger of a phrase. In fact, Jeff Meek of Carry On Colorado sums it up this way, "Don't try to think about reasonable too hard, you can pull a muscle." Having said that, we're going to have to put your brain on a treadmill for this one: If you're the kind of person who likes simple, carved-in-granite, this-means-that-and-that's-all-I-need-to-know definitions, reasonable is going to drive you fruit bat guano crazy. You'll be running around your house opening closets and lifting couch cushions to find this imaginary reasonable person.

Let me give you a shorthand way to describe reasonable: Would they *have* done the same if they were in your Size 10s? Another way to describe it: Can they be convinced—given the circumstances and potential danger—your choice of action was *appropriate?*

On one side, you have a reasonable man from Texas who believes "he needed killing" is the height of reason. On the other, you have the suburban pacifist who believes that violence never solved anything. These two people—and ten others in between— sit in the jury box. Regardless of their individual standards and how different they are, they are *all* reasonable people. These are the people to whom the lawyers are trying to sell the concept your use of force was reasonable—or not. Some of them are going to be a harder sell than others. Unfortunately, most of them will be prone to buy the prosecutor's version.[26]

Why am I talking about reasonable in terms of selling? If you pleaded SODDI, your defense attorney's job is simple. Attack the state's case and create reasonable doubt about whether or not you did it. If you didn't do it, there is no need to talk about whether it was justified.

But let's look at reasonable doubt with SODDI. To get a conviction, the state *must* prove beyond a reasonable doubt that *you* committed

---

25   The actual terms are production of evidence and preponderance of evidence (not the same thing). But anyone who is not a lawyer says, "Huh?" So you tell them the burden of proof, and they say, "Oh, I understand."

26   Sitting in the defendant's chair creates bias. Lines from the movie, *The Three Musketeers* (1971) sums it up: "I'm innocent!" "You're in the Bastille, you must have done something."

the crime, and that it meets the criteria of the charge (murder versus manslaughter). That means if the jury is 90 percent sure you *did* it and this is how odds are you're going down. If they're teetering at 50/50, you'll probably be acquitted (there's reasonable doubt). Where conviction versus acquittal is a real crap shoot is when they're around 70 percent convinced. The doubting 30 percent can vindicate you, convict you, or ensure a hung jury (and if that happens you get to go through the entire expensive, mind-draining, emotion-charged experience . . . again). In some folks' minds, their being 70 percent sure it was you is beyond a reasonable doubt, in other jury members' minds it's not.

But affirmative defense is a game changer. By claiming self-defense, you've confessed it was you who did the deed. The task before you and your attorney becomes to sell the jury on the fact that what you did was reasonable *given the circumstances*. The prosecution's job is to sell the idea it wasn't. Think of it as role reversal. You have to present evidence and build the case that it *was* self-defense; the prosecutor gets to attack your case.

Even though the roles have changed that 90 percent is still there. But it's now you convincing the jury you were in danger and it *was* self-defense—therefore, reasonable. That's how sure they need to be to guarantee you are acquitted. If they're 50/50 that's *not* beyond a reasonable doubt. You'll probably be convicted. Once again, 70 percent is a crap shoot. And since you confessed to the crime already . . .

Those people *aren't* going to take your word that it was necessary self-defense. It's not going to be plain as sunset to them. Your lawyer needs to convince twelve people—with completely different standards of reasonable—your actions were acceptable given the circumstances. Truth is a very good product, but you *still* have to sell it; it's not going to sell itself. Because the other side is going to try to sell to those same twelve reasonable people the idea you *didn't* act in self-defense. That what you did was in fact a deliberate crime.

The prosecutor's strategy depends on what he or she thinks will work best with the jury. Is it going to be you crossed the line out of self-defense? It never was self-defense? It was a fight you started? Or you're a murdering bastard who's trying to get off by claiming self-defense? Who knows how he'll try to sell it. But it will change anytime he or she thinks 'this one' isn't working.

Here's where things get tricky. Reasonable people's decisions are only as good as the information they are allowed to see. I'm going to give you an insider's tip about our legal system. There's a big fight between the lawyers—in front of the judge—over evidence the jury is allowed to see or hear. The judge and two lawyers know more about the case than the jury ever will. And the jury *never* knows what information they *weren't* ever allowed to examine. It sucks, but there it is.

This becomes doubly problematic if the defense attorney doesn't know to introduce the kind of information you're learning *here,* the evidence that proves your case. Unfortunately, this is more common than anyone—especially lawyers—wants to admit. Later, we'll discuss 'edjumakating' your attorney. Or—better yet—retain one who knows how to defend a person who acted in self-defense.[27] We'll also cover forcing the introduction of evidence in your statement.

But right up front, you need to accept that *after reading this book,* you'll probably be more knowledgeable about what constitutes self-defense than your attorney. You'll need to lucidly express this information to your attorney—so he will know to introduce it in court to use to your benefit. And that above all means *fighting* like hell to get it introduced as evidence.

Information needed to help the jury make reasonable decisions can be shown by a simple example. One of the common effects of adrenaline is spatial distortion. That's a fancy way of saying that "threats look bigger." I often joke I've never had a knife pulled on me. I have, however, been attacked by machetes and swords. (Those knives looked as big as swords.) In the same vein, I've never looked down the barrel of gun. I have, however, looked down the barrel of cannons being pointed at me. By hyper-focusing on the threat—common under adrenal stress—it looks *bigger.*

Another common form of spatial distortion is distance. The threat looks *closer* to you than it *actually* is. In our unconscious, bigger means closer. Let's take a shooting for this example. An attacker pulls a knife and charges. When shot, he is fifteen feet away. But to the adrenalized, hyper-focused defender, it appears he is closer. The police ask, "How close was he when you shot?" The shooter responds, "About five feet." This is *not* a correct answer, but *it is* an honest one. To the shooter—influenced by spatial distortion—it *looked* like five feet (again, bigger equals closer).

This is going to come up in court. In fact, the prosecutor is going to use it as a trap to undermine the defendant's credibility and his claim of self-defense. He will ask how close the victim was when the defendant killed him. (Notice the subtle manipulation of terminology?) When the defendant answers "about five feet," the prosecutor is going to run the video showing the fifteen-foot distance. Then he's going to ask why the

---

27   The Armed Citizen's Legal Defense Network is an organization that keeps a countrywide list of attorneys who know how to handle self-defense cases. It's much better than these other insurance programs I've run into. If you're not into paying membership fees, you also can stop at local gun stores and see if an attorney dropped off his business cards.

defendant is *lying* about the gap. Is the defendant lying? No. Perceptually, it *did* look like five feet to him, but there's the video. The defendant is going to stutter, stammer, and try to explain. To the jury, it looks like the prosecutor caught the defendant in a lie. If he's lying about that what else is he lying about? Hmmmmmmm?

That's what happens when the jury doesn't know about spatial distortion—or other effects of adrenaline. Why don't they know? Because the defense lawyer *didn't* call in an expert to explain it. Why? Because he didn't know about it himself.

Once the defendant's lawyer introduces spatial distortion, however, the discrepancy between the video and the defendant's statement is no longer a gotcha! The defendant's perception and the actual distance are *not* mutually exclusive. The discrepancy not only becomes reasonable, it turns into a no brainer. The jury can look at the prosecutor and say, "Of course that fifteen feet looked like five! Haven't you heard of spatial distortion?" *Without* this knowledge, it is reasonable to believe the defendant is lying.[28] With the data, the jury can make a more informed— dare I say reasonable—decision.

I give you this tour of how subjective, slippery, and unreliable 'reasonable' can be so you can mentally prepare to justify your actions to others. Pinning down what is reasonable is kind of like trying to nail Jell-O to a tree. But if you're forced to try and hang gelatin from that tree with a spike, you now know to also bring along a Zip-lock™ bag and some string.

But we're not done with reasonable, yet. Once again, a short and easy summation of reasonable: Although you believe they were appropriate at the time, your actions *must* be understandable to others. 'At that time' is another place where things get tricky. Remember adrenaline? Yeah, the same stuff that makes fifteen feet look like five? When it has you by the scruff of the neck, it's going to whisper that all kinds of things are reasonable.

There's three versions here. We'll go into them much deeper later, but let's give them a fast once over. Starting with what you thought was reasonable at the moment. You might have been convinced he was going to beat you to death with a kumquat. But that's going to be a hard sell

28   Or, and this is often the case, if the interviewing officer confronted you with the discrepancy, and you didn't introduce spatial distortion in your statement. Introducing this as evidence is something you need to discuss with your attorney *before* you make a statement. While it's advisable to have an attorney present during questioning—in the higher level uses of force, you *need* to have an attorney present. You also need to seriously consider not making a statement to police unless it's being videotaped. Yes, this means going down to the station, but all kinds of things get left out of written reports about statements. Fewer important details slip through the cracks when your statement is videoed. But this can work for you or against you—so again check with your attorney.

to the jury. At that exact moment, you firmly believed in the danger of tactical fighting fruit, but the jury won't. It just isn't reasonable—even to a Texan.

Another hard sell is that someone of your same size, age, and physical ability, who was unarmed, posed enough peril to justify pulling a lethal force weapon and using it on him in a bar fight. That *especially* isn't going to fly with the suburban pacifist sitting in the jury box. She hates macho blustering and posturing, much less fighting. But if you're losing a fight, it's *very* easy for your adrenalized monkey to suddenly believe you're about to *die!* So you reach down and pull out that cool tactical knife you bought and trained to use . . . and you go to prison.

It isn't enough that you *believe* or *feel* something. There has to be good, solid, explainable reasons *for* that belief. External circumstances and reasons you can point out. Reasons other people will hear and say, "Ooooh, that *was* dangerous wasn't it?" That's one of the meanings of reasonably believes. The other version of reasonably believes can work more in your favor. That is, given what you know—at the moment under the *circumstances*—was the belief in danger reasonable?

Let's replace the kumquat with a toy gun. You might not be old enough to remember, but back in the '80s toymakers got the idea of making plastic replicas of real guns. The Retard Special really pulled into town when they decided to make them the exact same color as firearms. Too many kids were killed because they pointed what looked like real guns at people—especially cops. (This is why today's toy guns have bright red or orange muzzles.) These shootings influenced changes in self-defense laws to include the term reasonably believes. If someone decides to paint the muzzle of a toy gun black and points it at you, in the seconds you have to assess and react to the danger of a gun in your face you *cannot* know it is a toy. Given the circumstances, it is reasonable to believe it's a real gun.

But what if someone pulls a Super-soaker™ and threatens to blow your brains out if you don't give him your wallet? Is it a reasonable belief that you are in danger of death or grievous bodily injury? No. How about if he tells you it is filled with acid or water mixed with HIV-positive blood? Well, that's a game changer—especially because of *what* he told you. Same Super-soaker, but you have just been informed of a danger and threatened with violence if you don't give up your property (the definition of robbery). What's reasonable now?

Two guys follow you down a deserted street at night. You dart around a corner and lay in wait. When they pass, you step out of the shadow and bust open one guy's skull. Was that a reasonable use of force? Reboot. Same two guys follow you. You try to take evasive action, but they counter and continue to close. Turning a corner, you discover you're trapped in a dead-end alley. Before you can escape, they block the alley and confront you. One of them does a two-handed action; one hand lifts his shirt and the other grabs for his belt line (commonly called a furtive movement)—and you bust his skull open.

Is it reasonable to believe he's going for a gun? Well, it's reasonable to believe he's *not* trying to show you the scar from his appendectomy surgery. And since the two-handed draw is common among criminals, it's reasonable to believe that's what he's doing—even if you don't see the gun before you react.

But notice what I did. I articulated facts, actions, details—including what you did to avoid an encounter—as well as their counter actions, your inability to continue to retreat, and a well-known criminal weapon-drawing action.[29] Your ability to articulate these kinds of details go a long way to convincing people your actions were reasonable and appropriate for the situation.

The third form of reasonable is based on the other guy. What does it take to stop him? What it takes to stop a drunken and adrenalized attacker does *not* seem reasonable to someone who doesn't know about the pain-numbing influences of alcohol and adrenaline. A reasonable person believes someone would fold after one good blow. (Remember, the jury and attorneys watch the same movies that gave you misconceptions about violence.)

That's why it is *critical* to introduce evidence about alcohol, adrenaline, and pain. It strongly influences *why* what you did might have been necessary to stop the threat. Not saying what you did was reasonable . . . yet. But the level of force it takes to stop a drunken and enraged person is a different from walking up and dropping a sober accountant with a sucker punch.

This really applies with what I call "professional drunks." These are people who can stand up and function with the same amount of alcohol in their systems that would guarantee a normal person would have passed out or been so impaired he'd be no threat. When these people go off, they can be berserks. I mean Viking, immune-to-pain, shield-biting, rampaging berserkers. We will come back and cover these types in depth in another chapter.

Moving on to something that is only slightly less clearly defined than reasonable. The term *minimum force necessary*. As in, you are "allowed to use the minimum force necessary" to resolve the threat or situation. Don't get a chubby about this idea. It's not as warm and friendly as you might think. In fact, it's best to think about it as a snake looking to bite

29   Criminals don't usually use holsters. They often are able to discretely throw away the gun before the cops reach them. But if the criminal is wearing an empty holster, the police know to look for a gun nearby.

you in the buttocks. It'll be how a prosecutor will try and sell the idea you crossed the line—especially with excessive force.

The term isn't in either of the two statutes I quoted (they use degree of force) but it might be spelled out in your state's statute. Even if it isn't, minimum force is a standard they are going to try to use to staple your dick (or tits) to the table. One of the ways they're going to try to cut the legs out from under your self-defense table is to try to set the bar for the minimum force necessary way too low. Then turn around and sell the idea that what would have been insufficient force is reasonable. By default, what you did was excessive.

An example? A meth freak on a rampage is a nightmare. That ninety-pound, toothless scuzbucket can become a berserker. In that state, the addict is so immune to pain that five rounds in the chest barely slows him down before he drives a knife into you. Is he dead? Yes, but he doesn't know it yet. So he's still on his feet and a viable threat. But because he weighs only ninety pounds, the prosecutor is going to condemn you for not trying to restrain him. You didn't have to shoot him—after all you're bigger, stronger, and in better shape. And speaking of minimum force, you could have outrun him . . .

What the prosecution is selling as a reasonable level of force *isn't*. (For safety reasons, professionals prefer using four- or five-man teams to control and restrain out-of-control *unarmed* tweakers. The 4:1 ratio ensures their safety and that of the meth head. Does he have a weapon? Game changer. All bets are off.)

I'm going to have to write another book about physical effectiveness in self-defense situations. But that's a can of worms I won't go into except to say, "There are quantifiable differences between insufficient power, minimum force, reasonable actions, and excessive." But they are all built upon effective delivery of force. If you can't do that, those other things are like making plans for when you win the lottery.

When it comes to sufficient minimum force, you have to add to the mix what you're facing at the time (an enraged seventy-two-year-old grandmother, a two-hundred-fifty-pound biker, or a berserk tweaker). At best, minimum force is a sliding scale. So the most accurate answer is "it depends." Burn these next three words into your brain: *The situation dictates.*

The problem is most attorneys only know the phrase 'minimum force necessary.' They have no idea what it entails and how variable it can be. Simply stated, if they were into getting punched, kicked, and beaten, they probably wouldn't have become lawyers. I personally have only encountered two attorneys to whom I didn't have to explain violence. (Both of them grew up in bad parts of town and went overseas into war zones.)

On the other hand, I have lots of experience with lawyers lacking the vaguest clue when it comes to violence. One of the most appalling moments I have had dealing with attorneys is when I was working a murder case, and the attorney said to me in frustration, "I just don't know why this case isn't going away (meaning the defendant takes a lousy plea deal)." I looked at him and said, "Because it really was self-defense." The attorney looked at me and said in amazement, "Really?"

News flash Mr. Harvard-Law-Degree, being strangled by a professional drunk bricklayer with a blood alcohol content of .35 qualifies as *immediate* danger of death. (When someone is that drunk, odds are good they won't stop when you quit kicking by passing out. You dead or brain damaged becomes the most likely outcome.)

There are many ways the minimum-amount-of-force line can be crossed. We'll cover them in chunks throughout the rest of the book. But for right now, I'd like to address a common mistake and something that will be critical in making an accurate use-of-force decision and explaining it. That is: There's a difference between an *incident* and *circumstances*.

Just being in an incident isn't enough. It's the circumstances that dictate the appropriate use of force. But those circumstances are *always* changing. To the inexperienced, it looks like a giant whirling ball of chaos. So I'm going to give you a beginner's tool to break it down into manageable chunks and parse things out. Think of an incident as the entire event, covering an arc of time. A lot of things can and do happen during that arc—most especially changing circumstances. If you take that incident and chop it into five-second chunks, you'll see snapshots of a series of ever-changing circumstances. This is important because what is *appropriate* for one set of circumstances is *excessive* or *insufficient* in another.

You can take a twenty-second incident and chop it up into four parts. More than that, you can be in immediate mortal danger for only one of those segments. Let's say the third one. In those *specific* circumstances, the use of lethal counter force is legally justified, but *not* during the other three stages. If you shoot, stab, or crush the throat of the guy during those parts, you've crossed the line.

An old friend of mine once said: "Just because something is dangerous doesn't automatically mean you will get hurt if you do it. I have found the young, inexperienced, and imagination-impaired often take this to mean there is no danger at all."

Welcome to where things gets tricky. Sometimes you can pass through that third stage, and absolutely *nothing* happens. Other times, you'll die. Odds are good the results will be somewhere in between with injuries ranging from slight to severe. There is *no way* to predict how things will go.

I'm going to give you three examples. First, you're engaging with someone. That's the incident. You're up on your feet for the first quarter (circumstances). You both go down in the second. In the third quarter, he gets on top and starts doing a ground-and-pound (sitting on your chest, punching you in the face). This causes the back of your head to rebound off the concrete. During the first two sets of circumstances, you really were not in immediate threat of death or grave bodily injury. Maybe if the stars aligned just so, it could happen. Under these new circumstances, however, the chances just went way up. The harder he hits, the more probable the injury.

Here's the problem. Let's say he hits you four times, and all that happens is your head bounces off the concrete. Then you throw him off and get up—danger passed without injury. Getting up is the fourth quarter, and the circumstances have again changed. Or your skull could crack wide open on the first bounce, and the next three punches are overkill because you're already dying. Another option is your head bounces three times and cracks on the fourth, leaving you a vegetable for the rest of your life. The last two results will significantly influence the fourth quarter action. While a strong case can be made for stabbing, shooting, crushing the throat, or popping an eyeball out during the third quarter, those same actions are *not* warranted during the other quarters—including the one where you safely got up.

Next example, you're on your feet engaging (first). You fall or are knocked down during the second quarter. The other person starts kicking and stomping you while you're down (third). The shod human foot against a downed person is legally recognized in many states as a lethal force instrument. The circumstances in that third quarter are immediate danger of death or grievous bodily injury. But he stops and steps back (fourth quarter). You draw your gun and shoot him. You cross the line because the circumstances no longer justify lethal force to protect yourself.

The third example is the murder case I just mentioned. The DA believed the defendant brought a knife to a fist fight. Giving credence to this is that earlier in the evening, the defendant and the deceased had gotten into a fight that had gone to the ground. They were rolling around wrasslin.' Those circumstances were different, however, than the conditions when the stabbing occurred.

In the first set of circumstances, they were rolling around on the grass, fighting, and trying to punch each other. In that situation, neither had a clear advantage. Nor were the circumstances particularly dangerous.

The fight was broken up; nobody was injured. During the second confrontation, however, the deceased had worked himself up to a fury through continued drinking. Upon seeing the defendant later that evening without warning, he leapt over a fire pit, tackled the defendant on concrete, knocked the air out of him, pinned him, and sat on the defendant's chest while strangling him.

The *circumstances*—at that *exact* moment—were such that the defendant was in immediate danger of death or grave bodily injury. He stabbed his attacker once under the armpit. Then . . . and only then . . . were people able to pull off the attacker, who summarily died of the knife wound. Would it have been self-defense if he'd stabbed him during the first incident? No. That's because the circumstances did *not* warrant use of lethal force. Would it have been self-defense if the defendant had charged around the fire pit and stabbed him? No. If the deceased had stopped choking him and tried to stand up would lethal force have been justified? Again, no.

But there was a perfect storm of circumstances—in those few moments—where lethal force was justifiable because of the immediate danger to the defendant. Until I got called in to explain why *these* circumstances were life-threatening *neither* attorney had the vaguest clue. Both of them were looking at the two incidents as basically the same. Was stabbing the minimum amount of force? In those exact circumstances, it was what was needed. In other circumstances, it would haven been excessive. Being both being strangled and asphyxiation through compression meant that stabbing his attacker was reasonable.

So let me clarify something. If you're losing a fight that doesn't mean you can pull a gun out and shoot someone. That is *not* using the minimum force necessary. It is crossing the lines out of self-defense, legal use of force, and of course minimum. On the other hand—and on rare occasions—shooting someone *is* the minimum force necessary.

But that only occurs if the consequences of *not* doing so exceed losing by light years. Simple idea, but real hard to get right during the heat of the moment. (This is why I tell instructors, "You're not teaching self-defense. You're training people to operate within the parameters of self-defense." That's a subtle but important distinction.)

Like I said, chunking an incident into blocks of time is a beginning concept to keep you from being overwhelmed by how things are always changing. Watch videos of incidents until you can tell the difference between what is occurring at :30 and :45 and :45 to 1:00 (four stages). Then move up a level to breaking it down into smaller chunks: :30 to :40, :40 to :50, and :50 to 1:00 (six stages). Then make it even smaller.

Identify the unique circumstances of each section. Being able to reliably do this is a prerequisite for the next, higher level. This is a critical skill for assessing probability and possibility (we'll discuss that later). But for right now, it's learning to recognize how the actions in :35 to :40 directly led to what happened in :40 to :45. For example, while the guy was shot in :40 to :45, the gun draw happened in :35 to :40. But if you know what to look for, you can see the other guy preparing for the draw in :30 to :35.

I'm serious about playing this game until you get the hang of assessing the circumstances on the fly. First, it's far better to learn to do it in the safety of watching videos of crime and violence instead of live-fire situations. Second, it will help you develop the ability to articulate what the circumstances were that resulted in your use-of-force choice.

Like I said before, there is *going* to be someone gunning for you over your use of force. The higher the level, the more they're going to try to nail you for it. A real common way the police and the prosecutor are going to come at you is by contending your use of force was not the minimum, but excessive. Usually, they frame it in terms of the incident, not the circumstances that led to your use-of-force decision. Their coming at you is *going* to happen. There's a lot of gray in the subject of minimum use of force. But the more you know, the better you are going to be at explaining how and why you stayed inside the SD square. You remained inside it because you reacted to the circumstances not necessarily the incident.

Okay enough of trying to nail Jell-O to a tree, how about something a little more solid? Texas calls it imminent. Colorado calls it immediate. Either way, it's not only the way many people screw the pooch, but outright fuck the dog. That's because when you act in self-defense, the danger to you must be *right now*. Such a simple concept—yet one so easily misunderstood. We're not talking about a feeling of danger—we're talking an actual threat. Some people claim you have to wait until you're attacked. Some try to contend the guy across the room was an immediate threat. Others decide to act on just a verbal threat.

So you want some nuts-and-bolts standards for immediate or immanent threat? I recently took a Law of the Gun class from Adam Weitzel here in Colorado. Instead of the old AOJ (ability, opportunity, jeopardy) he uses the NRA's (National Rifle Association) JAM:

- Jeopardy
- Ability
- Means

One of the reasons I use JAM in this book (instead of AOJ) is because "you're in a jam" is easier for the average person to remember. AOJ came from an old law enforcement model.[30] Look for more on both later—but for right now, we're going to look at these points in relation to immediate. For this example, we'll presuppose jeopardy—using a specific definition of "a person acting in a manner consistent with known dangerous behavior." (Again, we'll go into other interpretations later.)

For the forthcoming example, we'll call known dangerous behavior as threatening physical actions, intimidating behavior, and verbal threats. There are other forms of threat displays, these are just the most common.

Short version of ability is: Does he have the capacity to do it? A six-four ex-football player *has* the physical means to kick your butt. So when he verbally threatens to do so (jeopardy) it's reasonable to believe he has the ability to do it. Whereas, a paraplegic with cerebral palsy? Not so much. On the other hand, a guy in a wheelchair with a gun, saying he's going to kill you *does* have the ability. So like so many things in this biz, ability is not a fixed point, but a sliding scale.

Means: Do the circumstances—as they *stand* right now—allow it? Is that six-four ex-football player threatening to kick your ass two or ten feet away from you? Is there a table between you two in that ten feet? It's real simple, the greater the distance the *less* the means for empty-hand attacks. Is that guy threatening to stab you to death on the other end of the phone? Hard to get killed by someone if he isn't there. Is there a brick wall and bullet-proof glass between you? Even if he has a gun (ability) he's going to have a hard time shooting through that brick wall (means).

Ability and means are closely intertwined with immediacy of the threat. The problem is there is no real fixed formula. So we're going to have to make one up. Also what I am about to explain, isn't something I want you to be literally trying to do in an incident. "Doing the math" is a figurative term. But the addition and subtraction of elements to assess the immediacy of the threat is not. I'm about to show you the fundamentals of the process using numbers.

Remember something I said earlier: *The situation dictates*. You won't know the variables until you're in the middle of it. That's why you must be able to correctly assess the circumstances and situation to determine the threat's immediacy. Perhaps the easiest way to introduce you to that is by setting a scale from one to ten. The value of every number is fixed. How you combine them changes the end sum.

- $7+2-5=4$
- $5+3-1=7$

---

30   AOJ (ability, opportunity, jeopardy) is of particular use when it comes to immediate threat. There are other ways to organize threat assessment, IMO (intent, means, opportunity) TOC (time of contact) and others. Different people use different models to articulate these ideas.

Simple, right? Now let's assign. Zero equals no threat. Ten, he's attacking. The higher the number, the more immediate the threat; the lower the number, the less immediate. (We're going to assume you can't retreat.)

Our ex-football player (ability) is back and threatening us (jeopardy). Let's overreact and call that plus-nine. Because *that's* what your adrenalized monkey is going to tell you it is. But is your monkey correct that you're in immediate danger?

The monkey says yes, but what about the means? He's ten feet away. That's a minus three. There's also a table between us. That's a minus two. He's not trying to move around it, a minus one.

- 9-3-2-1=3

Yelling and threatening aside, three is a pretty low immediacy. That's why knowing some kind of threat assessment model is so important. Ability and means add or subtract from the immediacy of the danger.

Now that we have a better understanding, let's play it again. Same football player is threatening us again from behind the table. We're starting at plus three this time (jeopardy and ability). He comes around the table, a plus three (developing means). He stops seven feet away (the means is not fully developed). That's a minus one. Okay, now we're up to five. That's a problem, but not an immediate threat. (Means are missing.)

Reset. He's back yelling from behind the table. So, we're at plus three again. But this time, he jumps over the table. That's a plus four. And he is charging. That's a plus three. This is no longer a verbal threat of violence. It's an *attack,* and it's taking place now! You betcha you act.

But what if he jumps over the table and pulls up short four feet away to yell and threaten some more? Let's call that a reasonable seven. Why? What was a ten (attack) loses minus three when he stops *out of range.* But if he takes another step, we can bump it to eight. Because even though he isn't necessarily attacking, you are now in his striking range. If he raises his hand, you're at nine—and closer to ten than three. Anything past seven and you can start arguing it was reasonable to believe the danger of violence was imminent.

Now you know how the circumstances of the situation *add* or *subtract* to the immediacy of the danger. You won't know the *specifics* until you're in the situation. Do you have to measure danger this way? No. Any threat assessment model is an important tool to accurately assess the immediacy of a threat.[31] And that is a huge factor in the red or green light decision to act.

---

31   Notice I talk about danger in this chapter. An often used legal term is immediate threat. I've generally avoided using this because the average person thinks of verbal threats when they hear this term. I want you to make a clear distinction between threats and danger.

Throughout this book, we'll relay more information so you can accurately assess the immediacy and level of the danger, which are scaling (determining the amount of force you will need) issues. But for right now, we're going to give you some quick examples of the way people make mistakes when it comes to immediate threat.

The biggest way people screw up is they create immediacy of threat by stepping *into* attack range. Yep, you read that right. They're so busy trying to scare the other dude, they move forward. They *create* the means. And that's seen as stepping up to fight, thereby blowing a chasm in their self-defense claims.

That's not the only action they take. The behavior that throws a monkey wrench into an immediate threat claim takes place when the other person is turning away from you. While we'll go into this in more depth later, the quick-and-dirty version is the guy attacked, but has decided to beat feet. Instead of stopping, you keep attacking because you still *perceive* him as a threat.

If you were a third party watching video of this event, you would see the initial engagement, then one person turning away. This turn is the person taking his means to attack off line. To understand that comment, you need to know that human beings are oriented on the 90s (degrees). (Zero degrees [left], 90 degrees [nose], 180 degrees [right], 270 degrees [directly behind].) We *attack* in the same direction our nose is pointing (our 90). In an overwhelming majority of attacks, nose, toes, and belly button are pointing at the target. When this orientation appears, it assists his means to attack.

When the attacker tries to flee, his nose and hands point in *another* direction. Think of a cannon aimed at a target, then turned toward another direction. Again with *most* people, he is taking his means to attack off line. Recognizing this change in orientation is critical. As long as he keeps turning away, he's trying to flee. But here's a hiccup: You're still oriented on the threat, but it is no longer oriented on you. Yet due to his proximity, your adrenalized and scared monkey brain *still* sees him as a threat.[32] So you keep on defending yourself. But because the immediate threat of violence he offered has passed, *you,* now have become the aggressor and are committing assault. You've crossed out of the SD square—especially if he's trying to flee and you chase him.

And yes—*until* you learn how to control it—your scared monkey will have you do exactly that. You'll do it without question and without thinking. In your adrenalized, fearful state, you still think you're defending yourself from immediate threat, but what the video shows is

---

32   I'll explain the three-brain model later, but for right now know that when I refer to the "monkey," I'm talking about the socio-emotional parts of your brain. This part of your brain takes control (drives the bus) and seriously alters your perspective.

you chasing the guy and attacking his back as he tries to flee.

The good news is you can train your monkey *not* to give chase. (We haven't gone into it yet, but the monkey is the socio-emotional part of your brain. It's also the part that wants to punish him for daring to threaten, much less attack you.) There are some simple and easy tricks to break the adrenal stress loop and take control back from those parts of your brain. In fact, I'll give you one now because—among many other uses—it's a fast way to spot the immediacy of a threat.

Stand in front of a friend and measure the distance from his or her eyebrows to the floor. Take that same distance and lay it down on the floor between you. That is pretty much an empty-hand person's attack range (weapons extend that range). That's the distance they can reach you with using an empty-hand attack without taking a step. Draw a line halfway through that distance. The half closest to you is kicking range (where they can reach you with a kick). The half closest to him or her is punching range where he or she can strike you. But to do that, one has to *step* closer.

Someone moving into attack range is not a good sign (our fuming ex-football player). But a good way to rupture the spatial distortion and hyper-focus of adrenal stress is to break eye contact for a second and check this distance on the floor. Are you in attack range? If not, is the person moving into attack range? If neither, the immediacy of the threat isn't that high—no matter how adrenalized and scared you *feel*.

Recognizing immediate threat is always important, but it becomes *critical* the higher the level of force. That's where you're most likely to cross the "didn't stop" line of the SD square.

An imaginary scenario for the shooters: You're at home asleep in bed with your spouse. You hear a crash downstairs. Quickly unlocking the gun box that prevents your children from gaining access to your firearm, you grab your gun. You hear swearing, yelling, and angry roars from the intruder. And you hear your children screaming. As you get out of bed, the door bursts open. A maniac with a shotgun charges in. You follow your training, and shoot three times before he falls—losing his grip on the shotgun. But he's not dead. You kick the shotgun out of his reach. As you pass him, he snarls, "I'm going to kill you and your family." You settle the matter by putting a round into his forehead and rush to check your children. Seems reasonable, right? He broke into your home. Burst into your room, waved a weapon, and threatened your family. And you defended yourself.

Except in *most* states, you crossed the line with that last shot. It is no longer self-defense, but—depending on your state—manslaughter, murder three, or the local version. Or if you come back from the kids' room and cap him, first degree murder. Why? Because the *immediate* threat had passed, and he no longer had means or ability to do you and yours any harm. (Just ask Jerome Ersland.[33])

Look up your state's version of the fleeing felon law. In most states, if someone sticks a gun in your face, robs you, then *turns* and *runs,* you *cannot* legally draw your gun and shoot him (or give chase). The immediate threat (circumstances) has passed. Something we'll talk about in a bit is how many people go to jail because they hit back.

We're rapidly approaching the biggest punji pit of them all. But to truly appreciate why it's a trap, we need to look at another concept. That is being offered unlawful physical force. At first glance, this looks simple. There it is in black-and-white—except in reality it's a hillside road covered with black ice. That's because we're *threatening* each other with violence *all* the time. This includes that suburban pacifist who believes "violence never solved anything." Later, we'll develop entire chapters about threat displays and what is violence.

But here's something to understand. People *are* being violent when they use threat displays. Three important facts about threat displays:
1) They mimic pre-attack indicators and danger signals;
2) Whether they are subtle or overt, they play a large percentage in *everyone's* communications and interactions with others;
3) They aren't communicating, "I am physically attacking;" they are saying, "I might."

Threat displays are designed to intimidate, warn, cow, or change someone's unacceptable behavior. They show how serious we are, and how if you don't do what I want bad things *are* going to happen to you. They're recognizable points on the road *of* violence. Notice I didn't say, "road to violence." I wrote, "road of violence." When we're snarling profanities at people, we're being violent. When we're red-faced, screaming, and throwing things at the wall, we *are* being violent. Farther down the road is physical violence and even farther is extreme violence. But it is all the same road.

Let me restate something because it's that important. Threat displays are not saying, "I am attacking now." They are communicating, "I *might* attack." They are designed to communicate how close to physical violence the person is—and what's going to happen *if* you don't change your ways. They would *not* work as warnings, intimidation, or bluffs if they weren't on the road of violence. The effectiveness and credibility of threat displays are based on the fact that's how *most* people build themselves

---

33   The Oklahoma pharmacist who shot and dropped one of two armed robbers. One of them fled, Ersland followed him out. Upon his return, he fired five shots into the downed robber—who turned out to be a sixteen-year-old boy. Ersland was convicted of first degree murder and sentenced to life without parole.

up to physically attack. We see them and think to ourselves, "I know where this is heading." This gives the *acting in a manner consistent with known danger* definition of jeopardy a whole new depth and meaning. The problem is although we use threat displays all the time, we don't recognize them. (Or we rationalize: "You're yelling." "Damn right I am! I'm mad!") As such, we *don't* know how far down the road of violence we are. That is until someone believes our threat display and punches us in the face.

It is here that you run into a serious whiskey, tango, foxtrot:
You: "I'm feeling threatened."
Him: "You ought to be! I'm going to kick your ass!"
WHAM!
Him: "Why did you hit me!?"
You: "You threatened me."
Him: "I did not!"

As ludicrous as it sounds, many people—who have *no* intention of physically attacking—are shocked and outraged when someone *believes* their threat displays and reacts physically. They create jeopardy, ability, and means, but are shocked when you take their threats seriously. (I'm not making this stuff up. Why do you think we started calling it self-offense?) They had no intention to engage in unlawful physical violence. Go ahead and ask them, they'll swear on a stack of bibles they didn't.

But they sure as hell intended to reap the benefits of creating the circumstances where you *believed* they were ready, willing, and able to attack. Basically, they expected you to cower in response to their threats of physical violence—not react with physical force. You big meanie head, you.

Not necessarily legally speaking, but from a real, down-to-earth, practical standpoint: You can't threaten unlawful physical violence and then claim to be the victim of it. But, oh baby, will you run into people who *will* try. It seems large segments of the population have forgotten that being verbally hostile, threatening, and aggressive *is* being violent. I guarantee you'll run into such folks. They verbally attack you and their actions threaten you with physical violence. But they will squeal like a speared pig if you respond with a physical reaction to their provocation and threats.

That's a big reason why doing the math of threat assessment is so *important*. Is that person developing the circumstances to attack or is he just trying to bluff you? The problem is that bluff looks like the real thing. Still if he's out of range, it's a bluff. If he's moving into range, then bluff or not he's bumped it to nine on the scale—because if it's *not* a bluff, he's going to nail you.

Another reason the math is important is because in court the prosecutor is going to downplay any aggression the other person was offering. At the same time, he'll blow up any on your part. You have to be able to articulate when, where, and why his threat display crossed over into actual danger.

The most blatant example of crossing this line is the so-called peaceful protestor screaming obscenities and making aborted lunges at a police officer—from just out of range. He or she is allowed to do so (six or seven) until *one step* brings that person into attack range (making it plus eight) and WHAM! Then the squealing about police brutality starts, and video clips go viral. Bad cop, mean cop, oppressive cop!

If you *don't* know about range, JAM, and immediate threat, it's easy to believe the cop just got sick of the protestors and decided to throw the one a beat down—particularly because that's what you're told by the folks who are screaming about it. On the other hand, if you know about JAM and immediacy of threat, you can see the closer the protestor gets—while acting this way—the more reasonable the belief of a pending attack. (Especially if you know how common this kind of escalation and tantrums are for someone working him- or herself up to physically assaulting you.) Developing JAM on police is an easy way to learn about what happens when someone takes your threat displays seriously.[34]

An empty-hand action when done seven feet away from you is a bluff. The exact same action when done within two feet could still be a bluff. Or it could be the attack starting. In which case, action is necessary. But would it be necessary if you could move from attack range? Believe me that issue is going to be explored in an attempt to undermine the reasonableness of your choice to use force.

Recognize everything I've just said also applies to you. If you look like you're going to attack, it *is* reasonable for the other person to believe you're going to use unlawful physical force. So be careful about throwing threat displays, especially in high-risk situations (plus five through nine).

Another concept we'll go into later is provoking another into acting so you can justify your own actions. Then claiming you were unlawfully attacked or "he started it." Would it have been necessary if you hadn't made the comment about his mother's oral fixation? And yes, the law is wise to this dodge. (We'll talk about it when we get to Subsection 3A and 3B of the Colorado Revised Statutes.)

Now let's go to an area that gets really gray about lawful or unlawful physical force—trespass. While the degree varies from state to state,

---

34   It's also something a cop understands about a decision to react to a growing threat, which can influence how the report is written up.

all states recognize the rights of an owner (or a duly authorized representative) to use reasonable means to remove someone from their property. While you have the right to physically remove a trespasser from your property, how you do it is limited to reasonable force. What is considered reasonable is again back in the hands of the Texan and the suburban pacifist (with the added complications of state law and how long it would take for the cops to get there). What is reasonable in Boston is different from rural Alaska. If the level of force exceeds what seems reasonable to remove the person, you've crossed into assault.

The flip side of this is if the person escalates the situation. Is it always unlawful force because it's on your property? It's not that simple. How much force were you using? Has it become self-defense on his part? Is it safer and easier to call the cops and report the trespass? Or has the person's escalation moved the circumstances into a legitimate self-defense need on your part? That's way beyond the scope of this book, but you'd be wise to look into local laws and property rights interpretations.

Your property rights give you an advantage. But know this is a double-edged sword depending on which side of the property line you are on. Your claim of self-defense is going to be seriously undermined if you refuse to leave another person's property when ordered to do so. (Remember the fighting neighbors?) That was trespassing and physically removing you was lawful use of force.

Oh yeah, an officer arresting you in the execution of his duty—that's lawful. Resisting will cause the use of force to escalate, which—usually—is a lawful use. You do not have the right to resist being arrested—which will get you additional charges. Aaaaaand if you think being offered unlawful force is tricky, we've finally arrived at the covered, camouflaged pit filled with punji stakes—*necessary*.

Up to this, everything in this chapter has been foreplay. Here is where you are going to get screwed if you *don't* have it all wired tight. Earlier I explained staying inside the boundaries of self-defense was like standing on a table as people try to cut the legs off. I also mentioned how much easier it is to pull you down if you stand by the edge and reach down. Now I'm going to add something to that. It's even *easier* for you to jump off the table, run across the room, and save them the work.

Your adrenalized monkey brain *will* scream at you to *overreact*. It wants you to cross the boundaries from self-defense into unlawful physical force. Whether that is assault, aggravated assault, attempted murder, or manslaughter depends how far you jumped off the table and ran. Your monkey is going to do everything in its power to get you to:

1) Not back down
2) Stomp the threat flat

3) Chase that other monkey out of your sight

4) Teach him a lesson (punish)

5) Show everyone else the cost of messing with you

Yes, you have to be able to jerk the leash. Your human brain must override the monkey brain. (There's another part you'll also need to leash—that's the lizard brain. But the lizard has a different agenda than the monkey.) Most mistakes about necessary force come from the monkey and adrenaline.

Yes, any *inability* to articulate what happened and why your actions were reasonable makes it a slam dunk for the prosecutor to convince the jury you were an out-of-control berserk.

Yes, the jury's bias against violence and ignorance about the subject is going to make the necessity of the level of force you used hard to sell. And *yes*, even the fact you're sitting at the defendant's table works against you. Because if you're sitting there, it means the good guys (cops and DA) think you did something wrong. But above all else that which will convict you for illegal violence is letting your monkey *goad* you into committing illegal violence.

Ever heard of a guy named Sisyphus? (The man punished by the gods to forever push a giant rock up a steep hill.) You already have a boulder to push up the self-defense hill. Overkill, excessive force, not knowing when to stop (or inability to do so) and your monkey forcing you into fights and conflict will send that boulder bouncing back down, crushing you in the process.

I'm reminded of my friend Alain Burrese's[35] story about his explanation to an outraged defendant as to why he was being prosecuted. His explanation ran along the lines of: "Look, I understand he attacked you first. That's *not* why you're being prosecuted. I understand you were acting in self-defense when you knocked him down. Again, that's *not* why you're being prosecuted. You're being prosecuted because you kicked him while he was down. That's assault *not* self-defense."

Now that you understand circumstances, JAM, and immediate threat that story makes more sense. Those kicks to a downed opponent weren't necessary. (It also really didn't help his case when he told the cops he wanted to get his 'licks in.') How much immediate threat was offered by that guy on the ground? Could he have backed away to reduce means even more?

That's an important question. As you can unconsciously develop means, you can consciously reduce it. Making distance gives you time to accurately observe what's happening. It's much harder to do while still standing in attack range. I want you to imagine trying to figure out the next few things from two feet away and from seven feet away.

---

35   http://burrese.com/

Yeah, that guy is down, but he's still moving. *How* he moves is what is important. Forget that he might get up to strike again. Sure, he could. But was it happening at that moment? (What were the circumstances?) *If* he got up and attacked again, you would have to do something else. But it's just as likely he'd get up and run away. Or get up, stand back, and yell, but not physically attack. It's still more likely, he's going to stay down and curl up. There is *no* jeopardy or means from a guy just lying on the ground. Therefore, kicking him is *not* necessary. Nor is it self-defense.

In case you've missed it: You have to know when to stop! What's going to get you in trouble is your adrenalized monkey yelling, "If he's still there, he's still a threat" (proximity). Or "he's moving, he's still a threat!"

What makes it even more complicated is if you were *trained* to overreact. That is an important concept. I already told you about seeing neck breaks from behind on a downed opponent taught as self-defense. I have encountered silat and kuntao martial arts systems where instructors routinely teach kicking and stabbing downed, helpless opponents. I've seen instructors at MMA schools promote ground-and-pound as self-defense. I've seen scenario and adrenal stress instructors allow participants to repeatedly stomp downed attackers. Shooting a downed opponent, especially upon your return from somewhere else, is *not* necessary force. (Again, ask Jerome Ersland.) Continuing to shoot or slash with a knife as the attacker is turning to flee means you are shooting or stabbing him in the *back*. In all of these cases, the force is *not* necessary; it's applied *after* the immediate threat has passed.

I know a lot of so-called self-defense instructors who pride themselves on their "combat effectiveness," brutality, and "shoot him to the ground" attitude. I know a lot of women's self-defense programs that encourage women to "tap into their anger" and go berserk. The same with all too many reality-based self-defense courses that encourage excessive force and stomping an opponent flat. You *must* review what you have been taught there in light of the information I'm giving you here. Make that a spray-paint-and-tattoo comment. These will be the standards your actions will be measured against, not what your instructor told you self-defense was.

Another common problem is when the force used in response is excessive to the threat. This is where 'necessary' is going to rape you in the prison showers. Someone punches you, and you respond by hitting him six times and he goes down. Someone is going to hit you with a club, you can shoot him right? Not necessarily. There's a difference in mass (and by extension danger) between a broom, a tire iron, and a baseball bat. Just like there's a difference between an empty bottle and a full one. Then you have the complication of is he going to hit you in the body or in the head with the greater mass? Shooting or stabbing is *always* deemed lethal force (even if you aim for the leg). Whereas, are those others excessive force—not always. They can be, but often aren't. You cannot gun down on the street an eighty-three-year-old woman because she threatened to hit you with her cane. You'd better have a damned good reason why you can't outrun an octogenarian, who needs support to walk.

It's *much* more complicated than these simple examples. But scaling force up or down depending on the threat is integral to use of *necessary* force. Again, that's in the other book I'm going to have to write—specifically about the relationship between effective force and necessary force. It's way too big a subject to go into detail here. Because it involves things like someone who can hit effectively (normally) achieving in one blow what someone who can't punch effectively won't achieve in six hits. Then mixing that whole wibbly wobbly set of factors with pain, injury, control, lethal force, and incapacitation.

For the record, I'm writing this book from the perspective that your physical self-defense strategies actually will work—which, sad to say, usually isn't the case with most commercialized training. But like I said earlier, you only have two problems with your self-defense training: One is it doesn't work; two is it does work.

We're fixing one set of problems of why SD training so often fails. That is torpedoing the one-size-fits-all marketing lie out of the water and into miniscule pieces. There's a time and place for what you know. The trick is finding out when it *isn't* time. That, more than physical issues, is what causes most SD training to fail in application. But by knowing this information, you're bumping up your chances for success.

This is where most people, who want to know about self-defense, fall down. They want solutions without understanding the problem. More than that, they think they *already* know the problem. Because they don't actually understand what's involved, they have a hard time telling what *is* legitimate danger and what *isn't*. Hard to find minimum force necessary if you can't do that.

Thus far, we've looked at different examples of how the wording of self-defense laws has very specific meaning. We've talked about ways they're going to try to cut the legs out from under your self-defense claim by using these definitions against you. We've also talked about some of the ways you can cross out of defense and into unlawful use of force. We'll talk about the human, monkey, and lizard brains next chapter, but for now know that *emotions* are usually the reasons we cross that line.

Now I want to show you how the law is set up to *nail you* if give into emotion.

This involves doing things that aren't even in the neighborhood of self-defense, yet telling ourselves we are defending ourselves. Hopefully, you noticed the ellipsis (. . .) that started my quotes of state laws. That's because there's something in front of both. In the Colorado Revised Statutes (CRS) it reads:

```
Except as provided in subsections(2)and(3) of this
section . . .
```

Subsection 2 of the Colorado Revised Statutes deals with using lethal-force weapons on another human. But we'll talk about that later in this book—along with how much trouble you'll get into for using strike enhancers. But right now, let's look at 3.

Subsection 3 in the CRS reads:

```
NOT WITHSTANDING THE PROVISIONS OF SUBSECTION (1) A
PERSON IS NOT JUSTIFIED IN USING PHYSICAL FORCE IF:
A) with intent to cause bodily injury or death of
   another person, he provokes the use of unlawful
   physical force by the other person; or

B) he is the initial aggressor; except that his
   initial use of force upon another person under
   the circumstances is justifiable if he withdraws
   from the encounter or effectively communicates
   his intent to do so, but the latter nevertheless
   continues or threatens the use of unlawful physical
   force, or

C) the physical force involved is the product of
   combat by agreement, not specifically authorized by
   law.³⁶
```

Right there is a barrel full of suck for anyone who is young, buff, and touchy about respect. A, B, and C are pretty much designed to hammer anybody who engages in fighting. And they do it well. It's a trap for anyone who lets his or her emotions run amok. It's also not real nice for anyone who feels they have the right to say or do anything and *not* be physically assaulted. That's because such people—who despite being proud of being nonviolent—have a strong tendency to attack verbally and even hit, thereby provoking counter violence. Yes, I said hit. There are a lot of people whose attitude about violence is "it all started when he hit me back." *Don't* be that person.

If you look at Subsection B, you'll also notice that hitting back harder if you begin to lose a fight you provoked doesn't qualify for self-defense.

---

36   Authorized by law is the specific exemption of boxing matches, martial arts tournaments, MMA bouts, and wrestling matches.

either. Kind of important that. This brings up a point specific to readers who are martial artists (empty hand) MMAers, and combatives students. In the exact way that the term self-defense has been skewed and twisted to mean whatever people want it to mean that training has screwed up your *definition* of fight. In martial arts, self-defense, combatives, and reality-based self-defense, people often use the terms fight, combat, self-defense, and martial arts interchangeably. They're *not!* We're going to take a good hard look at that hot mess. There are so many false and fuzzy personal definitions in the SD world, we tend to forget that out in society at large these terms already *have* definitions.

Thus far I've talked about legal definitions, but now I want to shift your attention to Joe and Jane Average Citizen's definition of fighting. For right or wrong, they have their own working definition of fights. Generally speaking, they're not sophisticated enough to use terms like combat by agreement or mutual assault. No, indeed no. Their definition tends to run more along the lines of "two jackasses slugging it out." Oddly enough, if you've sat down with enough cops over the 3Bs (beers, brats, and BS) you discover a remarkably similar perspective. They know a fight when they see one, too. The difference is the police have a lot more first-hand experience walking into such situations.

Experts and agenda drivers have lots to say about violence and—to the uninitiated—it *sounds* good. But after you've seen enough of it, you gain a different perspective. Even though the paperwork has lines listing victim and offender, in real life that's not how it normally works. To be more accurate about most violence reports should read jackass number one, jackass number two. This isn't the movies where you have good guys and bad guys. Violence is seldom that clear cut. Even though we want to believe, "I'm the victim here," our adrenalized actions often give lie to that.

Take a close look at Subsection 3 and *all* the ways "participants in violence" could qualify for violating A, B, and C. When we're calm, it doesn't take much imagination to see how provoking, attacking first, and fighting take actions way the hell out of the self-defense realm. But it's harder to do when you're in the situation. Remaining calm when threatened with violence takes *practice* and *self-control.* That is something entirely too many people coming into self-defense training don't want to hear. In fact, many seem to want training so they'll have the ability to flip out more effectively with too many taking action not necessarily in response to aggression, but rather from fear and outrage over past wrongs.

As you will see in the human, monkey, lizard chapter, we are designed to emotionally infect each other. The three-brain model is useful because—

when we're emotional, adrenalized, and in our monkey brains—it's the *opposite* of forgetting. We don't *forget* violating sections A, B, and C is a bad idea. It's that violating them seems so much the right thing to do. Forget? Ha! We're talking charging over that line hootin' and hollerin.' The problem is the monkey starts taking control of our thinking way before we recognize it.

Even just sitting and reading this you might think to yourself, "Why is this twit repeatedly telling us how easily we can lose control and cross the line? I won't do that. I'm a mature rational person." *That's your monkey talking.* Yes, it starts that early. It's telling you you're too smart to do something that stupid. You're too cool and calm to blow it that way. You only need to be told once. Yada, yada, yada.

Be aware of that trap. Also how right and appropriate you feel while the monkey is guiding your thoughts and actions. You'll have rational, nonviolent reasons as to why you walked off your property to talk to someone, got out of your car and approached the other car at the stop light, why you couldn't leave, and why you had to _____(fill in blank) that led to the violence. This is how regular people get involved in violence and think they're acting in self-defense. They tell themselves they weren't fighting, it *was* necessary. It's also why they get reamed in the legal system for participating in illegal violence.

And for the record, this doesn't apply just to men, either. There's a video of a mother of three, who was involved in a brawl at the 2014 Sugar Bowl. After confronting some young men, she was hustled away (supposedly) by her husband. She slipped past him, returned, and didn't just attack the young men—she literally dove into them. Later when interviewed, her reason for the initial confrontation was she claimed someone taunted her son then insulted her. And this justified her flying guillotine act.

Later, we'll go into the nuts and bolts on how to spot the monkey reaching for the steering wheel. For right now, I just wanted to start that idea percolating for a bit. Moving on, it isn't just excessive force in the incident itself that crosses these lines. Your words and actions—*before* the first physical move is made—will cut the legs off your SD table. Here's a bit of a paradox. The most effective saw for cutting those table legs off is your mouth. The most effective way to keep from having the table legs sawed off is your mouth.

What you say (and do) *before* the first punch is thrown is going to be seriously examined with an eye to misconduct, provocation, and hostility. (Subsection 3A:

. . . WITH INTENT TO CAUSE BODILY INJURY OR DEATH OF ANOTHER PERSON, HE PROVOKES THE USE OF UNLAWFUL PHYSICAL FORCE BY THE OTHER PERSON . . .)

Often when that first punch is thrown, it's already a fight—and it has been one for a while. It just hasn't gone physical yet. That's because you participated in the creation and escalation of the *conflict*. Saying those things about his mother isn't going to help your claim that your actions were self-defense. With the other guy and any witnesses reporting every antagonistic, aggressive, insulting, and threatening thing you did, these *pile up*. They stack up until your self-defense table collapses. Even though *inside* your head the monkey is convinced it is defending itself, *you* are the only one who believes it.

Everyone else is seeing you provoke, intimidate, insult, threaten, and even physically assault the other person—who just so happens to be doing the exact same thing to you. (And for the record, he's probably telling himself he's defending himself from you.) About this time you might be asking yourself, "Wait, I want to know how to defend myself against bad guys and muggers. Why is he wasting my time with all this talk about interpersonal violence?"

Well let me ask you this: When was the last time you had a mugger stick a gun in your face?

When was the last time someone shot at you?

How about the last time someone tried to stab you?

Tried to rape you?

These are the scenarios people normally imagine when they consider self-defense. By contrast, when was the last time you got into an argument with your spouse? Had a conflict with a coworker or had to yell at your kids? Let's try this, when was the last time you flipped someone off, honked your horn, or yelled an obscenity at another driver? That's how *easy* it is to slip into your emotional monkey brain and do something resulting in physical violence! You may be thinking of self-defense in terms of robbery, but raw numbers tell us your chances of being in a situation that escalates to physical violence far out number your chances of being robbed.[37]

Fortunately, most people choose not to react to emotional outbursts. Or if they do, they keep it limited to verbal violence, threats, and insults, especially when it comes to strangers. I mention this because, although the exact percentages vary from year to year, you consistently have over a 75 percent chance of being murdered by someone you *know*. Of the 14,827 murders and non-negligent manslaughters in 2012—well, that's a lot of angering people you *know*! Homicide numbers don't exactly

---

37   *FBI Uniform Crime Report*: In 2011, there were 1,203,564 *reported* violent crimes. Robbery numbered 354,396, making up about one-fifth of them. While most robberies are against a person (usually one on one) that one-fifth drops farther down when you subtract business robberies. So your odds are greater of being involved in kind violence other than then a robbery.

translate to assaults—partly because violence between intimates is filed in a different category (domestic violence). That is *not* to say that strangers commit the remaining 25 percent of murders, *including* all the unsolved murders—so we don't know what relationship the killer had with the deceased. We know the actual numbers are much higher than 75 percent, but we can't say for certain.[38]

Oh, yeah, something else we don't know: How many of those killings by 'strangers' are murders by proxy? Whether contract murders, organizational killings (one of the gang kills you while the guy you crossed is sitting in public and smiling at the security camera) or a family vendetta murder (you did her wrong, so an uncle you don't know walks up and shoots you in the back of the head). Contract or organizational killings are really important to consider because a majority of so-called murder victims have criminal records (depending on the source between 67 percent and 90 percent).[39] Gangs and drugs make for high murder rates. The bad news is we have a heavily armed criminal class. The good news is they are more prone to kill each other.

The other thing we don't know is how many lives are taken by women through proxies. She finds a violent guy, gives him a sob story, maybe sucks his dick, and then sends him after you. It's rude and crude, but proxy violence is not uncommon in socioeconomic levels where sex is a commodity open to barter and a means of influence and control. This behavior is especially common among the young.[40]

Now the really bad news, violence between people who *know* each other is what the cops roll up on the *most*. With people who know each other (and those who don't) it's usually participatory. So law enforcement is predisposed to believe that's what happened. They *don't* assume self-defense. Is it a friend? Is it a family member? Is it someone in a close relationship? Is it a co-worker? Is it a neighbor with whom you dispute a property issue? Nobody can accurately predict *what* the circumstances will be when you find yourself dealing with a physical assault. And while we're at it, there is no magical standard where violence suddenly becomes

---

38   Source *Uniform Crime Report*. As a consideration, cases of homicide where it can be established the killer didn't know the deceased tend to hover around 13 percent. We don't know if the same percentages apply to unsolved cases.

39   It depends on if the numbers are local (city) or national. Some cities are 90 percent, but the murder stats of Podunk, Iowa, reduce the national numbers.

40   If you know a hotheaded young male who is the sort to want to get on his charger and right wrongs, you might want to take him aside and have a chat with him about this kind of woman. Often before he charges off to go do stupid, there will be stamping, snorting, and blowing snot. A crude but effective line of questioning is: "Is she sucking your dick?" Often the answer is no. I then say, "So you're working on spec. You're thinking about going out and doing something that can get you thrown in prison for the promise of a blow job? I wouldn't expect her to show up at the jail to pay up . . . or to bail you out."

real. The popular martial arts slogan, "Well in a real fight, I'd . . ." is complete hogwash. All violence is real.

Moreover, there will be situations where you might be called upon to physically intervene. These hardly ever involve self-defense. They may be justified uses of force, but call them that. Do *not* call them self-defense. Is getting drunken Uncle Albert out the door without hurting him self-defense? No. Is jumping on a drunken friend, who is about to get into trouble, and dragging him out the door self-defense? Nope. Is breaking up a fight self-defense? Not really—especially when it's between two family members at your cousin's wedding. Therefore, don't try to claim self-defense when the police show up. (We'll discuss dealing with the cops in another chapter.)

Those situations are *all* uses of force. Circumstances where you need to scale the degree of force you use, understand the goals, work toward them, and not cross the line into fighting. Oh, yeah, and be able to articulate what you did and why—in case the cops show up.

As an aside, I am going to recommend you finish reading this book, give it a few weeks to percolate in your head, then read it again. At the very least reread this—admittedly long—chapter. Much of the information later in this book will significantly influence your understanding of *this* chapter.

In closing this chapter, I want to give you a professional's perspective about why so many people are arrested for supposedly "defending themselves." I have seen this pattern thousands, if not tens of thousands, of times in my life. Once it is pointed out, you will see it, too. But until you have the information you've read in this chapter, you won't see the clear and systematic logic that goes into your arrest for fighting.

On the Internet, you can watch countless clips of violent behavior filmed on cell phones. While this behavior doesn't appear in every instance (for reasons we'll explain later) you will see a specific pattern in the majority of physical conflicts. This pattern constantly repeats itself—across ethnic and national lines and across continents. In short: It is a *human* behavior.

The first time you watch any clip involving violence, *mute it.* Turn the sound off and just watch. Words—especially the emotional commentary of the camera person—distract and induce bias as does the title the poster gives the clip. In the longer, unedited versions, you will see a loud and escalating conflict between individuals or groups, including yelling, posturing, threat displays, and other hostile actions. (And yes, you can see the body language of someone yelling—but you have to actually look for it.) This is what Miller refers to as the monkey dance.[41] This pattern of behavior is as human as falling in love.

It is so universal, it's why I say we're wired for conflict and violence. It's almost a default behavior for the common forms of conflict, a factory setting if you will. Until we can replace it with other strategies, it's nearly universal. It's also most obvious in young males. But in all honesty, I can't say if it's male behavior or if females learn to replace it with something else earlier in their lives. Because I've seen women do it, too—especially with people with whom they're intimate.

You can tell by either the distance or if they are still shouting that neither side really wants to engage. But they have too much ego, pride, and fear invested to back away. They're hoping their threat displays will work so they *don't* have to use physical violence. (That's the reason for the threat display.) Another common behavior—especially in the U.S.— is one of the participants staying in place while the other 'chicken struts' away and back again. On the return trip, the strutting person renews the verbal tirade and threats. And the dance continues. A technical point on this moment in the process: On second viewing when you turn on the sound, you'll often hear the taunts and jeers from the other side. These bring the person back.

On one hand, it's often the guy standing there who is taunting. Remember Subsection 3A about provoking? Even if the guy comes back and without another word swings, the baiting that brings him back *undermines* the taunter's claim of self-defense. This is important because your monkey wants to insult, degrade, or verbally punish a person, who is trying to withdraw for having dared to challenge you. *Get that monkey a ball gag!* If the guy is walking away, let him go! *Shut your mouth!*

On the other hand, taunts often come from a third (or more) party. While some in the crowd try to either pull the participants back or keep them from advancing, others do the direct opposite. They want to see a fight. These others—especially with larger numbers—will be egging on the participants. (Keep an eye on these types because after someone goes down, they often jump in and rat pack whoever is rendered helpless.)

Still others mill around. While you can say they are watching the show, often the reality is different. They are excited and emotionally distressed, but they don't know what to do and are looking for cues from others on how to act. And since everyone else is standing around with their thumbs up their butts . . . Having said that—and as you'll see in a later chapter—the crowd has a big influence on stupid decisions. Plus you have the whole witness and filming issue.

---

41   *Meditations on Violence* and *Facing Violence* by Rory Miller; *Scaling Force,* Miller and Lawrence Kane

In these videos, what often occurs is one party deciding the yelling, posturing, and threat displays are *not* enough. This individual will throw a single punch, open-hand strike, or will shove.[42] At this junction, it's *important* to note the distance between the two participants. Often the assailant does *not* press the attack. It's not an outright blitz and beating. Usually, the person struck reels back, and the assailant stands posed and threatening—but *not* attacking again. Sometimes, the struck person reels back and the striker *steps back* doubling the distance. Regardless of who creates it, distance is the important part.

For a split second, the means to attack is missing. The distance is too great. And usually the attacker is *not* winding up for another attack. (He's too busy striking a tough guy pose.) If you can freeze the video at that moment, you will usually not see an *immediate* danger or continuation of intent to attack from the primary aggressor. What you *will* see is the original attacker puffed up and threatening—from a distance. (Like I said, pose.) Then when you hit the play button, what you'll often see is the person struck rally, close the distance, and attack.

This is *not* a counter punch! Counter punches occur at the same time as the initial punch. But more than that, it is *not* a defensive action, which also takes place at the same time as the initial punch. At best, it is a counter offensive. But you have to turn your head and squint to see it as such—mostly by ignoring the circumstances and looking at the entire incident as a homogenized whole. In reality, it is an *independent* offensive action. At worst, it's revenge.

If you've ever been in this situation, your thoughts aren't "he's attacking me." They're more along the lines of "you sunnofabitch!" It is pure outrage and anger. Often less about the hit, but the insult of being hit. Later when you have to justify yourself, you start claiming self-defense. But at that moment, it is all fury and indignity. How dare this bastard hit me! The person's expression may show shock and pain as he reels back. But on the way *back in,* he has an entirely different appearance. He wants payback for the insult and indignity of being hit.

Again, this won't describe every incident of violence you see in clips. Depending on what your search history throws up and the length of the clip, you may have to look for the longer clips. (Many are now edited to show just the final engagement where one person blitzes the other and stomps him flat.) You want to see the full unedited version—or failing that the longest clip available.

Even in cases that are resolved with extreme beatings in the longer clips, you'll usually see this behavior *before* the final beat down. The

---

42   Men tend to punch men. Men tend to strike women with an open hand. Women attack either sex using punches and open-hand attacks—but with women open-hand attacks often involve clawing.

end often overshadows this mutual and retaliatory behavior. But this is very much part of the build up to *that* ending. Usually beat downs only come after lesser force has failed. Now stop and think about what I just described in the context of what we have discussed in this chapter.

You can run these scenarios through the standard of JAM (and some other factors I'll give you). You will be able do a much better job of assessing the threat than you would before reading this. In fact, let's do so now. Taking such a clip, what did we see?

Both parties were engaging in verbal violence, insults, and threat displays (contributing to the creation, participation, and escalation of verbal conflict). In order for threat displays to be credible, the other person must reasonably believe the primary aggressor is about to attack. But both parties are developing JAM on one another at first so they can *convincingly* perform threat displays.

Second is the strike as part of an escalated threat display. Third, they let it sink in for the other party (after the hit) exactly how serious they are. (See! See! That's how serious I am!) While retaliatory blitz attacks happen, just as often the struck person does the exact same pattern as the person who punched first. That is to say, step up, hit, and then puff. This pattern continues until it escalates to a blitz. Both parties are deep under the influence of adrenaline. Both operate under intense emotion and deep in their monkey brains.

What's keeping them there is *not* being physically trapped. They are mentally ensnared. Instead of withdrawing, the presence of the crowd is adding to their "I can't back down" positions, as well as "I can't run away." They are what I call rattlesnake cornered.[43] Use of force is a *choice* both parties are making, as well as choosing to stay and participate. The situation can be peacefully resolved by one or both parties walking away, especially if each can avoid throwing parting verbal shots that cause the other person to chase him or her.

The immediacy of the threat could be negated by either party walking away (thereby eliminating the necessity of physical force). Neither is in a position to offer lawful use of force. Both seek to provoke, antagonize, and intimidate the other through the threat of unlawful physical force. The initial aggressor engaged in assault (thereby rendering a claim of self-defense untenable under CRS Subsection 3b when the other person counter attacked.) Whereas, the person hit rendered a claim of self-defense untenable when he *chose* to return to attack range and commit his own assault.

In other words—when that person returned fire—the situation became

---

43   The American rattlesnake is so stupid it can find itself cornered in the middle of an open field.

combat by agreement in Colorado or mutual assault or consensual combat in other states—better known by normal people as a *fight!* These charges are further supported by *all* the behavior occurring before the first punch was ever thrown. If the police choose to do so, they can justifiably charge both parties. And both sets of charges *will* stand up in court.

If the police want to save themselves some paperwork or cell space, they'll only charge the winner. Not who threw the first punch, but the one with the least damage. When they do that, the loser of the fight is magically transformed into the victim by virtue of placing his (or her name) on that line in the police report, regardless of who initiated the physical violence. Keep that last part in mind. Usually, it's a safe assumption that the winner of the fight is the one who used the most excessive and unlawful physical force. It's been that way for the last ninety-nine calls the officer responded to, and it's an easy bias to develop. A bias you—having acted in self-defense—will have to contend with. Never forget: *Successful* self-defense looks a lot like you're the aggressor.

Lucy, you have some 'splainin' to do. Having said all this, let me repeat myself. If you lose your cool and engage in this behavior, then what you did was *not* self-defense. Or if you blow it some other way, then: *Shut up, lawyer up, and let your attorney do damage control.* Trying to talk your way out of being arrested—especially by claiming self-defense—will hoist you by your own petard. Or as a law enforcement friend of mine often tells people, "Nobody ever talked me out of arresting them—but a lot of people have talked themselves *into* it."

CHAPTER 4

Until you make the unconscious conscious, it will direct your life, and you will call it fate.
— Carl Jung

Three-Brain Model

Brace yourself—this is a big, bad chapter. More than that, I'm about to tell you the biggest lie to children of them all. I've been alluding to this model for a while, now it's finally time to explain it more completely.

No reflection on your sex life, but every night you go to bed with a human, a monkey, and a lizard. This an analogy for different parts of your brain.[44] And each part handles different aspects of life.

Understand that I have taken the fields of neurology, medicine, psychology, physiology, and biology and reduced them to nursery rhyme level. There are hard core sciences and lots of soft science telling us about the workings of our brain. (To anyone in those fields, I apologize for such a gross and incorrect oversimplification of massively complex topics.) The problem with those scientific fields while they're great in the classroom and lab, they don't do you much good out in the field—as in they *crash* and *burn*. But when someone is screaming in your face, you can remember human, monkey, and lizard. You also can keep them in mind when a predator is closing on you.

A couple of quick points. One, for communication purposes it's easier to talk about human, monkey, lizard, and *you* as individual entities. These are parts of you. *You* are not these parts. At the same time, we've tricked ourselves into believing this is who we are. So much so, we don't even recognize how much we've let these parts run our lives. Ursula Le Guin once wrote, "Fear and fire, good servants, bad lords." Think of the human, monkey, and lizard as advisors to the king or queen (that be you). A lot of people let the advisors run the kingdom while they slack off. When we're talking about self-defense, it is *you*, not *they*, who must rule the country.

---

44   Neuroscientist Dr. Paul D. MacLean first posited the idea of a "Triune Brain" in the 1960s. That model was often explained using human, horse, and crocodile. (*The Triune Brain in Evolution*, 1990.) The human, monkey, lizard model is what Rory Miller and I use in the Conflict Communication program. www.conflictcommunications.com

Two, the three-brain model is a road map of where you need to go to safely handle crisis situations. Circumstances like that are when we need to get out of the monkey. We do this by first remembering the lizard and human, then listening to what they have to say. They're *way* more competent at handling these emergencies. While there's a time and place, we need to keep the monkey and lizard within reasonable (human) boundaries—especially when they are screaming at us to react on a nuclear level. Because I'll give you good odds that the monkey is telling you to overreact to a situation. And *that* is a fast track out of the self-defense square. This chapter will help you get them to work together, instead of against each other and you. I'm going to start at either end and work toward the middle.

The lizard is the oldest and most primitive part of our brain, the hind brain. It handles deep survival issues such as breath, movement, spatial relations, proprioception, sex, escape from predators, and other primitive survival processes. Think of a real lizard in a world filled with creatures trying to eat it, things it's trying to eat, as well as have sex with. Got it? That's a pretty good picture of what the lizard is about and what it's good at.

It also handles complex processes at a nearly unconscious level—once you've learned and ingrained them. For example, driving. Simple act, right? No. The act of driving is really complex. But after you've done it for a while, it becomes easy, but that's not because it's effortless. It's simple because all the complex movement, subconscious processing, spatial assessments, and reactions are handled by your lizard brain at a down deep level way below your conscious thought process. If—while driving—you were to consciously think about everything you see, try to decide the right reaction to the circumstances, then implement it, you'd be in an accident within minutes—if not seconds.

Anytime you see what is called "unconscious competence" in performing a task, you're seeing someone's lizard brain at work. Whether it's playing the guitar, cooking, or participating in sports, the person has done these actions so many times the lizard now takes care of it, freeing other parts of the brain to focus on . . . other stuff. I mention this in passing, but ingraining this unconscious competence of movement is a *huge* factor in the ability to function in a crisis. By letting the lizard handle executing the movement effectively, you free up much needed consciousness to handle other issues.[45]

Something else the lizard is real good at is spotting immediate physical danger. In the first part of his book *Emotional Intelligence*, Daniel

---

45   Let's say you only have $10 worth of conscious thinking. During an incident, you want to invest all $10 into threat assessment, tactical considerations, and scaling the amount of force you use. The lizard handles the other stuff. What you *don't* want is to invest $2 in what technique do I use? Another dollar in is he in range for this move? Yet another $3 in how do I move to effectively generate force? Plus $2 toward what if it doesn't work? The only thing scattering your money around like that is going to do is cause you to fail.

Goleman talks about Joseph Ledoux's discovery of a back alley in our brain, to a part called the amygdala. Ledoux's finding helps explain the mechanism for emotional hijacking. (That's the term Goleman uses for our loss of control when perceiving emotional danger.) The amygdala holds our definitions of threats and dangers and controls the reaction button. It perceives danger and—faster than consciousness—hits that button. By the way, I do recommend you add Goleman's *Emotional Intelligence* to your reading list. It will help you apply a lot of the information from this book. Having said that, I'm going to identify three related points.

One, in our safe modern world we have very little experience dealing with physical danger. This is radically different from the way our ancestors lived when countless physical dangers were facts of daily life.[46] In ye olde days, our amygdalas were set for more than just emotional perils.

Two, it's *not* that we don't see physical danger or its approach. Many people have conditioned themselves to focus more on emotional dangers. In essence, they perceive physical danger as less important (or nonexistent). And why not? We live in a safe world. The result is the monkey controls the amygdala's action button. It has no problem pushing that button for its own reasons. But it slaps the lizard's hand away when the reptile is trying to sound the alarm. (This simple idea has huge implications for instructors, students of self-defense, and those involved the safety field.)

Three, when it comes to physical danger how much experience you have, how well trained you are, and how much you *trust* that training determines if what's pushed is the panic button or the time-to-get-it-done button. Important safety tip: If you don't have faith in your training, you *won't* commit to doing it. Again, a topic way beyond the scope of this book, but real important for acting in time, effectively, and within SD lines.

We like to think we're rational beings, but everything is built on top of the lizard brain. Down deep, we are animals and those animal concerns are the lizard's priorities. It's what has kept our species alive for the millions of years it took to develop the other parts of the brain. I tell you that because the lizard has its own . . . well . . . let's call it consciousness. When that part of our brain is up and running (usually during sex, sports, and in a survival situation) you are *not* the same person. This consciousness can range from blind, survival mode panic

46   Getting on a horse and riding to town was risking death if the horse spooked. Before they redesigned switches for safety, even turning on those new electric lights could kill you, as opposed to the danger of burning down your house with oil lamps. Then you had spiders, snakes, and scorpions in the pre-pesticide and pre-suburb world.

(crisis) to totally calm effective action (trained response) to having an orgasm. (That is species survival.) Lizard consciousness doesn't play much of a part in our modern lives. (When was the last time you fought off a sabertooth tiger?) As such, it usually lies mostly dormant. At the same time given a long-term shift in our circumstances, lizard brain consciousness can—and will—wake up. The comfort and stability of our modern lives keep us from discovering what appalling savages we can become when it boils down to survival.

As a side note: Don't think that you'll be able to snap into your lizard and do ruthless self-defense and mayhem because you've taken some self-defense training. Socialization is strong; it takes time to break it down and sink to this level. Many people do *not* survive long enough to reach the point of being ready to unleash the lizard. This is a lot bigger than you. Yes, millions of people died in the Nazi concentration camps. But they and millions more allowed themselves to be herded into those camps and ghettos rather than take drastic (socially unacceptable) measures. By the time they reached lizard consciousness, it was too late. The situation had progressed too far.

Often in the case of self-defense, people fail to consciously override a lifetime's social prohibitions and act effectively and quickly enough against someone with years of violence behind them. It's not impossible, but it requires a conscious act of will—especially the first time.[47] The trick to accessing lizard consciousness in time is not to try to abruptly teleport there. You don't try to suddenly morph into a god of destruction when unexpectedly ambushed.[48]

The first step is to learn that you have it. Second is to learn how to access this consciousness within you. (Hint: It's not all about violence, savagery, and conflict.) Third, start listening when that part of your brain tries to warn you about something. Fourth, when you see a situation developing wake up the lizard. Not before it needs to swing into action, but to help assess the situation. For most people, it takes time to get to lizard consciousness, allow plenty of time for traffic.

Moving on, the human brain is your rational, logical, problem-solving part. It's roughly equated with your neo-cortex. It's the part that handles things like math, language, and problem solving. Evolutionarily speaking,

---

47   The hardest part is having your human and lizard work together to override your monkey

48   For the record, the ability to flash into your lizard sucks. It's not cool, it's not powerful, it usually makes you a paranoid, violent jackass. While it saved my life in times of shit, it nearly destroyed it, too. It took me decades of hard work to learn how to live with what was inside me. It cost me a relationship when I came out of a dead sleep and threw my girlfriend across the room. My wife dealt with nightmares and me being triggered many times before I got it under control. This is one of the reasons why I tell people being able to stop is more important than being able to go.

the human brain is the new kid on the block. Hence, the term neo (new). The human also is very slow. Despite this, I really like the human. It comes up with all kinds of cool things like engineering, medicine, construction, math, written language, computers, and toilet paper. Basically, the human has solved many of the problems that bedeviled our ancestors . . . like plagues. But those solutions took time.

Where the human brain falls down is coming up with fast, on-the-spot answers. I'm not talking about answering unexpected what is four times two questions. (That's mostly memory.) I'm talking about "what do I do given these immediate circumstances?" answers. Situations in which you don't have time to think, but you need an answer *now!* More than that, you need to put that answer into action *fast.*

Okay. if you need a fast answer to a tiger charging out of the bush that's lizard's turf. But what about which fork to use? What person do you introduce first at a party? How do you handle a cranky boss? Okay to make it more macho, what do you say so as not to get punched? Welcome to the monkey brain. I also call the monkey our socio-emotional brain; it keeps a long list of social behavior and timing. A list of "this is what you do when this happens" and "that is what you don't do." (The latter can be more important.) Usually, these do and don't do lists follow socially determined rules. These behaviors are de rigueur and are so formalized that they become *scripts*. If you do something for someone, they say, "Thank you." In return you respond, "You're welcome." You perform this behavior without hesitation—or to be more accurate without thought.

You don't have to figure it out. It's rote. Here's the stimuli—*boom*—you simply follow the known script. Interaction complete. If the script is followed, everyone is satisfied—and each can go about his business. If the script is *not* followed, we are left emotionally dissatisfied. Or putting it another way, the monkey is discontented. An emotionally dissatisfied monkey is usually an angry critter on a crusade to set things right. But that anger is a *secondary* emotion. It follows the monkey's confusion and realization that its perceived needs, expectations, standards, and beliefs are *not* being met.[49]

I often demonstrate these ideas in a seminar by walking up to someone, extending my hand, and saying, "Hi, I'm Marc." Automatically, the person extends a hand and introduces him- or herself. This is an example of a social monkey script. They are so ingrained that even out of context (in a seminar) we *follow* them. I then explain what I did, and everyone nods sagely about how automatic this scripted behavior is. (Keep this

---

49   It has been postulated that anger has three core sources: 1) preservation of essential needs; 2) preservation of self-esteem; and 3) preservation of core beliefs. This is a very simple but profound model—especially when you start mixing and shading the three.

in mind, it's critical for understanding bad guy strategy.) Later, I have someone else walk up and introduce him- or herself in the same way. Except instead of responding in the normally scripted way, I blankly stare at them, turn, and walk away.[50] I ask what their internal reaction was to my behavior, my breaking the script. It's universally confusion followed by negativity.[51] I say negativity because anger is one of the choices. There could be confusion, embarrassment, shame, and other emotions. With many people, though, anger is a habitual choice. So too is verbal aggression.

In the short run, this reaction calms the monkey (self-southing). But it also works in a different way to satisfy it. *Anger is a script, too.* The person's behavior forces the situation into a known set of circumstances, behavior, and results—a comfort zone. Granted an uncomfortable comfort zone, but at least one that's predictable and familiar. The monkey is all about that.

Another thing the monkey holds is our beliefs about how the world works, who we are, how we identify ourselves (especially tribally) what others should expect of us, and how others should treat us. If those standards aren't met, the monkey can go on the warpath. Or drive you into depression and despair. Or coerce you into self-southing behavior (including drug and alcohol addiction). Or turn you into a narrow-minded, self-righteous boor. Any and all of these are possible responses, including engaging in harmful and destructive behavior that you—and your monkey—know is wrong (e.g., punching someone in the mouth). But to an offended monkey, *all* of these reactions are right and reasonable behavior.

The monkey's priorities are *entirely* emotional and social. Once you start thinking about behavior in human, monkey, or lizard terms, all kinds of things start making sense—including behavior that doesn't make sense. Would a rational human do that? No. Would an irate monkey? Oh yeah . . . That is actually an advantage on many levels. Once you learn to recognize the monkey's presence, you can make a conscious effort to soothee it—both within yourself and others. You do this so you can *get it out of the way* and return to finding a human solution to the problem. Because the monkey is so script-driven, it is predictable—even in its unpredictability. You can't always accurately predict that it will jump, but if it does, one of these four ways is most likely. Take for example the common defensive reaction to mentioning the responsibility of southing

---

50   Then I turn around and immediately apologize for what I did to them—this is important because I've just kicked their monkeys in the nuts. Remember to apologize if you want to try it out.

51   That's the need for an apology. It puts the situation back onto a script and soothees the monkey.

another person's monkey. The human understands it as a good idea. But the monkey often reacts with a "Why do I have to do it? He's the one who has the problem!"

While emotional and social mix together, there's also another set of factors—internal and external. Internal includes how you feel about yourself. How you view yourself? (E.g., I'm a good person.) How you identify yourself? What roles do you have (e.g., mother, father, boss, employee, student)? What groups do you belong to (e.g., national, ethnic, religious, ideological, social, etc.)? What do you do? What behavior don't you do? (E.g., I don't steal.) At first glance, these don't seem like much, but these labels *strongly* influence our thoughts and behavior. External is how you behave toward others; how others treat you. Who are your circles of friends and family? How well do you follow social scripts? What do others think of you? There are countless other outside elements.

Things get complicated when the monkey starts internally telling itself what external conditions are. While we all take in external data and process it, there is a particular socio-emotional monkey filter for certain kinds of information. Ordinarily, you don't get excited by the presence of a wall; it's there. Whereas, the expression on someone's face can and will stimulate the monkey. It's going to start writing, directing, and starring in its very own movie about what that other person's expression meant—a movie that *will* affect your behavior. Here's the question: Is the movie it's writing a documentary or science fiction?

Where this internal movie turns into outright fantasy is when it comes to the monkey deciding what other people *think* (or will think). Wait, we've gone from internal to external and have now passed into someone else's internal? When did this turn into the Psychic Hotline? The monkey not only believes it's psychic, it *knows* it is. It will tell us how to act based on its amazing psychic abilities. The monkey's biggest, sneakiest trick of all? Convincing you that *you're* doing such a thing not *it*. You *know* what that person meant by that comment. You know this person has it out for you! You know that person always . . . Actually, you don't know, but your monkey is sure it does.

It's a powerful motivator of our behavior, especially when it comes to being an offended monkey. The monkey fears what people *will think* if it does or does not do certain things.

Notice I italicized will think. That's because you are *not* a mind reader nor are you a fortune teller. Although it doesn't believe it neither is your monkey. You're reacting to a guess and a *story* your monkey tells you about what is going on inside someone else's head. This habit is so engrained our monkeys have us so convinced, we *don't* recognize when we've taken this turn. Because it happens on a subconscious level, most of us are functionally blind that we came to a crossroads and made a left turn.[52]

I'm going to give you a real important safety tip. I want you to take everything I've said about doing this and *apply* it to others. Recognize it's not just you, this is what happens inside other people's heads too. This is a very human mental process, one that guides huge chunks of our behavior. In 95 percent of conflicts, it's a person driven by their monkey who's coming at you. Knowing about it is a simple but powerful concept. A tool you can use to keep your monkey from freaking out and also to deal with another freaked-out monkey. I will go into this further in my forthcoming *Conflict Communications* book.[53] But recognize when we take this turn, the monkey *movie* becomes our *reality*.

Why do we believe it? Odds are good it's going to kick in emotions and adrenaline to cement the validity of this interpretation. Getting hit with thoughts, perceptions, emotions, *and* physical sensations create our reality. This is how the monkey movie becomes our reality, our Truth™.[54] This emotional and adrenalized reality occurs over an imaginary conclusion you've decided will happen (or is happening) externally. While the emotion and adrenaline are real—they are *internal*. As are the subjective realities they create within people.

Having done it all our lives, we don't realize how screwed up this is until it's laid out on the table. The fear results from an internal conclusion based on potential external results, which are based on psychically knowing another person's internal conclusions. Conclusions you didn't bother to reconfirm. Naaaaaah, nothing could go wrong there . . .

To be fair, yes it may be an accurate prediction. Those *may* be the actual results and consequences if you do or don't do something. But the fear is entirely inside your own head. If we do not double check for accuracy against what is actually happening externally, we can—and often do—chase ourselves down the rabbit hole.

52   An example of subconscious decision making: "When people meet, copulation is on their minds." I call this sex, yes, or sex, no? When we look at another person, we subconsciously go through a fork in the road. Would we want to have sex with him or her? This *strongly* dictates our behavior. Assuming you're mono-sexual, half the human race is an automatic no. Then there comes age, size, and countless other personal standards. No equals find another script. An overwhelming majority of people are filed under no so fast you don't even know you've made a decision. The only time we are conscious of this fork in the road is when the answer is yes. Then come all the reasons to bump-it-back to no (e.g., you're involved, he or she is involved, it's inappropriate, and other similar situations). This is a deep lizard process, we don't recognize we're doing until it's pointed out.

53   Miller also has a book on conflict communications. (We co-developed the system; we apply it differently.)

54   In the second chapter, I mentioned the difference between reality (your subjective interpretation of events) and actuality (what shows up on the video). This is the mechanism for that effect.

As an example, Miller once told me a story about a young man walking at night with his girlfriend along the beach. He saw a bunch of loud, drunken toughs partying up ahead. Part of him screamed danger, and he listened to it. He told his girlfriend they weren't going farther, and they turned around. It chewed on him. He felt bad about his decision. He believed he'd wimped out. For months, he felt awful about it. He went to Miller and told him this tale of woe. Miller did a tactical assessment of the situation: Lonely beach, a pack of drunken rowdies, his being outnumbered, and wanting no harm to come to her. Turning around and withdrawing was a good choice. So then, why was it bothering him? He thought he was not a man. He went so far as to plan on breaking up with his girlfriend. He reasoned that no woman would want to be with such a coward. Miller asked him, "Have you talked to her about what she thinks?" Well, no. "You might want to do that." It turned out she barely remembered the incident. When she did, her take was entirely different from his. She praised him for his good—not stupid, not macho—decision. She had in fact been very proud of his choice. It took a real man to put aside the macho and be smart. Yet he was about to initiate a bad plan of action because of what his monkey *thought* she was thinking. That is the best story I know for demonstrating how the monkey can control our reality and be totally off base.

It's when we do *not* double check our perceptions (our reality) with the external world (actuality) that we make our worst mistakes. We go rocketing over that cliff absolutely convinced we're right in our interpretation of the situation. After all, it's reality. Let me give you two points about this. Point number one even though I'm ripping on being psychic, the monkey is very sensitive and aware of body language. We can read a lot about someone's internal state by his or her external signals. But it's *not* an exact science.

If I see a certain set of signals, I can accurately assess that a person is in an emotionally agitated state. I can do this at a glance. And as a general assessment, it's pretty reliable. Yep, that guy's livid. This man is going about his business. She's sad. He's excited in a good way. He's excited, but not in such a good way. More specific than that? Not so much. Unless I spat in his face, I cannot know what upset a complete stranger.

This is where the monkey leaves conclusions based on observable signals and starts going all Hollywood. Often the monkey starts making up elaborate stories about what's motivating the other person. "He's mad because. . ." At the farther reaches of this thinking, it's somehow about the other person making things up, "he's enraged because I . . ." Even farther out, it becomes a whole, complex story line of "he's infuriated because I . . . so I should . . . that will make him feel . . . and it will make him . . ."

This kind of thinking can seriously spin out of control. As happened with Susan Smith, the mother who murdered her two children in 1994. She had decided they were the reason her extramarital lover didn't want to run off with her.[55] He, the boss's son, wasn't thinking about running off with her, he was trying to break off the affair, and that added to Smith's spin-out.

Point number two, if you know what to look for you can see this spin-out happening.

There are subtle—but sometimes obvious—signs of this process, visible signs long before the screaming, yelling, and stupidity start. You can observe certain behavior, patterns, and ways of talking that make no real sense until you realize the person's monkey is twirling his or her reality out of control. Three sub-points about this:

1) It takes *time* for someone to get this spun out. Now whether you're standing and watching someone trippin' or he or she steps around the corner in front of you, there has been prior build-up. In Smith's case, it brewed for years.

2) People want to ascribe a single cause to this kind of stuff. No, usually it's a cocktail of messed up. Yeah the person may claim it's about something specific, but that isn't the whole cocktail; it's only part of it. Often that specific thing is the cocktail being shaken—not stirred. Do a little research on Smith, and you'll find she was as screwed up as a soup sandwich with a long history of problems. All of those elements added to her conclusion that killing her kids would get her the man of her obsess . . . errr . . . dreams.

3) People don't take the time to look. The reason they say that "it came out of nowhere" is because they weren't looking—especially when it came to seeing the developing pattern.

First a gross overgeneralization: Because of advertising, media, and constant stimuli, our monkeys have developed the attention span of gnats. Second, we're going to count to ten. Patterns like counting to ten take time. That's where our modern attention spans bite us in the butt—in multiple ways. In one of those, a single incident of weird behavior is often dismissed, ignored, or minimized. (She always says things like that.) In doing this, we fail to see a gradual increase of behavior (the progressive count). The time between five, six, seven, eight, and nine allows us to forget and reset. Then we're shocked and appalled because ten just came out of nowhere. Uh, no, no it didn't.

Another way is when we assume the steps will be consistently

---

55   Smith pushed her car with the children fastened in their seats into a lake in South Carolina. She claimed a black man had carjacked the vehicle with the children in it. The police felt something was off about her story, and it fell apart during extensive questioning

incremental, one, two, three, four, and so on. We don't expect (and are confused) when someone goes one, three, six, ten. So we stand and watch the progression with our thumbs up our butts as we try to figure out what's wrong with this picture. As we'll discuss in other chapters, someone breaking patterns this way is a *bad* sign.

A third way we get teeth marks on our posteriors (and not in a fun way) is because our knowledge of the pattern, our comfort zone, or experience stops at a certain point. Let's say five. Sure we can spot one, two, three. We're good at that. But there's something after five? Six? I saw that happen once. How about seven? Uhhh, heard about it. It's bad, right? If it hits eight, nine, or ten what the hell is that? We're talking deer in the headlights. But again, we *stood* there, watching the whole time. As often as not by not seeing these patterns, people's monkeys assumed everything was hunky dory. They claimed they didn't see it, but more often their monkeys have been standing and telling them everything was fine, so they didn't have to be bothered. (Keep this idea of progression in mind, you will see this information again.)

Changing tracks, while both the monkey and lizard can override the human brain, the monkey has a unique power to hijack and enslave the human to its agenda. A hijack is different than an override. One type of override can be summed up as FEAR (fuck everything and run or false evidence appearing real). Total out-of-control panic, an emotional melt-down, or other highly charged emotions functionally shut down the human brain. That's an *override*. Same with fury. Same with passion. Same with obsession. The key point about overrides is while they may have a focus, they don't have reasons. They are what they are.[56] With a hijacking, the monkey orders the human to come up with logical-sounding reasons and excuses to validate what it believes. And the human brain *does* it.

Have you ever had an argument with someone who rationalizes something that has no rhyme or reason? Or they have a monolithic sticking point that counts more than everything else?[57] My favorite (not)

---

56   If anything, what they have at the moment are excuses (e.g., why it's okay to do it). Later, these are rationalized into justifications (and not in the legal sense of the word).

57   The most obvious target is religion. Say "religious fanatic" and everyone knows what you're talking about. What is less obvious is when someone has taken a secular cause and turned it into his religion. These new sets of "thou shalt have no priority before me" have their own dogmas and fanaticism. In the same way that a religious fanatic draws his or her authority from an invisible force, secular zealots draw their authority from the compassion, nobility, humanity, or monkey appeal of their cause (e.g., save the children, stop oppression, save the planet, and other causes). The behavior is the same; the focus and reasoning behind each is different. But what religious and secular fanatics have in common is not only do they live their lives by these standards, they are hell bent on making sure you do, too.

is when they use 'facts,' studies, and authoritative sources you never heard of to support a complex—often unrelated—conclusion. (E.g., "We must pass this draconian law because this study proves . . .") Another ploy is using words that both explain it all and are above question. These days my personal favorite is ". . . have or has a right."[58] (People who believe their rights are sacrosanct often turn into hostile and violent aggressors when things don't go their way—and they have literally talked themselves into this belligerence.) Another common strategy is the monkey demanding an explanation—but a very specific kind of explanation, not one of facts, science, or cause and effect. Instead, the monkey demands an explanation that satisfies it—except some people's monkeys will never be satisfied.

What I'm going to do is show you the common, everyday version of the monkey hijacking the human brain. You see this all the time. Those rationalizations meet five criteria:

- One, they protect what the monkey believes. While that's important, it's beyond the scope of this book.
- Two, no matter how irrational or unrelated these arguments are to everyone else, they make *sense* to that person.
- Three, it lightens the workload. That's all they have to do intellectually. I believe it, so that settles it.
- Four, a canned argument confirms they've met our modern monkey standard. That is the self-certified identity that we are smart, intelligent, rational, and informed. It allows for the pretense of reason (and self-justification). Knowing 'those words' and using 'that argument' prove we've done research and critical analysis of the situation. (No what it really means is by reading blogs, watching the news, and through other questionable means, we can tell ourselves we're "in the know.") But most of all, it shows that we're numbered among the right-thinking clique. This isn't a belief, dogma, or incorrect—this is Truth™. Except . . . often these points don't make sense at all. When you actually sit down and try to figure out what their arguments prove—much less what they have to do with the issue at hand—you end up more confused. To be fair, this turmoil can come from your monkey trying to defend its position by rejecting contradictory information (avoiding cognitive dissonance). It also can be because outside the other person's head, the argument *isn't* logical at all. Much of the time, it's both.
- But the fifth and biggest criteria is that the rationalizations serve

---

58   I often say, "A lot of people don't understand that rights are a starting point. They're good ideas that must be taken and the details worked out with other rights, responsibilities, and limitations. These days too many people use the word rights as a both a conclusion and an unquestionable defense of their position."

as a verification—an excuse, if you will—for that person's *bad behavior* whether that's a prefabricated, long-term response or one made up on the spot. (I've seen 'em both.) Believing this and the other person doing that is the excuse to whip out your dick and engage in unseemly conduct.

Before we get to the point of someone busting open the back of your head with a baseball bat, this behavior has been *occurring*. We see it every time people talk about political and social issues. Ordinarily nothing much happens with it, but sometimes it spins out of control. This process is how we get to batting practice territory. You're really familiar with the subtle forms of this—since you run into it on a daily basis. When it's subtle though, there are all kinds of checks and balances we take for granted. Socially, you don't do this, you don't do that. Taking away those checks and then progressing farther down that same road is how you get that person quietly coming up behind you with a bat. Learn to recognize this process and when it's beginning to spin out. Being able to do so can both save your life and keep you out of prison. (Because remember, you're capable of it, too—especially in the heat of the moment.)

Slight change of direction, we're taught to think that aggression and violence are wrong. We were raised to play nice. But let's say someone is a hostile, aggressive, mean, and petty dirtbag. I'm not talking about temporary self-southing. I'm saying their standard operating procedures are angry and hostile. In order to justify acting out, such a person will latch onto a term, idea, or philosophy that substantiates not their anger but their attacks on others. That's their *green* light! Spend some time in social media and look at the polarization and hate speech between liberals and conservatives. But their bad behavior is okay because ... You see the same mechanism with a gang member spinning out of control about you dissin' (disrespecting) him as you will with a radical feminist snarling about your "male privilege."[59] Both are justified by ideologies, the only real difference is whether he or she will shoot you for not living up to their unrealistic expectations.

This is where overriding and hijacking blend. It actually *is* an override, but it's spurred on by an already well established, long-term hijacking— often one that both perpetuates and justifies the person's anger. This

---

59   At the time of this writing, there is a trend in certain circles to scream about
_____ (fill in the blank) privilege. Basically if you are born _____(fill in the blank)
you automatically are bestowed with privileges that oppress others. There's nothing you
can do about it except be wrong. As in go sit in the corner and feel bad about being
privileged. Use of privileged, like many other terms, is endemic in certain movements to
explain everyone else's behavior and thinking. Except if you're everyone else, your first
reaction is usually, "What the hell are you talking about?" as the crusaders demonstrate
their psychic abilities and tell you what you think, believe, and how you oppress others.

can manifest in many ways. Hate speech about a group, verbal and emotional attacks on anyone who doesn't share the ideology, validations for excursions to go out and attack random members of a hated group. But usually, it's that person snarling specific words that make no real sense to you. Whatever it is, you're guilty of it. For the record pure, one-sided spin-outs are rare. While someone you've never seen before might walk up, snarl, and punch you that doesn't happen too often. Far more common, you engage in something that fed into the whirlpool. Here's a hint: If in the two minutes prior to you getting your teeth knocked out, you've thought "what a jackass" or said, "Screw you," you probably had something to do with his monkey spinning out like that. Keep that in mind because *your* monkey's gyrations are what are most likely to end up involving you in violent situations. Not robbery, not active shooters, not terrorism—your monkey going off on someone else. Remember, emotions are contagious. Until you learn to vaccinate yourself and not respond to monkey signals and threat displays, you're going to be *part* of the problem.

Letting the monkey take over in conflict will not just throw away your self-defense claim, it will catapult it over the hill—no matter how justified or correct you *believed* you were in what you did. Too many people get in these spin-outs and then try to claim self-defense when the stupidity whirls out of control.

But let's get back to telling ourselves how reasonable we are. "Because I don't wanna! And if you try and make me, I'll lay on the floor, kick, scream, and hold my breath" is *not* a socially acceptable reason for adult behavior and decisions. Instead, we have to pretend that *isn't* what we're doing. So the monkey hijacks the human brain to come up with what we think are rational and logical reasons for behavior and beliefs. The somewhat alarming thing is the smarter someone is the more likely that person is to both fall for this and do it. While that comment is again beyond the scope of this book, again look at the polarization, rhetoric, and media circus that has become our social and political ~cough, cough~ discourse.[60]

The issue with hijacking is that when it happens, people can talk themselves into what they deem 'good' decisions. If that good idea is to gut you like a fish for insulting them, you have problems. We'll talk about deniable malice later, but know now a common form of hijacking is the meticulous set-up of ways for that evisceration to happen. Oh yeah, this really shows up after the incident. Can you say vendetta, boys and girls? Can you say running to the cops and trying to get me arrested? Can we say suing me in civil court? I knew you could.

---

60   The two fields worth looking into are logical fallacies and heuristics or biases. The latter sounds way more intimidating than it is. A book, *The Art of Thinking Clearly*, by Rolf Dobelli, is a great bathroom read (really short chapters and clear, concise examples).

These can be the long-term problems brought to you by monkey hijacks. But let's talk about something that will get you in trouble in the first place—that's the short-term hijack. If you've convinced yourself you *can't* leave because he'll follow you. You *can't* apologize because you'll look weak. You *can't* let that insult go unanswered. Or that it's safe to walk alone through a dangerous part of town. Or that it's safe to verbally tear into a two-hundred-fifty-pound tattooed biker because he wouldn't dare do anything. These on-the-spot hijacks and overrides cut the legs out from under your SD claim. (Oh yeah, they don't do your personal safety any good, either.) But more than that, they are *seemingly* logical reasons why you have to stay and verbally engage.

See, it sticks in the monkey's craw to be treated like this. It wants to win, to 'even the score,' to get its own back. But often it's not confident (or mad) enough to step up and throw this cretin a beating. So you end up being high-centered by that part of you. It won't let you leave *or* attack. Instead, it keeps you there and talking trash. Until things go physical (and it can claim it didn't cause that to happen, it was that other goon's fault). This monkey mechanism is what torpedoes most self-defense claims. Because the monkey is convinced it *is* defending itself—when in fact it has turned you into an aggressive, hostile jackass. (Usually one of two.) That is not only likely to lead to violence, but everyone but you will know it *wasn't* self-defense.

Here's something else that's an aftermath factor. Someone who has convinced him- or herself about something may or may not be able to convince others. But they'll be real vulnerable to people who can speak convincingly about the subject—especially when that supports what they want to believe anyway. As humans we are susceptible to people who reconfirm our biases. When someone is saying what our monkey wants to hear, we functionally shut off our bullshit detectors, including our human brain. It's not bullshit because we know it's 'true.' This applies to self-defense in three ways.

One is the way most people approach training. This seriously influences the market. Most programs pander not to the actual complexities of self-defense, but merely reconfirm what people believe they know about violence. This is how you end up in ultimate fighting styles, all you need is _____ (fill in blank) and "I'd rather be judged by twelve than carried by six" training.

The second way is when someone talks the guy—whom you had to physically deal with—into suing you in civil court. This goes beyond my saying: *Never ask a barber if you need a hair cut; never ask a lawyer if you should sue.* Usually, this happens off stage. But factor into your plans the guy's family telling him he should sue you for what you did. That's if the booster club isn't telling him to do something worse. For example, someone tells him he should come back and beat you with a tire iron for the insult you gave him. Or burn down your house while you're in it. Vendetta can develop all on its own, but often it has outside help And gawd help you if they're willing to pay someone else to do it.[61] The third way is when it's a prosecutor selling the idea to the jury that you didn't act in self-defense. We're going to dedicate a whole chapter to that particular problem.

I'd like to take a look at this same monkey mechanism, but applied in a different—often dangerous—way: Blind spots. Something I heard decades ago is: A blind spot isn't just an area you can't see—you don't know you can't see it. That's an important safety tip. This goes beyond flaws in our logic. When your monkey buys into certain ways of thinking, associated beliefs will seem as obvious as sunlight and as natural as breathing. We simply assume this is *how* the world works. These truths are self-evident. Oh, in case you're getting bored with all this psycho-babble consider that for some folks a self-evident truth is that shooting you is a reasonable response for insulting them whether a lifestyle standard or a in-the-heat-of-the-moment decision. When someone is enraged and coming at you, they are functionally blind to the degree of danger they're putting you in. That's an ugly bend of committed and stupid.

There's a hole in that truth. I won't say it's always big enough to drive a truck through, but there's an opening the human would ordinarily see and say "wait a minute" about. The reason this doesn't happen is the human part of the brain never gets any other information—especially something that allows him or her to see the hole. That's because the monkey is distracting the human. This is a very subtle but important point. The human *never knows* what it didn't see. In daily life, this shut down, this distraction, this inhibitor happens so quickly we don't normally recognize it took place.

It's like you're riding in a car and looking out a window. But there's something in an alley ahead the driver doesn't want you to see. So as you come to it, the driver says something that gets you to look at him instead of down the alley. You don't know what was down that alley, but more than that you don't know you missed something. When you check your memory log, you have no recollection of even passing an alley. So when someone says you drove past it (missed the hole), you are utterly

---

61   I'm not joking about this. There is a completely over-the-top movie called *Baytown Outlaws*. While the movie itself is a spoof of *Road Warrior* meets *Waterworld* meets *Fast and Furious* meets anime—these kind of guys exist. If you cross them, they will set your house on fire—after they screw the doors shut. And guess what? Like in the movie, they often work for someone else.

sincere in your denial. This is how you can get someone who swears they brought the gun along only for self-defense. That's what their monkey told them. Or how they didn't mean to shoot, they just waved it around to scare the other person. It isn't they conveniently overlooked alternative interpretations of what they did, their monkey *literally* blinded them to the significance of their actions.

But this goes even further. I cannot tell you the number of times I've seen shocked looks on people's faces when they either realized what they've just done or when their monkeys' plans go off the rails. First is when they've committed violence. It's hard to believe that someone would be shocked about shooting someone, but I've seen it happen. Second is when it's committed against them; the look of shock on their faces when they get slugged for what they just said about the guy's mother. The monkey is real clever about shutting off the human brain until the moment has passed. Then—hopefully—the human brain will be allowed to kick back in.

Variation number two on this mechanism: If your monkey doesn't agree with the other person's position, those holes—invisible to that person—are going to look like the Grand Canyon to you. The monkey will set the human brain to find any weakness, any flaw, anything that doesn't make sense. Another common strategy is that it will dismiss and minimize key points that give credence to someone else's position. If you're in danger of something making sense, your monkey will drill holes and throw away parts until it doesn't make sense anymore.

These protective strategies give us no reason to doubt what the monkey is telling us is the truth. The monkey's interpretation becomes our reality—a reality that blocks conflicting information. That's a level deeper than doubt; it's a pre-doubt inhibitor. This is a common simian protocol that keeps your human from seeing something that would challenge your own monkey beliefs. Failing that, the monkey will turn it into an ad hominem attack.[62] The information is wrong because of who said it. In more extreme cases it's judging not the other person's monkey-driven rationalizations, but *anything* another person says as complete twaddle. More than that, the person is wrong, ignorant, pig-headed, and—if the monkey really believes its own biases—evil. This allows the monkey to utterly discount him and anything he says. It also gives you permission to be a dick to that person.

Here's where this applies to violence. Ad hominem attacks are attempts to change the script. They are efforts to alter the dynamics, to veer things away from dangerous facts that could threaten your beliefs. They do this

---

62   "To the man" or "to the person," a logical fallacy that something is false because of who said it. An example, depending on which side of the political spectrum you're on, is anything Fox or MSNBC says is automatically a lie.

by taking it into a known conflict script. Straight up, this sucks enough when it's in a situation where verbal violence is the norm. Yeah, you get mutual "screw yous" and hurt feelings. This behavior while not a pleasant experience is something we can do if things look like we can lose at a lower, verbal, emotional, or factual level. But you know what? It's actually *safe*. You know you can survive and handle getting your little duck feelings hurt. That is until we pull it on a physically violent person. Or have a physically violent person running this program aimed at us.

You have to know about this program before you can spot it—no matter what side you're on. Once you start looking for it, it's easy to spot.

I'd like you consider what we've talked about in this last section—in light of a prosecutor trying to put you in prison. The prosecutor will try to give the monkeys of the jury *legitimate-sounding* reasons to convict you, reasonably articulated ideas to dismiss your version of what happened. Revisiting something, knowledge of the monkey hijacking the human portion of the brain shows you how you (and I) fall into the same trap. It's easy to convince yourself how right you are, how your actions will solve this problem. Yet this behavior often provokes violence. Often, the only person surprised you got attacked is you.

I'm going to give you a short list of things that will help you recognize when your monkey is taking over. And it does so in some very predictable ways. The monkey is driving the bus when you find yourself:

- Using the word 'you' a lot
- Using the proper noun 'I' as much
- Not listening (instead, preparing what you're going to say next)
- Having a sense of *not* being respected
- Taking something personally
- Feeling the desire to punish or even the score
- Feeling territorial (whether over possessions or your job)
- Excusingyour(oryourgroup's)badbehaviorordenialofmistakesthat minimizes other's feelings
- Dismissing or minimizing facts
- Minimizing or discounting other's opinions because they are _____ (fill in blank)
- Escalating a situation
- Feeling the need to be right
- Having a sense of immediacy (it has to be fixed *now!*)
- Fear
- Feeling trapped
- Engaging in black-and-white or limited options thinking (especially regarding potential solutions)

- Feeling you can't back down
- Experiencing hurt feelings
- Engaging in insulting or condescending comments or behavior
- Doing 'freight train thinking' (bringing in other issues)
- Engaging in criticism, not complaints

The last two take explanations, but they are closely linked. Freight train thinking is when issues unrelated to the subject are connected in someone's mind and are then brought into the quarrel. Often these subjects are vague, overgeneralizations, accusatory, and omniscient. (For example, proclaiming someone is a racist or sexist based on a single comment.) The disagreement is *no* longer about the original issue, but about this greater wrong and how the person is guilty of it. While these are often examples of how the person thinks, such tactics often are red herrings to the issue at hand. In fact, they're commonly delaying tactics and ways to sow confusion. The user has learned to employ this tactic as a subtle (or not so subtle) threat or to elicit an emotional response or trepidation in order to get others to back off. For example, at work the simple mention of racism or sexual harassment from a problem employee triggers intense monkey brain fear in the corporate structure. What if the person lodges a complaint with human resources or sues? Being accused is scary because the company will often throw someone under the bus rather than risk being sued.

Other times, freight train thinking is an excuse to work oneself up to committing physical violence. By piling on offenses and past grievances, the anger builds—overwhelming the knowledge and prohibition that violence is wrong. Once again, it's a green light.[63] The monkey brain *loves* freight train thinking. When you hear it, it is a solid indicator the human brain's logic has been hijacked by the emotional monkey brain. Specifically, the human brain back-engineers and rationalizes what the monkey has already decided.[64]

That brings us to the second point. There's a difference between a complaint and a criticism. A complaint brings up a legitimate issue about circumstances that can be addressed and resolved. For example, "You're standing on my foot; it hurts." A criticism is condemnation *of* the person. One that *cannot* be immediately resolved—*if* it can be fixed at all. (E.g., "You always hurt me! You're so insensitive!") While a complaint is *communication* about an issue, criticism is an *attack*.

On the core level, we know the difference. In practice, it can be hard to

---

63   There's a specific tantrum strategy some people us to give themselves permission to attack. The speed of the acceleration makes it very recognizable—and articulable. You'll get the tools to spot it later in the book.

64   See Dr. Drew Westen's *The Political Brain* and Goleman's *Emotional Intelligence*.

distinguish between these two. Often like a snowball built around a rock, the criticism is disguised as a complaint. ("You clumsy idiot, you're on my foot!") More often complaints are followed by criticisms. "You hurt me" is followed by "you're an insensitive jerk." Criticism is absolute and eternal. There is no argument or defense to the jerk comment that is not black or white. "I am not." "You are, too."

Criticism also is why people become hypersensitive about admitting to mistakes or errors. When they hear a complaint, they automatically assume a criticism (and punishment) will immediately follow. Others presume any complaint—no matter how legitimate—is an attack and will automatically go on the offensive while maintaining they are defending themselves. It *is* possible to verbalize a complaint without it turning into a criticism. But there are some self-southing, verbally violent people who seem to be incapable of doing that. There also are people who either attempt to drive everyone away or seem only comfortable in the middle of trauma-drama.[65] They seem incapable of opening their mouths without spitting venom. Recognize this behavior for what it is, they're trying to *trigger* your monkey brain. Now you have a choice about responding.

At the same time, self-monitoring for you doing criticisms instead of complaints is a nice skill to develop.

Ordinarily, I don't make a big deal about sex when I'm talking about violence, self-defense, and personal safety. These are human problems and behavior, they are not specific to a particular sex. What also are *not* sex specific are threat displays; we all do them to get our way. Having said that, there *are* tactics more common to a specific sex.

Without going down that mouse hole, any strategy works by 1) having the means to back it up and 2) knowing the rules and limits of its use. If you don't have those, it's at best a bluff and at worst a disaster. The last is more common in extreme situations—especially those involving predators. A scared monkey is too proud to run, but too scared to fight. What it's most often going to do is try to bluff. This mistake is common to humans, regardless of what position they are in when they pee.

In discussing the correct signals to send out to deter a predator, a feminist self-defense instructor wrote: Women, lacking the innate and learned social responses of male aggressive interaction, may try to "out aggression" a predator by using displays of what they assume to be powerful male behaviours (sic, she's Canadian).

I'm torn about this. On one hand, I want to say, "A healthy message, wrapped in ideology and deep fried in agenda." On the other . . . I'm not quite sure what to say. "Right church wrong pew?" "Close, but no cigar?" "Half right?" Perhaps the most accurate response is she:

a) Points out a response common to some women;

b) Gives an understandable and partially right answer that falls short of the bigger picture;

c) Has components that are spot on, but for the wrong reasons;

d) Provides an answer that is *really* important for women to consider about their behavior in threatening situations.

That's because display aggression involves more and bigger issues than a person's plumbing. It starts with modeling behavior. This is something we humans do. In fact, it's a big part of how our monkeys learn to behave. We first watch someone else. Then we think, "Okay, that's how it's done." So we mimic it—usually not so well. If it works, we practice and learn how to apply it. In doing so, we learn the rules, requirements, and the appropriate time to do it—but if we don't practice, we kind of suck at it. Then there's the whole ability and means issue.[1] With modeling behavior in mind, you can take threat displays, plug in her statement, and it—technically—works. Still it skips over the fundamental problem.

Another female instructor responded that monkey threat display or display aggression is the *wrong* strategy to use against predators—no matter if you're male or female. So

---

65   It's often a means to keep from having to engage in introspection. If you're constantly in a crisis, you don't have to look at what's wrong with your life.

1   A nine-year-old modeling aggressive behavior he learned from his bad-ass biker father will work against a seven-year-old. But will get him an educational beat down if he tries it against a bunch of seventeen-year-olds.

why was the first writer pointing it out? The response was, "Because I think that it is not often pointed out to women. I think many women misunderstand display aggression." Okay, *that's* a good point. So let's consider it pointed out.

But there's a bigger issue involved here. Although puffing out your chest and looking like a bad dude may appear powerful and aggressive to you, it *doesn't* look that way to a predator. An entirely different set of signals scares him. But to prove how picky I can be, I'm going to add to it. *People*—not only women—have to be careful about not trying to ape this stupid and aggressive alleged male behavior. I use "alleged male behavior" because I'd like to point out that more and more young women engage in this very same conduct. Up to and including attacking and fighting . . . well . . . pretty much anybody.

Female violence is a taboo topic and off limits for study. The narrative is that women are only the victims of violence, not the perpetrators. Despite massive reporting to the contrary, deniers claim no study supports these reports. I know the plural of anecdotal is not evidence. I also know if studies aren't done and no data is collected, the information isn't available—especially if there's pressure *not* to ask certain questions.[2]

I've always reacted poorly to being told I can't ask certain questions—especially about things I have witnessed myself. So skipping academia and organizations, I asked individuals, police officers, security professionals, emergency room personnel, and teachers. There is a consensus from those on the front lines that women are becoming more aggressive and physically violent—especially young women. Here's something they also agree on. It's happening in exactly the same macho, stupid, aggressive threat displays escalating to physical violence way. Is it still stupid and macho if women are doing it, too? This isn't female-on-female violence, either. A great many men I have spoken to tell stories about being assaulted by women. A consistent interpretation of this behavior is that these women assume they will not be hit back because they are female.

There are all kinds of monkey thinking, beliefs, and biases about the topic of women and violence. It's a can of worms I don't want to open. But when we get to the "What Is Violence" chapter, things will take on a whole new perspective. But let me tell you now: It doesn't matter what your sex is, violence *provokes* violence—especially monkey brain violence. The differences really boil down more to strategy and style.

---

2   About ten years ago, I was responsible for a Bureau of Justice Statistics table on the targets of female murders: How many victims were male, female, or children? Until I specifically asked for those numbers, they *didn't* track them. Odd, because they tracked those numbers for male killers. I don't know if they're still tracking these or if it's tracked, but not generally available. But it can be a hard table of numbers to find.

You get better reactions addressing complaints. Criticisms seldom go over well, and mostly they're about self-southing in public.

If you can spot this dynamic and this behavior, there's a good chance you can keep from falling into this trap. Whenever possible, address the complaint and ignore the criticism. (This takes it off the monkey script.) Better, you can soothee your monkey, the other person's monkey, and resolve the situation *without* using force. This, believe me, saves you all kinds of paperwork, time, and expense. Additionally instead of panicking when social scripts don't work to de-escalate a situation, you'll be able spot when you're dealing with an out-of-control monkey. Or something else, something that isn't a monkey issue, something you might have to use force against.

But how do you know this? You double check that what you *think* is happening is *actually* taking place. Believe me when I say this is critical on the decision to act and articulation in the aftermath. You can't spot non-monkey behavior *until* you know monkey behavior. Nor will you be able to explain why you weren't engaging in aggressive monkey behavior when you're trying to account for your actions.

Remember I said the human part of the brain is slow? Your human brain thinks about as fast as the voice inside your head talks. Your socio-emotional monkey is as *fast* as an emotion. In fact, emotions show the monkey is already up and running. How fast does that feeling—that burst of annoyance, anger, frustration—hit you? I ask because monkey behavior *starts* showing up about a half second behind. Your expression, your body language, and physical actions (e.g., flipping someone off) or your words *follow* that adrenalized, emotional surge. Pay close attention to that order because it happens within two seconds or so.

I've talked about adrenaline affecting our feelings and altering our perception of reality. Our adrenalized emotions often dictate what we do next. When this happens, we're *deep* in our monkey brain. I will point out a small but subtle difference. As of this writing, it's coming onto seventeen years since I was last shot at. That night, I saw a laser pointer paste the client, I tackled her a second before the guy opened fire. Next thing I knew I was up on my feet returning fire. While I was completely focused, I wasn't emotional. I tell you this so you know I'm talking from experience. When you're functioning in your lizard brain, emotions tend to come *later*. Either after you're already moving *or* when you fall apart *after* the situation has been dealt with. Action first, emotions second. That's how you recognize the lizard is running things. Restating an important point, the lizard has absolutely no problem with running fiercely. The reptile will look at something, assess the danger, and haul ass if that's the best option. Later when the human has time to review the data, it will confirm the lizard's assessment and decision.

It's the monkey that has a problem with running. It will keep you there in the name of pride, fear of social embarrassment, and—much too often—winning. Not just in the face of growing danger, but you watering and tending it. If you do the smart thing, it will rag you for being a punk pussy coward. I'm not just talking beat feet, either. It can tear you down for finding a peaceful nonviolent resolution. That is open season, too, you wimp. After the danger is past, it will tell you all the things you should have done, what a loser you are for not whipping out your dick and beating Godzilla to death with it.

If you take no other message away from this book it's this: It's the monkey . . . with its socio-emotional agenda . . . with its pride . . . with its fear (especially of what others will think of you) that's going to put you into the greatest danger. Not fear—danger. Because the monkey fears humiliation more than it does death. The human and lizard know death is real—albeit from totally different ends of the spectrum. To the monkey, however, death is an abstract. It kinda knows it could happen, but it hasn't so it's not really real.

What *has* happened to the monkey was the shame, mortification, and emotional pain of humiliation. A pain made real by the adrenaline dump that comes with the emotion. *That* is what the monkey knows is *real*—and fears. *That* prompts most people into acting in a manner that creates, escalates, and causes a situation to go physically violent. In some cases, it's so extreme that the monkey becomes homicidally terrified of being shamed, of losing face, of being disrespected. *That* is what makes it hard to walk away. *That* is what makes an otherwise rational, reasonable, nonviolent person whip around and yell, "Screw you!" to an obnoxious stranger. *That* is the part that says you *must* get in the last word. You *have* to win. It isn't over until you get even.

This is why understanding violence dynamics is so important. Knowing violence dynamics helps you stay inside the self-defense square. Engaging in out-of-control monkey behavior is *not* self-defense—even though your monkey is absolutely convinced it is defending itself. You cannot put anything the monkey is defending into a wheelbarrow. Emotions, self-esteem, pride, social status, and other such feelings have no physical existence. But those are exactly what the monkey becomes violent over, usually in a very loud, obnoxious, and predictable way.

Now let's shift attention to the jury. These kinds of out-of-control monkey dances are what people remember seeing. Because of availability bias (what we most easily remember *must* be the answer) people assume this bad behavior is what *took place* in your case. What did you say or do that provoked it? You won, so you probably were the aggressor.

This bias is exactly what the prosecutor will try to exploit in the jury members. Putting it in these terms what he's selling is, "It wasn't self-defense as you claim, it's another case of out-of-control monkey violence!" Knowing all of this, what I'm about to tell you will make much more sense.

That is when you're presenting your information about the circumstances of the situation, it's crucial to also communicate *all* the monkey-inflaming behavior you *didn't* do. For example, you need to communicate that you weren't verbally abusing, insulting, threatening, challenging, or engaging in any other verbal violence. Don't worry about having to work it into the conversation. If you're talking to the cops, the subject *will* be broached. You'll probably hear it again from the prosecutor, too.

"Did you insult him?"

"No, sir. I said or did nothing a reasonable person would interpret as insulting."

"So you didn't say, 'Screw you?' "

"No, I did not."

"He says you did."

"Sir, you're going to have to ask the other witnesses about that."

Simple truth *not* engaging in this escalating monkey behavior *is* the best way to reduce the chances of violence. I would say avoid violence, but that is not guaranteed. Some people are just looking for a target to vent their hatred of the world on. Still others are operating on a whole different spectrum. Monkey behavior fails there, too. To a predator, nothing screams safe target better than someone dropping into their monkey brain. This includes macho posturing and anger threat displays. Knowledge is a key element to keep you out of illegal violence—and by that I especially mean—preventing you from engaging in threat displays and violence-escalating behavior. Knowing about the monkey becomes especially important in the next few chapters.

I've been bad mouthing the monkey this whole chapter. You might believe it is a bad thing, it's not. In closing, I'd first like to remind you of the Ursula Le Guin quote: "Fear and fire, good servants, bad lords." Our monkey brain responses work for us—in normal life. That's why we default to them. It's the right answer 99 percent of the time meaning the monkey's responses are good 99 percent of the time. A whole lot of what makes people good, what makes us better people, and what makes us humane comes from the monkey. It's just that in some situations, you need another part of your brain driving the bus.

CHAPTER 5

Amateurs talk tactics. Professionals study logistics.
　　　　　　　　　　　—Gen. Omar Bradley

Five Stages

Many years ago, I was teaching a self-defense class in California. During a break, a Little Bunny FooFoo-type came up to me. Eyes wide, she asked what to do if someone tried to rob her. I answered. She responded with an appalled, "Oh noooo, I couldn't do that!"

Okay, Plan B, do this. "Oh noooo, I couldn't do that!"

Annoyed, I suggested Plan C. "Oh noooo, I couldn't do that, either!"

Frustrated, I snapped, "Then you better not get mugged."

"How do I do that?"

I held up fingers as I fired off, "You look for predatory intent in his body language. You look for him interviewing you to see if you're safe to attack. And you look for him moving into an attack position. If you see these things get the hell out of there! You're being set up."

"Okaaaaaaay!" She happily turned and left.

Thinking, "what a dingbat," I turned to get a cup of coffee . . . then it hit me. WHAT THE HELL DID I JUST SAY! Instead of getting my coffee, I ran into the office and scribbled my words down before I forgot them. Thus was born what would become the Five Stages of Violent Crime. All because I didn't blow off a New Agey ding-dong's questions.

What came out as an annoyed and frustrated utterance was an articulation of behavior patterns I'd subconsciously learned. A collection of identifiable behaviors that had sent my hand to my weapon for twenty years before and still will in the twenty-plus years since. The five stages fill in a gaping hole in what was—and often still is—taught about self-defense. That teaching void is learning how to recognize when you're being set up to be robbed or assaulted.

I spent the next year running this idea past violence professionals. I threw this out to be peer reviewed, tweaked, refined, and tested. I spent a year being the intellectual chew toy of people who knew the subject. I asked these experts, "What's wrong with this model?" And they answered, "Hey, Dipstick, you forgot . . ." And that was before it was tested in court.

Before I tell you the five—remember I mentioned JAM? JAM (jeopardy, ability, means) is a spin off from AOJ (ability, opportunity, jeopardy). While we'll talk more about these in another chapter, I want to say two things. One, the five stages *aren't* exclusive. In fact, they're extremely complimentary with JAM and AOJ. Cross referencing them gives you a deeper understanding of both. Or if you're into animal husbandry crossing them gives you hybrid vigor. Two, once upon a time it was AOI (ability, opportunity, intent). Intent was eventually changed to jeopardy. Why? Because you can take the most widely understood and easily recognizable circumstance, get lawyers involved, and the next thing you know, you'll doubt the sun comes up in the east. The reason I mentioned the lawyers beating each other up over details and terms is I still use intent in the five stages. I do this *knowing* an attorney is going to attack me about being psychic. Bring it on . . .

I'll see your "you're not psychic" and raise you physiology, body language, known and describable behavior, and jeopardy. With a hat tip to Supreme Court Justice Potter Stewart,[66] I'll also throw in, "You know the highway to hell when you see it." With that last, you don't need to know which level of hell he's heading for. Someone manifesting these physiological leaks is way closer to physical violence than someone who isn't sending those signals. What kind? Don't know. At whom? Let me check some other things, and I'll get back to you. But we're on the highway . . .

With that in mind, let's look at the Five Stages of Violent Crime. The stages are:

- Intent
- Interview
- Positioning
- Attack
- Reaction

Intent: Short version, the person crosses a psychological boundary and moves closer to physical violence—and his body reflects it.

We'll go into pre-attack body language leaks later, but right now I want to introduce an important element of communication. Most communication is *nonverbal.*[67] We send millions of unconscious signals every day. Not just facial expressions and tone of voice, but through our

---

66   In the famous *Jacobellis vs. Ohio,* 1964, obscenity ruling, Justice Potter Stewart wrote in his concurring opinion: "I shall not today attempt further to define the kinds of material I understand to be embraced within that shorthand description (hard-core pornography); and perhaps I could never succeed in intelligibly doing so. But I know it when I see it, and the motion picture involved in this case is not that."

67   Depending on how a particular expert defines nonverbal, the estimated percentages range from 70 percent to 90 percent.

clothing; how we move; how close we stand to people; how we move with someone. (You can tell with great accuracy if a couple is married by how well they subconsciously move around one another.) All of these communicate something to others.

I'm going to give you dual points regarding intent. One is an important overview. Two is the counter to the dismissal of this idea. Although I separate them for ease of communication, they are so blended together as to be two sides of the same coin.

First the overview. That is: A single brick by itself is insignificant. Even collectively, a bunch of bricks is . . . well . . . just a pile of heavy rectangles. It's the *shape* the bricks form when mortared that's important. The individual bricks and how they are fitted together make the whole. Until we train ourselves to see the individual bricks and how they interact with each other—at best—all we're going to see is "a building." But that *isn't* good enough.

"Huh? I have to describe it? It's a brick building. Oh you want more? Uhhh . . . errr . . . " That's where most people fall down. The problem they face trying to describe intent is they aren't used to articulating the way specific bricks work together. They see a building, but when questioned about the details they fall apart. Often they try to describe a particular behavior rather than how that element worked with other mannerisms. This allows someone—intent on dismissing what the person saw—to discredit any particular behavior that is noted.

"How did you know he was going to attack you?"

"He narrowed his eyes."

"So you killed a man because he squinted at you? Could it not have been sun glare or a bit of dust in his eyes?"

"We'll no, but he looked at me really mean."

One detail by itself sounds like you're grasping at straws. In contrast to: "He moved into attack position, he bladed his body toward me, took a deep breath, reached for the area on his body where an appendix-carry gun is kept, inhaled deeply, leaned forward, and narrowed his eyes." "So you shot him because he narrowed his eyes?" "No sir that's just a detail in a collection of other behaviors that led me to believe he was pulling a gun."

Articulation transforms the details (specific bricks) into part of a larger pattern. That's the second point, the other side of this coin. Being able to explain how the smaller bricks fit together to form that larger pattern is how you justify (remember that means something specific in legal terms) your actions. Being able to spot when someone is about to go not only helps keep you safe, but helps explain why what you did was the right choice, especially to someone who is looking for wrong doing on your part.

Those bricks and patterns looking a little more important now? When someone is close to committing violence, their body (not just their body language) undergoes certain physiological changes. The body of a person who is ready to commit violence alters in certain subtle ways. Here's a short list:

- Skin color changes as blood pulls back from it.
- Breathing changes.
- Pupils in the eyes change size.
- Muscle tension alters (especially in the face, affecting expressions).
- Hands clench or flex.

All these occur along with many other small signs, and mostly it depends on how close the person is to attacking. Take for example someone who is red-faced and screaming versus someone who goes pale. The pale person is closer to action than the red-faced one.

At the beginning of the attack, there is a lowering of the jaw to protect the throat and to present the armored parts of the skull in anticipation of counter force. Shoulders rise to protect the neck. Eyes narrow to protect them. These all come from the lizard brain, and we're not aware we're doing them. So when the guy is in attack range and they all happen within two seconds . . . whup . . . here we go!

Four things about this:

One, just because someone doesn't consciously notice them doesn't mean these physical manifestations don't exist.[68] This includes knowing certain groupings of these subtle changes commonly reflect a dangerous mental state. These combos are recognizable, even if they are difficult to articulate in exact detail. The more individual 'bricks' you can contribute, the better you'll help your lawyer build your self-defense case. By the way, ordinarily we're pretty good at subconsciously reading these, but when the monkey is on a rip this skill can become . . . a little wobbly. Consciously learning this skill not only enhances your ability on a daily basis, but helps stabilize it during times of stress, adrenaline, and high emotions.

Two, some of these changes are beyond our ability to control. Things like the skin color altering or eye pupils dilating.

Three is that there are still other signs that are default behavior. They are associated with specific kinds of violence and normally appear when certain parts of our brains are active. Things like puffing up, jutting jaws, and throwing arms back in display aggression. Other behavior like yelling, facial contortions, leaning forward and into someone's face, or cocking back as if to hit someone are a hybrid of communication and

68   Old saw: An absence of evidence does not constitute evidence of absence. Tweaking that idea: Just because you didn't see it doesn't mean it didn't happen— especially when it comes to seeing the superficial without noticing details.

preparation for violence. Usually landing more on the communication end of spectrum (threat displays). While we can train ourselves out of doing them, they *normally* appear among the untrained before they fight.

Four, some signs are a matter of culture and personal style. There are cultures where a person becomes loud and aggressive. There also are people who rock back on their heels, pull their heads back, and look down their noses at you before they attack. Others purse or narrow their lips, hunch their shoulders, or drop and shake their heads in a no signal.

Again, these are often culturally influenced. This is different, however, from the signals projected by a person experienced with extreme violence. Often such people will be unnaturally still and meticulous in their motions, growl instead of bark, and subtly shift into an attack position before exploding on you. If you aren't used to that level of violence, you're about to wake up in a hospital—if you're lucky.

When I talk about intent, I am first and foremost discussing witnessing a collection of physiological and behavioral manifestations. No *one* element is the whole story. But the collective whole tells you this person is closer to committing violence or a crime than someone in a different state of mind. This isn't psychic. This isn't woo-woo vibes. This is body language, unconscious behavior, physiological changes, and deliberate action. You can tell this at a glance—although breaking it down into the exact components takes more time and attention.

In the original five stages, I described *intent* as crossing a mental boundary where the person is willing to commit a crime. I've expanded that. It's now not *just* being okay with the idea and giving oneself permission, but how close or far from acting. Again, the closer someone gets to physical violence, the more signs he presents. This includes the criminal trying to hide his intent behind a guise of normalcy. That creates some odd hybrid behavior. Depending on the predator, these range from stilted to smarmy to overly charming to way too accidentally-on-purpose (deniable malice). Once again, how it will manifest depends on the predator.

With all the available video on the Internet, you can watch the first three of the five stages develop. With a little practice, you can spot who has predatory or hostile intent before anything physical happens. If you are watching closely, you can see the change in a person's body language when they shift from planning or thinking about what they are going to do to a decision to act.

Here's a hint, that's who you don't want close to you. A lot of self-defense goo-roos really screw up when they preach situational awareness by telling you never to let anyone get close to you. I've had these deadly urban commandos brag about how nobody with a weapon would be able approach them—as I'm standing next to them, the waiter walks up with a knife, a seminar attendee walks past them carrying a weapon, or they're talking to a cop. That's not just someone getting close, but someone with a weapon. Now what were you saying about your urban warrior awareness? News flash here, we're constantly being crowded in our daily lives. It's less about not letting anybody near you than it is not letting someone, who's leaking danger signals, near you. Otherwise, you're going to end up kung-fuing the waitress, who was trying to serve your steak dinner.

One last thing about intent, part of the reason I use both the highway to hell analogy and say, "I'm not psychic," is because I really *don't* know what this guy plans. And neither do you. But there's a legal concept called mens rea (guilty mind[69]). You may not know exactly what crime he plans, but his body language is going to reflect mens rea. So, final destination? Don't know. But you do know bad things are down the highway he's on. So that's a highway you want to get off of.

Interview: Like intent, interview also has been expanded from the original definition. Originally, it meant the time and how (by the behavior he used) the criminal checked to determine if you were safe to attack. This was a last minute double-check before committing himself. That still very much applies, but there are two new tweaks.

One is interviews can blend. A good example is casing the joint before robbing a business. The robber pretends to be a customer and scopes out the security and layout. The criminal may even buy something and later come back and rob the place. (This would be a regular mixed with prolonged interview.) Or the robber pretends to be a customer, but having assessed the situation decides to act then and there (this qualifies as a regular mixed with a silent interview).

Tweak two is when it comes to attacking and robbing individuals, I used to say the interview was exclusively the aggressor checking to see if you were safe to attack. I've noticed something else, the interview is very much a time to trigger social scripts and monkey behavior in the *intended* target. This will make a whole lot more sense later, but it isn't just checking if it is safe to attack you—it's almost guaranteeing it. We'll go into this tactic a lot more later in the "Asocial Violence" chapter (resource predation).

There are five basic types of interviews:
- Regular
- Hot

---

69   Fundamental criminal law is based on the principle that a crime consists of both a mental and physical element. *Mens rea* is the mental part. That is a person's awareness of the fact that his or her conduct is criminal. *Actus reus*, the act itself, is the physical element.

- Escalating
- Silent
- Prolonged

Regular interviews are attackers pretending that everything is normal in short 'micro-scripts'—usually well under a minute. In robberies, this often manifests as the person approaching and asking you for something. I've heard it postulated the reason for asking is to see if you're willing to give. I think there is a large degree of truth in that. But when you include the second tweak, it becomes more than that—a lot more. It's priming you to give up something.

There is specific interview behavior, and that is the pre-assault touch. It happens in escalating and certain other interviews. Robbers are less likely to do a light touch before they commit. Where it happens most is when the goal is some kind of a physical assault.

This touch is a *test* to see how you will react. It's not exclusive to or mandatory for assaults, rapes, or stompings. But that's where the pre-assault touch crops up the most. (At the same time, these can take place without you first being touched.) While it can be an aggressive shove or poke, it *doesn't* have to be. Many a time, I've seen a pat on the back or shoulder precede a beat down by either individuals or wolf packs. Someone attempting to touch you during the first three stages is a sign things are going to get real ugly. As in odds are good the person is going to use physical violence—not just threaten you with it.

Hot interviews are barking, drooling mad dawgs popping up in your face. This kind of interview starts out with warm fuzzy opening lines like, "Hey, muthafucka!" They are designed to see how you react to overt and unexpected aggression. Do you fall apart? Do you cower? Do you freeze? Do you fumble trying to find a proper social response to the situation? Or do you simply proceed to try to rip their throats out with your teeth? Like the pre-assault touch, the aggressor is checking to see how you react. If you fold or try to bluster, he knows he can get away with what he's planning. If you give the—to him—wrong response, he breaks off. The wrong response is that you are ready to rock 'n roll—at whatever level it takes to stop him.

This is radically different than responding with bluster. A bluster response is when he barks, "Hey, muthafucka," and you snap, "Fuck off!" That's the wrong response for you because it's a green light to attack. A wrong response for *him* is when instead you say nothing, but reach for your weapon. Or you simply snarl and start to lunge at him. Oops, wrong target. (Of course there was the time I was in a bad mood, looked up at the sky and proclaimed "Thank ya Jay-ZUS!" Then I gave the guy a homicidal smile and moved toward him—now that was a funny reaction.)

Two interesting points about hot interviews: What separates them from war cries is they're usually done *outside* attack range. Granted, they often occur while he is moving into attack range, but if the wrong response is received the would-be assailant is far enough out he can retreat. Second, inexperienced humans seem to be one of the few animals who respond to unexpected loud noises by freezing. Most animals just beeline away, while some will drop first running is still on the schedule.

Humans—especially those *without* lizard brain experience—will often stand and look to others for cues as to what to do. Another tendency is to stand and stare at the source of the noise (threat). I liken the last to the difference between a cat jumping off the counter when you walk into the kitchen and a child freezing when caught with her hand in the cookie jar. This freeze allows the attacker to develop positioning (attack range and circumstances). This especially applies to standing and blustering. The key point is standing. Your words are aggressive, but your actions aren't indicating an attack, running, or demonstrating you're a bad target choice—again allowing him to develop attack positioning.

Escalating interviews are a combo, basically they start out as regular and then escalate to hot. If you weren't caught up inside it wondering "WTF?" you'd recognize a couple of patterns. Take a normal conversation, micro-script or normal exchange between two people. Also take an argument between two people that escalates to physical violence. Both of these are known to you. Now comes the imagination part. Take both and edit out one person. Then splice the two different halves together. What you have is a weird combo, one half trying to converse, the other half working up to a fight. That's the essence of the escalating interview.

Escalating interviews have three hallmark traits. One, you're confused. You stand there and say to yourself, "Wait. What? No, that's not what I mean!" I'd say they put you on the defensive, but often you don't even have time for that. You thought you were in a normal conversation when all of a sudden the person goes off into left field—usually accusing you of doing something wrong. Two, the speed at which they escalate. Basically it goes from a friendly greeting then thirty seconds later it's as if you gang-raped his mother. Three, demands, accusations, or standards are unreasonable. Basically, you're being set up to fail. Whether it's you not meeting his impossible standard, the claim you're criticizing him, or you insulted him—you're doomed to fail. It's that failure that is used as an excuse to attack.

Back in the days when many people smoked, I would use the following example of an unreasonable escalation. "Hey man got a cigarette? Gimme a cigarette! Gimma a Kool! Man, you're disrespecting me!" How the hell did it go from trying to bum a cigarette to you've given him mortal offense in four sentences? It was an escalating interview. It is in essence a tantrum thrown when someone doesn't get his, her, or their way. But it's also more than an excuse to attack. (Does all that time I spent on the monkey hijacking the human make more sense?)

Escalating interviews are very common among the young and with packs. It's often how they work themselves up to attack. Most importantly, escalating interviews are classic examples of "I don't know where it's going, but nothing good is down that road." Escalating interviews are a common tactic for both strong-arm robberies and group stomping of a stranger (we'll talk about these in social violence). At neither one do you want to be the guest of honor.

Silent interviews are simply the guy looking at you and deciding if he can take you or not. These can be as simple as quietly following you or watching you for a few moments before stepping into your way. Or they can be complicated *shadow dances*. That's a series of complex and subtle moves and counter moves two experienced players do to gain the tactical advantage in a situation—all the while pretending nothing is going on. To the uninformed, it doesn't look like anything is happening—except they both know what they're really doing. Literally, all the uninformed see is: She's standing and smoking a cigarette. He comes walking along. He changes directions to come at her. She steps out of the way, and there's a change in her body language. He turns and continues on the direction he had been going. She goes back into the building.

This is a shadow dance that happened to my wife. Back when she smoked, she was outside her office, having a cigarette. The building entrance was in a small attached pavilion. Basically, the doors were in a mini-wing that extended out from the main building. If you weren't going into the building, you had to walk around this outcrop. If you were going in, you approached the doors not where my wife was standing. Being as smokers were becoming social pariahs, they were banished fifty feet from the door. Along the main facade of the building were alcoves where smokers could shelter from the wind. An individual she describes as having a "jackal walk" came along. He was originally angling to avoid the pavilion and walking wide. But he saw her, targeted her, and changed course directly toward her. Not toward the door, *her*. The way he walked combined with changes in his intent and path made her step back into the alcove and bring her hands up into a fighting position. (She has a black belt.) Her thought was "I think not!" Seeing this, he broke off, changed course again, and walked off—around the pavilion. She skedaddled back inside. Move, counter move, abort, withdraw—all without a single word spoken. That was not only failing a silent interview, but a complete shadow dance. A dance that unless you understood the dynamics of the situation, you'd never notice even happened.

Prolonged interviews can take minutes, hours, days, or weeks. Other interviews can be over within a minute while a serial date rapist will spend an entire date (or several) interviewing (and setting up) his intended victim. On one hand, it is easy to understand prolonged interviews. The person develops intent and under the guise of other activities (e.g., work) observes, assesses, and plans how to successfully commit his crime.

A friend of mine, Terry Trahan, had just started his shift at a store he managed. A man wearing a hoodie came in. His head was down, and he was turning his body this way and that as he approached the counter. Terry immediately recognized his movement pattern as a way to prevent the security cameras from getting an image of his face. Obviously, the would-be robber had cased the store at an earlier time. Terry snarled at him, "Can I fucking help you?" The guy stopped, looked at him, and realized Terry was better armed, not afraid, and just *not* in the mood to get robbed. The prospective robber turned and left the store. When had he cased the joint? Who knows. The camera dodges probably spoke of pre-existing knowledge. Apparently, it hadn't been when Terry was on shift.

Of all interviews, prolonged are the hardest to spot. That's because the signals are spaced out over time and are subtle. At the same time, they're not—if you're paying attention. In the movie *Open Range*, Kevin Costner's character makes a profound observation. "Weren't the only thing he said. Most a'time, a man will tell you his bad intentions if you listen." In *Open Range*, the conversation was in the form of a story about bad things that happened to another outfit, a group of free grazers exactly like Costner and Robert Duvall's crew. Such pointed stories have a strategic goal. In the movie, it was to get them to move on so they'd be far from town when the bad thing happened (thereby giving the rancher who threatened them plausible deniability[70]). Costner's character knew how to listen in those circumstances. Let yourself hear.

While that can happen to you, what you're more likely to run into is it's a test to see how you react. If you get nervous and scared, but don't do anything else—you've passed the interview. (Five stages interviews are the only ones you *want* to fail. If you pass, you will be attacked.) Common to prolonged interviews is joking about doing it to you. You make a witty remark and get a comment like, "Ha, ha. How about I rape you? Ha, ha." "Excuse me? What did you just say?" "Oh, nothing. It was a joke." Uh, no. You don't joke about those things.

And then there's the ploy when the person reveals his intent for a

---

70   I'm fond of the "RSA Animate" clips on Youtube. Steve Pinker's "Language as a Window into Human Nature" introduces some important concepts. https://www.youtube.com/watch?v=3-son3EJTrU

second, them passes it off as a joke. "Ha ha! I scared you. Isn't that a funny joke?" Now, that you mention it—no. Again, you don't joke about those things. And you keep an eye on people who do. Lover Boy doesn't know it, but the slack you'd cut him has suddenly become a whole lot shorter.

Especially frequent to this joke strategy is his trying to turn it around onto you if you react negatively. You're the one without a sense of humor. You're too sensitive! Wow, he didn't know you were so up tight.[71] The exact nuances of mind games are beyond the scope of this book, but sociopaths excel at playing them. Having said that, sociopaths are real good at avoiding attacking people who won't hesitate to disembowel them because they know the sociopath isn't joking. Most sociopaths really aren't that good at violence, they rely on surprise not skill to get it done. Take that away and . . .

I picked up a term from my friend Irene, who does Internet security. You're probably aware of the term phishing scam. Those are the e-mails you get seemingly from the Bank of America or some other well known financial institution, telling you your account number and other information has to be submitted because your account has been frozen or for some other ostensibly legitimate reason. Mostly you know they're a fraud because you don't have a BofA credit card. But if you do, you might fall for them. Then there are the general scams sometimes telling you of money that will be released to you and which are addressed at "whoever is stupid and greedy enough to fall for this." But the new term I learned from Irene was spearphishing. That is a scam directly aimed at *you*. These are the scam e-mails I get addressed to Mr. MacYoung. Someone took the extra time to get my name and e-mail address and tried to phish me.

I tell you this because overwhelmingly the other interviews are phishing. In them, you're nothing to the person doing them except—hopefully—an ATM with legs. If it ain't you, it'll be someone else. For the individual, prolonged interviews are spearphishing. *You* are the target. Something happens that makes it specifically about you. Whether it's scamming, ripping you off, grooming, rape, assault, or murder, you're in the crosshairs.

Stalking also can be considered a form of prolonged interview. Something a stalker and any criminal, who uses this strategy, have in common is knowing when and where you'll be most vulnerable. Why?

---

71   This can come in two forms. One is gaslighting where the person says it and then denies that's what happened. It's you who interpreted it that way. Two is what Gavin deBecker dubbed typecasting. It's a common predatory behavior with such charming strategies as "I thought you were different. I didn't think you were like those other stuck-up bitches."

Because he's learned your routine and knows it about as well as you do. That's what prolonged interviews are for: Intelligence gathering.

Positioning: These are the processes of setting up the physical attack. Yes, moving into range is very much a part of it. But so, too, is stepping into a specific location to improve the attack and reduce the person's ability to resist. As is turning one's body to conceal (or more readily access) a weapon or generate more power in the attacking limb (blading). It also can be moving into an ambush position to wait.

Inherent in the interview is the criminal watching for your reaction to his development of positioning. What you do about his trying to develop an attack position is a huge factor in whether you pass or fail the interview. (Remember fail is preferred.) If you start shadow dancing to counter his set-up, odds are good the criminal will break off—especially if you develop your own tactical advantage. Because he's trying to set them up on you, he'll recognize when you're doing it back at him.

There used to be four, but I've changed it so there are five types of positioning:

- Closing
- Surrounding
- Pincer
- Cornering or trapping
- Surprise

While each has aspects in common, it's the differences that make them unique.

As an aside, I tell people crime is a process. It's not only knowable, but

Many years ago, I sent my ex through culinary school. Shortly before graduation, she asked me to talk to her friend. A fellow female student was having trouble with a male classmate. The classmate was behaving obsessively toward her. My girlfriend didn't like what she was seeing, but her friend was more furious than scared. She brought her classmate over to talk about the situation. The red flags started going up immediately. I was told of an incident earlier that week when he stared at her all night. He disappeared for about twenty minutes, then one of the male students reported he was jerking off in the bathroom. The rest of the class treated it like a joke. The friend was furious. She'd confronted him about it, and he'd laughed in her face.

I nearly had kittens when she told me that. I told her if she *ever* ran into him loitering in a deserted area, if he'd been drinking, and if he tried to talk to her—*get the hell out of there.* Instead of listening, she kept going on about how furious she was, and how she really wanted to give him a piece of her mind. I told her *bad* idea. Getting into his face would cause things to blow up. That's another case of "I don't know where he's planning to go, but nothing good is down this road." She was still more angry than scared.

Next week, the male classmate was absent one night. The senior students were shutting down the school. My girlfriend and she were two of the four remaining people in the building. My girlfriend walked out into the dark parking lot, and there *he* was. Drunk. Waiting. He "just wanted to talk" with the classmate. My girlfriend pretended she'd forgotten something, promised him she'd tell her he wanted to talk, and hightailed it back inside. She grabbed her friend and hissed, "____ is out in the parking lot. He's drunk, and he wants to 'just talk.' This is exactly what Marc warned you he'd do before he raped you!" Her friend started to brush it off—again—until girlfriend reminded her that Arizona allowed concealed carry. While she didn't have a gun, *he might.* That's when my girlfriend finally got through to her, and she blanched. She at last recognized the danger her anger and embarrassment had blinded her to.

Happy ending to this story. They got a large male student to escort them. He distracted the drunken classmate while they drove away. Turns out, he'd missed school for a legitimate reason. But he'd gone out and had a few too many at a conveniently nearby bar. He'd decided it would be a good idea to go to the school to talk to her.

I tell you this story because after it happened, I came up with a term: *Deniable malice*, which goes with prolonged interviews like peas and carrots. It's another reason why prolonged interviews can be hard to spot. Unlike embezzlement or a bank robbery (where mens rea is present) with deniable malice, the person is lying to him- or herself about it. Often to the point they convince themselves they're doing something else. The person is literally blind to the fact he or she is systematically setting up a crime.

The person is in denial about what he or she is doing while subconsciously, methodically setting up the circumstances for the attack. Lots of simple seemingly innocent steps are taken until the event 'just happens.' Even if the person is conscious of a particular act, there is a rationalizing, excusing motive for it. (E.g., I only took the gun along for self-defense.) When the event ensues, the person is shocked. They didn't mean for it to happen. They had no intention of doing that! They didn't plan for it. It just happened! Yeah, right . . .

Another example of deniable malice I use is someone who cheats on his spouse and then claims, "It just happened." No, jackass, you didn't just trip and your dick fell into her. There was a long pattern of (not so) innocent flirting. Time spent together in more intimate and isolated circumstances. And then came that bottle of wine . . .

The thing about deniable malice is—as the person is setting it up—he believes what he's *telling* himself about what he's doing. *His* reality is that these actions weren't malicious. There was no intent. Interest? Well yeah, but not intent. There is a huge disconnect between what he's doing and what he is telling himself about *why* he's doing it. With sincerity, he will claim he wasn't consciously setting up the perfect circumstances for violence. The methodical nature and orchestration of circumstances means some part of the person was up to no good—even if that part is hidden from that person's conscious thoughts.

Intent, interview, positioning are a unique combo that don't appear *anywhere* else. It's a slow drift, but unacknowledged intent moves the person to build circumstances until they are just right. Then all it takes is a little push for something bad to happen.

predictable. The closer it gets to its goal, the more predictable it becomes. It's like driving to a friend's house. At first there are many routes you can take to get to the general area. But the closer to your destination, the more you have to turn here and go down a certain street. Otherwise, you won't reach your destination. While this analogy applies to the five stages, it really is relevant to positioning. In order to successfully attack, there are definite things he *has* to do—certain conditions that *have* to be in place.

Closing is the most common form of positioning criminals use. It is simply walking up to you. They're not hiding. They're not creeping. Evident as white paint on a black shirt, they stroll up to you. The use of a regular interview (invoking a social script) is what pins most people to the spot and allows the criminal to close. What makes this strategy so effective is the victim's monkey is triggered in some way—whether by the criminal or the person doing it to him- or herself. With the latter, "They'll leave me alone" or "If I cross the street, he'll think I'm _____."

The basic counter to closing is to set a boundary. Tell them, "That's close enough," followed by a pseudo-social script. I say pseudo because it's actually a test. How that person reacts to you setting a boundary is both a test of his intentions and articulable—especially when things aren't kosher.

We'll talk later about attack range and how to spot someone developing it. But for right now, I want to add another dimension to closing positioning. That's his standing in a choke point, which is a narrow place you're forced to pass. It could be a doorway (entrance or exit) a breezeway, an underpass, or stairs. Bottom line, someone standing there isn't a good sign. But why is this in the closing section? Because the person doing the closing is the victim. Instead of going around, they walk right into the choke point and try to slip past. When you walk up to him like this, at most all it takes is the mugger making two steps

Surrounding is pretty simple: One person distracts you while the rest of the group encircles you. This strategy is really common with strong-arm robberies, but it is not exclusive to them. A common element of surrounding will be that the person who distracts you stands in the middle of the group's front line. This allows the wings of the group to quickly encircle you. With surrounding, there's again a triggering of your monkey. Usually, one guy will be doing the talking so you don't pay attention to what the others are doing. Or if you do, you're too polite to break off the conversation with the first person.

The basic counter to surrounding is for you to draw an imaginary line between you and them then enforce it. They stay on their side, you stay on yours. Once you establish that boundary, anyone trying to cross that line announces hostile intentions.

Pincers are a two-person form of surrounding. They come in two basic forms. The first is two guys who move together, then split up and come at you from different sides. An example of this is you walking to your car with two guys walking toward you. It looks like they're going to pass on your left. One cuts wide as if to pass on your right side, the second stays on course. When you're in the right spot, they close in. Sometimes one distracts you, other times they just silently close.

The second way is when they split up and wait in a place where people walk. When you walk into the trap, they close in. An example is you walk along and pass a loitering guy. About fifty feet up ahead is another guy, hanging around. Either he waits until you approach or starts to approach you. He says something and that's when you find out the first guy, his partner, followed you. Now you're caught in a vice. This tactic is especially common with two guys standing on opposite sides of an entry, walkway, tunnel, or other choke point. Anytime you see two people positioned so you have to walk between them—be careful. As in there are no macho points lost for turning around and leaving—instead of putting your (name a tender part) into a vice.

The basic counter to a pincer move is to either move to the end of the line or make it a triangle. Imagine three dots in a line. You don't want to be the dot in the middle. That's a pincer. Someone moves to put you there you dance out to the end of the line. Seriously never mind martial arts training, ballroom, waltzing, ballet, or even line dancing allows you to quickly and gracefully move to the end of the line. While dancing out of there may not seem like much, what they do next either ends the situation (they know you're on to them and abort) or is both your green light to act and articulable as to why force was necessary.

Another counter when you find yourself in the middle is to break the three-dot line by turning it into a triangle. You want to move as far out of line as possible. Then draw another mental line between you and them. They stay on their side, you stay on yours. If they attempt to cross it, they've tipped their hand.

Cornering and trapping use the environment to keep you from escaping. The criminal uses something in the environment to:

a) Keep you from leaving

b) Limit the directions you could leave, forcing you to go past him

In case you haven't noticed, usually it's the monkey that roots us to a spot and keeps us from leaving. I call this effect "rattlesnake cornered." (While most snakes will try to escape, a rattlesnake considers itself cornered in an open field.) This is why closing before brandishing the threat or attacking often works. But someone can flee from a closing criminal. Surrounding and pincers keep that from happening by the assailants placing themselves as barriers to your escape.

With cornering, walls, cars, fences, areas with only one way out are used to pin or trap you. Some examples: You stand between your car and another vehicle in a parking lot. You only have two ways you can go. You're in the apartment's laundry room. There's only one exit, the door. Depending on where you sit in a bus or train, there's might be one, maybe two exits. You're walking along the side of a building. Someone approaching you perpendicularly functionally pins you between himself and the structure. The basic counter to this type of positioning is a four-parter.

First is playing pool. Look at the angles, lines, and where they intersect. I would have said geometry, but I hate math. And there's another reason I used pool. *He*, not you, is the cue ball. He's coming in to knock you where he wants you. It's the ability to look at someone and recognize when he is intentionally moving in a way to corner or trap you. Someone moving hard and fast is one thing. He could be moving away from you. Someone moving hard and fast at you to pin you against a surface is another. Also not good is someone trying to sneak into a position where with only one hard and fast step, you could be pinned.

Second, when you see it develop, you move. Change course. If you're going to be in a corner with your back against a wall, then it happens *by your choice*. That can be part of your defensive strategy. Ordinarily the ability to move is your best bet, but that can change according to circumstances. Here's a hint: If you change direction and he attempts to re-establish an intercept course, that's—again—an articulable danger sign and removes doubt about the need for force. (It's not a green light yet, but things are definitely not kosher.)

Third, learn to consciously recognize timing. Our lizard brains understand a very basic physics concept: Two items cannot occupy the same space at the same time. Our monkey brains recognize social protocols about not crowding each other. The two combine to create complex subconscious dances of timing, sequential action, speed increase and decrease. For example, two people can't go through the door at the same time. Ordinarily we're out of sync enough that this isn't an issue. When people realize they are converging on an intercept course, one or both parties adjust speed to make passing through the door sequential. This is normal. What is *not* normal is a person increasing and decreasing speed to intercept you.[72]

Fourth, set boundaries as far out as possible. Don't be afraid to call the ball with comments like, "That's close enough. What can I do for you?" Again, what the person does next either adds or subtracts from the danger level—and your use-of-force decision.

There are forms of closing and trapping what I call the reverse or lopsided pincer. These are real common in areas where there is limited mobility, like apartment laundry rooms, convenience stores, and laundromats. A reverse pincer is when two guys come into a place through the main entrance, and one hangs back at the door. This is categorically a bad sign. That guy at the entrance is there both to keep people out and to stop you if you try to bolt. If there's only one entrance, the mobile douche-nozzle will approach you directly. You're not inside a pincer, you're outside it. A lopsided pincer happens when there's a back door. Often the mobile guy will swing wide, pass you to get between you and the back door, then hook around and come at you from the other direction. With this, you're trapped in both a one-sided pincer and against walls or other large surfaces.

Surprise comes in many forms. Basically, though, it's the attacker taking a position that allows him to see you first and move, but keeps you from seeing him until it's too late. This could be his waiting in an ambush position. Or it could be you turning a corner and unexpectedly running into someone ready to commit a crime (waiting for someone to turn the corner). Or he could quietly follow you and attack from behind.

---

72   People's monkeys can get triggered about who goes through a door first. A common behavior is one person races to the door. This is a mistake when it comes to dealing with predators. Among other problems, do you really want him behind you where you can't see him?

Sometimes, he moves to you. Sometimes, you move to him. Usually, you're both moving (like him following you to your car). Real common is when the guy ghosts up behind you, says or does something that gets you to turn around, and you find yourself looking down the barrel of a gun. The shock and surprise causes you to freeze. File his coming up to you unseen under El Grande Sucko. Why? Because surprise positioning isn't just a robbery strategy, it's also an assassin's strategy.

When you reach a certain level, violence changes: It becomes much more effective. No matter what, it's going to be over fast. But in those few seconds, it's going to be either really boring or really terrifying. There's *no* in between. That's because you get so good at spotting violence, the way most people try to do it becomes . . . "Really? You think that's going to work? Seriously?" When someone's at that level, attacking him is not going turn out the way the out-of-control guy wants it.[73] That's the boring type.

The terrifying type is the guy who is as good (or better) than you. He's not screwing around. He's coming in to kill you. And he knows how. Usually it's over before you know what hit you, but for those few seconds it's terrifying. If—and this is a qualified if—you're lucky, he's trying to overwhelm you. I say qualified because raping, robbing, or killing you after he tortures you might be on the table. The luckiest of them all is if he's only there to arrest you.

Surprise positioning and a blitz attack are hallmarks of professional hits. When it was up, moving, and making noise, the newly manufactured corpse angered the wrong person. Whether or not you're at the same level of violence, this kind of attack is terrifying—for a few seconds. Thing is, even being at the same level or better doesn't guarantee your survival. That's why surprise positioning and ambushes are so dangerous: Someone put some thought into it.

When I say ambush, many people think, "Oh, hiding spot." Well, not exactly. Unless you're using a sniping rifle, actual hiding spaces take too long to leave—and doing so makes too much noise. Most of the time, he's not exactly hiding. He's standing in plain sight, but it's somewhere you don't normally look. I like using parking structures as an easy example. Normally, when you step out of the elevator or stairs, you look toward where your car is parked. That's where you're going, so that's where you look. You don't look the other way. This isn't mystic, cloud-your-mind, ninja malarkey. You don't look into the corner or around the stairwell— because ordinarily nothing is there. Except this time, that's where the robber is standing. Again odds are good, he's not hiding. He's standing

---

73   Contrary to what you might think, people on this level tend to be extremely polite, calm, and reasonable. Right up to the moment they demonstrate they're *way* better at being unreasonable than you are. Like, you blink and you're in the hospital.

in plain sight, but because you don't even look in that direction you don't see him. Then he quietly follows you to your car. (By the way, predators tend to loiter not at the back of parking lots, but near the entrances.)

Another variation is when—from a certain perspective—you won't see him until you're in proximity. You turn the corner, and there he is. You pass a dumpster, and there he is. You pass doorway that's set back into an alcove, and he steps out. This kind of 'hiding' is like cover or concealment in shooting. It only works from one direction. Take four steps to the side, peek around the corner, and he's right there. Coming from the other direction, he's standing in plain sight. No matter what, someone loitering in that exact spot is neither a coincidence nor a good sign.

Surprise positioning works hand in hand with both silent interviews and blitz attacks. If you're lucky you hear, "Hey," turn around, and look down the barrel of a gun belonging to someone who just wants your money. Or you're standing at an ATM and suddenly you find yourself way too close to someone with a hoodie, mask, and gun. As long as he's only after the money, you're *lucky.*

If you're not lucky, you might hear a scuffle of feet just before you're knocked unconscious by a baseball bat. Another version is after being knocked to the ground, you are beaten and raped. Unlucky just keeps getting worse from there. If you've messed with the wrong person, you'll be standing at the urinal as a construction grade zip tie is dropped over your head and cinched around your throat. Your killer then walks out of the bathroom, leaving you to choke to death. Or as you're getting out of your car, someone steps out of the shadows with a shotgun and pulls the trigger. If you have people gunning for you (what I call a hot situation) odds are good you know it. If you haven't figured it out, there's not much hope for you. Knowing someone is gunning for you, you operate at a higher level of readiness. Guy with a shotgun? The lizard takes over. Zip ties are avoided by drawing your weapon before you pee and looking over your shoulder when someone comes into the bathroom.

The roughest of all surprise positionings to deal with is the blitz—especially when mixed with a hot interview. You hear a war cry and look up to see someone charging. His positioning is a surprise and closing and he's yelling his fool head off. The reason the hot surprise blitz is so difficult to deal with is because it *triggers* your monkey. Your greatest impediment to dealing with this kind of attack is *you!* You're being yelled at! He's running at you, looking real mad! Monkey either stands there trying to figure out why he's mad (what's happening) defaults to "hey diddle diddle, straight up the middle" fighting tactics, or tries to back pedal (hey diddle diddle straight back . . .)

Remember, we have *default* monkey responses to monkey violence. They're the train tracks, and you move forward on those tracks. You can travel backward. You can stand, looking at the approaching train. Not because you want to, but because your monkey *won't* let the lizard drive. Remember your lizard has no problem running. It's only the monkey who thinks running is for sissies and that if you start you'll never stop. (Notice the hijacking of the human to justify its beliefs?) Standing in your heroic, tough monkey pose is exactly what is going to get you run over.

I know any number of tacti-douche gun fighting goo-roos, he-man combative and self-defense instructors who claim to teach you how to survive these scenarios. You're ambushed and in a blaze of (insert) a) gunfire b) knife fighting prowess c) kung fu awesomeness, you dispatch your attacker. Join me in a little reality break about surprise positioning. It works. It *works* really well. That's why people use it. If you're blitzed like this, what you are most likely to do is lie down and bleed—especially if you try to stay there and fight. (We'll return to this later.)

The basic counter to surprise positioning is to *buy* yourself time. Develop habits that allow you to see it coming soon enough that you have time to shift mental gears; time to prepare; time to start doing something that will reduce the danger to you. Start by simply looking around now and then. This is not that hard. You look around when you enter a fringe area (there's a whole two seconds). Near your destination (e.g., your car parked in a lot) look around again. Wow, these seconds are just stacking up. If it's a long trip through the area, look around midway (another two whole seconds) to see if there's someone following you or trying to close the distance. It's not hard. It's not paranoid. It's not tacti-cool. It's just looking around. If there's nothing dangerous in the environment, relax and go back to what you're doing. If there is something askew in the environment, you've bought yourself precious time to assess and find the best solution. If you see trouble far enough out, the best answer is usually to leave.

Here's where people's monkeys start chattering and finding excuses— usually phrased as questions—as to why it won't work. "Won't he just turn and follow me?" "What if there's something in the way?" "What if I'm with my crippled, eighty-seven-year-old grandmother?" But let's tie this back to a surprise attack you didn't see coming. What if you just stand there, trying to get your superior weapon out—or deciding which technique to use— and you get hit by a frigging train? Lying there on the ground, bleeding out, you're not going to be much use to Granny now are you? Dodging buys you time! Here is where we tell the monkey to have a nice big cup of S.T.F.U. We're going to do so because it's going to get you killed if you listen to it in these situations.

Do you remember the quote attributed to Gen. Omar Bradley that started this chapter? *Amateurs study tactics. Professionals study logistics.* I used it for several reasons. One is if you look at the five stages as his developing what he needs to attack, you make an important paradigm shift that applies to you, too. What do you *need* for something to work in a situation? What do you have to do to get it on line?

Something that annoys the hell out of me is people who research military tactics and tell themselves, "That's what you do." They must think the following, "Hell elite special forces don't dodge for cover, they turn and attack! Since they do it that's what I'll do." The problem with this is people assume they have the resources necessary for this tactic to work. They don't. Never mind the whole trying to bring battlefield tactics to civilian engagements thing. I want you to look at it from the perspective of logistics. What do you need in order for a military tactic to work?

For example, I know many guys who were ambushed while out on patrol—guys who turned and attacked back. Wanna know what they had in common? First, they all had weapons in their hands when the attack *started*. Second, they all had time to psych up before going out on patrol. They were on the clock from the moment they left the base. Third, they had lots of people around them who were wearing the same color clothing . . . and who had guns, too. Fourth, they all had training. Fifth, they all had experience, a particular mindset, and were deep in it as in *this* was their lives. Sixth, they not only expected to be ambushed, they were looking for it!

As a civilian, you *aren't* bringing the same resources to the table. Starting with you're not on a battlefield, you're taking groceries to your car. While it is possible to whip around like a furious badger in a nano second, normally that takes some very specific resources. If you don't have those, it *ain't* likely to happen.

On the other hand, odds are good you *can* jump out of the way. That's a good strategy to keep from getting hit by cars, trucks, trains, and livestock. It also works really well when you're unexpectedly attacked. Mostly because if you can walk and chew gum at the same time, you can dodge and block, too.

Just because you dodge the initial attack doesn't mean you're forever doomed to run. Let the lizard get you out of the way *first*. That buys you time to decide what to do. Do you run? Maybe. Do you turn into a werewolf and lunge back at him? Maybe. Do you pull your own weapon? Maybe. But no matter what, *now* you have time to do it! By throwing the monkey out of the driver's seat—difficult to do because the hot, surprise, and blitz tactics are specifically designed to get the monkey to grab the wheel—you've bought yourself time.

I'm going to take a detour here before I tell you the second counter to surprise positioning. After you've practiced what I'm about to tell you, the second counter is a cakewalk. I have a game for you to play. For a week, you get to be a bad guy.

In the areas where you routinely go, how would you rob someone there? Start with surprise positioning. Where would you stand so you could see them before they saw you? Where in an environment do people normally not look? Where would you hide to ambush someone coming to your door or car? Where would you stand so you could follow someone to their car unseen? Get a friend to help you double check. You'll be surprised at finding how many places you initially thought made great hiding spots really aren't. And vice versa. Five feet over that way is a good spot that you wouldn't have thought so. Once you find these spots, you'll become extremely aware of anyone standing there—like "nothing good can come of this" aware. When you see someone there, you'll know it's a bad thing. That ruins the surprise positioning.

Bumping this game up to the next level find the fringe areas—the zones between safe spots. Places where it would take between fifteen seconds and a full minute for help to arrive. These are your hunting grounds. Start looking for places that have multiple escape routes. Places not in the crowd, but near it. Places where you can get back to the crowd and disappear in it. Places where you can disappear around the corner and dart down any one of multiple streets and allies. Places inside a crowd where you're separated from and out of view of the crowd (e.g., bathrooms at the mall or an isolated room at a party). All of these are fringe areas; you *don't* want to be in them with a predator.

Once you can spot both a fringe area and an attack spot take the five types of positioning and start planning ambushes. You can bring along imaginary friends. "Okay, here, we'd lean against both sides of the entryway …" "Here, I'd approach from that direction to pin her against the wall …" "Here's where I'd stand and follow someone to their car …" "I'd hide there, jump out, and force her into her car (spearphishing)."

Okay, now for the second counter to surprise positioning. Develop habits that *buy* you time—habits that do not negatively affect your lifestyle. In fact, cultivate habits that serve purposes other than spotting an assassin or mugger. Things like not taking blind corners tightly, instead of hugging the wall and turning the corner take two extra steps to swing wide, so you can see what's around the corner. If you're walking in a parking lot or alley move down the middle of the driving area. That way, even someone coming out from hiding will have to cover about ten feet. Learn to weave like a drunk with a purpose. That means weave when you walk, steering clear of those good ambush spots you've learned how to spot. It doesn't matter if you're walking on the sidewalk or a path when you see a good ambush spot put some distance between you and it and take a peek as you pass. Exploit things like hearing when you're in a fringe area. (Surprise, you can get information in ways other than your eyes.) When you hear something, check it out *before* it gets to you! When you're standing at a urinal and you hear someone coming in look over your shoulder to see who just entered the area.

Here's a news flash: Except for the last one, these habits will go miles toward keeping you from getting unpleasantly surprised, bumped into, hit by shopping carts, knocked on your butt, or run over by cars. Yes, even walking down the drive—if you're listening—you can hear cars coming. Walking in the middle also keeps you from being hit by a smaller car backing out when your view is blocked by a truck or SUV (sport utility vehicle).

These simple habits will do wonders for disarming surprise positions by garden variety muggers. If you're the target of a spearphishing rapist or robbers—or you've enraged the wrong people—you're going to have to do a whole lot more. Those strategies are beyond the scope of this book.[74] Something that is not, however, is what I'm going to say next. It is a combination of observation of, rant about, and criticism of what you've been taught about how to handle surprise positioning. Remember I mentioned the tacti-douche instructors who claim to be able to teach you how to defeat surprise positioning? But the reality is if you're blitzed, you're most likely to lie there and bleed? I also said we'd return to this later. This is later.

In the movie, *The Avengers,* Thor says, "Your work with the tesseract is what drew Loki to it . . . and his allies. It is a signal to the realm that Earth is ready for a higher form of war." The reason I spent so much time on surprise positioning is because it is a higher level of war. When you see someone coming out of an ambush spot, the kimchi has piled deeper. *How* you react is going to make all the difference in the universe.

Many years ago, I ran a correctional center that was far away from where I lived. Circumstances developed one day when my girlfriend had to come by my work. One of the inmates was there when she came in. After she left, he approached me, and the conversation went like this:

"That your wife?

"My girlfriend."

"She's fine."

---

74   After I wrote that paragraph I had what I call a "weird shit-o-meter moment." Those are the times you casually mention something you accept as normal. The weird meter pings when you realize that normal is back that way—*way* back that a way. Garden variety mugger? Normal people don't say that kind of thing. Having the weird shit-o-meter helps keep things in perspective by giving you a base line to compare your thinking to. It may be necessary given the circumstances, but it's not in any way normal.

"Thank you."

"Maybe when I get out of here, I'll go up where you live and pay her a visit."

<pause for mental gear shift>

"If I ever see your ass up there, I'm just going to assume self-defense and start shooting."

"Man, I was just joking!"

"I'm not."

When I was growing up, my parents had a saying, "That's not a threat—that's a promise." The inmate was threatening, I was promising. Technically, he was conducting an interview, but it went deeper than that. He was a convicted felon, who was testing my boundaries. My response, although phrased in legally acceptable terms, conveyed to him I knew The Life and how the game was played. In essence, I told him if he ever made a run at me (or mine) he'd better be good enough to kill me before I killed him. Thing was, we both knew he wasn't good enough to safely get the drop on me. Even if he did—while I might not live through it neither would he. (Okay, fair deal to protect my loved ones.) But the odds were far better I'd see him coming before he could surprise me. That was a can of suck he simply didn't want to open.

I tell you this because I had the resources. At that time in my life, I saw more convicted felons in one day than your average cop sees in a year. Not only that, but I was just barely out of The Life myself. While it had been a couple of years since someone had tried to kill me, there were a few more incidents still ahead. At that time of my life, I was changing, but I still had many of the Animal attitudes, reflexes, and responses. That is to say, I could go from zero to one-hundred-twenty in a blink. I could turn a corner and deflect a knife attack. I could walk a client to her car and tackle her, a split second before her stalker opened fire. And the next second be charging and shooting back. I could go from sorting my socks in the laundromat to disarming a mugger. I could go from walking through a doorway to dodging the hatchet a burglar tried to bury in my skull. I was really good at moving to cover after the first shot while drawing my weapon. I could survive a surprise ambush by tearing into the ambusher. *All* of these things—*and more*—I have done and survived. And I was complete jackass, too.

Yeah, I had panther-like reflexes. Because I had to! I was in such screwed-up and nasty circumstances that being surrounded by felons on a daily basis was a step *up!* Those are the conditions where you develop the ability to handle an ambush. You don't cultivate that aptitude because you want to; you develop it because you have to. Because you have no choice! But mostly what you develop are awareness and hard-core paranoia. When you are routinely infuriating violent and dangerous people, you learn to look into every shadow. You ingrain habits that keep you alive. You freak out over the smallest things. You can't live a normal, happy life. Most of all, you become a complete, paranoid, violent prick.

This is one of the reasons I hold such contempt for the tacti-douche instructors, who claim to be able to teach you—the average citizen— how to explode in a blaze of what-the-hell-ever and become an ultimate killing machine. If you're not routinely in high-stakes environments or a complete, paranoid bastard that *claim* is hogwash. The ability to do this comes from operant conditioning, being in the right mindset, and the intent and skill of your attacker.

Let's start with the last. I don't care how good you are, a pro coming up from behind you and putting a bullet in your skull isn't going to give you time to react. You'll also be hard pressed when while standing at the urinal, someone comes up, drops a construction zip tie around your throat, and throws you to the ground while cinching it—then calmly walks out the door. Same against the guy who steps out of the shadows swinging a crowbar. Two-man tag team or sentry removal? Same, same. People use these techniques because they *work* against armed and dangerous people.

Good people can't flash into Shiva destroyer of worlds fast enough to defeat a committed bushwhacker. Your safety comes in *one* of two forms. One, you see it coming so you have time to shift gears. Two, run like hell (either to escape or to buy yourself time to shift gears). It's simple logistics. Unless you're in The Life, you don't have the resources to counterattack as your first move. This is a no-win situation for citizens. Hell, it's a crap shoot even for those *with* the resources and in those professions.

There is a less-than-common third option that is unfortunately the basis of much training. That is it is assumed you do get a chance to mentally shift gears and react. This is dependant on a very specific condition—your attacker isn't good enough to control your options or immediately render you helpless when he's coming in to beat, rape, rob, or kill you. Having lived through these situations that is a big assumption.

You *might* be able to counter-ambush or get your game on with four significant drawbacks. One, unless your ingrained response includes something that jams his ability to attack all you'll do is trade damage. (This is my number one complaint against much of what is taught.) Two, when all you're doing is trading damage it's a total crap shoot as to who is going to the hospital and who's going to the morgue. Three, if your ability to stop such an attacker is entirely weapon based there's a damned good chance you'll never get it out. Four ties one and three together. That is any action that doesn't jam his attack means while you're drawing your weapon, all you're doing is taking damage. Even if you're able to get it up and out, you're starting with a trade deficit.

Part of the reason I'm telling you this is because I've lived through what scares you the most. I know what it takes to survive, and I know what's missing from this tacti-cool ambush survival training. That's awareness and assholeness. The technique doesn't matter. Really. Every one of them is as likely to fail as any other. They all are Hail Mary passes. That's because if you find yourself in a surprise situation ninety-nine times out of a hundred, you messed up. And it's not just one mistake, but a string of them. These errors have put you miles away from where you need to be to suddenly explode into extreme violence and overwhelm a surprise attack.

The most common mistake? Someone got too confident and sloppy. Examples are the career woman, who believes nobody would dare touch her, and who walks through Ambush Central while she's talking on her cell phone. The hustler who thinks he's good enough to burn heavy hitters and get away with it. The correctional officer who short-cuts his way through security protocols. The policeman or bouncer who assumes he's so good he can handle it when someone moves against him. All of these are people who aren't doing the little things that will keep them safe—the things that will buy them time and let them see danger before its right up on them. Surviving a surprise assassination attempt isn't about knowing some cool Hail Mary technique. Like I said, they all work or *fail* equally—heavy on the failure if you don't have what I'm about to tell you. What makes any and all of them work is: Do you have what it takes to *rally?*

What it takes is *not* just knowing some Hail Mary pass technique. Contrary to what many believe, knowing (even practicing) such a move does not automatically instill the ability to do it while under attack. Unless you:

a)   Develop the knowledge to recognize the degree of danger you're in
b)   Develop the ability to morph into a werewolf
c)   Develop good habits that keep you safe
d)   Ingrain the mechanics of the movement, so you don't have to think about doing it
e)   Work or live in situations where violence is a constant danger—

Learning these tacti-cool ambush counters is a waste of your money. Yeah, they're fun to learn. Yeah, they're exciting. But they can be extremely dangerous for you. They're risky because when we think we have something that is guaranteed, we get *sloppy.* Get spray paint and your tattoo kit out: Never, ever forget, *these moves* are predicated on the fact that you screwed up. There's *a price* for that screw-up. These techniques are *never* plan A. They are what I call "omega solutions." They are for last ditch, you-didn't-just-screw-the-pooch-you've-outright-fucked-the-dog situations. And even if they work, the cost to you still will be serious blood loss.

This is why I have such a problem with uber-cool techniques where the names start with "The" followed by _____(fill in blank) or close combat shooting programs. In the empty-hand world, these are often taught as a *primary* tactic. Not good. Not good at all. I find the unintended consequences to the attitude of "I know The _____(fill in blank)" is that people sloppily walk into dangerous situations and make all kinds of mistakes. But hey, why should they keep them selves together? They know The _____(fill in blank). I've seen this arrogance kill more reliably than *knowing nothing*. Because someone who doesn't think he or she has the ultimate silver bullet for when it all goes to hell is much more *cautious* about keeping things *from* going to down there in the first place.

Whether civilian, cop, bouncer, violence professional, or primary contact professional,[75] a far better and more reliable safety measure is to *develop* your knowledge of *what* certain signals mean—so you can see it coming and have time to shift mental gears. If you can see it far enough out, you have more options—reliable options. Including those which won't result in the cops giving you the hairy eyeball about your self-defense action.

My main reason for writing this is simple. It's not that you can't get into the mindset to do what you need, it's that it takes *longer* to get there than you think. That's why you need to *buy* time; that's any measure that allows you to shift gears and get up to speed. Think about it like booting up your computer—it takes time before you can start working. You buy that time *before* you need it. (Imagine you have a report in your computer. The boss will fire you if you don't hand it to him the second he demands it. One scenario is you're at your desk, and he pops up to demand it. Problem is your computer isn't turned on. Second scenario: You see him walking down the hall. You trot to your desk, turn on the computer, and start printing it out before he reaches you. Which scenario lets you keep your job?)

I only mentioned it once and that a long while ago. But in case you missed it huge parts of this book are about situational awareness—the ability see problems looming on the horizon. And I'm not particularly fond of the term "situational awareness" for a few reasons. One is people say, "Be aware!" I say, "Of what?" If you don't know *what* to look for being aware isn't much help. This book is filled with what you need to look for in situations.

---

75   The people, who have been dealing with the OOK (out of (k)control person) before the first responders arrive.

Two—and the other side of that coin—I have a saying, "Awareness without knowledge is paranoia." In our modern world, personal safety is as much about quality of life as it is about self-defense. How do you sync being safe with the rest of your life—without becoming a paranoid survivalist nutcase? Part of the answer is accurate knowledge. What are common dangers you can do something about versus what are imaginary boogeymen? Learning to deal with the boogeymen created by your mind (fear management) is beyond the scope of this book. Knowledge alone isn't enough to slay those dragons. But it *is* a critical element of what you can do about it.

FEAR is sometimes represented as "false evidence appearing real." When you feel fear, first thing to do is to *check* the validity of the message regarding the external situation. Is there an external danger? Or is it an internal message? In both cases, the message is real. The question is: Is it accurate? If not (or if it's questionable) then the challenge becomes learning how to take control back from your monkey.[76]

Three is something that hacks me off about most self-defense instruction. That is the hand wave instructors give to situational awareness. I call it that because while everybody says they teach it, they *don't.* They give it about as much attention as the rent-a-cop gives to residents of a gated community as they drive by (hence the term hand wave). They say they teach it, but then spend all their time doing the cool chop socky and pew-pew-pew stuff. If they do teach something about it, it's usually a simplistic cliché—a sound bite that's about as useful as tits on a boar hog.

In this chapter alone, you've learned more about what to look for about being set up for an attack than most black belts will ever be taught. Situational awareness? Look for these signs in your environment. If you see them, pay attention. If not, *relax* and go back to what you were doing. I tell you this because what most people call situational awareness is a fast track to burn-out. And that's the other mistake. As in the second most common blunder that keeps people from reacting in time is becoming *burned out* from clinging to paranoia.

Personally, I want to backhand the "aren't I so tacti-cool because I know the Cooper color code and call myself a sheep dog? I am *always* tactically alert and at code yellow unlike you ignorant sheeple—who are at the code white or transparent crowd." Shut. The. Hell. Up. If these guys were that aware, they'd recognize how they come across to people. There's a reason citizens get nervous about folks being armed. As annoying as those folks can be, I want to stomp the tacti-douche instructor with his

76   Here are two links to pages I wrote about this topic: http://www.conflictcommunications.com/abuse.htm http://www.nononsenseselfdefense.com/FEARvsDANGER.html

"you can be as incompetent and unaware as you want—my patented, guaranteed, anti-ambush move will save you!" Both student and teacher live in fantasy land. The reason for the bitch slap versus the beat down is the former is simply annoying. The latter is endangering other people's lives by presenting a flawed product.[77]

Way too often, I see middle-class, weekend warriors who insist on tactical awareness for everyone. This is why they are such a turn off for most folks. At the same time, their paranoia is like their vampire-repelling talisman. When you tell them it's not necessary there aren't any vampires, they'll respond with, "Yeah, I know there aren't any around here. See how good it works?"

Constant tactical awareness is not healthy, it's paranoia (in the actual meaning of the word). There's more to life than danger. But obsessing on it makes life simpler.[78] This goes double if you're not in circumstances where you deal with violence and criminals daily. In which case, it's almost their religion. Here's something to consider: Dark and deserted parking lots are the boogeyman of the self-defense world. You have to be on guard when you enter one! Be alert! Be vigilant!

Do you know what I *like* about deserted parking lots? There's no one *there!* That's what deserted means. It's when a parking lot is *not* deserted that there *could be* a problem. What's that person doing? Is the guy trying to develop the five stages on you? No. Then there is no problem. But for the tacti-kool, wannabe an operator there could be a horde of ninjas lurking behind every car! He's not going to be caught off guard! Like the uber-operator he is, he's going to tactically check every shadow and be ready for ambushes around every corner. Dude unless you've irritated some seriously dangerous people, you don't need to be this paranoid. Hell even people who live in bad parts of town aren't this uptight.

The problem with the paranoid is their obsession becomes not only their hobby, but all they can talk about. They isolate themselves from normal people and in doing so stress themselves more. Then they surround themselves with the like-minded, who reconfirm their fears. The scary thing is how folks like this seriously overreact when challenged *or* miss the real thing when they're being set up. Here's an example of the latter: I have a friend who used to rob armed guards of their guns then

---

77   There are people who teach a more realistic version of Cooper's color codes that won't burn you out. My friend Alain Burrese, for example, likens code yellow to driving; doable without burn out.

78   Years ago, a drug addict said something very profound to me. He said I didn't understand about addiction. His life was only about *one* thing: Getting drugs. It simplified his life in that all the other things people have to think about, worry about, and deal with—he didn't. His life wasn't easy, but it was simple, cut down to what he could cope with. You will find this same attitude in people who try to reduce life to only one thing. This includes being obsessed about danger.

sell the weapons to other criminals. (This is part of the reason I'm not a fan of routine open carry of firearms.) His strategy? Silent interview, surprise positioning (walk up behind them and hit them with a tire iron or brass knuckles). Nothing like a security professional being knocked out and robbed to give you faith in situational awareness, right?

Until you factor in burn-out. Too often the person has been *so* busy obsessing on being tactical, he or she doesn't recognize it when he or she is slipping. They don't see the little mistakes creeping into their constant surveillance. They're often bored and tired from staying at high alert all the time when nothing happens. Because they've tired themselves out by watching for everything, they've shortened the watch-for list to a convenient length—a list that doesn't include them being the target.[79] In this state, they don't see trouble moving in on them because it's not banging a drum. Burn-out turning fatal is a problem if you've actually crossed the wrong person or group. How do you function in the short term (say three months) until you can resolve the situation? And if necessary, the long term (maybe years)? You can only be alert for so long before you get tired and make mistakes.

This is why it's so important to know when—and be able—to scale back when you're not in a high-risk situation. Bump it up when you need to, but be able to scale back just as fast. You're on the clock when you need to be, but otherwise chill. Dark and deserted parking lot? Not seeing some dastardly person skulking in the shadows, I *can* relax. I don't have to be at any code just because I'm in a parking lot.

Reality is any time I'm entering a fringe area, I'm going to be a little more aware of my surroundings. That's just habit. But not as much as I'm going to be when I see someone who pings my radar in that fringe area. And I'm definitely bumping things up if I see him start trying to develop the five stages and JAM. If not, I'm simply going to keep on doing my business as he goes about his.

It's all about learning how to scale it up or down to your location and situation. Think of situational awareness as a muscle. You exercise it by tightening and relaxing it. But the purpose of exercising a muscle is *not* the exercise. It's so you can do other things with those stronger muscles. You build endurance so you can last longer. You use situational awareness so you know when it's safe to relax or when to buy yourself time when you need to shift mental gears. With this in mind, I'm going to suggest you do something when it comes to practicing situational awareness. It's a long-term, anti-burn-out strategy.

79   Unfortunately, this goes double for police. Cops are really easy to kill if the person coming at them treats them like just another armed person they plan to take out. It's beyond the scope of this book, but dealing with dangerous people who choose not to act is different from being someone dangerous people know not to act out against.

That is: Look for beauty. Every time you do a visual sweep (look at the far, middle and close ranges) reward yourself by using that same awareness to find something beautiful, cool, interesting, or even someone whom you consider hot. I don't give a damn what it is, but find something positive to counter balance the negative. "Anybody trying to sneak up and kill me? Nope. Okay. Hey, she's cute. Ohhhh, what a pretty sunset. It's a critical long-term survival strategy—especially if you've been through some bad situations. Learning to apply situational awareness to *all* circumstances—and not just focusing on the bad—is the counter to burn-out. Besides if you practice being aware of what's going on around you, life can be a lot better (including your love life).

Bringing this back to the five stages, I've spent a lot of time on surprise positioning and stuff that is related to it. There's a damned good reason. Realistically, surprise positioning isn't that common with run-of-the-mill robbers. They're more likely to run a regular interview and closing combo. This gives the criminal(s) a lot more time and leeway to decide if you're safe to attack. It also makes it easier for you to see him or them coming.

Where you *do* need top-of-the-line awareness is when you've messed with the wrong people. I used that Thor quote because surprise positioning is common among heavy hitters. In short, it's more of a professional move. But it's also common with someone who is going to be landing on you hard. I'm not talking about sticking a gun in your face and robbing you. I'm talking about slamming into you, knocking you down, and raping you. I'm talking about the success of the person who is gunning for you.

People don't just accidentally end up lurking in the best ambush spot in the area. Someone doesn't innocently and accidentally move silently within two feet of your back in a parking lot. When you look up and see this something is *way wrong*. It's time to get your game on. And yes this is how you buy time to shift mental gears, even if it's just a second.

Before we move on to the fourth of the five stages, I want to point out some things about the first three—factors that wouldn't make sense until now. First, even though you need all three for a crime to take place don't get married to the order I put them in. That's not fixed. Many crimes of opportunity track like this: Positioning, interview, and intent. Example: A guy is walking along, glances into a car, and sees a camera on the seat (positioning). He looks around to see if anybody will see or stop him (silent interview). Intent is him deciding to smash the window, grab the camera, and run. Despite the claims of the rape industry advocates that all rapists are serial offenders (who planned their attacks) this pattern of a crime of opportunity can be applied to a lot of drunken rape charges.

Another variation is positioning, escalating interview, and intent. In case you missed it, I've just described a fight—an argument that escalates into physical violence. The person didn't mean to attack, but things got to a point and it happened. In many situations, intent won't show up until the other elements have been created. Then, this 'good idea' pops up like a jack-in-the-box from hell.

Second, the five stages are court-tested because they are articulable factors of jeopardy, no matter what definition you use. (I'll explain more in a later chapter.)

Third, there is a model called the fire triangle composed of fuel, air, and heat. These are the things a fire must have in order to burn. Although firefighters later replaced the triangle with a more complicated shape, the triangle still works for laymen.[80] I like the triangle because it collapses when it loses one of its sides. Take away one of the components, the fire goes out. But if you get two and add the third, you have a fire. Intent, interview, and positioning form another triangle you want to stop from completion. If you see someone trying to develop it deny him one of the components he needs to successfully attack.

If possible, this is done during the shadow dance. I'm going to say something followed by a caveat: This is where the willingness to use force is more effective than use of force. Your willingness to use force to stop an attack (mixed with being savvy about playing the shadow dance) is a great way to fail an interview. Interview fails, triangle collapses. Withdraw from the situation or don't let the guy develop an attack position. Positioning fails, triangle collapses.

When I talk about shadow dancing with the guy to convince him to go away and pick another target, I am often asked, "But what if he attacks anyway?" Oh, you mean what do you do if he changes from regular close to a hot close, attempted blitz? Personally, I'm a big fan of defending myself. I've said it before, I'll say it again: I am negotiating until I pull the trigger. I'm trying every reasonable means to avoid having to use force. His attack means those reasonable, nonviolent strategies *didn't* work. How do you know? You tried them before using force.

That by the way is a useful tip about states with duty-to-retreat laws. I'm all for a good faith attempt to withdraw (even in states without duty-to-retreat laws and those with stand-your-ground laws). They often solve

---

80   The triangle revolutionized the way we train firefighters. Its use allowed instructors to explain some counterintuitive things. Like how when using a hose, recruits want to aim a stream of water at the fire. It's actually faster and safer to put out a fire using a wide spray waved over the flames and work your way down. (It takes away the heat, whereas water directly on the fire temporarily takes away the oxygen—until it evaporates. Then you get the steam and burning bits being blasted about because of the water pressure.)

the problem without violence. On the other hand, when the cops and prosecutors ask, "Why did you stop retreating?" the answer "because it wasn't working" *is* reasonable. More importantly, a retreat failure removes doubt about why you had to act.

Finally, the fourth of the five stages.

Attack: This is either an actual physical assault or the credible threat of violence to achieve a goal.

A refresher, according to the Bureau of Justice Statistics: *Robbery is the completed or attempted theft, directly from a person, of property or cash by force or threat of force, with or without a weapon, and with or without injury.* The difference between theft (stealing something) and robbery is force, whether it's used or just threatened. Robbery is treated more harshly than theft. The more force used, the higher the level of prosecution.

At this point, I'm going to throw in something for you to consider: Criminals know the legal system better than you do. More than that, they also know what crimes are going to encourage the cops to look for them. Do *not* think this doesn't affect their strategies. If three guys surround you and suggest that unless you want to pick your teeth up off the ground you should donate to their college funds that's a strong-arm robbery. If they just take cash, they're pretty safe. Even if thirty seconds after they've gone, you flag down a cop car, it will be a hard case to prove. They've never seen you before. You didn't give them any money. It's their word against yours, and there are three of them. The cops are going to need some kind of evidence that justifies an arrest (like their taking your wallet and still having it on one of them). Your word alone *isn't* enough. But let's say they get away. A single strong-arm robbery? Unless you're the mayor's wife or have some kind of serious political clout, your being robbed this way is not going to be looked into too deeply.

What is going to get attention when it comes to robbery is when the robber threatens someone with a weapon in order to rob her. Same if he jumps a store clerk, beats the hell out of him, grabs the cash, and splits. The cops are more likely to take an interest in such shenanigans. The punishment for that crime goes up, too. But they won't be looking for the guy threatening with the weapon as hard as they will for the guy who jumped the counter and cracked the clerk's skull. Pull this stunt—armed or unarmed—several times in the same area, and they'll definitely take notice. If he uses that weapon, they'll be looking hard. Kill someone and he definitely catches their attention, as well as the fact he's facing more serious charges if caught.

Hint: In most states, kill someone while committing a felony and it's an automatic murder one rap (or whatever they call it locally). Oh yeah, it doesn't matter if you were the get-away driver and one of your partners pulled the trigger. Felony with a death equals murder one charges for *everyone* who was involved. News to you not news to criminals.

To plant a seed that will become important later, after murder kidnapping is the most seriously prosecuted crime. A number of states have laws that read if you force someone to move during the commission of a felony, it's kidnapping. Again, criminals *know* this. So a criminal telling you to move—to, say, open the safe or go to a secondary location—is *never* a good sign.

So there's your attack. Is it physical or is it the threat of violence with instructions on how to avoid force (give him your purse, wallet, or car keys)?

I ask because if it's merely the *threat* of violence, it's scripted. And if you cooperate in a well run robbery, you'll be relatively safe. You're standing in line in a liquor store, waiting to pay for the booze. A douche bag (silent interview conducted by looking in from the outside) rushes in (surprise positioning) and waves a shotgun (threat of deadly force). He's screaming and yelling at everyone not to move (no kidnap charge) and to put their hands up (so the clerk can't push the panic button and you can't pull out your concealed gun). He points the shotgun at the clerk and demands the money from the drawer. Cashier forks over the cash. With a final, "Nobody move," the dude books out the door (no kidnapping, no murder one). Elapsed time, maybe twenty seconds. Everything goes according to script; nobody gets hurt.

But let's say someone tries to be a hero. After all, this is what he's trained for! The guy tries to kick the shotgun out of the criminal's hand or goes for a concealed pistol. Now the situation is totally off script. *If* that douche with the shotgun isn't taken out before he can pull the trigger, things are going to get . . . complicated.

Where it's going to get real complicated is if the douche bag isn't following the script. He runs in, butt strokes the clerk with his gun, and orders him down on his knees while pointing the shotgun at the clerk's head. Sorry, that's not how a safe robbery script goes. People who've spent a lot of money on training and equipment often get upset with me for suggesting not acting. Well, now we're on a road where action is not only a reasonable response, but likely the best one.

The incident I just described happened. A customer carrying a concealed gun shot the robber—who was out on bail for another robbery (where he beat another clerk). Remember when I said no matter what somebody's going to be unhappy with your decision? A relative of that robber said the citizen had no right to shoot him. Her reasoning was he wasn't threatening to shoot the customer, but the clerk. (Do you see the monkey hijacking the human to justify what it believes?) But Stud Muffins there was so drugged up, off script, and violent it was only a matter of time before someone put him down.

Realistically, a majority of robberies are very much about threatening extreme violence rather than doing it. Even if the numbers are 90 percent, there's still that damned 10 percent wild card. That's the idiot robber who thinks he's got to do something more to get what he wants (like clubbing the clerk) or who gets violent at the first sign of perceived resistance.

Of course, there're all those damned attacks that aren't about robbery. But moving on . . .

Reaction: This is the fifth stage. Unfortunately, it's often not the last— because it's what the person thinks, believes, and feels about what was done. Often, the reaction is to decide to continue with this course of behavior.

If you're familiar with the domestic abuse cycle, this is the "hearts and flowers" stage. If you're familiar with psychology, this is where operant conditioning sinks in (it worked once, do it again). In terms of vendetta, this is where the person works herself up to backing up on you or patting herself on the back for siccing the cops on you. Another common reaction—especially with people who lost—is to sit and blame you for their misfortunes. It's entirely your fault. They were the sweet and innocent Little Bo Peeps and you . . . you big meanie head . . . overreacted. The best reaction of them all is when the person goes back to his or her social circle and tells his or her tale of woe. There is great wailing and gnashing of teeth, but nothing happens. Yay! I like it when that happens.

It's when he decides to back up on you and get his revenge . . . awwww sunofabitch . . .

CHAPTER 6

I think that lawyers are terrible at admitting that they're wrong. And not just admitting it; also realizing it. Most lawyers are very successful, and they think that because they're making money and people think well of them, they must be doing everything right.

—Alan Dershowitz

If Your SD Works . . .
Part One: Your Lawyer

Remember I said there's a difference between the law and our legal system? Let's start with both that and a big problem—your self-defense works. Why's that a problem? Most defense lawyers *won't* know how to present your case when you really *did* act in self-defense. Truthfully, they don't see valid self-defense pleas that often.

I've already told you about the attorney who asked me, "Really?" when I told him his client's actions were truly self-defense. Stop and think about that. This attorney was defending someone charged with murder. His client had claimed self-defense not SODDI (some other dude did it). He faced at least twenty-five years for murder if it went to trial. He wasn't about to take the bad plea deal the prosecutor offered (manslaughter for fifteen years). Until I told him, the defense attorney didn't understand why his client was risking a longer prison term by *not* taking the plea. But most of all, the lawyer had no idea about the "immediate danger of death or grave bodily injury" his client faced when he *killed* his attacker. It hadn't even occurred to the attorney that if his client hadn't killed his attacker, he'd die. Basically, the lawyer thought the prosecutor was correct in her summation that his client "brought a knife to a fist fight."

Before I explained *why* it was self-defense, the lawyer was simply *going through the motions*. It wasn't just that he expected his client to go down, it was that he too thought his client had illegally killed another person. This case was business as usual for the attorney. But to his client, it was his life. A life for which he'd taken another's to protect; a life the legal system now wanted.

This book isn't just to teach you about how to stay in the SD square. It's also defining what you need to tell your attorney, to educate him if you will. Education he *needs* to have in order to defend you for having defended yourself. So with that in mind, you need to know what you're dealing with. Start with the assumption that if there's a body, there's been a crime—especially when that body has been manufactured by violence.

It's bad enough that the public thinks a body implies crime, but this becomes almost a dogma in the legal professions. After all, this is their bailiwick. They deal with it all the time. But here's the thing *not* questioning the assumption that a body equals crime saves lawyers a step. It means they can get on with what *they* consider important—prosecuting or defending the case.

This leads us to another big time saver for the legal professionals. Assumption number two: The winner and not dead guy is the one who committed the crime. Dead guy victim hence living guy committed the crime—simple. Guy with the least amount of blood loss and bruising is the aggressor. While indeed this is often the case, it's unwise to automatically assume it. But look at all the time saved if they take this easy-peasy formula for granted. The attorney skips two bothersome and time-consuming steps so he or she can swing into action.

Understanding the assumptions that body equals crime gets your head around something important. I started this book by telling you when you claim self-defense, you're confessing to a crime (an affirmative defense; i.e., "Yeah I did it, but here's why . . .") The first reason was to get your head in the game. Self-defense is *not* a crime.[81] It is a right you are legally granted when someone attempts to commit the criminal act of illegal violence, murder, or mayhem against you. The problem is the results of SD happen to look *exactly* like the crime he was trying to commit against you. And that's what you just apparently confessed to.

You're not ever going to get rid of the assumption in people's minds—especially cops and lawyers—that there was a crime. Your new task is to guide their attention to the fact there was a crime. A crime committed against you, not by you. This is where it starts getting . . . complicated. (Side note: Everything I'm saying here applies to every level of physical force—whether your attacker lives or not. But for grammar and simplicity's sake, I'm just going to talk about things as if it was a lethal force incident.)

In self-defense, a crime *was* committed. But it was carried out *by* the dead guy. It just didn't work out the way he planned. Since he's dead, he can't be prosecuted, and he certainly doesn't need a defense attorney. So

81   Except in New York, where it's deemed justifiable or excusable homicide. So, yeah, there self-defense is a crime, but they claim they won't prosecute you for it. ~Me: Lighting a cigar and squinting~"Wanna bet?"~

guess who everyone is going to be looking at? This also applies if he's not dead—except you have this bloody whiner, pointing a finger at you and saying *you* perpetrated the crime.

Because of the time-saving assumptions by those in the legal professions, one of the first people you need to convince you aren't guilty of a crime *is* your attorney. This step is critical to avoid the most common reason people go to prison for actual self-defense. That is when someone claims SD, most defense lawyers adopt a damage control strategy. They're not trying to get you off; they're trying to get you the *lightest* sentence possible.

In fact, most will recommend you accept the plea bargain the DA offers (copping a plea). This is when the prosecutor offers you a chance to plead guilty to a lesser crime in return for a lighter sentence. For example, instead of being tried and convicted to a sentence of twenty-five years for murder, you accept the deal of fifteen for manslaughter. A plea settles the case for *both* attorneys, and they can move on to the next case. If you actually committed a crime, this can be a pretty good thing. You murdered someone and got caught. Oops. But now instead of life, you only do ten years by copping to manslaughter. The defense lawyer is brokering a better deal for you. Yay!

But if you are convinced you acted in self-defense, this is a hard pill to swallow. As I said before what you believe *isn't* relevant; what matters is what you actually did—especially when you're about to claim SD. Reviewing your actions in that light is step one. Step two is your ability to effectively communicate that you acted in self-defense. And it's here we need to have an important reality break. Being treated like a criminal is a big part of that hard pill to swallow, but so too is accepting the fact you stepped outside the SD square. This is why *before* you say anything to the police, you take a good, hard look at your behavior. If you crossed the line, *shut up* and let your lawyer handle damage control. His existing strategy *is* your best chance. In most cases of illegal violence think of your attorney as a negotiator trying to lessen the punishment for your misbehavior.

But let's say you aren't off in your own private Idaho, and it really was self-defense. Copping a plea is the *last* thing you will want to do. Being treated like you broke the law much less being charged *will* enrage you. But what's downright infuriating is when your attorney tells you to admit guilt for something you *didn't* do. So I'm going to say it again—and I'm going to tell you it isn't exactly correct—but you need to get your head around it up front: The *first* person you have to *convince* that you acted in self-defense *is* your defense attorney. This is a game changer for several reasons.

First, it gets your attorney out of damage control mode. Or at least helps him or her put the case into perspective. (There will still be a degree of damage control, but for different reasons.) Second, it prepares your attorney for a fight. Realistically, most defense attorneys would prefer negotiating a plea deal. They don't want to go into a courtroom to defend a self-defense plea. It's long hard work, it's expensive, and there's a good chance of losing. Truth is the greater the chance of it going to trial, the more they'll demand to be paid up front. (And to be brutally honest about the commercialization of our legal system, trials cut into their profit margin.)

Having said that, there's something you *need* to know. Let's say you don't take the plea deal. You'll go to court on the original charge. *If* you lose, the court will throw the book at you. They're going to go for the maximum penalty for making them work for the conviction and spend money getting it. Right, wrong, fair, or not that's how it works in our legal system—deal with it. This is the damage control most attorneys try to achieve. The lawyer knows what will happen if you are convicted, and he is trying to minimize the amount of time you'll spend in prison. Accepting the plea makes sense—when you've stepped out of the SD square. It doesn't when you didn't. But not taking a plea deal confuses any lawyer you haven't convinced that your actions really were taken in self-defense.

The third point has two versions. Know I'm channeling Massad Ayoob here. The first version is as he told it to me. That is (if it goes to court):
1) You defend a guilty person differently than you do an innocent one.
2) Using the strategy that gets a guilty person off will convict an innocent person.

Got that? This is seriously connected to *why* the first person you *need* to convince is your attorney. Because I often work with lawyers, I have altered Ayoob's version. Although his is a much better sound bite (and easier for a layperson to remember) lawyers tend to gag on the terminology. My version:
1) You defend a SODDI or an innocent person (he really didn't do it) differently than you defend a person who legitimately acted in self-defense.
2) If you attempt to use the normal defense strategies, you will convict someone pleading self-defense.[82]

---

82   The reason for this tweak is a layperson thinks self-defense equals innocent. Innocent means something different to an attorney. (In layman's terms guilty—he did it and the attorney is trying to get him off. Innocent—he didn't do it because some other dude actually did it. I had to modify the original because when speaking to lawyers misusing legal terms makes you look like an idiot. Not only does it hurt your credibility, they know how the opposition is going to rip you apart.

Got it? An actual self-defense case is *not* business as usual. Again, this is why the first person you need to convince is your own attorney. You do this by providing enough evidence that he or she knows *beyond* a reasonable doubt your actions were necessary given the circumstances. (Information he or she also will use to defend you in court.)

There's a fourth reason why your lawyer believing you acted in SD is a game changer. All jokes about lawyers aside, an attorney fighting to protect an innocent person is a *joy* to behold. Really. Long ago and far away *that's* why they got into law—not to become highly paid negotiators. Having right on their side gets them all kinds of riled up and willing to open a can of whup ass on your behalf. A case he or she believes in is a case he or she is going to fight to win.

Another expert witness, Roy Bedard, has a saying I really like. He says in self-defense cases, the defense's "job is to prosecute the dead guy." You're the victim, not the dead guy. Marty Hayes from Firearms Academy of Seattle puts it in terms of tort and civil law—as in think of it as you're going to sue the dead guy. Your attorney must bring forth the tort for assault and battery *against* you. That's where 'the preponderance of evidence' about why it was self-defense makes lots of sense. (Oh yeah, in case the guy didn't die this attitude will really help you if he tries to sue you for damages.) You need your fired-up attorney showing the jury the other guy *wasn't* a victim, he was the *bad guy.* (Challenge the victim assumption.) The real criminal was the person who forced you into a position where it was either him or you.[83]

Fifth, it allows your attorney to introduce all kinds of other evidence. Information the prosecution probably has never heard of and doesn't know how to defend against. That's right, defend against. Things like adrenal stress, conscious use-of-force decisions, good faith efforts to withdraw, the pain inhibiting effects of alcohol, and other pertinent facts.

All of these make the prosecutor's attempts to make you look like a blood thirsty, out-of-control lunatic (who needs to be punished) less and less credible. And believe me, he or she will try.

How will your attorney know about all this other stuff (e.g., spatial distortion)? Because you told him to look into it. You're not just giving him ammo, you're giving him armor-piercing tracers and bunker busters.

Sixth—and finally—it's a litmus test to see *if* you *need* a new attorney. There are a lot of half-assed, sloppy lawyers out there. Hell, I worked a case where a guy was attacked and stabbed eight times by his 'professional drunk' and abusive girlfriend. Forensics and crime scene investigation support what I'm about to tell you. He knocked her back ending the

---

83   If your defense attorney is a former prosecutor (and a number of them are) this strategy should be easy.

first assault and stabbings, collapsed, got up, and staggered toward the phone. She went into the kitchen, got another knife, and attacked him again. He pulled the knife *out of his own chest* and fought her off. She died, he got medivaced out. He's in prison for second-degree murder. He's in prison because his attorney *didn't* call any witnesses or do anything else but go through the motions. Why? The lawyer thought he didn't have to. He figured "the jury would just know it was self-defense." (I was called in on the appeal.)

Nimrod the Magnificent also screwed the pooch because he told his client, "We're going to take the high road," and *not* besmirch the victim's reputation. Because they didn't bring it up, the prosecution downplayed her long-standing pattern of domestic abuse, mental instability, violence, and chronic alcoholism. So instead of the jury understanding the death was the end of a long series of out-of-control drunken rages, the prosecution led them to believe he murdered his sweet innocent Little Bo Peep girlfriend. Then stabbed himself eight times to cover up his crime.

Nor did the lawyer know to pick up and run with what I call "reveal statements." These are often casual small comments that reveal a huge, underlying dynamic. For example, the defendant testified, "When she started attacking me, I covered up like I normally do."

Wait . . . normally do? She attacked him so often he not only had a strategy for handling it, but it was so routine it was *normal?* As in, the guy mentions it casually? Hello! That's a pattern of ongoing domestic violence and abuse. The guy was stabbed eight times before he realized it wasn't her normal attack!

A lot of lawyers I've dealt with talk about the importance of jury selection when it comes to SD cases. True . . . to a point. They talk more about can the state prove it's case? With the last, I encourage defense attorneys to adopt a yes and . . . strategy. That is instead of attacking the state's evidence (like you do when someone else did it and you are innocent) agree, "Yes, that's what it looks like—and normally is—but . . ." Then add evidence and mitigating factors that *change* the significance of the state's evidence. This is not disputing the state's evidence. It's not discrediting it. Nor casting doubt on its source. It's changing the conclusion *by adding more evidence.*

Instead of trying to argue six plus three equals nine, acknowledge and add. "Yes, six plus three equals nine. But four also was present. So the actual situation was six plus three plus four. That equals thirteen." You're not arguing against the six, three, nine, or the addition. Nine would be the right answer *if* it weren't for the fourth element.

Example, the ninety-eight-pound knife wielder was shot five times. Prosecution claims this was excessive. An expert is brought in by the prosecution to point out at least three of the wounds would be lethal by themselves. Given *just* that, five shots seems excessive—except there is a difference between lethal and incapacitating. A person who is lethally wounded can remain up and a viable threat for a very long time. Also the dead person was a long time meth addict and in the middle of a berserk rage (common among tweakers). It wasn't until the fifth shot that the danger the addict posed ended. Five shots would have been excessive for a normal person, but a berserk addict is *not* a normal person. (I cover some of this in my e-book, *Writing Violence #1: Getting Shot.*[1])

With a little research, a good attorney can turn the state's expert into his or her own. For example, he or she can get the prosecution's medical expert

---

[1]   Although written for fiction writers, screen writers, etc, there's a lot of useful information about what to expect when someone gets shot—especially important if you carry a gun for self-defense.

to testify about a chronic alcoholic's ability to function at incredibly high BACs and the pain suppression effects of adrenaline and alcohol. A) Your expert reconfirms it. B) It's not going to look good if the prosecution tries to tear down points his or her expert confirmed.

Another strategy is rebutting *parts* the prosecutor's formula. The idea is selectively questioning aspects of the prosecutor's formula: "Yes, six plus three equals nine. While the six and three are correct that is *not* a plus sign, but a times sign. A symbol that is the same, just turned slightly. That makes this six times three, which is *not* nine, but eighteen."

Example: Two guys roll around on the ground fighting. One pulls a knife and stabs the other. Given those circumstances, yes the prosecutor would be right about it being manslaughter (+). Same two guys on the ground, but one is sitting on top and choking the other. That's not a fight anymore, that's attempted murder (x). *That's* when the knife was used making this self-defense.

The "yes and . . ." strategy doesn't try to debunk or refute the state's evidence. Nor does it look to the jury like you're trying to wiggle out of anything. It adds to and changes the significance of the evidence. This strategy is a very useful arrow in the attorney's quiver for defending someone who acted in self-defense.

And the dipshite attorney didn't pick up on that?

Another Spongebob move was when the attorney failed to call a doctor specializing in alcoholism as a rebuttal witness to the prosecution's medical expert, who testified that she with a .32 BAC (blood alcohol content) would be physically unable to attack him. Pffffft! Wanna bet? But more than that, the defense's rebuttal witness could have testified *that* BAC had more to do with the amount of force required to stop her.[84]

But before all of that, his defense attorney didn't even try to get the police interview—conducted the next day when the guy was sedated in the hospital—thrown out as inadmissible. Hell, I'm not a lawyer and even I can see the wisdom of challenging that evidence. That kind of bozo is *not* the lawyer you want to defend you.

There also is a really ugly financial reality. It's one of those unpleasant "the difference between theory and practice is in theory there is no difference . . ." issues. Morally and ethically the following is 'wrong,' but we live in the real world so think about it. When you're operating on limited funds, you have to take the attorney's advice to not call in experts to help your case with not a grain, but an entire block of salt. Experts are expensive. Let's say the most you can come up with is $20,000. If the attorney is thinking you're going to go down anyway, it is not beyond human nature for him to look at the cost of multiple experts going for $5,000 each and . . . well . . . you do the math . . .

But let's stick with you having a meritorious case for self-defense. You're going to have to fight to prove what you did was SD, and you need an attorney who *knows* that. You need an aggressive, offensive defense for a self-defense plea. So you want an attorney who believes in you and is willing to fight using whatever ammo you can give him or her.

84   Ask any cop, EMT, ER nurse, bouncer, or addiction specialist about what professional drunks (perma drunks) can do in an enraged state and with even higher BACs (blood alcohol contents).

Another type of attorney you don't want is the ' know it all.' Too many attorneys get caught up in the game and are too impressed with how well they play it. Lawyers fight with words and ideas all the time. They're pretty short when it comes to first hand experiences of spitting blood. Therefore, an attorney who *isn't* willing to listen to you (dismisses what you know about this subject) or is convinced his old strategy will work is likely to get you convicted. You *don't* want a lawyer who won't listen to you when your actions really were in self-defense. After reading this book, you'll have more knowledge about how violence occurs, what is involved, how to articulate it, and why it's important your attorney knows that. Your first test of articulation is your ability to communicate information to him or her.

CHAPTER 7

People don't understand what it's like being interrogated by the police. It's like defending your Ph.D thesis.

—Randy Carpadus

JAM and AOJ

If you're trained in empty-hand self-defense, you might wonder . . ."AOJ? JAM? What?"

For the record, this is a *major* hole in what you're taught. A hole that's way more scary in weapons systems, like Filipino martial arts. Important safety tip, campers: Using a knife (and certain other kinds of weapons) is lethal force. You will face charges just as high for using a knife on someone as you will for shooting them. Depending on what you're using and where you hit them with it, the same goes for strike enhancers, clubs, and even bottles. If you have *something* in your hand, the SD square shrinks and you're facing greater charges if you step out of bounds with its use. The presence of a weapon is a *game changer*—in many different ways.

JAM versus AOJ is a big debate in the shooting world where they *have to* plan for success. What do I mean plan for success? Simple, you pull that trigger and it's use of lethal force. More than that, pull that trigger and physics *will* happen. There will be some unhappy people demanding answers about that use-of-force choice.

In the meantime, Five Stages of Violence in one hand. In the other, pick either JAM (jeopardy, ability, means) or AOJ (ability, opportunity, jeopardy). Whatever one you pick combine it with the five stages, and you get all kinds of yummy goodness. But before you mix 'em know 'em independently.

That brings us to the debate about JAM versus AOJ. A debate over legal application and emphasis—and it's really among lawyers. But way too many camp followers of shooting gurus figure it's their argument, too. So they squabble over who's right.

Reminder, AOJ was formally AOI, (ability, opportunity, intent.[85])

---

85   AOI (ability, opportunity, intent) was originally a police tool to used explain why Officer Friendly had to shoot someone.

Lawyers contend that you are not psychic. You cannot read someone's mind; you cannot know for certain what someone plans to do. This is how they attacked the other side's case. Intent fell out of favor because of this tactic. It morphed into jeopardy, a word that was easier to defend than intent.

A similar squabble by lawyers exists over JAM and AOJ. In layman's terms, JAM and AOJ mean basically the same thing with much of the same information, but with different perspectives, different emphases, and different categorizations. So why the lawyerly slug-fest? From a legal perspective, the *order* matters—at least as part of your legal defense strategy.

Just so you know, the word jeopardy has the legal meaning of peril, danger. Ability and opportunity or means have also been court tested. Put in this order, AOJ means he has the ability and means thereby creating peril (jeopardy). Pretty easy to follow the logical progression there—in a courtroom.

On the other hand, JAM is an easy way to teach the average person three ways to assess and articulate peril. But with JAM, the jeopardy is not the conclusion instead it's part of the equation.

I tell you about this flap because nobody's 100 percent right or 100 percent wrong in JAM versus AOJ. Both are good ways to communicate to people that you were in immediate danger. Knowing this, I suggest you find proponents of JAM and AOJ, get some popcorn, get comfy, and ask, "Okay so why is _____ (fill in blank) better than _____ (fill in the other blank)." Then sit back and listen to the debate. At the very least, you'll learn something. I will go so far as to say listening with no dog in that fight is a great way to learn about the complexities of the process.

See, a big part of the flap is it depends on how you define jeopardy. I already gave you the legal interpretation. But I'm going to throw out a few other—useful—interpretations. Here's one popular definition: *Would a reasonable, prudent person in the same situation knowing what you know at the time have reasonably believed that the assailant intended to use his ability and opportunity to kill or cripple?* As in, were you in jeopardy? Using this definition, AOJ makes perfect sense. Ability is he has a knife. If opportunity is the same as means, then both are about his being in range (or closing range) to use it. And he does look kind of cranky. Yes, a reasonable person would believe he was in peril. Oh yeah, notice how they slid the word intent in there. (Those sly devils.)

Great, except I first heard jeopardy defined (non-legally) as: *A person is acting in a way consistent with known dangerous behavior.* Ohhhhh that's good, too. That definition still works, but not as *well* with AOJ. What if the person closing on you with a blade is a waiter carrying the new knife you just asked for. Nope, no peril, no jeopardy. Without calling it intent, this definition of jeopardy is kind of . . .weak . . . in AO equals J. "He's coming at me with a knife!" "Dude, he's our waiter."

On the other hand *that* definition works real well with the Five Stages of Violence, and takes on a whole new depth when added to JAM. Now you have three elements that combine to show there was peril. This without ever using the word 'intent' in a psychic sense.

Let's see that would mean if he tries to develop the five stages, he behaves like people do before they attack someone. That looks like jeopardy (legal definition, as well as behaving in a known way). And his trying to develop positioning is him developing the means. Now JAM isn't just checked, but double-checked. So if you see them being developed, it is reasonable to believe you're in immediate danger. Right? Uhhhh, yeah, but not so fast—especially when it comes to thinking you have a green light to slaughter the guy. There's a hiccup. Ability is when real life runs into the dog-and-pony show that is our legal system.

Generally speaking, when someone means to kill you, they're not down the street, waving the gun around, and saying, "Helloooo! I'm coming to kill you!" In fact with those pesky surprise assassinations, you probably won't see the knife until it goes into your gut. And that's kind of the bitch about ability. When someone is out to kill you, it's in his best interest *not* to show you he possesses that ability until he's in the *process* of killing you. Personally, I don't want to wait that long before I figure out I'm in deep kimchi.

In contrast when you're in the middle of escalato and the monkey dance, it is common for someone to pull their gun out and wave it around so you *see* his ability and *hear* him tell you how serious he is. Usually, he's waving it around so you *will* run away. You gone solves his immediate problem.

Robbery is a mutant mix of these two. Muggers can't display the weapon too early. (It's that whole you-running-away thing.) They like to get close and pull their weapon—so you can see it. Then, they tell you what you can do to keep it from being used. In essence, it is their being close enough to control your options. A big part of their credibility is *showing* you they have the *ability* to carry out the threat if you don't do what they want. The clear demonstration of ability is the "threat of violence" in the definition of robbery (as opposed to nonviolent theft).

This delay screws up both models. JAM morphs to JMA. AOJ switches to either OJA or AO you're dead. The reason for OJA is you were in jeopardy, but the degree wasn't clear until he displayed the ability.

This shows us two critical elements about the AOJ and JAM debate:
1) Both models can be messed up by circumstances.
2) No matter which one you ascribe to the map is *not* the territory.

Re-stressing: The bad guy can't show his ability too soon or you'll run before he can control the situation. That's the bitch about ability when it comes to weapons. Unless you're arguing with someone, odds are good you ain't going to see the weapon (increase in ability) until it's way late. Yes, things are tense, but the very next moment someone is trying to gut you like fish.

That's a situation the tacti-cool guys touch themselves about. Yet that same situation scares the hell out of us who have actually been there. It's also why we feel like Cassandra when we talk about the importance of environmental knowledge, circumstantial assessment, and awareness.[86] We learned the hard way about this cover up and delay in showing ability while developing means.

Let me give you an insight, I grew up around gang members. Now gangsta's aren't really big on holsters. It makes ditching the gun harder. ("If you weren't carrying an illegal gun, why do you have a holster?" "Uhhhhh." "Have a seat in the back of the patrol car while we look in the immediate area for a gun with your fingerprints on it.") Lacking holsters, the preferred carry-spot for their guns were under their baggy shirts and in the waists of their pants with the barrels pointing at their dicks. If it started slipping, they could easily and subtly adjust it. Gangsters are part of the reason I don't like appendix carry.[87]

The thing about this type of carry is the

Preclusion is another, "I'll get you my pretty! And your little dog Toto, too!" Some people add it to AOJ, some to JAM. Preclusion basically means that there was no other alternative than use of force. It's especially bandied around when it comes to lethal force, but you'll hear it if you hit someone with something, as well.

Like minimum use of force and duty to retreat, preclusion sounds nice, but it's *not*. That's because, while it's promoted to save lives (~coughcough-bullshitcough~) it's been turned into an assassin's weapon for prosecutors. It's easy for a prosecutor to use it to prey on the attitude of an uninformed jury with, "Well couldn't you have done something else?"

Cops face it in the form of, "Why'd you have to shoot him? Couldn't you have just tasered him?" Well, no. "We didn't have a taser, and the bastard was trying to run us over. While we're at it even if we had one, taser barbs don't go through car windows bullets do." I'm paraphrasing the response to comments about an actual incident where police officers shot a guy who'd stolen his father's truck and trailer, rammed a police car, engendered a high speed chase through the streets and onto a university campus (I counted nineteen circumstances where he endangered the lives of others) lost the trailer, rammed a police car, and was trying to run over another cop at the time he was shot. The commentators whinged, whined, and condemned the police for not first trying tasers. I tell you about this because if the cops face it, you can bet you will, too.

Preclusion, minimum force, and duty to retreat all fall under the category of good ideas make bad laws. Should you always be looking for a viable alternative to physical violence? Yes. Does *your* ability solidly influence your viable options? Yes. Does the other person's ability strongly influence your options? You betcha. If there are viable alternatives to physical violence should you take them? Not only yes, but hell yes. Are there always going to be good alternatives to physical force? *No!* Sometimes violence *is* the best answer. At times, violence is the fastest

---

86   In Greek mythology, Cassandra was given the gift of prophecy. But she was cursed because nobody would believe her. When you're dead, it's kind of hard to say, "Hey, you know what? Cassandra was right."

87   And then there's the whole thing with the gang banger who shot off one of his balls, but I gotta be drinking to tell that story.

and safest answer given all the other considerations. Is that going to be the case in every situation? No.

Like everything else in this business, *it depends*. The incident and circumstances dictate what's most likely to happen, what options are viable, what variables are involved, and what is the fastest, safest, most effective, and reliable response. Given the *circumstances*, you're looking for viable options that scale from good to better to best. What's a good answer? What's . . . etc. At the same time—in the negative—you're throwing out options that scale from bad to worse to awww hell no. Except "aww hell no" is kind of hard to explain in court. You need something a little more . . . solid.

Instead of hell no, the scales you use are *time* and *safety*. Do you have time to use that option? Can you safely use that option? Those are both excellent means to assess your viable options (given the circumstances) *and* the counter to the prosecutor using preclusion against you.

"Why didn't you _____ (fill in blank)?"

"That was not a viable option because the circumstances were A,B, and C."

"Yes, but you didn't even try."

"A,B,C didn't allow the time necessary for _____(fill in blank) to work. Also given D,E, and F attempting to _____(fill in blank) would have been too dangerous to safely try."

Remember, there is always going to be someone unhappy with your use-of-force decision. That *right there* is reason enough to always try to find alternatives. The most common strategy to attack your use-of-force decision is through preclusion. You need to be able to justify your decision—not only why you had to do it, but also why other options were not viable at that moment and given the circumstances. (By the way, the irony of starting this sidebar with misquoting *The Wizard of Oz* (1939) is that real quote is: "Just try and stay out of my way. Just try! I'll get you, my pretty, and your little dog, too!" It often seems—even if you do try other options before using force—a career prosecutor should be green and wear a pointy hat.)

draw is basically a two-handed operation. The left hand hooks and lifts the shirt while the right hand draws the gun. The action is not unlike someone lifting his shirt to show you his appendectomy scar. And showing you surgery scars *isn't* normal behavior for a stranger in an alley and at night.

I tell you this because a few people have been introduced to unconsciousness for this behavior. In *none* of these situations did I ever see the gun until after it was over. In those circumstances, the two-handed motion is what triggered my response *not* a visual confirmation of a weapon. (The other reason I don't like appendix carry is there's a damned good chance the other guy with a weapon knows what you're up to when you go for it. If he has his gun out expect to eat some lead when he sees you trying to draw.) Yet I know of numerous self-defense cases where the prosecution pounded the defendant for acting *before* he saw the gun.

Let's go back and remind you of three things:

1) Someone's going to be unhappy.
2) The monkey hijacks the human brain to come up with reasonable-sounding excuses for what it *wants* to believe.
3) The prosecution will do everything in its power to make it look like it *wasn't* self-defense, but you overreacting.

The district attorney hammering you for acting when you saw the draw, not the weapon, is a common tactic in such circumstances. Basically, he's selling the idea that the dead guy's draw was the actual self-defense act—*not* what you did. (You shot him in cold blood, you evil bastard.) This is why being able to articulate what that two-handed claw means in the circumstances is *so* important.

Okay, so there's some background and perspective. Now I'm going to tell you how far out I am. My use of JAM in this book does not come from the legal, much less lethal force aspect. (To be honest, I lean more toward the AOJ argument—especially when it comes to lethal force). I use JAM in this book because of the ~ hack, gag, ralf, barf, puke ~ *tactical* application. Yes, I said it. I said "tactical." After I finish typing this, I'm going to go wash my hands. And just because I said tactical doesn't mean I'm going to start touching myself when I watch *Roadhouse*.

But it does point out there's a different way to look at both JAM and AOJ. You're not going to hear this elsewhere, but:

1) It tracks back to doing the math equation I gave you about JAM

2) Assessing the degree of force necessary for a non-lethal situation

News flash here, children, making up numbers to give you an idea with about 98 percent of the kind of violence the average citizen is going to be involved in, *lethal force is not justified.* You can fiddle those numbers with gang members on one end of the spectrum and Amish on the other, but there is *no* group where lethal violence will ever be the majority of what they face.[88]

While martial artists may ask, "What's AOJ?" Shooters ask, "What's scaling force?" Both questions are fast tracks to prison. This chapter is an introduction.[89]

I *don't* look at JAM as "am I in danger?" Instead, I look at it from the standpoint of: Am I in a situation, and if so what *degree* of force is *necessary?* This is my unique spin. I don't know anybody else who does it. If you look at jeopardy in the definition of *acting in a known pattern of danger*, you can start using JAM as a way to scale your use of force up or down.

Starting with: Do you have to use force? But I especially scale it when it comes to the combo of jeopardy and ability. See, the five stages don't just apply to robbery. You'll see the same core elements used to set up a physical assault in a fight or argument. They just manifest differently (escalating and closing with intent somewhere in the mix). The five also apply to a developing sexual assault whether it's a jump-out-of-the-bushes type or a date rape. Wolf packs, knock-out games, and stompings have their own flavors of the five stages. If you swap interview

---

88   Raw numbers from the FBI Uniform Crime Report. In 2012, there were 14,827 murders, 354,520 robberies, 84,376 rapes. Remembering these are *only* reported crimes that's 1,199,635 to 14,827. That's roughly an eighty to one ratio of other violent crimes to homicides. Now, when you add in all the unreported violence that ratio really climbs.

89   A book specifically dedicated to the subject is *Scaling Force* by Rory Miller and Lawrence Kane.

with build-up, it even applies to the abuse cycle. Each is a unique set of manifestations. While each of these forms of violence comes with its own particular differences, dangers, and goals recognizing the core similarities is important.[90]

Once you get them out of the way, you can start looking at the differences. All violence is not created equal nor is all equally dangerous. In some situations, lethal force is on the table, with most it's *not*. But you can't come up with an appropriate response until you know what kind of threat you face. How do you know that? Why, by his behavior of course. (The *other* definition of jeopardy.)

At the same time, each comes with its own sets of probabilities and variables. Behaviors tend to come in clusters. If you see A, B, and C, there's a high probability of D coming soon. If you see one, two, and three watch for four. For example while anything can escalate to the point where weapons are likely, there's a *much* higher probability of a weapon being involved in a robbery as opposed to a basic fight, rape, or domestic violence.

Being able to accurately assess possibilities and probabilities is beyond the scope of this book. But before you can recognize different flavors of jeopardy, you first have to know that it's possible. Then as a learnable skill, you can go out and learn how.[91] Equally cool, you can start figuring odds, possible responses, and counters much farther out. If you can read body language, you know when trouble has walked into the area. Stud Muffins there doesn't necessarily have intent, but he's a lot closer to it than my nursery school teacher ever was. We're just going to keep an eye on him to see what he does next.[92]

Kind of a sideline, but also germane: I often tell people not to be hot to trot about jumping into the middle of a situation. For that I get a lot of people who whine at me, "Are you telling me not to get involved?" Or the ones I really want to back hand, "Are you telling me I should just sit back

---

90   I often find myself at odds with proponents of identity campaigns against specialized violence. Take for example, rape. If—as advocates contend—rape is a specialized, stand-alone act, different from all other violence, then what they say about it is incontrovertible and their contentions unquestionable. If rape is a subset of violence, however, then much of the so-called education they provide on the subject flies in the face of what we know about the way violence materializes.

91   Part of the reason I recommend Desmond Morris's *Manwatching* is it introduces you to the fundamentals of human behavior. Knowing those, you can start working on environmental knowledge. From that platform comes situational awareness.

92   Various operators call it different things. My dad and I used to call it 'pinging.' (i.e., a radar ping). We'd know when a heavy hitter walked into the environment just as he knew we were there, too. And everyone knew we all knew. It wasn't a shadow dance, but we all knew to behave. Behaving qualified as everyone quietly going about his or her business and not making a fuss.

and let them get away with misbehaving?" The question of involvement starts with: What is his behavior most likely to be heading toward? More specifically: Is it headed en route to you or one of yours?

If no, it's not your problem. If you have no skin in the game, the best answer is usually don't get involved especially over someone else's bad behavior. Use the wheelbarrow standard to get you out of your monkey brain about his not acting according to your standards and expectations.

If yes—it is heading for you or one of yours—then it becomes a matter of scale and appropriateness. Again apply the wheelbarrow standard, especially if someone you know feels it's his or her right to get up in someone else's face about his behavior. You'd be well advised to put your person's posterior in the wheelbarrow and roll it away.

I worked in a lot of situations where it was my job to keep people from aiming their bad behavior at others I didn't personally know. The counterbalance to that is I was getting paid to care about someone's bad behavior toward strangers. Bad behavior of any level from obnoxious drunk trying to pick a fight to someone trying to kill a client. It was my job to tell them no. (And if they insisted, keep it from happening.) I tell you that for an important reason, something I learned a long time ago. The average drunk looking for a fight and sans weapon really isn't that *dangerous*. Yes, he's obnoxious. Yes, he's making a scene, and he may even go so far as to hit someone.

Whoopity-bloody-do. Odds are good you've been hit harder in training. For a lot of guys, you've probably been hit harder by a girlfriend or wife. You don't want to unleash your killer kung-fu, draw your knife, or shoot him—especially if it's drunken Uncle Albert at a family gathering. So what is the appropriate level of force to use on an obnoxious drunk? Well, it depends on the circumstances.

If you have to act and are in a safe situation, then minimum force means one thing. Unless you have a really screwed-up family, grappling and submission are good, safe ways to control drunken Uncle Albert without hurting him. Grappling and submission in a place where the crowd is likely to throw in some kicks for fun and games? *Not so hot.* It's really *not* good if while you are trying to grapple the drunk, the people standing around are on his side. Safe or not safe to go to the floor? Safe or not safe to go for submission and control? These are variables in what constitutes minimum force.

Pretty much the *last* thing you want to do is fight a drunk. The same alcohol that is screwing up his mechanics and ability to punch hard is *jamming* the pain signal. He has a lot more commitment, and that pain message isn't getting through like it would normally. Often a blow that would stun a sober person won't even get through to a drunk.

Okay, sidetrack coming from years spent wrangling drunks. When it comes to *not* fighting drunks think of the nervous system like the Internet. You get e-mails really fast. But when someone's drunk that person's nervous system becomes the Pony Express. It's going as fast as it can, but it takes longer for the message to get there. You can see this when cops put down a drunk and are cuffing him or her. The drunk is screaming, "You're hurting me!" If you know what to look for and the cop usually isn't—the source of the pain took place during the take down (or landing). But the pain message arrived ten or fifteen seconds later. Relying on pain to stop a drunk? Forget it. Often they end up fighting harder.

Conversely, drunks are *really* susceptible to being spun, twisted, twirled, off balanced, and pulled down. Ever been so drunk the room spins? You can induce that *same* effect in drunks. This is a really helpful thing to know if you're trying to control them without injuring them. Drunk swings, falls down, and there you are kneeling on him, using an arm bar. "Hey, how's everyone doing? I'll let him up when he calms down." What neither the drunk realizes nor the witnesses saw is you spinning him like a top and helping him fall down.

Everything I've said about drunks being a low level threat *changes*, however, when you have two specific conditions. One is a drunk with a weapon. You might as well put a weapon in the hands of a chimpanzee. Nothing good ever comes of it, and the danger goes way up. Two is a professional drunk. There is no unified term for these people. But anyone who's ever stood the line, worked in bars, as a first responder, or in the emergency room (ER) *knows* the critter.

These are the perma-drunks, chronic alcoholics, bottle coveys or—as Clint Overland calls them—tush hogs. (Sweet little piggies when they're sober, but wild boars when drunk.) Kasey Keckeisen, a police officer I know summed them up this way: These are the people who need a .20 blood alcohol content (BAC) simply to *function*. They sound like fairy tale creatures until you run across them. For example, I know of a house painter, who buys a fifth of vodka every day before he starts work. He chug-a-lugs it, then goes and paints houses. Moreover, he does a good job.

Professional drunks have such a high tolerance for alcohol they are still up and—I use this term loosely—functioning when they have a BAC where normal people would pass out (.30 and above). No lie, there is a term among medics and emergency room folks—the 500 Club. These are such severe alcoholics, they've survived having a BAC of .50. *Half* of what is in their bloodstream is alcohol. Death normally starts showing up around .40. I've read reports of professional drunks surviving .60 BACs.

When such people go off, they are a hard core problem. Here are some—among many—issues with professional drunks. They are in *black-out* conditions. They usually will have no memories of their actions, but they are still up and offering viable threats. But being that drunk means there are *no* stops—either externally or internally.

Externally, there are no social scripts, things you can say, actions you can perform that will calm them down. When they're that far gone and they go off, you can't offer to get them another beer to distract them and get them to stop. Once you have that run-away train, you either get off the tracks or you crash the train.

Internally, the stops, checks, and safeties normal people have are *gone. They won't stop*. Until that run-away train either runs out of gas or you derail it in a fiery crash, it's going. Most people stop a beating someone when that person quits resisting. A professional drunk *won't*. He won't just beat you into unconsciousness, he'll beat you until he runs out of gas. Dead? That was two counties back.

The second issue: Tush hogs are berserks. I'm talking biting their shields, psychotic supermen. Pain that would drop a normal person usually just makes them angrier. You cannot stop them through pain, you must either injure them to render them incapable of attack or dog pile on them for the same effect.

I've worked two cases where deceased attackers had BACs of .32 and .35. In both cases, the prosecutor found (medical) expert witnesses to testify that someone *that* intoxicated couldn't function well enough to be a viable threat. Hey, you know what? With a normal person that's *true*. Normal people can't function worth a damn past .2 and change, so it's not reasonable to believe they would pose a viable threat—except we're talking about perma-drunks. The new standard of reasonable threat includes one driving a kitchen knife into the chest of the defendant and the second, tackling and strangling the defendant. (This is where the no internal stops become a problem.)

Add to this an alternative definition of reasonable: What it takes to stop bottle coveys from killing the defendants. With one, it took nineteen stab wounds. The other kept on attacking even after he'd been stabbed in the heart. (The defendant survived only because other people dragged his attacker off after he'd been stabbed.) Both only stopped when dying got in their way. Clint, a six-foot-four power lifter, hit one with a table so big it would have herniated you or me. He had to hit that tush hog with it to stop the guy from killing some young guy he'd muckled onto. (The professional drunk put the kid in the hospital's intensive care unit in under thirty seconds.)

This spectrum of drunks shows you why I look at JAM differently than most people in the biz. Okay you have a run-of-the-mill drunk acting up. His misconduct is the problem (jeopardy). Yet his .23 BAC seriously impairs his ability to produce a serious threat. Now the question: Is he directing his impaired ability at you or one of yours? If yes to the latter, then the jeopardy and his ability are going to seriously influence whether you're even going to use force or how much.

First off—and this is why we're spending so much time on violence dynamics—you may not have to use force at all. Remember I said you can't reason with a drunk, but you can lie to, con, trick, and bullshit one pretty easily? If you can keep *your* monkey out of it, you can get him to solve the problem for you—like sending the drunk to the state capitol to complain about the public intoxication laws. (That story is in the footnotes.)

Second, if there is no weapon and he isn't a professional drunk, he's not much of a threat. As long as I don't try to fight him—I don't have to injure him to end the situation. In those circumstances, any level of force likely to cause injury is *off* the table.

Hell, something else that's *on* the table: Call the cops. Take a hit and get him arrested for public drunkenness and assault. Pffffft! Situation resolved. If I fought him, I'd get hit anyway. But this way he's out of my hair. His anger is aimed at the cops. He has charges to deal with. I go home to be with my wife. (I mean, hey, man, if we have a screwed-up legal system, why not use it to your advantage?) Even better if the wife is there and videotaping the incident. On the other hand if I see him go for a weapon, that's a *game changer*. His ability to offer me serious threat just went up—as did the level of my response.

Ability is a huge issue when it comes to your scaling force to appropriate levels. Someone is about to hit you with a club. You can shoot them, right? Well, it's an eighty-seven-year-old great-grandmother about to hit you with her cane. (Hint, the presence of a cane probably means you can outrun her.) A guy in a wheelchair threatens to punch you. Again, mobility is probably your best way to reduce the danger. By simply stepping away, you have reduced that person's means of attack. (Gee, preclusion.) On the other hand, wheelchair or not that gun in his hand extends the range of the peril. (Ability and means are much bigger.) A six-four, two-hundred-eighty-pound power lifter? Let me tell you, your McDojo karate isn't going to work against him. Your MMA training isn't likely to succeed, either. While giant slaying is possible, it's a lost art in most empty-hand training. (Blame weight divisions. Most of what you are taught these days is sport fighting for same-size, same-skill opponents.)

But what if *you're* the eighty-seven-year-old grandma, the guy in the wheelchair, or the power lifter? I ask because an often overlooked aspect of ability is your *own*. What are you capable of? Your ability affects other people's abilities to offer significant danger. For example, the average woman is smaller and weaker than a large man, but she's bigger and stronger than a small child. What if she's bigger than most men? One of my step-daughters is six feet and grew up bucking hay bales. Yep, she's bigger than me. My friend Clint is bigger and stronger than both of us. Hell, I know mastodons smaller than he is.

Because of my experience and training, someone who may be a danger to you isn't much of a menace to me—until that person picks up a weapon. Even though I have greater than average ability, so, too, does that person with the weapon.

I tell you this because there's a big disconnect between two worlds. Worlds that *should* be gradients on the same spectrum. Empty-hand martial arts are one end of the spectrum of self-defense and firearms are the other. Realistically, the spectrum needs to run from one to the other and not be exclusive. You should have the ability to control without injury, stop a low-level threat, use less than lethal force, utilize injurious, and if necessary lethal force. Focusing all of your attention on one end, much less one aspect, of the spectrum is a guaranteed failure when dealing with anything outside your area of *specialization*. You lack the ability to deal with things outside your training zone. Empty hands against someone trying to kill you with a weapon? Forget it. Firearm against a homeless drunk? Overkill.

The greater *your* ability across the spectrum, the *safer*—and more *confident*—you will be. Not feel, be. But wait! There's more! Order now, get two free gifts! One, the less likely you are to use excessive or insufficient force. Two, overwhelmingly trouble will go find an easier target.*

Supplies subject to your azzholeishness.

In case you missed the gist of this the greater your ability to handle all kinds of different problems, the lower someone else's ability to harm you. Funny how that works isn't it?

Another aspect of both jeopardy and ability is to look and see if someone is trying to hide ability. We'll go into that more in the threat display chapter. But there are certain key signals. And if you see them in combo that thing you see poking above the water is a shark fin. That fin is *all* you're going to see because he's actively trying to hide his ability until it's too late.

But I'll give you two indicators of a higher level of danger. They are the weapon pat and the witness check. Commonly this is before an attacker starts the interview and positioning, but not always. A predator usually adjusts, confirms, and pats his weapon as he approaches. Although he's pretending to be casual about it, it's more than an accidental brush or simple movement. It's reassuring himself it's there, memorizing its location, and—if necessary— adjusting it. That way when he needs to pull it fast, it's ready.

The witness check is a very specific glance around the area to see if anybody is close enough to stop him. It can happen before he approaches or when he's close enough to attack you. Or it can happen twice at both distances.

These are often pre-interview behaviors for robbery. And as if it needed to be worse, they're pre-attack indicators in other, more immediate situations. In a robbery, the thief usually starts before he gets close enough to launch into the interview. For the other situations if someone is confronting you and he unexpectedly looks around or does a weapon pat it's time to get some distance. Odds are good, they are getting ready to go off on you.

As mentioned in the intent section of the five stages, individual elements are part of a collective pattern. A big part of that is: Given the specific circumstances of the situation is that behavior *appropriate?* You and a friend talk about his or her surgery. Given the circumstances, a pulling up of the shirt makes sense. A stranger asking you for directions, then pulling at his shirt to show you his appendix scar *isn't* appropriate given the circumstances. If he did the witness check and weapon pat before starting the interview, that shirt lift means only one thing. I'm telling you all of this because after you read Desmond Morris's *Manwatching* your ability to assess body language will increase dramatically. With enough practice, you'll be able to spot when someone really doesn't have ability versus when they're trying to hide it.

Someone trying to hide ability is indicative of one of two things:
1) He or she is capable of a higher level of force, but is trying to not scare people.
2) He or she is planning to use a higher level of force—and doesn't want to scare off the target.

You'll be able to determine which one it is by the other behavior. (Remember the bricks? Look at the whole pattern. What else is he doing?)

I'll tell you the truth, a lot of heavy hitters—people capable of incredible violence—walk around out there. Missing are intent and jeopardy. They're just going about their business. You leave them alone, and they'll leave you alone. Most of them don't advertise, but if you know what to look for the signs are there. If you have to interact with them follow the rules of whatever social script you're in, and you'll be fine. (Here's a hint: If you recognize that someone's competent at violence being polite is a great way to keep him from deciding to demonstrate his skill.) Except for young punks and mad dogs *most* people, who are skilled with violence, have pretty reliable codes of conduct about its use—especially with strangers. Unless you've gone out of your way to get in their way, they aren't likely to go off.

A lot of people are scared of the screaming berserk, who charges from across the room. These out-of-control monkeys are poster boys for jeopardy, ability, and means. Personally, I don't find them to be that much of a problem. Usually, they're trying to trigger your monkey, to intimidate, or to force some kind of ineffective response. Reminder: Default monkey violence is a whole lot like train tracks. The triggered monkey either moves forward on the tracks (fights) stands there (freezes and braces for impact) or tries to back away. The last is a bad flight attempt in lieu of an outright turn-and-run.

The hardest part about teaching the physical aspects of self-defense is helping people break out of these patterns. It's not physically difficult, but it's mentally hard to override what your monkey is telling you to do. I tell you this because it's a two-way street. That howler monkey bearing down on you is *caught* in the same trap. As such, he or she is really susceptible to you stepping off the tracks at the last minute and either knocking him or her into next week from the side *or* stepping off line (moving at an angle from the line of the attack), grabbing him or her, spinning, and throwing them over a table. The monkey can't change from attack mode fast enough to handle being t-boned.

Sometimes showing your greater ability is the game changer (especially if you create distance and give him a chance to think about it). People relying on their berserk to intimidate tend to wet themselves when you turn into a werewolf and lunge for their throats. If you start early enough or lunge slowly enough, you give them a chance to turn tail and run. Do it right, and they'll be running like hell to deprive *you* of the means to hurt them.[93] Their running is a great option because you don't have to do paperwork.

What's indicative of a *greater* level of danger is someone trying to *hide* his ability while slowly and methodically setting up the means and positioning to attack. That's a form of jeopardy you jes' don't want to see aimed at you. Unless you can convince them to pick another target before they attack, you're going to have to put in a little overtime to handle those guys.

Earlier I described JAM in terms of "the attack happening at ten." Then it was a case of plus and minuses (threatening to kick your butt with a table between you). I want to tie a number of other concepts to this.

93　　My street name was Animal. I cannot tell you how many potentially violent incidents I ended by snarling. Thing was, I wasn't faking it. I had no hesitation about biting body parts off.

Starting with, let's talk disparity of force. Three against one changes the ability. That's an automatic bump up on the danger level. A small, angry woman may not have the ability to cause you much damage . . . until she picks up a knife. In which case, her size becomes irrelevant; same thing with a fourteen-year-old boy. That gun in his hand supersedes his age and inexperience. A guy brandishing a knife across the room is still not a kosher situation, but it's not time to end his life. (I highly recommend you either withdraw or have the means to exterminate with extreme prejudice in your hands.) If and when he starts to charge—different ball game, he's going for the means.

Let's change the scenario a bit. You had a run-in with someone. One night you're walking to your car, looking over, you see him closing on you without saying anything. And he looks kind of crabby. Whoops. Silent interview and attempted surprise positioning. Pretty safe to assume ill intent. Do everything in your power to keep him from developing range and means and watch for his going for a weapon. By the way, this kind of scenario is real common if you're a bouncer or primary contact professional (after you've told a customer no).

While we're at it, let's talk about the problems faced by primary contact professionals. These people's jobs are to deal with the public. I object to the mystique built around 'first responders.' Starting with by the time they're even called everything shit has been rolling downhill for a while. Also by the time they show up, the folks at the scene have been dealing with the yahoo for a while already. Or the shit has already happened, and the first responders are there for the clean up.

Primary contact professionals sit behind counters and are the targets of wrath. (Hell, I've been the person in that chair.) Whether they did anything or not, something infuriated Numb-Nuts, and he goes off on them. Oh joy, oh rapture. They're the focus of his or her rage.

Problem one with this sort of situation is often people, who are howling, barking OOKs (out-of-[k]control monkeys) with primary contact folks morph into Little Bo Peeps when a uniform arrives. Problem two, Jag-off there knows the police response time. He hangs around, howling, barking, and threatening until he figures the police should be arriving. Then he jets out of there. Leaving you with the adrenaline dump and the jitters. Problem three, a lot of these jerks get off on behaving this way. They're a lot less scary when you imagine them skipping down the street afterwards chanting, "Attention, attention, I got attention!" And that's pretty much what they're doing.

Five things about this: First, a lot of the time people wait too long before calling in back-up. It is the threat of the cavalry arriving that usually ends the problem . . . so why wait?

Second, don't tell him you've called the cavalry. That just tells him how much more time he has to misbehave. Third, telling him you're calling the cops is a threat display. In general don't make threats; they often just make things worse. Now, you have an even angrier person and a wait for help to arrive. Fourth, have code words or phrases among your co-workers that communicate various options. "Is Wilson here?" could mean "call the police." "Josh, have you seen the file for so-and-so" is the call to the establishment's heavy hitter that his presence is necessary up front. Fifth, *don't* be afraid to call for back-up.

Unless it's part of your strategy don't let him know you did. Let him figure out he miscalculated when the cop unexpectedly taps him on the shoulder. The two best examples I know of these strategies come from my days of event security.

The "not letting them know" was from Silas keying his radio and saying to the guy, "Yes, I know you can kick my ass here at Ale Five. But see this radio? There are fifty guys in it who can kick yours." It wasn't fifty of us who immediately showed up at Ale Five, but it was enough to end the confrontation.

The "letting him know" as part of the strategy was my friend Randy asking them if they wanted to see a magic trick. He'd call for beef to the location, Code Three, then drop the radio, and tell them they had about a minute because some really big, irritated guys were about to appear. (Beef was internal terminology for the Goon Squad. Code Three equalled "it's hitting the fan.") This usually was a show stopper. They either had to commit right then and there or back off. The longer they thought about it, the more refugees from Jurassic Park showed up. (Randy is no small puppy—around six-three— but Goon Squad guys made him look petite.) I would say they'd just magically show up, but like Godzilla coming ashore you could see the crowds part as the Goons ran toward a code. Now imagine about six of them closing in from different directions. Sometimes it helps to let folks know they've bitten off more than they can chew—after you've called it in.

Having said that, if after such a flare-up you're walking to your car and Laughing Boy shows up, it's usually a sign things are about to get ugly. I'm not going to tell you not to bother to try to talk your way out of it if possible, but be prepared for things to immediately go sideways. That's a set-up for a higher level of violence. I've *never* had a warm and fuzzy meeting under those circumstances. The only thing I can attribute to those few situations that didn't get bloody was me morphing into a werewolf, and the guy changing his mind. But that's because I recognized the jeopardy inherent in that kind of behavior. Quite often the bozo was too committed to stop.

If you use the JAM model—and I'm not saying it is the only interpretation—the first three of the five stages are articulable jeopardy. You're looking for signs of hiding ability; don't allow him to develop the means; and if when you try to prevent it and he forces the situation, then AOJ is in play.

Now after everything I've told you, go out and ask other people about JAM or AOJ. In fact, try taking a class from Marty Hayes at the Firearms Academy of Seattle. He's probably gnashing his teeth over how badly I've screwed up AOJ. He'll set you right.

CHAPTER 8

Law is an imperfect profession in which success can rarely be achieved without some sacrifice of principle. Thus all practicing lawyers—and most others in the profession—will necessarily be imperfect, especially in the eyes of young idealists. There is no perfect justice, just as there is no absolute in ethics. But there is perfect injustice, and we know it when we see it.

—**Alan Dersowitz**
Letters to a Young Lawyer

If Your SD Works . . .
Part Two: The Prosecution

I'm going to take excerpts from a blog I wrote called *Four Lies: You, Our Courts, and Claiming Self-Defense.* It was an introductory piece I wrote to get people thinking about the post-incident consequences of defending oneself. We've covered one of the two lies already and part of a second one. I want to have you look at the two lies most germane to prosecutors.

Bear with me about leaving the lying to children part in (I have a fifty-dollar bet with an attorney about when I'll get hit with a variation of, "Mr. MacYoung is it okay to lie?") Lies to children unfortunately become a necessary strategy to help people leave behind what they *think* they know about our legal system.

———

Four Lies: You, Our Courts, and Claiming Self-Defense
©2012

I'm going to start by lying to you. In fact, I'm such a big liar I'll tell you four falsehoods about our legal system, self-defense, and what to expect when you are caught in the meat grinder. Well to be more precise, I'm going to tell you four "lies to children."

It's funny that I use the word precisely because a lie-to-a-child is: *A statement that is false, but nevertheless leads the child's mind toward a more accurate explanation, one that the child will only be able to appreciate if she has been primed with the lie.* Those are Terry Pratchett's exact words in his book, *The Science of Discworld* (a very funny fantasy series). I got the term from him.

But let's expand on the concept. The Discworld Wiki adds: *Any explanation of an observed phenomenon which, while not 100 percent scientifically accurate, is simple enough, and just accurate enough, to convey the beginnings of understanding to anyone who is new to the subject. There is always time to fill them in on the fine details further down the road. This describes the sort of axioms we tell young children when they are beginning to get to grips with science.*[94]

Got it? Lies to children are teaching tools. Not exactly true, but true enough to prepare you to understand more complex—and nuanced—information. So here are the four *lies* about what you will encounter in court when you claim self-defense. These four lies help you understand what you face and keep you from being traumatized by what happens after a self-defense situation. And they are:

1) Most attorneys don't know how defend an innocent person.

2) The burden of proof is on you.

3) The roles change.

4) There are prosecutors who think if someone died there must be a crime.

1) Attorneys don't know how to defend an innocent person. *(We already covered this. So a large part snipped before we get to what is relevant to defending guilty and innocent—and even then there's a bit of a redux.)*

Simplifying an incredibly complex process, it is up to the prosecution to prove it was the defendant, not some other dude, who did it. This is due—partly—to burden of proof. The state's job is bring evidence to prove to the jury it *was* the defendant who acted, how he did it, and why (mens rea). It is the defense's job to tear down the state's case. And in doing so, convince the jury the state is wrong—erroneous because the wrong person was charged, witnesses were mistaken about what happened, or due to blunders in how the police investigated and collected evidence. Often this is done by tearing apart evidence the state brings to meet its burden of proof requirement.

Without opening a huge can of worms let me give you another gross simplification: What the evidence is (read, what the jury is allowed to see and hear) and what the jury decides the facts are will either convict you or set you free. Each side is going to try to *sell* the significance of the evidence to the jury. If the prosecutor can get them to believe 'this' means 'that,' you're going to prison. If your defense attorney can convince them the prosecution's 'this' means something else, you'll be acquitted. The version of evidence the jury accepts *will* become the facts of the case. Too

---

many people go into the courtroom thinking their versions of events are the facts. No! It's going to be a fight over interpretation. This is all done in an adversarial process. Keep that in mind because fighting the legal system will be the second attack on your life (and freedom).

Snip a bunch of stuff about confessing to a crime and defending an innocent person. Until we get to 2) The burden of proof is on you. *(Still more snippage of stuff we've covered, until . . .)* Once you claim self-defense, you're going to have to show up with a boatload of evidence why it *was. Why* what he was doing was dangerous enough to warrant the level of force you used. *Why* your response was both reasonable and necessary. *What* you did to try to avoid it. And most important: *Why* you aren't some homicidal maniac, a dangerous idiot with a weapon, a vigilante, or some douche bag trying to escape justice.

All that is a lot harder than you think. Prosecutors have a lot of experience convicting violent offenders and lying criminals. That's their job, after all. If they decide you're one of those undesirable types, they turn their not insignificant skill and experience on *you.* They'll do everything in their power to convince the jury you are a lying, violent, douche who was just itchin' to kill someone—including this poor innocent mugger.

Let me give you fair warning: If you know the person, it's even *worse.* Some bad news here, a majority of murders are between people who know each other. If you had to defend yourself against someone you know *don't* think the prosecutor won't try to turn it against you. (It's complete and total hell if it was a domestic situation.)

Once again, snipping out a lot of stuff about spatial distortion, adrenal stress, and your attorney getting said information to the jury, which we've already covered, but now this important thought, 3) The roles change. This is another big lie to a child. But there's a really simple way to understand it. You know the actual burden of proof is on the prosecution. You know ordinarily, the defense is going to try to pick apart the state's case. Taking a massively complex process and reducing it to the silliest image possible, it means the defense's role is to chant, "Liar! Liar! Pants on fire! Neener neener!" about everything the prosecution says.

When you claim self-defense, the prosecutor *gets* that role. He is going to pick apart your story. He's going to nitpick each inconsistency, every poorly stated phrase, and all details to try to sell his story. I'm not even going to say it's his version of the story because often what he is selling is an entirely different account of events. That would be self-defense versus a conflict that escalated too far. No, odds are good what he tries to sell is that it was cold-blooded, premeditated murder. The only two things those two stories have in common is the body on the floor and you. To tell you the truth, this is *not* a hard sell. Remember, you confessed to the elements of a crime—but you've said there were good reasons for it. He's saying there aren't, which makes it a crime. Another let's-watch-lawyers-twitch-and-drool explanation is, "The prosecutor doesn't have to prove beyond a reasonable doubt, all he has to do is *create* reasonable doubt about your story." Your affirmative defense has already done most of the heavy lifting for the prosecution.

Even if the prosecutor isn't promoting the proposal that you're a cold-blooded murderer, you're still in trouble if he's selling that you overreacted. A common version of this is *imperfect self-defense*. Yes, it started as self-defense, but you went too far. (Author's note: Imperfect self-defense is why I came up with the SD square.) Because of the bias against violence and the fact he has decided to prosecute, the jury is *already* skeptical. You admitted you did it. The jury thinks there had to be something wrong with the situation or you wouldn't be sitting at the defendant's table. The burden for the prosecution is showing your reasons *weren't* good enough. All the prosecutor has to do is hyper-focus on a few inconsistencies, blow other points out of proportion, plant the seed of doubt in the jurors' minds, and—voila—you're convicted.

You are going to get hit with "liar, liar." Your attorney needs to know how to counter the very tactics he often uses to win cases. At the same time, your attorney also needs to know to prosecute the dead guy. There is something else you need to know. And I mean tattoo it on your forehead in reverse so you see it in the mirror every morning: *The higher the use of force, the more microscopic the examination of the case.*

On a cable TV show, other experts and I were shown recreations of crimes and self-defense scenarios. (It's called *Stop the Threat* with James Towle, and you can see episodes on line.) We watched the crime and SD videos once, then commented. The key word in that last sentence is once.

As an expert witness, I have spent not only hours and days, but weeks, poring over video of incidents (security or cell phone). I'll take a two-minute clip at one-quarter speed, slow motion, *again* and *again* to pick out tiny details of the event. I look for details that—unless you know *what* to look for (and its significance)—you won't recognize as dangerous. Translate that to the fact the jury will not see or understand the danger unless it is pointed out. Nor will they understand why the level of force response was appropriate or inappropriate. The prosecutor is going to do the *same* thing—except he's looking for things to translate as your criminal behavior. He'll look for things you did, mistakes you made about your use-of-force decision, any action, any detail, or any decision he can use to make you look like a cold-blooded murderer or an out-of-control vigilante. In short, he attacks your self-defense justification. If and when that defense is undermined, you will be convicted of the crime you confessed to.

This is why you and your attorney need to show up with a boatload of evidence to prove it *was* self-defense. But even with cargo containers, *your* side must weather the storm of "liar, liar." You will have to face your credibility being challenged, endure sneers, insinuations, and being called a liar to your face. If your side fails to provide this mountain of evidence, you're going down. I don't care how obvious you think it is or your belief the jury will see it your way.

Snipping verbiage about the guy who was stabbed eight times and had a lousy, going-through-the-motions lawyer: 4) There are prosecutors, who think if someone died, there must be a crime. This lie is going to be the one that has prosecutors screaming for my hide to be nailed to the cabin door. In fact, I'll bet it will even be brought up in court that I dared put these words in writing. Well, even I have to admit there are all kinds of things wrong with this particular lie to a child. But it's an important perspective to take. It will save you *all kinds* of emotional distress about the aftermath of a self-defense situation. But more than that, it can help keep you from going to prison.

This is a critical factor. You may think you're a good guy. You may think the prosecutor is a good guy, too. You may have nothing but respect for the police. But that does *not* automatically mean you're all on the same side—especially if you've taken another citizen's life.

That's a very important point I just slipped in. I'm going to give a hat tip to the Armed Citizen's Legal Defense Network[95] here and bring up an issue they like to remind folks of: *When the police arrive, they don't see a self-defense situation as you versus some dirt bag. Legally, it is considered two citizens in dispute.* That means you *and* the person you consider to be a douche-bag-criminal-low-life have the *same* rights to life, liberty, and *not* being gunned down in the street. It is the district attorney's job to take umbrage at citizens killing citizens. Death is the purview of the state, not its citizens. That you've come to his attention for doing so . . . well . . . let's say he might be suspicious. Until it is proved you did not wrongfully take a person's life (as in that person was going to wrongfully cause your death if you didn't act) the prosecutor is *not* your friend.

Add to that, there is a big difference between it being proved that you acted in self-defense (e.g., found not guilty in a trial) and the prosecutor *not* having enough evidence saying otherwise to win a case. Your case can be closed if the investigating officer presents it as self-defense and the higher-ups agree. If he or she doesn't, your case *isn't* closed. It will be

---

95   www. armedcitizensnetwork.org

left open and hanging, even as it goes cold. That's an *ugly* limbo. A limbo you'll need to learn more about in a seminar on legal use of force. But know to ask about it—because it *will* last the rest of your life. (Murder is one of the few crimes that has no statute of limitations.)

Remember, I said earlier there's also a difference between the law and our legal system? The latter is strongly influenced by factors that have nothing to do with the law. This is the elephant in the room people pretend has no bearing on what happens—especially with whether or not a prosecutor decides to act. Ours is one of the few countries where the district attorney is *elected* (or the appointee of an elected official). As in if the DA's office doesn't have an impressive conviction rate, there's a good chance that the boss man is *out* of a job. The more convictions and plea bargains the DA's office chalks up, the better they look for being tough on crime. Incidents that make it on the news really need to be actively pursued to show the public that the system works. Political pressure, public outcry, and—of course—internal pressures from the boss *are* factors that will determine how the prosecutor's office will act.

(Snip of the rest of the article because you're getting more in-depth versions in the book.)

———

Even in the article, I said my speaking for what prosecutors think was a stretch. For the record, I am not psychic. I cannot read anyone's mind. So I must confess I cannot accurately know what actually goes on in the minds of prosecutors. I will further admit that perhaps the cases I take create a confirmation bias. Perhaps, I've just run into a few bad eggs when it comes to over-prosecution. All of which I will *admit* are possibilities.

What I also can say is, "If it looks like a duck, quacks like a duck, and floats like a duck, it's not a peacock . . . no matter what someone claims."

I have met some prosecutors who sure as hell act as though theirs is a holy crusade. God is on their side. They are the smiters for justice; the punishers of the wicked. I also will say this bias is understandable. *Overwhelmingly* in the cases the prosecutor is going after, the suspect did what he is accused of—if not worse. Yeah, yeah, I know innocent until proved guilty. But I grew up in the streets. There is way too much crime and illegal violence going on out there. Prosecutors are doing a much needed service. Having said this, it's time for serious reality break.

Although you might be walking into it for the first time, our legal system is an ongoing game that has been going on for a *long* time. There is a lot more going on in this game than just the law. Let's start by expanding it past the courtroom to say: Our justice and legal system is a *big money* topic. If you include law enforcement, corrections (including private prisons) lobbyists, lawmakers, lawyers, and related fields, we're talking trillions of dollars and millions of careers.

I'd like to give you an Upton Sinclair quote that'll help put that into perspective: "It is difficult to get a man to understand something, when his salary depends on his not understanding it." And as with any major money game, you have players, who don't make the big bucks if they lose too often. Success, career, and by extension money depend on numbers. So they develop tactics, tricks, and sleazy practices to improve their chances of winning.

While it's easy to think all the greed is on the defense side, misconduct is a two-way street. Suppressing or withholding exculpatory evidence from the defense, allowing testimony the prosecutor knows to be false, prosecuting for purely career and political reasons—these are obvious cases of misconduct. More of a gray area is stonewalling or dragging their feet about providing exculpatory evidence and full disclosure (while pressing hard for a plea deal). Or fighting to exclude a witness or expert, who will prove damning to the prosecution's case.

I've personally experienced prosecutors doing some over-the-top things to win. In one instance, I had to sit in the witness box and explain how a photo had been tampered with (in an attempt to discredit me). I knew it had been edited because the prosecutor got it from my Web page. He tried to paint me as a racist after someone cropped the black guy and Indonesian I was standing next to out of the photo. I'm on record for saying the photo had been tampered with. Three lawyers (including the judge) in that courtroom and not one of them said a word . . .

Then comes what could be called institutional credibility—although another word is infallibility. No matter what really happens behind the scenes, the public face is one of complete certainty about being right. God is not on their side, the Law is. The Law they represent is infallible—and by extension so too their decision to prosecute. During an interview, I've seen a prosecutor (who lost a flimsy case) state with *absolute* conviction the man he prosecuted *had* committed the murder. That statement would have been a lot more credible if someone else hadn't later been arrested and convicted using DNA evidence. But he *knew* he'd prosecuted the right man.[96]

As an aside, this is the same officious certainty the prosecutor will bring to your case. You didn't carry that knife as a self-defense weapon, *you* were itching to stab someone. You didn't try to avoid conflict, *you* were looking for an excuse to murder him. You weren't defending yourself, *you*

---

96 The case had been bungled by the podunk sheriff's department. That led to the first trial. After that, the case was bumped up to the state police, who had the temerity to check the DNA of their suspect.

went out looking for a fight. You had mens rea (Latin for guilty mind). The irony is how hard the same prosecutor peddling your mens rea will fight *against* the idea of you knowing the intent of the other person.

That's what the prosecutor will try to convince the monkeys of the people sitting in the jury box. He's selling them an appeal to authority (logical fallacy). He is the authority, as well as what he knows. But to sell that, he must first convince himself that you're an evil-doer, who deserves to be punished. Going back to an analogy from the three-brain chapter, he doesn't want the jury looking down the alley to see that at the time, the deceased was trying to kill you. To convincingly sell his version, he *too* must not look down that alley. Knowing this, you'll have a deeper appreciation for the need of enough evidence to support your self-defense claim. Your lawyer has to call attention to what's down that alley. But first, he has to get the jury to look down an alley the prosecutor and their own monkeys don't want them to see.

Another common problem is prosecution of someone—anyone— because of political and media pressure. The self-righteous DA and the person later convicted I just mentioned is a good example. Although the local small town PD (police department) didn't have the resources to properly investigate, that murder needed to be cleared off the books—so grab the nearest suspect. This hurry-up-and-arrest pressure is the source of many flat-out wrong convictions. (I include arrests from the attitude of 'someone has to go to jail.')

Like I said, winning is important in this game. Winning not just by outright misconduct, I also mean throwing people into the sausage maker to keep up conviction numbers. It's easy to understand wrongful conviction in the sense of someone sitting in a prison for a crime he didn't commit. But over-prosecution is way more common. Need more felony convictions? Go for felony instead of misdemeanor charges against someone you already have in custody.[97] Also common is bringing charges against someone who acted in self-defense—because it's a slam dunk. (Hey, he confessed to doing it.) The question *isn't* how many people are sitting in prison for crimes they didn't commit. A much bigger question is: How many people are sitting in prison because they acted in self-defense, and their lawyers didn't know *how* to prove it? Especially if they went to court against an overzealous prosecutor, someone who justified his or her prosecutorial decisions with the assumption that if someone died a crime was committed.

I've worked on cases where my primary reaction was, "Why the hell is this even being prosecuted?" It's almost as if some prosecutors believe self-defense *doesn't* exist. Or if it does, their standards are so

---

97   Although the official position is denial, there also is the very real correlation among funding needs, fines, and enforcement.

high it is functionally impossible for anyone to legally act in self-defense. They acknowledge it exists (in theory), but in practice try to prosecute everyone who pleads to it.

I've also seen them throw the book at "low-hanging fruit" (easily prosecuted cases) while refusing to act against worse crimes (and coincidentally suspects who were much harder to convict). They get ten felony convictions or pleas for the same amount of time and money it would take to try and convict the monster that's still walking the streets. Is this wrong? Is this injustice? Get over it. It's reality. And you need to know that's what you face if you act in self-defense. Stop and think about this from the standpoint of someone whose boss is an elected official; a boss whose re-election is based on how many convictions his or her team brings in. What kind of pressure is he (or she) going to put on you? That's the prosecutors in the district. Never mind the idea of an assistant district attorney advancing and becoming the DA one day. I'm talking the pressure of *keeping* your job so as not to be out on your butt for not bringing in convictions, not keeping up the numbers.

There's an incredible pressure on prosecutors *not* to lose. If you were in a situation where your job, your livelihood, the wherewithal to feed your children depended on sending people to prison—where most of the people you prosecuted were indeed guilty—what would that do to your interpretation of innocence? Of self-defense? Especially when you see so many guilty and toxic SD claims? Seriously, stop and think about it from this perspective. What would you do? Now add the fact good conviction numbers mean a successful career after you've left the DA's office. A successful stint as a prosecutor means you can move on to big-money positions in the private sector.

There are good, honest, and decent people in the prosecutor's office. There are self-righteous crusaders. There are savvy legal animals (who choose not to order your arrest because the case would be too hard to win). There are complete career animals who would prosecute their own mothers to boost their numbers. It's a total crap shoot. You don't know what kind of prosecutor's desk the police report will land on. But whatever number is rolled, *that's* what you have to deal with. This is why your pre-incident behavior and keeping your actions within the parameters of self-defense are so *critical*. They not only have a strong influence on whether you're arrested, but play an important part in becoming the wrench in the works of this well oiled machine.

First, you want to do everything in your power to stay *out* of this game. That's the best win of all. Second, if you still get dragged in your behavior is what loads the dice in your favor or rolls you snake eyes (including pre- and post-incident). The correct behavior is what you and your lawyer can use to jam the meat grinder so you don't get chewed up and spit out. The best outcome is when the incident report is written up as self-defense, and you *don't* get arrested at all. Third, if you are arrested you have what your lawyer needs to get the charges dropped or failing that to keep you from being convicted.

When these possibilities are exhausted is when the defense attorney's common approach of damage control needs to become a viable option—even assuming you stayed in the SD square. If not, damage control needs to start at the second stage. Seriously, sometimes $20,000 in fines, legal fees, and time served is better than the $60,000 it will cost for an acquittal.

Slight directional change here: Once certain steps are taken, the *process* takes over. Simple to say—real important to remember. Once an arrest is made, this juggernaut starts rolling. It's *not* about what happened anymore. It's *not* about what you did; it's *not* even about you. It's about the *process*. What is the system going to do about it? You can take this as far you want. From a simple once the ball starts rolling the process must be completed to institutional face saving to calling it evil gub'ment conspiracies. *None* of that matters. What does matter is that past a certain point it's *out* of your hands. You don't know how far it will go or where it will end. You have no control; all you can do is strap in and hang on.

I'll point to the George Zimmerman case. Reminder of some key points: On the night of the shooting, the Safford police contacted the DA with the evidence they collected from the scene, including statements from a cooperative Zimmerman. They asked, "Do we arrest?'" The DA said, "No, insufficient evidence. Keep on investigating." That's what the police did, including interviewing Zimmerman multiple times—even returning to the scene and videotaping him telling what happened that night. (This incidentally played into why his attorneys chose to not have him testify.) Why did the DA say don't arrest? Why didn't the cops arrest on the spot? It *wasn't* a clear case. A big part of that was Zimmerman. Arguably (except for not having an attorney present during questioning) he did *everything* right in the aftermath. He cooperated, he articulated well—his injuries and crime scene evidence made his story credible.

Had the media *not* become involved, there's a very good chance that case would have been left open, hanging in limbo. But once the national media got hold of it and pundits fanned the flames with claims of racism, police incompetence, yada, yada, yada, it all went political. The case was taken away from the Safford PD and the local DA, a special Florida prosecutor was appointed, the feds sniffed around for civil rights violations, and the U.S. president himself gave tacit approval to the lynch mob mentality—all on a *local* homicide. It could be argued—once the media became involved, once racism was invoked, once it became political, or once a special prosecutor was appointed—charges *had* to be brought. *Any* of these could have been the point of no return, but collectively? There was *no* way Zimmerman would *not* be arrested and tried. There was too much attention, too much coverage, too much money, too much emotional investment, too much political face, and too much institutional credibility at stake—there *had* to be a trial. [98]

Odds are good your situation won't become a media circus or get presidential commentary. But that's not why I mentioned that case. After an officer decides to arrest, other influences, other factors, and other priorities *take over*. Included in this are professionals with a totally different emphasis from what you had when you acted. From the moment your attacker hits the floor, you're in a whole different world. You have to mentally shift gears for these new circumstances.

All of the above are *gross over-simplifications* of things that are much more complex. But it's for a very specific reason. It's to prepare you to understand something important, another lie to children: Our justice system *isn't* about *justice*, it's about *resolution*. Resolution in that: *Something* was done about what happened. Does it matter if what was done was right or wrong? Good or bad? No, not really. What matters is something was done, and there's a paper trail to *prove* it. That problem is done, dealt with, and finished (in their area). The case then goes somewhere else where it is no longer the cop's or the prosecutor's problem. It's better (at least in the prosecutor's mind) if it's both done and a check in the win box.

The win side for the prosecutor's 'somewhere else' means prison, alternative sentencing programs, mental health care, plea bargain, fines, penalties, and similar solutions. A loss for the prosecutor ensues if the defendant is acquitted. A draw occurs if the prosecutor chooses not to pursue legal action or drops the charges (not the same thing). In those cases, the prosecutor has to explain to his boss why he or she chose that course.

I give you the win, lose, draw scenarios because the time has come to embrace the suck. It's *not* in a prosecutor's best interest to let your case go. It has nothing to do with justice, fighting crime, morals, or making the world a better place. It's about numbers—a whole lot of really bad men (who are skilled at getting away with crime) walk away from major crimes with low level plea bargains for time spent. Why? They're too expensive to prosecute. Then there's a damned good chance of the prosecutor losing if the case goes to court.[99] So time spent or a minimum sentence plea turns a loss (or a draw) into a win—granted a

---

98   Arguably, there was not enough evidence for it to be proved self-defense or illegal homicide. Even so, Zimmerman's acquittal did not change many people's minds about what he had done.

99   Add double jeopardy. You cannot be tried twice for the same crime—even if you did it. If acquitted, your case walks out the door forever.

minor victory, but still a keep-the-boss-happy win. This also requires the prosecutor to make up for lost felony numbers by over-prosecuting minor crimes and—unofficially—coming down hard on self-defense cases. Self-defense is low-hanging fruit, hence easy felony convictions. Assuming body equals crime makes it easier to sleep at night for doing the latter.

Looking back on that list, there's more wins for the prosecution. So if it looks like they can bag you, they're going to proceed, especially with gawdawful plea offers. Keep this in mind because often until they can get something, they *won't* let it go. Careerism and costs are just two of the unmentionable elephants in the room when it comes to our legal system. (There's an entire herd.) I'm not talking about prosecutorial misconduct, I'm talking about the everyday attitude of "I hold all the cards, why should I be reasonable?"

There are systemic checks and balances, but most of them are out of your hands. Having said that, there are three checks you can do to this otherwise unrestricted power: One is have lots of money to hire the best lawyer you can find. (Better yet have a good one on retainer.) This strategy works because a good lawyer costs the system lots of money if it proceeds with a prosecution. Two is understand and stay inside the self-defense square. Three is being able to articulate that's what you did, and why it was reasonable.

Truth is you *need* all three. But the last two are the cheapest of what you can do to make it expensive, time-consuming, and risky to try to prosecute you. Someone who shows up with that boatload of evidence that shows why violence was justified is a fight the prosecutor *does not* want. Having said that, most of the cases I work on *do not* go to trial. The mere presence of an expert and a report showing why the defendant's actions were in self-defense encourage prosecutors to find a resolution that is the least damaging to his or her numbers. And that's where your lawyer is going to earn his keep.

Coming back to the idea of resolution, even losing a case is a form of resolution for the prosecution—as is dropping charges. The matter is finished. Not what the prosecutor wants, but you do. What is neither a resolution *nor* something you want in a self-defense case is for it to be left open. That's when the prosecutor and police don't clear it as self-defense, but don't have enough evidence to arrest and prosecute.

Open cases are common with "we don't know who did it" killings. They're big in "we know who did it, but we just can't get the evidence (and he's claiming SODDI)" cases. These often go cold and are never solved. If you're a professional criminal, this is simply the cost of doing business. For a citizen living with an open case is a sword of Damocles hanging over your head. Odds are good if they don't come after you in the first year, nothing is going to happen. But it *never* goes away. You need it to be cleared as self-defense by the police investigation. This is extremely useful for any civil proceedings that might follow, as well.

Harsh Truths time. Harsh Truth A: The better the quality of your attorney (and yes that usually means the more money you pour into this) the more options you have. That means he or she will know how to navigate a system where the wins are stacked toward the prosecutor.

Harsh Truth B: In the introduction, I mentioned that prosecutors will sometimes try to punish you. When you're facing a raft of incidental charges, it's really hard not to believe "if they want to get you, they will." Because heaven knows it'll feel like he's out to get you. Knowing about the prosecutor's win, lose, draw situation "wanting to get you" makes a lot more sense. Stacking charges means on top of murder charges, reckless endangerment, and others, they tag on a discharging a firearm within city limits or some kind of criminal negligence charge (which often is still a felony). The real hard one to wrap your head around is being charged with firing a gun near a dwelling or inside city limits when dealing with a home invasion. (Yep, it's happened.) What makes more sense is: These kinds of smaller charges are common when there's a good chance they don't have a really strong case for the bigger ones.

The more they throw at you, the better the chance *something* will stick. This allows the prosecutor to put some kind of check in his win box. He didn't get you on the big thing, but he got you for something else. So he can show his boss he at least accomplished something. Stacked charges also make it look like it's suuuuuch a big concession when he offers you a lousy plea.

Another common—and seemingly petty charge—when it comes to weapons is brandishing (or menacing). It's *not* petty. In Colorado, the use of a weapon makes it felony menacing. It is a serious trap—particularly to anyone who has a concealed carry permit. That's because it can be used to pull your permit, as well as your right to own arms. Do you want to be a convicted felon caught carrying a gun? (Or in some states even a knife, but that's a talk to your attorney issue.)

If you carry a self-defense tool, a very real danger is when you pull it for a legitimate reason and then the trouble evaporates. Someone calls the cops to tell them you brandished a weapon, and another problem shows up. In these days of cell phones, it doesn't have to be the person you pulled the weapon on who makes the call. If the cops find you, you need to be able to articulate that it *wasn't* brandishing, but a reasonable response to circumstances that changed when the attacker realized you were armed. As such, it was an act of self-defense. In short, you need to justify pulling the weapon even if you didn't use it.

Here's a dose of bitter medicine that will do you good. I've worked on some extremely high profile cases. I've also worked cases that never made the news. I've seen some hard-core monsters walk free, and I've seen average people thrown into the sausage maker. I've seen cases become media circuses, and I've seen horrendous crimes just quietly disappear and never be heard about again. You can say that's for all kinds of reasons—whether it's money, politics, connections, racism, or proof of a corrupt and elitist system. I've heard all those accusations and more. I'm not going to say those don't have influence. But having been involved in it, I'm going to suggest another factor. We've commercialized our justice system. That's what you're going to be up against if you act in self-defense. The system is (mostly) *not* corrupt, but business interests, funding considerations, and attitudes are part of the process. Believe it or not that can be turned to your favor.

In closing this chapter I want to recap some things I've said. Andrew Vachss, the most brutal and nasty lawyer I have ever met,[100] once commented, "Do you know what the most common injury for prosecuting attorneys is? Repetitive stress injury from throwing in the towel."

Here is a raw fact. The bigger monsters, the professional criminals, the hard-core organized predators have the game *wired*. They're good—and their attorneys are even better. (I've known some who keep $100,000 cash 'legal defense fund' squirreled away, this over and above having a lawyer on a $5,000 permanent retainer.) Getting a conviction on these guys is hard. Translate that into more expensive. Put that into bookkeeping terms, and you get a whole different perspective. From a career protection aspect, a prosecutor pouring hundreds of thousands of dollars into a case he has a good chance of losing is not a good way to win the favor his elected boss.[101] It also makes investigating, charging, and prosecuting them more expensive. I'm not just talking about convicting mafiosos, gun-running bike gangs, drug king pins, or cartel members, either. Practiced predators are expensive and time-consuming to arrest

---

100   I am not kidding, this guy intimidates even me. His crusade is putting away sexual predators, serial rapists, murderers, and other two-legged monsters. His disgust with prosecutors is from their not prosecuting the extreme, but hard-to-win cases. This is over and above the facts of his growing up in the streets and spending time in a war zone.

101   The obvious exception to this is if a case goes viral and doesn't go away. The George Zimmerman trial itself cost taxpayers $900,000 (UPI, Aug. 22, 2013). It's estimated that the investigation cost the city of Safford alone over $600,000 (*Orlando Sentinel*, March 11, 2013) A special prosecutor was called in to take the case away from Safford PD. So now you have to include the investigation costs from other state and federal agencies. And in the end, the state lost. Now imagine what would happen if they did this on every case.

and convict. And the better they are, the less guarantee of the conviction. That's where the "throw in the towel" comment comes in. Vachss is a monster hunter. He knows all too well that if it looks like it's going to be a hard and expensive fight, how often prosecutors back down rather than risk their sterling conviction records.

It's cheaper and easier to let the real monsters roam free and rack up felony convictions on easier cases. Those are still felony convictions. The latter give the prosecution the numbers it needs to show they're doing their job, especially when they throw the book at easy cases. A murder one conviction is a murder one conviction. More common is prosecutors offering what I call the "plea bargain from hell." Wow, isn't the prosecutor being generous to offer you a deal of manslaughter (or murder in the third degree) and fifteen years, instead of going after first-degree murder charges and thirty years?

Here's where you face a really hard choice. There's still a fight in front of you. But the question is which fight will it be? Many of the tactics are going to be the same, but the goals are different. Offering you a bad plea is an easy win. A lot of people don't realize a plea is negotiable. More than that, you *don't* have to take the first one that comes along. If you decide to take a plea—not the plea, but a plea—your lawyer still has to hit the DA with the self-defense evidence to get the *best* deal. If not, there's no reason for the DA's office to make a better offer. Guilty plea with a suspended or deferred sentence? I'd cop to a murder charge for that.[102] Or—and this often happens when the prosecutor won't budge—are you going to take it to trial? In which case, you either win or go to prison. In either case, it's up to you and your attorney to not only make it a hard fight, but expensive to prosecute you.

You do this by staying inside the boundaries of self-defense, being able to articulate what you did, why you did it, why it was self-defense, and then showing up with the evidence that supports it. You pay for experts to show up who can testify on this kind of stuff. You may not win in the way you want, but it goes miles for keeping you from losing as badly as you could. Your claim of self-defense is going to be considered an easy case by career-minded individuals. Well, let's introduce that pumped up chihuahua to a junkyard dog.

Throughout this book, I've stressed the fact that self-defense is *not* fighting. That is still true. Where a fighting attitude is not only appropriate, but necessary is you and your attorney coming at the prosecutor with the attitude of "it *was* self-defense, so we'll not only fight you, but we're going to kick in your tender bits for starting it!"

---

102   Especially because these often can be expunged from your record.

CHAPTER 9

People who haven't been there learn from those who have
The problem is when they decide they're smarter than their
teachers. They think they can improve the information so they
change it, adding what they think will work better. Then they
teach that.

—**Sam Walker**

Adrenal Stress

My response was, "More than that, they promote the new untested version as combat proven." When Sam said that, he and I were talking about misconceptions and the dangers of untested ideas being taught as unquestionable truths in the martial arts. (At worst, this is an outright lie; at best, it's false advertising based on an argument from authority.) That statement also applies to what you've been told about the effects of adrenaline.

Basically, half of what you think you know about the effects of that particular cocktail of hormones is wrong. The question is which half? This is made even more complex by the fact the more experienced you are with operating while adrenalized, the more the effects change—*as do their magnitude.* So now on top of everything else, you have a sliding scale depending on circumstances and who's involved. That is why *any* flat statement about adrenaline is wrong. Example: "You can only do gross motions while adrenalized." Or: "You can't think while adrenalized."

Nope.

It's your butt if you listen to instructors who pimp the juggernauts of adrenaline and emotion in self-defense. Because if you buy into either, you'll be sitting in front of the jury, saying that when you acted you were out of control or in an emotional freak-out. Gee, a prosecutor would never be able to turn that against you . . .

In the movie *Black Hawk Down,* there is a scene where the troops come under fire. The crusty colonel walks around, barking orders as bullets whiz by. He comes to a young, cowering soldier [103] and demands to

---

103   For the record, the movie made them out to be young, fresh-faced innocents. Bah! They were Rangers. You don't get into the Rangers without being a serious meat-eater.

know what he's doing. "They're shooting at us!" His answer? "Well, shoot back!" At seminars, I tell people about that scene, then I ask, "Which one of them is under adrenal stress?" Most people say the young kid. They're half right. The correct answer is both. The difference is how much experience each has had operating while under the effects of adrenaline. Both had the same training; one had more experience. That experience allowed him to move, think, assess, and communicate—even in life-threatening circumstances. Once the kid had orders, he could operate, too.

Now let's add something else. That same colonel might fall apart in completely different circumstances, say, fighting a fire. He's less likely to, but experience in one field doesn't necessarily translate into other fields or other circumstances. As you'll soon see, a big part of being able to function under adrenal stress is having a goal and reliable skills. Are you beginning to understand why there are no absolutes about what adrenaline does?

Now for the real wobble. That lack of absolutes include what it's going to do with you. The effects of adrenaline don't follow a specific check list. While some things are pretty consistent (increased heart rate, change in breathing patterns) it's more a selection of *possible* options. You may get auditory exclusion (you go temporarily deaf) you may get time distortion (Massad Ayoob calls it "tachypsychia") you may develop tunnel vision, or you may see the world in crystal clarity. You may see in color or it may shade toward black and white. Where this gets weirder is that the next time, you might experience an entirely different set of manifestations. One time, you get tunnel vision with auditory exclusion; next time, crystal clarity, hearing, and time distortion.

Studies are underway about the effects of adrenaline and what Peyton Quinn dubbed "adrenal stress" (a kind of umbrella term for all the different things that happen to people while adrenalized). The findings indicate certain combinations of symptoms seem common (e.g., auditory exclusion and tunnel vision versus tachypsychia and crystal vision). But science is slow, and definitive answers aren't in yet. In the meantime, exactly how adrenal stress is going to hit you remains a crap shoot. Furthermore, the more experienced you get, the less adrenalized you become. The less adrenalized you are, the better you can think, perform complex tasks, and achieve specific goals. This doesn't just sink, but blows the current dogma of "you're adrenaline's bitch" out of the water.

Before we go any farther, there's an important concept you need to know. That is: Training is *not* the same as doing. Such a simple concept, but one so many people screw up. Often I suspect, intentionally. A corollary to that, the best training in the world still lacks one critical element for application in the field—you.

I use the analogy of building a bridge over a canyon. Too many people think their training is a complete bridge that allows them to just stroll across the abyss, especially if they've done some adrenal stress training. Man, they're ready to rock and roll. They're hard cases. No. The best training in the world is *not* a complete bridge. You are the one who has to complete it. You're the one who has to make that jump to get to the other side—especially for the first time. The better and more diverse your training, the shorter the jump. But *you* still are the one doing it.

Your training *isn't* going to carry you across that abyss. Not the first time, not the last time, not all the times in the middle. But it will *help* you make the jump. Adrenal stress training won't allow you to stroll across, knocking bullets out of the air with your dick when the time comes. It'll just make that jump shorter—especially useful when there're bullets whipping past you. In the end, it is your commitment and an act of will that changes everything. You are the one who will have to decide to act *not* your training.

For the record, this also includes simply turning and walking away from a situation, instead of progressing to physical violence. That, too, is an act of will and commitment. It's channeling adrenaline and overcoming your monkey.

I'm going to let you in on a little secret: The monkey tends to be a coward. Fear is one of the big drivers of the monkey. But where things get downright goofy is that the monkey—especially when adrenalized—can make you do suicidally aggressive and inclined toward dangerous acts because of its fear.

But "the monkey fears humiliation more than death" seems hard to believe until you realize soldiers in combat could not be relied upon if they didn't fear the shame and humiliation of abandoning their brothers more than they feared dying. To lose the respect and status of the group is a fate worse than death—to the monkey. So, soldiers risk their lives by staying under fire and fighting complete strangers. But that same mechanism can rattlesnake corner you. It can send you walking into the lion's jaws with complete pride and confidence. It can make you think that cussing out the president of a motorcycle gang in front of his crew is a brilliant idea. It can make you haul off and punch a cop. Most people's only experience with functioning in an adrenalized state is in the *context* of their monkey. They get all kinds of excited and adrenalized over their emotions. This colors their perceptions and makes them susceptible to the twaddle about what's going to happen to them under adrenaline.

The first step in being able to function under adrenal stress conditions is to learn to apply the wheelbarrow test to whatever you're stressing over.

Does whatever you think is in danger have a physical existence? (To be redundant: Will it fit in a wheelbarrow?)

The second step is to have faith in what you know. I'm not talking pie in the sky, I believe _____ (fill in blank) so I have faith in it. I'm talking about something you're *willing* to bet your life on.

To demonstrate this in seminars, I hold out a closed knife and ask someone what will happen if I open my hand. He or she tells me it will fall. I ask, "Are you willing to bet your life on that?" No tricks, no BS, no me pulling a sneaky. Are they willing to bet their life on gravity working? Typically after some hesitation, they go with gravity. When I open my hand, gravity works. We *know* gravity works. It's what keeps us from trying to walk on thin air off the top of buildings or bridges. It's what sends you scrambling to try to catch your plunging laptop, i-Pod, android, Ming vase, or other falling object. Beyond knowledge, this bedrock faith dictates our behavior.

What things in your training are you willing to bet your life on? What parts of it are you willing to commit to with the same conviction you have about gravity? (Conviction that keeps you from stepping off the edge of a cliff.) What in your training will you engage in completely during a crisis? Uncertainty is a huge part of why people fall apart under adrenaline. They don't *trust* what they *know* to work.

Conversely, this often creates a self-fulfilling prophecy. Gen. George S Patton once said, "A good plan violently executed now is better than a perfect plan next week." I tell you that because a good plan executed half-heartedly and with trepidation will reliably fail more than even a bad plan executed with commitment. Unsure something will work, too many people try to hedge their bets and move with half-assed commitment. When it fails—and it will—they claim their training won't work at all. Using something you *don't* trust is a huge factor in how much stress and, by extension, adrenaline you'll be trying to function under.

Another source of both stress and actual failure is the false belief a single thing *will* do it all. The most obvious example is a punch. One punch or a lot of them, that's still *one thing*. But I'm going to take it further because that misconception is endemic to what is taught as self-defense. It extends into over confidence in one thing. I'll point to extreme close quarter shooting. The idea is get your gun out and pump as many bullets into him as possible. All those shooters' belief is invested in pulling the trigger will keep them safe.

Fundamental problem about when you are legally justified to use lethal force: It's used when someone is trying to *kill* you. Assuming you can even get your gun out and deployed in time if all you do is shoot, you are simply trading potentially lethal damage. And by the way, getting it out is one hell of an assumption. But even if you do manage at that range, you need to do things other than just shoot. You need to deflect incoming damage. (Again, this applies to empty-hand SD, but your ability to take punches masks this gaping hole—you have to go to weapons to see it.)

And still another problem. People's expectations may be too high for what a move will actually accomplish. When it doesn't work as expected . . . more stress, more adrenaline, more panic. Again in seminars, I ask people "Why do you hit?" It's a simple question, but the answers people come up with are too complicated. They're also aimed at imaginary results. "I hit so he'll stop attacking me and go away." "I hit to cause enough pain so he'll stop attacking." Yada, yada, yada. They look at me like I've grown a second head when I tell them, "I hit to deliver force to create a certain physical reaction." Then I continue, "Whether that is to create shock that will slow him down or so I can move or to knock him into where I want him to be. It depends on the circumstances."

The difference is they're hoping one move will create a domino effect, resulting in a specific end goal. ("I hit so he'll stop attacking me and go away.") I, however, look at a hit as one step in a process of reaching that goal. It will be something I do aimed at a small, specific purpose that is part of a strategy for reaching a larger goal. Here's a news flash for folks who train for empty-hand combat: A single hit somewhere in a four-step process works faster and more reliably to end the threat than six hits and the hope he'll go away. I told you all this to now ask: *Which approach is more likely to reach the goal of stopping his attack? Hit and hope? Or hit as part of a methodical process?* (Say: 1) Grab. 2) Twist, put him off balance. 3) Hit down and diagonally. And 4) pull him over in the same direction I hit or knocked him.)

More than that, I *trust* my punch to work for that smaller tactical goal. I don't expect it to be the entire strategy. If it actually does create that domino effect, I'm tickled pink. But I expect to have to do a lot more. In fact, I plan for it. That hit is a building block, a stepping stone for my next move. Knowing this, I can use my adrenaline to help me reach my goal, instead of letting it get in the way. People who expect a hit to do it all tend to freak out, fall apart, and flail when—instead of turning and running away while crying—the person they punch attacks *harder*. This unexpected response jacks up their adrenaline even more.

Oh incidentally, for martial artists a big source of this lack of trust when it comes to striking comes from point sparring. You tell yourself, "If I just hit harder, it would work outside the ring." Simultaneously, you *have* stable data about hitting people, getting hit, and it *failing* to make someone stop. It happens all the time during sparring. Yet the few times a blow lands hard enough to stop the round, it reinforces the idea violence will stop if you only hit hard enough. There's a self-eating watermelon for you. The same goes for shooting paper targets. Yeah, there's a hole in it, but:

a) It's still there.
b) You can cause more damage to paper by sticking your finger through it.

To reiterate: Not trusting what you're doing to work (especially if you have stable data about it failing) increases your stress and adrenaline, causing you to fall apart to an even worse degree. This brings us to something else—the difference between fear and panic. Basically, the disparity boils down to knowing what to do.

When people talk about "no fear" when it comes to violence, I want to reach out and slap them. Fear of legitimate danger is a *good* thing. It is your ally. It's your inspiration. Your muse, if you will. Strength increases, reflexes are faster, pain sensitivity drops, and you can run faster. In those circumstances, adrenaline becomes the get-it-done drug.

Panic, however, sets in when you have nothing you can use that you trust to solve the problem at hand. Your brain goes into vapor lock. This can engender a freeze, doing the absolutely wrong thing (like throwing water on a grease fire) flailing, or a complete melt-down. In short, with panic you disintegrate. The problem with a lot of what people in the self-defense world *think* they know about adrenal stress and response is closer to panic, not fear.

Here's a seminar question any parent can relate to. After establishing how many parents I have in the class, I ask, "How many have had an injured child and made a hell run to the emergency room?" Immediately, hands shoot up. Then I ask, "In the middle of this crisis, how many of you forgot how to drive?" I've *never* had a single hand raised. While they may not have driven as well as they normally do, everyone remembered how, was able to drive a vehicle, and transported the injured child without accident. During a crisis and while adrenalized, they did not lose this complex skill. Then I ask, "How many of you fell apart afterward?" I get another parade of hands.

I want you to recognize driving a child to the ER is a complicated mix of actions, reactions, calculations, assessments, adjustments, and planning, all accomplished in ever-changing circumstances. And those are *all the things* some people contend you're *not* supposed to be able to do while adrenalized. Yet, here is a room full of parents—untrained about adrenal stress—who managed to take care of business during a crisis.

The key elements of why they could:

a) They had a plan and knew what to do (get the child to the hospital).

b) They had ingrained the physical aspects of driving into their lizard brains.

c) They trusted both their plan and ability to drive.

d) They overrode their monkey.

e) They were committed to the plan.

These are enormous game changers. This, however, does open some doors to important considerations about training. A whole lot of people, who spent years in the martial arts, go through scenario training (adrenal stress-inducing scenarios) and crumble. I mean the wheels come off. Often this results in wailing and gnashing of teeth about how they wasted so many years . . . blah, blah, blah. This is *normal. Nobody* does well the first time out when they are *not* the aggressor.

Often unscrupulous instructors with reality-based self-defense training programs (including trademarked techniques that start with the word The) swoop in from the wings and show them why, yes, their previous training was wasted time. Whereas, Stud Muffin's ultimate fighting system is *so* much better. Except what makes this new studly system 'work' is the foundation built during all those years *wasted* in a good martial arts program. All the new system is doing is boosting an existing engine.

Learning how to function under adrenal stress is a lot like learning how to swim in the ocean. Just because you learned how to swim in a pool doesn't mean you're ready to swim in the ocean. The fundamentals of swimming *do not* change, but you have to learn how to apply them under the conditions of waves and tidal pull. Adrenaline is like those waves— you need to learn how swim before you try to body surf.[104] It's better if you can learn to swim in a pool. Then practice the elements of body surfing in a pool that has a wave machine (adrenaline-inducing scenarios), but:

a) You still need to have the fundamental skill sets involved in swimming.

b) You need to trust them.

c) You need to be able to perform them effectively without thinking (lizard brain competence) while under the influence of stress and adrenaline.

d) After developing C, you need to be able to perform them (or switch to another strategy) when someone is actively trying to stop you (e.g., water polo).

e) You have to realize the pool with the wave-making equipment is still *not* the ocean.

---

104   For those of you who live farther than a hundred miles from the ocean, body surfing is like surfing except the swimmer uses his body as the surf board.

A lot of training collapses because it focuses on one or maybe two of those items. The instructors and Kool-Aid drinkers of such programs dismiss, ignore, or downplay the significance of other systems (e.g., MMAers bagging on traditional martial arts). Or they assume their focus automatically instills the necessary abilities to function in a crisis. (Two examples: Traditional martial arts practitioners believing their training prepares them to function under adrenal stress. MMAers assuming they're instilling good body mechanics because they immediately start competing).

Is the repetitive motion of kata good for ingraining neural pathways and developing good mechanics? Yes, *if* done correctly.[105] Is that *all* you need? No. You need to have someone actually try to hit you in one-step drills so you learn the importance of moving off line and the need for correct structure against incoming force, among a variety of other things depending on the training and teacher. *Then* you can tweak your kata so you train yourself to perform it effectively against another person. Will throwing someone who doesn't have these skill sets ingrained into sparring or full contact "aliveness" training going to help him? No. In fact, *that* will instill bad habits, weak mechanics, and an over-reliance on using muscle. Does someone who has had years of training in a traditional martial art school need to go through adrenal stress or scenario training? Yes. Is it helpful for shooters to go through low-light, fun house training to learn how to function under adrenal stress? Yes.

In case you missed it, there is no such thing as one-stop shopping for all your self-defense needs. You should go out and find other schooling that covers what is missing from your existing training (especially if you're in a high-risk profession or situation). I also strongly suggest that anyone who is trained to act within the lethal force spectrum find some less fatal training. (Personally, I recommend a basic familiarity with throwing arts like Danzan Ryu, Judo, Jujitsu [not Brazilian] or even Hapkido. If shooting someone is illegal under the circumstances, throwing him and running like hell is a nice alternative.[106]) Then add a dash of something that punches and kicks. Flip side of that if you're into empty-hand get some weapons training.

Is it important for anyone taking any kind of self-defense training to get legal education on use of force? It's critical for *everybody* who might be forced to use his or her training. That's something that isn't covered in

---

105   By that I mean moving with process, muscle tension, timing, and structure. Otherwise, all you are doing is waving your arms around.

106   I'm not talking grappling, wrestling, or submission fighting. While it is useful to be able to function on the ground, it's far better not to go there for self-defense. I didn't put Aikido in the list of throwing arts because . . . well . . . even though I know some amazing aikidoists, who can throw someone through a wall, way too much of what is taught has been watered too far down to work in a self-defense situation.

most punch, punch or bang, bang training. But it's knowledge you need to guide your actions by when you're adrenalized.

Side track here: Many people natter on about "analysis paralysis." That's the alleged freeze you experience when you have too many options. Another common interpretation of the same phrase—and I wish to hell I was joking when I say I've heard people utter it—"if you know the law, you'll freeze instead of act." After taking a slug of bourbon straight out of the bottle to calm my nerves, I do have to say freezes are possible, but not in the way people think. They exist with or without adrenaline. In fact, adrenaline usually is blamed for something it didn't do. It just happened to be in the room when the inability to act struck. It's been my experience that this break-down is more a combination of not being able to accurately assess the dangers of the situation, not trusting your tools, and, most of all, not leaving your monkey brain.

When you can accurately assess physical danger—other than what your monkey deems as dangerous to *it*—you get a far more limited selection of appropriate options. That's actually a good thing. Shooting drunken Uncle Albert is off the table. On the other hand, when a predator is closing on you in a dark and deserted place options that work for Albert are inadequate. In case you haven't noticed it, this book is chock full of ways to assess a situation. Depending on the circumstances, the number of viable options is reduced to a more manageable size. Instead of legal issues getting in the *way*, they become a factor in your use-of-force decision—especially about not crossing the line into excessive force.

So now I've talked about all the stuff that other people who to talk about adrenaline don't mention, let's look at some of the things that you're likely to have happen to you while adrenalized. The most common effects of an adrenaline dump in response to violence are:

Pain tolerance and delay—Things that would normally cause you to squeal in pain don't. The damage is still done, but you don't necessarily feel the same level of pain. Some people don't feel it at all. (This is why it's important in the aftermath of an incident to examine yourself for injuries. Run your hands over your body, checking to see if you're bleeding. Often you won't know you've been wounded until you do this.) Under adrenal influence, people can take fatal wounds and *keep on* attacking.

Depth perception and visual distortion—Things appear closer or larger than they are. For example, the person across the room, waving a knife at you, suddenly looks like he's only inches away, grows ten feet, and waves a machete in your face. This distortion occurs because you are entirely focused on the threat.

Tunnel vision—Closely related to visual distortion, your peripheral vision can drop away and *all* you see is the threat. "Elephant? What elephant? All I saw was the guy with the gun."

Auditory exclusion—Hearing can just go away because every brain cell you have is focused on the threat. To the point you often won't hear gunshots within just a few feet of you.

Speed and strength increase—Under adrenaline's influence on your body, you can accomplish amazing feats of strength and speed. Unfortunately, this doesn't make you invincible. While stories of mothers lifting cars off their children are true, what you don't hear are the fact that they tore muscles and tendons and ruined their backs doing it (see pain tolerance).

Changes in blood flow and heart beat—Not only will your heart beat and blood pressure shoot up, but inside your body veins will constrict and expand to divert blood to where it is most needed to oxygenate your body. (Don't get too caught up in the whole optimum heart rate thing.)

Time distortion—Time slows or speeds up. On one hand, this is the proverbial slow motion effect. On the other, there are gaps in time. It's like you're going so fast you're skipping ahead to two seconds in the future—a result of your entire consciousness laser focusing on the danger.

Fine motor movement decay—Although you will be able to run faster than you ever did before, forget twirling a quarter in your fingers. Anything that isn't ingrained isn't likely to happen as fast as you want it to—or as well. Even with ingrained movement, there will be *some* decay, but there are two other elements:

Trembling and fumbling—This is a bigger reason for the myth that you can only do gross body movements while adrenalized. I have something you can try: Pick up the phone in one hand; extend a finger on the other hand; extend both hands away from your body. Shake both hands erratically and in different directions, then try to push the number nine. Seriously, try that . . .

Two bases *moving at once* is the primary reason behind the myth about inability to carry out small precise movements while adrenalized. When everything shakes and trembles, it's like trying to tap dance on ice during an earthquake. You can resolve a lot of these issues if you develop practices to stabilize one of the trembling bases (e.g., instead of trying to dial 911 with your hands out in front of you, tuck the arm of your phone hand against your body, then dial).

Timing problems and movement drop—Two more sources of the gross movement-only myth. These are where the consequences of not having ingrained neural pathways (unconscious competence) steps up and says, "I'm heeeere!" They're also the other big reason behind the myth that you're adrenaline's bitch.

Let's say a move has three gross movement elements. We'll use a block that involves moving your arm out and back in an arc, rotating your wrist, and dropping your elbow. All of these are *simple* gross moves. (Do it right now. Start with your arm at your side, palm up or down, it doesn't matter. Extend your arm out in a loop and bring it back while tucking your elbow to the side. At the apex of the loop, flip your wrist . . . that is a *very* effective block against an incoming punch. That's all it is! Very simple.) But unless you ingrain correctly executing all three moves and then practice them *under adrenal stress conditions*, you're likely to drop one, maybe two. Or mess up the timing. These are the dreaded complicated moves you supposedly *can't* do under adrenaline's death grip. If you can't do them, it's because you haven't practiced proper movements while calm, then worked them while adrenalized and under pressure. Here's a news flash, running is a far more dynamic, variable, and complicated process than you know. Yet you can do that while adrenalized. So don't mistake lack of experience and ingrained neural pathways (wrongfully called 'muscle memory') and flawed training for 'what's impossible to do.'

Changes in respiratory rate—Breathing patterns change. Anything can happen from a fast, sharp inhale then forgetting to breathe to hyperventilation.

Unconscious muscle tension—Some muscles will clench, others will relax. And afterward, you'll ache in places where you weren't even hit.

Mono-emotion and emotional detachment—Usually there will be one overwhelming emotion (e.g., fear or anger) blocking every other feeling. The reverse also can be true, however. There can be a sense of emotional detachment as the body functions to achieve an end. The latter is more common among those individuals experienced in operating in crises.

Rhythmic motion and rocking—In the intent section of the five stages, I talked about watching someone's hands open and close unconsciously. It doesn't have to be a full clench. You can see someone's hands rhythmically pulse. Another common sign of adrenaline is a slow sway or rocking back and forth. Other people bounce, still others—especially when sitting— look like they have restless leg syndrome.

Bladder or bowel release—Although not exactly an adrenal response, your body jettisoning extra weight (feces and urine) *is* common when someone faces danger and is adrenalized. This is part of the fight-or-flight response influenced by adrenaline.

Erection—This commonly occurs among men in response to a violent conflict with another person.

And now for something completely different . . . post-adrenal stress effects. While most people are concerned about what will happen *during* an adrenalized moment—having been in a number of life-and-death situations—I'd also like to inform you about the aftermath. Again like the effects mentioned above not everyone will have the same reactions or undergo them to the same degree.

Short- or long-term memory loss—You won't remember some very important things until the adrenaline wears off. Other things, you'll never be able to remember.

Nausea—Post-action vomiting is common.

Post-incident soreness—Remember I mentioned how some muscles will tighten up? You'll be achy. This will be over and above the bumps and bruises you took.

Hypo-mania—Remember I said that the adrenaline remains in your system? After an incident, the adrenaline doesn't just go away. Its presence manifests in many different ways: Some people get the jitters, others fidget and pace, others rapidly babble, some yell, shout, and whoop, some laugh maniacally, and various people experience all those aspects (hopefully at different times). This is part of the winding-down process.

Horniness—There is nothing that reinforces the fact you survived danger better than wild monkey sex. This is one of the reasons people chronically in dangerous situations are often hypersexual. Throughout history, camp followers, hookers, whorehouses, and armies have been linked.

Crash and exhaustion—-After running on high octane for a long time comes the crash. If at all possible, I suggest you sleep through it. (Although for the record, cops get pissed if you try to take a nap on the interview room table.)

Dreamless sleep or nightmares—A number of people fall into a deep, exhausted, dreamless state. Others toss and turn all night after they've encountered violence. These people often report bad or weird dreams.

Post-incident resurgence—It is not uncommon that anywhere from twenty-four to forty-eight hours after an incident, you will suddenly and unexpectedly find yourself in the middle of an adrenaline rush. This may be triggered by some small incident or it may just seem to come out of nowhere. Generally, it's best to ride it through and let it pass.

Although I don't go too far into PTSD (post traumatic stress disorder) here's something you need to know: *Violence rewires the brain.* Graffiti, tattoo time. Past that is where things get a little less black and white. There is a concept called neural plasticity. If you're a nerd like me, it's a really exciting concept because it means even though violence alters the brain, you aren't necessarily stuck there.

The old neurological model claimed the brain once developed was fixed and unchangeable. If you're a victim, you're victim forever; if you're a criminal, you're a criminal forever; yada yada, yada . . . Except evidence kept cropping up that people *can* change. Oops. Well bad ideas die hard, so then it became, "Okay, you only get one change. So if you're an okay person and you have a traumatic event, you change into a victim forever perpetually doomed to suffer PTSD." Uhhhh, no. Our understanding of PTSD has come a long way from the early days. A lot of the advancements are bad news for the victim industry. In ye olde days, it was assumed if you experienced a bad thing, you'd automatically be traumatized. And, boy oh boy, those highly paid grief counselors and crisis experts would swing into action. The new approach to PTSD is to first ask, "How're you doing with this? Do you need help?" It turns out, not everyone's automatically traumatized. In a giant case of "oh, gee, that's kind of embarrassing," it turns out professionals automatically assuming distress and pestering people about it *create* trauma. Like making the person wonder and doubt about him- or herself because he or she hasn't collapsed into a helpless, quivering pile of Jell-O.

More bad news for the victim industry: Post traumatic stress disorder is temporary with most people. Damn neural plasticity! Yes, the brain is rewired by an event, but after a while it resets itself. Think of the neural pathways in your brain as a river course. There's an earthquake, and the river temporarily shifts (short-term PTSD). After a while, the river reverts to the way it normally flowed. Will there be differences? Yes, but in an estimated 85 percent to 90 percent of people with PTSD, the river reverts to its normal channel.

Third item of bad news for that particular industry: Most people get better by themselves—as in without the help of experts. Funny thing, humans survived in a rough and dangerous world for millions of years. Somehow, we muddled along before Sigmund Freud started asking about our relationships with our mothers. We humans are an amazingly adaptable species. While it may sound like I'm telling you to "sack up, princess!" or I'm bagging on the field of psychology, I'm not. Most psychologists acknowledge these new developments about treatment of PTSD as a *really* good thing. Also acknowledging it's usually temporary, the emphasis of treatment has shifted to getting people through it as effectively and quickly as possible. Doing this allows patients to avoid many of the negative, secondary problems that often develop (e.g., alcoholism, drug abuse, and mood swings). Conversely, there are anti-anxiety drugs and other medications that truly help people through the process. Add the statistic that there are between 10 percent to 15 percent of people who don't get over it; the river stays permanently shifted.

Professionals and support groups—as long as they don't try to make you redefine yourself as a permanent victim—*can* and *do* help. You might think you're a freak because you retain some elements of PTSD. I cannot begin to tell you how much stress relief there is in having someone say, "Oh that? It's normal. Here are some things you can do about it." If you're having problems after an incident *don't* try and tough it out. Seek professional help. The odds are good, it's a temporary phase and finding help will get you through it faster.

Now how does this relate to adrenaline and the aftermath? You've heard of menopausal hot flashes? After an incident, you'll probably experience adrenaline flashes similar to those hot flashes. You'll be going about your business, and something in the environment makes the monkey or the lizard hit the amygdala's response button. Ohhh goody, instant adrenal stress . . . while you're standing in line at the supermarket. Yep, that eighty-year-old woman who gets too close to you while reaching for a pack of gum suddenly morphs into a ninja assassin come to kill you. Remember me talking about the difference between reality and actuality? For your information, that great-grandmother? She's not a ninja. But at that exact moment, every adrenalized nerve in your body screams that she is. Bumps in the night will bring you out of a dead sleep in either a blind panic or monster rages. You'll freak yourself out with the idea you're about to be attacked while standing naked in the shower.[107] You glance into a parking lot, see someone who looks like . . . get a whiff of blood or cordite, and you're right back there.

In case you missed it, been there, done that . . . I'm going to give you some helpful hints for dealing with this kind of stuff and working your way through it.

First, *assess* the actual danger and identify the source of the trigger. When adrenaline screams that you're in danger, *confirm*. Danger, yes or no? The five stages and JAM are checklists for that. They are your external confirmation or shut-down standards. Once again, we're talking the difference between fear and danger management. If something triggers you, look for the *other* elements. Are they there? What is missing? Check before you react! One of the acronyms for fear is 'false evidence appearing real.' Reconfirm the evidence is real.

At the same time, look for the source of the trigger. Once the source is identified, it's easier to deal with the emotions and adrenaline. For example, last time I was shot at a laser sight was used. I saw the dot paste the other person and move toward me. I have 'issues' with red laser dots near me. Recently, I went into a bowling alley that had a light and sound show. A red dot pasted someone and moved on, I started to move.

---

107   No kidding, I once was involved in a women's self-defense forum where someone asked, "How can I carry a gun in the shower?" And these so-called experts in self-defense tried to answer the question! At first I was dumbfounded, then I got mad. "There are these things called locks! I suggest you use them. There also are things called alarms and dogs for early warning. I highly recommend those, too."

Then I saw another and another, all moving the same way. Not hearing screams, shots, or seeing people running, I knew there was no danger. Still I looked and saw a disco-ball producing these lights.

In case you didn't know it, stuck in the medial frontal cortex are parts of the brain that suppress when other parts are firing and telling you, "Do this." *Get to know this part.* It can be a great servant. Right next to the Panic Button, install an Abort! Abort! Abort! button.

Second, identify the *trigger.* This sounds like a repeat of the first coping method, but it's different in a small but significant way. Focus strictly on that particular trigger, and you begin to take its power away. Yes, that person looks like the person you killed. But it's not. Yes, this parking lot looks like the area where it happened. But it's not that place. Yes, this smell was in the air when it happened. But it's not happening now. Yes, that old lady just moved into my blind spot, but she's not trying to stab me. By looking for the specific triggers, you collect a list of these are the things I react badly to. That will become important for the fourth strategy.

Third, *disengage* the power train. I call adrenaline the *do it now!* drug. But it's not just chemistry, it's a whole lot more. Lies to children and imagination time: I liken the whole neural pathway, adrenaline, habits, ball of behaviors, and emotions to a flash flood in an arroyo. For those who haven't spent time in the desert, arroyos are deep mini canyons created by periodic rainwater run-off over thousands of years. Most of the time, arroyos are dry, weed-infested channels in the desert. When a heavy rain hits, the deeper the arroyo, the more likely a flash flood is going to be created with a high wall of water rolling down a very narrow space at speeds between 10 to 30 miles per hour. We're talking enough water surging with enough force to pick up cars and uproot trees. Your neural pathways are like the arroyo, adrenaline and your thoughts are like the water. They combine to create the flash flood.

A lot of people hit by an adrenaline surge try to dig in and fight it. These strategies have limited success. (And if you ever have been there, you'll understand this comment, "It bloody well hurts.") In arroyo terms, this is like trying to brace against a flash flood or swim against it. You're going to get blasted and knocked over. In other words, fighting that rush is going to knock the crap out of you.

I'm going to give you another analogy. In driving terms, it would be like your accelerator sticking. Fighting or resisting the adrenaline surge is like trying to slam on the brakes or steer your vehicle while the engine revs and your car's still in gear. If the brakes fail or you steer wrong—instant accident.

Instead of trying to fight the flood, *get out* of the canyon. Instead of trying to brake, shift the car into *neutral.* When I say disengage the power chain, I mean *don't* try and fight the feeling. That's the flood, that's the engine red lining. Let the feeling pass without acting on it. Break the *habit* of believing a feeling automatically equals action. You do not *have* to react to either emotion or adrenaline—doing so is habit. A habit we've had for so long, we don't remember that we don't have to act. Flash floods pass in a matter of minutes. If you're not in the canyon, you won't be carried away. A revving engine with your foot on the clutch is not rocketing you toward an accident. I tell people to have a cup of coffee while watching the flood go past. With your foot on the clutch, you can safely coast to the side of the road and turn off the engine.

Still another analogy: In my youth, I used to body surf at Venice Beach. Swimming out past the waves that had broken was simple. Instead of trying to swim through the white water, you either jumped over the turbulence (when shallow) or dove under water. You let the bulk of the turbulence pass above you as you swam against the current. There were some days when instead of the gentle spilling waves, there were 'close outs.' This was when the waves crested and came crashing down all at once. Only the bravest and stupidest folks went body surfing on those days. (Naturally, I was one of them.) With close outs, there was no swimming below the turbulence or jumping over it. Turbulence went from the top all the way down to the bottom, and even the strongest swimmers would be sent tumbling. To handle the terrible power of close outs, I swam to the bottom and dug my fingers, like plant roots, into the sand. Then I relaxed my body. I became like seaweed that flowed and swayed with the turbulence, but was not uprooted. When the white water passed, I popped up to the surface and kept swimming to get out of the close-out zone.

It doesn't matter what analogy works for you—or if you come up with your own. The key element is to *not* fight the adrenaline surge and emotions. Let them pass *without* controlling your actions.

Fourth, once you've learned what sets you off develop *habits* to keep from being triggered so you can relax. My wife-to-be was tickled pink that I was such a gentleman when I pulled her chair out for her in restaurants. While I still do this, we'd been dating for nearly a year before she realized that it also always allowed me to sit with my back to the wall. Learn to look into reflective surfaces to check what's happening behind you. (Hell put a mirror on your desk or work station so you can see anyone innocently walking up behind you.) Rather than risk being triggered by ninja great-grandmothers in the check-out line, I'd lean up against the check-out counter or a stand with my back to a display. This was not tactical. It wasn't that I was such a hard case I was ready to be ambushed anywhere. It was so I didn't wet myself when someone's nanna wanted Altoids.

CHAPTER 10

The less you know, the less you think there is to learn.
—**Kathy Jackson**

What Is Violence?

"Violence never solved anything!" "Violence is bad!" "Violence is the last refuge of the incompetent." I get all kinds of cross-eyed looks when I point out how often people, who *use* these clichés, are violent. Where the reactions diverge is when I add, "How judgmental, elitist, extremist, and bigoted the people saying these words can be." One set of folks nods their heads with an attitude of, "Well, now *that* I've seen that (but I'm still not sure about the violent or extremist)." The other group goes postal. Generally, they're the ones using those clichés. The reason for the crankiness is because I've revealed their dirty little secret.

Before we go there, I say, " 'Violence never solved anything' is an extremist—and unsupportable—statement." Worse, it's a contention that if left unquestioned *will* put you in prison for acting in self-defense. That's why it needs a swift kick in the nuts. Violence never . . . is *easy* to say. Proving that it's true . . . not so much. It has to meet some tough standards. As in, extraordinary claims require extraordinary proof. That's because despite only having five letters, *never* is an awfully big word. First, have you met everyone on the planet and asked, "Has violence ever worked to resolve a situation for you?" If the claimant hasn't, then how does he or she know it *never* works? That's just an introduction to how big 'never' is. Second, assuming the claimant gets past that first round, she or he would have to build a time machine, get in, and ask the same question of everyone who *ever* lived.

With the time machine notion, we know we've moved into the ludicrous. What we fail to recognize is that we've been there from the *start*. The word never is an absolute, one that stretches into infinity and all of time.[108] But, boy, doesn't it lend credibility and conviction to the

---

108   A more accurate and incontestable version would be, "In my perceived experience, violence has never solved anything." You can't say the person is wrong for his or her subjective experience. Be forewarned though, allowing for personal experience, many people will try to respond with a tale about their victimization by violence. (Free tip, replying, "Apparently you suck at it," does *not* win you friends—just trust me on this one.)

rest of that statement! I'm talking holy word, right-with-God fanaticism (Some people's monkeys love that kind of certainty.) This conviction, this *moral certitude* triggers our monkey and keeps our human brain from looking down the alley to see what's obviously wrong with this statement.

Problem is, most people have been buffaloed into just being quiet when barking moonbats are tossing extremist clichés around. Think I'm making that up? How many times have *you* kept quiet when someone boldly makes this unsupportable proclamation? Or starts going on about the evils of violence? And my personal favorite, "Violence is *never* acceptable?" Why? Simply by reading this book, you're demonstrating you disagree.

Here's something else. Do you resist mentioning your interest in personal safety in polite company? Have you ever revealed your involvement in the martial arts or that you own a firearm and felt you'd receive a better response if you'd come out and said you're into something kinky? Do you just keep quiet about these because of the typical reactions you get? Have you ever had someone have a melt-down over the fact you're armed? That is how strong the bias is and how well people have been conditioned in our modern society to avoid the subject of violence. Never mind actually going physical, simply refusing to toe the party line about the evils of violence is likely to get you verbally attacked and berated. You know about that response already. So why am I wasting your time telling you about it? People are hidebound against violence; you're going to get reamed if you defend yourself. So why bother?

Well don't lie down and die, yet. I'm telling you this so you have the ammo to fight this particular battle. Instead of it being a massive ball of suck you are helpless against, you have the understanding, the background, and the knowledge to fight it. Behind all the noise and outrage about how bad violence is, there's very quiet resistance. And it's that resistance that gives you a *chance* to keep from being arrested or going to prison for defending yourself. Play it right, and it's a damned big chance.

When it comes to violence, I like to use the punch line of an old joke, "We've already established that, now we're haggling over the price." If you sit down over a cup of coffee with folks, you'll find that nearly 100 percent agree that *sometimes* physical force is the answer—at least to certain situations. Ask the right questions, they'll admit, "It's not how I want the world to be, but yes there is a time and place for violence—even extreme violence." And now, we're haggling over the price.

What are those times? How much use of force is acceptable? Under what circumstances do we allow it? In what circumstances is it unacceptable? What should the consequences be when these standards are violated? And perhaps most importantly, who should be allowed to use it? That is one hellacious argument and debate—*as there should be*. What are we—as a society, as a whole—willing to accept? What rules do we agree on that guide, restrict, limit, and *allow* use of force? When does force transition into violence? Negotiate furiously on these, folks, you're going to have to live with the decisions. I'll include not shutting up when a barking moonbat is holding court over how evil violence is at a social event. (I mean c'mon, man, you're thinking you're going to be able to act in self-defense when you can't even stand up to someone preaching an attitude that will put you into prison for self-defense?)

For the record, I'm all for living in a society where these standards are high. I've resided in, worked in, and dealt with people from places where those standards are low. They are *not* nice places. Yay, high standards! Yay, us! So why mention this? If there is anything that will give you hope about getting through both a self-defense situation and the aftermath, it's knowing we're simply negotiating the price.

Despite the extremists and idealists screaming it's *never* okay, there is a ray of hope. And that is—most people do *understand* that sometimes force is necessary. Self-defense is one of the times when it is okay. In fact, that's the gap you're trying to shoot through. You have to be careful and *aim* for that gap. Let's make that gap a little wider. People also know there are bad places, areas where prohibitions against violence are real low. Locations where nasty, brutish, violent people lurk . . . usually from *somewhere* over there. Somewhere nice people don't regularly frequent. Locales where violence goes down that are far away from where they live. The challenge you face is convincing people that—even though violence never occurred where they live—you were confronted by someone from such a bad place or found yourself in such a place. Given those conditions even though you too have high standards against using violence, it was necessary. That's something people can understand.

When it comes to talking about violence, the trick is to not let the extremists control the conversation. More than that, you cannot automatically assume people will understand *why* force was necessary. You have to communicate to them why it was essential in your particular situation. Pointing out this not-so-intellectual 'bias against violence' has five reasons:

One is that's what's probably on the mind of the prosecutor and the jury. Ignoring this bias is like trying to ignore gravity. You can't see it, but it is *there*. And the effects are most definitely present. (I'm giving you the tools to deal with it.)

Two—and this is good news—the knowledge you're merely negotiating the price is another paradigm shift. An alteration that gets you out of the judgmental monkey while recognizing its presence in those you tell your story to. That puts you ahead of the game. You go in prepared to present why what you did was necessary (the legal definition of justified). This will be in direct contrast to the prosecution's story that it *wasn't* self-defense. But that's not the most important element.

Three is that this paradigm shift *takes it out* of the subjective right or wrong and a moralistic and judgmental good or bad. Let me expand on that. It doesn't look like much, but it is. With this shift, violence is no longer categorically bad. It's just violence. It is what it is. Start with that, then start adding layers and other considerations—including whether or not we believe it was a bad use of force. Why is this important? The monkey tends to be moralistic and judgmental. Remember, the monkey can hijack the human part of the brain to rationalize its previous decisions. Or in this case, shut off incoming data that would challenge its previously determined mindset. (Monkeys don't like cognitive dissonance.)

If you don't ever have to apply them in the real world, morals tend to be kind of absolute. Put another way if you don't ever have to go out and get dirty, it's easy to have high and noble standards. They'll never be tested by real life considerations. Like oh . . . say . . . about violence. The problem with a moralistic, judgmental approach is once people have decided "it's bad," most people *shut off* their brains about the subject—especially when it comes to something that isn't a daily issue for them. That philosophy summed up is: It's not an issue in my life, but this is what I believe about it. That settles it for me. A less common, but more pernicious direction is any follow-up human brain activity is dedicated to collecting evidence and proving why it is evil and must be stopped. These people are hell bent on 'educating' everyone about the evils of violence against _____(fill in blank).

Part of your task—and your lawyer's—is to kick start the other parts of people's brains. To get them to look down that alley and see what's there. To get them to make an informed assessment based on the evidence, not a judgment based on what an ignorant monkey 'feels' is right or wrong. It's not uncommon that the only thinking people want to do is to rationalize and defend their positions. Life is simple when the extent of your thoughts is it's bad, it's wrong. (This allows them to reject any complicating information that may require more thinking.) How deep inside the monkey someone is depends on the person. Some on the jury are looking hard for some little detail to justify their prepackaged decision that you were wrong, what you did was illegal, and you need to be punished. That's not the kind of person you want in the jury box when you're in the defendant's chair—whether you acted in legitimate self-defense or not, but *above all* when you did.

The kind of person you need sitting there is someone who can step away from his or her judgmental, unconscious biases; someone who understands that when it comes to violence, we need to negotiate the price. Was this situation in the percentage of violence that is acceptable, if not essential? (And yes, I just slid in a message for lawyers.) But wait . . . didn't I just say if you sit down with folks you can get them to admit sometimes violence is necessary? Yes, I did. I also said you'll have to ask the *right* questions that take them out of an emotional, moralizing, and judgmental monkey mind. Questions that get them thinking along the lines of, "Okay, how would *I* solve this problem?"

But also know those folks sitting in the jury box *believe* in justice. More than that, most of them—arguably wrongfully so—believe our court system is about justice. While they may agree what you did was necessary, they might want to hang a lesser charge on you to satisfy their need to know that justice was served. Knowing and accepting this and how it also applies to the prosecutor are part of embracing the suck of self-defense. (Remember poison and antidote?)

There's a reason I waited so long before flopping the monkey's moralistic, judgmental bias onto the table like a dead smelly fish. It was so you could go back and review all the things I've said in this new light, a beacon that can do wonders to keep you out of prison. Often when we take in new information, we review it through our existing standards. How well we understand it is based on what we already know. We try to integrate new information not with existing information but with beliefs. We believe this to be true so to be deemed true, the new information must fit with this.

Now you know a lot more about violence. But even then, it is judged by our monkey. How much of what you've read so far has irritated you? Bored you? Made you feel like it's hopeless? Confused you? Made you want to just say screw it? *All* of these are monkey reactions to the world not behaving the way it wants; to information not meshing with what it believes or wants to believe is true. But the more you know, the more you understand, the easier it is. As this happens, your perceptions change. Not necessarily in huge ways or at least big ways that happen all at once. Often, the biggest changes come about through lots and lots of small steps.

Reading this has already changed how you look at this subject. As of right now, odds are good you're less likely to become involved in unnecessary violence than you were when you picked up this the book. Not that you were wanting to go out and find trouble, but now your understanding of 'unnecessary' is different.

Getting back on track . . . Well, sort of. To spoof The Who song, *Won't Get Fooled Again*: "And the monkey who spurred us on sits in judgment of all wrong."

Earlier in this book, I mentioned that the majority of violence erupts over feelings. I also talked about the difference between physical sensation, emotions, and how we mistake our feelings for reality. People have seen the monkey spur other people into violence (hell, it might even have been them). That's their default assumption about *what* causes violence. In fact, many people can't themselves become violent with another human without strong emotions—so they assume the same about you. The assumption is you had to be an out-of-control monkey. Here's another assumption: Violence is wrong and only bad people engage in it. Ergo, your out-of-control monkey was at fault. Shortened down, it means one thing: You are *bad*. So now it's an offended, bigoted monkey that sits in judgment of you over something *it* believes was actually bad monkey behavior. Oh yeah, then there's this little Catch 22: Anyone who can do violence without emotion must be a monster. So if you weren't an out-of-control monkey, you're a monster. ~sigh~

Some of these people *will* sit on the jury. Your boatload of evidence isn't going to sway them. What *will* be more likely to sway them are the ten other jurors. The ones saying, "Damn it, this was self-defense!" Many studies have been done on the effects of peer pressure. It's hard to be the hold-out in a room of people who—having seen the same evidence— came to different conclusions. It's those ten people whom you need to convince

Kitty Genovese was murdered in 1964. The mythology is thirty-eight neighbors looking down from their apartment windows, witnessed her murder, and did nothing (condemning so-called good people for letting an innocent woman die). Not only did the media misreport what actually happened, but movies, popular fiction, and nonfiction references cemented the idea of 'by-stander effect.'

The details of the case actually were quite different—including the fact there were two attacks, the first occurring outside in the street. This was only witnessed by a few. More than that, they didn't realize it was a knife attack. Her soon-to-be killer fled, thereby apparently ending the incident. The actual rape and murder took place inside a building, in isolation at about 3:30 a.m. Kitty had managed to get into the building and collapsed in the hallway. Her attacker returned, searched the area, found her, and attacked her again. Thirty-eight people? If they weren't standing in the hall, they didn't *witness* the rape and murder, much less do nothing. But that's the story we believe about her death.

Let's fast forward to your case. Eventually, after consideration of evidence the jury is going to have to make a judgment about the appropriateness of your use of force. Sooner or later, morals, ethics, and judgment will come into the process. But you *don't* want them to start from a close-minded, prejudged (violence is always bad) perspective.

Our monkey judgments and assumptions are like looking out the windows of our apartment building. They distance us from actual events. They color our perceptions of what we think we see. (E.g., the few who did witness the first attack on Kitty assumed it was a domestic dispute.) Looking from one particular building also limits what we can see. But we *think* we've seen it all and know what happened. Yet, that one perspective doesn't let us know what we didn't see. For example, it's easy to mistake a stabbing for a punch if you don't know what to look for *or* if you don't see the knife because you are too far away. Also because of different perspectives, people in different buildings will see different aspects of an event. As an example of different perspectives, someone can hold a knife in a way that it's unseen by the person in front, but someone standing behind can see the blade clearly. Yet, people are convinced that—from their perspective—they see and understand the whole truth about what happened.

Working with this building analogy, you and the person who lives across the street both think violence is bad. Your perspective, however, allows for people acting in self-defense. The person across the street thinks only stupid and evil people use violence.

If that person were ever to get involved in a self-defense situation, he's going to want you on his jury. But you probably don't want him on yours. In the meantime, the prosecutor will to try and run up to his apartment, knock on the door, and tell him what happened. Now he 'knows' what happened without ever leaving the comfort of his apartment.

The defense's challenge is to go into that apartment building, take the elevator, knock on his door, get him to come out, ride the elevator down to street level, look at the raw (nonjudgmental) evidence, then walk him over to other buildings, get into the elevator, and show him a different perspective. This is all done so he can make an informed decision not a monkey judgmental one, like the prosecutor wants him to decide.

because they'll sway the other two. This is also why—during the aftermath—there's going to be nitpicky examination of your actions beforehand. The monkeys are looking for a reason to confirm what they already believe. Knowing this will help you recognize how your actions *before* the incident can be used as a means of bias confirmation. Anger, aggression, hostility, threats, they'll *all* be used to undermine your claim of self-defense. Use awareness of this bias to guide your behavior in all stages of the process. Let me count (some of) the ways and at what stage:

Before: First, try to prevent it altogether. Second, encourage yourself to do everything in your power to avoid it. Third, by trying to prevent or avoid it you create witnesses and video to corroborate your version of events.

During: Fourth, this will influence the degree of force you use (to help you to be effective and to keep you from crossing out of the SD square). Fifth, it will motivate you to end it quickly. The longer an event goes on, the more it looks like a consensual fight or a beating.

After: Sixth, when dealing with the police it helps you recognize common pitfalls. Seventh, it bumps up your credibility with the police. Eighth, it helps you communicate to your attorney and the jury that your actions were within necessary levels. Ninth ties back to the second point, you can provide evidence that shows you sincerely tried to avoid the situation.

Some of those connections can seem a little vague, but they are very real. Let's talk about the points in the middle of a situation for example. Knowing about the bias can help you choose to use an open hand instead of a closed fist to deliver force. Why? It's not merely to protect your hand from breaking; a closed fist used to punch is perceived as more violent than an open-hand strike—even though open-hand strikes deliver more force (when done right).

Back in my bouncing days, I often used well targeted open-hand strikes. The video showed the other person swinging on me. It also showed that all I did was put up my hands to block as I moved out of the way. My attacker was so drunk, he fell down. I gathered him up and walked him to the door. The only person who was seen to throw a punch was my attacker. In truth, he felt like his brains had exploded. He really needed to be helped to the door. But I was never seen to throw a punch—much less multiple strikes. What the investigating officer (and his attorney) didn't know was I'd hit him effectively and accurately in a spot that causes the nervous system to temporarily shut down. Because it was over so fast, it greatly reduced my chances of being arrested and sued. I was not seen to be beating the guy or fighting him. A well placed, open hand was a strategy I used in a professional capacity—a profession where in a bad month, I had more violent encounters than most people have in their entire lives. Although I talked with the cops quite a bit, I was *never* arrested or sued doing that job. A big part of why is because I knew how to play the game. I knew the limits and biases and how not to run afoul of them. It. Can. Be. Done. But you have to invest the time and effort.

My fourth reason for telling why you need to know how to play this bias game is because it *will* be played *against* you. I have seen people who were absolute out-of-control berserks during the incident suddenly turn into the most cooperative, meekest, butter wouldn't melt in their mouths, sweet, and innocent Little Red Riding Hoods—when the cops showed up. Three guesses who they pointed at and said was the Big Bad Wolf?

First the good news, the cops have had this act pulled on them before. Now the not-so-bad news, you're going to have to come up with *truths* that make you look good faster than your opponent can come up with lies that make you look bad. (If you kept from going all monkey, it's not hard to do.) Now more good news, if you were planning and operating with bias in mind even facing the Lil' Red Riding Hood act is easy. Like asking him to explain certain evidence, "If that's true, then why . . . ?" Now the bad news if you gave into your monkey, you're hosed.[109]

My fifth reason for telling you about that not-so-intellectual bias comes back to something I alluded to earlier—people's dirty little secret about violence. And that is: People are *constantly* violent, they just don't want to *admit* it, *especially* to themselves.

I mentioned this in passing earlier. But when someone's monkey has

---

109   Another thing you need to know, until an actual arrest is made the police are under no legal obligation—or duty—to tell you the truth. In building a case, they can lie like rugs. They can (and on occasion will) tell you stuff to trigger an emotional monkey reaction. Even if the guy is around the corner swearing, "Damn right I hit that mofo. Bring him back here, and I'll kick his butt again," they'll often tell you, "Well, Little Red Riding Hood said . . ." Keep your monkey on a leash, before, during, and afterward.

defined them as nonviolent, you'll be amazed at the back flips and other mental gymnastics they perform to keep from admitting they've been screaming, feces-throwing, biting, clawing, violent monkeys. Some people believe violence is never ever acceptable—except oddly enough when they're the ones doing it. Because of the attitude that violence is bad—but I'm a good person—there are some wildly violent people who tell themselves they aren't violent. That can make handling them a bit tricky. Keep this in mind because it is a huge element in the fact that someone is going to be unhappy with your use of force. There're a whole lot of people who apparently don't really object to being in a violent situation. What they object to is *not* winning—beginning with their it-all-started-when-he-hit-me-back attitude. This is commonly accompanied by minimizing and outright dismissal of their own physical violence. "That didn't hurt" is one common version; "you deserved it" is another.

But you don't normally see that until after the *denial* that they hit you doesn't work.

"You hit me."

"No, I didn't."

"Yes, you did."

"I did not."

Third person, "Yes, you hit him."

Pause, "Well, it didn't hurt." Or "Well, you deserved it."

I wish I was joking, but I am *serious* about this. I tell you that because the same people also will go all out with a threat display and then squeal loudest when you take them seriously. As far as they were concerned that *wasn't* an attack, it was simply showing you how serious they were. How dare you punch them in the face when they lunged at you! They weren't going to attack you! You attacked them! (Never mind, they developed JAM to nine—in their *minds* they weren't attacking you.) And the people they are crying to are often the police. It's from the violence-is-bad folks you get the worst mental gymnastics about their own violence. I mean bends, twists, and flips that would make parkour free runners gulp in disbelief. Gloria Steinem summed it up beautifully, "From pacifist to terrorist, each person condemns violence—and then adds one cherished case in which it may be justified."

Stop and think about that for a few seconds. How have you seen that manifest in your life? I also want you to consider it in the context of how someone can farm out violence to third parties—because that's a biggie with the 'I'm not violent' crowd. Nice, civilized people rely on the police to do the violence for them and take this bad and evil man away. This allows the person to agree that violence is sometimes necessary, but that concurrence includes some wiggle room—specifically to rationalize since they're *not* the ones doing it, they aren't violent—even when they sic the cops on you. Not just to enforce their will, but to win, as well as teach you a lesson. They won't stoop to kicking you, they'll have a 'servant' do it for them.

But I want you to look at this from a bigger perspective. What does farming out violence do to one's perceptions *about* violence? If you don't have to do it yourself, how easy is it to tell yourself you're not violent? If you don't have to do it yourself, you have no idea about what is actually involved. In farming it out, what you think you know about violence is never challenged. If you've never been hit or hit someone, how easy is it to believe it's the end of the world? How effortless is it to believe someone who tells you that violence is a trauma a person will never move past (particularly important with Little Bo Peeps and campaigns to raise awareness). How many people believe their personal safety is someone else's job? And perhaps most troublesome, how many people believe they can physically assault you and then have you arrested if you respond?

These can be the same people sitting on your jury. The people you are going to have to convince with a boxcar full of evidence. Switching analogies, your lawyer is going to have to get them out of their comfy apartments, down to the elevator, and walk them over to other perspectives.

I'm going to expand on something. There appears to be an attitude out there that goes like this: Violence is bad. I am a good person. Furthermore, I believe anyone who uses violence is bad, ignorant, and wrong. Therefore, what I am doing is *not* violence. It can't be violence because I am a good, nonviolent person. Laid out like this, it's really stupid and obvious. Welcome to the advanced mental gymnastics part of the evening.

If you categorically deem violence bad, you have to come up with some nifty ways to exclude yourself from it. It seems like a great many people's definition of violence is: Any level of force *beyond* what I am comfortable using to get what I want. Got it? If I win, it's not violent. Basically, violence is anything past my comfort zone. That's scary enough, but let's start with the caveats: Caveat A—It's violence when the same level is used against me. Caveat B—When I'm really emotional—maybe what I did was violent, but I get a free pass because of my feelings. I can still call myself a good person. C, and the biggest caveat of them all—It's okay for me to act in 'self-defense,' but not you—even if I'm attacking. (If you effectively defend yourself from me that's violence and wrong.)

Flopping these rationalizations onto the table like this is important. Like your life may depend on it important. That's because people who use violence against you or engage in dangerous—even life-threatening—behavior often *don't* see it that way. Why? Their monkeys won't let them see what they're doing in that context. It's hard to believe that someone who just threw a bottle at you doesn't believe he or she is being violent. But it's true. You'd think someone screaming obscenities in your face and mimicking pre-attack indicators would admit that he or she is acting violently. No, there is a huge disconnect between an emotional person's actions and what she or he thinks they are doing. Violence is bad, they're good; therefore, what they are doing *isn't* violent.

Look at Caveat B. That only comes around after they've admitted that maybe what they did was violent. In the heat of the moment, it's *all* about their emotions. Violent? Putting you into danger? Who cares! They're furious; you deserve to die. Okay, so what about situations that are still emotionally hot, but not homicidal infernos? It still applies. Whatever happens to you, you *deserve* whatever pain you suffer. What about moments that aren't really hot at all? Again, same thing.

I used to ride a motorcycle. On numerous occasions, I had a driver look directly at me and intentionally pull into my lane. This was *not* a case of their not seeing me. As often as not, they looked me in the eye before forcing me into evasive driving. The impression I got was, "I'm bigger. Get out of my way." Intentionally cutting into a biker's lane can be construed as attempted murder.[110] Yet if you were to ask any of these people if they'd ever tried to kill someone, they'd answer—with complete perceptual honesty—no. Pretty much anybody who has ever ridden bikes has these stories. While it is easy to imagine it was some redneck truck driver doing it, the biggest culprits were usually affluent middle-aged women, driving nice cars. Again if you asked them, these women would deny they endangered someone. ("He changed lanes, he wasn't in danger.") They would emphatically deny they were trying to kill anybody.

If we define lying as the conscious supplying of false information with the intention to deceive, they would *not* be lying. Their intentions were focused on other goals, other objectives. That is what their monkeys are judging their actions on and—more importantly—as. For the sake of this example, let's assume "I want over" was their primary intent. The "get out of my way you disgusting, dirty biker" was a much lesser motive for their aggressive driving. (Of course, the latter was much more emotionally satisfying to their subconscious monkey. "I scared him, tee, hee, hee.") But trying to kill me? No, never. They're good people. They'd never do

---

110   Although now days, it would be easier to get a road rage or reckless endangerment conviction.

that. So, they tell themselves they were only switching lanes. As such, they are literally *blind* to the dangers their deliberate actions created— even though they directly benefited on multiple levels from the threat created by their actions. Yet by focusing on what they intended to do, they allow for a subconscious disconnect between themselves and their actions. They don't think they've ever tried to kill anybody because that was not their *intent* when they acted.

The significance of this is threefold. Too often this blindness to the danger they're creating is what's going to come flying at you. Part of *why* they are coming so hard (and with such commitment) is they don't recognize the extent of the danger they are creating, especially if someone is just trying to scare you. Next even if they were trying to hurt you, it was to punish you for hurting their feelings. They weren't expecting *that* much damage or for you to die. Still another is what happens if you successfully react. If that person lives—a teary eyed, innocent Little Bo Peep is going to sit on the witness stand.

Once again, it's not their intent, it's the action (jeopardy) that you base your force decisions on. *Don't* try to argue with their story. That will be colored by what they thought their intent was. And that's another reason you need to show up with evidence that Bo Peep's story *isn't* what happened. You want the cops to give that story the hairy eyeball. This is a lot easier to do earlier on (because at the scene, his act isn't usually perfected yet). This is important to keep from being arrested. And this still applies if the situation is so serious, you have to wait to make a statement.[111] It's doubly important if it all goes to trial because by then the Little Bo Peep act will be well entrenched.[112]

There's something you need to be aware of. It seems an attitude many folks have today is: If I didn't *intend* it to happen, I *shouldn't* be held accountable for unexpected and negative results. That's what you will deal with. I'm not going to speculate where this attitude came from. But you can see it in action when people yelp things like, "I didn't mean to shoot him; I just wanted to scare him!" Hang on. You went out of your way to bring a loaded gun to a situation you knew was going to be confrontational. When things became heated, you didn't try to withdraw. Instead, you pulled your gun, pointed it in his direction, screamed some more, and pulled the trigger. Now which part of that are we supposed to

---

111   I like Massad Ayoob's advice to tell the cops your name, point them toward evidence and witnesses, then shut up until your attorney gets there.

112   Here's a hint, do full disclosure with your attorney about anything that can torpedo your case. Lawyers *hate* being blindsided. At the same time, an effective torpedoing of someone's Little Red Riding Hood act works on a deeper level than just presentation of the evidence. People, who felt compassion and empathy for Ms. Hood, feel betrayed and suckered when they find out they were lied to.

ignore in order to believe you didn't act intentionally? Laid out like this, it sounds like a lie. Your human brain isn't going to believe that any more than if you claimed the gun magically appeared in front of the person and went off by itself.

But our monkey is good at assigning the absolutely *best* motives to what we do. So bringing the gun for self-protection et al is exactly what the monkey tells that person happened as the person was consciously doing it. Their monkey honestly believes—and by extension so do they— that they were only trying to scare the guy. They literally did not intend to shoot the person. In their *subjective* point of view, it *just* happened. Five points arise from this attitude:

1) You'll often deal with people who believe they are not acting violently.
2) They'll be coming at you hard and fast with this 'nonviolence.'
3) They *won't* see the signs and warnings that would scare off a person familiar with violence—so they'll keep on coming.
4) Your decision to act must be based on jeopardy, ability, and means *not* what they intend.
5) They'll squeal like a guinea pig when things go wrong (like calling the police, suing you, seeking vendetta, or other vindictive actions).

Let's look at number three's 'won't see.' That comes in many forms. In descending order of frequency: Usually they are so emotionally invested in winning, they'll ignore everything else. They actually see it, they just cognitively block it (are mentally blind to it). Less frequent, but very common is the belief you won't act—whether they think you *won't* react to what they're doing, expect you to act a certain way, display raw inexperience about different options, or believe they have a right. (I've seen them all.) Occasionally, they legitimately won't recognize the danger. (Lacking environmental knowledge, they don't recognize an 'ahhh hell' signal that would cause an experienced player to back pedal.) Often, you'll get a hybrid mix of these various types of stupid. Be aware of and ready for this *kind* of person. They are more common than professional muggers. And if they target you for their nonviolent fury, they *can be* more dangerous. Why? Because what they're doing is subjective—especially about what qualifies as winning. Some will stop, some won't.

A professional mugger sees you as an ATM with legs. Accept the deal he's offering and the robbery script is pretty safe. It's also very predictable—especially if you don't try to personalize it. (People worry about muggers on drugs becoming violent. For the record, that does happen. But more often, the victim breaks the script and antagonizes the mugger. That—drugs or not—is what provokes the violence.) The reason out-of-control monkeys can be more dangerous is because they are playing for a subjective monkey win, an emotional victory that is *entirely* dictated by their emotional satisfaction—at the moment. This is not crazy, but it *is* out-of-control emotions.

News flash here, the majority of murders take place between people who know each other during emotionally charged circumstances. A melting down monkey with a knife is just as dangerous as the common self-defense boogeymen (e.g., a crazy person, someone crashing from drugs, or a sociopath with a knife). It doesn't matter if the melting down monkey is a family member, friend, or spouse. The reason such a person can be more dangerous is—being emotionally invested—we make bad threat assessments and tactical errors.

My next point requires two qualifiers. Qualifier A: We personally tend to think in terms of intent. This is a twofold philosophy. One, we're lax about assigning ill intent to ourselves, yet fast to assign it to certain others. Our monkey tells us, "I didn't mean anything by what I said, but he did." (That simple qualifier is a doorway into a universe of psychology, people skills, and culture, but we'll just let it stand.) Two, intent also plays another important social function about forgiveness. Both play an important part in what I'm about to say. Qualifier B: Legally, sometimes intent matters—usually not. With said qualifiers in mind, overall the law doesn't give a damn about what was intended. You are accountable for the *results* of your actions, irregardless of your *intent*. Knowing this simple fact puts you miles ahead of the other person.

Going back to the second half of qualifier A: Socially we use judging intent to cut people slack, so we can get along. This is a bit of an availability bias. It's easier to remember the times we assigned ill intent, so we overlook how often we allow intent or it's *lack* to sway us. This tendency to forgive is an important element in the ability to function socially. It influences our choice of reactions to a situation. Yeah, he said it, but he didn't mean anything by it. Yes, he broke it, but he's six. It was an honest mistake. So as often as we condemn with intent, more often we are giving people the benefit of the doubt.

This is the direct opposite of how it works legally. There, the only thing intent does is make it worse. In certain crimes, *intent* plays a big part in the degree of the charges filed. It's called mens rea (literally, guilty mind). This can be the difference between murder and manslaughter charges. They're still going to try to hold you liable for an illegal homicide, but it's from bad to worse. Overall, when it comes to assigning responsibility, action is *more* important than intent. It doesn't matter you only intended to scare him, you threw the bottle. You are the one who, while drunk, got behind the wheel. It doesn't matter that you didn't intend to attack the cop, you lunged at him. It doesn't matter that you were only firing a warning shot, you discharged a firearm within the city limits. It doesn't matter that you were scared, you shot the guy as he was turning away from you. You are *responsible* for your actions regardless of your *intent.*

This can be a blessing in disguise. And the reason is JAM. Again, don't argue with what the person meant to do. *Stick* with JAM. What was their behavior (jeopardy)? When it came to developing the means to attack, jeopardy was important as it changed the significance of his getting close. You can only assess the situation from what you see them doing, *not* what you think they meant to do. The factors that made for the assessment not just your internal state are what you *have* to communicate. Why is this important? When someone's violence doesn't work out, you can usually set your watch by two things:

One is—unless it failed spectacularly—how fast they'll crank up the action. A common phrase in the shooting world is "stop the threat." It's an attitude that many in empty-hand self-defense need to look into. If your use of force is ineffective to stop the threat, it's going to enrage him more—and you end up fighting him. Without going into the subject too deeply, you want any conflict to end as soon as possible. If things jump to a physical level, you want that part of the program over *now!* You do not want it to turn into a fight. The longer physical violence extends (as in the less effective you are) the more it's going to look like you were fighting. This is a big reason why many empty-hand self-defense claims are scuttled. Knowing where and how to hit, other moves to combine with a blow, and a this-ends-now attitude are extremely important. (Again, it's past the scope of this book, so I'll cover it in another one.) Instead of a long, drawn-out brawl, you need to tailor your moves so it's over as soon as possible.

Two—when it does fail—how fast they go into "I'm-the-victim-here" mode. In case you haven't noticed, I call this behavior the Little Bo Peep act. Because they're going to run around, looking high and low for people who believe their tale of woe. They'll gush about their innocence, what they weren't doing (e.g., attacking you) and what they meant to do. They weren't trying to hurt you. Oh, that? They just wanted to _____(fill in blank).

You counter this narrative with statements about jeopardy. *That's* what you focus on. This little shift in focus makes a big difference. Number one, you *can't* argue his intentions. Again, you are not a mind reader. Remember this because when talking to the cops, his story of his intent will totally change. Changing, for example, from "going to kick your . . ." to "I was defending myself." Number two, instead of trying to articulate his intent, you describe his actions that led you to the reasonable conclusion you were in immediate danger. This is the difference between you saying, "He was going to kick my butt" versus "first, he said he was going to mess me up; then he closed the distance into attack range and raised his shoulder and fist as if to punch me." The first detail is easy for the other person to deny. The second one, however . . .

I tell you this because I can guarantee you after someone loses, his intentions are to go straight into Little Bo Peep mode, especially if the cops *aren't* called. Let me tell you, a co-worker who takes a swing at you will look for allies after the incident. He's going to run around and tell everyone his side of the story. This is common monkey behavior. Basically, it's an attempt to embed oneself further into the crowd in hope of:

a) Not being kicked out of the group (fired)

b) Possibly getting you fired

You have a choice, either play the same game or tell the boss what happened and remain mum about it to co-workers (don't forget to tell the boss this is your plan). Or just pull back among your own crew, let them know what happened, and let them handle the gossip and office politics. No matter what option you take—keep your work production *up*. If someone has to be fired, make sure you're the more valuable employee. And that includes *not* making waves by telling everyone else what a jackass he was. (In other words, be very careful about playing the same game as Lil' Bo Peep.) Because such people *honestly* believe they weren't being violent, they'll be convincing when telling others how it's completely your fault. They become really good liars—due to the simple fact they believe they are telling the truth.

I say that with a caveat. Unlike Officer Friendly (who has just arrived at the scene and doesn't know anybody) and the jury—often there are other people who have a history with the Bo Peep. And that history weighs heavily for or against whether or not they believe his story that it was entirely your fault. Something I read many years ago: Of ten people, two will love you, two are going to hate you, the other six don't care.[113] Peep's people are going to believe his or her story no matter what. Your people aren't going to believe it, no matter what. It will be how both of you have treated (and behaved around) the other six that determine what tale gets any traction. If you're known as calm, friendly, and professional—while Bo Peep is renowned for a bad temper and acting up—her or his story *isn't* going to fly. Those six will look at Peep and say, "No, I know so-and-so. He wouldn't do that." Now Bo Peep has an additional rep for lying. But if you're known as an jackass even *if* Peep is lying, people are going to say, "Well, maybe it did happen like that."

I also can guarantee you that all information about pre-attack indicators, violence, and aggression is going to be left out of Peep's

113   Bob Burton, *Bounty Hunter*, 1984

version of the story. That's why you have to supply the details he (or she) won't want el jeffe (the boss) to know. If you aren't expecting this, it can be shocking how fast some will run to the police, your boss, human resources, or whatever community both of you are in. If they can't win one way, they'll win another—by having the other entity punish you for them (farming out the violence to a third party). While I attribute this as another version of winning, I've seen it most often among people who don't believe they're violent—specifically middle-class, white folks. As in it doesn't matter that they tried to hit you with a bottle, *you* committed assault when you punched them. They also are really damned fast to threaten you with a lawyer before and after things go physical. I tell you this because people who have successfully defended themselves (after the aggressor has left) are often surprised when a police car pulls up. Or when they get served with notice that they're being sued. Or when they get called into the boss's office. *Don't be.* Call it vendetta. Call it a need to win. Call it revenge. People whose monkeys need to win are a reality. Now whether that is tattling to the cops or to his six friends (so they'll come back with him to stomp you) . . . well . . . that's kind of the luck of the draw.

I'm about to help you make a huge paradigm shift regarding violence. To do this, let's start with the *Random House Unabridged Dictionary* definition:

Violence: 1) Swift and intense force: *the violence of a storm.* 2) Rough or injurious physical force, action, treatment: *to die by violence.* 3) An unjust or unwarranted exertion of force or power, as against rights, laws, etc.: *To take over a government by violence.* 4) A violent act or proceeding. 5) Rough or immoderate vehemence as of feeling or language: *the violence of his hatred.* 6) Injury, as in distortion of meaning or fact: *to do violence to a translation.*

This is another reason I waited this long. I wanted you to know about people acting violently without considering what they do as violence. You can see from definition three on that someone can be extremely violent without *ever* using physical force. Someone who is mean-spirited, aggressive, hostile, and verbally lashing out at others *is* violent. Someone going off on a clerk for giving incorrect change *is* violent. Someone who runs to an authority to get you into trouble *is* violent (farming it out, mind you, but still violent). As is someone who uses force without physically attacking you (slamming things down, hitting walls, or throwing things against the wall while screaming and yelling). That *is* violence.

And this is where the mental gymnastics start. (Remember? Any level of force beyond that with which I am comfortable . . .) This belief allows them to maintain their self-identity as good, nonviolent people. But there's more than that. Even though they do not recognize it as violence, they *reap* the benefits of their aggressive, hostile, and violent behavior. This goes beyond simple denial (although that happens, too—particularly when it's pointed out to them.) With their new and improved definition of violence, they sincerely *believe* their behavior *does not* qualify. That makes them right with God. And when the Almighty is backing your play, you have *no* hesitation about it.

Such folks 'know' what violence is. What they do is not that (or so they tell themselves). Except, by acting this way:

a) They get what they want (which encourages further bad behavior).

b) They don't know—or follow—the 'rules' of violence.

c) They are more reckless, sloppy, and unpredictable than someone who knows he or she is being violent.

The reason I'm spending so much time on this issue is because out-of-control monkey violence is what you are *most likely* to run into. Mugger, robber, serial rapist? Not so much. Someone who'll bust a bottle over your head or take a swing at you? Yep. Lots of them out there.

For the record, there are all kinds of people in this world who have absolutely no problem with you dying so they can get what they want— whether they farm it out to others or pull the trigger themselves. As long as they get what they want, they're cool with whatever it takes. More common is someone who doesn't *think* what he or she is doing is (all that) dangerous to you. Because it's not dangerous, they're *really* committed to doing it. See, he and his five friends were just going to stomp you a little bit. She's only waving that knife around to scare you. His ground-and-pound with your head on concrete is simply to teach you a lesson. The list goes on and on . . . That kind of behavior is, however, way down the road. By the time it manifests, odds are good you've made several mistakes along the way.

First, the good news: An overwhelming majority of out-of-control monkey violence can be resolved without having to go physical. There's only one tiny catch, *if*—and that is a big if—you can keep from turning into an out-of-control monkey, too. (Also known as the source of your making several mistakes along the way.) If you can remain calm and polite, you can usually bring someone's torqued-off monkey down and find a reasonable compromise.

Now the bad news—until you train it to do so—your monkey couldn't care less about finding a reasonable compromise, developing a win/win, determining legal consequences, or finding the smart thing to do. The jell with that. What it cares about is *winning*. It's all about showing this other monkey where it's at. This is a biggie. You may think you can remain calm and in control of your monkey, but a really good analogy is trying to drive in heavy traffic with a kid screaming and kicking the back of your seat. The monkey's desire to win influences your behavior.

That's why it's a smart idea to reframe your monkey definition of winning. (For example, a win becomes how slick you were about monkey wrangling and resolving the situation without violence.) Remember I told you acting in self-defense is a choice? That choice has consequences. The reason most people get arrested for defending themselves is because they *weren't*. And that comes from letting their monkey define things. Like, oh, say, what is violence and what is self-defense. Their monkeys drive them toward goals of violence—not self-defense. At the same time when an out-of-control monkey comes screaming down on you, it's *hard* not to react the same way. Simultaneously—if you don't know how to check that reaction—acting the same way will demolish your self-defense claim. (And yes, I'll show you how to do this in a bit.)

Knowing about out-of-control monkeys is why it's critical to look at conflict and violence divided into thirds—before, during, and after. First, this overarching perspective keeps you from falling into it from that mindset (and making mistakes that take it out of the self-defense square). Second, if you find yourself in out-of-control monkey head space, you grab the leash and jerk yourself out of it. Without knowing the stuff you know now, it's nearly impossible—when things move at 120 mph (miles per hour)—to safely get the steering wheel away from the monkey. (By that time, the monkey has been driving for a while.) It can be *done*, and again I'll show you how. But when you're going 120 no matter who you are, it'll be rough. It's far better to take control of the monkey when things are moving much more slowly. You do this, so things don't speed up.

But let's get back to someone's monkey telling her she's not being violent while she throws things at you. Four significant problems arise from this attitude that denies violence:

- One: Violence is a collective set of behaviors.
- Two: Violence provokes violence.
- Three: Experienced people—who knowingly use violence—also acknowledge it can be used right back against them.
- Four: Inexperienced people are overcommitted.

We're going to spend some serious time here. These four components are deeply intertwined. They also tend to feed off each other and escalate situations. In fact, let's make them their own chapter. But before we do, we're going to take a trip into some nuts-and-bolts stuff about recognizing when you're in danger.

CHAPTER 11

What is perhaps most remarkable about "aggressive," "agonistic," "fighting," or "contest" behaviors is that the violent examples given above are exceptions rather than the rule. In most cases, contests are settled through the use of non-injurious aggressive behaviors such as displays and trials of strength.

—**Mark Briffa**
Territoriality and Aggression

Threat Displays and Pre-Attack Indicators

Before we start, know that posturing and threat displays *don't* have to be loud and obnoxious. A parent gives a misbehaving child a stern look. A boss jabs a finger at you while making a point. A cop asks someone, "Do you want to go to jail?" A lawyer sends a letter. These all are threats we recognize and use. We often don't consciously and rationally notice threat displays. Most of the time, we're just too damned busy reacting to them or throwing them at other people. But there's another reason we miss them: They aren't the ones we're used to.

In a functional group, someone giving you 'a look' can be sending a big enough threat display or posture to cause you to change your behavior. A subtle but pointed comment sends the message to knock it off. Our bosses do it, our spouses do it, our parents did it, our teachers did it. In less functional (or more committed situations) voices raise. Truculent glares and body postures are employed—jaws jut, hands wave, items are slammed down on tables. If the person responds with similar behavior, the situation escalates—usually growing louder and more excited. Eventually, things *might* cross over into physical violence. But here's the important part, usually it doesn't.[114] If you send the *right* monkey signal, the situation de-escalates.

That's where things get a little tricky. The question is: What's the right signal? Is it, "Mine is the bigger wee-wee, you are an underling?" (You will

---

114   There's a third type. They're a bizarre mixture of subtle signals, but extreme violence. This gives the false impression such people act 'without warning.' No, the warnings were there. It's just the target didn't recognize the significance of the signal. Starting with how quiet (and often polite) it was. A common source of bloodshed is how often people from the second group mistake quiet and polite of the third for weakness and fear (assuming it to be first group behavior).

do the job this way.) Or is the signal, "Okay! Okay! I'm not a threat. I'm not challenging you." (Either I submit to your authority or I don't want to fight about it.) Or is it, "You don't belong here—leave" (territoriality)? Or is the right signal, "Okay, I'm leaving?" Or is the signal, "Stop what you are doing or I will rain hell upon you?" (Knock it off, right now.) Or is it, "I will stop the unacceptable behavior and behave?" (No need to get cranky, we can all co-exist.) Or is it, "Let's solve it using other scripts?" (Empathy display or redirection)

Generally speaking that depends on the circumstances, the personalities involved, the relationship, and the environment. Any of those seven strategies or signals *might* work given certain circumstances. In other circumstances, there's a good chance they'll cause things to escalate. For example, as an underling at work, you don't try to cow the CEO using the same dominance displays that he does. You don't walk into another person's home and treat it as your own. You don't try to order an equal around. A cop doesn't treat his or her spouse the same way he or she handles a quarrelsome drunk. The signals themselves are not wrong, but the *use* is. They are the same signals, but can be used in wildly inappropriate times and circumstances.

It's tricky enough to figure out the correct response given social situations. But there are times when *none* is the right answer because the situation *isn't* social in nature. In fact, there are times where those monkey signals are not only the wrong answer, but a green light for a predator to attack. Ohhh big scary! But that's less common than your fears tell you. A far greater basis for physical violence is when two people throw monkey signals and decide, "Back down? Oh hell no!" Viola! Instant escalation! When someone throws aggressive threat displays, they hope that the other person will respond with *non*confrontational counter signals. You go, "Grrr, grr." The other person backs down (and communicates this by throwing the appropriate signal). If *not*, the situation escalates —occasionally to physical violence.

Remember, the primary purpose of threat displays is to *avoid* physical violence whether by bluff or communication of actual danger. Yes, threat displays show how serious someone is. At the same time, balls-to-the-wall violence looks like the pen in the throat attack from *Casino*. (Part of why it's so 'scary' is because Nicky attacked without any prior communication). Things get real serious when both sides are going at each other at that level—there is *no* showing, it's doing. I tell you this because we are so accustomed to threat displays working, we fall into two common traps:

   1) We default to them.
   2) We assume specific ones will be present.

The reason they are traps is that the monkey throws them out or expects to see them without our even knowing we're doing them. By defaulting to that behavior, we fail to think of likely responses or possible consequences if they *don't* work. (And bad news, they often don't.) Assuming specific ones will be displayed, we think we're safe if we don't see them or think they'll be in a recognized order. Not necessarily . . . Later, I'll talk about the road *of* violence and the mile markers. Threat displays play a big part of it. As do those two (speed) traps.

To keep from making either mistake, we need to make the subconscious conscious. Failing to do so is a fast track to noticing lost teeth the next morning. To keep your dental work in place, you have to:

a) Not act out threat displays *without* thinking
b) Recognize when what you're dealing with is different from your *normal* expectations.

In his book, *Ape in the Corner Office* (2007) Richard Conniff made a simple but brilliant observation about threat displays: "They are not saying I am attacking, but rather I MIGHT (emphasis his)!" Keep that in mind because it differentiates between the communication of a threat display and when an attack is starting. Oh by the way, although they are commonly called pre-attack indicators, it's more accurate to call them stage one of the three stages of an attack (beginning, middle, and end). So-called pre-attack indicators are very much stage one of the attack. Unless you do something to abort the process, you're going to experience stage two.

There are many threat display behaviors, and they are both foreseeable and easily recognized. That takes us back to the bricks, JAM, assessment, and articulation. But like adrenal stress, it is not a check list, it's a list of possibilities.

Change of voice—Three main options: 1) Shouting, yelling, and screaming (common monkey threats) or 2) condemning, hostile, and contemptuous tone or 3) lowering of the voice, making it growly or more monotone or some unique combination specific to that person.

Change of word choice—This especially applies to insults, slurs, belittling terms, and (if you know the person) use of acknowledged hot button words. Profanity is a common sign of escalating hostility, anger, and contempt. The question is whether the profanity is used for emphasis ("what the hell is going on here?") or in a personal attack ("what the hell is wrong with you?") One is the sign of anger, the other of directed hostility.

Speech cadence or word emphasis—Speech either speeds up or slows down. ("WhattheHELL is happening here?" versus "What. The. Hell. is happening here?")

Facial grimaces or expressions—Frowns, open-mouth snarls, or barking expressions, narrowed eyes, bug eyes, pursed lips, thin lips, flaring nostrils, beetled brows, and similar facial contortions are the most obvious. With others, however, flat, deadpan, deliberately neutral are the warning signs particularly with those people experienced with committing violence.

Lean—The person either leans forward (toward you) or rocks back in a specific way. Don't mistake this backward lean for running, backing away, an "I'm submitting" signal, or any indication he is scared of you. There's a certain form of rockin' back that is him winding up. (If you don't get out of his face, he's going to hit you so hard you'll get a speeding ticket in El Paso, Texas.)

Chin jut—Man, if that thing was sharpened, it could put out an eye. He's sticking it out so far, it's almost as if he were trying to poke you with his chin. This is very common in combination with forward lean and facial expressions.

Chin lift—A subset of chin behavior. Chin lifts are strongly cultural and done in combination with other signals. One set of the chin indicates a greeting, one set is an insult and dismissal (looking down his nose) one set a challenge, and one set a threat. Recognizing which is which involves what I call environmental knowledge.[115] The chin position works closely with the body lean and facial expression.

Puffing—Like a puffer fish, this is inhaling and not exhaling. Angry and confrontational people often try to swell. This isn't just sucking in air and straightening up. In many cases, it's also going up on the balls of one's feet to gain extra height. Arm position and movements also tend to become bigger and fill more space. It's almost as if the person has a giant, invisible beach ball they are moving around. The classic monkey dance example are two monkeys with puffed-up chests, standing chest to chest with arms thrown back, each challenging the other to swing. (This is where the chin jut or lift becomes funny because with a puffed chest, it's hard to jut the chin. But they do try . . . my how they try.)

Change in breathing patterns—Faster breathing is the sign of an adrenaline rush and excitement. In and of itself, it is not usually a threat display. Although it can be used as a threat signifying someone is barely in control ordinarily changes in breathing accompany other signals, especially in tandem with changes in speech and volume.

Aborted lunge—This is a common strategy among the young and inexperienced. It's also a great way to get shot if the person takes you seriously. The lunge differs from the lean in that it is a sudden forward

115   Environmental knowledge is the foundation of situational awareness. In general, what are the rules, behavior, and standards of a situation. In this specific what is cultural 'language' of chin movement for this individual?

charge that stops or jerks back before it becomes a fully committed attack. Often, it is done with just the upper body and *without* the feet moving. This is an intimidation tactic, pure and simple. When done outside attack range, it is a threat display, but it's also often used as an interview technique (to see how you react) and part of a build-up to an attack (he creeps closer with each lunge).

Drawing back an arm or raising the hand to hit—We've all seen this. But the more I research, the deeper and wider this particular ocean turns out to be:

- Someone pulls their hand back near their shoulder, threatening to hit you. On the surface, it's just a simple threat display, right? That is until it's embedded in another gesture. He cocks back as if he is going to hit then drops his hand from his shoulder sideways and down. So now the threat signal is *still there*, but deniable. Was that a threat to hit or not? (These are called compound gestures.[116])

- Raising the hand to strike tends to trigger a freeze response in the target. Many people when they see that hand up acquire a bovine expression and *stand there*, watching that hand go back—no matter how aggressive they were previously. If the blow doesn't come, they reboot back to aggressive behavior—often at a higher level because they were threatened.

- Aside from the intimidation factor, it also seems as if there's some kind of a 'this is social violence' signal and trigger embedded in the movement. (Drawing back this way decreases effectiveness, slows down the attack, gives the target time to brace, and actually robs you of striking power). Does it trigger some kind of a violence-limiting switch? Kinda looks that way. (There are far more effective ways to attack to cause injury and death.)

- Another indicator of how deep this goes is teaching people how to strike with power. Next to getting off line, getting people *not* to draw back is the second most difficult unconscious behavior to break. Cocking back is *deeply* embedded in our psyches and in some weird ways.

Baton gestures—A baton gesture is when you use a limb or finger like a conductor's baton or drumstick. Most baton gestures are *not* threat displays, they are enhancements and exaggerations. They're used more for emphasis or direction. In this context, they're mostly with just the hands and forearm. A person whose hand keeps the beat of driving home his points is not necessarily displaying threat (e.g., a politician, "We must A [beat] and B [beat] and most of all C [big beat]). A person giving you

---

116   *Believe me* this is going to come up in court if your 'go signal' was his cocking back to hit you.

directions by pointing is not threatening you. The greater the distance, the bigger the gesture (e.g., pointing where to park, right there or on the other side). Baton gestures turn into threat displays when they begin to mimic a club rather than a baton—commonly fast, wild swings, and gesticulation with the entire arm. It doesn't take much imagination to see how closely they resemble a strike—which is kind of the point.

Vacuum attacks—Vacuum attacks *are* attacks. They are clearly acts of physical violence (like punching, choking, clawing, slapping, and kicking) but done *out of range* and to the air. These are completed moves that fail to have a key element—you. They fall into a vacuum because you are not there, they're not touching you. These, however, communicate what will happen to you if you don't change your behavior.

Environmental attacks—These too are completed attacks. Except the person attacks the environment as a display of how angry and close he or she is to violence aimed at you. These range from slamming things down, throwing things (in a direction other than at you) punching walls, to breaking stuff (like windows). The interesting thing about environmental attacks is how *loud* they are. Swinging a baseball bat at a bush is nowhere near as strident as slamming a book onto a table. The noise and damage to the environment are designed to intimidate you. (As a side note, don't laugh when it fails. Punching a hole in a wall is supposed to be intimidating. Cracking up when the person accidentally hits a wall stud and breaks his hand doesn't go over very well. Same thing when someone hits a brick wall in frustration and anger. Let them realize they're hurting themselves then allow them to make a production out of storming off. Resist the impulse to scornfully throw out, "Elvis has left the building." Just trust me on this one.)

Looming—This is something that is really common with big guys. It's arguable that a lot of them don't recognize they are within their attack range while still outside that of a shorter person.[117] But when a larger person moves into range to loom, it can be intentional. What many of them don't seem to understand is they've not only moved into a location that allows them to easily attack, but have shifted into the shorter person's attack range, as well. You get a really unsubtle version of looming when people loom over you while you are seated. This is particularly common in office situations when a co-worker or customer leans over your desk. Although beyond the scope of this book, head level is significant in dominance and status displays. (Again read Desmond Morris's *Manwatching*.)

Invading space—Take your arm and extend it. That distance is

---

117   If you're a big guy and are getting a bad reaction, check your attack range you might be looming. If you're a short person getting uncomfortable, check attack range. Usually, you'll find he's in his attack range while just outside yours.

commonly deemed your space. Think of it as a giant bubble surrounding you as you walk. We only let certain people into it and only under certain circumstances. Realistically if someone means to punch you, he has to be close enough that you can reach out and poke him in the nipple. That's *not* what I'm talking about when I say invading space. The invasion of your space is mostly by an antagonist's limbs (baton gestures). They reach into your space. Again, extend your hand as though you were trying to poke the person in the chest. With most space invasions, you would not be able to reach his body nor he yours. What would happen *if* there was physical contact is they would hit your extended hand or forearm. Now take your hand down and recognize—while there is no physical contact—such a person is reaching this far *into* your space to intimidate you.

There is another thing you actually already know. But like so much about this subject, we need to hook it, drag it up from the depths of your subconscious, and make it conscious. You subconsciously know there are two common sets of responses to threat displays, one of which is fear and intimidation (your threat works). The other is anger, insult, and aggression (it doesn't). To further muddy things up, the two are not mutually exclusive. Funky hybrids are a common third reaction (usually leaning toward the fail side). So—looking at just those raw data points alone—you have a one in three chance of threat displays working the way you want them to, and two in three chances of things going wrong. A typical monkey reaction when a threat display fails is to do it again, but bigger and louder.

As humans, we tend to respond to certain kinds of internal distress with threat displays. Given that most often the provocation is another stressed-out human, *odds are good* our threat displays are in response to his or her threat display. Now you have two stressed-out monkeys emotionally infecting each other with threatening behavior. Nahhhhh, nothing could go wrong there. This is more a Conflict Communications thing, but the way you break this cycle is to either give the other monkey the signals it wants (thus fulfilling the script and settling the issue) or with a hat tip to the other monkey, you politely change scripts. Again, this is way past the scope of this book. But for here and now, the short answer is: When someone is throwing monkey brain threat signals at you *don't* throw back more monkey threat displays.

That right there is a script changer. I'll give you a hint: If you can relax—because you know the guy is out of physical attack range—and let him vent odds are good the situation *will* calm itself. It's a sad truth of our times that—with all the communication that daily bombards us—we've stopped listening. This stresses the monkey. There are a lot of people who are screaming to be heard. Often just listening satisfies and calms the person. (I've had great success with the strategy of telling the person the price of my listening is to keep their distance [outside attack range] and then I let them rant. I don't have to fix it; I don't have to defend [myself or others]; I don't have to come up with any answers. I just let them rant and self-soothe.)

Before we move on to pre-attack indicators, let me make five things *very* clear. First, while there is a difference between threat displays and pre-attack indicators, there is a lot of *overlap*. Like I said elsewhere, displays would not be credible threats if they didn't mimic the common ways humans work their way up to violence.

Second, where threat displays—normally—shade over to pre-attack indicators depends on range. Get your graffiti and tattoo kit out, that was a biggie. The same behavior that is credible danger from two feet is *not* dangerous when ten feet away, which incidentally is a good range to have arguments. It's a whole lot easier to calmly let someone say their piece at that distance than when they're up in your face, barking, and drooling. The problem with close range is while the person might mean it as a threat display enhancement, it's way too close and easy to finish the move as an attack. What is an obvious threat display at greater distances creates reasonable belief that you're under attack up close. Why? Because he's in attack range. Duh! (Do yourself a favor and don't add that last when you're explaining your actions to a cop or the prosecutor. Again, just trust me on that one.)

Third, when someone's threat displays don't have the desired effect, the monkey figures the answer is to get *louder* and more in your face. Yeah . . . that works out well. If your imitation of an attack isn't working, do a more credible version by moving into attack range. This is your classic 'peaceful' protestor, screaming, lunging at, and gesticulating at the cops while creeping closer and closer until . . . *wham!* Again, the problem is often in that person's subjective reality, he or she isn't intending to attack. So when you react, they'll claim you attacked them—without cause or provocation.

Fourth—and fatally—these kinds of up-in-your-face threat displays are widespread in places where weapons are *not* common. Where weapons *are* common if you get up this close into someone's face, they'll kill you where you stand. I tell you that for five reasons:

- One, range becomes vital when weapons are involved. Distance equals time. The farther away he is, the more time you have to respond appropriately to the greater danger.
- Two, where weapons are *not* common people tend to aggressively encroach on each other's space without hesitation. I witnessed a

few jams in the United Kingdom and Europe. These guys were doing in-your-face threat displays at a range that had me having kittens. I was freaking out because in the 'hoods, barrios, and ghettos I roamed, even trying to get that close would get you shot or eviscerated on the *spot*. So, you really have to be firm about setting your boundaries when folks try to crowd you.[118]

- Three, while citizens fear street people getting up in their faces, the truth is street rats are cocky about dealing with them because they know civilians *aren't* armed. More than that, nice people won't kick their butts on the spot. This isn't just safe, it's a green light, allowing many rats to act out. (They know they have the time to do it before the cops show up.) At the same time, if they sense danger to themselves that kind of behavior evaporates faster than a drop of water on a hot griddle. A big indicator of such danger is someone who knows not to let anyone crowd him and shows a willingness to enforce that boundary.

- Four is predators know the "weapons equal keep your distance or bleed" rule. Remember, they are from places where weapons are *common*. So when a robber (an asocial predator) closes on you under the pretext of a social script, one of the things he's looking for is *whether or not* you know that rule, too. This is why setting boundaries way outside of surprise weapon deployment range is an express lane to failing the interview.

- Five expands on four in that a common element of assassination is to get close enough to jam the target's ability to resist or flee. In situations where you know the target is armed, you jam his weapon arm. No matter what, you pin him to the spot to make sure he stays put while you finish the job. In the streets and especially in prison, you don't let enemies get close enough to do that.

118   Geoff Thompson came up with what he calls "the fence." This is where you put your hands out to create a physical barrier between your opponent and you. I have some problems with the way it is commonly taught by all these other 'experts,' who picked it up and ran with it. (Another case of people thinking they're smarter than the guy who'd been there.) Mistake one is many people hold their hands up too high, putting them in the other dude's face. This provokes rather than deters. Mistake two is that there is a time to leave it out and a time to pull it back in. Many people leave their hands hanging out too long—thereby turning it into another provocation. Three is a combination. If you need to keep it out there I prefer keeping the hands at chest level or lower. Four, I actually like using my hands to set boundaries in a more subtle but intimidating manner. My words are saying, "That's close enough," but my hand isn't acting as a fence. It's shooting out and pulling back like a whip crack—at his groin. It's amazing how fast thinking of getting their pee-pees whacked will cause men to pull up short. If the guy starts to try to creep into range again, I bring my left hand up in a baton gesture and leave it out in a fence position until he either backs off or commits to an attack.

And now time for the fifth point about threat displays that needs to be made clear. That is while threat displays intimidate, they are *less* dangerous than what else is out there. I don't care about someone huffing, puffing, and threatening me from 'over there.' What's going to send me straight for a weapon is someone breaking the social scripts in specific ways. Ways I'm about to tell you.

Miller and I were talking about a study he'd love to see done on the parallels of behavior of bikers and samurai. It's a good idea because it would demonstrate how dangerous people interact among themselves . I threw in, I'd like to see a study done about how dangerous people from different tribes interact and what protocols they follow so as to *not* trigger violence. While both he and I know these social scripts exist now and in the past, lacking accredited academic studies the general public doesn't believe they exist. *They do!* These scripts and behavioral protocols are what keep the gutters from running with blood. Here's a news flash, people from dangerous environments have as many if not *more* social scripts, rules, and ways things are done than you do (e.g., not coming up behind someone and if you do, make noise—while out of range—to attract the person's attention before coming close).

This especially applies to dealing with strangers who might be dangerous. Where I'm from, we unleashed intense violence on people who *broke* these social scripts—especially strangers. That's because such behavior is common in set-ups for robberies, assaults, or murders. Your survival was strongly dependant on showing a bunch of dangerous people you knew how to behave. And a big part of that was *not* throwing around threat displays to show how tough you were—especially when it came to what citizens commonly thought made them look scary tough. The locals know what dangerous looks like. It's quietly watching everything and sitting in the corner.[119]

We're going to go into it a whole lot more in the next few chapters, but you will *not* see these kinds of threat displays with the worst kinds of violence. The greatest danger will come gliding at you under the disguise of seemingly innocent social scripts. But these normal scripts and behavior will be broken and off kilter in certain, *easily* identifiable ways. This faux behavior is something you don't want to see coming at you.

So let's talk not about pre-attack, but the first stage of an attack. I'm going to start with the most important of them all:

---

119   Again I'm going to have to go wash my hands for typing the word, but there are 'tactical' seating arrangements that dangerous people tend to automatically take. Again beyond the scope of this book, but it's more than just 'back to the wall.' One of the ways to gather environmental knowledge in a new area is to look at the scarred old boars who are sitting in such positions—and watching the room.

Developing range—Fast or slow, someone moving into attack range is a bad bloody sign. I talk elsewhere about recognizing the distance needed to pass information versus the distance to pass something. Here's another hint: In order for someone to rape you, he has to be closer than length of his dick. You don't want him that close. I mention this because maintaining that distance also is necessary for him to kill you with a knife. And there's something a lot of people apparently don't know. An amateur will start his attack and develop range *simultaneously*. This is the dreaded howling berserk charging down on you and—oddly enough—cocking back his hand to hit you. If you can get out of your monkey (not freeze on the tracks) these guys actually are real easy to handle. If you can remember to dodge, there're all kinds of really tender bits to grab, as well as funny ways to make them squeak. They're also loads of laughs to snatch and throw face first into walls or out windows. (Oops, that was my inside voice wasn't it?)

It's the professionals you need to be wetting your pants about. These are the bastards who slowly and methodically develop range and attack positions. This is the ambusher, who's in plain sight and drifting into attack range so slowly that he doesn't trigger your danger alarms until you're looking down the barrel of the gun or are already bleeding out.

My advice to you if you're approached in a strange situation is to assume the presence of a weapon and become a control freak about setting boundaries. Set them fifteen to twenty feet out for people who make you uncomfortable. At those distances if he goes for a weapon, it's a race as to who has the quicker draw. That's a contest in which most bad boys don't want to partake. And if there aren't weapons involved when Bozo decides to come kamakazing in instead of you falling apart, it gives you time to come up with the best way to make him scream and collapse.

Sticking with the pro theme, I'll first address the not-so-obvious, but predictable behavior of someone who knows what he's doing when setting up his attack. If it lands, this attack will put you in the hospital—if you're lucky. Then we'll work down to the more common, plus the physiological signs of an attack.

Attack positioning, strong side, weak side—This involves more than moving into range, it's getting into specific attack position *and* location. While someone closing on you hard and fast from behind is grounds for unpleasantness, watch for someone sliding to the angle in front of you. Remember, humans are oriented on the 90s, someone trying to quietly snake to a 45-degree angle on you is an experienced player—particularly if he's setting up his power (next section). He is trying to move to your weak side to attack through it or trying to get into position to jam your strong side. It's better for everyone if he stays right in front of you and in a neutral pose. You calmly countering his developing attack positioning—as if nothing is happening—is another express pass to interview failure (remember, you want to fail).

Setting up a power strike or attack stance—Did you know that one of the worst places to get hit *hard* is right under the ear and behind the jaw? It's kind of like you've been kicked in the nuts and your knees buckle, except when you're drilled under the ear your entire body gets wobbly. I tell you this because it was one of my favorite targets when I saw someone trying to set me up like this. The safest pose to communicate that you aren't setting up to drive someone's nose through the back of his skull is feet and shoulders on the same line, hands in plain view, and—if you were in range—you could reach out and put your hands on his shoulders. This is a neutral stance. It's really hard to effectively generate force from this pose without moving to another. That's what you *want* to see standing there, out of range.

What you *don't* want to see is someone in range, in a bladed or wound up pose. That's one where he's close enough to reach out and touch you, but with only one hand. That rear hand is his power or weapon hand. The front is his speed or grabbing hand. He doesn't have to move into an attack position and pose, he's *already* there. All he has to do is move. By sliding into attack range, positioning, and turning his body to develop an attack stance, he can launch an especially powerful attack.

When someone did this to me . . . well . . . sometimes I'd move out of where I was standing. Sometimes, my expression about being set up like that changed his mind. Other times, I'd move first. And at still other times, I'd wait for him to attack, move, and hit him under the ear; then I'd get real cranky. For a professional, justifications to use that much force are hard to come by. His sliding into attack range, positioning, and taking an attack stance just gave me what I needed.

Shoulder raise or drop—There are certain things you simply don't want to do when you stand close to a heavy hitter. If you ever get to see two serious players negotiating about *not* going violent, watch how still they get. Major movement becomes very slow and deliberate. Extraneous, fast movements stop. That's because neither of them wants to make *any* move that can be interpreted as an attack being launched or a weapon draw. If someone manages to end up in your range, fast movement of his shoulder is articulable and a reasonable cause for what happens next. (At the same time, keeping your body movements to a minimum sends a distinct message.)

Sudden weight shift forward or rotation—Once you understand attack range, it's a no brainer to spot where an attack is coming from. (I'll give you a game to play to improve this skill in a few.) If he's standing there, the fastest attack is with that limb. All he has to do is reach out with it. To put power behind it, he has to shift his weight. So *watch* for that shift! To bring his heavy guns into play, he has to rotate and bring that part of his body forward. When you see that part of his body coming at you, that's where the attack will come from. There are certain, predictable movement patterns you can learn to recognize that precede knife draws, gun draws, punches, and kicks. Once you know what they look like, they are easy to spot. Watch for the shoulders and hips moving in that specific way, whether he has empty hands or a weapon.

"Ahhh fuck" moves—I know of no official term for these. But anybody who's been around the block knows 'em when he sees 'em. That's what you say when you see these calm, small, seemingly insignificant moves. And it's what you say when you see these particular moves done in this manner. It's a sick sinking feeling in the pit of your stomach because you just got the memo that what's coming is going. to. suck.

These are actions experienced fighters take, like casually turning his baseball hat around (to keep the hair out of and the brim from being knocked over his eyes.) The old guy who takes out his false teeth and sets them on the bar. The guy who—when someone is in his face—calmly takes a small backward step to develop attack positioning and stance and just waits for the other guy to step into range. The guy who carefully takes off his prized hat and sets it aside. The guy who takes his glasses off or expensive sunglasses out of his pocket and sets them down before moving forward. The concealed carry guy who sees three gangstas pull up their hoodies as they approach the cashier. He pulls ear plugs from his pocket, puts them in, then stands calmly with his hand under his vest. (They changed their minds about robbing the place.) The guy who is sitting in a chair, turns, shifts his butt forward, and puts one leg underneath him (so he can use it as a piston to come out of the chair). The guy who leans back and puts his hands under the table or casually leans against a car and crosses his arms. The guy who is wearing armor under his clothing. The list is long . . . and they're like the tip of a shark fin leaving a wake on the surface. Something ugly is in the water with you.

If the guy is calm enough to attend to these little details in the face of violence, he is someone with whom you're going to have to put in overtime to handle. It's a damn good reason to reconsider your plans. If it goes (even if you win) he's going to get a piece out of you. In such situations, winning means you wake up in the hospital. If it's going to happen no matter what, all you can do is embrace the suck.

Hands—This is a three-parter. Here's the . . . well . . . I guess you could call it good news. People who are accustomed to dealing with weapons immediately understand the significance of you establishing rules about hands. And it's articulable if someone refuses to cooperate. Refusal both qualifies as jeopardy and indicates a higher level of ability (danger).

1) <u>Hands disappear from sight</u>: Remember that I said in places where weapons are common, you just don't do certain things? One of them is let someone's hand drift out of sight. You don't know what's going to be coming with that hand the next time you see it. If in certain circumstances someone's hand drifts from sight, you call him on it. You do it in a way that communicates if he doesn't bring that hand slowly back into sight, extreme violence is imminent. That's because his hand disappearing is just cause for yours to disappear, too.

2) <u>Hand position</u>: Watch the hands of people walking when they have nothing in them. You'll see a kind of loose, stringy, relaxed, bouncy movement. You'll also see them swing their arms back and forth around the body in a rhythmic sway. This is a happy sign. Get a warm fuzzy when you see it. That's because when someone is holding something concealed in his hand, his hand position, muscle tension, and way of walking change—often in the form of keeping that hand out of sight, which gives him a walk that would be comic if a weapon weren't involved. Here's the thing like concealment in shooting, a palmed weapon is only invisible from one direction. All you have to do to render it ineffective (to see what's in the hand) is move. If you see someone walking at you with these kinds of muscle tension, hand position, and changes in gait, move to where you can see that hand. If he counters that's articulable, too.

There are three stages a person goes through to employ a weapon: Draw, deploy, and use. The draw gets the weapon out and puts it in the hand. The deployment readies it for use (e.g., opening the knife, taking the safety off, putting your finger on the trigger and aiming the gun, moving the club into position to swing and adjusting your grip.) Use is actually utilizing the weapon. Whether that is to intimidate, brandish, menace, put holes in, or crush parts of the other person. While they all have to happen, they do *not* have to happen quickly.

Two points about this. One, when they happen quickly they are very *recognizable*. Three and a half subpoints on that:

- Distance equals time in this biz. Often the guy will get close enough before he draws, deploys, and uses, so he can rely on your confusion or weak and ineffective response to keep you from successfully jamming his attempts.
- Flipping that same idea over, distance and time strongly influence *preclusion*. The less time and distance you have, the fewer alternatives you have against extreme violence when someone is going for a weapon. You're forced to either let it happen or commit

extreme violence yourself. Since most people aren't capable of going to that extremity at the drop of the hat, they submit. That's why his strategy of getting up close before pulling a weapon is so effective.

- If you space the draw, deployment, and use out, it's less obvious. The result is the draw already accomplished, the guy approaches you with the knife in his hand. All he has to do is get close, deploy, and use it—whether to threaten or stab. (A slight variation comes with things like brass knuckles. These are slipped on [deployed] in the pocket, drawn from the pocket, and then comes the attack. Someone carrying a gun in the pocket also is deploying it there. If it's an assassination, he might just shoot through the jacket instead drawing out the gun.)

Point number two is more of an aside. This three-stage process is why emergency quick draws so often go awry, particularly if the adrenalized person tries to do all three in the same second. Again, train, ingrain, test, train, ingrain, then train under pressure. And pray to God you never have to use it.

3) <u>Hands going to the body</u>—I've already talked about the gangster or appendix draw. In these days of folding knives and pocket guns, watch for the hands going to the front or back pocket. Sudden urges to scratch his armpit or crossed arms also are bad signs. There're too many ways to conceal and carry weapons, so I'm not going to go into them. But I will warn you: Be careful. The first guy I ever stabbed only saw me cross my arms. Since I was wearing a t-shirt, it didn't look like much, but I had a short knife strapped to the inside of my upper arm. When he went for his gun, he was surprised to discover I already had my hand on my weapon.

Sudden changes in direction, speed, or an intercept course—Think about all the people you pass every day, pass being the key word. How many of them are going somewhere? Somewhere else. We're really good at passing and avoiding each other. So, someone on an intercept course isn't normal. But you won't know what isn't normal until you consciously know what *is*. There are certain predictable turns, timings, and destinations we find ourselves in with others. While you might converge with strangers for a short time, after a crunch you're going to go your separate ways in pursuit of your goals. Say for instance, people converging at a crosswalk, an elevator, entrance, or exit. Even then, people make subtle tweaks to pass and avoid.

For example, entrances and exits. Ordinarily when approaching a door at the same time as someone else, we speed up or slow down to adjust the timing. Adjusting speed instead of trying to pass through this choke point simultaneously, we pass sequentially. If you know this is normal, someone who speeds up, slows down, and changes direction to *intersect* with you at the door will stand out like a nun in whorehouse, especially if you change your direction and speed and the person adapts to still meet you.

Checks—I've mentioned someone checking his weapon while at a distance and then closing. I also mentioned witness checks. That's when the person looks around to see if there's anyone close enough to interfere with his plan of attacking you or testify in court. Another check that stands out is someone looking for cameras—especially if after looking, they start doing a funky chicken dance to keep their face off camera or pop up hoodies to block their faces and ears from recognition software.

(Another aside: A big concern about self-defense is the misconception that you have to wait until you are physically assaulted or see a weapon before you act. What we're talking about here is shifting your perspective about when the attack *actually* starts. Think in terms of incident, instead of attack. The attack is just one stage in the whole process. You're defending your actions in regard to the entire incident, not just the circumstances. If you see him developing the five stages, you try to avoid, he counters; you set boundaries, he blows past them when he finally does the double-handed claw at the front of his shirt—gutting him like a fish *is* reasonable and justifiable. Those circumstances didn't just pop out of nowhere. You'd have been in a shit storm for a while. The shooting or stabbing was a long time coming, and you did *everything* you could to keep it from happening. Just as he did *everything* in his power to make it happen.)

Fake submission—While this can happen when a resource predator decides not to come at you head on, it's far more common with the asshat crowd. That's someone who decides he objects to you telling him no, but you've shown you're too ready for him to come at you straight on. So he'll fake a social script of cooperation and peaceful intention to get you to lower your guard, then he'll turn on you.

I used to deal with these pricks all the time when I was bouncing. These are the people who figure they can't take you head on, so they'll fake submission or calming down and then try to sucker punch you. One of the more ham-handed versions is the guy who insists on shaking hands to prove there're no hard feelings. (Not going to happen, Precious.) A little more common is the guy who says it's cool and starts to turn away. You can see this one coming because he's watching you out of the corner of his eye. He starts to turn away then whips back around. His supposed turn was to hide his development of a power stance to attack from and usually making a fist.

The more advanced form is shown by the guys who will measure where you are, turn completely around, and then flip back on you. Except for one thing, you've left that spot. Don't close the distance, *slip to the side.* A major reason you moved was to get into position so you could see if his turn was to cover his hands going to his body. I mentioned earlier the experienced player who will step back and set up a power, positioning and then wait for the other guy to step into range. Same thing. As long as he doesn't whip around and try to attack where you were, he's safe to leave.

Backing up on you—For the record, I hate this. This is the jackass, who goes out the door, then comes back in with a gun. (If you can, you *always* leave through another door after an incident.) Back in my bouncing days after I got someone off the property, I'd spend some time standing by the blind side of the entrance. Come in looking right, and I'd be standing to the left. Another, oh joy, oh rapture, was stepping outside and seeing the guy waiting for me in the shadows by the dumpster or in the parking lot. When someone does this, it's never pleasant. Odds are pretty good the guy brought a weapon—or even worse, friends. This vendetta behavior is not uncommon. It's why I tell people if at all possible after an incident get the hell out of there, and don't come back for a while.

Skin color change—When the body gets the "go" signal, blood is pulled from the surface of the skin and into the muscles, which results in a change in skin color, a pallor. We ordinarily associate this paleness with fear. We think the flush-faced, angry person is more likely to attack. *Wrong.* This pallor is one of those physiological changes we can't control. It happens with both fear and anger because either can result in physical action. Think of it as going from fourth to fifth gear. In fourth, that person is adrenalized and ready for action (red faced). The skin color change occurs when they slam it into fifth, whether it's fleeing in panic or trying to tear your throat out with their teeth.

Adrenaline rock, sway, tremble—I'm going to take this out of order so you can understand the next point. I've already talked about how someone who is adrenalized can rock, sway, or tremble. Anyone doing this is very close to attacking (fourth gear), but they haven't given their body the go signal yet (fifth gear). Expect violence sometime real soon. (Some people have certain tics, twitches, and behavior that tell you they're about to go off. I know of one mental patient, who would start wringing his hands. I get an unconscious tic in my face. I once knew a guy who'd hum. I know someone else who smiles and laughs. While they're signs of adrenalization, you have to know the person to recognize which particular one means he's about to go off.)

Adrenaline shake or jerk—Not everyone gets the rock, sway, tremble, or tics from adrenaline. What is common is when they slam it into fifth gear, they do a super fast jerk or twitch. They do this because when it's time to go, they get the extra adrenaline dump. I call this the 'that's it' twitch. Stand in front of a mirror and pretend you're angry. Imagine someone saying something that you're going to kick his butt for and say "That's it!" Watch your body movement, especially hands, head, and shoulders before you finish saying "it." That's adrenaline hitting the system. Someone who is experienced will use this extra burst as part of his attack. But most people throw it away in an unnecessary jerk or extraneous move (like cocking an arm back). Look for this turbo boost in movement, especially if it's spent going for a weapon.

Sharp inhale—A lost aspect of most martial arts is breathing. Without getting woo-woo, there are all kinds of important elements of breath control when it comes to violence. Most people have lost that, so they revert to taking a deep breath and trying to hold it while they fight. If you're paying attention, you can hear them suck it in. Kind of like hearing a train whistle, you know what's coming down the tracks.

Chin drop, jaw clench, shoulder hunch—Remember the chin jut of threat displays? Well, a nearly instinctive protective action is to drop the chin (protect the throat and face) and hunch the shoulders when attacking or being attacked. The human body is designed to take impacts from the front. By dropping the chin, we project our armored forehead and cheeks and protect our more delicate central facial features. That and clenched teeth lessen the chances of a broken jaw Oh yeah, it also lessens the chances of getting punched in the throat. When you see this hunkering, things are about to get interesting.

Sudden silence—While war cries herald many attacks, usually the attack itself is done in silence. He may be snarling, "Screw you," as he charges, but when he gets to you, he's not saying much. In cases where the guy decides beforehand to use extreme physical violence, he may not say anything—he'll just come at you from the shadows. It's hard to describe, but among experienced players there's a kind of 'roaring silence' before they launch at you. (Again, watch the pen-in-the-throat scene from *Casino*.)

Grabbing—Someone grabbing you is categorically a bad sign. Many people think this *is* the attack. The reason I put it among pre-attack indicators is because it's not the grab that's dangerous, it's what comes next. The grab is to hold you in place or to set you up for what is coming. Yes, it's part of the attack, but it's not the damaging part. Grabs are a go sign. Hell's coming your way, and you need to do something *now*. If you're lucky the guy will be sloppy enough that his timing will be grab, then (insert damaging next attack). These are the grab and punch. Grab and drag you over. Grab and pick you up to slam you down or into something. Grab, stab, and other forms of mayhem. You either need to do something about that grab (part A) *before* part B shows up *or* jump ahead to deal with B *then* break the grab. B is the danger. (Any time-consuming complicated action against the grab—as is commonly taught in martial arts—will fail to keep you safe from B.)

Making a fist—Pay attention to the fact this is at the bottom of the list. That's because while empty-hand folks consider it a big deal, just punching someone is one of the least effective ways to attack. It's mostly non-injurious monkey violence. Often—but not always—the fist clenches just before he swings. But if you haven't figured out you're in deep trouble by then . . . Where a fist is a serious problem is when it forms immediately after the hand comes out of a pocket. That's often an indicator that something is in his hand. Of course, that bandana with a padlock tied to it he just pulled out of his pocket is a pretty good indicator, too.

Okay, so we've covered the behavior that allows you to drink a cup of coffee and take a smoke while someone exhibits their little threat display. We've also covered the 'ohshitohshitohshit!' behavior of an attack being initiated. Now is the time for the pain-in-the-behind middle ground. That's when Nimrod the Magnificent takes his threat displays just a little too far.

These can come in five basic ways. One, he's working his way up to an attack. Two, he doesn't think his threat displays are working. Three, he's drunk, drugged, or mentally ill. Four, he's getting off on it. Five, he's just too damned young, stupid, and aggressive to know when it's time to turn down the volume. Now to really piddle in your Post Toasties, these are not exclusive. Odds are good, it'll be some combination. Oh joy . . .

Threat display too close—Really, seriously, it'll be better for everyone if you threaten to kick my butt from across the room. The closer you get, the higher the JAM numbers, and the more likely I am to take you at your word. "He was threatening to beat me up, I tried to leave, he got close enough to do it, then he . . . and that's how it happened officer."

Lunging—Yep, that one again. Except the rule of thumb is that *up close* you treat a fake, feint, or lunge as an *attack* because by the time you determine it was fake, an attack has already landed. And if he didn't know not to lunge at someone when he's that close, well he learned an important lesson didn't he?

Throwing things at *a person*—This is no longer an environmental attack, it is a distance attack. The problem is Numbnuts may think it's only another step in monkey escalato or a threat display. The good news is that most throwing or ranged attacks are easily dealt with by leaving (which coincidentally is what the assailant wants anyway). The bad news is that experienced attackers often throw stuff into people's faces as a cover for their next—potentially lethal—attack.

Slaps, weak or single hit—The first book I wrote I wanted to title "It All Started When He Hit Me Back." The publisher's editorial staff, however, felt it sounded too much like a book on domestic violence. (Which if you think about it has some scary implications.) Unfortunately, it all started when he hit me back is a classic example of monkey brain threat display, conflict behavior—and I use the term loosely—thinking. Too often in escalating threat displays, stepping up and smacking someone is viewed as just another chip in the pot. A pot that you keep raising the stakes on until the other side folds, and you rake it in. Where this gets a gold star stupidity award is how often the striking monkey—*honestly*—doesn't perceive this as an assault. I wish I was lying—particularly about how many women believe hitting someone when they're upset *is not* violence. Sorry, folks, women are human beings. That means they can be just as stupid, aggressive, and violent as the other half of the species (men just tend to be more effective at striking).

But I didn't tell you this to start a debate about sexism. I told you to illustrate—*if* a stressed-out monkey can rationalize that striking another person in anger is *not* violence—how easy is it for that same monkey to convince itself it's not engaging in threat displays and aggressive behavior? Remember the term self-offense? A lot of the time, *that's* what you'll be facing. This is why you don't want to argue someone else's intent, your use of force is based on JAM.

As aside but related, if you aren't careful that aggressive and threatening person can be *you*. I tell you this because of what I call the monkey slide. And this is not uncommon after people have taken Conflict Communications training. Fresh and ready, they're aware of their monkey and proud of themselves for staying in control. Then they get into an incident where their monkey flat-out hijacks them. I'm often told, "I knew what the monkey was doing. I just couldn't stop myself." It's like unexpectedly finding yourself on a slide, and you don't know how to stop. You'd think this monkey slide would be first hand experience about how powerful the monkey can be about hijacking our actions. Truth is, it's probably the first time you're consciously aware of it. We've actually been letting the monkey take control like this throughout our lives. But ordinarily, we don't try to stop it. Add to this, we're not consciously aware of the difference between our human mind and a monkey hijacked emotional reality. The monkey slide is just becoming aware when it's happening. Now the good news it takes a little practice, but you can develop the ability to stop yourself from sliding.

Brandishing—We'll cover this more in another chapter. Still, I'll repeat myself: The presence of a weapon is a *game changer*. But too often the monkey's response to a weapon is to think of it as another raise in the poker pot of escalation.

By now you're probably hoping I'll tell you what the right answer is to these circumstances. Bad news, Punkin, I can't. *The situation dictates.* You won't know the circumstances, factors, and environment until you're in the situation. All I can do is show you how to assess the danger, scale the extent of your response to the circumstances, and then articulate why it was a good use-of-force decision. Realistically, I've also given you (on the sly) all kinds of information, tools, and tricks you can use to get the situation off what I call the road of violence. The biggest factor? Stay calm and use all parts of your brain to come up with workable options.

Okay, I promised to teach you a game on how to spot when you're being attacked. I call it the "One, Two, Three Game." That's short for "one move, two moves, three moves." *Important safety tip*: This is done *slowly* and with *no* intention to inflict pain. It is a *learning* exercise that enables you to recognize what developing attacks look like.

With a partner, stand close enough to reach out and touch each other's heads and bodies with your palm. Then with minimum body movement find different ways you can attack (empty handed) with only *one* move from that position. (Turning your body counts as a move.)

For example, if I'm standing with my left shoulder forward and my weight on the lead foot with just an arm movement, I can jab, hook, uppercut, back fist, and hammer fist with my left arm. But I can't reach him with just an arm movement with my right. (It would require pivoting and raising my hand). If I pivot, however, I can do a short swing kick with my right leg. That still qualifies as only one move because I didn't move my leg.

Take different locations and positions (hold your body this way and that) and see all the ways you can successfully attack in *only* one move. In the meantime, the person who is receiving watches how the attacker's body moves and learns to assess where the attack will come from. For the moment, he just watches.

Two moves introduce distance and moving into range. Now that you know where the body has to be in order for an attack to succeed, you make one of the moves by getting into that position. For example, let's stick with the left lead. A cross can require rotation of the body (1) as well as extension of the arm (2). A left jab from out of range requires stepping into range (1) and the punch (2). A distance kick requires a weight shift (1) and a kick (2). Go slowly, but play with the distance. Work different locations, different techniques. Again, the purpose of the exercise is for the attacker to consider what movements are necessary to successfully attack and for the receiver to learn to recognize what these attacks look like when they are being developed.

To play with this, go back to one-move attacks. Have the attacker take different positions and stances inside attack range with an attack in mind. The target starts saying where the attack is going to come from. Then bump it up to two moves. As the attacker shifts into a new position to attack, the target calls where the attacks will come from. (It's important for the attacker to have a planned attack while doing his set-up move) In a very short time, the target will be able to easily predict where the attack will come from.

The third move is the attacker stepping back farther out of range. So one of his moves is obviously coming into attack range and doing everything else he needs to. Again, the attacker identifies where the attack is going to be as soon as he or she is able. Remember this is done slowly, so everyone can see the elements of different attacks, what they look like when they are being executed, and what it looks like when such attacks close in on you.

Have fun playing this . . . jokes and laughter just seem to be attracted to this exercise. It also is important for the attacker to not cheat. By that, I mean he's comes in with a left jab, and it gets identified. Don't switch to a cross. You're helping your friend learn to identify the attack that's coming at him. More than just seeing when the attack starts (as opposed to seeing a fist in front of your face before you realize you're under attack) you're learning how to see—and articulate—how you knew you were under attack.

Remember I talked about two traps we fall into when we default into monkey brain threat displays? There's a third I call, "Too little, too late." At the beginning of this chapter, I talked about possible responses to threat displays. One of them was sending a "hey, I don't want to fight" set of signals. I didn't want to mention it until now because without understanding (all the other things we've been talking about) it doesn't seem like a bad move. In fact, it seems like a reasonable idea. In reality, too little, too late often serves to infuriate the other person and provoke him to *much higher* levels of violence. That's because he thinks it's a chicken's excrement move. Now the bad news: Too often, he's right.

When I talk about sending a "hey, I don't want to fight" set of signs, people automatically assume I'm talking about submissive signals. Those are only *one* specific set of these kinds of signals. (And again, I'm going to point to Desmond Morris's book, *Manwatching*, for you to learn these and many other body language signals.)

The raw truth is too many people are more than happy to jump up and be complete, screaming miscreants toward others. I mean they're spitting, snarling, insulting, belittling, and calling the other guy names you reserve for someone who gang raped your mother. They've weaponized words and don't hesitate to slash others to ribbons. *Yet* when the other guy stands up to kick their butts, they—suddenly—switch to, "Oh no, I don't want to fight." They start throwing these signals faster than someone trying to bail out a sinking boat.

Thing is they usually don't show actual submission signals, which is why they get thrown a beating. Too often, they try a "nobody here but us chickens" act or "I'll just look at the ceiling until he goes away." Commonly, they break eye contact, look away, or lean back. It's almost like they've put the other person on hold and are thinking to themselves, "I'll just wait until it passes." The next two concepts work together. First, I liken what they do to being on the phone.

Basically, what they've done is put *their* bad behavior on hold. It's not gone, it's just waiting to come back on line. If the other guy were to back off, they'd push that button and be right back at it again. Second, they aren't really submissive signals. They're an "I'm perfectly okay with being a dick, but I don't want to get my butt kicked for it" signal (e.g., looking away). Actual, sincere submission signals *might* work to prevent a whuppin', but these aren't them. Submission signals usually include trying to make oneself look smaller, raising hands, backing away, and verbally communicating. Just looking away isn't enough. (In fact, it's kind of an insult.) The other guy knows too little, too late behavior, and it infuriates him even more.

For example, I saw a subway stomping video where one guy was talking smack to three dudes off camera. As long as they were safely seated on the other side of the train, he was happily talking trash (to the laughter of other passengers). When one of the dudes jumped up and got in his face, trash talker (who was leaning back against the doors) just looked away. Not a submissive signal, an insulting cut-off gesture. Then he tried to push the other dude's face out of his. Not an attack, a push away. They beat the hell out of the guy.

In their comments, many people whinged and whined how he'd tried not to fight. No. First off, three against one is not a fight—it's going to be a stompin'. Second, if he actually tried to avoid it, he *wouldn't* have been talking trash in the first place. Third, he was more than happy to play as long as he thought he was winning using verbal abuse. Fourth, when the first of the three jumped up, his reaction was 'oh shit.' Arguably it was already too late, but *that* was when he should have started trying to throw legitimate submission signals. Fifth, when he looked away, he had a look of contempt on his face. Sixth, trying to shove the dude's face away was technically the *first* physical assault. In reality, it's what opened the flood gate to physical force.

Don't wait until you're going 119 miles an hour before deciding that 120 is too fast.

CHAPTER 12

*The nation that insists on drawing a broad line of demarcation
between the fighting man and the thinking man is liable to find its
fighting done by fools and its thinking done by cowards.*
—Thucydides

The Road of Violence

There was a load of nuts-and-bolts considerations dropped on your
head after being all airy-fairy and psychological. Believe it or not, those
nuts and bolts will help you better understand the next dose of psycho-
babble. And that so-called psycho-babble teaches you how to apply this
information in an unfamiliar environment. The ability to do this is what
will keep you from dying on one hand and sitting in prison on the other.

And here's an additional thought, and it's something I want you to
think about because it's really important. There's a critical weakness when
it comes to self-defense—even with scenario training. When a young
police recruit comes out of the academy, he is paired with a field training
officer (FTO). This is where he serves his apprenticeship. (Medical grads
do residencies in hospitals. Same thing.) With law enforcement, under
the FTO's guidance the recruit makes the transition from school to
learning how to calmly function in live-fire situations, including stressful
and often bizarre circumstances that weren't covered in her training.
How do you respond to the naked, masturbating man who asks if he can
finish? Believe me when I tell you that isn't a situation where you want
to go hands-on. But respond wrong, and the situation *will* go sideways.
Nuances of effective behavior are modeled by the experienced FTO. This
helps teach the recruit how to function in ways that just cannot be taught
in classes.

But for self-defense students, there's no such thing as an apprenticeship
under a street experienced pro. Worse, there's a whole lot of people who
believe they can step straight out of training and swing into action in
the streets. Neither your instructor nor I will be there with you when—
God forbid—you find yourself in an unexpected situation that was
never covered in your training. The best I can do—by explaining all this
psycho-babble stuff—is to help you understand how things commonly
go wrong, so you don't end up wrestling that three-hundred-fifty-pound

naked guy because your response to the situation was technically correct, but tactically wrong.

Now, restating five significant elements of violence:

- One: Violence is a collective set of behaviors.
- Two: Violence provokes violence.
- Three: Violence usually comes with instructions on how to avoid it (warnings).
- Four: Experienced people—who knowingly use violence—know it can be used right back against them.
- Five: Inexperienced people are overcommitted.

Let's add a sixth: People experienced with violence set it up *before* they go, so when they move they're a lot more effective and intense (the five stages).

By setting up, I'm not talking about someone engaging in self-offense and increasing the JAM score when their threat displays don't work. (We'll address these types later in this chapter.) I'm talking about people who slowly, methodically set you up for a physical attack.

Although it's kind of funny to watch an experienced person set up a self-offense person. That's to say, someone who is huffing, puffing and doing threat displays. The experienced person just shifts into everything I talked about in the pre-attack indicator chapter and waits for the self-offense person to step *into* range. The latter doesn't have a clue he or she is about to get dropped like a prom dress and walks right into it.

With those six points in mind, I'd like to give you an analogy to help get your head around many of the concepts presented in this book. It's a big paradigm shift: *Violence is not a destination, it's a road.*

There's not a city limit that once you cross it, you're being violent. Remember, violence is a cluster of behaviors, not just a single act. Some people apparently think there's a sign, "Now entering Violence. Population XXXX." (Or if you're West Coast, "Violence city limits.") This explains why, while they're screaming obscenities, insulting, and threatening you— *to them*— that's not violent. They haven't crossed their self-created, subjective definition about what violence is. (Any level of force beyond . . .) According to them, violence is still miles away from what they are doing. This allows them to reap the rewards of violence without accepting the costs.

The most common tactic is to present the threat of greater violence. That's a warning that wouldn't be credible if they weren't already violent. They're not threatening you *with* violence, they're threatening you with *more* violence.

Remember, violence is a cluster of behaviors *not* a single act. If we think of violence as a road, we get a broader and better understanding of this behavior—including how things escalate to physical conflict. Additionally, we learn to ask a critical question: How *far* down the road is this situation? That simple question can be a life saver because the distance the situation has gone tells you the appropriate, legal, and effective response. The flip side of that same coin is what responses *won't* work? What are ineffective, inappropriate, and often illegal responses?

But perhaps the best thing thinking of violence as a road does is help people—who have no real experience—recognize both the absence and presence of physical danger. Some things that are scary *aren't* dangerous. But some things that are real dangerous don't look scary until it's too late. I call recognition of the danger and appropriate responses "mile markers."

I'm originally from California. Back in the day, the highways didn't have mile markers. The only way you could know where you were during a drive was by knowing the route. As in if you see this landmark, you're about a hundred miles out. See that terrain feature, and you're halfway to your destination. My mentors knew the route violence would take. Even lacking mile markers, they knew where a situation was along that particular highway that ended at physically acting, maiming, and possible death. At a glance, they could tell what the guy was most likely to do; they subconsciously read if the guy was merely woofin' or if he presented a real danger.

What they couldn't do was explain *how* they knew. When you asked one of my mentors how he knew the guy was going to act in a specific way, his answer was to shrug and say, "I dunno, I just knew." This frustrated the hell out of me. They taught me a lot, but I had to learn the landmarks on my own (often bleeding when I missed them). That frustration is what motivated me to start writing and teaching after I'd learned the indicators, signs, and behavior (the landmarks) they'd seen, but couldn't articulate.

I found out things like seeing this particular landmark behavior meant stay cool. Or if you saw another series of actions and verbalizations, you're way close to bad crap happening. Now that I had the route and landmarks mapped out in my head, I realized how many people were clueless about the road of violence and its danger signs. But most of all, I found how hard it was to communicate exactly where you were along that road.

Then I moved to a state with mile markers on the highway; all of a sudden I had new ways to give directions. "At around Mile Marker 175, you'll see Castle Rock. It's a big rock that looks like a castle sitting on top of a hill. You'll know it when you see it. It's actually at 182, but you'll see it long before you get there."

Mile markers play a big part in determining whether you stand and let the guy bluster to save face before he walks away or whether you shoot him in the face before he does it to you. Basically, how far down the road things have gone determines your viable options.

Not all behavior is equal. Normal rudeness is below the 50 mile marker. Certain things you'll commonly see at a hundred miles out, meh, no big thing. He's just talking smack, trying to intimidate you with verbal violence and threats. Other things pop out two hundred miles down the road. These you better pay attention to. Okay, he's getting closer and madder. But these kinds of landmarks only show up past Mile Marker (MM) 300, and the situation is becoming worse when you see them— like, his hand just disappeared into his pocket.

How did I learn these? As a professional, it was my job to keep bad things from happening. If they did, I had to handle them. I learned early on that by looking at violence as a process and finding its predictable patterns, I could recognize the early stages. This allowed me to intercede before things escalated to where I got stuck with the power-washer-and-wet-vac detail. This isn't magic, it's just *paying attention*. After you've seen enough violence, it's depressingly predictable and easy to spot— especially verbal and emotional brutality that are speeding toward physical confrontation—in contrast to two guys just making low mileage noise. After enough experience, you know what will happen if things aren't stopped early. But also what it's going to take to stop it if it all gets up to speed. Because as the *miles* increase, so too does the *speed*.

Let's make up a situation to show you how this road of violence idea works. John is feeling internal distress over something. For this story, it's at a social gathering, and Jim is the person who John has decided is the source of this distress. John is already at Mile Marker (MM) 5. But he tries to self-soothe by making a snide comment to Jim. (Let's call that MM 10.) Jim gets infected by John's emotions and fires something back. Now we're somewhere between 10 and 30 miles (depending on whether Jim's response is a barb hidden in jest or outright nasty). Even more distressed, John blazes back, 30 through 50. From there on, any pretense of civility is gone. From 50 to 100, both Jim and John start throwing verbal slings and arrows at each other and are pulling subtle threat displays. Nobody's backing down. We're now speeding down the highway between 100 and 149, the threat displays become more obvious, voices are raised, and threats are vocalized. At MM 150, John steps forward and pops Jim in the mouth.

What happens next depends on other factors. Having shown how serious he is does John step back and try to stay between MM 145 and 149? That's to say huffing and puffing. Does Jim curl up and cry? (Whereupon, John scales it back to 110.) Do people rush in and intervene, pulling it back to 130, and heading them back on the highway? (Both parties make face-saving noises as they're being pulled apart.) Or does Jim step up and pop Jim right back and start making more noise to show he's just as serious (bumping it up to between MM 160 to 175)? Does it turn into a mutual punch-out (ranging between 200 and 250)? Or does Jim just go full-on ballistic and throw John a beating on the spot? Or is John's hit the first in throwing Jim a beating? Either kicks it up to MM 300. Or does John do something farther down the road (like going out and getting a gun and coming back)? That's somewhere around Mile Marker 400 or 500. Given the circumstances, any of these can be a possibility.

Where this gets scary is I wasn't describing young people at an inner city party or rednecks at a bar. I was depicting were multiple events I know about that occurred in a rather affluent neighborhood, a place where house prices start at six figures. This also includes two separate incidents that went to Mile Marker 150 and 175 in a gated community. (One was just a single punch, the second escalated into an outright fight.) When I tell you violence is part of human behavior, I'm not making it up. It's not exclusive to sex, race, income, or culture. We *all* do it, what changes is the style. At the same time, as shocking as these cocktail party punch-outs may sound, these are still very low numbers on the road; there are still many more miles after things go physical.

I have to tell you something else, seeing Jim and John act like this might be shocking, unnerving, and really uncomfortable for you. Given my past and experience with violence, it's not only extremely minor, but it's about as common as a house fly. But we can learn a lot from this common pest; vermin you've seen or perhaps been involved with.

Using the basic idea of Jim and John, we're going to spend the rest of this chapter examining the ways your monkey can put you into conflict before you 'know what's happening.' Then we're going to expand beyond these low mile markers on the road of violence and follow the same dynamics out to where they can get you or someone else killed.

Start with this raw truth: In *any* violent conflict, there is the chance someone will die. Even the smallest, pettiest, and most stupid reason for conflict *can* escalate to this level. I have seen people die for some extremely idiotic reasons. That death might be yours, it might be the other person's.

But having said that, most of the time this is *not* the case. Making up a number to convey the idea in 99 percent of all situations involving physical violence (including the threat of extreme violence) *nobody* dies.

258 IN THE NAME OF SELF-DEFENSE

Death is neither the intent nor the result of violence.[120] Yet accidents happen, and sometimes when someone intends they succeed. An example of the former would have been if when John hit him Jim fell and cracked his skull. The second can be an intentional murder or a rage decision in the heat of the moment. (E.g., "I'll kill you, you son of a bitch!")

The significance of this is how many people—who don't want to accept this final outcome—still happily jump into the lower mileages of the violence road. They do this *without* hesitation because they not only don't expect certain actions, but down right rely on their belief of things not going that far.

When I said violence is a collective set of behaviors, I meant do *not* think of violence as one act alone. It's not just a strike or pulling the trigger. It's not just a word (it's that and how it's delivered). Think of all the other behavior present last time you saw someone get punched. What else was going on? What led up to that punch? How long did it take to get to that point? I guarantee you, it's pretty predictable. Those behaviors *are* as violent as actually hitting someone. Ordinarily, the more of them you see and the harder and faster they're coming means someone is that much closer to getting hit. These behaviors are mile markers that also indicate both speed and commitment. They're why violence is a process (collective, road) *not* a single act.

Let me re-stress something: It is rare to see a physical assault occur *without* conflict and verbal and emotional violence playing their parts in the whole process. Those facts alone should tell you something about those actions—even when performed separately. When you see these actions, you'll immediately recognize you're *traveling down* the road of violence. So start looking for the mile markers and the off ramps.

The flip side of that statement is just because something's rare doesn't mean it doesn't happen. Specifically, that normal build-up *doesn't* always happen. Physical violence can occur without emotional hostility nor is there necessarily a lengthy build up. Someone can go from Mile Marker 25 to 150 in a heartbeat.

In other cases, you're dealing with someone where 300-plus is the norm. The landmarks are *very* different. But those tend to be very specialized circumstances. Two examples are:

1) You're an outsider who has violated a rule and decided to argue about it.

2) You're dealing with—but not necessarily confronting—someone who routinely deals with higher levels of physical violence.

---

120   Amazingly enough, often when death *is* the intent due to many other factors it is often not the result.

Before we get to the specialized, let's look at how much control you *do* have in normal situations. If you accept the fact there are various types, degrees, and levels of violence, it loses a lot of its stigma. We can look at the situation from a rational human perspective. This includes closely examining what the monkey tells us to do. Snarling obscenities at someone *is* violent, it's just not as far down the road as slugging someone. Slugging someone isn't as far down (or going as fast) as beating the hell out of him. And throwing someone a beating *isn't* killing him.

I have a really bad bit of news: Your ancestors, hell, even your grandparents knew this. But today, we have seriously lost sight of it. How has this affected how you think? How you behave? What topics or behaviors do you subconsciously avoid and are afraid of? Seriously, stop and consider this for a moment.

As an example, I, as a Conflict Communications instructor, won't talk about you spanking your children. Instead, I phrase it as, "How many of you were spanked as children?" We can't ask people in a public forum if they ever physically disciplined their children. Few if any will admit to it because they're afraid of being accused of child abuse. That's how ingrained these modern attitudes about violence have become, and how out of touch we've become about the levels violence.

Even I find myself affected by this current taboo. A few years ago, my wife and I were standing in a line in the store when a child started acting up over wanting a doughnut. His mom warned him, he kept on throwing a tantrum to get what he wanted. Mom casually reached out and popped him lightly on the back of the head. My first immediate emotional reaction was a sharp inhale. Then I realized: A) It wasn't a hard hit. B) As a kid, I would have been smacked a lot harder. C) How conditioned I'd become by the constant barrage of information and editorializing about child abuse.

Once I got over this sensitized and knee-jerk response, I slowed down and looked. The kid was clean, well fed, well dressed, and showed the normal response to being disciplined and frustrated. So I relaxed. My wife, who raised four ranch daughters, didn't bat an eye. The cashier (who it turned had adopted and raised foster kids) didn't have a problem, either. The person who *did* have a problem was the middle-aged, upper middle class woman standing behind us. She was appalled. Aghast at this child abuse, she looked around for allies. Upon seeing that nobody was willing to become as outraged as she was, she stormed off.

The point of that story is teaching and being surrounded by middle class people for the last fifteen years, *it even got to me.*[121] So what has

---

121   Where would I put smacking that child on the road? Probably around MM 75 since the child was throwing a tantrum. Words and warnings weren't working, and the single smack was proportional (unlike the way she would have hit another adult).

it done to your perspective? We've been so over-sensitized to the idea that violence is bad, we've lost perspective. How many people have lost understanding of why violence sometimes is not just the best, but the fastest and most effective answer? Or even allowing that sometimes it is, what has this taboo done to our standards? Again, *these* are the people who will be sitting in the jury box.

Knowing that, we have to consider:
1) How do you know when violence *is* the answer?
2) How do you know when violence is the wrong answer—but you're doing it anyway?

With the first, I'm not talking articulation yet. I'm talking threat assessment. I'm talking about how do you reasonably and logically decide when it's time to go? What process do you use?

With the second, I'm talking about a problem most people have. It's a problem that's more than *not* recognizing they're on the highway. They also fail to realize how far along a situation has gone. Usually this blindness is caused by the fact their feet are pressing down on the accelerators. (We talked about the monkey slide in another chapter.)

Violence, hostility, and aggression are usually not okay, but they are things we have to deal with. It's *how* we deal with them that will either get us off the highway or send us farther down it and picking up speed. Also thinking of how far down the road an incident is (or can go) gets you out of your monkey brain. Not only about violence in general, but even when you're in the *middle* of it your train of thought becomes more, "Okay, so how bad is this particular incident?"

Once you're out of your monkey, reading the mile markers is actually pretty simple: The higher the number, the more landmarks, the farther along the situation has gone. The lower . . . Is this person just talking trash? That's a lower number (including on the JAM scale). Is this person talking *and* getting closer (higher number)? Is he close enough to be considered developing attack range (much higher)? There are mile markers and landmarks when things start to go toward physical conflict. Let's say someone is dithering about closing or does something physically to create distance. Like, say, pushing you back. Is that the same as Mile Marker 150 when John punched Jim? No. It is around MM 120 even though physical contact has been made. Even though your monkey will be screaming you're under attack, there's *still* a lot of road beyond that point.[122]

---

[122]   I often have to tell people, "This may be the worst thing you've ever seen, but it's not the worst I've seen. This often offends people who are selling how traumatic and horrible violence is. With all the sturm und drang they make about the evils of violence, they miss an important point. My litmus test for bad starts with did the person live? If yes, my response is, "Good, we can work with that." (This is where the outrage starts.) If the answer is no, my response is, "How many parts was the body found in?" Having dealt with monsters and freaks, I have a whole different scale of bad.

As the numbers go higher, the violence gets more intense and damaging. There are many different levels and degrees of force. I tell you this because a situation degenerating to the physical level does *not* mean it's a green light to nuke someone. (Jim wasn't legally justified to pull a gun or knife and do John on the spot for punching him.) Again, how far up or down the road a situation is dictates the viable options—including your chances of peacefully getting off said highway.

Take for example someone shoving you back, but standing there. Even though there's been physical contact, he's trying to *create distance* between you (that's why I said Mile Marker 120). Is he just standing and barking? He's trying to take it back to lower mileage. You returning into range to avenge the insult will be what bumps it to 150 (and turns it into a fight, undermining your SD claim). Or is he advancing? That could bump it up. If he's coming in to hit you, that's MM 150. If he's moving forward and drawing a weapon, it's jumped up to the 400s.

Here's something else to consider, there are lots of people who constantly zip up and down the lower numbers of this highway. They are verbally and emotionally attacking other people all the time. This is their *comfort zone* when it comes to violence.

When I use the term comfort zone, many people think I'm talking about ease, comfort, enjoyment, and—most of all—good feelings. I'm *not*. Our comfort zones are what we accept as normal and acceptable. It's not only what we can live with, but what we *expect* from others. People comfortable with lower mile marker violence are often quick-draws about insulting, degrading, backstabbing, yelling, and screaming at others. If this intimidation doesn't work, the worst they expect is people to yell and scream back at them. This is a known cost, a price they *know* they can handle. Despite the brouhaha about emotional trauma, negative emotions *do not* kill.[123]

That is a simple but profound concept. Being yelled back at and having their feelings hurt are stakes verbally and emotionally violent people are *willing* risk. In their pursuit of getting what they want it's acceptable. You may not enjoy engaging in this kind of violence, but you *and they* know it's survivable. Some folks do not hesitate to unleash verbal and emotional violence because it usually grants them a win.

Yet there's a step beyond that. Negative emotions and trauma drama *can* become someone's comfort zone. The process, feelings, and results of their behavior are predictable, acceptable, and some of them get off on

---

123   Negative or psychological traumas do not kill you. It's what you do about them that kills or causes problems. Depression may drive someone to suicide, but what killed him wasn't depression—it was overdosing on booze and drugs.

it. This goes beyond chronic self-soothing.[124] Some people are perfectly fine with getting in a screaming match because it makes them feel 'high.' Forget adrenaline, you can get addicted to dopamine.[125]

What these low-mile people are *not* prepared for is when—instead of responding to their emotional attack with counter verbal violence—someone tries to drive their noses through the backs of their skulls. Surprise! Different people have different comfort zones about violence, particularly when it comes to how they will react to your violence toward them.

When you get slugged for being verbally violent, odds are good either: a) *That* person came from a place farther down the road and is comfortable with a different level of force. b) The situation was farther down the road than your monkey thought it was.

Both touch on the point of violence provokes violence. Yet, the first statement (a) bears a closer look. When you're operating in your comfort zone, it's easy to think that if you throw the dice, these are the stakes you're playing for because, hey, you're in a known comfort zone, dealing with people who follow the same rules.

Here's a bit of a hitch, people can begin to assume their comfort zone extends to *anywhere* they are. So if they are comfortable verbally attacking people with little to no negative consequences, they won't hesitate to throw those dice. This is particularly common among people from civilized areas of society where the common response to rudeness and low-level aggression is to do nothing but pretend it didn't happen (as such, John never progresses past Mile Marker 5). In particularly egregious events, one might even work up to making a comment or an

---

124   The best way to describe chronic self-southing is in terms of addiction. An old model of addiction held that there were two kinds, physical and mental. Modern medicine has found that distinction is less and less valid. A big part of the physical aspect of addiction isn't feeling good, it's not hurting. Often, the person isn't getting high for euphoria anymore, but more for stopping what has become chronic pain caused by the absence of the substance. This is analogous to miserable people, who constantly verbally lash out to soothe their internal distress. It's not about feeling good, it's about not feeling so bad.

125   Although not officially recognized by the DSM V (*Diagnostic and Statistical Manual of Mental Disorders*, Fifth Edition) there are folks I call "rage-o-holics." These are people who employ tantrums and rage like an alcoholic uses getting drunk. They utilize fits of rage as a way self-southing, acting out, and releasing tension. Not to fix or change what they believe (what's creating this distress) but to regulate it and release the pressure so they *don't* have to change. I use an analogy of a pot of water on the stove. Most people are half filled; when heat is applied, there isn't any boiling over. Other people are pots that are filled too high. When heat is applied, they boil over. Instead of reducing the water level (changing what they think causes such strong emotions) they rely on routine boiling over to self-regulate their emotional distress.

obscene gesture. This is beyond Jim's MM 10, it's more like a one-sided 75. Nice people—who if they really get worked up can get to 50—often are intimidated by this 'extreme,' so it usually ends there. The verbally violent person wins and goes on his way. Except being verbally violent with strangers (or people they just know in passing) is throwing the dice *without* knowing the stakes. You don't know where that other person's comfort zone is or how fast he can accelerate to get there.

A good example of this—and a situation found in a fair number of cases I've worked on—involves getting into a dispute with a neighbor. Sure, you've lived next to that person for a while, but what do you really know about him? Add to that mix the fact people get strongly territorial when it comes to "my property." If something doesn't go their way, they can become very verbally aggressive. If things go way wrong, the situation goes physical. I've seen a lot of situations where two neighbors start swinging over a property dispute.

Recognizing that violence is a road—a collective set of behaviors—gets you out of the simplistic and moralizing mindset of "that is violence, and it's bad." It also takes you out of the false assumption that you don't engage in it. It shows you how easy it is to fall into this behavior. It also gets you looking at how commonly people use violence and the threat of physical violence to *get* what they *want*.

You can start seeing the whole process. This allows you to see how things escalate to extremes. And this will help you get off the road before the situation moves into physical aggression. Failing that, you learn to recognize when physical violence will happen *no matter what*, as well as the kind of violence you'll probably be dealing with. It doesn't seem like much, but this is a critical element in being able to mentally shift gears and do what you gotta. Uncertainty is a huge element contributing to the dreaded freeze.

The real benefit of learning how to recognize when we're on the road is the ability to get off it. There are off ramps you can take before things get too bad. But you won't know to take them if you don't *recognize* when you're on that road.

This brings us to significant problem number two: Violence *provokes* violence. This is especially important when it comes to recognizing our own violent behavior. Remember, we are designed to emotionally infect each other. Most people become violent when they are emotional, insecure, or feeling hurt. There's a term for people who a) can use force while calm and b) don't freak out when others throw emotions at them. The word is professionals.

But most of us aren't pros. Nor do we practice to be. When we are hit by a violent emotional tidal wave, we tend to react violently. Here is where we can fall into the same trap. When we get triggered this way, we tell ourselves we're *not* being aggressive. We're defending ourselves because this asshat . . . We're justified in acting this way, because . . . I'm feeling . . . He wronged me when he . . . You get the idea. It is important to remove moral judgment—strongly linked to emotions and 'deserving'—from the assessment of am I being violent?

When you're emotional, this is a lot harder to do than you might think. It's hard to see when you're being violent. And the people who have the hardest time seeing this are those who categorically think *violence is bad.* The monkey is damned good at blinding us to what we actually are doing—especially when it comes to our own low mileage violence.

Don't worry, you'll still be able to see when someone else is being violent and aggressive. Take Jim and John woofing at each other. I mean it's right there in front of you, *even* the low mileage stuff. Your monkey is damned good at spotting it—even the subtle stuff hiding behind a smile or joke. This goes double when it's aimed at you.

But more than that, the violent person is usually going out of his or her way to attract your attention and communicate their violence. That person *wants* you to notice, even if they're trying to be subtle enough to create doubt.[126] If you don't recognize the threat, how is he (or she) going to win?

Most overt verbal violence is—later—justified as: "He hurt my feelings," "I was warning him not to mess with me," "I wanted him to back off," and other rationalizations. Again, commonly *not* a hogwash answer. These *were* the person's monkey goals. The problem is the monkey decided the best way to achieve these goals was through verbal aggression. Better known as . . . an . . . attack. This pushes the gas pedal and farther down the road we go.

I'll give you two side points to this behavior. Side point A starts as a question: *Why* do people become violent? Come up with an answer before we proceed. Got one?

I prefer asking that question in a room full of people. They come up with all kinds of reasons why someone can become violent—fear, anger, frustration, jealousy, and various other reasons. That's the point of asking a group, I want people to hear other people's answers. That's because, they are *all* correct! People *do* become violent for all those reasons, not just the reason you came up with. But collecting all them into one unified answer, we come up with consistent point: *People become violent because they want something.*

---

126   Start with the people who slip in sly digs to insult you, but leave the wording vague enough that you're not sure they've just taken a shot at you. Then upgrade it to people who insult or threaten you, and then play it off as a joke. Then you get the real asshats who misbehave and then try to blame you for being too sensitive.

Look at the answer you came up with and ask, "What did the person want?" This brings us to a "wow, I never thought about it that way" realization. Overwhelmingly, violence *has* a clear goal. It's a goal, even if it can't be put into a wheelbarrow. It's an understandable goal, even if you think it's as screwed up as a soup sandwich. It's a goal even if you think it's stupid. Even if you think violence is the absolute worst way to get there, there's a clear goal—usually a pretty simple one.

After you read this, I want you go back and read the previous paragraph. *All* of those judgments get in the way of *understanding* violence.

The monkey wants to make up complicated narratives about violence and why those who engage in it are stupid, evil, wrong, and broken. In short, the reasons we're superior to them. Who cares if that conclusion is wrong? It's more emotionally satisfying than an actual understanding of violence dynamics.[127] These judgments also keep us from recognizing when we are infected or are infecting others. (Free safety tip: If the word deserve is anywhere close to your thinking, you're infected.) When you take away monkey brain judgmental thinking, violence is actually an easily understood subject. If you can accept this idea not just your understanding of violence increases, but so does your ability to make good use-of-force decisions.

Bar none, the most common goal of violence is to *get* people to *change* their behavior—starting with wanting a certain behavior to stop or another behavior to start. Now the question is: Are they going to tell you to do it (threat) or are they going to do it for you (physical violence)?

Gee, another tattoo, scrawl it on the wall, potentially life saving bit of information: Violence comes with *instructions* on how to avoid it. You might recognize it as element number three about violence. Ninety-nine percent of the time, the guy is going to *tell* you what to do to keep from being hurt. That's because physical violence is *not* the goal. Violence—and the threat of it—is a means to his goal. He wants the *results.* Yes, someone who says leave or he will kick your butt is more interested in you leaving than kicking your posterior. Yes, someone saying shut up or he will throw you a beating is more interested in your shutting up than beating you. Yes, a mugger will use the threat of violence to get what he wants. Guess what? As he's pointing a gun at you, he'll tell you what he wants. It's a simple deal: Give him what he wants, and he won't shoot you.

But what about someone who hits you? Say, he slugs you for saying something. Odds are good, he told you to shut up before he punched you. And if you got slugged, odds are better that you *didn't* shut your

---

127   "You don't want to understand violence you just want to judge it." Start with juries. Move on to the victim narrative, policies, programs, ideologies, and lobbying. That's what you're up against when you claim self-defense. Factor that into your decision making.

mouth—most of the time. Remember too little, too late? But even more common is you told him what he could do with his telling you to shut up. Stop and think about that, though. This behavior *isn't* a one-way street. By telling him to back off, *you* were trying to get him to *change* his behavior toward you. ("Listen, jackass! Don't you tell me to shut up!") We communicate what we want—including relaying the message that *you* don't get to tell *me* what to do.

Here's something to try, go to YouTube or some other site where videos of violence are posted and find the longer ones. Not just the clips that start with it going physical. Then *listen*. Yes, you'll hear threats, but try listening to them as warnings. Often in the earlier stages, the communication about how to avoid conflict is quite clear. (Although often these boring parts are edited out, so in those clips it just looks like violence explodes without warning.)

After the primary idea of wanting something, there comes all kinds of other stuff (e.g., teach someone a lesson, prevent future events, getting off on their fear, and other factors). But those are mostly details, versions of what someone wants. In all that variation, it's easy to miss that main point of wanting something.

By taking it down to this fundamental level, you remove moral judgment and the need to rationalize why your behavior isn't violent or aggressive. Violence is just a tactic. You also greatly increase your ability to keep from being infected when confronted by violent behavior. So if you need to act, it isn't out of such monkey motivations as punishing the guy, teaching him a lesson or he deserved it.

Use of force is a means to an end. It's a fundamental mechanism we humans use *all* the time. It's not good or bad at this level. It just is. Higher up the intellectual ladder, we add moral judgments about whether it's good or bad. The problem is how often we do that without thinking?

Remember, I said a big part of this book is showing you how to avoid situations where you have to physically defend yourself? That our subconscious and unconscious reactions happen *faster* than we can consciously think. Okay, cool. We get a stimulus and react. Usually the right message is sent, and it's a good thing—until it isn't.

When you're dealing with someone who routinely plays farther down the road than you are accustomed, things can seem to spin out of control at an amazing speed. He says something, you say, "Screw you," and—out of nowhere—he punches you! No that *wasn't* out of nowhere. You got slugged because of (among other things) what you said. It only came as a surprise because you're probably from a place where immediate physical violence isn't the common response to verbal violence. There's supposed to be a drawn out build up of verbal abuse and threats. (Think, Richard Jeni.)

Here is where you *can* take control back from the monkey. Just because the monkey is screaming at you to do something does *not* mean you have to do it. We respond to the monkey's commands from *habit*—not because we have no choice. We've been listening to the monkey all our lives. It's telling us this is the right thing and because it's right, we don't question it. Add the fact, we've been doing it for so long we've come to believe that feeling equals acting. In fact, we perceive them as simultaneous. They. Are. Not.

Were they simultaneous, there would be *no* way to control them. It would be a single beat. One and it's over. If that were true, there is no approach the human brain could take to catch on, catch up, and intervene. Again, a lie to children, but think of your reactions as a four-stage process that goes from external to internal and back out to external:

1) See and hear (this is the external incoming stimuli)

2) Perceive (interpret the stimuli and assign a value or intent)

3) Adrenaline dump, emotion triggering an habitual monkey response

4) Act (going back out to external) [128]

For the record, this is a damned good system—when it comes to surviving in an environment where there are lions, tigers, and bears are trying to eat you. Something jumps out of the bushes and BOOM! You're up a tree before you even think about it. Except, I don't know about you, but I haven't had to wrestle any saber-toothed tigers lately . . .

So let's look at this in our modern world. Steps one, two, and three happen faster than the human brain can kick in. You're triggered, and it looks like nothing will stop the landslide. Well, not exactly. You can stop the process. But, if you *don't know* you can take back control of the process just past three, four *will* happen. This loss of control has become a conditioned response for a lot of people. Not having control of themselves is a *habit*. A habit that the more they engage in, the stronger it becomes.

Have you ever found yourself in an argument and wondered how it happened? Much less, how did it happen so fast? Well, now you know. Odds are your monkey responded so fast, you don't even know that it made you go off (e.g,, a facial expression of contempt). Being so insulted, you hardly remember you told him to go do unnatural acts. Basically, you wake up and find yourself speeding down the violence highway. You're left wondering, "How the hell did I get here?"

Breaking this habit of non-control is an important life hack. But there's more. The more we tell ourselves we're helpless before our emotions, the more of a self-fulfilling prophecy it becomes. That's to say, the stronger

---

[128]   If you're into such, this is a classic OODA loop (observe, orient, decide, act conceived by Col. John Boyd) except decide is changed to habitual.

the habit becomes. The faster we speed through these steps as though there is no way to break the process, the truer it becomes. It's hard to stop because we're *out* of the habit of stopping. And that's why knowing about these stages is so important. No matter how fast we go through the first stages, it *is* one, two, and three. Once you reach three, there your monkey is with revving engine and ready to slam it into gear to send you speeding down the highway. But four is *not* inevitable. The human brain *can* step in and abort the process. Remember the arroyo and body surfing analogies? Pick one or design your own.

I'm going to get a little woo-woo and philosophical here. You are not your monkey. Believing that is who you are is another habit. Nor are you the monkey's bitch. Just because the monkey tells you, "This is reality," you *don't* have to believe it. In fact, double check it. That simple statement can save you all kinds of problems not just regarding violence, but in all aspects of your life.[129]

The other thing is just because the monkey is screaming at you to do something doesn't mean you have to act. More than that, your own screaming monkey is being violent with *you*. It's threatening you with horrible visions of what will happen if you don't change your behavior. Yeah, *that's* violence. First, that doesn't mean it's true. Second, the monkey cannot make you do anything. You and *you alone* have that control. Let me restate that because it is important: Just because you're feeling something doesn't mean you have to act. Your monkey cannot make you do anything. Thing is, if you've developed the habit of automatically doing what the monkey tells you, it seems like you have *no* choice. But it is you, who is actually acting on the monkey's imperious commands. Remember not having a choice is a *habit*. Therefore, the question is how deeply ingrained is that habit? Then comes, how do you break it? But that's a whole different can of worms—and once again beyond the scope of this book.[130]

What is not beyond this book's capacity is how easy it is to snap, "Screw you and you're your ancestors" at someone. How easy it is to react from habit instead of conscious and considered thought—especially when you're angry or scared. Acting in this manner will catapult you out of the SD square—as so many people sitting in prison for illegal violence found out the hard way.

---

129   A simple life hack: When you feel insulted instead of reacting to your decision that you're under attack, ask the other person, "What did you mean by that?" You'll be appalled at how many times something you interpreted as a deliberate attack wasn't that at all. But even more fun is watching the way someone—who disguises their digs under vague comments—has to dance, stumble, and pretend they weren't attacking.

130   A good starting point is Rick Carson's book, *Taming Your Gremlin: A Surprisingly Simple Method For Getting Out of Your Own Way* (2003)

It doesn't matter how much the monkey is revving the engine or what gear it's trying to put you into. Your human foot on the clutch means that vehicle isn't going anywhere. You're not going to do anything until *you* choose to. This gives you and your human brain time to think and find a better option than telling this guy to go commit incest with his mother, which is *exactly* what your monkey will be screaming at you to say to him. There are all kinds of complicated stuff about self-identity, comfort zones, and learned behavior tied to these habits. "Well, I always react XX." Really? Have you tried to break that habit? But again, those are way past the scope of this book.[131]

I can't tell you how many cases I've worked where someone was arrested because they'd gotten into a fight with a neighbor. Cases where the defendant walked out of his house, off his property to complain, and things escalated. Or road rage incidents where the defendant got out of his car to confront the other guy, who jumped out of his. Or where the defendant said or did something that provoked a physically violent response and then—quote—defended him- or herself.

To a person, they *all* considered themselves good, non-violent people. They were stunned at how normal habits exploded in the face of abnormal circumstances. If it can happen to them, it can happen to you. It's critical you learn your human brain is fast enough to intervene by stage three to keep you from going to stage four. Not only will this save you from all kinds of unnecessary violence, but as you will see in another chapter, it also can save your life.

That's because predators want to trigger your monkey brain reactions. Doing so gives them the advantage. A huge advantage. It's a tactic they consciously use against you. We'll discuss that in greater depth later. For right now, let's stick with dealing with you getting emotionally infected in everyday situations that can lead to violence. An even bigger problem is when the initial monkey brain reaction doesn't work. So what does the monkey do? It does it again . . . but louder and more aggressively. Worse is when we see things are going downhill, but the monkey gets stubborn.

Monkey, "Damn it! I'm handling this!"

You, "Yeah, but it's going downhill fast."

Monkey, "I know what I'm doing, now shut up, and let me drive!"

You, "Monkey, that guy is getting seriously angry at your telling him to shut up."

Monkey, "Shut up! I said I'm handling this!"

And what your monkey is doing is speeding you down along the road of violence. Your human and lizard brains have no problem with *not*

131   Do a Google search on breaking bad habits. Start small. For example, if you become uncomfortable when someone compliments you, and you make deprecating remarks practice saying, "Thank you," instead.

throwing gasoline on a fire. In fact, they're really cool about not doing that. But not the monkey. Its attitude is, "This is how things work! And if it isn't working, do more of it. And louder. A cup of gasoline on the fire? Oh no. But when I pour the whole gas can on, the fire will go out!"

This is monkey logic. More than that, the monkey can be damned stubborn about having its assessment of the situation questioned. Remember back in the lawyer chapter where we talked about having to get across the fact that the prosecutor is wrong about his interpretation (six plus three, when in fact it's six times three)? Well, you also have to do that with your *own* monkey.

Now that last paragraph might not make much sense now, but in another chapter you'll get another piece of the puzzle that I mentioned earlier. That is how predators turn social scripts against you in order to set up their attacks. The monkey's stubbornness about letting go and having another part take over is—*overwhelmingly*—what allows people to be successfully attacked by predators. (Basically, the monkey insists it's six plus three, while the lizard and human know that's a multiplication sign.) Coming out of the monkey brain—its goals and definitions—is the best deterrence to violence and gives you a better chance if things still go physical. And this brings us back to the original subject, finding yourself on the road of violence.

If you don't counter verbal violence with more verbal violence (which your monkey will be screaming at you to do) you greatly reduce the odds of things escalating to physical conflict. Because not only does violence provoke violence, but—as often as not—violence *escalates* violence, too! Remember Jim and John? Both were infected. Yes, your verbal violence is likely to elicit equal counter verbal violence. But odds are good what you're going to get back is louder and more aggressive, which in turn can prompt you into the same. This dynamic can push things farther down the road, including allowing the situation to escalate into a physical confrontation.

In your rational human brain, you *know* this. You've seen it. You've experienced it. Sitting here calm and reading, it is so obvious that it might even seem insulting to talk about it. But your monkey is even *more* convinced that's how you handle another monkey. And when you're adrenalized and emotional, it's real easy for the monkey to grab the steering wheel, slam the vehicle into gear, and hit the gas. Not responding to verbal violence with verbal violence breaks the escalation script.[132] It is literally turning and getting off that road or at least doing a U-turn and heading back the way you came.

---

132   Now how you do it is up to you and a matter of style. I would advise caution when it comes to humor unless it is self-deprecating. (E.g., "Screw you!" Response: "You wouldn't like it. I'd just lay there and sweat.") Do a Google search on de-escalation and de-escalation techniques.

While the monkey is utterly fixated on winning (whether it's dominating the other monkey, chasing it away, changing that monkey's behavior, or impressing watching monkeys) it ignores the fact its behavior is escalating the situation. This is why claims of self-defense are given the hairy eyeball. Way too often both parties were busy pouring gasoline onto the fire—simultaneously—and are absolutely convinced they were defending themselves. I cannot stress this enough: Engaging in this behavior *decimates* your self-dense claim.

And this brings us to another overlooked issue: The *threat* of physical violence is many times *more* effective than actual physical conflict. (Man, your forehead and walls must be running out of space to write things . . .)

Once again, going down to a fundamental level to take out judgment, humans have imagination.[133] When we feel threatened, it is our imagination that tells us what could happen. That's why threats *work*—especially if we don't think we have the means to counter the danger. When it comes to threats: We are the ones doing most of the work to make them effective. We are the ones choosing to alter our behavior when we feel threatened.

Bringing something back from the threat display chapter, they are not saying, "I am attacking." They are saying, "I *might*." As such, this is more about *communication* than actual danger. If we look at it objectively, most are in fact very low on the road of violence, much less JAM.

Tying this back to violence is a collective set of behaviors. I can be a very scary person—as in, I've had bad guys on three different continents hit high gear to get the hell away from me when I go werewolf. But when I'm teaching, the entire room cracks up when—in the ultimate Casper Milque Toast, nerd body language, facial expression, voice tone, and volume—I squeak, "Excuse me, but I'll kick your ass if you don't stop doing that." It's just *not* credible. But change the body language, and the threat becomes all kinds of believable.

When the threat becomes credible, people's imaginations take over. Tone of voice, a certain type of look, or just the presence of someone who has threatened them with physical violence can make someone freak out. This can go on for days, months, and years. But in comparison to all these mind games, physical violence occurs in only a matter of seconds. (And, boy, does that statement apply to both bullying and stalking.)

This is another reason why thinking of violence as a road is such a critical paradigm shift. That person may not think he or she is being

---

133   I suspect imagination is a survival strategy that has done very well by our species. It's arguable if we have instincts (behavior that doesn't have to be taught). We don't have the blind instinct to gather nuts for the winter, like a squirrel, or to gorge ourselves, like bears before hibernation. But apparently our ancestors were able to imagine that winter would return, so maybe it was a good idea—while everything was green and there was lots of food—to store enough for lean times.

violent, but they are definitely on that road. And he or she is trying to get you to imagine them going farther if you don't change what you're doing. Consciously knowing about that gives you a huge spectrum of other options than just getting emotionally infected.

And this brings us to the fourth significant element about violence (about damned time). Experienced people—who knowingly use violence—*know* it can be used right back against them.

I've lived much of my life according to the creed: Be prepared to kill or die over your words. This is neither hyperbole nor macho posturing. I've *seen* people die over their words and actions.[134] Add to this, I've had people try and kill me over mine. I've certainly spit enough blood. Contrary to what one might think, this creed has made me particularly careful about using verbal violence and hostility. As in, if I'm not willing to bleed over it *don't* do or say it.

We're heading to a point where road of violence analogy can start getting . . . well . . . a little quantum; a place where different points on the highway can end up interacting. Or to put it another way, a churchgoer, who only attends on Christmas and Easter, and a fanatic can be sitting in the same pew.

Much of what is said about violence is by people who either suck at it or farm it out (have others do it for them, e.g., the police). This seriously screws up what you think you know about it. To the violence never solved anything cliché, I've heard a retort, "Then you're doing it wrong." There is a degree of truth to that. But it's based on something so fundamental, we seldom think of it. That is much of what we hear about the subject is predicated on the assumption that violence is always a *one-way* street.

What does the word victim imply to you? What do you think you know about bullying? Abuse? Domestic violence? The significance of asking is to show that most of what people think they know about violence comes from this one-sided perspective.[135]

This includes the proposed solutions, and often no other resolution is allowed. For example, the horror of an active shooter incident only continues as long as the shooter is the only one firing a gun. One way or the other (including suicide) active shooter situations are overwhelmingly

---

134   What is appalling is how often the dieing person has a look of shock on his or her face about the fact it's happening, despite what they just said or did. Seriously, what did they expect? The answer is their monkey expected it to work, for them to win, or at least to get away with it.

135   Google quotes about violence, and you'll mostly get quotes about the evils of violence and superiority of pacifism.

resolved by firearms.[136] The sooner they get there, the fewer the people who die. As such, you'd think having armed personnel at a school makes sense. Yet, I cannot tell you how dead set against this solution the same people, who fear school shootings, are.

This one-sided approach affects our perceptions about the way violence occurs. Worse, it negatively impacts our understanding of what it takes to stop it—starting with the guy who is running up to scream in your face. Often, he has no conscious idea his actions put him at somewhere between Mile Marker 200 and 300 (high JAM). Subconsciously, we have to consider both deniable malice and a learned habit he relies on for success—as in part of him knows exactly what he's doing.

Add to that, with his actions he's traveling at 100 miles per hour. It never occurs to him as he charges that a reasonable and defensible action is for someone to whip around and straight arm him. After he gets up, he's going to squeal like a stuck pig, so be prepared. Yet, if he were to crack his skull open when he hit and die, someone—who could articulate the danger his behavior normally represents—could walk on manslaughter charges. That's *if* that person was arrested at all.

If they were to know about the road, way too often such screamers would claim they're only around Mile Marker 100 if that. So they get hysterical when someone pulls a gun or knife on them. That is assuming they're fast enough to recognize the danger they've put themselves in and break it off before you blow their brains into a fine pink mist. But always remember, when they break off the behavior, you *do,* too. The threat has passed. Still if you don't kill them, expect histrionics and outrage.

I tell you that to add: People who are familiar with the full extent of the road of violence are—in many ways—much easier to deal with, especially when they recognize you are familiar with it, as well. It's the amateurs, the one-way streeters and the *I'm not being violent* deniers who are the real pains.

I spent many years dealing with extremely dangerous people. I'm talking you-dead-without-hesitation dangerous. Oddly enough, these people were the easiest to deal with. They were calm, respectful, predictable, and—in many ways—*far* more trustworthy. Trustworthy? Yeah. You knew there were certain lines you didn't cross with them. If you did, bad things happened. If you didn't cross those lines, you were basically safe. If they set up a deal, odds were they'd stick to it. The thing

---

136   Despite the media coverage of Antionette Tuff talking down school shooter Michael Hill (2014) there's more to that resolution than talk. The police had arrived and exchanged fire with Hill. He'd taken refuge in the office where, facing death if he continued, he allowed himself to be talked down by Tuff. It doesn't take anything away from the bravery of Tuff's actions, but it debunks the contention that words alone solved this incident.

about truly dangerous people is they know they are *not* alone. They know there are equally, if not more, dangerous people out there. People who are just as of good shots as they. Just as fast to shoot or stab. Just as sneaky and just as able to break bones. They know the higher ends. They know the rules and the warning signs of who not to mess with without good reason. They knew life at MM 300-plus and how dangerous it was. When you're dealing with people as dangerous as you are, you'd damned well better know how to behave.

Where they were the easiest to deal with was when it came to finding ways to keep things from going to physical violence especially when they knew you'd not only shoot back, but if it came to it, shoot first. The average person has *no* idea how much compromise, negotiation, and peace keeping goes on at these levels.

If there's violence in these leagues, it comes in two common forms. One is it's off the radar . . . until someone discovers a body. And usually it remains an unsolved homicide. In these leagues, you probably won't die right then and there, but in a few hours, days, or a week your old haunts will take on a whole new meaning.

Two is that people who play at the 200-plus mile markers begin to lose the lower mileage signs. Three hundred and beyond, you hardly ever get the posing, posturing, and noise of overt threat displays or the drama of build-up. If it happens in public, it seems to take a quantum leap from 75 to 350-plus. Again giving rise to the belief that it came out of nowhere.

Sure you might get a dangerous situation with an out-of-control punk, screaming and waving a gun. But with that kind of behavior, the odds are good he's the only one with a gun—and he knows it. Pull that in the wrong place, and the punk would be shot by five different people from around the room.

Again, too much of what we *think* of as how bad guys behave is based on movies and incidents where the violence was one-way streets or a macho fight. But people who survive in environments where high level violence is common don't make it a habit to engage in grandiose threat displays. They've transitioned into pre-attack indicators, and they're not about to consciously tip their hands. The cost of doing so is too extreme.

While John and Jim were disregarding the signs they knew,[137] this is different. It's why so many people claim it came out of nowhere or that the guy just went off on them. No, the mile marker signs and landmarks of this level of violence were there. The 'victim' just didn't *recognize* their significance and kept on misbehaving.

Here is where the road of violence analogy gets quantum. Hell, it gets

---

137   Not ignoring and actually not disregarding them either, but reacting to by escalating via, "Oh yeah? Well, I'll show you . . . !"

downright science fiction-like. And that is two points hundreds of miles apart are right next to each other through a fold in space and time. That means you can be at Mile Marker 100 traveling at 90 mph, and the guy you're cussing at is at 450. Mix in, you're going 90 mph, he's moving at 250 mph, and it gets real wobbly analogy wise. In real life, three guesses whom that isn't going to turn out well for?

That's why it's important to recognize the landmarks and mile markers. Not just of where you are, but *where* the other guy is and how *fast* he's going. You may think the situation is at 100, but it's *not*. That's why you also have to look for landmarks. There are certain behaviors that *only* show up at the higher mile markers. (The "Ahhh fuck" signs from the pre-attack indicators chapter, for example.)

The higher the mileages, the faster the landmarks and signage come into view and flash by. You're not ready to shoot someone, but he is. It's not really quantum at all. *That's* where the situation is at even if you aren't there yet. In the same vein, let's say throwing someone a beating is at Mile Marker 300. Let's also say this guy habitually roams between mile markers 250 and 350, and what you're throwing at him is the equivalent of you being stuck in traffic at MM 75. That low mileage behavior is going to irritate him. So we're back to three guesses whom . . .

Coming back to something I said earlier. Normal people not understanding—in these leagues—how often things are resolved with just a look or a quiet word. Or so it would seem. To be more precise, issues are resolved with a quiet word and a whole lot more *left unsaid.*

My friend Sam was called in on a situation. A guy had been misbehaving around a bunch of women, one of whom ran and got Sam. Now Sam is a truly sweet, caring, and loving man—who also happens to be able to break someone in half (high mile marker stuff). Sam calmly walked in to where this man was intimidating everyone and quietly told him it was time to leave. The man looked at Sam, assessed that violence was an option—just not a really pleasant one for him—and quietly left. When the amazed women asked Sam what he had done, he replied, "I just talked to him." Technically, Sam told the truth. On one obvious level, all he did was talk. But it was all those unsaid elements that did the work.

While the guy was running around at Mile Marker 100 and intimidating nonviolent people, Sam appeared not to be on the road at all—at least to the nonviolent. Yet 250-plus was on the table, and the troublemaker recognized it. Put in terms of this analogy, he recognized the landmarks and knew not to trust the seemingly low number signs Sam was projecting. He knew something was off in such a situation. Starting with the fact, Sam calmly walked into the room. Then came the talking quietly and politely. The unspoken message was Sam was good enough that he wasn't afraid of him.

The problem is people—who don't recognize the unspoken—think words *do* all the work. Such people have unrealistic expectations about the power of words. While it is true, language has power, it *only* has power if someone is listening. Quiet words also have a whole lot more power if they're backed up with mile markers that read 3-something-something, and the landmarks are of pending and extreme violence.

That brings us to the problems of when one person (believes he or she) controls all the violence and doesn't want to listen. These people tend to require a lot more force to stop. *Not* because they're so dangerous (e.g., that guy who runs up hard and fast on you could only have been planning to scream at you) but because they're so *committed* to their course of action. They:

a)   Often don't acknowledge they're being violent
b)   If they know they're being violent, think they have a monopoly
c)   Have gotten away with going that much further than everyone else (out of control)
d)   Miss the signals when it's not working
e)   Often can't stop in time.

These people are speeding up and down the road being all kinds of low-level violent. But they often don't recognize violence can be used *right back* against them. Thinking it's a one-way street, they blow past the warning signs that they're about to get their heads caved in.

The ones who tend to be the most dangerous—not because they're good, but because they're out of control—are the people who *think* they have a monopoly on violence. This especially means the young, stupid, aggressive, and insecure. I'm talking the mad dawgin', truculent sneer punk, who glowers at every citizen in the place. I'm talking about the high school bully, who relies on everyone else to behave, while he's being a complete goon. I'm talking about the guy who thinks his waiting for you in the shadows with his knife or gun over an insult is the proper response. These are the guys who swagger in making noise and daring anyone to mess with them. They're damned fast at committing assaults, but actually suck at fighting.

Here's where you get a unique form of mental disconnect. A whole lot of people don't actually think they have a monopoly on violence. Commonly, what they usually have is a *limited* definition of who they think is dangerous—at least more dangerous than they think they are. This is a very special brand of stupid. One that is going to get a lot of innocent people hurt before someone hands this jackass his liver.

But let's look at when violent people know violence can be used against them. You see a pack of gang bangers in an area. Here's an important exercise: Take a close look at the environment when they *don't* act up. You notice them when they are making noise. But here's a hint: When they're making noise something is *missing* from the environment. When they're not, something *is there.*

That's what I want you to start looking for, some detail that keeps them in line (or at least not acting out). Often it's over something like the fact they're in someone else's territory. They're with family. They're doing something mundane, like laundry, shopping, or school. They're alone. Whatever, they're choosing not to 'represent.'[138] But often there's something way bigger and more dangerous than they are in the area, something or someone who isn't making noise, but is enough to shut them down.

Decades ago, an old brawling buddy and I had to take a bus to a sporting goods store. This was the only store in the area that carried boxing wraps (cloth to wrap around the hand to protect it while working on a heavy punching bag). We were on the way back and the bus was crowded when five gang bangers got on. Looking at us, they didn't like what they saw.

They looked around, at us, at the other commuters, and one did a test. "Woof?" No reaction. Another joined in, "Woof! Woof!" Again, no reaction. Knowing they could get away with it, they all joined in and it got bolder and louder. "Woof! Woof! Woof! WOOF!" People were getting uncomfortable and even scared. My partner and I just kept looking at each other. The lil' gang bangers were getting more confident. They hadn't crossed the line yet, but they were working their way up to getting froggy. Up to that point, it was just general noise, but it was only a matter of time before their behavior specifically targeted us.

I reached into the bag, pulled out the wraps, and opened the package. I tossed one to my buddy. Without a word, we started wrapping our right hands. As we did this, the woofing subsided. When we finished, we just kept on looking at each other . . . waiting. The gangstas all got off at the next stop.

That story is background to get you to look at an unconsciously ignored element, the other commuters. While this was happening, there were a

138   Although represent means to stand up and show outsiders why they don't cross your gang, this has become more of a life saver. Back in the bad old days, simply crossing into another gang's territory was enough to get you killed. Representing or *not* are really goofy compromises of "I'm really a big, bad gang member, but since I'm not acting up, please don't shoot me because you're from another gang. I'm not on the clock right now." Crossing another gang's territory during school hours and along designated routes is *not* representing. Odds are good, you won't get shot. Driving down the same street with eight of your friends that night, throwing your gang signs, and raising hell *is* representing. This can get you shot. As silly as this may sound, it actually does work to keep the body count down.

lot of nervous people. After the guys got off the bus, everyone relaxed. Stop and think about that for a second. The people had their *attention* on the troublemakers. Like mice in a locked room realizing there's a cat in there too, they were paying attention. Yet despite the fact they were supposedly focused on the noisy group, they *did not* see what had chased them from the bus. They were too focused on the noise and perceived danger to actually see what was happening in that situation. But the real wait-a-minute observation was people were scared of five gang bangers, but not scared of the two guys, who scared them off. Why should they be frightened? We weren't doing anything, we were just sitting there.

You could say, "What the commuters were focusing on were their feelings not what was happening." By this I mean while supposedly focusing on what was happening, mostly what they were paying attention to were their emotions and hoping they wouldn't be drawn into a mess. They weren't paying attention to what was actually *happening*.

That's a simple but profound thought. In heuristics and bias study, there's a thing called attentional bias (what we think about and focus on influences our perceptions). I've also mentioned the difference between fear and danger management. (Fear management is about soothing your emotions over an imagined danger. Danger management is about reducing the actual danger.[139]) It's too easy for people to focus on their fears and discomforts. In essence even though the commuters were paying attention, they didn't know what they were seeing. It wasn't obvious enough for them.[140]

That same discomfort is going to strongly affect *what* the witnesses tell the cops. They won't be lying, but their discomfort influences what they saw. So don't be the one they remember as being a total louse.

Moving on . . . It's not uncommon when two are people in a conflict that one is more committed. One is more willing, more invested in using physical violence than the other. That's basically because he thinks he can *get away* with it. (Although that sentence was phrased in the masculine, women do it, too.) The other person is not as willing, not as fast to use, not as committed to winning by physical violence. In such situations, the person who makes a bigger *display* of being out of control and violent wins.

This leads us to the assumption that *all* violence is wild and out of control. That's the behavior people see (although technically *notice* is the right word). This myopia blinds them to other options. Through this

---

139   Entirely too much training is fear rather than danger management.
140   This dynamic becomes very important when it comes to understanding what witnesses will tell the police. It's important they see you engaging in behavior they *recognize* as you trying to avoid physical confrontation. In fact, that's just as important as their not seeing behavior they recognize as you pouring gasoline on the fire.

filter, they conclude there's *nothing* a normal person can do to sto_r when such a person is acting out. That is what they believe they know when they think of violence. There is some truth to this. In reality, someone who has come to rely on the threat of violence tends to be more committed—when he or she chooses to act out. But a big part of that commitment is the belief he or she *can* get away with acting like this.

Here is where things get really stupid. In the same way I wanted you to start looking for the danger in the environment that you didn't see before, I want you to start looking for something else. Start looking for: How often people don't see danger signals outside their own perceptions.

This goes beyond not knowing something is dangerous. For example, years ago my boss and I came around the corner to find a co-worker smoking a cigarette while working with a chemical that had a flashpoint of 500 degrees. (In her defense, the co-worker just didn't know.) Without knowing about the flash point, there was no perception of danger. What I'm talking about is a person from one culture not recognizing the danger signs of a person from another. This is especially problematic when someone from a loud demonstrative culture confronts someone from a quiet, but explosive culture.

But this can happen to you. Years ago, I noticed something I started calling "cartoon tough." It came about because I noticed people's behavior changed toward me depending on how I was dressed. So-called tough guys—who would scramble to get away when I was in my leathers or work clothes—would either not see me at all or swagger across my path when I was wearing a suit. Far worse were the ones who would come up and try to get in my face. It was almost as if they couldn't see beyond the suit and—often—my skin color. Nice clothes and a haircut somehow jammed their radar until I turned into a werewolf right in front of their eyes.

Sex and age can also jam these idiot's radar. This can be a serious problem for women, older people, and concealed carry people because the problem child doesn't recognize your warning signals over your clothing, age, and social class. That's why you seriously need to focus on communication, preparation, and commitment, instead of threat displays.

We'll talk about his over-commitment in a bit, which is part of the problem. Another part of the issue is what body language you present. (Again, start by reading Desmond Morris's *Manwatching*. Then on the second reading, study the threat display chapter.) Partly, it's your learning how to set boundaries. A big part is developing the commitment, so your body is throwing "I'm about to do serious violence to you" signals and *not* throwing out scared monkey signals.

no way to fake these. When they are real, it doesn't matter ming from a five foot nuthin' woman Ask your instructor to practice how to present the right signals and avoid the wrong t most of all, it's making the mental shift that you are willing to serious violence to stop them. That shift is what takes it out of a blustering threat that you hope will scare him away and turns it into a subconscious 'leak' of intent.

Here's where we come to a crossroads. A person who is both acting out and has experience with physical violence as a two-way street *knows* he can lose. So when he encounters resistance, he has two main options:

1) Back off

2) Crank it up

Number one is where we revisit a point I made in the "What Is Self-Defense" chapter. He *has* to know that it's safe for him to back off. As goofy as it sounds, you're going to have to communicate to him that it *is*. Hell, sometimes you have to walk the guy through the process. "The door is over there. Back away slowly, keep your hands in plain view, and you'll get out of this alive . . ."

Number two is the problem. That's when he decides to try to escalate the level to the point where the opposition folds. This comes in three common forms:

Option A is the person who has never really lost, so he cranks it up incrementally.

Option B is the person who has lost and who rockets.

Option C is the person who panics.

Option A occurs when someone *without* experience with being physically bested often cranks it up, but within limits. Sure, that person was acting like John and Jim at around MM 100. But when he or she runs up against someone who says, "Knock it off," he or she either goes emotionally and verbally ballistic or ~gasp~ steps up and strikes the other person before returning to verbal abuse and threats. Oh, he bumps it from 75 to 100. This often results in fights.

Option B is the person who has been physically defeated before. He knows the escalation must be fast enough and of sufficient force that the target has no chance to rally. This isn't going from Mile Marker 75 to 150, this is a turbo boost to 300. It *has* to be a big burst. If the target can get it together in time, the escalation turns *against* the aggressor. The last thing he wants is to crank it to 200, and the guy not only doesn't go down, but comes back at him at 210. He called the tune, now he has to dance to it at that high a level. And that's a price he doesn't want to pay.

Option B or nothing happening is real common in rough places. The violence and commitment of someone, who knows violence is a two-way street is distinctly different from someone who doesn't believe it will be used against him or her. With the former if he doesn't think he can get away with it, he'll back off the majority of the time. I've seen this in action many times. I've seen predators turn on their heels and leave. I've seen bad asses put up their hands and back away. I have seen people—in a full-on attack and at a dead run—look as though they ran into a force field. I'm talking about flying backward without physical contact. They did this when their target turned into a werewolf right before their eyes. They knew—if they kept coming—the absolutely best result would be their going to the emergency room.

But be careful if you don't have the means to bump it up, too. You may be willing to jump up to Mile Marker 200 (empty hand self-defense) but if he can win by throwing you a blitz beating (MM 300) or using a weapon (400-plus) odds are good he *will*.

Option C is another one of those giant pain-in-the-tuchus situations and that's when the guy panics. In these situations, he's attacking you from *fear*. Again, this is one of those you gotta be kidding issues, but you can be too convincing in your warnings—especially if you have a weapon. Remember give him instructions on how to avoid being hurt.

It's when you encounter someone who thinks they have a monopoly on bad behavior that things really become a pain in the butt. When they encounter resistance, they crank it up, too. But with some, there is literally *no* warning they recognize as reason to back off. It's going to go down.

The person is an out-of-(k)control monkey (I call them OOKs.) As we'll talk about later, they are utterly *committed* to this course of action. Not necessarily good at it mind you, but, man oh man, are they committed. I tell you the last because OOKs are in many ways the real-life boogeyman people fear. And well they should. OOKs are intimidating and appear dangerous to nice people (who don't want to be violent). To professionals, they are a pain in the posterior because you can't just shoot the idiots. The greatest invention ever for handling them is the taser. Letting OOKs 'ride the lightening' of a taser is the easiest and safest way to deal with them.

They're dangerous *not* because they're good at violence, but because they don't know when to *stop*. They are *all* about winning. Use minimum force, and they escalate. You try and control them, and you end up fighting them. You fight them, and it goes all to hell. Chances of injury go through the roof. They'll injure you without thought or hesitation. They'll hurt themselves fighting a restraint. And even if they lose, they *won't* stop. They'll run to the cops or sue. It's your fault, and they won't quit until they win—one way or another.

OOKs hurt you not because they mean to, but often as an unintended result. They're so caught up in their emotions and monkey goals, they don't recognize the danger they're really creating. Because of it, they'll come at you full steam ahead. And they don't care that they've crossed the line into violence. They're coming to hurt you, to punish you, to make you pay for daring to cross them. The only question is how far down that road of violence are they going to go? Where will this OOKs's monkey be satisfied? The answer is it depends on the OOK. Sometimes, it's when you leave. Other times, it's when you're humiliated. In some instances, it's when you've been sufficiently beaten. And at the farthest extreme, it's when you've died.

I told you about those who will stop because I have seen people change course in mid-behavior when they recognize danger. But I have also seen OOKs so committed to their stupidity they charge weapons. There is no viable *threat* that will stop them. I've also seen people—who are fatally wounded—keep on coming.

There is no one-size-fits-all answer to this problem and what to do. That's because until you are *in* the situation, you won't know what you are dealing with. Is it a pro? Is it an OOK? Is it someone who has reason to be infuriated? Can it be deterred? De-escalated? Or is it going to happen no matter what? Will throwing him into a wall stop him? Will knocking him down stop his physical attack and any other aggression? Or will he then divert and run to the police, thereby changing his method of attack? Or is nothing short of lethal force going to work? Until you are right there on the spot, you will not *know* what circumstances, much less the right answer.

I have a saying, "I am negotiating until I pull the trigger." That means until the very last instant, I am looking for another *realistic* way to end the situation without blowing someone's brains out the back of his head. In a lifetime of dealing with violence, this attitude has saved me from wrongfully pulling the trigger many times. At the same time, it has also helped me act when negotiating was not an option. As in, "Nope, negotiation isn't working." WHAM!

As a side note, look at the emphasis on the word realistic in my search for a non-violent solution. One of the bigger problems you'll face with those unhappy with your use of force is the—often stupid—ideas people have about other options. The best summation I ever heard of this issue was from Eric Yip, a friend and shooting enthusiast—"The 'you could have been less violent' is a variation of 'you could have shot them in the leg' line of reasoning. It's an attempt at applying untested personal solutions to real-world problems you have no experience with. It's like trying to put out a structure fire by smothering it with a wool blanket.

It might sound good in your head, but lack of experience or knowledge will ensure you're in for a rude awakening. However, most people will never deal with a raging house fire so it's easy to go around telling folks your opinion is valid."

Now back to our regularly scheduled program.

The closer you are to acting, the more you *need* to look for signs the danger is abating. Whether it is the attack breaking off or the guy—still talking trash—backing or turning away. What matters in the latter is his actions, not his words. Most importantly, learn to spot the difference between an attack and aborted lunge (it looks like an attack, but pulls up short and out of range). These are signs that your warning signals, your commitment to act are getting *through* the guy's thick skull.

Yes, I'm talking about shoot and no shoot decision making. This is a big issue in firearms training, but almost universally ignored in empty-hand training. And that is one hell of a dangerous hole to have in your education. When is it time to go? More importantly, when is time *not* to go? When you see the danger abating do *not* pull the trigger—or use them again if hands are your weapon. Conversely, when you don't see danger abatement, when the only signals he's putting out indicate he's coming at you, this has moved from threat displays into attack indicators. The attack is occurring. It's time to act. (This is jeopardy developing means.) But it isn't just about the attack.

I'm going to put this in gun terms, but scale it according to what you do. It is incredibly useful to be able to list off to the cops, your attorney, and the jury what you *did not* see that would have led to a no shoot decision. Instead of "he whirled toward me and raised his pistol," let them know there were options where you *wouldn't* have acted. Like what? How about him turning and running? Looking at you, freezing, and dropping the weapon. Lowering the weapon and retreating. All of these were things that person could have done *not* to get shot.

But he didn't choose to do them. How do you know? Because you were looking for them. (You may not have noticed that elephant off to your right, but you certainly were focused on the danger.) Consult with your lawyer about introducing this kind of evidence. The prosecutor will try to undermine your interpretation that the guy followed you outside. Throw back the contention he could have stayed inside. He could have left through another door. Coming out of the same door, he could have turned left or gone straight ahead. Instead, he turned right and sped up. With those other four options available and not taken, as well as his speeding up, odds are seriously against it being something other than him following you.

Here's the caveat to everything I've just said, and it is specific to non-lethal use-of-force situations. I have seen OOKs suicide out because they refused to stop attacking the wrong person. What I've seen a whole lot more of is them—not exactly snapping out of it—but pulling back and trying to figure out what to do now that plan A failed. Waiting for them to decide is a seething ball of suck.

Here's the scenario, a guy comes charging forward, and you knock him on his butt. He could get up and immediately attack again. Or he could get up and keep on flipping out, but this time just out of reach. Or he could get up and run like hell (often yelling that he'll sue you). Or he could get back up, yell, snarl, snort, blow snot, and then work himself up to attacking again. Putting this in the highway analogy, the first is he tries the 150 mile marker and it doesn't work, so he tries to accelerate to 200. The second, he gets up and waffles about going farther or going back to a lower mile sign. The third is he's running back down the highway to safety. Fourth is he first waffles, then tries again.

The reason this sucks is while he's deciding what to do, the *immediate* threat has passed. The damned incident isn't over yet. But these circumstances are just flat-out awkward. Etiquette books just don't cover what to do here. At the same time, it is a real delicate situation. One where there are lots of ways it can go bad, and only a few ways that it can end well.

First off—if you just stand there—it's a complete and total coin toss if the guy is woofing to save face before backing off or if he's working his way up to attacking again. (Which way you going to go pal? Back to MM 70 or up to 200?) While standing there doesn't seem like you're adding to the problem, it *can*. On one hand, the guy can interpret your presence as an attack—or at least a continued threat. This can influence him to work himself up to attack again. On the other hand, the cops and prosecution are going to want to know why you didn't leave. And that's a *good* question.

The problem is leaving the wrong way from an OOK you've just knocked down *is* a good way to have him get up and chase you. Just turning and running increases the risk of the guy thinking that somehow his polishing the floor with his butt scared you. It can result in him getting up and chasing you. (Give your monkey a banana as a reward for being half right.)

Conversely, I'm a big fan of turning this around. "Yes, officer, I tried to leave. He followed me. He first attacked me there, I tried to withdraw. He followed me and attacked again. I only stopped trying to retreat because it wasn't working."

The odds of him following you are less if you back away while giving him instructions to stay down (or away). Odds of a second attack are even less if you sent him ass over tea kettle into a chair or table before withdrawing like this.

The key point here is your *trying* to pull back. It doesn't even have to be a big withdrawal, what's important is you're shown on camera as backing away. By not outright leaving, the prosecutor is going to try to make it sound like you were just waiting around to throw him another beating. That interpretation holds less water if you're seen on the security recording as trying to back away.

Second, if you get hyper-aggressive about not leaving, you risk another coin flip. Will he run or will he attack in his *own* self-defense? (Remember, we covered this in the legal chapter.) And if he attacks believing it was SD, you're going to have to do some explaining because now it looks like you were fighting.

The third option is *you* have to supply the social script for him to follow. Yes, I've mentioned this before, it's *that* important. Sure, you've sent him flying into a wall, dropped him like a prom dress, or sent him tumbling with a chair. But now, you have to *give* him a map of how to get out of this mess he's put himself into. And—this is where most people screw up—it *has* to be conditional. Otherwise, you're just threatening him.

In my non-professional capacity, I'm a big fan of throwing people across the room. (Professionally, I had to close and control.) Non-professionally though, I want to create distance between us. Now granted there might be an open hand enhancing his trek across the room (and an odd table or wall in the way). But the primary goal these days is to create distance between him and me. Remember *distance equals time*. An OOK attacks and the next thing he knows he's crashing into a distant wall. This is a derailment of his plans. So *use* that time to your advantage.

Commonly my snarled response ran, "Do *not* attack me again! If you do, I *will* hurt you! Now you can walk away and it's cool. You'll be safe, I won't chase you. I won't come after you. But do *not* come at me *again*. Now what's it going to be?"

I don't want you to mimic my words. I want you to *understand* what I was doing. Notice I told him what to do. Also notice I said that anything bad that happened to him would be *conditional* on his behavior. That is a small but important legal issue. It's not a blanket threat. The only way he will be in danger is *if* he offers me more danger. This makes it a conditional threat. Also I offered him a safe retreat *without* consequences. If he chose to attack again, however, it would hurt (vague, not specific threat). I also gave him limited choices: Attack *again* or leave. I did not offer him the opportunity to stand around barking, drooling, and working himself up to another attack.

The other thing I have done is called "witness grooming." *Everyone* heard me say, "Don't attack *again*." They heard me say that if he didn't, he would be safe. They didn't see me baiting or antagonizing him. And most importantly, they saw me irritated, but not attacking, closing the distance, threatening, or endangering him. Any OOK behavior from him after that is going to look *real* bad. At the same time, the witnesses are now looking for the elements I pointed out. If the situation goes physical again, what will show up on their phone's video is the conditional warning and then him getting up and attacking again.

Another important point of this is it shows that I'm *trying to control* the level of force I use. Man that goes all kinds of miles toward helping establish minimum level of force. The first time, I wasn't trying to hurt him (mile markers between 150 and 200) But, if he comes at me again, then he's coming with increased force (250 to 350). This in turn justifies a greater degree of force on my part. After all, the lower level of force didn't *stop* him, and he committed himself to attacking again with a greater degree of force.

All of this is to get you thinking about scaling force to the situation. Why is this important? First because—after articulation—scaling force is one of the most overlooked aspects of self-defense training. Second, if *mixed* with other elements, there is a *good* chance of lower levels of force working. Working in combo and in situations where the lower use of force alone *wouldn't have!*

If I just hit him or throw him across the room or even tell him to back off, odds are good he'll come at me again. But if he somehow get whacked upside the head, tossed across the room, and told not to come at me *again* . . . well, that combination has a good chance of working. See, he has stable data that attacking me kinda hurts. Now I'm telling him that there doesn't have to be a next time, but if there is it'll hurt a whole lot more. And while we're on the subject I'm offering him a safe chance to leave.

Will it always work? No, that's why we call them OOKs. But I guarantee you, you'll have an easier time convincing Officer Friendly who the out-of-control blockhead, who needs to go to jail, is.

Tying this all up into one neat little bundle. Don't ever monkey dance with an OOK. Don't insult them, challenge them, threaten them. That will only encourage them to escalate and undermine your self-defense claim. You want everyone unanimously pointing to him when the cops ask who was the violent, out-of-control aggressor. Using JAM *don't* let them develop the means (especially the range and positioning). If there's one element you need be absolutely adamant about is them keeping their distance. While actively trying to get the hell out of there, you have to be ready to flash into sufficient violence if they try to close the distance.

Do everything you can to avoid going physical. But with that, know that some OOKs are going to go off no matter what. So what you're doing is building articulable evidence about you trying to avoid, de-escalate, and make a good faith attempt at withdrawing before resorting to physical force.

OOKs are what give people the impression that violence is dangerously out of control. At the same time, true OOKs are actually very rare. These are the people who will attack a werewolf without hesitation—and they will die for it. This kind of imbalance is self-selecting. What you're going to encounter the most is that this kind of out-of-control behavior is almost exclusive to situations where one side believes they have a monopoly on violence (including "you can't touch me for acting this way"). Most faux-OOKs are relying on other people following society's prohibitions on violence. They act out believing you can't (i.e., lack the means) or won't (e.g., are afraid of) hurting them.

I tell you this because the fundamental flaw in violence-never-solved-anything is it ignores one of the biggest realities about violence. That is: *The willingness and ability to use force overwhelmingly means you don't have to.* Talk about an ultimate paradox of defense.

For criminals, those engaged in most social violence, resource predators, and even process predators, a large portion of their strategies revolve around the fact that violence *can be* a two-way street. The simple fact that you're willing to go means it's a good idea to find another way to resolve the issue—even if it's don't try to rob you, go rob someone else.

A fundamental assumption underlying the strategy of OOKs is nobody is as violent, fast, and intense as they are. And as long as you respond to their out-of-control monkey behavior with your own monkey behavior, they're *right*. They're hauling down the violence highway, and you're trying to catch up.

I'm going to take a side track and give you information that is a key element of willingness to use violence paradox. Starting with, I have a problem with how many people approach self-defense. That is, they both learn and teach it in a fashion I consider backward.

When I talk about lethal force, a whole lot of people get hairless. Oh mah gawd! They don't want to kill anybody. They just want to be safe. Okay, understandable attitude, but kind of problematic. The monkey and it's ~cough cough~ logic aside, there are three critical flaws in this approach.

The first flaw is based on use of lethal force as the most restricted and narrowly defined circumstance in the self-defense world. Remember the SD square? The self-defense table? Stack a much smaller one on top, then put an upside down bucket on that, and stand on the bucket. *Those* are your lethal force standards for SD. They are damned high, small, and shaky. If you're going to carry a weapon (especially a gun or knife) you *need* to know these standards. But that's *not* the flaw. It's a big one, but not *the* one.

The flaw is that lethal force needs be a starting point to work your way *back* from. It's not addition of force, it's *subtraction*. Oddly enough, it's a form of subtraction that adds options. Do the circumstances warrant lethal force? No. Okay, it's off the table then (take away the bucket). How about this level of force? No. Not that either (take away the smaller table). This level? Ummmm, close, but no cigar (stop leaning over the edge of the table). How about this level of force? Yes. That works. Better still, that puts you firmly in the middle of the SD table. Now what are the means to achieve this solution?

With this approach, you can articulate why B was the right amount of force. "Why did you use that level of force?" "Because A would be too little. C, D, and E would have been too much and were inappropriate for the situation."

But more importantly, it allows you to *stay* calm and make better use-of-force decisions. Once you get the hang of thinking like this, you can skim through the options with the same speed you do making decisions about driving. Apply the brakes? Yes. How hard? This hard. There's your answer.

I can't stress how important this way of thinking is. Here's something to consider, the monkey is going to freak out for its *own* reasons. If you don't develop the habit of questioning your monkey-reasoning, it's going to tell you that self-defense is going into another room during an argument, getting a gun, coming back, and shooting him. Your monkey is convinced that was self-defense. The cops won't be. In fact, they'll ask the one question the monkey doesn't want to answer. "Why didn't you just keep on walking?" "Uhhhh . . . errr . . . ummm."

More than helping you keep *out* of all kinds of danger, knowing what constitutes a lethal threat keeps your monkey from convincing you your life is in danger when it *isn't*—especially when what is in danger is to your monkey's pride. Since pride alone isn't a good enough reason, it will throw imaginary good reasons at you—like, "He's going to kill you!" No. You just got punched. It hurts, but you *will* survive. And you are certainly not justified in pulling a knife on him—much less using it.

The second flaw is summed up in something Sean Connery said in the movie *Rising Sun*: "We're playing that most American of games. Catch up."

Imagine you're walking down the sidewalk, you turn a blind corner, and there is a guy in a track outfit and hunkered down on running blocks. As you turn the corner, someone yells, "You're in a race, GO!" The runner takes off. How likely are you to catch up to him, especially if it's a short dash?

That's the problem with how most people approach self-defense. They're trying to play catch up with a violent person. Wait, you're trying to catch someone who has a head start and who determines how far he wants this race to go? Will you ever catch up in these circumstances? Not likely.

Conversely, what happens if you turn the corner and are told you have to run, but the person is down at the other end of the block? Now instead of running the same direction, you run *toward* each other. You're not trying to catch up anymore. Running *at* each other, you're going to meet somewhere in the middle, no matter how fast he's running.

Look at these two examples. With the first, you can try to catch up before he gets to lethal. Or with the second, you can scale *down* from lethal and meet somewhere in the middle. Coming at it from this direction, odds are good it'll be a better use-of-force decision. Also one that is sufficient to stop an OOK, instead of escalating him.

Put in the context of the highway of violence, you're speeding *back* from the higher mile marker areas. And there's *not* a speed limit coming from that direction. So you can come back from extreme violence as *fast* as you want. Talk about turbo charged Ferrari on the autobahn!

The third flaw with how self-defense is normally taught is you aren't given the means to spot *bad* advice about use of force. I guarantee after you sit through a self-defense and the law class, you'll *never* look at training in the same way—especially in martial arts, weapon systems, and combatives training.

When your silat instructor says, "Then you pull your knife and stab him before he gets up," you'll *know* better. That's manslaughter. When your combatives instructor tells you to do a head stomp on a downed opponent, you'll say, "Uhhhh, no. That's attempted murder." When a gun-fighting guru tells you to shoot him to the ground, you'll be thinking, "Not so fast . . ." (especially when you find out the most common response to someone getting shot is to turn and try to walk away).

When the threat stops, *you stop.*

All of those are foundational concepts to help you understand why the willingness to use force usually means you *don't* have to. See, that guy whom you're trying to play catch up with is controlling the race. He's the one who determines how far he wants to go. And why shouldn't he? With you running behind him, the harder and faster he runs the more his win is guaranteed. Oh, you don't want to take it this far? Hee, hee, hee.

But if he sees you coming back *at* him, the only thing his running harder and faster is going to do is make your collision happen out at a higher level of force. Guess what? He's seeing a known landmark coming hard and fast *at* him. That landmark means he's heading toward a level of force where his safety *isn't* guaranteed. By working back from lethal force, you've undermined the most popular strategy there is when it comes to violence—him coming at you hard, fast. You coming back means that isn't an easy win anymore. Ninety-nine percent of the time for him that's a slam on the brakes *now!*

I've spent nearly 300 pages priming you for this. An OOK who is relying on people's hesitation to do violence has no *reason* to stop. Any monkey signal you throw back at them is going to encourage them to hit the gas pedal harder—especially threat displays. I'm not encouraging physical violence or constantly being an aggressive jerk, but when most out-of-control monkeys see you high speeding it back down the highway to meet them, all of a sudden they *get* all kinds of self-control.

That is when you need to be able to slam on the brakes, too. When that SOB flips a U-turn and speeds away, screaming obscenities, threats, and making an exit, *let* him go. When he slams on the brakes, *don't* you attack. When he tries to back away, *let* him. When he's talking trash as he's backing away, keep your mouth *shut*. Don't you pick up the role of a violent, out-of-control monkey when he drops it.

It's time to add another concept to the violence as a road analogy. I've alluded to it several times and that is: The farther down the road you get, the faster things are going. First off, it has taken time and effort to get that far down the road. Also the farther you go, the fewer off ramps there are, and the *harder* it is to get off without blood being spilled. What I'm saying is effective options become more limited, require more investment (to make them work) and involve greater risk. That last point takes some explaining.

When you're doing 10 mile per hour, you can easily make a 90-degree turn. You do it all the time when turning left or right on city streets. There are lots and lots of places to turn. Take for example driving down the street where you live. Staying at a lower speed, how many driveways, alleys, and intersections can you take to get off that street? Now, imagine trying to do a hard right at 120 mph. Not going to happen.

Let's look at where speeds are decreased, specifically freeway or turnpike off ramps. First, off ramps are a lot rarer. Not only do off ramps require more distance, they also have speed limits slower than the highway. If you try to take them at 120 mph, there are going to be problems. The *faster* you are going requires more distance and a gentle arc or degree to the curves in combination with banking of the road. If these conditions don't exist, you crash and burn trying to get off the road.

This is what I was talking about when I said the more you subtract, the more options you have. As the mile markers reduce, you slow things down. You may speed like hell when you're coming back from the boonies, but when you get into populated areas you slow it down. Lethal force? No, now I have more options. Slower, lower miles? Even more options. It's the direct opposite if you increasing speed and trying to play catch up.

Want something less theoretical and more practical? Try this: You accidentally walk into a biker bar, and one of the patrons tells you to leave. Looking around, you see a number of similarly dressed people who are watching. But nothing has happened (so lethal force is off the table). Saying, "No problem," turning around, and walking out the door is a pretty simple and effective way to avoid violence. Low mileage, low speed, easy to get off the road. It's not galling or a blow to your ego because you know what can happen if things accelerate.

Telling the guy that you have a right to drink anywhere you want and asking who the hell is he to tell you to leave increases both speed and how far down the road you are. And you're the one who pressed that gas pedal. After you've done this, you *might* be able to get out of there without getting your tender bits tromped on by just turning and leaving, but odds are you're going to have to do something else, too. Like when the hostility goes up, holding up your hands to show you're not aggressive, telling them you are not arguing, apologizing, and backing out of there.[141] Another potential life saver is having a friend who grabs you by the scruff of neck, turns you around, and pushes you out after you started up about your rights. (Hint, don't be afraid to be that friend.[142])

If on the other hand, you've slept with one of the biker's old ladies, ripped off another in a drug deal, and you pour your beer over a third guy's boots . . . there is no way just saying, "No problem," is going to work. A social script is *not* going to save you. This may seem like one of my now famous 'no shit, Sherlock' issues. But you'd be appalled at the number of people who try it. They go racing down the highway and then think flipping over and trying a social script will keep folks from throwing them a beating. That off ramp was two hundred miles back and when they *weren't* going 150 mph.

Now that's kind of theoretical, and I made it so to put it in a social

---

141   There are other ways to handle this kind of situation, but they require intimate familiarity with certain lifestyles. Unless you are experienced, you won't be able to navigate these kinds of minefields. Besides, it's beyond the scope of this book because, at that level, it's not exactly self-defense.

142   This is a very powerful psychological and social tool. While again beyond the scope of this book, the short version is you handling your friend means they don't have to.

context. But the same idea applies for explaining to Doubting Thomas's why it isn't reasonable to ask why didn't you just kick the knife out of someone's hand. Or why you had to shoot a charging person four times when the prosecutor is using the coroner's testimony that any of the three wounds would have been lethal to sell the idea you overreacted. The farther down the road and faster things are going, the more limited the options.

There is another kind of monkey brain mistake that people—who don't routinely deal with violence—make. When they find themselves speeding down the highway, they press the gas peddles harder. Apparently they're doing this in hope of finding an off ramp sooner. This is a very subtle but important point. Instead of slamming on the brakes, pulling a U-turn and heading back, they try to accelerate to the next off ramp.

Now I should not have to tell you saying to the mugger, "What are you going to do now? Shoot us?" isn't smart. But how many of you have heard the full quote of what Nicole du Fresne allegedly said before she was shot? That is: "What are you still doing here? You got what you wanted. What are you going to do now, shoot us?"

In her defense, that kind of confrontational, challenging strategy commonly works at lower mileage situations—especially against someone who is concerned about negative social consequences. You can see how she was trying to accelerate the situation to a conclusion. The idea of wanting the situation to end it makes *sense*. But that approach is just not an option when things have gotten that far along.

These are some of the problems people, who don't have a lot of experience on the highway, can have—*starting* with not realizing they're on it. Then how often they don't recognize where they are and how fast things are going.

That last especially includes the out-of-control monkeys. That's what makes OOKs such a pain to deal with. Most OOKs *know* they're on the highway. But they assume they have a monopoly on the danger and that *you* have no options other than:

a) Running and hiding
b) Some kind of ineffective noise making
c) Taking the butt kicking they're going to hand you

They're just fine and dandy speeding down the highway toward kicking your butt. They're committed to that idea and not really thinking about exactly how much of a threat they really are offering you. So they're not thinking about collisions, only winning. And that doesn't make them functionally blind to warning signs, but they just keep on charging at you. The only way to stop them is to make them crash. And yes, that's the moron you're going to have injure—possibly kill—to stop him from doing the same to you. ~sigh~ I hate paperwork.

On the other hand, people with experience know how easy it is to crash when going up against someone as good as they are. If you know how to handle yourself correctly, people experienced with violence are safer and easier to deal with. They won't be stupid about it, but when it goes, it's ugly and fast.

The problem is that most of us are only familiar with dealing with the slower, low mile marker forms of conflict. Situations where there are lots of off ramps. And circumstances where bluffing, confrontation, and calling someone on something works. Often, all it takes to get someone off the lower end of the highway is a slightly higher level of response. They think, "Uh oh, that didn't work," and they change their behavior. This by the way is what convinces the monkey that the best response to verbal aggression is bigger, badder, verbal aggression. ("I might attack!" "Oh yeah? I *will* attack!") Again, it works on the lower levels—higher mileage and speeds, not so much.

Where this gets problematic is that some people have learned that if they go speeding through the lower levels real fast, it's an effective strategy to get what they want. This can be like someone driving 60 mph on a surface street. They think it's impressing everyone, but most people think he's a jerk, a knothead it's not worth the risk to confront. Here's a strategy tip. Against these street racers, the confrontational and threatening strategies people use against lower level folks usually fail. If you yell at someone to slow down doing 40 in a 20 mph zone, he's going to flip you off. If the guy is going 60, yelling is of no use at all. But isn't he a big bad driver for moving that fast on the city streets?

This creates two pain-in-the-butt conditions. One, the person thinks speeding is a good strategy. It works, so he gets comfortable using it. Two, when it *doesn't* work instead of backing off, the person goes at it even harder. This accelerates how hard and fast he's coming at you. He was doing 40 mph in a 20 zone, but when you confront him he floors it. Now the dumb son-of-a-bitch is doing 70.

The problems with this are:

A) He doesn't see the warning signs that he's heading for a wreck;
B) Because he doesn't know to stop, odds are good you're going to have to injure him;
C) If you don't, he'll injure you.

About point C: Not intentionally, mind you, but out of sheer stupidity, lack of thought, and aggression. Yes, he intended to hurt you some, he just didn't mean for you to fall down on the ground and crack your skull when he was doing it. He wasn't trying to kill you when he stomped you when you were down, he was just getting his licks in to teach you a lesson. He doesn't care that you're a sixty-year-old man. You disrespected him, so he'll throw you a beating like you were his own age. ~sigh~ I loathe these idiots.

Usually pain alone won't be enough to stop such people. While if you're really good, you might be able to grapple them into a hold, odds are good it's going to take injury to stop the threat they present—as in injure him to get him to stop before he injures you.[143] Years ago, I read a perfect summation of this kind of situation: They were too young to know any better, but too big not to be taken seriously.[144] And yes, this behavior is particularly common among young men.[145] Especially when they've been drinking, often when they're in groups and are being territorial.

As a bouncer, I had to deal with these retards all the time; same with working event security. And as a private citizen, too—including being a home owner. They're out there, and they don't react well to anybody telling them what to do. But where they really get snippy is when you tell them to *stop* doing something—no matter the fact they're big idiots for doing it. Once again, non-violently handling situations with these jerks is beyond the scope of this book. But I will give you two important elements:

First, putting your pride aside, backing away from these kinds of people often allows you to avoid violence. More often than not, all they want you to do is to go away and leave them alone. If you can, *leave*. It'll save you all kinds of grief and unnecessary violence. Besides this is the perfect situation to back off, call the police, and let them handle the obnoxious twit(s).

Second, someone high speeding it through the lower speed limits of the violence highway is an articulable form of jeopardy. For example, "I calmly said (insert reasonable request) and he reacted by becoming extremely aggressive, threatening, verbally abusive, and moved into attack range." These are not reasonable responses to polite requests (or your good faith attempt to withdraw.) Use their aggressive behavior patterns to your advantage; use it like the police sequence of 'ask, tell, order' to establish a pattern of noncompliance justifying increased use of force.

"I held up my hands, said, 'I don't want any trouble. I'll leave,' and tried to back away. When I did that, he aggressively advanced into attack range and raised his hand to strike." (This one works even better if there's video

---

143　Contrary to what most people think, there's a difference between pain and injury. I have serious problems with the idea of stopping an attack through pain alone. It's horrifically unreliable—especially since I'm the kind of guy, whom if you kick me in the balls, you'll just piss off. Pain won't stop me; a broken leg will. I've gone skull-to-skull with a number of people like this. Here's a bad news flash, people who can take pain and keep on coming are disproportionally represented among the violent. That's why injury to stop is more reliable. Although not legally accurate, a rule of thumb I use is that pain may mean you gargling with warm salt water and spitting pink into the sink; injury means a trip to the emergency room.

144　*Phule's Company*, Robert Asprin, 1990

145　Although this behavior is rarer among women and strangers, it is not uncommon with women in privacy and with people with whom they have a relationship.

supporting your side of the story.) Both doing and articulating reasonable behavior on your part establishes a pattern of aggressive behavior on his. That pattern is necessary to explain why self-defense became an option. (Remember, defending yourself is a choice you have to justify.)

I tell you all of this to bring up another issue when it comes to people either denying they are being violent or giving themselves permission due to emotions: Commitment.

Remember number five—over-commitment? At long last, here it is. Most people need to be emotional before they engage in violence, the same with the threat of violence. This is what allows them to overcome their internal monkey brain prohibitions against it. Professionals, *not so much*. That's because they are using a different scale about when it's time to use force.

And that's what can make amateurs harder to deal with than pros. Having the subjective definition of what they are doing isn't violence really helps with giving themselves permission to act. But so, too, does the lack of clear goals. What constitutes a win? You leaving? Them beating you senseless? Their killing you for disrespecting them? Quite often, OOKs don't see the danger they are putting you in. If this weren't bad enough, they're really committed to doing it. Whatever their goal, they are *all in* about getting it. It takes a high level of force to stop them. You literally have to crash through their commitment to get them to stop. The old term "get it through your thick head" applies here.

Unlike professionals—who know that a violent reaction to their own violence is possible and factor that in (through either preparation or careful victim selection)—self-righteous amateurs often ignore warning signs and come charging in. I'm talking full steam ahead. An insufficient response from you sets off OOKs more (including, by the way, just inflicting pain.)

A sufficient response is one that ends the physical danger right then and there. If it doesn't, it wasn't sufficient. Usually a sufficient response involves more than just physical force. Communication is very much a part of getting someone off the highway—even after things have gone physical[146] especially if it looks like it's going to escalate to physical

---

146   I tell people, "Often witnesses don't see the first punch." They're looking elsewhere. When they do look, the first thing they see is you defending yourself, which they interpret as you attacking him first. That's an important element of what's called witness grooming. Not only in making sure everyone sees you try to avoid the situation, it is why you have to do a TV trick. And that is telling them, "previously on . . . ." On many occasions, the first words out of my mouth to someone I'd just tossed across the room or was trying to control were, "Don't attack me again!" Notice that sentence tells people what happened. Even if people didn't see his attack on me, they heard me tell him not to attack me . . . again. You also are setting conditions on the danger. By standing back, you are not advancing. The danger to him is conditional on his closing the distance and attacking. If the guy gets hurt, it's because he got up and attacked you again. That's what people will tell the cops, and that's what's on the video.

conflict again. Use a sufficient response and—odds are—they'll start squealing like piggies, especially if you didn't use those other elements.

You see this behavior all the time when someone is acting out against the police, both the acting up more and more against insufficient response and squealing. They're going great guns until the cops put them into cuffing position. Whereupon, they start screaming, "You're hurting me!" Expect the same behavior.

Way too often people are convinced of their right to misbehave. And they're going to fight to defend that right. Not just formally committed amateurs screaming at *you* about what a mean and horrible person you are for stopping . . . excuse me . . . hurting them, but also running to the cops and suing you. (Oh and in case you haven't guessed, civil suits can be another form of vendetta behavior.[147])

People's belief in their right to misbehave extends into places you wouldn't believe. I mean stupid is back that-a-way. No lie, one of the biggest, baddest men I know was called in to handle an out-of-control bar. This dude is a six-four, power lifting, former enforcer for the mob. He does strong man competitions and drags around trucks and vans. He's not just big, he's mean, and experienced with extreme violence. Walking into this bar, he sees all kinds of problems, not the least of which is drug dealing. I'm not talking about going into the bathroom to sell, either. There are drug deals not under their tables, but exchanging drugs and money *over* the table.

His response was to spend the next two weeks, telling these guys he'd taken over the bar business. If they were going to deal drugs at *his* bar, they'd have to pay him a $1,000 a week. This was actually a good plan. Most of them looked at him, pulled out their calculators, figured they couldn't afford that, and left. But some puffed up and demanded to know who he thought he was to tell them they couldn't deal drugs there. That lasted until he smashed their faces with his brass knuckles. You would think word would get out fast, but it took five or six incidents before these penny ante drug dealers stopped trying to sell in his bar. What's amazing is the number of them who—stumbling out, holding their teeth—were muttering about suing him. Really? You're going to run to the cops complaining this big ol' meanie head beat you up for selling drugs in his bar?

My point in telling you that story is to show you exactly how far from common sense some people's monkeys can take them. There is no 100 percent guaranteed-will-always-work strategy to prevent violence. There are always going to be some idiots. But that is not permission to

---

147   The good news is that the same information and articulation that will keep you out of prison in a criminal case works to win civil cases, too.

throw up your hands and say, "Then, I shouldn't bother trying at all." Especially because there are strategies that—with certain people—are almost guaranteed to escalate it. Try actively resisting lawful orders from cops. Try and argue with my friend about your right to deal drugs in his bar. Violence *will* occur.

What I'm telling you is don't let it be your monkey, but don't be surprised when you run into an OOK. The trick is when you see an out-of-control monkey don't let your monkey out to play, too. That right there greatly reduces the likelihood of violence. It will save you all kinds of problems with paperwork, court costs, vendettas, and having to hide the body. At the same time, you'll recognize when despite your best (and most reasonable) efforts to avoid violence, that monkey is so out of control you *have* to act.

Another problem with letting your monkey loose is OOKs usually provoke ineffective, emotion-based counter force on your part. This results in an insufficient response, which—if it doesn't break through their commitment—will cause further escalation. So you end up having to use more ineffective force, which looks like you're fighting (with the witnesses, cops, and jury assuming those motivations).

Sometimes a punch in the face does interrupt a person's commitment—but not enough. They charge in and get nailed. Then instead of turning tail and running, they step back and start yelling and screaming even louder. How it's going to go from there is anybody's guess. But don't you be guessing, pay attention to what's happening. It's going to dictate what you do next.

Start with the fact their strategy has failed. Now what? Play your cards right and there's a good chance they won't physically attack again. But there's as much of a chance if you do nothing else, they'll work themselves up into taking another crack at you because while they're yelling and screaming, they convince themselves the first time was a fluke. Say the wrong thing, and they're going to come back in. There's also a very good chance that with all their huffing and puffing, you'll get excited (or just fed up) and tell yourself they're attacking again. What the video will show is you closing the distance to assault the other person. That's stepping outside the SD square.

Knowing these options are on the table, you can take control of the dynamics of the situation. It's a higher skill level, but while that guy is huffing and puffing, you can do all kinds of things to end the situation. For example, telling the guy you are leaving and starting to back away. And if the he starts to follow, you make a slight forward lean that conveys, "I thumped you once, I'm willing to do it again." When he falters, you keep on backing up. Even if the guy decides to have another go at you, this looks good for you. Both on video and with witnesses telling the cops you were trying to leave when he decided to go off on you again. Remember if somebody has to go to jail, you want it to be him.

The challenge when it comes to dealing with out-of-control monkey commitment is to use both enough *and* effective force to break the person's commitment without drawing out the physical circumstances of the incident. Again, this is something I'm going to have to address in another book, but basically it's not about using lots of force, you get better results using effective force and not wasting so much energy, time, and opportunity. That's what draws out the physical altercation and makes it look like you're fighting instead of defending yourself.

Here's something for you empty-hand self-defense people to consider, punching—by itself—seldom breaks someone's commitment. Even hitting someone five or six times might not be enough to stop the person. But it will be enough to convince anybody watching that you were either fighting or beating him. (This is the basis of so many 'police brutality' headlines on YouTube.[148]) It's also a slam dunk for the prosecutor to sell that you overreacted. But while effective force can and will stop an attack—without looking like you're beating the person—it's more than just punching.

Commitment isn't a mile marker, it's *speed.* Learning to gauge how much someone has is important. First, it can be a sign that things are farther down the highway than you thought. Second, it takes you out of thinking, "Well, if *I* did this, *I* would stop" and then deciding that's the right course of action (insufficient response). Third, it keeps you from assuming you have to nuke anyone who looks mean at you (excessive response). Fourth, when you can read it even during physical action, you can see it wane or increase. This allows you to scale your force to a justifiable level—including stopping and letting the person run away. Fifth—and this is where things get almost woo-woo, but are in fact issues of body language and behavior—people who use violence will look at you, realize your commitment is higher than theirs, and leave you alone whether a hissy fit, an emotional physical attack, or professional criminal violence.

---

148   Important safety tip: If the 'left hand turn' has been made and you are about to be arrested, *do not* resist. Your part is done. It's now between your lawyer and the court system. Another lie to a child: It doesn't become police brutality until after the handcuffs go on, and they keep beating you. People who are resisting being handcuffed are disobeying a lawful order and demonstrating that use of a higher level of force by the police is necessary. Worse, you're just adding extra charges for your attorney has to contend with. And if it's on film, odds are you're going to lose—regardless of the comments on Youtube and Facebook.

After reading this book, you're never going to look at violence the same way again. Knowing about the road, you're going to see emotional and verbal violence everywhere. One of the last places you're going to want to see it is with your spouse, friends, and family.

Realistically, that's where self-violence deniers will be your biggest problem. While it's never fun to have it directed at you in terms of self-defense, violence deniers can get you into deep waters. They go off on someone, and you're left with options that range from suck to worse.

Some of the tensest moments in my life came not from my actions, but from someone I cared about going off on the wrong person. Here's the problem, I'd be the one going to jail or the hospital for what she was doing. While there are such things as redneck feminists (they'll treat a woman the same as a man, they'll punch either) most of the time when women are being verbally to physically violent on other males, those men will usually turn to the man who is with the woman to keep her in check.

For some odd reason, this pisses women off. I'm being tongue in cheek about calling it an odd reason. It's very simple and understandable that women get flamed off at this. They consider it disrespectful and dismissive. But that's because they are thinking in terms of verbal violence, not along the lines of broken jaws, police, and handcuffs, which is more what the guy who is with her is thinking about.

As such, it's important that you and anyone you're involved with have a code word (a safe word, if you will) that communicates: "Stop what you're doing, shut up, and back off, *right now!*"

Now for the bad news, Punkin . . . when the spousal unit says it, you have to listen to it, too.

See those last three words, professional criminal violence? We've come to something that will make sense now. Thinking of violence as a highway is a good way to avoid many pitfalls of the subject. How far along are things? What is the appropriate level of counter force? Articulating what was going on that makes what you did reasonable and everything else we've talked about. All of these are important for effectively defending yourself.

But there's more than one highway and you need to be able to tell which one you're on. Most violence between people is because of social issues. That's the main highway. That's most violence you've seen in your life. And yes, it can—and does—escalate into extremes resulting in death and crippling injury. But it's still about social issues.

What I'd like to introduce now is a fork in the road, an interchange where an entirely different highway branches off where the mile markers jump to a new—and very dangerous—high. This road is particularly dangerous because right up until the moment extreme aggression explodes, it doesn't look like violence at all or looks like the other highway, but begins with much lower mile markers.

It's the difference between social and asocial violence. But before we go there, in the next chapter, we're going to deal with talking to Officer Not-So-Friendly about the guy whose arm you just broke.

CHAPTER 13

When the cops show up, I want to be able to articulate exactly what they have walked up on. Did I do this quickly enough to show my innocence. Speed equals innocence. I take him out fast and hard enough, then no one goes on and on about how brutally the downed man was beaten.
—Clint Overland

Problems If Your SD Works
Part Three: Cops

Let me start this chapter by pointing out that I teach cops. I respect the profession and the men and women who step up and do the job. Having said that, no way in hell would I want to do their job under the restrictions and pressures placed on them by modern society, the administration, the courts, social media, camera phones, and the "blogsphere." On one hand, never in our history have we had such professional, well trained, high quality police. On the other, never have police had to perform under such screwed up and draconian circumstances. While there are bad cops out there, a bigger problem—for you, too—are the circumstances under which they have to do their job.

Six things to put this chapter in perspective:
1) By claiming self-defense, you are confessing to—hopefully, just the elements of—a crime.
2) If you had chosen SODDI (some other dude did it) the simple advice of say nothing, let your lawyer do the talking applies.
3) By claiming self-defense, you *have* to talk.
4) The self-defense pool has been polluted.
5) Depending on the severity of the incident, the first or second batch of reasonable people you have to convince your use of force was justified are the cops. (The first might be your lawyer.)
6) Like the jury, the cops *are* suspicious. Unlike the jury, cops are professionally suspicious.

No matter how sure you are that you acted in self-defense, it's smarter for you to proceed from the belief the police and prosecution are going to assume a crime has been committed. That's to say they probably *don't* think there is a good reason for the violence. Assume they will do everything in their power to build a case against you and prosecute regardless of how justified you *think* you were. In fact, you might want to add that to the graffiti and tattoo collection.

When it comes to self-defense, one of the most suicidally arrogant and stupid things someone can say is, "I know that already." It's the intellectual equivalent of saying "Hey everybody, watch this" as you hand someone your beer. You've lived in a society with police all your life so it's real tempting to say you already know about cops. Trust me, you *don't*. There are serious reasons why we're not going to try to remodel that old house. Instead I'm 'scraping' it, and we're going to build an entirely new one from the ground up. We're pouring a new foundation and everything.

First and foremost police are *safety officers*. Read that again. It's important. Safety is their profession.

Putting aside any argument and attitude about how well they do this job—politics, selective enforcement, preferential treatment, potential abuse, yada, yada—ensuring people's *safety* is their primary job. They enforce the laws that keep people safe and secure. When you stop and think about it, this makes sense. A number of our laws revolve around this fundamental safety issue (e.g., speed limits and laws addressing traffic and other misdemeanor crimes). The big violations are for such things as muggings, murders, and rapes, of course. Other laws prohibit behavior *known* to be potentially dangerous, nuisance, and problematic (e.g., public drunkenness, drunken driving, underage drinking, drugs, prostitution, and similar crimes). Many safety violations occur when this behavior is present. Do these behaviors cause them? No. But they usually occur in tandem. (Here, hold my beer.)

Police protect and serve the public by enforcing these public safety laws. That's their job. When they roll up and there's a body on the ground or someone is hunched over bleeding, they're going to be suspicious a safety law was violated.

The officers' second job is investigation. They investigate to find out what happened during an incident. They do this specifically with the view to determine if a crime has been committed. Let's say they show up and there's a body on the sidewalk. Was it a natural death? An accident? A suicide? A homicide?

In theory, they're not supposed to automatically assume there was a crime. A dead body in the street with no indication of foul play? The coroner will tell you heart attack. A body lying among collapsed scaffolding? Accident. Open window and note? Suicide. When two people (or more) were involved in a violent confrontation, however, and one ends up dead, *odds are good* a crime has been committed. Still, the team of law enforcement officers who examine the scene work in the *homicide* (the killing of one person by another) *not* the murder division.

If in the process of his probe of the circumstances resulting in death, the investigator determines a crime has been committed, then the nature of the investigation *shifts*. Specifically, it shifts to building a case for the prosecution. This especially involves building a case against the person who the police think committed the crime. Once sufficient evidence is gathered, an arrest is made.

This can occur in one of two ways. One is the patrol officer (first responder—the first law enforcement official on the scene) acquires sufficient evidence and arrests a suspect on the spot. Drunken driver, car crash, there you go. Two, the case is transferred to a specialized investigation department (generally a detective). This individual is trained in more advanced investigative methods and said skills are put to use gathering more evidence. Often these cases involve consulting with the district attorney or grand jury (citizens specifically called, like a jury, to consider whether the case should be prosecuted or not) before there are arrest(s) of a suspect(s).

Sure, this is very simplistic, but I give you this step-by-step run down to help you recognize a pivotal point in the process. Remember I wrote *determines?* It's actually more the first responding officer who *decides* if a crime has been committed or not. This is an important crossroads. Turn right and you're cleared. To the left, he's building a case against you. Straight ahead, more investigation is needed to figure out what happened because the evidence isn't clear enough at the time. That's one of the reasons why I say decides, not determines.

Silver lining versus cloud time: Straight means left or right has *not* been decided. But odds are good, he'll be in either the left or right lane as he drives on. When he gets there, he'll be ready for that turn. Similar to you not being able to predict what the prosecutor will do, the same goes for not knowing which way the first responder is going to go.

Sometimes, you'll get an open-minded officer who is going to investigate to find out what happened. At other times, you'll get the attitude that his presence means a crime has been committed (he wouldn't be there otherwise). Then there's the officer who's looking to hang a charge on someone and wrap the incident up. Sometimes, you'll get an officer who will change his mind once he investigates. And there are times if god and twenty angels show up and testify, his mind will not be changed about your guilt. There are still other times where the policy is someone *has* to go to jail.

Welcome to self-defense. You knew the job was dangerous when you took it. Still, you want to do everything in your power to keep the officer from deciding to *take* that left turn. And that involves providing him with enough information to help him take a right. It also includes patiently waiting and cooperating if things drag out longer on the straightaway. Knowing this is a big paradigm shift. So too is knowing *you* influence— but don't necessarily control—the direction things turn.

And a huge part of this is: Do *not* fail the personality test. It shouldn't be, but that is *as* important as the evidence. Let's look at some of the ways folks fail. Many people come roaring into the crossroads, assuming an automatic right hand turn. They're the good guys. The other guy is a violent douche who deserved what he got. What the hell is wrong with this stupid cop for not seeing that! (Personality test failure.) So they're shocked when things turn left.

Other people approach it with the attitude that the cop is automatically going to make a left hand turn because they assume their race, sex, or socioeconomic level guarantee it. The police are against them. The police are racist. The cops are oppressors. The police are trying to . . . yap, yap, yap. Unfortunately, these folks' attitudes often turn into self-fulfilling prophecies—the officers should have turned right, but instead turn left. (Again, personality test failure.)

A real fast way not only to step on your tender bits, but to pogo stick on them is to self-righteously and aggressively start ranting about your *rights*. I'm not going to go down that rabbit hole except to point out six things:

1) Rights are something that are to be argued over in court—*not* at the scene.
2) Rights are a starting point—with a lot of complication, shading, considerations, and interpretations following that.
3) Rights are *not* the *only* thing. Nor are they the beginning, end, apex, conclusion, proof, or ultimate answer to the situation.
4) If you start shouting about your rights, you're going to get labeled an jackass—in that special way only cops can say it.
5) Odds are good as you're hooting about your rights you're going to be getting in the way of the cops doing their job (another way to get oodles of love from them).
6) It they arrive at a situation where significant violence has occurred and you get self-righteous with them . . . well . . . let's just say that could have negative consequences.

That's from a practical point of view. I'll give you a cop's perspective. This is taken verbatim from a career law enforcement officer I had fact check this book:

. . . if a potential assailant begins shouting aggressively at me about his civil or constitutional rights while I'm 1) trying to investigate the potential crime (which, in this context, includes collecting or preserving evidence, keeping all witnesses separate so they don't taint each others accounts, and

attempting to determine if there's more going on here than a simple assault)
2) render or summon first aid for the injured party, 3) notify dispatch and
the appropriate supervisory personnel, 4) stabilize the scene to make sure
a bad situation doesn't become worse and, 5) make sure I'm safe from
harm, that's the point where I'm going to look at "Mr. I Have Rights" as
an impediment or obstruction to me fulfilling my obligations as a public
servant—and possibly think of him as an asshole.

Still another—unique—breed comes charging into this crossroads with
such an aggressively self-righteous attitude he or she *forces* a left hand
turn. I call these the I'd-rather-be-judged-by-twelve-than-carried-by-six
crowd. Colonel Jeff Cooper is popularly attributed as the source of that
twelve-six saying. Others say he merely popularized it. Having never met
the man, I don't know how he meant it. I've heard it argued that it was a
well thought out and rational conclusion. Unfortunately, it's been picked
up and run with by a whole crowd in the self-defense world—folks who
apparently think learning use-of-force laws is for pussies. In fact, they
use twelve-six as a slogan to reject learning about the legal aspects of self-
defense, much less scaling force. We have a term for such people: Loose
cannons. Cops refer to them by a word that starts with the letter "A."

What they ascribe ultimate importance to is their survival. On the
surface, their contention that "nothing else matters if I survived" makes
sense. But if you scratch the surface, it's not only selfish but scary. They're
willing to sacrifice the lives of others for their survival. While that might
seem to make sense, the problem is they also actively resist stepping out
of their fantasy training world to learn about scaling the amount and
type of force they use. *Every* situation is a life-and-death matter and is
about surviving a self-defense armageddon. That's not the kind of person
you want to have a fender bender with or get into a dispute over his dog
crapping in your yard.

The twelve-six crowd is often too busy running and gunning, learning
knife fighting or deadly combatives to bother with the fact that killing or
crippling someone has some serious consequences in the real world. Such
people cling to simplistic, sound bite responses to complex situations.
(E.g., "All you have to say is I was in fear for my life.") And too often, their
behavior is outside the SD square. Mix that with a lethal force instrument
and you 'got' yourself a problem.

Take for example Raul Rodriguez, the Texas man who filmed himself
leaving his own property to handle his neighbor's noisy party. He'd
already called in a noise complaint to the police. But he decided the
police weren't acting fast enough and figured to take matters into his
own hands—bringing his gun for self-defense. He was on the phone
with the 911 dispatcher when he confronted the partygoers. After

antagonizing and monkey dancing with three guys, he's shown on his own film claiming, "I'm in fear for my life" and "I am going to have to defend myself"—right before he shot three of them, killing one. He was sentenced to forty years for murder, after pleading not guilty under the stand your ground and self-defense laws of his state.

The reasons he's sitting in prison cell? Let me count the ways. He left his own property, confronted the neighbors and their guests, and escalated the situation (self-offense). He brandished his weapon. Then instead of retreating back to his home, he opened fire. That's *way out* of the SD square—even for Texas. All of these undermined his claim of self-defense and cost him the protections of the stand your ground law.

But by golly gum, he knew all the right clichés. He had all the simplistic sound bites.

Worse, he filmed himself doing it all with a running commentary. He'd really screwed the pooch by telling a different neighbor (who testified) how to avoid prosecution for shooting someone by simply claiming "I was in fear for my life." Those were his exact words on the video, too—repeatedly said while everyone was out of attack range. Those old and worn out alleged SD phrases blinded him to the significance of *his* actions, starting with walking toward that fatal—and illegal—shooting.

Here's an important safety tip: Your actions have to be *consistent* with your claim of self-defense. If they aren't, the cops aren't going to have to do much investigating to discover you committed a crime. The evidence is going to help them build a case for the prosecutor. This is also why I say: "You need to come up with truths that make you look good faster than the other guy can come up with lies that make you look bad."

Evidence has to match your version of the story. If there are witnesses and video, you have to be seen trying to *avoid* violence. Be assured that the police will be talking to witnesses and reviewing any film to see if your behavior comes close to your story. And once again, don't take it personally—this is their *job*.

The 'I'm the good guy,' 'the cops are against me,' and 'I'd rather be judged . . . ' crowds often collapse in this area. During the investigation, their horrid pre-incident behavior is revealed. That's why I've spent so much time on psycho-babble about good social skills and keeping your monkey on a leash. Those play a critical part in both avoiding violence altogether and post-incident articulation. But let me add that a good habit to develop is to be polite, calm, and articulate with the cops. They shouldn't, but cops judge your credibility on such things.

Changing tracks, here is something else that you need to write a note about, scrawl on the wall, and tattoo onto your forehead: *The higher the use of force, the more you need your attorney present during questioning.*

I told you this because of something called the Reid technique. Many police forces are trained in it, and it is a very popular form of interrogation. The results have stood up in court many times. Wikipedia describes it as:

The Reid technique is a method of questioning subjects and assessing their credibility. The technique consists of a non-accusatory interview combining both investigative and behavior-provoking questions. If the investigative information indicates that the subject committed the crime in question, the Reid Nine Steps of Interrogation are utilized to persuade the subject to tell the truth about what they did.[149] (Naturally the Reid Institute has a different summation of the technique.[150])

Now, I'm not going to bad mouth the Reid technique. But I will point to the same Wikipedia link. The first part tells of a provincial Canadian judge who ruled in 2012: *Stripped to its bare essentials, the Reid technique is a guilt-presumptive, confrontational, psychologically manipulative procedure whose purpose is to extract a confession.*

Followed by: *John E. Reid and Associates maintains that "it's not the technique that causes false or coerced confessions, but police detectives who apply improper interrogation procedures."*

Bad technique or bad application?

To you, it *doesn't* really matter. What matters is the officer:

1) Decides if there was a crime or not
2) 'Holds the pen'
3) Stands with the power of the legal system behind his or her decisions
4) Answers to his or her superiors for decisions.

You may remember that last point from the prosecutor chapter. Cops are the low men on that same totem pole. If they don't arrest, it's their nuts that are going to be held over the fire.

I'm going to share with you two other terms when it comes to being interviewed. One is excited utterance. Two is spontaneous exclamation. To understand how problematic these terms can be add the following words behind them . . . of guilt.

Excited utterances and spontaneous exclamations are the exceptions to the hearsay rule in court. Ordinarily, "he told me" or "I heard him say" are not allowed as evidence because they cannot be substantiated and there is no direct experience with the crime. That is unless it's a cop—basically—saying, "The suspect engaged in an excited utterance or spontaneous admission of guilt when he said _____(fill in the blank)." If you say anything (especially when you are adrenalized) the officer interprets as evidence it was *not* self-defense, it's going to be deemed a

---

149   http://en.wikipedia.org/wiki/Reid_technique (as of March 2014)
150   http://www.reid.com/

confession of guilt. Utterances and exclamations are what they call it to make it sound official.

This is one of the many reasons with higher level of force incidents you *need* your attorney present while making a statement. He can body slam any questions an investigator asks that are designed to create an excited utterance or spontaneous admission. And yes, *any* interrogation technique can be abused this way.

Changing tracks, something that has the self-defense world all in a kerfluffle is the contention that the U.S. Supreme Court has "overturned your right to remain silent." We'll talk about Miranda rights in a bit, but right now know this misconception arises from the case of *Salinas vs. Texas.*[151] In essence what happened was the police were questioning Salinas, and he was cooperating—without the presence of an attorney. When a certain question was asked, he quit answering and behaved a certain way. This behavior was brought up in court. Salinas was convicted of a murder. The appeal was based on Salinas's Fifth Amendment rights being violated.

Here's hitch number one, Salinas *never* invoked his rights, he just went *silent.* Hitch number two, he had neither been arrested nor detained. These may not sound like much, but they're important elements of law and were reasons why his appeal was denied.

But back to the immediate aftermath, when you're adrenalized and freaked out it's *real* easy to say the wrong thing (hence the quote at the beginning of the chapter). But you're pogo sticking across thin ice when someone is looking for an excuse to take a left turn. Police unions have fought for (and won) a specific departmental policy that legally helps officers all the time. That is after a shooting incident, officers *do not* have to make a statement for up to seventy-two hours.

Here's another important safety tip: If the cops don't have to make a statement immediately *neither do you.*

In fact, it's better if you don't. Remember the adrenaline chapter? Most of all, do you remember that adrenaline is a drug. When you're in its grip, you're high and not thinking straight. It's *too easy* to say the wrong things that can—and often will—be interpreted as excited utterances and spontaneous exclamations *of guilt.*

Another reason to hold off saying anything is because memory loss is common with an adrenaline dump, especially short-term memory. I worked a case where the defendant remembered a sense of panic while being pinned up against a car and beaten. When questioned at the scene about why he stabbed the guy, that's what he told them. It was only later

---

151   Salinas v. Texas, argued April 2013, decided June 2013. http://www. supremecourt.gov/opinions/12pdf/12-246_7l48.pdf

he remembered the guy's forearm across his throat, cutting off his air. A common reaction to strangulation—air chokes—is a survival level panic response. That's why waterboarding works and rescuing drowning people is so dangerous. (And by the way being strangled is the immediate threat of death or grave bodily injury that is used in a self-defense plea.) Later when he remembered the forearm across his throat, it sounded like he was lying. The cops testified, "He never said anything at the scene about being choked."

So from an added adrenaline standpoint, you do yourself a favor by shutting up and *waiting* for your attorney. The down side is you'll be waiting in a cell or an interview room while you're coming down off the adrenaline rush.

There are three points I want to make. One re-stresses something I already said: You never know what officer you're going to be dealing with. Things can change *very* quickly. I worked on a case where two officers were fine with the situation and about to arrest the other guy. Then a sergeant showed up and took an immediate dislike to the defendant. It was partly a personality test failure—the defendant got frustrated. The sergeant ordered the defendant arrested, despite evidence the other person was the aggressor and had committed a class five felony.

Two, you don't know when things are going to change. In the case I mentioned before, it wasn't until the sergeant showed up that things took a left turn. And here's where it gets complicated, you *don't know* where that point is going to be.

This brings us to three—you have to *watch* for the turn signals. You don't know where it's going to be, but the turn *doesn't* come out of nowhere. There are signs that it's about to or is happening. As there are signs when it's been made (aka [also known as] it's time to shut up now.) For example, there are certain questions where if you answer 'wrong,' everything turns left. The question *itself* is the turn signal. I know I'm harping on the fact in high level force situations you need an attorney present during questioning. One more log onto that fire, an attorney can spot such set-up questions.

I had a use-of-force incident that started with the cops pointing their guns at me and my partner. In their defense, I was on the sidewalk and kneeling on the guy's head at 1 a.m. My partner was controlling his legs. It was legitimate use of force, we were protecting clients whom he'd attacked. Then he'd attacked us.[152] The officer interviewing us asked, "Did you hit him?" See that flashing light? *That's a turn signal.* On the police use-of-force scale, strikes are *hard hands* and imply a higher use of force.

152 Looking down the barrel of the cop's gun, my response to his order of get off the drunk was to hold up my hands and say, "We will comply, but this guy is on the fight. If we let him up, there's a good chance he'll attack us again."

"No sir, we did a prescribed take down so he wouldn't hurt us. Once he was on the ground we only controlled him." Turn signal seen, lane change accomplished, wreck avoided. That little situation was resolved by him being arrested. [153]

The interrogation is a game of chess where often the little moves are a set up for a greater move. I know of cases where when—in self-defense shootings—the detective asked, "You didn't mean to kill him did you?" The interviewed shooter honestly answered, "No" (because after all who wants to admit to wanting to kill someone). That person was then arrested for manslaughter. The *no* answer was deemed a spontaneous admission. It wasn't self-defense, instead it was written up as an unjustified killing. Why? Because *no* was interpreted as proof the situation didn't warrant the need for lethal force. (And yes, I learned of this trick from the defense attorney who defended that guy.)

This is a deliberate flip of the advice, "Do not say you meant to kill him. Say you meant to stop him." This is common advice about how to answer questions about intent. Let's look at that a bit more. To start with, too many people used the word *kill* in their self-defense statements, and it was interpreted as proof of intent to murder. So people teaching about use of force in their self-defense training started advocating, "Don't use the word kill, instead say, 'I meant to stop the threat.' "

Well, so far so good. But even good advice can be watered down to nearly useless sound bites and clichés. That's what many people started doing. That stop-the-threat response became nearly robotic, including in situations where it was questionable if it had been actual SD. (Google the terms Raul Rodriguez, shooting Texas, video.)

Here's the problem with dealing with thinking people. They *tend* to think. The cops after getting slapped in the face a few dozen times with "I didn't mean to kill him, I only meant to stop the threat" figured out a way to flip the general idea around. See when Officer Friendly asks, "You didn't mean to kill him, did you?" people jump at the chance to support their position that it wasn't murder. And in doing so, fall into this reverse engineered trap. Oh you didn't mean to kill him, so it was an accidental homicide . . . that's manslaughter. Probably better to stick with the whole, "What I meant to do was stop the danger to myself" approach. But since your attorney is going to be there anyway, *consult* with him.

I'm going to take a slight side trip here. The truth is the law, legal strategy, and tactics are *always* changing. I liken this to the history of

---

153   One of the responding officers was female. She and two others were interviewing the drunk. The situation ended when we heard the drunk shout, "Fuck you, cunt!" The officer interviewing us blinked and told us to leave. As we went back inside we saw the drunk had new friends who were kneeling on his head. And that female officer was *really* working that knee.

warfare. Some new invention, some new tactic is developed and—for a while—it is wildly successful. Then someone comes up with a counter, and it becomes less successful. In time, enough counters evolve that it becomes old and is left behind. This is why there is no "you just do this" answer. There is no, all you have to say is _____(fill in the blank) simplistic cliché or sound bite that works every time. Unfortunately, too many people are looking for these. And because that's what sells—*too many instructors are teaching them.*

Don't drink this Kool-Aid. Your best legal advice comes from lawyers— not self-defense instructors, especially not martial arts instructors. Oh yeah, add me to that list, too. I *want* you to go out and double check this information with legal sources. (Seriously, go take a class.)

Let's extend that. Too many people out there are talking out of their butts when it comes to advice about dealing with the cops. The Internet is full of, "Say this because if you don't the cops will _____(fill in the blank)." Go to another site on the Web, and you get the direct opposite advice. "Don't say (the same 'this') because if you do, the cops will think you _____(fill in the blank)."

There are *no* hard and fast rules about making a statement to the police. You need to go into questioning with full situational awareness of that statement. There are lots of guidelines and it-depends-on-the-situation rules of thumb. But these *aren't* carved in granite.

Hell, George Zimmerman violated what I would consider the closest thing I have to a granite rule about talking to the cops, which is *don't* talk to the cops about a lethal force situation *without* an attorney present. Yet, he did okay until the situation went political, but even then it worked. Turning a frown upside down, the videos of his cooperation with the police were played by the prosecution so many times that he didn't have to take the stand. The jury had already heard his side of the story.

Making a statement to the police is like crossing a mine field. You have to go slowly and carefully. And depending on what you run into, you have to be ready to stop or change direction. There is a time to talk, a time to shut up, and a time to call in the verbal and legal bomb squad. Conversely, a whole lot of people talk themselves into waking up in a jail cell the next morning. They do this as much with *how* they say it as *what* they say. It's that personality test I mentioned.

I've dealt with a lot of cops. I've done this from both sides of the law. I've stood in handcuffs surrounded by a whole lot of police who were just looking for an excuse to arrest me. And I've walked away. I've also watched people open their mouths and infuriate the police so much, they basically arrest themselves. Hell back in the bad ol' days, I saw people volunteer for a beating. Not in a "gee, the cops overreacted" way, but a "give me a club and I'll help you beat this bastard" manner.

So, if there is going to be a second do-not-violate rule about dealing with cops: *Be polite. Be professional. Be calm.*

Yes, you've probably just gone through the most traumatic experience in your life. But screaming obscenities at the cop because the blockhead can't see you're the victim is *not*—*I* repeat *not*—going to help. It certainly isn't going to convince Officer Friendly you acted reasonably and weren't involved in the creation and escalation of the situation. In fact, it's going to convince him of the direct opposite. Your bad attitude just gave him a reason to want to nail you. "But he's trying to arrest me!" *Get over it.* "He's trying to ruin my life!" *He's doing his job.* "He's against me!" *Grow up!*

Tattoo and graffiti time: It's *not* between you and the cop. He or she is just doing the job. The officer is investigating and trying to determine what happened. Don't make this task harder by being obnoxious. Don't treat the officer like a servant come to clean up your mess. Don't treat him like the enemy. Don't try to be slick. Don't be indignant and obnoxious about your rights. And most of all, you damn well better *not* lie to him!

At the same time, the officer is *not* your friend. He is *not* there to rescue you. He is *not* your mommy (whom you go running to tattle on what the other kid did to you). He *is* the five-hundred-pound gorilla who has just strolled into the situation and asked, "What's all this then?" And you better have a good answer and the ability to articulate it.

The third point I want to make about the police is they *do not* make the laws. Nor—despite what many would claim—can they select which laws they enforce.[154] They operate within specific guidelines and limitations.

We can expand that to include pressures from above. One of the biggest ones is what could happen if they *don't* make an arrest. I'm talking about a serious demand on the patrol officers and detectives. See, they have their own version of a win box they must check off. Every time they make an arrest, they get to put a little check in the 'cleared' column. Clearance rates on violent crimes make the brass happy. They delight the city council. They keep chief of police in high spirits. They please the mayor. And they make the happy little taxpayers feel all warm and fuzzy. The easiest box to check to keep their bosses cheerful is 'arrest made.' If they *don't* check that box, they'd better have a damned good reason.

That's for everyday stuff. But the more serious the violence, the more they're going to have to justify to someone why they *didn't* make an arrest—and that person in turn is going to have to explain to someone higher up the ladder. If it hits the news, the ladder goes even higher. Somewhere up that ladder, the person demanding the explanation will

---

154   At least lower down the chain.

have more interest in an arrest (that relieves the media and political pressure) than that justice is served. Political problem solved via it's now someone else's problem. And by someone else, I mean the prosecutor.

There are also these things called crack downs and mandatory arrests. These, too, come down from above. Crack downs come around now and then. Usually to show the good citizens someone is tough on crime, although there's evidence of other factors.[155] Mandatory arrests are the result of strong lobbies and legislation. The end result of both is that— in certain circumstances—officer discretion is removed. Arrests are *compulsory*.

This has had unintended consequences. See in ye olde days when it came to a fight, the officers could say, "You guys can each go home right now or I can arrest both of you." This kept the number of people sitting in cells more manageable. If this new pressure to arrest was equally applied, the police would be undermanned, jails and the legal system would be in a log jammed, and half the nation would be a prison. Mandatory arrest and equal treatment are simply *not* economically feasible. Under the circumstances of somebody *has* to go to jail, the easiest way to manage numbers is to only arrest one person.

That statement is not entirely accurate. But you'll have a better chance of it *not* being you if you approach the situation accepting the philosophy that someone has to go to jail. If the officer doesn't arrest someone, hell will be demanding its paycheck from him. So, you must do everything within your power to make sure it's the other guy who's arrested. (Starting with what he did to prompt you to act in self-defense.)

There are two important lines marked on most police report forms. One reads "offender" and the other "victim." When one person assaults another (a one-sided attack) and beats the hell out of that person, it's pretty much a no-brainer as to who broke the law. Put the name of the person doing the beating on the first line, the name of the person taking the thrashing on the second. Arrest the first.

Walk in on the aftermath of a fight, the winner is the guy with the least number and severity of bruises. Odds are good, he's also the worst aggressor. Put his name on the offender line and arrest him. Put the other guy's name on the victim line and let him go. So what if the loser started the conflict and attacked first? It's *easier* to arrest the winner! The officer gets to transfer his paperwork to the 'cleared' folder. The brass is happy. There's no more pressure on him. The paperwork is in order. And most importantly, it's now officially someone else's problem.

---

155   There is often a correlation between crack downs and pre-elections, budget crunches, bad press, and public outcry. During these times it seems the officer's discretion to arrest for minor infractions evaporates. When these are the times, just assume it's going to be settled in court.

But here's where we run into a problem. If you'd just let yourself be beaten senseless, the officer could easily determine who the aggressor is. Who goes to jail is a no-brainer. The problem is when you successfully defend yourself, it *looks* like you were the bad guy. It's up to you—and your attorney—to keep your name off the report's offender line.

I'm not going to go into it, but one of the most horrible places where mandatory arrest can get ugly is with domestic violence.

***** Insert Side bar *****
***** End Side Bar *****

Now, you're probably getting sick and tired of me talking about all the stupid ways you can screw up. Or maybe you're thinking I must think you're stupid. You'd never do that; you're smarter than that.

But I want you to remember two things. One, cops are professionals. Tripping up bad guys is their job. *They're good at it.* You're not. Think of the cop trying to do your job as well as you do it and you get the idea of how well outmaneuvering a cop in his job works.

Two, as I said earlier, "*Adrenaline is a drug.*" You're crashing from (or are still in the grip of) adrenaline. You've just been through a horrible event, and now here's this cop treating you like a douche.

Call 911 or not to call 911. That is the question. The answer is "it depends."

In case you haven't noticed by now, once the process is put into gear, you have less and less control over the situation. Think of the 911 call as turning on the engine to begin the vehicle that is the criminal justice process. How you deal with the cops is putting it into gear. Getting arrested is pulling out into traffic, but you *ain't* drivin'! That 911 call brings you that much closer to being a passenger on that roller coaster. And sometimes you gotta take that ride, other times you don't.

If you know how to get away with crime, you've already got things set up. There's no way in hell you're going to call 911 (unless it's part of the set-up). If you don't have things set up, 911 is a crap shoot—especially at the lower levels of force. It's a crap shoot because it can be a race to the phone. As a rule of thumb—and remember when your thumb isn't being used as a ruler, it's up your butt—the *first* complainant gets his or her name on the report's victim line. I mention the alternative use of your thumb because if you have two people equally incompetent about making statements, the rest of the sentence applies. If you are good about statements and your use of force was clean, then the person who gets his or her name on that line is *not* automatically the one who called first.

If you have two idiots engaging in illegal violence, it's a popularity contest with the loser going to jail. Normally, the first caller has a slight advantage, but not always. (As a professional, you'd be amazed at how many times I've watched people who called the cops on me talk themselves into getting arrested.)

If the other guy *doesn't* call them, you've just called the cops and perhaps announced you committed a crime. (That goes double if you can't articulate the

Let me give you an example where people—in an adrenalized state—screw up. They get tired, cranky, and angry about having to repeat themselves. They've already told the story twice, and now this third cop is asking the same damned thing. Why the hell doesn't he just go ask the other two?

Here's why: Those three different interviews are to see if your story changes, if you trip up, or if you're lying. Forcing you sit in the interview details of the incident.) This is why the advice of it's a race to the phone deserves a response of "wait a minute, let's think about this."

I cannot give you a *yes or no* answer to the "Do I call nine-one-one" question. I can, however, point out some considerations:

1) The higher the use of force, the more likely it is that the cops will be called—by someone. Factor that into your decision.

2) Not calling them will require certain answers from you if they are called (e.g., why didn't you call?)

3) What you say on the 911 recording *is admissible* as evidence.

4) Some folks recommend you look at the 911 call as witness grooming. The farthest I'm going to go is to say, "The call is like talking to the cops." It's also very much part of your defense strategy.

5) If you have to deal with a problem person on an ongoing basis, calling 911 can kick it up to a new level (vendetta or feud). Conversely, it can have the opposite effect and let the person know you *will* call for back up. This can be an important consideration in dealing with bad behavior.

6) Staying with the on-going basis theme if you know and are having problems with a person, he or she is more likely to call the police than a mugger. It's now a race to the phone.

7) In a drawn out feud or stalking situation, a record of police involvement can work for or against you.

Like everything else about this subject, it's your call. But make the decision based on the circumstances not a simplistic sound bite that some 'expert' told you.

room for a long time repeating yourself is part of that strategy.

Remember they are *investigating*— with emphasis on seeing if a crime was committed. They are watching you for any sign of deception, aggression, or hostility. They'll get together and compare notes—outside your hearing. Getting hacked off and losing your cool about being questioned supports the suspicion that you probably *didn't* act in self-defense. It also reinforces the idea you were part of the problem.

It's important for you to know that police are under *no* legal obligation to tell you the truth during an investigation. This is a serious double standard. They get hacked if you lie to them, but they have no problem lying to you. Once again, *get over it*. In fact, an officer lying during questioning is *not* uncommon. For example, say you had an altercation with your neighbor, the officer says "Well, he said you _____ (fill in the blank)." This inflames your anger, and you react.

Did that person really say that? Or is the officer trying to gauge your reaction? More than that is the officer trying to deliberately provoke an excited utterance or spontaneous exclamation? Furious about the lie, you say something that qualifies as an admission of guilt. BAM! Investigation done, you're under arrest.

You can occasionally see the same kind of testing for an aggressive response from animal control offices. They want to see if the dog you just put back on leash is aggressive; if so, they'll cite you. Prove that you're smarter than a dog and *don't* react aggressively to a cop testing to see if you will lose your cool.

Another common technique is Good Cop, Bad Cop. Most people, when they hear that think, "Oh I know that one. The bad cop makes me want to run over and talk to the good, friendly cop." That is one way it plays out. The other is you react to the cop in your face while the other officer quietly stands there. That way they *both* hear your 'spontaneous' admission of guilt.

An aggressive cop accusing you is an *act* (similar to outrage and anger displayed in that courtroom by a prosecutor).[156] It is a tactic to elicit a specific emotional response. It's designed not just to get you on the defensive, but to get you talking. When people are feeling threatened, they commonly try to explain and justify themselves. The aggression, threats, show of disdain of the bad cop triggers your emotional monkey brain. You can find yourself getting excited, babbling, and saying stupid stuff. (Basically, being accused comes with its very own adrenaline dump.)

Four points about this strategy. One, it is seldom played in presence of your attorney. That's because your attorney will shut it down pretty damn quick. Two, it's not likely while there's a camera rolling. If this behavior is caught on film, it's a great way for your attorney to get your 'confession' thrown out. Three police are professionals. They literally see this stuff *every* day. Odds are they've seen worse, too. They also know they have to meet certain standards and achieve certain goals. So what's with all the emotion? Where's the professionalism? Unless it is a tactic to achieve certain goals. Hmmm. Ya think? Four is human beings tend to get 'excited' around aggression whether they too become aggressive or profoundly uncomfortable.

A good way to tell if it's an act is look over at the good cop. This is a great litmus test for other things, too. Is that person displaying aggression as well? (Is he ready to jump in and stomp you, too? Ready to back up one of his own?) Is that person looking profoundly uncomfortable about a superior officer's lack of professionalism. Or is he ready to swing into action, too? (The look of someone who is about to pull an out-of-control partner off someone is different than the one of someone who is going to join in throwing you a beating.)

Or—and this is a dead give away it's an act—is he or she displaying little to no emotion? Basically, is the good cop acting neutral about his or her OOK partner swinging from the tree branches? *That is not normal!* Check the reactions of other officers present. See if they are calmly letting this officer take the bad cop role. If you can calm yourself enough to see this as acting, it's a good way to keep from falling for it.

While we're in the neighborhood, I encourage cooperating with the police after a self-defense situation, but *use* common sense. And this

---

156   Unless you're being a complete douche bag, have just killed his brother, or punched him, too. Like everything I say, there are limits and exceptions.

includes accepting advice from anyone who is *not* a lawyer about what to say to the police. (And yes, that includes me. I don't want you to think that just because you read this book, you're now an expert.)

Some self-defense gurus tell you to "say nothing." Others contend, "Let your lawyer do all the talking." Then there are those who advise, "Don't even call the police." Still others say, "Tell them you will cooperate and give them a full statement—but only in the presence of your attorney." Then there are those who suggest you only give them your name and that you're waiting on the presence of your attorney, but to point out witnesses and evidence that will be helpful to you later. There is *no* one right answer, it depends on the circumstances you find yourself in.

But there is a critical point to communicate. I'm going to write what is printed on attorney Adam Weitzel's business card:

"If you are involved in a shooting the only three things you will say to the police are:

1) My name is _____

2) I am the victim.

3) I will fully cooperate after I have spoken to my attorney."

That last line is important because it clearly invokes your Fifth Amendment rights. And yes, you *do* have to clearly state that you are exercising your right to remain silent until your lawyer arrives (*Salinas vs. Texas*). Just remaining silent is not enough. Simply saying, "I know my rights" is not enough. You *must* say you will *only* make a statement in the presence of your attorney.

Let's come back to something I mentioned in passing. Rights are a starting point. When it comes to practical application, a whole lot of other stuff *follows*. Unfortunately, there's a whole crop of people who think their rights are the beginning, end, apex, conclusion, juggernaut of any debate and are carved in granite to boot. The whole of their—and I use the term loosely—argument is they have the right to do this, you don't have the right to do that.[157] Most people have no clue what rights really mean in a practical, everyday application—much less a legal one.

In case you slept through civics, the Fifth Amendment in the Bill of Rights states: *No person shall be held to answer for a capital, or otherwise infamous crime, unless on a presentment or indictment of a Grand Jury, except in cases arising in the land or naval forces, or in the*

---

157   It should tell you that the idea of positive and negative rights is popular in philosophy and political science not legal circles. When talking with Joe Blow on the streets, you'll run into the assumption of positive and negative rights all the time. But these folks don't know that's what they're talking about. They folks also don't know positive and negative was proposed for the first time in 1979 by Karl Vasek. They've also never read John Locke writings about rights, but, man, are they experts on rights— especially about their own.

Militia, when in actual service in time of War or public danger; nor shall any person be subject for the same offense to be twice put in jeopardy of life or limb; nor shall be compelled in any criminal case to be a witness against himself, nor be deprived of life, liberty, or property, without due process of law; nor shall private property be taken for public use, without just compensation.

Wow. It's more than "I don't gotta say nuffin,'" ain't it?

Personally, I am tickled pink to live in a country where we have rule of law, especially when it comes to the Fifth Amendment keeping that process in check. The police and courts have to operate *within* those boundaries. They may play fast and loose with those boundaries, but they have to stay inside them. If they're caught stepping outside, they're in deep trouble.

But when you're the one facing the dragon's flames, it hardly feels like there's any hope. That's not surprising, because a lot of time and effort by some very smart people have gone into ways to investigate cases and check off the cleared box. Recognize, too, a lot of the same has gone into getting the defendant off.

Because of this, due process is an amazingly complex field. So don't even pretend you understand it. It's far above your pay grade. There's a reason you're paying a lawyer. Due process is the game your attorney knows. But what you can do is help him or her not only defend you, but keep you from being arrested in the first place. That's right. If you've landed yourself in some next level hell, you want your lawyer sitting there *during* questioning. (And that means having one on retainer or picked out *before* you ever get your butt into a crack.[158])

This brings us to the Miranda warning and rights. Depending on the state you're in the wording may change slightly, but the points covered will be:

You have the right to remain silent when questioned. Anything you say or do can and will be used against you in a court of law. You have the right to consult an attorney before speaking to the police and to have an attorney present during questioning now or in the future. If you cannot afford an attorney, one will be appointed for you before any questioning, if you wish. If you decide to answer any questions now, without an

---

158   I'm a big fan of having a lawyer on retainer. Consider it an insurance payment. If you never use it, great. Straight up, professional criminals have their lawyers on speed dial. Rich people pick up the phone and call their attorneys. Despite what you see on TV about the show's hero talking to a mob boss, in reality the investigator is talking to the bosses' attorney, too. *Take a lesson!* The reason the professionals and the rich do it is because it *works*. Do your homework now! You don't have to pay a retainer (that just gets him down to you quicker), but at the least leave the lawyer's name and number with someone who can drop cash off ASAP (as soon as possible). In the mean time—expect to sit in cell.

attorney present, you will still have the right to stop answering at any time until you talk to an attorney. Knowing and understanding your rights as I have explained them to you are you willing to answer my questions without an attorney present? [159]

Before we look further at that, I'm going have to point some things out because of the number of Internet lawyers out there. (Well, that means . . .) Start with there is a difference between being detained, questioned, taken into custody (being taken in for questioning) and being arrested. Why is this important?

Well to start with if you're in handcuffs or sitting in an interview room at the police station, it *does not* mean you are under arrest. Until the cops announce that you are under arrest, it's all part of the investigation. Once you are placed under arrest, the legal process starts, certain rules apply, and conditions change. Until that time, they are the lead-in to that procedure (the left turn has been made, but not the arrest).

Officially, the officers have to Mirandize you when you are in custodial interrogation, they are arresting you, and you are *'otherwise deprived of . . . freedom of action in any significant way* (detained).' In practice, sometimes it's hard to tell where that point occurs. But the confusion can be cleared up easily by asking, "Am I free to go?" If yes, "Hey, what a great idea; see you later." If no, "Tell you what let's get my attorney in on this."

Here's your warm fuzzy for the day: Your rights are there throughout *any* interaction with the police. This especially applies to *not answering* questions without legal counsel present. By the time most people start thinking in terms of Miranda, the cops have long ago made that left turn and have been building a case since. By that time, it's too late. The damage has been done.

Adam Wietzel's third line of "I will fully cooperate after I have spoken to my attorney" doesn't seem all that important, but it *is*, both in the legal process and during the investigation. It informs them (without you being a jerk about it) that you are invoking your Fifth Amendment rights. That takes it down a very specific route. Anyone who is involved in that process *knows* what it means, what the limits are, and what standards they now have to meet.

Invoking your Fifth Amendment rights also is a serious sign that you are ready for a much higher level of the way this game is played. You rolling that out means you're as *serious* about this part as you were about physically defending yourself. Having said that:

1) Use common sense

2) And—again—*don't* be a jackass.

In fact, consider those important safety tips.

---

159   http://en.wikipedia.org/wiki/Miranda_warning (2014)

Before we get as far along as you talking to cops while standing over the body you just manufactured, let's cover some basics: You *do* have to identify yourself to the police when asked. The easiest and fastest way is to show an ID. In a routine stop, you will be asked your business. If you're not breaking the law, there's no real problem in answering truthfully. If you're driving, showing your license and registration *is* mandatory. Other states add proof of insurance.

The officer also *will* ask certain questions and *request* actions that indicate any level of intoxication. Drunks have a hard time multi-tasking. That's why you'll get questions during actions—like the officer asking you a question while you're looking for your registration. He's looking for safety violations and impaired judgment (significant because adrenaline flowing through your system can make you look like you're on drugs).

An officer in the legal execution of his duty can tell you to do something. (Stop, show me your ID, step out of the car, and other such commands.) And you *legally* have to obey.

Before you get your knickers in a knot, let me remind you: Police are primarily safety officers. Odds are if a cop tells someone to do something, it has to do with that or with nuisance behavior. Even more likely, the person he is interacting with was doing something that violated safety or nuisance laws.

I feel it's almost retarded that I have to mention this, but there is an endemic attitude in our society about people's rights to violate safety and nuisance laws (e.g., speeding, breaking traffic laws, wandering around in public drunk and stoned). People actually get angry when they're pulled over for speeding. In fact, they often demand an explanation for the officer's actions. ("Why do you want me to step out of the car?") Worse, many want to argue with the cop about their rights and tell the police what rights the police *don't* have when it comes to them.

Six points:

One: The cops have a better understanding of what they can and can't do than you do.

Two: They also know tricks and ways around the limitations they operate under. Most people don't actually know their rights or what will or will not stand up in court—if it is brought up. Cops do.

Three: If a cop *does* cross a line or break legal precedent, the time and place to deal with it is in *court*. Tattoo and graffiti that one. For non-arrest incidents, there's also contacting the officer's supervisor and filing a formal complaint. You're not going to win by arguing with the cop then and there. The only thing you'll achieve is his stacking charges and undermining your claim of innocence. Yeah, he crossed the line. You still resisted arrest. Guess which one is going to stand up in court?

Four: Cops also know the tricks and dodges people use to stall and interfere with them and their duties. These are pulled all the time by actual criminals and lowlifes. Guess what your doing the same thing is going to get you classified as?

Five: When you're standing over a body, it is *not* the time to argue for your rights, insist how you want to be treated, toss around weasel words, or demand information from the coppers.

Six: While it may not be high on *your* list of priorities, officer safety is right near the top on the cop's list. Guess what? By being the victor, you've just demonstrated that you're dangerous. Officer Friendly isn't going to be pleasant until he has secured his or her and everyone else's safety. This is first and foremost. Be patient and cooperative until this status is achieved, no matter how freaked out and scared you are. Remember the cops just got there, they don't know what's going on.

Let's have an in-depth look at number four, tricks and dodges. While self-righteous, drunk, and stupid people often engage in this behavior, *so too do* professional dirt bags. Constantly asking the cop why about his questions or wanting an action performed is a form of evasion and passive resistance. It's designed to interfere with the officer performing his duties. Unlike outright lying, though, the criminal can't be easily caught at this kind of deflection. A professional and experienced criminal will make the stall seem to be all sweetness, reason, and not a confrontation. Stupid, aggressive people make it a challenge. This not only encourages the cop to use physical force, but legally justifies it. (We'll get to ask, tell, order in a second.) *Don't* be that guy!

Why is knowing this important? Because stating you are invoking your Fifth Amendment rights should be as about as exciting as the news the sun will rise tomorrow. You know the stakes that are on the table, they know the stakes. And now they know you know, too. It's a simple fact of life. So, everybody can calm down and be professional about the situation.

There are a lot of people who give sound-bite advice about dealing with cops. "If you ask for your lawyer, the cops will think you're 'lawyering up' and are guilty." Or, "Shut up and don't say anything!" Or, "You don't have to tell them a gawddamned thing." Or, "Let your lawyer do all the talking."

The problems with simplistic solutions are: One, they're simplistic (therefore not really reliable). Two, lacking other information too many people insist on adding their own dash and style. Like becoming an obnoxious aggressive lout while snarling at the cops, "I know my rights. Get me my lawyer, you dickhead!" Right, that's real smart when you're using an affirmative defense where you must talk to the cops and justify your actions.

The closest thing to sound-bite advice I will give you is: If you don't want to convince the police you're guilty, *don't* act like a jackass, weasel, or professional douche around them. They are doing their job. Accept that, deal with it, and learn to be patient about it. Because you're accomplishing your new job assignment: While cooperating with the investigation, you need to be doing everything in your power *not* to go to prison. Hopefully, you started this process by trying to avoid physical conflict. If so great, keep on working that strategy. Convincing people you acted in self-defense is a whole lot easier when you actually did!

Include in this new job description not getting shot or slammed into a wall by responding officers—particularly in the immediate aftermath. Trust me, if the cops roll up and see you standing over a body, they're going to get . . . excited. Don't give them reason to be any more nervous than they have to be.

I will remind you about compliance. The normal pattern is to ask, tell, order. "Sir, could you please step out of the car?" "Sir, step out of the car." "Sir, I am ordering you, step out of the car *now!*" Having established an articulable pattern of noncompliance (often videoed) Officer No-Longer-Friendly is justified to use force. In other words, your butt is coming out of that car. Don't fool yourself. Sugar and spice and asking nice aside, these are *lawful* orders. Ignoring, arguing about, or resisting ask, tell, order establishes a pattern of resistance and noncooperation to lawful orders that will stand up in court.

However, when the police roll up and you're standing with a weapon in your hand, there could be some tense moments. That is not the time for *any behavior* other than:

a) Telling them you will comply

b) Comply

Notice the order I put those in. Something people who have just been involved in an incident tend to forget—the officer is *really* interested in his or her own safety. When the officer rolls onto the scene, he or she doesn't know what has happened. Who is the bad guy? Is this a case of two bad guys and now only one is standing? That person still standing is still there for a *reason.* Is that person actively aggressive? With the other person down and bleeding or dead, it's a reasonable conclusion there is danger present.

So the first thing officers want when they arrive is to secure anything that could injure or kill them—after you've defended yourself that means *you.* And this usually means you're going to end up disarmed, searched, and handcuffed. That's just the way it is.

I would say deal with it, but *how* you deal with it has a lot to do with whether the investigation turns left, right, or continues on straight ahead.

While we're at it, your reactions also have a lot to do with whether or not you are killed by the cops for being stupid.

So *do not* squeal, "After an incident I'll be emotional and traumatized. I'll be unable to remember all this." That is unless you want your emotional brains splattered on the concrete because you did something the cops interpreted as aggressive. Something that is way too easy to do if all you're concerned about is being emotional and traumatized.

First things first, if weapons were involved *don't* have them in your hands when the cops roll up. While we're at it, don't holster it.

Your life may depend on not screwing up here, If, for gawd knows what foolish reason you haven't, *before* the squad car stops rolling, *put your weapon down.*

If it's not a firearm drop it. If it's a firearm, do *not* turn toward the cop car, hold the gun in a non-firing position, put it down (if you can, preferably by holding it with two fingers) and keep it *pointing away* from them. As you step away, show them your hands by holding them open and away from your body. Do this *before* they get out of the car.

So why not holster your gun? You may think you're going to let the cop disarm you, but that ain't going to happen. They're not going to be hot to trot to approach an armed person. Do you really want the added complication of pulling a weapon when the cops already have theirs out? Think about it.

Know you're going to be looking down the barrels of their guns when they do get out. Wait for orders about what they want you to do. Don't worry, you won't be waiting long. Personally I've found repeating the orders as you do them helps. "I'm stepping away. I'm turning around. I'm getting down on my knees . . ."

Accept this truth: You're going to be cuffed while they check on the other guy's condition. While you're waiting is a good time to practice your meditation and breathing and get your brain cells front and center, starting with do you need medical attention, too?

Even if weapons weren't involved, a calm, open, nonaggressive stance *is* the way to go. Personally I like to openly show my hands out to the side. If I'm wearing something that is common to the attire of people who legally carry concealed weapons (like a vest or baggy shirt) before they even get close enough to start talking, I do a slow, two-finger lift and pirouette to show I'm not carrying. (I'm still going to get searched and probably cuffed, but cooperation is a good precedent to set before I tell them they're going to have to wait for a statement.)

Here why I am such a big fan of first telling the officer you will comply, then demonstrating it. Your actions match your words. It communicates to the officer that you are *not* a threat to him or her. That's a real good precedent to set. Telling the officer step-by-step what you're doing keeps you from accidentally moving too fast and in a threatening manner. This lessens the chance of the officers freaking out and using force against you. Believe me when a cop has a gun drawn on you, you *don't* want to freak him out. This standard does not change, regardless of how freaked out *you* are.

Equally important *after* you tell the officers you will comply—if the other guy seems still to be a potential threat—you can communicate that information, too. I mentioned previously an anecdote about the last time I looked down a cop's gun (he was a little cranky because I was kneeling on some other guy's head). My first words were, "I will comply! But this guy is on the fight! If I let him up, there's a good chance he'll attack us again!" The cop's response of "I'll take that chance" didn't win him any brownie points.[160] But us doing the 'tell and show' routine won us some.

Your cooperation also is recorded on tape by the dashboard camera mounted in the police car. That's one more bit of evidence that you *weren't* belligerent—pretty useful when claiming self-defense. So—when Officer Not-Interested-In-What-You-Have-To-Say-Until-The-Situation-Is-Secure shows up—don't start trying to explain your position until he has the situation *secured*. You'll get a chance to say your piece. Be patient. Granted that can be hard when you're adrenalized, but this is part of your new job assignment. *Slow down* so you don't make mistakes.

Another reason to take this opportunity to be quiet is it gives you time to bring your adrenaline under control and your rational thinking brain back on line. While you're sitting handcuffed is a good time to do some deep breathing exercises to calm yourself. Chant your mantra. Find your inner harmony. Find your tranquility. Un-torque your 'wa.' But most of all: Get your brain cells *front and center*. You can make serious mistakes when you're excited and going fast. And one of the biggest effects of adrenaline is you'll *want* to babble. You'll want to tell this authority figure what happened—as fast as possible. Again, *slow down!*

The severity of the situation (level of force) is the measure you should use when it comes to talking on the spot to the police about what happened. Again the higher the level, the more I suggest waiting for an attorney before making a statement. If you do decide to talk to them at the location—*from the start*—assume the following: *You have the right to remain silent when questioned. Anything you say or do can and will be used against you in a court of law. You have the right to consult an attorney*

---

160   Realistically, if the guy is dumb enough to try to get a couple of free licks in can you think of better proof that you weren't the aggressor? The cops witnessed him attacking you. Three guesses whose name is going on the offender line.

and to have an attorney present during questioning . . . Ahhhh, the *old* Miranda warning. We've seen it before.

If you do choose to talk at the scene, *watch* for left turn signals indicated by questions like: "Did you hit him?" "Did you try to retreat?" "Did you have anything in your hand when you hit him?"[161] If you hear queries along these lines, it's best to be able to honestly give the right answer. If you hear too many of them, it's time to stop and call in the lawyer. (And be sure to tell them that's what you're doing.) Remember, invoking your Fifth Amendment rights kicks the situation up to a higher level of play. But if things are taking a left hand turn, you're going to need a lawyer anyway.

Here again we have a lot of Internet 'lawyers,' people who think they understand what invoking the Fifth Amendment means. They contend that once you've invoked it, they can't ask you any more questions. Not exactly. They just can't ask you any more questions *about* the case. If they ask if you'd like some water, "I want my lawyer" isn't the right answer. Don't laugh. I've seen it advised by Internet 'legal experts.' The real bozos are the ones who think, "After I've claimed the Fifth, they can't use anything I say against me." *That is flat-out wrong.*

They can use anything you've said up to that point. And *if* you decide to waive your rights by starting to talk about the case after you've invoked the Fifth, *you're no longer exercising your right to remain silent.* (We'll look at this in more depth in a bit)

Also numbered among the bozo brigade are those who claim the Supreme Court overturned the Fifth Amendment's right to remain silent by upholding the *Salinas* conviction. No. What that ruling did was establish you *must* articulate you are exercising your Fifth Amendment rights. Just going silent is *not* enough.

So for the record, once you've asked for counsel, the police cannot legally ask you any more questions about the *investigation.* Not that they'd want to, but they *can* talk to you about football. Here's the catch, they can't ask you any more questions about the case as long as you don't waive your rights by starting to talk about it again on your own. (Gee, I've mentioned that twice now. Think maybe it's important?)

<u>But first let's look at why it is important to communicate that you will</u>

161   Incidentally, I don't like strike enhancers. First, they limit your versatility (hint, a grab is just a hit that hangs on). Second, learn how to hit (that skill is with me always). Third, they don't extend you range like a club or a gun (that means you gotta be close). Fourth, they *are not* defensive weapons, they're only good for increasing the effectiveness of your offense (not something that you can use to protect you from an incoming attack). Fifth and finally, they automatically bump charges to aggravated assault, felonious assault, or assault with a deadly weapon (however the law reads in your area). If that's what you intended, fine and dandy, but a set of brass knuckles seriously sinks your self-defense claim.

cooperate and give a statement with an attorney present. I cannot stress enough: Get that established *right up front* for a variety of reasons:

A) This takes the pressure off the cops. They're going to get a statement. You are going to cooperate with their investigation. It may not be as fast or as soon as they want, but they're going to get what they need.

B) It gives them something they can use to explain to the boss why they don't have a statement (or an arrest).

C) It is a formal and legal statement that you are invoking your Fifth Amendment rights. And that *legally* sets the guidelines for what comes next. The police know they have to stay within certain parameters or they are going to blow any case they might hope to bring to the prosecutor.

D) If after you've explained what happened to your attorney and he tells you to shut up and say nothing, you have not tried to deceive them. The situation has changed. You are now acting on the advice of your lawyer. (And you haven't confessed to a crime by claiming self-defense when it wasn't.)

E) It informs them you aren't a complete amateur, which means the tricks they use on such novices are less likely to work.

F) Knowing the above, keeps them more professional. They know they need to clearly stay inside the bounds. And finally . . .

G) Knowing you will give them a statement reduces the chances of their trying to *provoke* you into waiving your rights.

That last one is way too easy for people to fall for. To quote comedian Ron White, "I had the right to remain silent—but I didn't have the ability."[162] Remember . . . adrenaline, drug, altered consciousness, babbling? First off, develop the ability to keep your mouth shut under the effects of adrenaline. (You can practice this by biting your tongue when someone irritates you.) At the same time know this, a part of you will be saying, "But . . . but . . . that's a policeman. If I explain myself to him, he'll understand I'm the good guy!"

This brings us to two common ways officers provoke someone into talking so they can testify you waived your Fifth Amendment rights and willingly talked with them. As you'll see in a second that conversation can be filled with excited utterances and spontaneous exclamations of guilt. Saying you waived them is the counter when you claim they violated your Fifth Amendment rights. To tell you the truth if you fall for these tricks, you *did* waive them.

The first way is ham-handed *and* illegal. That is after you've invoked your right not to say anything at the time, the officer can ask, "What?

---

162   *Blue Collar Comedy Tour: The Movie* (2003)

Do you have something to hide?" When confronted this way—by an authority figure—part of you will want to justify yourself and explain. *Don't fall for it!* This crosses a line about continuing to question after you've requested a lawyer. Most cops won't do it. But for those who do, it *doesn't* go into the report. Nor will their saying this be on film or recorded. So if they say it, it won't be near the dash cam. Since few of them are dumb enough to let themselves be recorded saying this, it's your word against theirs. If it's brought up, it's put down as you waiving your rights and talking. Remember, they are the ones with the *pens*.

The second way to provoke you relies on the same human mechanism to justify and defend yourself when accused. Except this one doesn't cross lines of conduct nor is it coercive or entrapping. In fact, they don't even ask you a question. Instead, they start talking about the case—in front of you. It is full of comments such as, "Well, I think he (you) did . . ." and "Well, the other guys says he (you) did . . ." When you hear this, part of you will just want to jump up and set the record straight. "They're getting it all so wrong! Oh mah gawd! What if they write that in the report?" You feel you just have to correct them! You start telling them what really happened.

And in doing that, you will be waiving your Fifth Amendment rights— *even if you already invoked them!*

This is why you *need* to slow it down. You've just been through a terrible ordeal. Adrenaline is still coursing through your veins. You're still *not* at 100 percent capacity, and you'll feel an overwhelming urge to babble and correct Officer Friendly about what really happened. Remember I mentioned the good cop being neutral while bad cop acts up? You know it's a set up because that's not normal. Well, same thing here.

Cops *don't* legitimately discuss evidence with each other in front of a suspect. Sure, they'll discuss what they think. But they'll do it while *out* of your earshot. If they're talking in front of you, they're *seeking* a response. And odds are good they're also lying about what they think.

Although not cop related, there is a third way you can waive your Fifth Amendment rights and that is via jailhouse snitches. These are often guys facing serious charges. They are looking for a chance to cut a deal with the prosecutors by giving over something they heard in jail—like your admitting it was murder not self-defense. Prosecutors know these guys are about as reliable as a Jell-O hammer. But they'll use them if they don't have a solid case. Basically, the prosecutor will try and throw all he can at you in the hope something will stick, starting with contending they have someone who will testify against you . . .

*Do not—under any circumstances—*talk about your case in the cell with a friendly douche bag. Since most jails and cells these days have cameras, it's best not to be filmed in prolonged conversation with anyone else. Again, no need to be a jerk, but ending polite conversations as soon as possible is important. Yeah, you'll be lonely, scared, and stressed sitting in jail, but consider yourself *alone* until your attorney gets there. (He'll be the only one who is totally on your side.)

You need to know something right now. Dirt bags, douches, and criminals know who belongs in jail. Odds are you're going to stick out like a nun in a strip joint. They're going to come up and check you out. Staying polite, but not engaging in conversations is an additional safety issue. In this context, jailhouse snitches aren't an issue when the prosecutor watches the video and sees you never spoke to the dude for more than ten seconds. Whereas, even if you were just exchanging tofu fruit dip recipes, the snitch and the prosecutor are going to try to sell it as that being the time you confessed.[163]

Knowing about cop tactics and jailhouse snitches will help you keep from accidentally waiving your rights. Whether you waive them accidentally, intentionally, or through provocation doesn't matter. *You've waived them.*

At the same time, knowing:
a)   slow down
b)   talk to your lawyer first
c)   make a statement with your attorney present
d)   let your attorney shoot down the set-up questions
really helps you not be a sleazebag when dealing with police after a self-defense incident.

It gives you a goal to work toward and a strategy. Knowing that you are engaging in your second job (staying out of prison) will help you remain calm and do things that seem impossible—like not freaking out about sitting in a jail cell or interview room while you're waiting for your attorney to arrive. And yes, they'll sweat you by leaving you alone in a bare room until they think you're cooked and ready.

I'm going to restate something, I am a firm believer in taking some kind of use-of-force education or training and keeping a lawyer *on retainer*. Consider both a self-defense expense. Skip a chance for low light, funhouse shooting. Skip a couple of seminars with big name goo-roos. Instead attend a use-of-force class. (How do you find one? Try calling a few gun stores and clubs.) Once you've taken such a class, you'll see the wisdom of saving up a retainer and finding a lawyer who can defend you.

---

163   Want to know your best strategy for staying out of trouble in jail? Sleep. A lot. Not hard to do because exhaustion is common after the crash of an adrenaline rush.

While I recommend use-of-force training for anyone doing self-defense training, it goes *double* if you have a concealed carry permit or carry a knife, which is a lethal force instrument. A knife's use—even if you don't slash or stab someone—has the *same* restrictions and limitations as using a gun (that upside down bucket on top of two tables in the SD square). It's also a smart idea if you carry any kind of self-defense item (especially something impact-based) as such automatically increases the charges and limits the legal use (smaller table on top of the bigger table).

Now about the lawyer on retainer. Police can detain you without arresting you while waiting for a statement. Yes, you are in custody (or are being held for questioning—sometimes called investigative detention, sometimes detained) but you are not necessarily under arrest. The *investigation* is *continuing*. The length of time they can hold you without bringing charges varies.

Think of a lawyer on retainer as an investment so you don't have to spend extra time in the county jail while your family finds an attorney before you even can make a statement. A retainer gets your attorney there faster, which means you get out faster. Fork over a big retainer and you can get your legal pit bull to the jail within an hour of an incident.

At the same time, I strongly suggest you don't just pick AAA Lawyers, Inc. out of the phone book. (Yeah, yeah I'm so quaint with my old-fashioned references.) Finding a lawyer who knows how to defend someone who acted in self-defense is no small feat.[164] If you're going to be carrying a self-defense item, it's not just worth it, but you're an idiot if you *don't*. You need to have an attorney present who knows what the terms you're using mean and that you've had training in appropriate use of force. (Hell, give him this book as a Christmas, Hanukah, Kwanza, Yule, Hogmanay, or birthday present.)

This brings us to something that is highly controversial. I've run it past numerous attorneys, who—when they hear my reasoning—agree. (Granted, being lawyers they all put their own spin on it. But hey, they're lawyers . . .) I tell you it is controversial because I want *you* to run it past *your* attorney before you accept it as a strategy. In other words, it's not a sound bite, but something you and your attorney need to discuss when you put him on retainer (hint, hint, nudge, nudge).

I am a big fan of video—especially when it comes to the police questioning you. In fact I am such a big fan, I heartily recommend you go to the police station to wait for your attorney. You want your entire interview to take place in one of those interrogation rooms with *audio* and *video!*

---

164   Oddly enough, use-of-force training is a good way to find attorneys who know how.

Remember I mentioned that the officer is the one with the pen? Well three things about that. The first is something you need to consider—especially when it comes to not being a bastard about the officer doing his job and investigating—that is: *How* the officer *writes* that report has a lot to do with whether or not the prosecutor decides to pursue charges.

Believe me *not* failing the personality test is critical here. If you irritate the cop, that report will be written with a slant that—without video—you can't prove or disprove. It's his word against yours, and he has the pen. That official report is a black hole that affects gravity all around it.

Second with video if it goes to trial, the jury can see your interview. They'll see your good behavior, your cooperation. And if there is something you say that the officer interpreted as an admission of guilt, the jury can *see* it for themselves. A testifying officer carries an odor of sanctity when he says, "Then the defendant uttered a spontaneous exclamation of guilt." But when the jury can see and hear that exact statement for themselves . . . well . . . they might not interpret it the same way. Best of all is when they watch the video and say to themselves, "How in the hell did the officer get that out of what he said?"

Third, I've worked a number of cases where the defendant claimed he told the officer something that *never* made it into the report. More than that, I've read depositions of witnesses filled with information—they *swear* they told the officer—that was not in the initial reports. That information would have undermined the prosecution's case and called into question the arrest itself. This 'absence' is not unusual *after* the left hand turn has been made. (Decides versus determines.)

Remember once that left turn is made, it's about building a case for the prosecutor. Omitting certain statements and details from the report is a convenient, subtle, and legal(ish) way to help him or her with the case. Evidence that could prove to be . . . troublesome . . . is somehow not mentioned. It's *not* suppressing evidence if it is never acknowledged to have existed. While a prosecutor can get in trouble for withholding evidence, he or she cannot disclose evidence to the defense he or she *never* had.

Why is this important? Because introduction of evidence that is *not* in the report can be a bitch. If it's not in your statement, it gives the prosecutor a leg to stand on to get it disqualified later.

This also is important for the memory loss common to adrenal stress (sometimes temporary, sometimes permanent). The delay and making a statement in the interview room can help you remember—and include—important details in your statement.

Remember the case where the defendant recalled his attacker's forearm across his throat? The prosecutor fought like a wildcat to keep that information excluded from evidence. Why? Being choked explained the panic and legally allowed for a higher level of force because of the danger of death or grievous bodily injury. (His assailant was drunk and out of control.) In addition, there was something wrong with the audio of the police cruiser's dash camera, so the defendant's statements to the police on the scene weren't recorded. The only record of the defendant's statement was in the written report. His fear *not* panic was the only thing written down.

The biggest reason I vote for interrogation room video is it puts into evidence all kinds of things that can otherwise be left out of reports. There is no he said, she said debate. The officer cannot claim he was not told something germane to the defense when it is right there on the video. Better yet, it's hard for a prosecutor to exclude troublesome evidence contained in your statement.

Another reason is that it opens the door for your side to call in experts, who can confirm your version of the story as credible. Example? In the adrenaline chapter, we talked about many of the perceptual changes that come with adrenal stress. But one of the most common ones is a hyper-focus on the threat. You literally won't see an elephant standing in the area when you're *hyper-focused* on the charging tiger. That's how our brain works under adrenal stress. We target danger as important! Everything else . . . wait there are other things there?

At the same time, when we are being questioned about the event— especially by an authority figure—we often feel we should know that as an answer to an inquiry. What triggers this above all else is when faced with incredulousness that we don't know something so obvious.

"Was it an African or Indian elephant?"

"I didn't see an elephant."

"I find that hard to believe. The *huge* pachyderm was standing right there!"

Truth is, we were too damned busy with the attacking tiger to notice any elephant. But, in our rush to be believed, we often *make things up—* with *dire consequences!*

"I find that hard to believe. The monstrous elephant was standing right there! And you're trying to tell me you didn't see it?"

"Uhhhh, it was an African elephant."

"Wrong! It was an Indian elephant! What else are you lying about?"

This is going to be sold in court as your being caught in a deception and proof you lied to the police. And it won't help you if it's on video. The prosecution will probably play it in court. And with no other information, it will *look* like you're lying.

Conversely, try this version:

"Was it an African or Indian elephant?"

"I didn't see an elephant."

"I find that hard to believe. It was standing right there!"

"I was being attacked by a tiger. I was adrenalized and hyper-focused on the threat. I didn't see the elephant."

"I think you're lying."

"No, I was under adrenal stress."

Okay, that too is going to be sold as you lying. Until your attorney calls in an expert, someone who—after he or she and the jury watch the tape segment—can testify, "Yes, that's the hyper-focus common to adrenal stress. Under adrenaline—without specialized training or extensive experience—it is extremely likely someone will undergo what the layman thinks of as tunnel vision. It's not just plausible, but probable, he didn't see the elephant at all." Not noticing the elephant now makes sense to the jury. Going back to an explanation from a previous chapter, that same video the prosecutor tried to sell as a six plus three becomes six times three.

Oh yeah side note: Personal incredulity is not a question, it is a logical fallacy. (Short definition of this fallacy: An individual asserts something's not true because he or she has a hard time understanding, believing, or ever hearing of it.) Someone stating that they don't believe you is *not a question.* You don't have to answer. But we fall for this all the time, especially when the disbelief comes from an authority figure. And it is very much a trick cops and prosecutors use to put you on the defensive.

Related to that, *do not* be pressured into trying to fill in the blanks of your memory. If you don't remember, *say* you don't remember. If you didn't see something *don't* try and guess. There's a cargo ship of neurological science and legal issues that come with this simple concept. I'm not going to waste time trying to explain the whys, *just don't!*

This is another reason I am such a big fan of articulation. The more information you can get onto these tapes, the more ammunition your attorney haves to help him win his case. "What is this adrenal stress he speaks of?" "Well, let me call in an expert who can explain."

Additional benefits of having video are:

1) It helps the officer explain why he cleared the case as self-defense.
2) The prosecutor can watch it and recognize what a fight he will have in court on his or her hands
3) Because the video is discoverable evidence if you face a lawsuit, you can use it—and the same information—in the civil case.

Okay, so I'm biased pro video. But I'm not going to say being filmed is the only or correct answer every time; it can backfire on you. Talk to your

attorney and get his take. Remember, it's your butt on the line. And you
have to do everything you can to protect it.

Let's look at ways people mess up about physical force and the police. And believe me, if
you act in high level self-defense cops using force against you *can* be an issue.

Rule number one, an officer arresting you is *not* using an unlawful use of force against you.
You *do not* have the right to resist arrest. In fact, the harder you defy the officer, the more
illegal your use of force becomes at the time of arrest. In addition to any force you used during the original incident. This includes fighting being cuffed. And once again, if there was a
weapon involved, expect that to happen. Handcuffs don't automatically mean arrest. Using
them is part of officer safety, and they're kind of tetchy about it. So save your breath about
being handcuffed. Besides if you were a cop dealing with someone who'd just been involved
in violence wouldn't you want to limit ugly surprises? Being who I was, I was cuffed on
numerous occasions until the cops figured out what was going on

Rule number two, you cannot refuse a lawful order. When a police officer gives you a lawful order, you have a *duty* to comply. Not doing so is a crime in and of itself.** Your active
resistance *is* an unlawful use of physical force, even if it is just jerking your hand away when
he tries to cuff you. No matter how outraged you are about the officer touching you, you must
comply. (Again, the time to argue for your rights is in court.)

Nor does it matter how self-justified you feel about your right *not* to do what the officer told
you or your demand the officer justify the order. (This includes your right to keep on doing
what he has told you to stop—very common with drunks and excited people.) By refusing
not to obey a law enforcement officer's directive, you are disobeying a lawful order. If it goes
hands on, *you* are the one using illegal force.

So remember if it's heading toward an arrest, it's not between you and the cop. It's between
your lawyer and the court. Same thing applies to trying to stop a cop from arresting someone.
That is interfering with an officer in the execution of his duty.

** Asking someone to comply with a lawful order (e.g., being pulled over for drunken
driving and the cop asking you to step out of the car) is different than an officer requesting
permission (e.g., "Can I search your car, backpack, or person." Or, "Can I come in?"). You
don't have to consent to those kinds of requests. It's beyond the scope of this book, but generally *don't* give permission (e.g., if a situation happened outside, don't bring the interview
inside your house or don't give permission to search your car). If the cops search anyway
and find something, it's not admissible in court. In an SD situation though, he has probable
cause to search your person, which is another reason why it's advisable to limit yourself to
legal self-defense items.

CHAPTER 14

If stupidity got us into this mess why can't it get us out?
—**Will Rogers**

Giving the Monkey a Weapon

Thus far, I've avoided talking about fight or flight because most people get it wrong. Starting with, in the animal kingdom, the survival pattern *between* species is freeze, flight, resist.

See the predator and freeze, hoping it doesn't see you. If it keeps on going, the danger is past. If freezing doesn't work and danger approaches, run like hell. If caught, try to resist. But if the prey *can* break free, it's back to running again. This is pretty lizard brain behavior.

In predation (also lizard level) there is *no* fighting. When it's about food, it's a quick and effective kill—after stalking or waiting for prey to come into attack range. Zap! It's done and over with. What we think of as fighting shows up when it comes to monkey brain violence—as does our resistance to running like hell. (You'll read more about that in the social violence chapter.)

Dave Grossman in his book *On Killing* came up with a four-part model when it came to possible responses *within* the same species: Flight, fight, posture, and submit.

Let's start with the fact these four are more common when you're talking about potential violence *between* members of the same species; specifically during dominance contests. This is not just among males trying to mate, but males and females over internal social hierarchies, status, the behavior of others and when people of different 'tribes' encounter each other. That makes it a game *everybody* can do and play. (The big question is "with whom?")

Grossman and I had a conversation about his model, and he told me he wanted to redo it to fight, flight, posture, and freeze. I told him *no*. He was right with the freeze idea—but as an addition *not* as a replacement. So the new expanded model would read fight, flight, posture, submit, freeze.

These are five common monkey responses to the threat of violence. I'm going to make another change, though. I want to replace fight (which is a specific type of violence) with attack. The nature of the attack depends on the situation.

Remember that cryptic the big question is "with whom?" When humans from *different* tribes go at it to kill each other, it's called combat. Fighting doesn't even come close to describing the intensity. Reaching out and smacking someone on the back of the head to enforce the knock-it-off order is *not* a fight, either. If you want to get technical, it's a one-sided assault. Two guys slugging it out to prove whose dick is bigger? Yep, that's a fight. *Attack* pretty much covers those physical options and a whole lot more.

As an aside, a 100 percent defensive action seldom stops an attacker. There are certain exceptions, but they involve very specific circumstances. Usually a defensive action done in such a way that it is part of a much bigger threat (e.g., when a guy throws a punch, you catch it, and do nothing but glare into his eyes.[165]) Ordinarily, just blocking doesn't work to stop an attacker. I tell you this because many people may attempt to block, but then *go on* the verbal offensive. Attack or posturing? I can make a case for it being either. But to keep it simple, let's say that attack is physical. (Posturing is usually verbal mixed with threat displays.) Still blocking and posturing doesn't end the situation, they usually escalate it—especially if your attacker is a woman.

Posturing is the most common monkey brain response to the *threat* of violence. I'm talking "screaming monkey in a tree throwing feces" posturing. Put in human terms: Two macho idiots bumping chests and talking trash to each other. (But that's not the only situation.) For the record, increased posturing behavior is also common in response to a single strike.

Here's a common scenario: Two guys posturing, one steps forward strikes (attacks), then steps back, and starts posturing again. This additional posturing is to allow time for the message to get through. He's shown how serious he is; he'll hit again if the other person *doesn't* back off. Same thing from the person struck, often he'll jump back and posture. But just as often, he'll stagger back, catch himself, step back up, strike, step back, then posture some more. Look closely at this behavior. Neither party is engaging in an outright blitz attack—nor are the strikes really meant to kill, cause injury, or cripple. Ineffective strikes are often used as *part* of posturing behavior to show you're willing to do more. So they are—in a sense—reduced to a high stake threat. "You don't think I'll hit you?" *WHAM!* "Now do you believe me? I'll do it again if you don't back off!"

---

165   This often has the directly opposite effect on women—especially drunken women. It often will trigger them into a berserk rage.

Whether or not this will work the way the striker intends is a total crap shoot. A big part of why it's uncertain is odds are good the person who just got hit is deep in his or her monkey brain, too. Often people in such a mindset are more outraged over the insult than the pain of the blow.

Remember in the "What Is Self-defense" chapter, I talked about those who have been struck once then claim to have acted in self-defense? The video shows them first out of range, but then closing the distance and attacking? This is that mechanism. We posture, hoping to scare off the other monkey. This is so we *don't* have to attack—or be attacked (especially again). While you might think the last thing we want is to get into a knock-down drag-out *fight* with an equally skilled opponent, the absolute final thing we want to do is get into *combat* with an equally skilled opponent. Because it could very well be the last thing we do . . .

Lies to children, most of which you've heard before:

Lie 1: Most of what has been said about violence comes from the people who suck at it. That skews our perception about the subject mostly because we're hearing about it from the loser's perspective.

Lie 2: Half of the people involved in violence lose.

Lie 3: In the current social ideology, the loser of a fight automatically transforms into the victim, which implies 'innocence.'

Number three results in people editing the narrative to remove any participation and escalation, much less active fighting, on the part of the 'victim.' Along these lines, the first person the victim must convince is him- or herself. Hence, that person did not verbally threaten and abuse someone, nor did he punch the other person first and get his butt kicked. He was little Bo Peep attacked for no reason by the evil aggressor.

The victim perspective skews our understanding of violence dynamics. On one hand it steadfastly ignores the mutual and participatory nature of conflict and violence. On the other, through judgmental and emotional rationalizations (e.g., nobody deserves to be hit) *that same behavior by the 'victim'* is dismissed and minimized — when it can't be outright ignored. So in our quest to find the victim of this wrong, we overlook his or her participation in the fight.

In empty-hand aggression, participatory behavior cannot only escalate a situation to physical violence, but catapult your self-defense claim right out of the square—and legitimately so. Monkey posturing is *not* self-defense—it *is* fighting. These same dynamics hit warp speed when weapons are involved. Self-defense square? Planet Earth? You're not even in the same solar system. The reason I say that is because of how often the person waving the weapon around claims to be the victim . . . *and actually believes it.*

But I want to step away from the excitement and adventure of physical violence for a second. Past the sturm und drang, I want to look at this behavior as part of a bigger strategy. When we face someone, who also is in his monkey brain, threatening behavior *can be* effective. It shows who the bigger, more dominant monkey is. Threats are thrown back and forth. Pee-pees are whipped out, wagged, and measured. Someone backs down, and the situation is resolved.

We act out this behavior *all* the time—enough so that we don't even notice when we're doing it. (Tell me you haven't been involved in a conflict at work like that.) And that is *why* it can explode in your face. Sometimes autopilot is a good thing. Other times, not so much.

There are a few ways this can blow up. The first and second are the most common. They are in essence, two sides of the same coin. In my first book, *Cheap Shots, Ambushes, and Other Lessons,* I swiped the term escalato[166] from Tom Lehrer. I likened escalato to a poker game where two players are drawn into a spiral of seeing and raising their bets to get the other to fold. In the original, I pointed out that each held a pair of twos—but "damn it, I'm going to *win* this pot!" So instead of doing the smart thing and folding, they both kept on raising their bets—and each other.

Years later, I came across the term escalation of commitment,[167] functionally the same mechanism. With both, the more time, energy, and money we've poured into something, the more it *has* to work. When it doesn't—instead of pulling back—you pour more time, energy, and money into it. (It's also known as sunk cost fallacy/bias in heuristics and bias study.) If you're familiar with Miller's works, you might think, "Oh, monkey dance." Yes. No. Not exactly. Sometimes. A lie to a child: Escalato is the engine *inside* the monkey dance. The monkey dance is one specific make of car, but this same engine goes into *many* different behaviors.

When you're caught in the escalato mindset, the monkey *is* driving the bus. Remember I mentioned justifying bad behavior? It isn't that you *don't* know what you are doing. You *do know.* It's that to the monkey, it makes *perfect sense*—at that very second at least. This includes overriding the part of you that knows your behavior is wrong. To the monkey, it all looks A-OK, even as it actively breaks its own rules. (Included in this are all the alleys your human brain isn't allowed to look down while the monkey is driving.) That enraged monkey is in

---

166   Album, *What a Year That Was,* song, *Send in the Marines,* 1965: "What with President Johnson practicing escalato on the Vietnamese and then the Dominican crisis on top of that, it has been a nervous year . . . "

167   1976, Barry M. Staw, *Knee Deep in the Big Muddy: A study of escalating commitment to a chosen course of action.*

control until another part of your brain kicks back in. The speed that the monkey will break its own carved-in-granite rules shows how subjective and conditional these rules—and who we tell ourselves we really are.

I recently talked to someone who—having read all our works, being aware of the monkey, hearing about how powerful the monkey can be, and priding himself on how well he could 'control' his monkey—had a little . . . incident. He found himself screaming at a guy, slamming him up against a wall by his throat, and, by his description was "unable to stop myself." He kept telling himself to stop, but he kept going.

I told him he'd just encountered the "monkey slide." That is when you intellectually think you understand the power of the monkey, but it hijacks you anyway. The first time you experience this, it's like unexpectedly finding yourself on a slide and not knowing how to stop. You discover how strong the monkey's control over you is as you're uselessly scrabbling, scrambling, and flailing while trying to stop.

While it *can* be stopped, intellect alone isn't enough. As the person who experienced the slide found, it takes an act of will. An act more ferocious and committed than what he was doing to the other guy. Stopping a monkey slide requires more commitment *not* to do something than the part of you that really *wants* to do it. In his case, slamming the guy against the wall was easier than stopping himself. With others, it's stopping from saying or doing something that is hurtful and wrong.

People monkey slide all the time then claim they *just couldn't help themselves*. Codswallop. The majority didn't *want* to. Even if they did, their monkeys wanted what they did more. When you see it in others, it's easy to spot. But now when you find yourself sliding, you have to acknowledge you are letting the monkey drive the bus—and the consequences will be yours.

So, why all this?

When you have the ability to end another human's life, *your self-control* **must** *be more powerful than your monkey's urge to do it.*

There's a time and a place to end another human's life, but living in a rule-of-law civilized society those times are few and far between. You *need* to have self-control greater and stronger than your selfish and darkest impulses. That includes shutting down the process that will result in taking another life out of pride, fury, emotional pain, selfishness or humiliation. That unfortunately is going to put you into the minority.

By learning self-defense, you're going to encounter an unpleasant truth. Many people fear those who are capable of physical violence because they assume that person is as selfish, impulsive and out of control with violence *as* they are.

That is a very simple statement, but it carries big implications. Many people who claim to be pacifists *aren't*. They're just afraid of losing at physical violence. Notice, I didn't say they're "afraid of physical violence." People adept at verbal and emotional violence won't hesitate to go physical—*if* they think they can act without retaliation. In other words, they are just very selective about whom they will physically attack and under what circumstances. If there's a chance of getting their butts kicked, they'll stick to routinely committing safer verbal violence.

This parallels something else. For many years, I was extremely confused by a common reaction while teaching self-defense. I'd tell people an important thing I'd learned being a professional, "Be polite."

You'd think I'd told them to cut themselves and jump into a shark tank. I swear they acted as if I was not only trying to disarm them, but telling them to lie down and be a victim. "Polite? Oh, hell no!" The attitude seems to be if they don't have verbal violence, hostility, aggression, and rudeness, they'll be victimized. They get down right aggressive about their right to be verbally and emotionally violent.

Then comes the other extreme. These are the nice people—usually women who've gone through a change of lifestyle (e.g., a divorce)—who buy a gun for protection. While I generally applaud this decision, I'm somewhat nervous about their attitude. An attitude Kathy Jackson sums up as it seems to be they'd rather shoot you than be rude. I thought about it more and realized that a better explanation might be *talisman thinking.*

I'll explain that phrase in a bit, but basically it boils down to they'd rather threaten you with death so you'll run away than be rude by standing up to you. Stop and think about this. People who've never learned to stand up for themselves and hate and fear conflict and fighting *now have guns.* Nahhhh, nothing could go wrong with their use-of-force decision making.

I seriously debated whether to put this next topic here or farther along in the chapter. Both placements have good arguments. Putting it here, the following subjects we cover will make a *lot* more sense. Putting it after could save your life. While making sense finally won out, the strong arguments for the second placement need to be remembered.

That's because, while what I'm about to tell you is wildly common with weapons display, do not *under any circumstances* think it's the only way weapon displays will occur.

Even saying there's a 50/50 chance "this is what you'll be dealing with" isn't right. Depending on the circumstances, it could be 80/20 of what you're facing (80 being behind the behavior we'll be talking about next) or it's 100 percent *something* else. Treating that 'something else' like it's what I'm about to tell you **will** get you killed. It gets even more wobbly when *you're* the one doing it. The topic is both a unique problem in and of itself and something incredibly intertwined with monkeys with weapons. That is: Talisman thinking.

Talisman thinking is wonderfully demonstrated in the original *Fright Night* movie (1985). A late night horror show host (who specializes in running vampire movies) holds up a crucifix to the vampire and—in a voice straight out of a Hammer film[168]—says, "Back you spawn of Satan!" The vampire calmly looks at him, reaches out, takes the cross out of Roddy McDowell's hand, and crushes it. His comment, "You have to have faith for this to work on me." Welcome to talisman thinking: The belief that the item is what does the work. It's having the item (or form) but *lacking* what makes it work. These are the people who have a weapon for self protection and who believe that simply waving it around will make the other person back off.

It's a weird twist on the paradoxical the *willingness to commit violence usually means you won't have to*. In one way, the danger of the weapon is *very* real, but in another it's not. They don't really intend to use it to kill anybody, but they very much want to use the prospect of danger to get a monkey reaction—mostly for the other monkey to back off or leave. Causing damage is neither the goal nor the intent. The weapon is a prop to achieve the real goal of threatening the other monkey enough so it will leave. So they wave it around like a cross, trying to scare off the vampire.

I'd like to say things get brainless when the threat of violence doesn't work, but the truth is it's been stupid—and illegal—from the beginning. With that in mind, let's look at the danger of weapons. Often they aren't used to level the playing field, they're brought in to stack the deck for monkey and predatory violence.

But let's stick with monkey violence a while longer, because that's where most mistakes happen. The reason I called escalato two sides of the same coin is because it manifests differently depending on which side of the weapon you're on. But both are uniformly stupid.

The first is from this side of the weapon. The monkey thinks pulling a weapon is the final bump to make the other side fold. *Monkey thought process:* Displaying that weapon will cause the other monkey to back off and go away, leaving it with the pot, giving it the win.

And in truth, showing that weapon *might* work. The other person could snap out of the monkey and run like hell—unless he or she doesn't.

That brings us to the *other* side of the weapon (also a person caught in the escalato mindset). Often in an emotional pique, the monkey sees that weapon not as a *danger*, but as another *step* in the bluffing process. Another see and raise—a challenge that cannot go unanswered. So instead of folding, you get another raise in the stakes. His, her, or your "Screw me? No! Screw you!" reaction results in a trigger pull.

---

168 Hammer Films is a British studio most known for its cheesy horror films from the '50s through '70s. Christopher Lee played Dracula . . . a lot.

Get your spray paint out—time for more graffiti on your wall. Animal's important safety tip: *The presence of a weapon is a game changer.* As in it isn't a game anymore.

Before you say, "No shit, Sherlock," and put this book down forever because I'm insulting your intelligence—know this: More than the danger of a weapon, the monkey sees another monkey trying to *win* the escalato process. Winning is the monkey's focus, **not** the physical danger. The monkey doesn't see the weapon as a danger, it *sees* a bluff—especially when it's another freaked-out monkey holding the weapon. Gee, a couple of freaked-out monkeys in the same room as a weapon. Once again, nahhhhhh, nothing possibly could go wrong with that.

Human thinks in terms of solutions. Lizard thinks in terms of survival. It's only the monkey that has the emphasis on winning. Your monkey is so focused on winning, you won't *know* you were caught in escalato until you're bleeding on the floor or standing there shocked that you pulled the trigger. (And believe me I have seen the look on people's faces of 'oh mah gawd, what did I do?')

There is a reason for all the italics in the last few paragraphs. This monkey behavior will get you killed or thrown into prison! I have *seen* people in escalato mindsets die and kill. I have scrubbed them out of the carpet. I have carried coffins, and I've helped people's families when loved ones were in prison. *That's* how powerful this monkey slide into escalato is. Do *not* under any circumstances tell yourself you're immune to it—especially if there's a weapon involved.

I tell you about this perspective for another reason. When you take cold-blooded murder off the table, *this* is the alternative explanation for so much violence. More than that, *this* is what all the antiviolence, gun control, prosecutor, and swayed jury members are saying and thinking happened. Their attitude is anyone who picks up a weapon *must be* an OOK. An out-of-control monkey with a weapon who *must* be punished for what he or she did. That's the story they *want* to believe. That's what they're telling themselves about you and your weapon. And most of all, that's how they're going to look at your case.

Lethal force options *change* how we approach conflict (especially when both sides can shoot back). This is a level of hell your sensei, firearms instructor, or self-defense goo-roo probably *isn't* teaching. That's because most of them haven't been there. They can't teach it because they don't *know* how important it is. That is seriously bad news because weapons are where *most* citizens fail.

Understanding escalato is critical for several reasons:
- So you can keep your monkey on a leash.
- An overwhelming number of situations escalate to physical

violence because *both* parties are in their monkey brains.
- While a small number of people will never come out of their rampage no matter what, *if* you change the dynamics of the situation by getting out of your monkey, there is a high probability physical violence can be avoided.
- Monkeys aggressively scream and threaten while trying to intimidate each other; this knocks the claim of self-defense off the table.
- Normal monkey violence is overwhelmingly non-injurious and ineffective.
- The pattern goes sideways when a weapon is introduced to the same equation.
- Way too often people aren't trying to kill someone with a weapon; they're just giving them an educational beat-down.

That last one is going to require an explanation. One type of social violence is what Miller calls the "educational beat-down" (EBD). In the most simplistic way, think of it as punishment. But most people's idea of punishment is exclusively past tense. In practice, EBDs are more on-the-spot behavioral correcting violence. They send the message, "That behavior results in pain. Stop doing it (or don't do it again)." In this regard, it's more about stopping unacceptable behavior now and preventing it in the future than it is about actual punishment.[169]

This kind of rule enforcement is very monkey, tribal, and survival based. It comes to us from a time when violating the rules *would* kill everyone in the tribe. Our understanding of the need for EBDs has been lost in the safety of our modern world.[170] But the pattern still exists in our monkey wiring and factory settings. It's a *very* strong monkey urge to want to reach out and smack someone for unacceptable behavior. The fact is it's now more a matter of style (how you do it) than that we don't use EBDs. (Hint, you can look at getting chewed out by your boss for a mistake as an EBD.) But we pretend we don't use them anymore.

The problem with this zero tolerance approach to violence *isn't* that it has failed to stop this behavior. It's going to happen no matter what laws or policies say. Not allowing conflict and physical enforcement of rules to be socially acceptable has raised a generation that doesn't know *when*

---

169   I know a horse trainer who referred to it as "making the horse uncomfortable with unacceptable behavior."
170   Hint, kosher and halah fool rules were great to keep everyone from dying of food poisoning in the desert without modern food preservation, refrigeration, and sanitation techniques and served on wooden plates. In our modern technological society, we don't personally have to deal with these issues. This has seriously affected our views of social violence and rule enforcement.

to stop or how to lose. Putting in other terms: They don't understand the rules of fighting.

Here's a short list of what youths don't know these days:

- You don't pull a weapon on one of your own over a minor beef.
- It's time to stop once you've won (you don't have to hospitalize him).
- If you fight and lose, you take your beating like a man. You don't back up and shoot a man who stopped before hospitalizing you.
- Winning isn't everything, and losing isn't the end of the world.
- After a fight, you make up.

Now this might sound like some old guy pining for the nonexistent good old days of bad street warriors. It's not. Those good old days sucked, and even then we had people who broke the rules. That's *not* the point. The point is, you currently have an entire generation of people who are terrified to lose—including a lot of people in self-defense training.

The significance is how often these folks will pull a weapon over something that thirty years ago would have been settled by punching. Instead of a fight that settles issues, now you have beating someone to the ground and stomping them into the hospital. Also how many of these people will try to throw you a beating with a weapon in their hand.

While an EBD from someone who understands 'social violence rules' is not particularly dangerous, it becomes so when there is a weapon in the monkey's hand. A good number of the knife cases I have seen were *not* the knifer trying to kill the other person, but instead *beating* him while holding a knife. Such violence has a very distinctive pattern, intent, and manifestation. These beatings were *not* how you kill someone with a knife (that, too, is distinctive). Yet, they were prosecuted as attempted murders or assaults with deadly weapons. That's because the use of a lethal force instrument (knife or gun) automatically bumped the charges to that level.

Let's put that on hold for now and look at another kind of monkey stupid. It's not only a pain, but also a forecast of stupid when someone looks at you and your weapon and says, "You ain't got the guts." That's a pure monkey challenge. By the end of this book, you'll know what it takes to communicate to him that he's *not* dealing with another enraged monkey. As such, guts are not a factor when it comes to you acting. What's going to determine if he gets shot or not is *what he does*. That's an important tactic for getting him out of his monkey brain.

While we're talking about cloudy and a 70 percent chance of stupid, let's add people who say, "Well, he might take the weapon away from you and use it against you." (Pregnant pause while I reach for a bottle of scotch to calm down.) Okay. That is possibly true. There *is* a chance of being disarmed—*when* you're a freaked-out monkey, trying to bluff the other monkey by waving a weapon. Conversely, trying to close and take a weapon away from the lizard is a great way for an attacker to attain that split second sensation of having his brains blown through the back of his head. Getting shot also is likely if he escalates and scares that monkey with a gun.

So the whole get-your-gun-taken-away rationalization has 3:1 odds of *his* being shot. Now let's talk about *you* facing a weapon. Because, baby cakes, you have those same 3:1 odds against you, which kinda torpedoes most martial arts weapon disarm techniques.

When I say, "A weapon is a game changer," it is to *prep* both your lizard and human brains to throw kidney and throat punches on your monkey. This especially about pulling a weapon in escalato or talisman thinking. Simultaneously, but from the other side of the weapon, we're not talking a "shut up, monkey," we're talking knocking it out in order to save your life—starting with you *not* trying to kung fu the weapon out of the other guy's hand.

In case you haven't figured it out, I have major problems with most of what is taught about facing weapons, but those are beyond the scope of this book. That's a physical book I have to write, but some key points are necessary . . .

Fundamentally, most of what is wrong with what is *taught* about facing weapons in commercial martial art, MMA, and combatives schools is that it's monkey driven. It's not about surviving, it's about *winning*. Mostly these techniques consist of attempting to control the weapon, whereupon you throw him an educational beat down for daring to pull a weapon on you.

There are problems with neutralizing his weapon with your hands. Listing a few:

1) It's still there; still a factor.
2) You're in range of it
3) Beating someone into incapacitation takes time.
4) You've lost the use of one hand when holding his weapon hand.
5) It's easy to lose control of his weapon hand while you're ineffectively trying to beat the hell out of him.
6) If he wasn't intent on hurting you before, he is now.

With any empty handed technique for facing a weapon, check for those 'little problems.' If that doesn't scare you, then count the number of times certain techniques—that originally knocked the weapon off line—draw the weapon back across your body. Short of sucking a shotgun to suicide, I know of no better way to get killed than using what is taught in most martial arts as bare-hand defense against a weapon.

That was background to get you to the next point: You do not fight a person with a weapon—*ever*.

Fighting is monkey brain violence. It has loads and loads of unconscious assumptions, baggage, and limitations that come with it—assumptions and behavior that will get you killed facing a weapon. I once yelled at a room full of cops I was training in knife survival because they were attempting control tactics and trying arrest the attackers—that's how deeply ingrained trying to follow social violence can be. If professionals default to it, don't think you're immune.

Conversely, an equally fatal mistake is to ignore defensive action at close quarters and only focus on offense. I call this trading damage. The results of which are, "HA! You only stabbed me three times. I shot you four. I win!"[171]

But if you *have* to engage with weapons, you are not in a fight, you *are in combat*. That individual has to be incapable of offering you a threat inside of three seconds. Whether lying on the floor unconscious, broken, or dying doesn't matter. Fighting takes too long. The longer you're facing a weapon, the more danger you're in. That's why you don't try to fight a person with a weapon . . . you have to end the immediate threat *now*! Unlike combat, though, you have another option to end the threat—run fiercely.

When you find yourself facing a weapon ask yourself—literally the most important question of your life: Do you *have* to engage?

Tattoo and spray paint that one.

Here's a free hint, if you have time to ask about having to engage, usually the answer is *no*. While many martial artists pay lip service to this idea, they always come up with grandiose and exaggerated scenarios where they are trapped and have to fight.

Remember, the lizard has no problem running. The human's okay with it, too. The monkey on the other hand has major problems with it—including all kinds of reasons as to exactly why you *can't* run. Like, "If I run, he might shoot me in the back anyway." So the monkey figures it's better to stand there, mouth off, threaten, and insult. It's going to show this other monkey where . . . it . . . is . . . at.

Wow, great plan—except your body gets perforated instead.

Another common mistake is thinking you can verbally chase off the monkey holding a weapon. But saying something like that to a person with a weapon? Not such a good idea. (Knowing this, Nicole Du Fresne's last words make a lot of sense.)

---

171   I also do a *Writing Violence* series for authors. These thirty to forty page booklets explain issues like 'Getting Shot' (Volume 1) and 'Getting Stabbed' (Volume 2).

But until you know about the monkey's need to win, this behavior makes absolutely *no* sense. Who'd be stupid enough to do that when facing a weapon? Well . . . lots of people. When you understand the monkey, you know how easy it is to get caught in a monkey slide. Also what a disaster it can be if you do.

All it takes for things to go horribly bad is a *wrong* monkey signal—especially in response to a threat. Believe me when someone is waving a weapon, the correct response is ***never*** "screw you." Here's a free safety tip: A monkey's holding a weapon on you? The situation is *already* far down the road of violence. Making the simian holding that weapon flip out even more doesn't tend to end well.

What's really hard to stomach is how this can come as a surprise—to both parties. And I wish to god I was lying.

Here is where I seriously considered putting the part about talisman thinking. What I'm about to say is where it really comes out. That is threat displays with weapons. Also known as brandishing, menacing, or whatever they call this crime in your state. When weapons are displayed, overwhelmingly, they are flashed in this illegal—usually a felony—manner.

This in contrast to when you draw a weapon to use it for self-defense, and he changes his mind about misbehaving, which is a legitimate and legally justified reason for drawing a weapon.

But know, the bias toward brandishing is what you're up against if you pull a weapon. Later if you have to explain yourself to the police, they'll be looking to hang a menacing charge on you. So in case you've been wondering what I'm doing wasting your time with all this noise about escalato, the answer is helping you *not* get a felony brandishing or menacing charge hung on you.

You have to know what brandishing *is* and what *not* to do so you can explain to the police why—what you did—*wasn't* a crime. That it was a legitimate weapon deployment in response to an immediate threat. A deployment that, upon seeing your commitment, the other person stopped offering you an immediate threat. Recognizing that, you, too, scaled it back (hopefully by withdrawing from the situation).

Despite what you may have seen in the movies, in real life a weapon in the hands of a freaked-out monkey usually ends badly for the simian. Whether it's in the form of a shooting, stabbing, bludgeoning, and an arrest for those or it's an arrest for brandishing or menacing. The latter tends to happen because another way an escalato-playing monkey can win is to run and tell the cops about you pulling and threatening him with a weapon. He doesn't win by beating you, he wins by getting you arrested.

Remember I said the race to phone can be speeding toward getting yourself arrested? Also remember I mentioned the reversal of roles in affirmative defense cases? Same thing. The cops need to arrest *him* for committing the crime of endangering you with death or grave bodily injury, a threat that was so immediate you drawing a weapon *was* a reasonable response.

Now what does that tell you about not drawing your weapon if what you're facing is penny ante? Low JAM? That weapon stays where it is, and your hand stays *off* of it.

Now I want to turn your attention to what you do when you're facing a weapon. Not in a kung-fu blaze or Mogadoishu-esque shoot-out way, instead in knowing what to do and assess if you have to move or not.

The bar none-biggest issue when it comes to assessing the danger of a weapon is range. Are you in range for that weapon? Is the person trying to create that range? That is foundational for everything else I am about to say here.

In teaching, I often tell people that before you can recognize the abnormal, you have to know what normal looks like. Your definition of normal may not include someone waving a weapon around, but let me assure you that for some of us it's not uncommon.

Remember the most important question of your life? *Do I have to engage?* Everything up to this has been the ground work.

Generally if you're seeing a weapon, it's a threat display. Granted a threat display on steroids, but there's a difference between seeing a weapon and someone trying to use it on you. That gives you time to consider your options.

Again the majority of the time—if he or she is communicating—you're probably being told how to avoid having it used on you. Unless it meets certain criteria I'll tell you later, I strongly advise you to take this advice.

The two most common social violence messages attached to weapon brandishings are:

1) Go away.

2) Change your behavior.

The most common asocial message is "gimme something." Socially the most common is "Stop what you're doing."

If you're getting something other than go, gimme and stop, the fecal matter is a lot deeper. This goes double if the person *isn't* talking anymore, but is coming at you, which is an articulable fact. An old Roman saying: "A barking dog isn't biting." I've told you that sudden silence is a pre-attack indicator. Well, nothing good ever comes from someone silently charging you while holding a weapon.

The good thing about someone who is still talking is *if* you take their advice, odds are good you won't end up dead or doing paperwork (much less prison time). Having said that, the odds for or against things working are strongly influenced by you and your actions. Once again it boils down to how well you can keep a leash on your monkey.

- *Communicate that you're leaving.*
- *Hunker over, reducing your size (it doesn't have to be much, but your body language has to be consistent with the message you're leaving).*
- *Don't look at either his eyes or the weapon, focus on his chest and indications of any movement*
- *Back away slowly, don't turn and run (once distance is established, then turn).*
- *Keep an open hand out, extended barrier, but keep it low.[172]*
- *Do NOT put in a monkey dig (parting shot).*
- *Do NOT react to a monkey dig while leaving.*
- *Do NOT make any fast movements*
- *If your hand is on a weapon or your weapon is out, **freeze** that part of your body—don't do anything that could be interpreted as a draw or deployment.*

Not all circumstances are going to be like this. Sometimes the withdrawal you have to negotiate is the other guy's. Unless you're a cop and have a duty to arrest, remember these additional points.

- Communicate to the guy that it is physically safe for him to leave.
- Communicate that you'll give him a head start on the cops (if you're going to call them at all).
- If necessary, step out of the way so he can leave (don't block the exit).
- Do NOT react to a monkey dig when you're holding the weapon.
- Do NOT throw a monkey dig when you're holding the weapon.

Something that most self-defense goo-roos don't tell you is the etiquette for when someone comes at you and discovers you're just as dangerous as he is. So you end up with two armed people standing there, looking at each other, and wondering how to get out of this mess. Awkward!

It says something about my previous lifestyle that I've ended up in several such uncomfortable situations. And you know what? Emily Post doesn't cover the etiquette for them. But in the middle of it all, I noticed there were three re-occurring concerns these people had:

---

172   Physical barriers are an important element. But unlike a lot of self-defense instructors, I tell people to keep you their hands low as though they were trying to guard against getting kicked in the groin. There's a good chance if you keep your hands high it can be interpreted as being up in his face. Low guard is less likely to provoke this monkey response.

1) They couldn't withdraw safely.

2) I was going to call the cops on them.

3) I'd come back and kill them later.

Now number three never really made much sense to me. After all, I could kill them right then and there, but there it was. They can be concerned about revenge, so be prepared to address it if it comes up. The first two, however, universally had to be specifically communicated. They'd gotten themselves into a mess and needed some guidance about how to get out of it. I had to provide that guidance.

In dealing with these guys, you'll find yourself making some odd concessions. One guy —who'd attempted to put a hatchet in my head— tried to talk me out of calling the cops. This was a sticking point in our negotiations. He was afraid that if he tried to leave, I'd call the cops. I told him of course I was going to call the cops, he'd broken into my house, but I'd give him that five-minute lead. He needed to be gone before they showed up. Also if he left the property by going over that particular wall, I couldn't see which way he went, so I couldn't tell the cops. He took me up on my offer. Since I'd gotten everything back from him (except the ax) I waited five minutes before I called them. The real win was I didn't have to scrub blood out of the carpet.

Here are a couple of other little details that can prove useful. But they are more advanced tweaks and not always possible.

- *Don't take your eyes off him until he's way out of attack range. You don't have to mad dawg him as he's leaving, but calmly watch.*
- *I learned the hard way when someone turns his back on you, move laterally from the position you were in when he last saw you (in case he whips around).*
- *If you must follow the person to the door (to make sure he leaves the property instead of getting a weapon from the car and coming back) give him a good head start for the door.*
- *If possible, leave the area immediately -- if necessary by another door.*
- *Like many self-defense issues this one is situational and highly debated by 'experts,' but I contend as the guy must trust that I will use the weapon if he attacks, he must trust I* **won't** *if he doesn't. I have found a good way to reward someone for their decision to retreat is gradually lower my weapon as they increase the distance. If he changes his mind, my weapon will come back up. If the incident is videoed it supports your contention you weren't needlessly threatening him or brandishing.*

Don't be a freaked-out monkey about pulling a weapon on someone. And that includes thinking that if you pull a weapon someone has to

This is specifically for anyone who carries a knife—but it won't hurt for folks with guns or any other self-defense item to stop and think about, too. First and foremost, a knife is a tool. The difference between a tool and a weapon is design. A dagger is a weapon. It has certain design elements that render it useless for any *other* purpose. (The double edge doesn't allow for thumb placement on the blade for leverage.) It also has other design features that improve its use as a weapon (e.g., double edge allows you to cut your way out in either direction). As such, a dagger's primary purpose is to be used on another human. I tell you this because if you are carrying a designed weapon, the sole use aspect can—and will—used against you in court.

So what does that say about answering the question, "Why do you carry a knife?" with "For self-defense." The same goes for any other defense item. "Oh, so you carry that around to stab (or beat or shoot) someone, eh?" They'll try to sell it as you carrying a weapon with premeditation.

A tool is something that can be used as a weapon, but that is not its primary design or sole intent. Furthermore, the design of the tool limits it's effectiveness as a weapon. A tool is what you *need* to carry. What you have in your pocket is a tool *not* a weapon.

I tell you that so you can understand my next statement. Avoid *anything* with the word tactical in the title, description, or marketing. While we're at it: Cool matt black, wicked lines, sweeps, and designed by famous knife-fighting goo-roo? Drop it faster than an annoyed scorpion. Because these sales and marketing tricks can—and will—bite you in the ass if you ever have to use that item on another human being. (This also applies to custom ammo and hot reloads.)

Remember, a knife is a lethal force instrument. *Any* use of one on another human must meet the legal (and very narrow) criteria for lethal force. The cops and prosecutors are going to be going over every detail to find some way to sell the idea to the jury that you weren't acting in self-defense, starting with the assertion that you were carrying a weapon.

die. You're not some mythical samurai with a sword that requires blood every time it is pulled.[173] As I tell people, "I am negotiating until I pull the trigger." And anything short of lethal, I pick up negotiating again after it has gone physical—just for slightly different terms.

I cannot stress enough that monkey behavior and weapons are a *bad* combo. Weapons are like power tools, mistakes from doing something stupid happen faster, are worse, and are always wet and messy.

If you in any way, shape, or form believe you are immune from falling into this behavior, I have some bad news, Punkin. That's the biggest sign you're *vulnerable*. That's your monkey whispering in your ear and saying, "I'm too smart for that to happen." After a lifetime of letting the monkey guide our behavior through social situations, we're really good at fooling ourselves about how in control of it we are. The last place you want to have a monkey slide is when you're holding a weapon.

If you don't practice awareness and control of your monkey in the day-to-day, you're going to have a snowball's chance in hell of keeping it collared and leashed when weapons are involved.

---

173   Yes, that is a myth you hear among "the katana were the greatest swords ever made, and samurais were the greatest warriors ever" crowd.

CHAPTER 15

Everyone knows what something means until there's a problem.

—Paul Spiegel,
Contract Attorney

Social Violence

In his book *Meditations on Violence*, Miller first introduced his social and asocial violence models. I took one look at it and tossed my method of categorizing violence. Miller's version is simpler, faster, and easier to explain. I also culled out a number of models from academics, psychologists, criminologists, and other so-called experts about the causes of violence. Not only do I feel Miller's model is more useful, but you don't need a Ph.D to understand it. (Kind of like the human, monkey, and lizard). Unlike a lot of the crap out there about violence, the social and asocial models don't require you to embrace ideologies or dogmas before they make sense.

Are these models perfect? No. Are there gray areas? Yes. Is there room for debate about taxonomy and definition? You betcha. (I'm going to do some here.) Where social and asocial shine—by far the best and brightest—is in *field application*. Out in the bush: If it looks like a duck, walks like a duck . . .

Most of all, the social and asocial models don't require you be a mind reader. You can look at behavior, and tell—with good on-the-spot accuracy—what you're dealing with by the behavior. As such, they're valuable tools for identifying the degree of danger you're in at the moment. Miller calls this the models' predictive qualities. I'll explain my interpretation in a bit. Either way, once you know these models, you can damned near set your watch by the different patterns and scripts.

But looking at it from both a training and expert witness perspective, I find additional values in using it. The two main ones are:

1) Helping you shift mental gears to what works (and is appropriate) for the situation.

2) Like a Google map, they tell you where you are

A little explanation about number two. First, imagine being a stranger in the city. This model is a map of different neighborhoods. But not just neighborhoods, it's a map with helpful hints like: Safe; okay to be there during day, but leave by 5p.m.; don't go there alone; and oh hell no!

The first value of such a map is it tells you where you don't want to go. The second, if you find yourself there, it keeps you from going the wrong way. Some neighborhoods, you need to leave quickly. But don't run from danger—instead head to safety. To do this, you need to know which way to go to get back into a safe neighborhood. Such a map tells you going that other way will put you in an even worse part of town. Third, this map is good for articulation purposes. It's like being able to say, "I found myself in (insert worst part of town)." Those who know that part of town understand what you did because they'd have done the same. As for the rest, it can be explained. They may never have been there, but they've heard of that neighborhood.

While I don't particularly agree with the idea of the social and asocial model being predictive, it's great for threat analysis. I look at situations in terms of probabilities and possibilities. The type of situation you are dealing with will dictate the three most probable courses of action someone will take. At the same time, what are two possible, but not probable directions? That's to say, they happen enough not to be uncommon, but they aren't feasible for specific situations. I won't know which way someone is going to jump until he does. But when he chooses one of these, I know what's coming. This model is the best way I know to assess the probable and possible actions you'll face and options you have.

Furthermore, with a little practice you learn how much your actions influence the other person's decisions. If it is social, if you do (A) it de-escalates such situations. Not only does that reduce the chances of violence occurring, but it helps with articulation. "I did (A), which if it had been a normal social situation should have caused (B). But instead he reacted by doing (C)."

And by the way, "I knew it wasn't social. I expected (C, D or F) all along. I didn't expect (A) to work. I was doing it both as reconfirmation and for articulation purposes."

While I will give you the basics of the social and asocial models, I highly recommend you go read Miller's works on the subject. There are a lot of details I'm not going to cover here because you should get them from the horse's mouth. Because of the way I look at these models, I'm going to cover a lot of stuff Miller doesn't. And I will tell you where Miller and I disagree on categorization. So, having said all that . . .

Violence can be broken down into two main categories: Social and asocial.

Let's start with social. But we're going to build that house from the ground up. A major factor in social violence is that humans are social primates. We are designed to function in groups. Our individual survival depends on the group (or society, if you will). For millions of years, an individual with no group was dead from starvation, exposure, accident, or predation from either animals or other groups. Got it? Alone equals dead.[174] So from an individual perspective—yay belonging to a group! In a group equals I'm alive.

Knowing this, let's step away from the individual and look at what a group needs to survive. In order for groups to function (especially over the long term) certain issues *must* be addressed. Numbered among a larger list are things like hierarchy, division of resources and labor, roles, standards of behavior, ways of doing things (customs) and maintaining tribal identity (what distinguishes us from them). Most conflicts (and by extension violence) are over these—social—issues.

But before we go there, it's important to look at when these group dynamics work for the individuals because that's *most* of the time. Again availability bias, we vividly remember the times when it didn't work, but overlook all the times when it did. Things work and people get along; basically they accept the group's and society's standards and go about getting through the day with as little fuss as possible, especially as they get older and have more responsibilities. More than that, these systems and standards dictate huge chunks of how we go about our behavior. To the point of it's arguable that we're wired—as individuals—to try to win and to strive to achieve stable status *within* group dynamics. With that in mind, a lot of seemingly selfish behavior actually perpetuates and stabilizes the group. That's if it doesn't outright benefit the group.[175] It is within this bigger group context that an individual moves around. And that includes conflict. Because the most common sources of conflict are when someone tries to dictate those dynamics, overreaches, breaks the rules, or messes with the status quo and someone else enforces them. Most of all, social conflict and violence occur among members *within* a group; it's us fighting among ourselves over how things are going to be.

That argument you and your spouse had over the toilet seat being left up? That's an argument over both how things are going to be done in your home *and* how you want to be treated in this relationship. These are social goals. The police officer taking down, controlling, and arresting an aggressive drunk and stopping unacceptable behavior? A social goal. Two young bucks in a dick-measuring contest that escalates into a punch out? Social goal. Spanking a child to deter future unacceptable behavior? Social goal. Locking up someone for committing a crime? Same thing,

---

174   This still applies today. The irony of this is how many people proudly declare they don't need others. These examples of chest thumping, mighty aloneness come from the comfort and safety of national unity, urban environments, cultural achievements, and social support networks regarding food, medicine, technology, rule of law, and emergency support services. Such people are paragons of self-reliance and achievement—except for the millions of people their lifestyles depend on.

175   You may see it as a fight over the leadership of the group. But winning the role of leader comes with the booby prizes of responsibility and lots of work to keep the group going.

social goal. A vendetta killing? Social goal. *All* of these are about how things are, the status quo, how things are done around here, how you are treated, and how others treat you.

As an aside, there's a subject important for you to look into, but way too big to go into here. That is how much of our behavior and presentation (how we dress, carry ourselves, and other social niceties) is to broadcast the message about who we are, our status, and how you better treat us. Once again, I'm going to send you Desmond Morris's book *Manwatching*,[176] this time to the clothing and status display chapters. By the way they act and dress, tough guys are actually presenting a "don't mess with me" message more than "I'm a predator hunting you" one. The former is a much more important social message in places where both challenging and predatory behavior are common.[177] In their local environment, people know this and basically everyone leaves everyone alone as they go about their business (e.g., nice people up front, bad boys to the back of the bus).

Trouble often happens in one of three ways, two of which are when these tough guys come out of their area. First is when the younger toughs, who often want to 'represent,' make a production to show everyone in a different environment who they are. If you see this behavior, my advice is let them pass through without responding. If they try to set up a situation, leave the area. Treat them like a monsoon, intense but just passing through. Go have a cup of coffee while you're waiting for them to pass.

The second way trouble occurs can almost be called an "it all started when he hit me back" situation—except it's the citizen who's claiming it. For the record, I, as an ex-street thug, routinely encountered this as I was in the process of changing social levels. As often as not, when a thug goes somewhere different someone gets so distraught with the tough guy's presence in *his* territory, he has to make a production about it, instead of just shrugging and going about his business. (There's often a very subtle but powerful "you don't belong here" attitude—even among those who don't act.) I tell you this because this is deemed as "messin' with me" by the tough guy. Serious bit of advice here if you find yourself in proximity to a tough guy in the second scenario, treat him like you would any other person of your social class. Basically, ignore him and go about your business while he goes about his. If you have to interact with him be polite with nothing to prove.

---

176   As it was written in 1979, *Manwatching* has gone in and out of print several times. Price is like the stock exchange, sometimes it's way up, sometimes way down. I've seen it range from $9 to $79 (collector's edition). Since I recommend it as easy bathroom reading get a cheaper used one.

177   Interestingly enough when they engage in actual predatory behavior, gang members usually strip off tribal identifiers because 'colors' make it easier to identify them, and they face higher penalties for crimes done while 'representing.'

The three most common mistakes citizens make dealing with tough guys are in order:

1) They treat them with contempt (*especially* women).
2) They try to drive them from their territory (you don't belong here).
3) They puff up. ("See how tough I am? I'm not scared of you! I'm tough, too!")

Fast note on point two: When I talk about territory, I am not talking about your property. Nor am I talking about your business. As a hard core biker and bad ass, I was treated better by staff in upscale businesses than I was by customers. This is not a matter of race (as is so often ascribed) but social class and territoriality. How dare I come into where *they* eat or shop and inflict my presence on them. If you find yourself in close to a tough guy in what you consider your territory *don't* engage in this behavior. He's not going to rob you in a store, but if you're a jerk he will punch you out there.

The third way people get in trouble with the "don't mess with me" signals is a double whammy. That is they go into the tough guy's territory and start showing how tough they are to the locals. This tends to end badly. It's viewed as an outsider, who doesn't know how to behave, getting up in someone's face. As an outsider, the normal rules and limits of internal social violence *don't* apply.

Other situations where these limits don't apply are when social violence occurs within the group, but it also can be about protecting the group from others (e.g., another group or individuals who threaten your group). Or it can involve a group activity, a rite of passage, and sign of affiliation to the group. (These are the breakdowns and subcategories Miller goes into. He has a good list.)

A source of social violence that is actually numerically small—but really sticks out in our minds—is the idiot trying to establish dominance *outside* his group. This is the clown we think of when we imagine some guy coming into a place and trying to push people around to show how big and bad he is. As an aside, we should not confuse that behavior with a public confrontation. That is to say, someone who is offended by actual misconduct (whether intentional or accidental) directed at him by the person he is dealing with. While it's easy to blame the confrontational person as overreacting or trying to prove something, more than we'd like to admit there *has* been some kind of misconduct on the part of the person being challenged.

Large sections of this book are about behavior that led to—and reasons for—social violence. Social conflict—and yes, violence—are so ingrained, we don't notice what we're really doing even when we are in the middle of carrying it out. We're so wrapped up in our emotions about the situation we *fail* to see the details. Particulars that can—and often do—cause the situation to escalate to physical violence.

Point one: The majority of violence that occurs between humans is social.

Point two: Violence between strangers is rare. Generally, it's between people who know each other. The most common form of violence between strangers is over territorial transgressions. (Managing these two greatly reduces your risk of being involved in a physically violent situation.)

Point three: Generally, social violence is *not* intended to be lethal. Nor is it intended to be injurious. Usually it's about inflicting pain. (You don't want to kill or injure your own tribe members because it weakens the group.)

Point four: Although it has served our species for millions of years in our *modern world,* social violence is hideously misunderstood.

Before we move on to five, let's look at this. Aside from being preached at about how bad, hurtful, and evil violence is (i.e., anything beyond our personal low mile marker is evil, traumatizing, and abusive) we've forgotten the rules about it. Worse, we've forgotten that there even are rules. For example, if your friend and someone else start to fight when do you and his friend step in to pull them apart? Not too early, not too late. But you do pull your friend out, especially when he starts losing. Due to this massive modern push against violence, we've lost the ability to distinguish between punishment and abuse, abuse and necessary violence. To the barking moonbats, they are *all* abuse, evil, and wrong. With that attitude floating around, how can anybody learn what are appropriate and necessary levels of force? And if you don't know it, how can you do it?

Point five: Social violence is usually very emotional and monkey brain driven. Since we are designed to emotionally infect each other, it takes practice and experience to be able to see the details.

Again, an expansion before moving on: Seeing the details is often made harder because freaking out about social violence also is contagious.[178] Unfortunately, a lot of those excited monkeys will be screaming for

---

178   I've mentioned witness grooming a few times. This is making sure the witnesses see and hear you make a good faith effort to keep the situation from going bad. It sounds Machiavellian until you realize the buzzed, stupid dude (or dudette) standing and making a running commentary is grooming witnesses, too. He or she is influencing what the witnesses think they're seeing, usually in an excited, ignorant way, and all too often egging everyone on. That commentary colors your perception, often to the point it's hard to see what is actually happening. (It's like reading 'police brutality' in a YouTube video title.) With many people, the narrative will be what they believe they saw. If there is cell phone video of the incident (and there often is) this excited nattering is going to be on the soundtrack. You can easily experiment with how powerful this grooming is. Spend about fifteen minutes watching different clips of violence. Watch the videos *without* the sound for the first time. See what you see. Then run them a second time with the sound on. Compare the commentary with what you saw happening.

blood. The next few times you see conflict instead of getting caught up in your monkey study people like bugs. Not just the participants, but the people around. Who is cheering it on? Who is trying to stop it? Who is looking at it in disgust? Who is nervous? Who is grinning like a teenage boy who just got his first blow job? Don't come to any conclusions. Just watch the whole thing before you start telling yourself what you're seeing. The monologue and judgmental decisions will be your monkey jumping in like a sports announcer. Tell it to have a nice big cup of STFU and *just* watch. Do this for the same reason I advise you to watch videos of violence with the sound off the first time. When you think you have an answer, you stop looking. You stop seeing anything other than what you already think.

Point six: OOKs overwhelmingly . . . well . . . . screw up social violence and scripts. Usually because they don't have a clue about how these work. But as you'll soon see, I suspect there's often another factor at play.

These points add to the challenge of choosing an appropriate level of response—especially if the OOK is a woman. It's even worse if the person is underage. Sisyphus would break down in tears of frustration if he were forced to defend himself against a woman or a child.[179]

These points are also the challenge about communicating *why* what you did was not just another case of social violence going too far, it was in fact inside the SD square. Or if it wasn't self-defense per se why it still was a legally justified and appropriate use of force (e.g., a bouncer removing a drunken, violent individual from the premises or you doing the same from your property). Remember that a common reason for use of physical force in social violence is stopping unacceptable and potentially dangerous behavior. If we didn't allow for this use of force, the police would be out of a job. Bouncers, too.

As such, when at a family reunion your mom asks you to deal with drunken Uncle Albert what you're doing is *not* self-defense. Handle him correctly, and it can be a legitimate and lawful use of force, but it's not

---

179   As a bouncer, I *loathed* dealing with drunken women. Hell hath no fury when they go off, and they don't know either to quit or surrender. The best analogy I know is that they're like trying to safely hold a very angry cat—claws, fangs, and kicks everywhere, as well as hissing and spitting. Yet, if you want an entire bar to turn against you, treat them as you would a man offering you the same level of danger. The challenge with holding this angry cat is you can't hurt it. Armbars and joint locks were literally the only way to go. Even then, there was the problem of knights in shining armor. Almost universally, once you got the woman under control and were walking her to the door, she'd start screaming that you were hurting her. Whereupon, up stepped some Galahad. The counter I developed was to turn toward the would-be rescuer and say, "Is she yours? Please, man, put her on a leash." The resulting explosion of fury, vulgarity, and fighting the control hold made Sir Lancelot hold up his hands and back away saying, "No, no. Sorry. My mistake. Carry on."

self-defense. (It is here that grappling, joint locks, and arts that move people around *excel*. They aren't that good for high-level-of-force self-defense, but they really work on lower level and necessary use-of-force situations.) If something goes wrong with Albert, think long and hard before claiming SD. What you are talking about is the equivalent of a cop justifying his use of force to control a suspect. It's not quite self-defense, but it's not exactly fighting, either. The attack is what warranted the use of force, but your goal was to contain the situation, not hurt anyone. This is why it is very important to *avoid*—using police lingo—"going hard hands on" with the person (punching him). They're looking for excessive force and when they ask if you hit him, you need to be able to honestly say, "No sir. I didn't punch him." Or if you did, why that was a necessary level of force.

While there are many similarities, there are some subtle differences between talking to the cops in a self-defense situation and a use-of-force situation. Overall, these are beyond the scope of this book because many of these differences are based in the techniques you use when your goals are different. But we can do a fast skim through . . .

In control, remove, or restrain circumstances, you have different goals. The first is to end the situation. That's the goal of all self-defense isn't it? To end the threat? Well, unlike self-defense, in-control running away isn't normally an option.[180] You have to stick around and deal with the person.

And that brings us to the second goal. That is a higher emphasis is placed on *not* hurting the person. You want to put an end to the behavior, not the person. After all, odds are good you know the person. But if it goes to extremes and the police become involved if the person is hurt, you must be able to explain: 1) Why the injury was caused by that person's actions (you didn't go in meaning to dislocate his shoulder; he dislocated his own shoulder when he tried to wrench free from your escort). 2) When and why it transitioned into self-defense. ("I was trying to walk Albert through the kitchen when he grabbed a knife . . .") In which case, yes, you needed to incapacitate.

Moving on, I want to talk about social behavior that can be lethal. Let's start with how it can get you killed. If you think about two young siblings squabbling over a toy, you can get an insight into the dynamics

---

180   Although tactical running can be fun. Back in my partying days, I led many a drunk on a late night jog. Instead of fighting them, I let them chase me. Just staying out of reach kept them going until they tuckered themselves out. If their interest started waning, a few choice words spurred them on. It got them out of the location where they were causing the ruckus. If they were friends or family, I'd bring them back after they'd settled down. If they weren't, I'd ditch them out in the night. Either way, the problem was resolved without me having to hit anyone.

of *most* social violence, especially about how quickly someone can cross the line from being right to being self-righteous about their own bad behavior. The difference is the 'toys' adults fight over often have no physical existence. Social status, rules, how someone treats you, what someone thinks, these are *monkey issues.*

I want to focus on a specific aspect of social violence for a second, something I call territorialism because it's actually different from territoriality. Even if the disagreement starts over a physical object, it rapidly leaves that arena and becomes a monkey fight over other issues. Again look toward siblings. One sibling goes into the other's room and takes an item without permission. This transgression is discovered, conflict ensues. Ostensibly, the fight is over the item. But it quickly morphs into being about *my* stuff. Going into *my* room without asking *me*! It's become about expected behavior and how you treat *me*! The fight started over the item, but it is not *about* the item. It expands past simple possession (which can be put into a wheelbarrow). It goes into territorial behavior (territoriality). It keeps going into respect, perceived status, being too good to be treated this way, a demand for certain behavior, the willingness to fight over it, and most of all self-image (territorialism). All of these are reasons for social violence.

Anyone who has siblings remembers and any parent of multiple children knows this pattern of fighting over more than just stuff. (And this includes the kids taking your stuff.) It is this very familiarity and acceptance that can make it dangerous. And it's a great way to get shot in a robbery (asocial violence). In fact, it's arguable this behavior is what—most often—gets people killed or injured in robberies, carjackings, and other incidents over property. When confronted by robbers, they *default* to this social script. It goes beyond simple possessiveness and becomes about self-image and being treated this way. "You're not taking *my* car!" "Do you know who I am?" "You don't do this to *me*!"

There are multiple problems with this. One is a robbery isn't social violence. It's a specialized kind of asocial violence. Two, the level of force used in territorialism is way too low and slow to save you against a mugger. Three, it's not just the ineffective resistance that is the problem. The contempt thrown out by the offended party also tends to personalize the situation for the mugger. By trying to turn it into a "screw you, this is *mine*" and "you don't do this to me" (territorialism) the chances of getting shot, stabbed, or brutalized sky rocket.

As an aside, there appears to be a correlation in injuries from robberies and social class. Oddly enough, poor folks—who are robbed more often—are less likely to be injured than middle class people. Speculation runs toward people in higher crime areas *knowing* how to get robbed.

This is to say that robbery is a fact of life. We can expand this to suggest they knew *not* to engage in monkey brain territorialism when it happens to them.

Moving on, while most social violence is not intended to be lethal, there are certain types where that *is* the intent. State-sanctioned executions are a prime example. We think of these in terms of punishment for breaking the rules, but the dynamics of the situation go beyond that. A dead person learns no lesson. Without going into the deterrence debate of capital punishment when individuals or groups use lethal force against those who cross them, it definitely sends a message—to *everyone* else, starting with the people inside the group.

Something beyond the scope of this book, but worth considering in discussions about justice and punishment: How much does our belief of bad things will happen if you break these rules tie into guiding our behavior, self-identity, and expectations? As in, do we follow the rules because we expect bad things to happen if we don't? Do we insist they happen and feel betrayed when they don't? As in, do we feel like idiots for believing that and following the rules when someone gets away with not abiding by them? If so, how does that influence our demands for justice—or our willingness to act? While most people have bought in to letting the system bring about punishment, not everyone has. This is an important question if you've burned someone, and you're thinking they won't back up on you.

But how likely are you to run across this? Yes, groups and individuals who will take matters in their own hands exist. But ordinarily they're not much of a threat to the average citizen. Years ago, I heard it summed up very well by a mafioso, "If you get killed by the mafia, you're doing something wrong." That pretty much applies to getting involved with and crossing any dangerous group. If you're outside your territory and . . . wait, I just had another sunuffabitch thought.[181]

Back when I grew up, I was from Venice. That was my territory. I knew the rules, I knew the ways, I knew the power dynamics and structure. Most of all, I knew the local players, power houses, and heavy hitters. I knew who you didn't tangle with without good reason. When I moved into other areas, I looked for and learned those standards for the new location. I also knew that when I left my turf the rules were different

---

181   This has been the hardest book I have ever written. I've likened it to trying to teach someone a complicated subject and discovering that you don't speak the same language. (If they do, it's appalling how many people want to argue over fundamental concepts—like you don't have a right to tell a biker to go screw himself without consequences.) I tell you this because now that you're reading this book, you'll be facing the same problem when it comes to this subject.

(learned that one the hard way). Most of all I knew when I wasn't in my home territory—this affected my behavior. What was okay back home wasn't okay here. What was acceptable here wasn't acceptable back home. The challenge was to learn the new rules wherever I went.

How many people have lost this? How many people believe wherever they go the rules are the *same?* I don't mean consciously thinking this way I mean subconsciously defaulting to this attitude in how they deal with people? In talking this over with my wife, she dubbed it the "hermit crab syndrome." Hermit crabs take their homes with them wherever they scuttle. It often seems wherever some people go, it's as if they take their own little territory with them. No matter where they are, their rules of behavior are the same. The keyword in that last sentence is "their"—what they think they can do, what is allowable. They also expect everyone else to leave them alone when they're doing it. Stop and think about this for a second. It's important.

Before I got hit with the sunufabitch thought, I was about to say, "If you're outside your territory and you're told to alter your behavior *don't* get up in that person's face." On the surface that seems so stupidly obvious that it's kind of insulting. It's like me saying, "Don't stop breathing." Really? Ya think? But I have seen blood spilled and teeth swept up off the floor due to the hermit crab mentality. I'm not talking about when some punk comes out of nowhere and gets in your face. The in-your-face behavior usually is done by the person being told to alter his or her behavior by a *local*. The punk behavior usually is coming from the hermit crab. I've seen this kind of scenario numerous times. Simply stated, if you're not in what you consider your home territory *don't* do a territorial monkey response. Don't act like you would if someone challenged you back home, especially don't do it in someone else's territory.

How will you know?

A) They'll often tell you.

B) If you can tell your monkey to settle down and pay attention, the signs are obvious.

The same bouncer who had the thousand dollar fine for drug dealing strategy had a run in with a bunch of hipsters at his bar. A pack of hipsters were standing so as to block the view of members of a motorcycle gang. Out of respect for my friend, the clubbers weren't flying colors, but you had to be really self-absorbed not to figure out who these guys were. Well, the hipsters were that self-absorbed. They not only were standing in the way of the bikers, but they were blocking the path to the bathrooms and fire exit. When the bikers asked them to move, they did for a moment then returned. Again they were asked, this time the hipsters responded with attitude. Again, out of respect and courtesy—not for the hipsters—

the bikers' sergeant of arms went to my friend and asked him to deal with it. Without hesitation, my friend threw the hipsters out of the bar. In doing so he saved their lives. That story had a 'happy' ending. Many such situations don't. Reacting as if you're being challenged at *home* is not just inappropriate, it's something that can get you killed—if not severely beaten. Mostly by the locals, but it can be the local mob. You're crossing them in their own territory. This, if anything, is how citizens most *commonly* get cross wired with bad guys. (Remember the *Casino* bar pen stabbing?)

There are some pretty simple rules for functioning while out of your home turf:

1) Make a good faith effort (this more than anything will earn you 'credit' [182]).

2) Be polite.

3) Don't be afraid to apologize or ask for help.[183]

4) Don't try to pick up their women or men.

5) Don't touch things you haven't paid for, intend to buy, or haven't brought with you.

6) Don't go in too deep (especially at first).

The last point takes a little explaining. Growing up in Los Angeles, I developed a taste for ethnic foods. I describe moving to the small town in Colorado as: "Do you have any ethnic food around here?" "Oh yeah, we got both kinds, Mexican and Chinese." My response was, "I've died and gone to Hee Haw Hell." To this day, I do a lot of my shopping in Denver in areas where my ethnicity stands out. I take my wife along, too. Thing is, we go at certain times during the day. We stay on the main streets and most of all, we go about our business.

At the same time, I can drive down the boulevard and point to places where it would be okay for me to go and others where it wouldn't. I'm tolerated in markets and shops. Places where I don't go are places of socialization (bars, clubs, pool halls) and businesses that can be a little bit dodgy (often having to do with cars, liquor sales, and specialized services). Before I would go into such places, I'd either be accompanied by a local or invited by the owner. While there, I'd play it extremely low key for the first few times (until the locals grew accustomed to my

---

182   People will cut you more slack when they see you are sincerely trying.

183   This follows a very specific social script. "I'm sorry I didn't know. What is appropriate behavior . . . ? Thank you, I appreciate the help." If the situation is *about* your behavior, the conversation will take some very specific directions (i.e., "that's okay, just don't do it again" or "that's okay, but you better leave"). Making this good faith effort to be polite and cooperative does three things. One, if it goes in another specific direction he's tipped his hand; it's about something other than your behavior. This tells you you're somewhere else on the social and asocial map. Two, it allows you to mentally shift gears. Three, it gives you articulable facts about how you tried to avoid a confrontation.

presence and could relax because they knew I knew how to behave). I'd behave this way because I know what happens when you don't. I know of many an incident where someone decided to go directly to such places (too deep) proceeded to violate the rules, and then got self-righteous when confronted. They didn't end well.

You *can* move safely through these environments, but it involves more than just your willingness to defend yourself. You need to mentally shift gears long before it ever gets to that point (leave your hermit crab shell at home). This is why I have problems with people who talk about situational awareness, but can't bang off a list of environmental factors that tell you what you need to know.

Here's a fast set of examples from a biker bar: Don't touch a biker's leathers, bike, or woman. Look for the pathways people follow (you'll see distinct routes to the bar, to the bathroom, to the dance floor, etc.) Be careful about crowding them. Recognize the hierarchy—if possible use it to your advantage (especially when dealing with prospects[184]). Remember if you mess with one clubber, you'll face them all. Most of all though, your safety depends on you demonstrating your ability to follow the rules rather than how tough you are.

Another big factor again beyond the scope of this book, but that needs to be mentioned, is what I call faux-politeness. It's basically having a thin veneer of politeness over a massively bad attitude. Mix in demanding something (e.g., a service, a consideration, or a change in behavior) from someone with whom you don't have a social economy,[185] and it goes bad real quick. An air of superiority and condemnation is not freshened just because someone sprays faux politeness, (e.g., adding please) to mask their inherent criticism and contempt. Always keep in mind that you're a guest in their territory, and you can avoid a lot of these problems.

Changing directions, a form of social violence you—as an ordinary citizen—*can* run into, whether misbehaving or not, is pack behavior. A Greek philosopher named Bion said the following. "Though boys throw stones at frogs in sport, yet the frogs do not die in sport but in earnest." And this applies to what Miller talks about as the group monkey dance. That's when a group gets together to beat the living hell out of someone. His insights into this dynamic come from his more than fifteen years spent as a correctional officer. His observation about not associating

---

184   People who are not a full-fledged members of a club, but are vying for admission, acceptance, and status.

185   In teaching Conflict Communications, I tell people that relationships are economies, win/win situations with exchanges of the goods and services everyone needs to get by. Like economies, there are fluctuations. In long-term relationships, there *should be* credit built up for when someone hits a rough spot. At the same time, there's a certain breed of people who come in demanding instant credit and services from others.

with or betraying violent groups is spot on. The unified responses are common in criminal and violent circles. Unified responses are . . . ugly.

What I want to talk about is when the group monkey dance meets Bion. Not too long ago, there was a flap about the knock-out game. Oh horror, oh terror. Packs of roving youths randomly selected and beat the hell out of strangers. First off, this is not new behavior. Five years ago, it was called flash mobs. In the '80s, they were wolf packs, earlier than that rat packs. Overseas, it was called happy slapping. I don't remember the Renaissance and Roman terms for this behavior, but I've read historical sources bitchin' about it, too. So this behavior is not new or news. Ohh, big scary. They go out and randomly attack people. Okay, these out-of-the-blue attacks do happen. Realistically though, you're more likely to be stomped by a group because you got into a confrontation with one of their members. (Ahhhh, the hermit crab syndrome again.)

Like the presence of a weapon, *numbers* are a game changer. The problem is your out-of-control monkey can dismiss numbers just as fast as a weapon. Furthermore—and you'll see this again in being set up for a robbery—all too often your monkey focuses on the person in front of you and *not* what the rest of the group is doing. This is especially common when the potential victim is either engaged with or tries to engage only one of the group. Now whether this is to try to fight only one or to reason with that person doesn't matter—it's usually a tactical mistake. Groups are dangerous because they team up against outsiders, often in the form of showing how much they are there for their own. As Miller points out, a group monkey dance can often turn into a competition to prove how much you are part of the group by the amount of damage you cause the victim. This is what makes this behavior social in nature. Although the violence is aimed at someone outside the group, the social purposes it serves are *internal*. While it might start for a legit reason, it can easily become a dangerous, out-of-control, "rah, rah, yay us" stomping. This sporting glee club activity is aimed at you, Mr. Ernest U. A. Frog. The physical danger of packs comes from what is called disparity of force. How dangerous is it? Here are two hints.

Number one, strong-arm robberies are neck and neck with the number of robberies committed with a gun. (I'll tell you the reason why in a bit, but strong-arm is dangerous enough to commit robberies.) Number two, disparity of force is one of the legally accepted justifications for use of lethal force in self-defense. Remember immediate threat of death or grave bodily injury? Three, four, or five guys beating and stomping you *meet* that criteria. What is most appalling about this is how many defense attorneys don't even know the term 'disparity of force.' More than that, they have *no* idea of the danger it poses.

We're going to play a little math game so you can explain to people, starting with your lawyer, *why* it's dangerous. This is the same danger that makes strong-arm robberies possible. We're edjumakating folks—who have seen too many movie heroes successfully fight multiple opponents—as to why that's complete bullshit. Mathematically speaking, you cannot have more than 100 percent. Knowing that, we're going to tell another lie to a child. But we're going to keep one correct element an *individual* cannot produce more than a 100 percent.

Let's say that two people get into a fight. Totally making this number up, let's say that in order to have a chance to win you need to exert a minimum of 50 percent. Then add whichever person has the higher percentage will be the winner (winner 70 percent versus loser at 60 percent). Here is where we're going to veer away from actual percentages. Let's also stipulate that—with empty hands—injury starts at 90 percent—with a very slim chance of death. A weapon or multiple attackers pops the lid off of the hundred level. Now we can say death becomes more of a possibility at 120 percent, really possible at 150 percent, probable at 180 percent, and certain at 200 percent. (Figure a parallel injury sufficient for a hospital trip around 110 percent.)

While ordinarily a person can't execute over 100 percent, let's say that weapons allow it. That person may be only operating at 30 percent, but that gun or knife adds another 100. Now that guy is running at 130 percent. (Certain techniques also bump it, but for ease of communication let's file that specialized knowledge under weapons.) So in order to reliably hurt another person, a single individual—with no weapon or training—has to be operating at least around 90 percent. Conversely, three people operating together each only need to operate at 30 percent of capacity to achieve the 90 percent necessary to injure an *individual*. If each of them is operating at 50 percent, they're way past what it takes for minor injury. They've moved into the area where death is a distinct possibility, and it's still a walk in the park for them. If you have three people going at 70 percent, the chances of death are high, but crippling injury is almost guaranteed. Ninety percent? He's probably dead.

Two more elements. One, unlike the movies, multiple attackers aren't likely to wait in line and attack one at a time. The closest you're going to get to this is with five attackers, two might be hanging back (three attackers) or not giving it their all. On the other hand, when one of the original attackers pulls back, the others step forward to take his place—so now you have four guys beating on you. (Three of the original assailants minus one plus two equals four.) Two, add the numbers having weapons—including strike enhancers and improvised clubs (bottles, tire irons, and such.) The suck factor is high. Hospital is guaranteed, chances of death are high.

But now, let's look at the equation from the other side. Let's limit it and say three attackers. Also that two the three attackers have 80 percent and one only 50 percent. That's still 210 percent aimed at the target. In order to beat three guys all at once, however, the target needs a collective output of 240 percent (90 percent, 90 percent, and 60 percent). Without a weapon, he can't achieve more than 100 percent. So it's *not* going to happen. The single guy goes down against superior numbers and gets maimed.

Beginning to see:

a)   Why disparity of force is a legal justification for lethal force?
b)   Why packs are so dangerous?
c)   And that I just gave you a way to articulate why use of lethal force can be justified in such a situation?

Now I'll be the first to admit that from a mathematical and physics standpoint, this explanation has more holes than Swiss cheese. But it gets across the idea of the danger multiple attackers pose. In fact, it's what I used to explain to an attorney why his client had acted reasonably (and in legitimate self-defense). When five guys tried to pull him over a fence from his own property to stomp him, he pulled a knife and slashed. The client had been the only one arrested—for attempted murder. (We won that case.)

What is most terrifying about these situations is how often those in the pack are unaware of the degree of danger they put the target of their Bion-esque romp into. I'm talking not even remotely aware. This is especially common among the young, who a) tend to be the ones behaving this way and b) believing they're safe have high commitment levels when attacking ('60s, '70s, and '80s). And I can damn near guarantee when arrested, the lot of them will squeal, "We didn't mean to hurt him . . ." You also get the same squeals about how evil their target was for pulling and using a weapon on them.

So be very aware about this type of social violence; consciously *look* for it developing around you. (Often, it looks like you're being set up for a strong-arm robbery.) If you see it, it's an entirely different game. One where the rules are different and you really don't want to play. At the same time if you find yourself in a confrontation with someone watch for growing numbers of back up. I tell you this because most of the time your monkey will be so focused on the guy in front of you, it blinds you to the growing danger as you are surrounded. When you recognize the circumstances or see it developing, *swallow* your pride, *forget* your outrage, and *get the hell out of there.*[186] Odds are that nothing short of coming in hard and fast with potentially lethal force is going to save you against a pack coming at you. And if they're committed, that might not even work.

Having said that, when dealing with a pack you have to be *hyperaware* when commitment falters and they attempt to break off the attack. Disparity of force dwindles as the numbers go down. So chasing the last remaining guy down and shooting or stabbing him in the back is *still* outside of the SD square.

In closing about social violence, this also is where we as groups, families, professions, and society get to negotiate the price. Acceptable levels of social violence will vary depending on where you are. Know that before you go somewhere and start making waves. Most of this book helps you keep from messing up when confronted by social violence. And that includes not getting upset about it (whether you're involved or not). Staying calm in a situation is critical. I'm not talking the macho movie stereotypes (steely eyed, lantern-jawed hero coolly shooting down hordes of attackers while under fire or the wise cracking martial arts expert beating a bar full of bikers). I'm talking about shrugging your shoulders, putting your coffee down, and calmly resolving the situation. When you can do that, you don't make the monkey mistakes so many people do.

I mentioned this before, but a big part of being able to do this is by changing your definition of winning. Once you change winning from that of an insecure monkey trying to prove something and into it's a win because of how well you averted that problem by soothing his monkey so you could achieve your goals . . . well . . . all kinds of good things start happening. Starting with how many conflicts you *don't* get into. Followed by how those you still have turn out. It's a small thing changing your definition of a win, but the results are amazing.

But back to the topic at hand: Simply stated, social violence can usually be de-escalated.

---

186   Martial artists: I don't *care* what stories you've heard about your instructor taking on multiple opponents using this style. I especially don't care about MMA gym stories and the spin about it. I'll point to dead pro and semi-pro MMA fighters, who tried to take on numbers. My all-time favorite was the professional MMA'er who got stabbed taking on a group, died on the operating table, and was revived. He claimed his MMA saved him. No you, stupid twit, the paramedics, the ER, and surgery staff saved you. Good physical condition helped. It's arguable that the only thing MMA did for you is convince you that being an athlete in a sport that mimics a certain kind of social violence makes it safe for you to go to dangerous places alone and do stupid things. Because someone *without* that training would have a) not gone there alone and b) run like hell. Instead you tried to fight a strong-arm robbery attempt and got stabbed for it.

Predatory asocial violence, however, needs to be *deterred*. And here's why. Asocial violence isn't about monkey wins. It's about something else. But before we go there, let's take a look at social en extremis.

CHAPTER 16

Some wars have been due to the lust of rulers for power and glory, or to revenge to wipe out the humiliation of a former defeat.

—John Boyd Orr

Problems When Your SD Works
Part Four: Vendetta

Thus far I have talked about the problems you might or will have with the legal system if you have to defend yourself. It says a lot about my past that down deep, I consider the police and prison to be a secondary set of problems. See, sitting in a cell after a situation means you're still alive. That *wasn't* guaranteed where I'm from.

Cops? A far bigger danger was that someone you'd left alive would come back and try to kill you later. Or a family member and friends of someone now deceased would come looking for you. In fact, one of the biggest indicators of it's going to *suck* was when someone you had just beaten looked you dead in the eye while telling the cops he didn't know who thumped him. Such a person would have a good chance of later success if :

a) You weren't on your game

b) He was slick.

Because when people back up on you, they come at you *harder!* Write that on the wall! What's coming back at you is *not* going to be a fight. At best, it's going to be a beating. At worst, an assassination. The best descriptor of any level is he's hunting you. When you're hunting something, you *don't* give it a chance. He's not interested in just winning, he's now looking to leave you bloody, beaten, hospitalized, crippled, or dead. While he can do it alone, odds are just as good he's bringing friends and family to help. If he's alone, he's probably bringing a weapon. With friends, who knows? It depends on the individual if it's probable or possible.

Living the life I did back then, I spent a lot of time looking into shadows, walking against traffic watching for cars driving slowly with windows rolled down, scanning the distance, periodically and randomly turning around (not just looking over the shoulder, but a slow, three hundred sixty pirouette). For years I didn't wear a seat belt while driving so I could bail out of the car fast. When I did, I wore it so I could easily access my pistol. I stayed in the left hand lane as much as possible to buy distance in case someone pulled up and opened fire at a stop light. I did these things so if anyone was coming for me, I'd spot them far enough out that I had more options. And by extension, a better chance of survival. I also made it a habit to vary my routines, routes, schedule, and—if at all possible—avoid the place where violence had occurred. Also places where I was likely to run into him or his. I did this for at *least* a week. Depending on a) the level of violence, b) who was involved, the length of time was often longer.

There are some folks who have long memories about what they consider wrongs done to them. Working with that fact, there also are people who believe their right is sacrosanct to attack you without consequence. They *do not* lose! They will go to great lengths to prove that. Therefore, waiting with a shotgun in the shadows by your car is to them a reasonable way to even the score. Your punishment for making them lose face is to die.

Time for some more lies for children. An easy starting point is to consider this kind of thinking as a perversion of normal social conflict and violence behavior. In case your mind immediately jumped into the gutter, here's the original definition of perversion: *The alteration of something from its original course, meaning, or state to a distortion or corruption of what was first intended.* Got it? They take something which is understandable and normal, something tempered by other things, lose those moderating factors, twist it, and blow it out of proportion. What is left is a warped parody of normal. What makes it so scary is it looks close enough to the original. At first glance, it should be predictable, but you don't know what's missing until it goes insane. Ohhhh eeek freak!

Truth is it really is rather predictable. It's more than just having certain, moderating elements missing; while that is true, other—*known*—motivations increase to fill the void. That's why it's important to start with that lie to a child. The parts *are* known to you. What's different here is the mix. It's simply, take away this, this, and that, then quadruple what's left.

When you do that, vendettas become understandable. The guy who you backed down coming back and hunting you makes sense. He's got toxic levels of shame, humiliation, and anger. What's missing are all the checks and self-governors we rely on other people to have so we don't have to be bothered by them.

For example, we all understand the urge to be free from the burden and humiliation of being shamed. At the same time, the checks and limits we *impose* on ourselves keep us inside certain boundaries. Most people can imagine the future and negative consequences; so shamed or not, they don't throw someone out of a fourth story window. Take those limits away and increase the humiliation and fury. Add a constant stream of adrenaline and coming back to murder someone—while it hopefully doesn't make perfect sense—it becomes understandable. What is a minor thing to you is a mortal insult to such a person.

Oh yeah and while we're at it let's talk about a weird middle class response I've run across when talking about these extremes. That is you're not a monster. Something isn't wrong with you, nor are you likely to blow a gasket just because you understand how someone could _____(fill in the blank). It really is just take away this, this and this, then quadruple what's left.

The hardest part of understanding vendetta is getting over your subconscious assumptions about the presence of what will keep the other person in check. This not just about what the other person will do, but what will actually work to prevent attempts at retribution. For example, you won't do it because you fear the cops. But to him, cops are just a problem to work around. Repeat of something you know, but with a new twist: Most conflict and violence are over issues that cannot be put into a wheelbarrow. But they become a person's reality. When that person *broods* on them, he or she keeps re-introducing adrenaline dumps and gets more and more worked up about it. Revenge seekers also tend to be brooders.

A repeat on something you already know, reality and actuality. Reality is internal. It is what we see externally, interpret internally (process), mix in some adrenaline, decide, and base our next actions on (react to). In a sense, it's like us watching—and reacting to—a movie inside our head. Our external actions are driven by our inner reality. Actuality is what shows up on the security camera. Another repeat, as social primates we are designed to function in groups. This has given us some unique wiring when it comes to our dealings with others. Status, how we appear, and the opinions of certain others are *powerful* motivators for our behavior. Final repeat: Most of what we think about our status is *inside* our own heads. We don't really know what other people think about us, view our behavior, or—more importantly—how much time they actually spend dwelling on us. Generally speaking, we imagine it's a whole lot more than it actually is. Also we tend to be horribly biased in what we think people think about us. Now throw in obsession, brooding, and adrenaline then take out normal checks and balances. For a real spicy dish throw in cultural standards of honor and the need to save face. Oh wait, that looks just like a crazy vendetta.

We're going to take a closer look at these repeats because they play a big part in vendetta and someone acting to avenge himself over a loss of face, starting with internal reality. Ever have someone say something that you got upset about? Something you were convinced they'd maliciously said just to hurt you? Then discover that's not what the person meant at all? That's an example of your (perception of) reality taking over. Actuality is what the person said. Your interpretation, emotions, and what you needed to do to right that wrong were your *reality*.

Ordinarily this mechanism is a really useful tool for people to get along in groups. If someone's wiring is normal, the result is common and predictable behavior. Things happen within the local social parameters. Interpretations and reactions are predictable and scripted. Everyone knows what to do and how to behave. "May I?" "Thank you." "You're welcome." A powerful internal motivation for staying *inside* these guidelines is 'what will everyone think?' This becomes both a chicken-and-egg issue and a deeply entrenched set of mental arroyos that dictate our behavior.

If there's a short in the wires or there's some bad software installed, the resulting behavior can be *way* beyond the norm. But it is normal reaction taken to the extreme. And now we've arrived at vendetta, revenge, evening the score, you deserving what happens, and winning. In extremis, the internal process about what everyone will think spins out of control. A physical loss, a perceived insult, a loss of face, failure, humiliation, terror over what will happen if word gets out about his pussification (loss) reduction of status, shame, and the fury over you doing that to *him* can—and with certain types of people—will result in extreme retaliatory behavior. Such folks call it evening the score, but their version of an even score is that they win, you lose.

This behavior can arise exclusively from what is inside someone's head. There are people who are just born screwed up, like those with anti-social personality disorder (a sociopath) for example. There are others (due to their history) where empathy, caring, and compassion have been ripped out of them. They are socially maladjusted and completely off the rails about what are appropriate social norms and even right and wrong. They honestly believe this is how things are done. Intellectually, they may know it's wrong. But in their emotional, adrenaline-fueled monkey brain reality, it is *right*—to the point it may have become a conscious creed, philosophy, and self-identity. ("I'm So-and-so. Nobody messes with me!") This is an especially common way for a shame-based personality[187] to try set right the great humiliation and injustice you have done to him or her by either direct or indirect means.

---

187   Look up via Google Shamed-Based Personality. This will mostly show you the human, suffering side of this type of thinking. Yet, while compassion and understanding are good, also realize such people can be explosively violent to a terrible degree. Whatever they do to avenge the humiliation, to lift the crushing burden of shame is 'right.'

Another way this behavior can come about is through cultural standards. Males from certain cultures will not tolerate being berated by strange women in public. Conversely, they'll tolerate their mother, grandmother, or aunts beating the hell out them—even in public. Their wives routinely rip into them in private. But if a female police officer berates or denigrates them in public, there's a good chance they will be honor bound to react.

Still another common element is age. There's a drive for humans to establish and maintain status— especially for teens and young adults. As people grow older, they usually establish and learn how to maintain their social niche. And they develop habits and rules about how to go about it with the least amount of fuss. Younger people are often ham-handed when it comes to how to do this. Lacking experience and finesse, they often resort to sledgehammer tactics. Young males can be particularly tetchy and violent when it comes to revenge.

Another reason things can go to extremes is when the person is a member of group. A group whose approach is "We are (insert name here)—don't mess with us." Straight up, anything you've ever learned about these kinds of groups from Hollywood is wrong.[188] One of Hollywood's biggest fictions is how predatory these groups are to any and all citizens. Robbery is only a small slice of their income. If you're the target of these predations, it's usually because you're in some kind of job involving value to them (like driving a truck loaded with cigarettes). Realistically, as a citizen if you end up cross wired with such a group, you've done something *wrong*. You're more likely to be hurt over gambling debts, encroaching on (or trying to stop) their business, or treating someone connected to them wrong. The way you're most likely to be killed by them is by being in business with them and misbehaving.

Reality break time: Depending on the source, numbers of murder victims range from between 65 percent to 95 percent having criminal records, same with their killers.[189] Basically, the high murder rates in this country come from having a well armed, professional criminal class, which instead of arguing for gun control suggests the need for citizens to be armed—especially those stuck in areas with a strong criminal presence.

So instead of focusing on the danger such groups might pose to you, let's look at how they operate. But I'm going to do something very

188   And by the way, if it says 'based on a true story' flush it down the toilet. *Texas Chainsaw Massacre* is 'based' on the life of Ed Gein.
189   The reason for the variation is whether it is city (e.g., Chicago homicide rates) district (south side of Chicago) versus national homicide rates. A murder victim in Podunk, Iowa, is less likely to be a crack dealer than a deader in South Central LA (Los Angeles).

specific. I'm going to start at the extreme—as in you've had to kill one in self-defense. Often such groups are forged in circumstances where the rule of law doesn't carry much weight. Rule of force, however, applies in spades. Since the law can't do it, safety and protection of the individual come from *involvement* with the group. It is a benefit of being a member. A whole lot of self-identity and comfort comes from being involved in a group with a reputation for violence. This especially applies if you injure or kill one of theirs. You've just violated two of their important standards—this is who we are and you don't do that to us.

But retaliation is not cut and dried. While there are groups that will seek revenge no matter what the individual did, *situational* is more common. That means who you are, who the individual was (status in group) and what the person was doing at the time of his death. I go to the extreme on this one (his death) but you should know when you are most likely to run into retaliation is over low-level, loss-of-face incidents.

To assess the chances of retaliation you face, we need to cover some points. There exists not only a hierarchy but all kinds of rules, boundaries, and checks and balances in violent environments. You just don't normally see them from the outside. The strongest tribe is often—by the number of incidents—the least violent. But when they act, it is with epic finality. Knowing this, troublemakers, criminals, and predators steer clear of crossing them or harming those under their protection. (Again, the pen-in-the-throat scene from *Casino*.) Their numbers of violent incidents are actually low because of their reputation for consistency. Messing with them equals dying reduces the numbers of small fry willing to take a chance.

Because of the degree of force involved, incidents between members of two powerful groups are a major concern—they could erupt into violence, blood feuds, and outright war. Those are not just costly and interfere with making money, but winning can be a pyrrhic victory. Another big factor with such violence is there are these people called the police. In most civilized countries, cops have teeth. While an occasional murder might go unsolved when the bodies start stacking up, the police take a more proactive interest in such behavior. This serves as another set of deterrents, checks, and balance. The end result is that violence between members of groups of equal size is extremely rare. But when it goes, it can often go big (like the Hell's Angels versus Mongols riot in Harrah's Casino in Laughlin, Nevada.) That's the influence of groups on not just whether or not violence occurs, but retaliation. You may occasionally hear of gang wars, but what you don't hear about are all the peace meetings that kept wars from happening after violence has occurred between members of different groups.

Whereas, individuals committing violence against a group member will often be met with extreme reprisals to show that you do not mess with the group. This message is not to you personally. Face it, you'll be dead or crippled. Instead the message is meant for anyone else who is thinking of making a run at them or any of their members. Their reputation and status *must* be protected.

Another contributing factor is what the member was doing when he died. For example, a biker who was killed while (or for) raping a six-year-old isn't going to get much sympathy, even from his own. On the other hand, if said individual was killed doing gang, club, or family business (even if it's illegal) reprisals are likely. In the most violent groups and in some families, it doesn't matter what the member was doing. ("He was trying to rob someone." "So? He must be avenged!") This attitude is especially common among the young, males, and certain cultures. Put those three and a criminal together and you better be ready to leave town. Or at the very least, get to another part and lay low for a while.

There's something I'm going to briefly touch upon. I mentioned places where rule of law isn't that effective, this can expand to entire cultures. Places with corrupt, ineffective police and legal systems tend to be very violent. In these environments, people band together into or accept the protection of larger groups. With the former, you become an enforcer or provide other benefit to the group. With the latter, you operate within their territory and protection (and by that I mean both safety and extortion). In such places, honor, face, and reputation are often very important to the individual. In order to protect these, an individual *must* be seen to be willing to be violent without hesitation when someone crosses a line with him. People from such cultures and socioeconomic areas are seen as hot-headed, touchy, violent, and dangerous. Again, that's from an outside perspective. What you *aren't* seeing is the checks and balances of such a system. In fact, if you come from a rule-of-law background, you won't even know to look for them. There are complex social roles and dynamics at play. Often rule of force places are very tribal, clannish, or neighborhood oriented. That keeps serious violence in check *inside* those circles.

What is most important for the individual is to be seen as *willing* to respond violently (providing the threat of violence). The actual peace keeping and problem resolution is done by others. For example, the younger ones pulling their own back while calmer (often older) heads negotiate a solution. A classic cliché is the two husbands huffing and puffing in the front yard in front of the whole neighborhood with sons, daughters, uncles, aunts, and neighbors holding them back. The next day, the wives are quietly solving the problem over the backyard fence.

Many of these 'old country' ways have been transplanted to this country, but with a twist. You have the same touchiness over honor and face, but *without* the same degree of social controls and safety. It's still there, but it's often less powerful especially when it comes to young males involved in criminal activity.

Recapping some old points with additions: First, you are an *outsider*. (We dealt with the significance of that in the violence dynamics chapter.) Second, don't go into such areas unless you have a good reason or local connections (preferably powerful). Third, if you do have to go there go there during the accepted hours (daylight, preferably early). Fourth, stay on the main routes and corridors. Fifth, *stay out* of entertainment or leisure venues (bars, pool halls, and other such venues) Six, be polite. Seven, be ready to sincerely apologize and admit you didn't know the local rules. Eight, be ready to change your behavior. Ninth be ready to withdraw. Tenth, do *not* flirt with the women or men. Eleventh, conduct any and all transactions legitimately and reliably (keep your end of the bargain). Twelfth and finally, *do not* reduce your capacity with alcohol or other intoxicants—especially in public.

I tell you these things because too many people with the hermit crab mentality put themselves into difficult situations. But specific to martial arts, MMA, and combatives training is how many people think their training makes them immune. A Tap Out shirt doesn't make you bullet proof. (When I Googled "shot, killed, mixed martial artist," I got 2,520,00 hits in .35 seconds.) Even sillier is they think they're going to claim self-defense.

The problem is being an outsider, they probably won't live long enough to do so. Once again, violence against outsiders *is radically different* than violence among members inside a group. Often in the form of it isn't one person moving against you, but a group. (With internal issues, it's usually an individual and not the group, even if the group supports the individual.)

If you see a group moving toward you with intent, your best bet, your safest strategy is to *withdraw*. Even if you have a gun, odds are there's more on that side than on yours. Equally important is that in some cultures if you shoot one the rest keep on coming, but even harder. Also I don't care how good an empty-hand fighter you think you are, numbers matters. In the long run, greater numbers will *win*.[190] That's why your goal against numbers is *always* to get out of there. Remove yourself from the situation—whether you call it a strategic withdrawal or running

---

[190]   I wish I could remember the name of the historian who went back and found the numbers where a significantly smaller army defeated a larger one in battle when both sides were equally armed. His findings were—if I remember right— this happened about 3 percent of the time. The rest? The larger numbers won.

fiercely, b*ug out*. If you have to engage, only do so long enough to break free and keep moving. (Oh yeah by the way, stop and think about how this strategy supports your claim of self-defense even if they chase you. They *chased* you. If you get away—good. If you can't, you can now justify a higher level of force because trying to flee *wasn't* working (instead of standing there and trying to fight). I took that little side trip to let you know that if you, as an individual, tangle with a member of certain groups—especially if that person loses—he will *return* with *company*. That is another good reason not to get involved in unnecessary situations.

Oddly enough in times like these, your best defense is to be down at the nearest police station doing your best not to get arrested. Why? Because it means the incident has gotten the attention of a much bigger gang, who will know where to look if something happens to you. This can—and often does—serve as a deterrent against vendetta violence. If nothing else, it sets up a paper trail you can use in defense of your actions.

Having said that, I'm going to have to take a side track here. There is a lot of crap out there in the self-defense world (especially the shooting side) that the police have no duty to protect you. I hate it when people mouth this platitude because they don't know what the legal definition of duty is. So this platitude is at *best* ignorant, in the middle misleading and wrong, and at worst a scare tactic so you will sign up for their self-defense course .... A duty is a legal obligation. Specifically, one for which you can be sued, fined, or imprisoned if you *do not* meet it. Take for example, child support that *is* a duty. Fail to meet it and penalties will be assigned.

The police-have-no-duty rulings are significant only in that the police cannot be *sued* if they do not protect an individual citizen while executing their other duties.[191] That doesn't mean they can drink coffee and watch you get murdered. (As many barking moonbats believe no duty means and will try to convince you.) Police *do* have a duty to protect and serve the public. The key word here is public. That means they must allocate time and resources across many subjects and across the whole city. That's the first step in the misunderstanding about duty to protect. The second step is if the police *aren't* present, they *cannot* protect you. It's not a matter of rights or a conspiracy, it's physically impossible. Step

---

191   *Castle Rock vs. Gonzales*, 545 US 748 and *Warren vs. District of Columbia*, 444 A.2d. 1, D.C. Ct. of Ap., 1981, are the two most quoted. The public duty doctrine holds that police have a duty to protect the public in general, they aren't accountable for individuals. Two exceptions are 'special relationship' (e.g., an elected official) and 'danger creation.' The latter has to involve a particularly egregious dereliction of duty. Having said that, danger creation has strongly influenced the removal of officer discretion. Say, for instance, an officer stops a drunken driver and lets him go. Then the drunk kills someone with his car. Now the officer and the department can be held liable (danger creation).

number three, if you end up tangling with a violent gang, the police *will not* post a twenty-four-hour guard to protect you. Not because they don't care, they simply do not have the money, resources, or manpower.

This puts the average citizen into a serious bind when it comes to dealing with groups and individuals who are into vengeance. On one hand, you are responsible for your own personal safety— especially when it comes to crime and violence. On the other, doing so might just get you entangled into a vendetta situation. This is especially problematic against a group. The problem with any vendetta (singular or group) is you are dealing with thinking hunters. If there are cops present, he or they will wait for another time. Sooner or later, the cops will leave.

After that point, there are basically two options for the targeted person:
1) Disappear
2) Become a hard target.

The second option is *much* harder for the average person to do. Not because it is technically that difficult, but it requires—among other things—a type of knowledge, a significant mindset shift, and committed awareness for however long it takes.

Knowledge— It's knowing how things work, what it takes to successfully attack or defend, and what constitute legitimate danger signals. Most of all what works and what doesn't when it comes to what you do to increase your safety. As an example, many years ago I had people looking for me. Where I lived there was a good hiding spot near the door. Not dark, just a blind corner where someone could wait in ambush. There also was a wooden fence. I kicked a hole in the fence so— as I approached—I could look through the hole and see if anybody was waiting in the spot. That strategy was based on my knowledge of what it takes to successfully bushwhack someone. That's just one example of the kind of knowledge I'm talking about. Another is instead of looking into every shadow you approach develop the habit of looking out as far out as you can see in a direction and then bring your gaze back to where you are. You do this sweeping your eyes left and right. This greatly increases the chances of seeing someone trying to approach and spotting good ambush positions. Yes that's a habit, but you have to know what to do and why to develop that habit.

Still more: Starting with does that person or group fall on the thumper or shooter side of problem resolving? (In other words, what level of force is likely to be coming back at you?) Then knowing if the person or group you crossed has the resources to send a proxy. In other words, do you have to worry about seeing that particular person or can that person arrange to have the dirty work be done by a proxy? While the actual source of the problem is smiling for the security cameras somewhere else. (Violence by proxy is a serious issue with groups.)

Mindset shift—Most of us go through life following comfortable routines. We all have habits. There are certain stores we shop at. We follow both set and unconscious schedules. (What day do you mow your lawn?) We take certain routes. Because we don't have to think about these details every time we do them, we can focus our attention on other matters. For example, when you are grocery shopping, you're busy getting the things on your list. But do you notice you (and everyone else) are subconsciously following traffic rules in the market? Oncoming traffic passes you on the left. The same goes with walking down the street. This behavior is so subconscious we don't even notice it until someone violates it.

Shifting one's mindset involves developing different habits. When you accept that you are being hunted, you develop habits and strategies that lessen the chances of someone gunning for you being successful. Things like sitting with your back to a wall (or toward a safe party) and always taking positions where you can see the entrances. Get into the habit of dropping your head and shifting to peripheral vision when you walk through dooways before doing the visual search pattern I just told you about. Learn to walk on the sidewalk against traffic so you can see approaching cars. (Know that a car cutting across traffic from behind means you're about to come under fire—and they're hoping they'll get closer to try for better accuracy.) Standing in the shadows watching the parking lot for movement before approaching your car. Taking different routes home while making unexpected turns to see if you're followed. I have a friend who had sandbags lining the street-facing walls of his front room and kitchen. While they used them as a shelf, the sandbags were for drive bys and multiple gunmen (specifically for the multiple shooter tactic of one shooter sending a few rounds high up through the windows and walls followed by the rest raking the house at floor level). These may sound like horrible ways to live, but habits like this are essential. As the person with the sandbags says, "The graveyards are filled with people who weren't paranoid enough." He's buried enough friends and family to prove that true.

Mindset also involves not whining about having to do stuff to stay alive. It's stopping yourself from wishing it would just go away and everything would go back to normal. It's accepting that this is the situation you're in right now, and this is what you have to do to get through it. Einstein said, "The significant problems we face cannot be solved at the same level of thinking we were at when we created them." That's a whole lot nicer than "Suck it up, Buttercup." But the biggest danger to you isn't how good the other guy is, but how your own self-pity, impatience, and anger that you have to deal with this can blind you and make you stupid when you need to be alert and on your toes when dangerous people are seeking revenge against you.

Awareness— Think of awareness as both intel gathering and early warning. We're going to spend some time on this before we move on to the other elements.

Dropping your head, using peripheral vision as you walk through a doorway immediately lets you know if someone is lurking beside the door, waiting in ambush for you. As you walk through that door, it combines the knowledge it's possible, a mindset shift that it's necessary, and immediate awareness that an attack is or *isn't* happening. Once the immediate is taken care of, you buy yourself more time. And in this business time is survival. That look-far-and-work-your-way-back gaze behavior does the same. You do this visual sweep pattern so— hopefully—you see him before he sees you. Failing that, you see him coming in time to do something other than bleed. You keep watch in the rearview mirror to see if anyone is following you. You check your mirrors whenever you're pulling up and stopping. You scan the parking lot for people waiting in cars before your get into yours. You do this to make yourself aware of any actual dangers as soon as possible. Again, all to buy time to react.

Now if this sounds like a horrible way to live, *it is*. It's also an incredibly fast way to burn out and start making mistakes. Mistakes that will get you killed or maimed if someone is hunting you because of a vendetta. This is why I have problems with people who claim you must always be in code yellow (Cooper color code). While you can maintain tactical alertness for short spans of time, trying to keep it on long term . . . well . . . that's a fast track to burn out. Awareness must be like a muscle you flex and relax. The trick is to know *when* to relax it and *when* to flex it. The problem for people who have just found themselves in a vendetta situation is they don't know which time is which. This is exhausting and crazy making. They are constantly adrenalized and worried. Every bump in the night, every second they are not behind locked doors, they are fearfully looking everywhere. For what? They're not too sure. Even behind locked doors, every bump and thump they hear is their doom approaching.

I have a saying "Awareness without knowledge is paranoia." It's way too easy to slip into paranoia when you're being hunted. Usually because people don't know how to set an effective perimeter and early warning system—much less effectively disappear. But throughout this book, I've been sprinkling little details that will not only increase your chances of avoiding crime and violence in general, but you can now knowingly apply in a vendetta situation to keep from burning out. Okay onto the fourth and fifth elements.

Willingness to use higher levels or different forms of violence—What's coming is not going to be a fight. It's not going to follow the same scripts, rules, or standards. At the very least, he's coming to give you a beating, to teach you lesson about daring to cross him, or make him lose face (even if the latter is entirely inside his own head). Way more often—even if he doesn't plan to kill you—what he's planning is to hurt you bad.

Getting up every morning knowing today you might die or have to kill— This is the roughest one for citizens. Your life, your home, your day-to-day environment—which you built who you are on—suddenly becomes a dangerous, shadowed-filled death trap. A place where you may have to violate a societal taboo that you've lived by your entire life: Thou shalt not kill (although the actual Aramaic better translates into murder). The rules, the safeties, the ways of doing things that have always worked before are suddenly *gone*. It is a horrible and exposed feeling—one that you desperately want to go away so you can get back to normal. Back to your life. Back to your routines. Back to how things are supposed to be. That is both the siren's call and where people burn out. In many ways it's easier to move to a completely new area because you don't have the spectre of what was once normal and safe in the back of your mind every time you look at a building. Or the knowledge that today may be the last time you see it or your loved ones.

How to function in a vendetta situation is beyond the scope of this book. Those are just a few of the factors. But the most important point is you *know* it can be done. It does, however, require some significant changes in both priorities and behavior. I tell you this because if you find yourself in such an extreme situation, the biggest danger to you is yourself.

Many years ago, I ran a correctional center. Through a paperwork slight of hand, a parole officer managed to get her cousin remanded into my custody. Basically, he'd ripped off the wrong people, and they were gunning for him. By having him violated (someone breaking his parole provisions and being returned to incarceration) and put into my custody, she got him off the streets (and into safety) while she arranged for him to be transferred to another district.

In speaking to him I found out the details. I told him that in order to stay alive, he had to change . . . well . . . pretty much everything. Just moving to a new area wasn't enough. He needed to stop doing certain things, stay out of contact with certain types of folks, and not fall back into certain patterns. My reasoning for telling him that was simple. Many years ago, Louis L'amour wrote something very profound about both hunting humans and life in the desert (in the Old West). He wrote that despite being so large, the desert is actually very small. There are only certain areas where water is available. There are also limited areas where humans gather. If you know where these are, you know where a person *will* end up.

In many ways 'the street' is like that, as well. Street people tend to congregate in certain areas, frequent certain businesses, and know the same people. I told him the desert analogy and how it applied to his situation. His response was a prideful, "I can take care of myself. I know the street." My, "So do the people hunting you," fell on deaf ears. Later, he was released and relocated to another part of the metroplex. A few months later word got back to me he was dead. He'd returned to the same kind of watering holes, gathering spots, and social circles where his hunters hung out at. Although in a different part of a huge urban area, his world was—in fact—very small. He'd been spotted and a phone call was made. His refusal to change his lifestyle got him killed.

Another analogy that is very common when nice people find themselves in such situations. There is an off-roading term, 'high centered.' Basically, it's what happens when you attempt to drive over an obstacle that is too high. Your front wheel goes over, but the obstacle acts as a jack. In lifting the vehicle's body, the wheels don't touch anymore. You're stuck unable to go forward or back. I tell you this because most people high center themselves when it comes to a vendetta situation. They engage in behavior that gets them into a situation and then freak out that it's not just over and done with. That their actions, instead of ending it, both escalated it and drew it out. Then they refuse to take the next step. Often people will refuse to 'bug out,' citing as their reasons financial, career, social, family connections, and other such circumstances. At the same time, they aren't willing to make the changes, take the measures, and pay the cost of what it takes to settle the issue in other ways. They become high centered.

They most often just want things to go back the way they were before. IT'S. NOT. GOING. TO. HAPPEN.

I cannot tell you what the right answer is about what to do in a vendetta situation. But I can tell you the *wrong* ones. Refusing to change your lifestyle. Assuming that nothing will happen. Assuming that your normal priorities are still more important. Assuming the police can, much less will, protect you (and this includes the reputation of the police scaring the bad guys away). Hoping that it will just go away. Wishing that you don't have to do anything. Believing because it's wrong somehow matters. And worst of all, that you are helpless and have no control.

All of those are great at keeping you inside your emotional comfort zone, but they do exactly dick about keeping you physically safe when someone is hunting or stalking you.

I bring up stalking for two reasons. First is when the stalking involves a woman, a majority of cases are post break up (or perceived scorning). Again, outside the scope of this book, but understanding vendetta really clarifies the subject of this kind of stalking.

Second, it can help you understand—and reframe your thinking—about how situations can escalate to your engaging in physical self-defense. Again, a lie to a child but: Stalking and 'bad blood' building up to violence are forms of vendetta. The reason for someone having a vendetta against you does not have to be because of physical violence. They usually start around a perceived loss of face or someone not getting what they believe they *deserve*. (There's that damned pesky word, again.)

This triggers an emotional part of the brain and this reality is further cemented with an adrenaline dump. Anytime that person sees you or thinks about you (and the horrible wrong you committed against him) these perceptions are reinforced and enhanced with another adrenal stress response. Although they often think of it in terms like evening the score or wishing you were gone, their strategy is that of winning. This win is defined by whatever is inside their head. These are the conditions that person is operating under when dealing with you. And—since emotions are contagious—odds are good you'll be triggered, too, just by seeing or thinking about the situation. The problem is when we're in our monkey brain, the absolute last thing we want to do is give them that win. In fact, we often actively reject any strategy that would give the person the *emotional satisfaction* that would resolve the situation. Let him win? Hell no! We often justify it by claiming if we did that, the situation would get worse. We rationalize it by saying the person would use it as a green light to escalate. In fact, the biggest green light to escalation is when the person *doesn't* get the emotional satisfaction of a perceived win.

Remember I said it's *not* being a victim that is most likely to get you killed, but instead being too confident? Well let me add something to that now. It's also a combo of not being willing to brutally end it and your own need to win. You aren't willing to act and you aren't willing to back down. That high centers you. Worse, it becomes a game of escalato.

Not too long ago, I had a friend contact me about a dispute she and her husband were having with a supplier over a piece of equipment. Their contention was the equipment did not perform up to promised standards. The supplier claimed they were just trying to get out of the contract. She was furious, but at the same time at a loss because the harder they fought the more the supplier dug in. It had escalated to the point of taking it to mediation. I should tell you this woman is not only a professional, competent in her field, a mother, a grandmother, and a black belt, but she routinely trains with SWAT and other high level tactical teams. So, physical intimidation wasn't going to work on her. (I suspected his inability to intimidate her is what added to this mess.) I listened to the details of the situation and realized the sticking point did not have anything to do with the equipment or the contract. It had become a matter of his need to win.

"He wants to see you cry" I told her. "He's not going to settle, until he wins on this front. You have to let him see you cry to let him think he's won." The heat of the reply would have put nuclear fusion to shame. (Sticking with stereotypes, on top of everything else she's a redhead.) I explained the reason this had escalated so far was that he needed an emotional win before he'd come to terms. If he didn't get it, he'd just keep on going—while pretending that he was doing it for business reasons. Finally—and oh-so-grudgingly—she accepted the idea. A week later she called me up and happily reported, "It worked like a charm. I broke down and cried, and he settled. It's done."

Okay reality break here. Having the standard of must see this competent woman cry is *not* professional. Conversely, it was her very competence, aggression, and (legitimate) complaint about his product that triggered his sense of having *lost face*. Even though it was in a professional environment until this was satisfied, professionalism went out the window. When he deemed he had won emotionally *that's* when he settled. This guy was going to continue fighting, continue raising the stakes, and continue with his behavior until he got what he wanted— which had nothing to do with professionalism. In fact, when you add it all together (including reduced settlement and mediation costs) the guy ended up losing more money than if he'd just settled up front. But that didn't matter to him. What mattered was he won. He was satisfied; the vendetta was over because he thought he could put a check in his victory box.

Stupid, but that's how vendettas work. Did it become violent? No. But the point is knowing the mechanics of vendetta. This helps you see how many *don't* become violent. And with that to understand why some do and some don't. This knowledge is an important element in understanding violence dynamics.

The problem is that when someone goes deeply into their monkey brain, we do, too—especially when it comes being insulted, humiliated, and frustrated. They infect us and our monkey starts playing for the same goals. We get into it as much for the win as the other person (although we call it "what's right"). As such, the easiest lesson—*when you find yourself in a hole quit digging*—becomes the hardest to put into practice. That's because your monkey will tell you, "We gotta get out of this hole boys, dig faster!"

While it is possible that no matter what you do the situation will keep on escalating to physical violence, that *isn't* the common reason for such an extreme. Most of the time, it's mutual and participatory. By that I mean both people are doing things to save face, to get in that last lick, to have it end on your terms. Satisfaction is the key element here not whether you're being aggressive or defensive (although counter aggression on your part does tend to escalate things faster). The more you engage in behavior that does not *satisfy* the other person's need to regain his loss of face, the closer the situation gets to physical violence. Depending on the degree of violence, it's either the final resolution or another step in the process. The latter especially if his attempts at violence don't work out.

Let's go back to John and Jim from the "Road of Violence" chapter. Yes, it went physical, but let's say it was broken up. Because it was broken up before there was a clear winner, it's just one more log on the fire for both John and Jim. Now they have another reason to nurse the grudge. Next time the two parties are in proximity, odds are things will go bad. How bad? Well it depends . . .

But just for the sake of example, let's say that Jim was losing when it was broken up. But Jim's ego doesn't allow for that. So now instead of accepting that he threw his hat in the ring and lost, he starts brooding and obsessing:

a)   On the loss of face he feels

b)   And blames John for

How is this going to turn out? It depends on how far Jim is willing to take it and how hard a target John makes himself to be. I want to remind you that one of the purposes of this book is to get people looking beyond the physical act when it comes to self-defense. To see before, during, and after as all part of a greater interconnected whole. Understanding how vendetta and someone's need to win (including your own) is usually present *long* before a situation goes physical. This is a big part of :

a)   Keeping things from going to where you must physically defend yourself

b)   Keeping you inside the SD square

c)   Making your attorney's job of defending you all that much easier

d)   Preparing you for the aftermath—especially if it isn't legal

CHAPTER 17

Information without the ability to apply it is useless.
—Dan LoGrasso

Social Violence
Real Life Considerations

Before we move on to asocial violence, there are three more things I'd like to cover about social violence situations. They're pretty nuts-and-bolts considerations. The first is exclusively a post-incident situation. It also scares the hell out nice people who have had a run in with someone.

In the first part of the last chapter, I spoke of staying out of places where violence had occurred. I also mentioned the desert being small because of watering holes and towns. Realistically, violent people have routines, habits, and schedules just like you. There are places they frequent, areas they consider theirs, and times they are likely to be there. This shrinks their world into predictable sizes. While it is possible for them to leave such an area, *most* of their time is spent inside these self-imposed circles.

I tell you this because often people will talk tough about avenging themselves against someone, but in fact, *do* nothing. They'll stay in their normal areas and haunts and go about their business. Basically, it's over. That is unless they see you walking down the street in their neighborhood. They see you and remember that you've infuriated them. If they also see you're not paying attention or are scared of them, it can result in their deciding to act.

This is not a vendetta, per se. They were not planning to act. They're not hunting you. They aren't necessarily prepared. Simply stated, the opportunity to avenge themselves falls into their laps.

Don't let that happen.

Also in the previous chapter I spoke of the traits involved in being hunted. Three points, knowledge, mindset, and awareness (KMA) headed the list. KMA is important—especially in the weeks after an incident—because they can keep things from happening at all. Starting with, they'll help you stay out of places where you're likely to run into the guy. Part of your brain will be saying, "I'm not going to do it. I have the right to go there." But KMA will weigh in as to why it's not a good idea. Then if you gotta go there, KMA allow you to either see him before he sees you or lets you see him coming at you. Impromptu ambushes or attacks of these kind tend to be sloppily executed. If you're even partly awake, you have a good chance of seeing it coming. You don't have to be paranoid, but being on the ball really helps.

This brings up the second to last issue. There is an advantage to this. Awareness and good habits make you a hard target—especially against impromptu retaliation. And that goes miles for *reducing* the chances of it happening. A reminder, someone who is looking for revenge (hunting you) is going to be coming at you with a higher level of force than last time. They lost last time; that ain't gonna happen again. Or they think you didn't get the message. Either way, that person is bringing more force to get it done. The problem with raising the stakes like this is that you might just call him. Worse, you might just see his level of force and raise him. The person who is considering raising the level of force has to factor in that losing at this new level hurts a whole lot more and that includes he might not live.

That's where deterrence comes in. The revenge-seeker has stable data that he's lost once already to that person's skills. Having lost at one level, it's easy to believe it was a fluke. It's easy to tell yourself that all you have to do is crank it up. That's why the guy comes back at you with a weapon or friends, this time he's going to *win*, damn it!

Still, there are very few people who willingly throw themselves into a wood chipper. Even with the plans for seeking revenge, there's that niggling voice that *maybe* it wasn't a fluke. So before he

There are people who try for 'rent free space in your head.' Such people specialize in street racing in the lower mileage parts of the road of violence. They find grave insult in the smallest perceived slight, and they'll threaten you at the drop of the proverbial hat. But most of all, they'll go out of their way to make sure an incident escalates to a confrontation. Then, they'll scurry away with the threat of horrible future violence hanging in the air like a foul fart.

I'm often contacted by people in a kerfluffle about experiencing these kind of events. Make no mistake, this is an interview, but it's post-dated. It's to see what you're going to do about that horrible smell he left in the air— *next time* he sees you.

Peyton Quinn makes a very accurate observation about punk strategy, "When a troublemaker walks into the area, he's not just looking for who's looking at him. He's looking for the fearful person, who's scared by his mere presence. He's also looking for someone who can hurt him and who has noticed his presence." (The former are going to be his play toys, the latter will feed him his liver if he misbehaves.) The rent-free crowd takes this strategy to the next level, the move to the fearful-victim farming.

The reason I use the passing gas analogy is because—to start with— you aren't special. He befouls the air all over the place, all the time, and with a lot of people. This is what I mean by farming. He's looking for people who will volunteer to be victims later. He's looking for people he's crossed before who will act like deer in the headlights when he walks in. He doesn't have to look for a safe victim, they'll *self-identify*.

Remember in the "Road of Violence" chapter, I talked about people who get off on conflict and trauma drama? This is one type. He didn't act last time because he wasn't certain enough. But if when you see him again, you fall to pieces—that's a power rush to him. *He* made you do that. *His* mere presence turned you into a hand-wringing, pantywaist. You start trippin' just because you saw him. *That's* the pay off for him. Is he going to act? Often yes, but not a physical attack. What he's trying to get from you is attention, so the threat of an attack is much more useful. Because these guys have highly refined radar about who's looking, the odds are pretty good he's going spot you freaking out over his presence. Act? Oh yeah. You can bet he's going puff up, posture, and go, "Booga booga boo!" The sight of you scurrying off is going to make his day. (We have a running gag of skipping around childishly chanting, "Attention, attention, I got *attention!*")

If he was going to kill you, odds are he would have acted the first time. Or he would have unexpectedly shown up in an ambush spot. Getting this kind of attention is a whole lot more fun. Even better, he can do it over and over again if you're local. Better still because he's not overtly threatening you anymore, there's not a damned thing the police can do about it—and he knows it.

The reason I say you aren't special is because he's threatened a whole lot of people. Now he's like a cat that has multiple scared mice to play with. His ego is the cat. A cat can't exist on only one mouse, it needs lots and lots of them to constantly feed itself. The more people he can collect who are scared of him, the bigger a man he feels himself to be. And every time one of the many little mice he's scared see him, he feeds off their fear. Is he going to ever physically act against you? Well, that kind of depends on how much of a victim you play by just seeing him. This is the 'rent free space . . .' part.

All for the cost of a burst of noxious air.

commits, he's going to look to see if he can get away with it. Seeing their target bump up the KMA is a powerful deterrent factor. It's not an 'oooooh, I'm a scared little mousey' bump, either. The over-the-shoulder look of someone who's raised KMA is the look of someone who is checking to see if they have to shoot someone in the face in the next thirty seconds. Lemme tell you, you really don't want to try your luck against someone whose body language signals while looking over his shoulder are, "Do I have to shoot anyone? No. Cool."

Also—while it might not say so to you—to a revenge-seeker a post-incident KMA bump means the person *knows* how the game is played. And that's not a good thing for the revenge-seeker. We covered it in the social violence chapter, but violence has rules, deals, scripts, and contracts. You break these conventions at your own peril. As a friend Ian Hogan summed it up, "You've got a knee on his chest, and you have to decide whether he's got the message or do you finish it."

Stop and think about that. There are all kinds of unspoken depths, dynamics, and details in that simple sentence. Before you read on, I'd like to ask you to find a few of the underlying elements that statement is based on. I asked you to do that so the following would make more sense. If the guy drubbed you and let you leave, he's giving you a chance to live and let live. It's a *deal;* a contract. Accept the social order and you're safe.

You break it by backing up on him, and it's a *betrayal.* An experienced player knows this and will react accordingly. With what he's going to do to you, you can find mercy between malice and mutilation in the dictionary. Except with a serious player at that moment, he's looking to see if you'll accept it or betray him. Send the right signals, and there's a good chance he won't maul you. Send the slightest indication that you'll back up on him, and he'll do you right there. And in doing so save himself the bother of you backing up on him.

I'm not going to tell you what heavy hitters use to decide to end it there or that the guy is safe to let walk. You trying to ape them without having the requisite abilities and street smarts is a criminal charge waiting to happen. Simply stated, deciding the deal's not going to work is consciously stepping out of the SD square and committing a crime. What you're going to do is not self-defense because the person *does not* pose an immediate threat. If it is lethal, it is murder. And that is not something you want to confess to by claiming self-defense.

As a side note, this is where most people screw the pooch and cross excessive or unnecessary force line—thereby leaving the SD square. Their monkey whispers, "What if he gets up? I better kick him to make sure he stays down." Yeah, except you've just crossed into assault—perhaps an attempted murder charge. (Remember shod human foot?) There's a big difference between an experienced player making the conscious decision, "Nope, this guy is going to back up on me" and a freaked-out monkey telling you to act on what it's says he *might* do.

Two points about this. One, I told you the hardest thing to do is to get your adrenalized monkey to stop when the threat stops, so you don't cross out of the SD square. *This* is that mechanism. Two is this is exactly the same thing that makes punks and OOKs so dangerous to the average person. They don't know *when* to stop because their monkey is driving the bus. They've never learned how to break the monkey slide and stop.

But let's flip this around. What about the person who doesn't know how the game is played? I'm not talking the idiot who's doing the revenge seeking. He knows what he's doing. While he may not understand the consequences of what's going to happen if he fails that's his problem. Nor am I talking about the sociopathic rage monster, who will come back, kill you, then sit down, and wait for the cops. I'm talking about the target of the return. That's *you* if you defeat someone and don't manage the aftermath.

Let's start with communicating about his safety—and the consequences of not taking the deal. I've already mentioned some dynamics I observed transitioning out of the streets, including verbally and emotionally violent people flipping out over my mere presence. I also suggested the idea of their assuming I was as out of control with my violence as they were. This scared them and they wanted me gone. Now mind you, the only thing that kept me from throwing them out a window was my self-control, but that's not the point. The point is projection. You're probably aware of the old saw about dishonest people see the same in everyone. Well, violent and emotionally intimidating people will often ascribe the same motivations to you they themselves have. Because they'd extract revenge or trick you, *they think you will too.* As such, they have to be convinced that you are sincere about your willingness to let them leave safely. At the same time, you need to communicate their safety *is* contingent on them sticking with the contract. This deal as it stands is a win/win. He can walk away with his head held high. Breaking this deal . . . would be bad.

It's not a threat, it's not escalato. It's a fact. But there's a fine line between communicating that fact and provoking him to either attack again right there or back up on you later for threatening him. Another fact is that you very calmly discussing options when breaking his arm is on the table sends a message that this *isn't* business as usual. That tends to discourage all but the most dedicated (or stupid) from taking a crack at you in the future.

Again, beyond the scope of this book, but people skills are paramount—especially when it comes to *not* having to kill someone or beat their ass. And for some people, you *really* have to work on selling them not getting their butt kicked.[192] But doing so a) reduces your chances of paperwork and b) is articulable about how you tried to solve it nonviolently.

Another case of aftermath management failure is that often when confronted with a return engagement, the targeted person makes the mistake of thinking it is just round two and it will be conducted at the *same* level of force. As such, they try to react the same way they did before. This is a bad, bad mistake. As an example, I worked a case where there was a road rage incident in front of a condominium complex. It ended with no decisive winner. Later, the defendant came out of his home to see the other person driving around *his* section of the development (the other person lived in another part with no connecting roads or reason to be there). Everyone I consulted with on this case said the same thing as what I initially thought, "He was hunting him."

When the defendant approached to confront the driver (again) the driver came out of his car with a stun gun and attacked him. Using a stun gun as part of an assault is—by itself—a class five felony in Colorado. The way things would have ordinarily played out is the pedestrian would be tased, then kicked and stomped. What made this complicated is the stun gun's batteries were dead. It turned into another physical go round. And because the pedestrian failed the personality test—guess who got arrested? The only person surprised by the presence of the stun gun was the defendant. He intended to just confront the guy, bluster, threaten,

192   Rory Miller, *Meditations on Violence.*

and tell the guy to get out of there. He was—if you'll excuse the pun—shocked at the new and unexpected level of force

Yet, his approaching the car was used by the prosecution as evidence that *he* was the aggressor. Especially because the person with the stun gun claimed the defendant just ran up, started punching him through his car window and then dragged him out of the car. In reviewing the case, my first question was "Is this guy an octopus?" In order for the victim's story to be true, the defendant needed at least four hands. Oh yeah, the 'victim' also claimed he had only brought the stun gun to defend himself.

Don't make that mistake! Someone unexpectedly popping up like this is *not* a round two of the same fight! It's a bad, bad sign! Someone backing up on you is engaging in some very specific and usually dangerous behavior. While it's unwise to assume just by seeing the guy that it's a lethal threat, so you pull your pistols and start blazing—it is equally unwise to assume that you're going to be facing the same level of force as before.

How do you tell? Start with the circumstances you see him in. Is it across the parking lot at the supermarket? Is it in a hardware store? Or is it him coming at you in a lonely and dark place or somewhere you routinely go? Is he stepping out of a blind spot and coming at you hard and fast? Or is he suddenly appearing right next to you in a place he shouldn't be? [193] Or when you're cutting down an alley where you don't normally go does he step out the door carrying a garbage bag? Does he look as surprised as you? I'll let you figure out which of those go on the deep manure list.

KMA will change your short term behavior. Change it in a way so that there's a good chance it will act as deterrent. I've seen many an occasion where a revenge-seeker changed his mind and retreated when he realized he'd lost the elements of surprise and confusion.

The third and last thing I want to address in this chapter is a restraining order. Many people say that a restraining order is "just a piece of paper." They say this to warn you a restraining order will *not* protect you. On the other hand, I have a joke, "Yeah, it's a piece of paper. It's a hunting license! See right there's the bag limit!" But that isn't 100 percent true, either. Like many things, truth is somewhere in the middle.

I'm okay with the basic sentiment about a restraining order *alone* not being enough, but not so okay with the reasoning or the conclusions following that attitude. Usually people who tell you a restraining order is useless are people who are selling something. That something is most often the fact:

---

193   Whereas, someone you run into at a social event and who sits over in the corner, drinking and brooding before he comes over to you again is very likely a round two. But, the dynamics of those two events are different. As is the guy who sees you, leaves, then immediately returns. In that case, odds are good he has a weapon.

1) You're helpless and only a change in the laws can save you.

2) You must become a killer kung fu commando.

Both believe the restraining order is useless. To both. I say "Bullshit." The first because it's politically driven. The second because it bolsters what they're selling. Conversely and unfortunately entirely too many people, who get restraining orders, have talisman thinking about their effectiveness. The problem with talisman thinking (whether it be a restraining order, a gun, or telling someone you have a black belt) is that's *never* all there is to it. The talisman alone isn't enough.

The following statement applies to more than just restraining orders: One of the most fundamental mistakes people make is they base their strategies on what would work on *them!* A restraining order would scare you off? That other person *isn't* you. It might not be enough for him. Remember, when someone is emotional and adrenalized, another part of the brain is driving the bus. Accurately assessing long-term consequences is *not* the monkey's strong suit. As in, "A restraining order? I'll show you!" Especially if alcohol is introduced to the process. Now you have a drunken, self-righteous monkey driving the bus. That's going to end well. Not.

Then there is the issue of different priorities. A restraining order *could* set such a person off. Realistically, this is why a lot of people hesitate to get a restraining order against someone. In a very real sense, this is still talisman thinking. Except now, it's what if the talisman doesn't work and it only infuriates him more? What if instead of repelling vampires, it attracts them? Ummm, that's what faith, garlic, sunlight, holy water, threshold wards, and the stake are for. No one thing works alone to keep you safe.

I'd like to help you make a paradigm shift. Instead of thinking a restraining order is the cross that holds evil at bay think in terms of a shotgun—one loaded with double-aught buck. For non-shooters, if you have a pistol every time you pull the trigger a single bullet goes toward the target. In order to send out six slugs, you have to pull the trigger six times. Bang, bang, bang, bang, bang, bang! Now the first time you pull that trigger and the bullet goes whizzing past his head, the guy *might* decide to pack it up and leave. Or he might just be driven into a rage and come at you anyway. Often when someone is relying on a talisman—that one bullet—to do everything, they are shocked and dismayed when the person chooses to keep coming—often to the point of shock, surprise, and freezing because their magic talisman didn't work.

Conversely, there are nine shot, pellets, or buck in a double-aught (00) shotgun shell. Each of these is the equivalent of a single .32 caliber bullet. So with every shotgun trigger pull, you send the same amount of lead at the target as pulling a .32 caliber pistol trigger nine times. Extending this analogy, someone might decide to keep coming at you anyway when a single bullet whips past his head. But let loose with a shotgun blast and you'll catch the attention of even the most thick-witted.

By itself a restraining order often *isn't* enough. In fact, think of it as a single .32 bullet. I tell you this because the restraining order works in tandem with everything else you're doing. It's all the other things you do that turn a single bullet into a shotgun blast. It's the combination of the restraining order, you installing cameras, taking photographic proof,[194] as well as KMA that will usually show him he'd better let it go. Or more importantly not escalate things up to physical violence.

Originally the subtitle of this book was going to be, "Essential Information Your (SD) Instructor Didn't Tell You." Here's something your instructor probably didn't tell you: Getting a restraining order *after* violence has already taken place is closing the barn door after the horse is already gone. First off, if the guy thumped you, there's a good chance he figures he's won. As far as he's concerned, it's over. Second if getting a restraining order is *all* you do, then there's a good possibility it's going to be interpreted as you continuing the escalato game. You're trying to take his victory away from him! You're too weak to win by yourself, so you've called in someone to bully him. If it is interpreted that way, then yes the vendetta is back on again. On the other hand, there's nothing that says you can't get a restraining order before violence occurs.

The exact ways to make a restraining order part of a shotgun blast is beyond the scope of this book. But know documenting vendetta, harassment, or threatening behavior (including date, time, and if possible making recordings) makes it *easier* to get a restraining order. The more concrete and complete your evidence, the better. After a restraining order is acquired if the person is still stupid, the same procedures make arrest and prosecution a slam dunk. If it's not too risky collect information on multiple infractions.[195]

But I want to specifically look at how a restraining order and police reports help you with your claim of self-defense. While it's not a hunting license (and as such, don't get stupid) restraining orders and an established trail of police reports are very helpful for getting your name written in on the victim line of a police report. With a paper trail already in place, it's a whole lot easier to support your claim of self-defense.

---

194   Cheap and easy to use electronics—such as cell phone cameras, motion-activated cameras, and caller ID (identification) really make it very easy to collect evidence of stalking and aggressive behavior.

195   If you have a stalking problem, I cover the subject extensively at No Nonsense Self-Defense http://www.nononsenseselfdefense.com/stalking.html On the nuts-and-bolts page, I explain specific tactics to use to deal with stalkers

In the aftermath of a self-defense situation there is another thing that *might* be an issue. The media. Short answer, *don't* talk to them. Tying this to vendetta if the family of the person you had to deal with sees the story, odds are they'll go off. Yeah, odds are good they'll try to sue you anyway, but appearing on TV is damned near a guarantee.

If you have to talk to the media:

• Make sure your lawyer is present. Your lawyer will tell you yeah or nay about answering certain questions.

• Wait for a moment before answering any question. This gives your lawyer time to speak first. (E.g., "My client is not going to answer that question the way it is phrased.")

• If the attorney jabs you in the ribs, *shut up*. (Think Reid technique without the legal boundaries. They'll ask you questions in a such a way that you can or will incriminate yourself if you try to answer them.)

• *Never* forget the media creates and sells narratives.

That last one takes a little explaining. With all the screeching and howling about media bias too many people overlook that much of what we think of as news has turned into info-tainment. And much of that is getting us riled up by telling us long-standing and established stories. Much of the so-called bias is based on which narrative or story type we buy into. We believe this—therefore, we think a source that supports our bias is unbiased. But that other source? They're lying, manipulative, rat bastards. Here's something to know about your source. All too often, the story will be tailored—by the source—to emotionally trigger you—instead of inform you. The same as the other side is doing for the people who buy into their version.

Now, I'm not talking about when the media get caught in an outright lie—although that happens, too. I'm starting with spin doctoring and using minor events to fill air time (making mountains out of molehills). But mostly, I'm talking about tailoring the story to fit a bigger, pre-existing narrative (e.g. gun control, war, politics, racism, and other issues). They do this to stir up public interest. For example, every mass shooting automatically becomes grist for the mill of the gun control narrative, which is not only a hot button topic, but brings the barking moonbats from both sides out of their caves. Moonbats the media knows and *repeatedly* puts on camera. Will they show for your situation? It depends. By tying the events of your story into these bigger narratives, the media keeps the story alive and can fill air-time or column space.

I tell you this because they are professionals at this—including getting you to believe they are on your side before raking you over the coals. They control the editing buttons when it comes to anything you say to them. Simply by adding or subtracting ten seconds of what you say, they can sell you as a monster, a criminal, a victim, or a hero. It doesn't matter which one.

No matter how they paint you, they make *money* and have grist for the mill. If they throw you into the grindstones, what happens to you is inconsequential. You are just another story. A story where they hope to keep that ball up in the air for as long as possible.

There are two ways this happens. First if the story progresses—new events, new developments, etc., etc. That's the 'news' aspect. Second if there is interest, much less outcry, the media will swoop down on such outcry and use that to keep the story going—often to the point that the outcry becomes the *story*. That outcry will be the motivation for progress in the story. It's not about the shooting, it's about the rallies, and the outrage over what is being done (or not) about it.

Again—and you'll probably be sick of the talk of it—the shooting death of a teenager in Florida would have been a one-day blip on the news feed— if certain people hadn't started screaming *racism* to the media. Once the pundits and media ran with that narrative, what actually happened that night became all but irrelevant.

I warn you about the media because—unless you're a twelve-year-old girl who's home alone or an eighty-year-old in a wheelchair—painting you as the innocent victim of an attacker *isn't* in the media's best interest. Those stories die too fast. But all you have to do is think of George Zimmerman, O.J. Simpson, and Bernie Goetz to know that stories occasionally catch fire.

I've already said it's not a good idea to talk to the media. Here's another reason: Know that anything you say to the press can be introduced as evidence against you (remember the monster spin and edits). But with that last paragraph in mind, ask your friends, family, co-workers, and neighbors to refrain from doing so, too. Well-meaning friends and family say things that can—indirectly—get you prosecuted. Statements by your people help feed the media frenzy. Odds are good they're going to find your dumbest, most obnoxious family member and put him in front of the camera. Who knows what Cousin It is going to say, much less your second cousin's ex-boyfriend, whom you went to high school with.

If the media is making a production out of your situation, the prosecutors, and politicians will feel compelled to do something about it—especially if the story has morphed into how they *aren't* doing anything about it.

CHAPTER 18

A street thug and a paid killer are professionals—beasts of
prey, if you will, who have dissociated themselves from the rest
of humanity and can now see human beings in the same way
that trout fishermen see trout.

—Willard Gaylin

Asocial Violence
Resource Predation and Protection

Asocial violence comes in two basic forms: Resource and process.

In his original model, Miller called it "resource predation." I added the other side of that coin, that of resource protection. In a nutshell, resource violence is over things— specifically, necessary resources.

Time to bring back an old idea with a new spin: Resource violence arises over things you can put into a wheelbarrow. It's not about 'issues.' You cannot put your pride, your status, or your feelings into a wheelbarrow. Those all have to do with social issues (especially imagining how other people should treat you). But *you* can climb into a wheelbarrow and sit in it. And that is the secret to knowing when it's time to act in self-defense.

What you are protecting is your physical body—not who you think you are, how you should be treated or how dare he . . . You can't set those in a wheelbarrow. Resource violence is what marks the difference between fighting and self-defense. Fighting is over issues that cannot be put into a wheelbarrow.

Resource protection is defense of self or others—notice I confined this to human beings, not things. Simple fact about American jurisprudence, except for *very* specialized situations life is given priority over property. In our modern world, you are not going to starve to death, die of exposure, or be stoned to death by your tribe if something is taken from you. So the other person's life is given priority over what he's trying to take from you. While force *can* be used to prevent theft, offering that person lethal force without his offering the same threat to you is pretty much a no-no for citizens. (The exact standards, interpretations, and exceptions are something you need to know for your state—especially if you're going to go armed with a lethal force weapon.) This is a very fine line and many people cross it.

An important concept comes with resource protection. Work with me for a moment. You're going to have to read this paragraph and set down the book. Hold out your arm. Then imagine there is a mosquito on it that's biting you. What do you do? Seriously, put down the book and run through that scenario.

———

I usually do that scenario in a room full of people. The sound of fifty people slapping their arms fills the room immediately after I ask, "What do you do?" Those imaginary mosquitoes are dead ... without hesitation ... without remorse ... and most importantly without emotion—just like you would kill real mosquitoes. But more than that:

- You didn't posture.
- You didn't threaten the mosquito.
- You didn't try to dominate or insult the biting insect.
- You didn't give it a chance to change its behavior.
- You simply killed that imaginary mosquito like you would a real one.
- Killing it is pure asocial *resource protection*.

You killed it to protect yourself. Mosquitoes carry diseases, and its bite is the way it transmits those diseases. To prevent that, you killed the insect in the fastest and most effective way possible—without warning, communication, hesitation, remorse, or second thought. What's more, you killed without suffering a moral dilemma.

Why is that important? Those are the purviews of social violence, as well they should be. They are integral and understood *in a social context*. They and many other behaviors are ritualized and scripted in social aggression. They take time; they slow things down. They are chock full of warnings, communication, and chances allowed before life is taken. They also are what we wrongly believe must be a part of violence. Not true, especially resource violence.

Humans kill in resource violence all the time. We kill to protect; we kill to gain.

In fact, humans are the *ultimate* resource predators on this planet. The most common form of resource predation is food. When it comes to killing animals for meat, you take its life, skin it, cut it up, and put the meat in the freezer. This simple fact of life has been removed from most people's daily lives; billions of animals are slaughtered, butchered, packaged, and sent out to stores and restaurants *every* day. We've industrialized this slaughter with meat processing and packing plants. They are literally factories to produce meat. The closest most people come to this kind of resource killing is the meat section at the market.

This distance from the realities of killing for food creates a problem with the way we've been conditioned to think about violence.

Now that the seed is planted, let's go back to resource violence— especially when it comes to dealing with human-on-human incidents. Effectiveness—*not* necessarily killing—is the hallmark of resource violence. The goal is to acquire a resource.

Once again for clarity, we're going to go to extremes and work our way back, this time using robbery. When dealing with a human-on-human resource predator, the danger level is high. But when it comes to citizens, the intent is *very seldom lethal*. Again, the threat is more effective than actual violence. Criminals know they won't be prosecuted as harshly for threatening physical violence as they will be for doing it. Yet in order to make the threat viable and to quickly achieve the goal, the perception of the degree of violence on the table *has* to be extreme. This danger encourages the target to make the 'right choice' (give over your property).

The simplest way to understand this is to think of an assassination. The assassin sets up the killing, closes the distance, brings out his weapon and aims it . . . and stops. Instead of pulling the trigger, he starts talking and offering the target a way to keep from being killed. In these circumstances the target making a mistake is costly. That is why it is critical *not* to confuse resource violence with other types.

Too many people try to find social solutions when facing asocial situations. Not a good idea. Worse, they often react with verbal and emotional hostility— outright *bad* idea. If you try to personalize it, you will be treated like a misbehaving outsider. Or, using the image I just created, the assassin finishes the job.

The flip side of this ignorance about handling resource aggression is people who want to turn *any* and *all* violence into a valiant life-and-death struggle against evil. They seem to be just itchin' to find an excuse to use their training. These are the idiots who run around and train to inflict extreme violence because they claim, "There are no rules in a street fight" and "We don't train for social violence." In fact, I've heard it proudly crowed, "We only train for asocial—which is always lethal." Like the prison showers do you?

There's always lethal force when these people are involved because *they* bring it to the situation. Here's a hint, before you scream about losing your concealed carry permit for brandishing make sure that *isn't* what you did. Before you whine about being charged with aggravated assault make sure that isn't what you did. While we're at it don't be like the moron who pulled a gun and tactically hunkered down in the middle of a firefight between cops and robbers. (It's a miracle the bozo didn't get shot by the cop, who reacted poorly to his armed presence.) Or the guy who opened fire on someone breaking into his car, using a busy highway as a backstop. And fer gawd's sake don't imitate idiot number one who shot idiot number two in the Florida theater when number two threw popcorn in his face. These are just some of the results of thinking every situation entails a battle for your life.

While people who react to *social conflict* as though it were *asocial* are a problem, trying to react to asocial as though it is social is what gets *most* people hurt in robberies. I already spoke of what I call territorialism.[196] That's where the fight over the item is actually about social issues. (You don't touch *my* stuff.) When you hear about people killed or injured by a robber, odds are great the person reacted with territorialism—*not* resource protection. With resource predation, the violence occurs over *obtaining* the item or resource. In its simple form, resource protection is to keep *that* from happening. At the same time, we already addressed life being given priority over property.

There is one resource, however, that you are allowed to take another life to protect. That is your life. But that resource must be under immediate threat, so protecting it is self-defense. That is the standard you *must* meet. Not protecting your property or pride or telling yourself you're saving your life because you're emotional. Neither form of resource violence carries the baggage, rules, and scripts of social violence—the unspoken rules, limitations, expectations, attempts to prove superiority, or the moral judgments and outrage.

You don't need to be angry or self-righteous to commit resource violence—you just git-r-done (like you killed that imaginary mosquito). Both predation and protection are done in the most effective and fastest way possible. It is not macho posturing. It is not filled with blustering warnings and communications about the approaching danger. Although with both, communication about how to stay safe occurs after the danger manifests.

I cannot stress this strongly enough, it's *not* a show or to impress anyone. It is about gaining or retaining control over critical resources as quickly and efficiently as you can. Another version is someone who is paid to do violence as an occupation. With the former think: Tag it, bag it, drag it home. The latter, it's a paycheck. Something else I cannot stress strongly enough is the speed and efficacy of this kind of aggression. You can go from a seemingly social situation one second to looking down the barrel of a gun the next. Nor can I stress the extent of the penalty for trying to resist *ineffectively*. When someone has a gun pointed at your face, it is not time to drop back into your karate stance. Slapping the gun

---

196   Territorialism is an obscure term (mostly) from history that I have hijacked. The way I use it has no relation to the original definition.

aside as your crush his throat on the way to pile driving his skull into the concrete has a much higher return on your investment.

Did that last line shock you? Time for the seed I planted earlier. You already know lizard consciousness isn't used much in our modern lives. Well, lack of direct experience of killing animals for food tends to screw up our understanding of violence—especially resource. Few people in our modern society have killed and eaten an animal. Fewer still have ever been in a circumstances where if they didn't kill, they *didn't* eat. It changes you—in ways that cannot be explained to those who have not done it. It is a form of consciousness, awareness, and knowledge that is a blind spot in what the majority of people think they know about violent behavior, much less life and death.[197]

The problem is that people who haven't done it often attempt to write dark fairy tales about people who have and can do it. ("You're a hunter? You killed Bambi's mother? You cruel, heartless beast!")[198] They fill in gaps in their knowledge with opinions and monkey judgments formed by these fairy tales. They especially go ballistic about someone who takes another human life—usually in declaring what a monster such a person is.

Once again an 'I can't stress this enough.' People try and frame resource violence in monkey terms. While I'm talking in general terms, I want you to also apply everything I'm about to say to the jury. We want to put violence in the context of a story. Instead of looking at it for what it is (getting stuff) many people start from the premise of right or wrong or trying to find justifiable reasons for it (e.g., poverty). They've *already* made an emotional decision. This is monkey thinking *not* logic, *not* knowledge, *not* understanding. Then they make up stories to justify this judgment.[199] They want to decry it or minimize it. (They become moral vegetarians. Or they are those who conclude, "They're just animals.") This is easy to do because our modern lifestyles allow us an emotional

---

197   I can tell it to you, but lacking a common frame of reference the significance will be lost. "It's a fact of life."

198   There is a current challenge to the universality of psychology and social sciences. Its premise is that these systems have overly focused on people who are WEIRD (western, educated, industrialized, rich, and democratic). These disciplines have come up with overly broad generalizations that humans all think the same way and have the same motivations and desires. The best introduction to the topic is in *Pacific Standard* magazine: http://www.psmag.com/magazines/magazine-feature-story-magazines/joe-henrich-weird-ultimatum-game-shaking-up-psychology-economics-53135/

199   This extends to all violence. Miller often talks about how good people need to create stories about how broken anyone must be who can do violence. The hard core detective must be a divorced alcoholic. Anyone who has served in a war must have PSTD (post traumatic stress disorder). In some way, the person must be broken so the nonviolent person can feel superior.

and intellectual distance from resource killing. You can have opinions and morals about killing for food because you're *not* going to starve if you don't have to do it yourself.

This lack of experience with resource violence makes it difficult for many to understand. Here's a thought—going out and killing a chicken for dinner was a *child's* chore. In an environment where food production is a family responsibility, it still is. It's not traumatic. It's not wrong. It's not icky. It's not sadistic. It's *dinner.* If you aren't experienced with it, the lack of emotion over wringing a chicken's neck, plucking it, and then frying it is intimidating. Our emotional monkey wants to drag the subject into its realm, frame it in its terms. Most of all, we want life to mean *something.* We particularly want *our* lives to mean something.

One thing that freaks people out is the idea of being eaten by an animal. Damn it! This doesn't happen to humans! We're special! We have rights! As such, we want resource predation to fit with how we think the world works. We want it to be about something more—especially when it comes to doing it to other humans. If resource predation occurs, apologists want to make up a story about it: Poverty, oppression, and frustration are the causes of it all! At the same time, we have another story going on: Our own. That's the "I don't get robbed. I'm special. I have rights. The police will protect me. You don't do this to me." (Notice the monkey and territorialism creeping in there?)

Despite this emphasis on individualism, "me," and "my" (whatever) remember how I said humans are social primates? That we're designed to function in groups? Well, the key point of that idea is *small* groups. Although we're capable of banding together in larger groups (say, along national, racial, religious, and political lines) these artificial constructs are not as *comfortable* as being in smaller tribal groups. So, we unconsciously try to reduce the size of our tribe.

Anthropologist Robin Dunbar came up with the theory that humans can only maintain a small number of stable relationships. Dunbar's numbers range between one hundred and two-hundred-and-fifty. The number works with tribal and small village situations. With smaller numbers, the idea is self-evident. But what about living among millions in a metroplex? It *still* applies! If you stop and think of—family, co-workers, friends, and other people you regularly interact with—those numbers aren't that far off. You reduce those millions of others to background color and noise. On one level, you know they're people. But on another level if you tried to interact with them all as people, you'd be overwhelmed.

Here is where I'm going to squirt something into Dunbar's numbers. Those we interact with on a stable, ongoing basis are our tribe (to varying degrees). These are the people to whom we show empathy, help, and effort and on whose part we are willing to contribute (share). All the good things of being human, we direct toward our *own* tribe. Outside our tribe? Not so much.

Here is where we run into a philosophy problem. Humanism and nationalism tell us we must think in large numbers. All those others are our uber-tribe. We are (insert nationality). Integral to this grand label are our beliefs in human rights, our beliefs in equality, and other values. News flash: These all are modern attitudes—only going back to the 18th century. Most of them only came into popularity in the last half of the 20th century, and if you look at humanity in terms of millions of years even three hundred years ain't nuthin.' Fifty years? Pfffft!

Personally, I'll be the first to admit that thinking this way has done us a lot of good overall. But it does run against how we're wired. That's important because a whole lot of people haven't fully made the shift to this new way of thinking. In fact, it's arguable that a certain percentage of the populace *can't* . . .

But before we address those who can't or won't, let's keep looking at the modern philosophy we've been raised with. And in case you're wondering why this is germane:

A) It puts you at a tactical disadvantage when dealing with asocial violence.

B) This is the bias your attorney needs to overcome to keep you out of prison.

Despite being raised with humanist ideals, the best most of us can do is sorta, kinda extend our tribe to our nationality or race. Still, you don't know everybody in said uber-tribe, and there's certain micro-tribes filled with people we loathe, disdain, and we wish we would really not have to deal with 'those people.' And this is within our own tribe. (Quick, name a family member you detest.)

In extreme cases, people are claiming that *all* of humanity is included in our tribe.[200] That's where most people's minds just shut down. Billions of people? Intellectually, yeah, sure, maybe. In practice? No. Most of us have to work hard to expand our tribal concept to millions. But that is the modern standard we believe is expected and often lie to ourselves that we do achieve it.

These are the standards we use to self-identify ourselves as civilized people. Why? Because that's how intelligent and civilized people think.

200   Humanism is often interpreted as a philosophy that all humans are in a giant uber-tribe. An interesting exercise is to consider whether or not the people in PETA (People for the Ethical Treatment of Animals) and Earth First have ideologically expanded the idea of who is in the tribe past even that extreme. They include animals and trees. If you think about it, this sort of explains the mental 'what the hell?' thoughts most people have with such ideologies.

(In that last statement did you notice the tribalism and elitism, as well as the ideological sleight of hand? The one that allows a practical separation from others while maintaining ideological unity and self-identity? Keep that in mind, it'll become important in a bit.) Thing is, we don't live up to these standards in our day to day. In urbane and civilized ways, we convince ourselves we are *not* tribal and elitist. We tell ourselves we don't look at others as 'less human than us.' Our monkey tells us we are better people because we generally think well of others.

Now obviously, the tap-dancing elephant in the room is racism. I must be talking about racism, right? No, I'm not. What I'm talking about is deeper, more universal, and more human than that. What I'm talking about is what we do *to* people—including those of our own race and sex. It's how we make divisions between us and people who don't think like us or make the same amount of money. Even if they are the same race and sex, we go out of our way to make mountains out of molehills to differentiate 'us' from 'them' and to make them less for not being part of our micro-tribe.

Yet, we believe we *are* kind and compassionate people—even as we fall short of these ideals daily. Even though we tell ourselves we are egalitarian, open minded, and democratic, we splinter into countless identity politics and divisions. We all have identifiers that separate us from them. And the truth is we're way more comfortable being around 'us' than 'them.' Often these identifiers turn into "yay us! boo them" behavior. In fact, we often take pride in our contempt for these other groups. (For example, if you were to replace the words liberal and conservative with the name of an ethnic group, a lot of the ranting about the other political positions would qualify as hate speech.) Our monkey doesn't let us see that we're exhibiting the same behavior we claim we hate—and accuse the other side of doing.

In centuries before, the my tribe equals human, other tribes less so attitude was an open and accepted fact of life—especially along national and ethnic lines. So, too, were social castes and distinctions. Hell, the rules of chivalry *only* applied to how nobility treated each other. (Don't feel bad, they fell short, too.) But peasants—especially someone else's peasants? Pfffft! Tribalism was a fact of life.

It has taken decades of propaganda to convince us that this tribal mindset is wrong. I don't want to say we've all bought into the idea, but because we've been force fed this philosophy for so long—to some degree—we have. And again let me state, overall this has been a really good thing for us in Western society. Yet the end effect is that now we must deny we're still tribal, elitist bastards who put our own tribe first.

People still think this way, but they don't talk about it in polite company. We have to engage in some complex mental gymnastics to rationalize why that's not what we're doing.[201] In a very real sense, we're caught between what we want to believe about ourselves and understanding— on some level—what this world can often be about.

That's the problem with trying to explain asocial violence (of any kind) to people who have never stepped outside their monkey—particularly to people who bought into the egalitarian, humanistic philosophy. Often these are people who have never experienced life outside the safe, modern WEIRD (western, educated, industrialized, rich, and democratic) lifestyle. Therefore, they attempt to interpret the situation through monkey scripts and high idealism.

I 'wasted' all of this time talking about intellectual tribalism so you could truly grasp what I am about to say next. Get you graffiti kit out because this is a big never-forget point: *A mugger doesn't consider you part of his tribe.*

He's doing the same thing we all do, but taking it to a further extreme. How extreme? To him, you *aren't* really human. You are—at best— an ATM with legs. When I say at best, people often think, "Oh how dehumanizing and horrible!"

No. You want him thinking it's *not* personal because such muggers are *predictable.* As long as you follow the robbery script, you're pretty *safe.* And *yes,* there is a mugging script. He finds some way to get close to you, brandishes his weapon, threatens you, tells you what you are to give him, he gets it, and leaves. That's it. Just like dealing with an ATM—walk up, push a few buttons, and walk away with cash. Again, a professional criminal knows that deviating from this basic script will *increase* the penalties he faces. The mark of a pro is that he follows this script.

So if that's the case, why is robbery the most volatile, unpredictable, and 'unnecessarily' violent crime? Basically because of the human factor.

For example, things start getting problematic when you have a young and inexperienced mugger who hasn't made the entire transition to resource predation. They often use excessive force because they don't know how much is sufficient. Because of that, they can overshoot the mark of the force necessary to rob someone and needlessly hurt people. Until they're in the middle of acting, you won't know what they're going to do (e.g., the guy who runs up and butt strokes the clerk or fires warning shots—especially at people).

Such folks, however, will be predictably and excessively violent *if* you attempt social scripts with them—chiefly if you try to get some

---

201 For the record, people who are decrying all the elements in society out to oppress them are doing the exact same elitist, us versus them, tribal identification. Whatever they do to those hated others is completely jutified.

of your own pride back through attempted intimidation, contempt, and superiority. ("What are you going to do now? Shoot us?")

Here's a life saving tip: Don't treat a mugger like you would an uppity busboy. Don't try to plead or make emotional contact. This is *not* social, so do not try to use your everyday social scripts with him. That will turn out badly.

Another way things go bad in robberies is when he considers you a member of another, hated tribe; a group he feels justified in and takes glee from preying on. Your people have done him wrong by wronging his people, therefore you deserve whatever happens to you. (There's that damned deserved word again.)

Far worse is when resource predation is mixed with process predation (the other form of asocial violence). These guys are total wild cards against whom you must be ready, willing, and able to flash into extreme resource protection *when* they start going off the resource script. (And yes, in the next chapter I'll show you how to tell when that is happening.)

But let's fall back to plain

Peyton Quinn of Rocky Mountain Combat Application Training (RMCAT) came up with five core mistakes made when facing aggressive people. It's a list of do's and don'ts for preventing violence:
1) Don't insult him.
2) Don't challenge him.
3) Don't threaten him.
4) Don't deny it is happening.
5) Do give him a face-saving exit.

I consider this list one of the most brilliant observations about violent behavior I've ever seen. I waited this long before mentioning them because you now have the foundation to know *why* they work. A critique of this system, however, came from Miller—who accurately—observed, "Those work to de-escalate social violence, they don't stop asocial violence." We are now two for two when it comes to profound observations about violence. So, here's my ante into the pot. "It's true these don't work to deter asocial violence, but violating them will categorically *make things worse*— whether social or asocial."

If you do them, you will cause a robbery to escalate into a shooting. You increase the savagery of a beating. You will give a process predator the green light to move on you. All because you *personalized* the process.

Earlier I said robbery can be the most volatile, unpredictable, and unnecessarily violent crime there is. Then I mentioned the human factor. There it is in a nutshell. Often that human factor is *you* and how you act.

Keep the monkey out of your dealings with resource predation.

unadulterated resource predation. While you're scrawling that part about you *not* being part of his tribe on the wall add: *Therefore, the rules of social violence don't apply to you.*

I tell you this because there is a strong link between tribalism and resource predation. Again, we're going to start at the extreme and work back. If you don't consider certain people as part of your tribe, you can *hunt* them. You can prey upon them. You can steal their resources, so they starve and die. And who cares? They're *not* one of yours. You can kill them without regret. And the only thing that does is bring glory to you and your tribe. You can enslave them. You can oppress them. They are lesser beings. You can use them. You can sacrifice them like pawns in a chess game . . . and you *will not* lose a night's sleep. If it is a member of a hated tribe, you can take sadistic glee from their setbacks and losses. Or you can actively work for that tribe's downfall and not only sleep well, but believe you're doing god's work by lies, sabotage, torture, and murder. (God's work even if it is in a secular cause.) Or you can ignore them, dismiss them and their plight, and profiteer from it. And again you will sleep *well* that night.

This is made possible by the process known as 'othering.' That is to say, you reduce anyone not in your tribe to being less than human.

Now comes an uncomfortable reality: We *all* do it. It's only a matter of degree.[202] If you live in a city, you are master of the subtle form of 'othering.' You pass thousands of people a day, who are just background color and noise. That wasn't a person you just cut off in traffic, it was a car. That's a cashier, not someone you want to maintain a relationship with. The trashmen are little more than nameless robots that come and pick up your garbage. If you consider yourself a corporate elite, those are accounts and workers, interchangeable numbers and parts.

About this time, your monkey might be rebelling. "No! I think of them as people." Nooooo, you think about them as people *when* you think about them as people. Usually, you don't think of them at all. If you do think of them, it's often in the form of a label. As in the jerk who cut you off. The twit who (insert annoying behavior here). Or you think of them as a role. The waitress, cashier, or cop (those are jobs, not people). At work, they're voices on the telephone more identifiable by address, phone, or account number than name. That's a customer. But mostly, humanity is a nameless, faceless background as you're going about your business—and they theirs. People *you* treat like moving lamp posts and obstacles as you move through an environment. People who return the favor by treating you in the same manner.

There is a stone cold survival reason why I keep nattering on about this subject. Your life depends on you to be able to recognize how *much* we unconsciously assume about human behavior. About our subconscious attitudes about the power and reliability of social scripts, and how *fast* we habitually revert to them—particularly when things go sideways. The predator is going to *turn* this against you.

A big part of this is how—when our subtle 'othering' of each other *doesn't* work—we default into *trying an established social response pattern.* Putting it bluntly, ignoring me hasn't worked, so you find an appropriate social micro-script to get what you want and go your way (including

---

202   When told about the universality of 'othering,' folks often respond, "I'm nice to people." While technically true, it's another case of availability bias (we remember the most recent events and assume that is the truth). Subconsciously, people usually mean those in my tribe. So yes, they have clear memories of always being nice to 'people.'

when what you want is me going away). I lie to you not, we do this tens, if not hundreds of times a day.

Think about this carefully. Much of our public behavior is based on avoiding having to deal with strangers—enough so that it's a mark of social status.[203] What social behavior do you default to when dealing with strangers? This incidentally is part of the reason we don't believe we subtly 'other' people to background color and noise status. We have availability bias of all the times we actually talk and deal with strangers … before moving on and never seeing them again.

The insidiousness of subtle 'othering' is it's a comfortable habit, one we aren't even consciously aware we're doing. It's what we *have* to do to get through the day.

At the same time, we accept this same behavior being done to us—within limits. We don't want to talk to that person passing us in the store—it's an attitude of leave me alone while you go about your business and I go about mine. 'Othering' also allows us to get through otherwise socially awkward situations. We're both stuck in this elevator for the next minute or so. I'm really comfortable with you pretending you don't see me as I pretend I don't see you. So we both stare intently at the floor indicator until one of us can get out of this cramped space. Guess what? *That's* a social script. In fact, it's become kind of the new 'manners.'

We accept this behavior until we become offended by it—usually when we consider it too extreme. We don't get upset by people in the elevator not making eye contact, but damn it that waiter has ignored me for five minutes! The irony of this is how often we become upset when people are not following the expected social scripts about 'othering.' We all understand and accept our comfort zones about 'othering'—and most of us tell comforting lies to ourselves about it. This is not a judgment; like I said, we *all* do it.

Where it becomes a problem is when it adds to our freaking out when we run into extreme 'othering.' Not knowing what to do destroys our calm, which is never a good thing when dealing with extreme situations. Like say, someone trying to mug you.

We claim we don't understand extreme 'othering.' How could an embezzler steal millions from people's retirement funds? How could management lie and then 'unexpectedly' lay off thousands of workers, destroying the economy of an area by shutting down a factory? How could that mugger stick a gun in our faces? How could a crackhead beat up an old lady for her social security money?

---

203   Jobs where one deals directly with the public are of lower social status than those where one deals with select individuals (waitresses, cashiers, police versus doctors, lawyers, account managers). Conversely, fame and status are given to those who entertain the masses—but who don't directly interact with them.

But on a monkey and a non-monkey level, we really do *understand*. Let's be honest, how much of your job relies on you 'othering' people— even if it's just beating out the competition for a bigger share of the market? Or processing as many people through as possible? Do you think the pilot of your flight wants to get to know you and everyone on the plane? Do you want to know him or the flight attendants? Just take my money and do your job. We even understand wide scale resource predation done on our fellow humans.[204]

It's when extreme 'othering' is directed at us that we freak out. It doesn't allow us to hide behind comfortable social conventions and lies. We are looking into the eyes of someone who doesn't consider us human, and it scares the hell out of us. And *that* is the biggest danger. This whole long, drawn-out explanation was *not* to point out what a hypocrite you are about 'othering" (we *all* do it). *It was to alert you to the danger of ignoring that you're doing it.*

Because, with subtle and polite 'othering,' we have a fall-back position. It's our back-up plan, our safety plan, an ace up our sleeves, a trump card if things don't work out. An escape pod we can use to keep things from going bad. And that is: *If 'othering' doesn't work if we're nice to him, he'll* **have** *to be nice to us.* We assume when we absolutely *have* to deal with this person, we can revert to superficial scripts, and an "okay, I'll treat you like a human until I can get what I want" behavior.

This point is *huge*. We rely on that safety net! Even if we absolutely loathe this person. If we engage in the correct social scripts, we can stay inside the confines and safety of social behavior. The underlying assumption is that we throw certain social signals out, and they'll respond a certain way. Is this realistic? Well 99 percent of the time, it *works*. But, recognize these assumptions work because of the *situation*. That person you despise at work? Keep it formal and polite to each other's faces and everyone will play the same game.

This safety net does not exist with asocial predators.

The assumption that there's a social script *he must* follow can get you killed when facing a resource predator—especially if you opt to resist. Because it works so well in our daily lives, we assume it also exists in extreme situations. We've seen enough TV where the hostage negotiator humanizes the victim or praises someone for humanizing herself to a predator. We know it works. If all else fails, we can connect with him and that will keep him from doing something we don't want him to do. Unfortunately, the way most people use this idea is like thinking that

---

204   Show me a genocide, initial invasion, or rebellion that—under the rhetoric, idealism, and propaganda—isn't about a land grab, controlling resources, or increasing these for one's tribe. While that may motivate the people on the front lines, these economics are very much part of it.

declaring bankruptcy will save them from a loan shark.

When we're confronted with extreme 'othering,' instead of shifting gears into resource protection, the common reaction is to try to select our responses according to the best possible social standard— including that safety net. A safety net that is normally our last ditch effort. In asocial situations, this puts you *behind* the power curve. We don't want to be rude to a stranger, so we allow the mugger to develop intent, interview, and positioning.

Folks, that civilized social safety net *isn't* there with extreme 'othering' and tribalism. Nor is it present in resource predation. But here is where the 'tacti-cool' and 'no rules in a street fight' crowd make a critical mistake. Their attitude is binary—it's either a social script or Armageddon. You're confronted by extreme 'othering' and resource predation? Time to whip out weapons and start blazing away (or slicing, kung fuing, yada, yada, yada).

No. Just because this isn't a social script is *not* to say there aren't protocols, behavior, rules, and negotiation. There are ways two members from different and hostile or predatory tribes behave toward one another. There are *in fact* numerous guidelines. These protocols are based on neither side wanting to start anything when the other side is armed, equally as tough, and as good a shot. And most importantly just as fast to shoot back. There are forms you *will* follow—unless you are looking to get shot in the face.

What *isn't* on the table is, "Well if I'm nice to him, he'll be obligated to be nice back to me."

What's even less effective is you trying to be a socially intimidating and aggressive monkey in hopes of cowing the mugger into submission. I'm dead serious when I tell people *they are not dealing with rude busboys*. In fact, it might help to think of him as a warrior from another tribe. And both of you have to decide whether or not to apply your craft—because this is a situation where both of you can die or be crippled if that ball starts rolling. Even if you can play for those stakes, intimidation isn't a good strategy against resource predators. There's no need to bluster, everyone knows death is on the table if things go sideways.

But the biggest high dive into an empty pool is when intimidating monkey behavior doesn't work and you want to be buds with the dude. No lie, I've seen it happen—it's a common tactic in low level conflicts. (The reason it's rare in high level stuff is because by the time the person realizes aggression isn't working, he or she is lying on the floor and bleeding). The people who are most likely to rely on "all I have to do to get out of this mess is to start singing kumbaya" are also the ones *least* likely to recognize how much they engage in 'othering' people. This especially applies to trying to use humanism as a way to wiggle out of bad situations. That *does not* work in these circumstances.

What works when dealing with a predatory, tribal mindset is the willingness to engage in resource protection. Your response needs to be based on the JAM and level of danger you're facing *not* some social ideal or script. You're *not* looking to take him out, but you won't hesitate if he tries to move against you. It's *not* to prove a point; it's *not* a threat; it is a fact.

Here's something to understand. For experienced robbers, stealing from you is not a statement. It's not social. It's not a challenge. It's not macho. It's not posturing. It's not to prove anything. And most of all, it's not about you personally. *It's a job.* It's a calculated and effective means to get something that can be put in a wheelbarrow. Again, you are nothing more to him than an ATM with legs. *Use that to your advantage!*

How? It doesn't matter which ATM he goes to. If you're too hard a target, he'll pick another, easier one—as long as you don't personalize it for him.

Also remember that resource predation uses the credible threat of a much higher level of violence than you'll find in social aggression. He's *not* there to psychologically or socially dominate you in the long term. It's about the immediate moment. The control is that physical failure to comply will result in injury if not your death. While muggings and robberies have their own scripts, goals, and unique tweaks on resource predation, this is *not* the time for your monkey's social agenda to pop up—especially territorialism. "You don't treat me this way" or "How dare you try to 'other' me! Do you know who I am?" Remember Richard Jeni's street fighting etiquette? It doesn't work in resource violence.

For the record, a social conflict between strangers can escalate up to a mugging as a final insult and punishment for daring to cross a person. But when dealing with a straight out resource predator I cannot stress enough how important it is to keep your monkey *out* of the equation. What most people think of as the 'cool and calm' of someone who is supposed to be a bad dude is simply the *absence* of the monkey.

I'm going to give you another set of reasons why you need to keep the monkey out of it. Starting with: The *biggest* tactical advantage the bad guy has *is* your monkey! Yes, I said the T-word again. But it's appropriate here. The most common tactic of asocial predators is to trigger your monkey so he can *turn it* against you. Yeah, tattoo and graffiti time.

Overall when it comes to violence between a lizard and a monkey the monkey loses. It is guaranteed to lose if it tries to fight the lizard like it would another monkey. Monkey violence has all kinds of subconscious rules, limits, and behavior we don't even realize we are following. For example, monkey violence tends to be face to face so the other monkey *knows* who beat him. That rule doesn't exist for the lizard. It has no problem striking from behind. Lizards don't fight fair, that's a monkey concept.[205]

So monkeys are easy prey. If he can trigger your monkey, he's *got* you. You will habitually and subconsciously do exactly the wrong things, starting with getting emotional and excited. The last thing a lizard wants is to go up against another lizard. But it won't hesitate to attack a scared, confused monkey. So the asocial predator is going to do everything in his power to trick you into your monkey. I'm going to give you a very easy image to remember. It's a particular Warner Brothers cartoon character, not stalking through the forest, but the city, saying, "Shhhhh! Be vewy, wewy quiet. I'm hunting monkeys. Huh-uh-uh-uh-uh-uh-uh-uh!"

Summing up everything I'm about to say in one concise concept: He's trying to push you into your monkey, so *you* need to be pushing yourself out of it. Turn that one into graffiti and a tattoo, as well. A refinement on the idea, resource predators use—and abuse—social scripts to *trigger* your monkey. This is how they hunt people. And it's why I have spent so much time talking about social behavior. You *have* to be able to tell a real one from a fake. The only way to do that is to know what the real ones look like.

Let's start with the criminal pretending they aren't hunting you as they approach. As I mentioned in the five stages, criminals very seldom *hide*. Most of the time, they walk right up to you. But they're *pretending* they're doing something else (like asking directions). It's appalling how many robberies are effective because they start out with the words, "Excuse me . . ." While part of you is screaming about the danger it's seeing, your monkey is saying, "He can't be a mugger, he's being polite." So you stand there and wait to see what he wants. He's turned your monkey and social scripts against you.

To the criminal, behaving like everything is innocent and normal (well at least normal-ish) before the attack serves many purposes:

- It doesn't spook the prey.
- It triggers a default social response and behavior *from* the prey.
- This response *reduces* the prey's ability to effectively physically resist.
- It triggers a sense of confusion and uncertainty in the prey (hesitation to act).
- Because the prey doesn't know what to do, usually he or she does

---

205   At the same time, "there are no rules in a street fight" is very much a monkey interpretation of what it thinks are lizard rules. There are rules of engagement in that kind of violence, including the knowledge that if it goes down it's going to be on this level of fecal matter.

nothing.

- It allows the predator to develop the conditions to control the situation (set up the attack).
- It is a litmus test—if something goes wrong with the interview and set-up process (e.g., the victim starts turning into a werewolf) it allows the criminal to *withdraw under the safety of social scripts.*

I want to look at "ability to effectively physically resist" for a second. When I say there are problems with effectively resisting, people often think I'm talking about physical ability, I'm not. I'm talking about *mindset.* Think of two cities in opposite directions, but equal distance from where you are now. Let's say one represents social violence, the other asocial violence. If you had to get up and go straight to either in a certain amount of time, you could do it. The mindset issue is that the criminal is deliberately trying to send you to the wrong city first. Once you realize the mistake, you have to turn around and try to get to the other city. All in the original time frame. Not going to happen is it? The issue is not that you can't get to resource protection city in time. If you head straight there, you *can.* It's that you won't make it if you have been tricked into wasting time by going to the wrong city.

That is why shifting into the right mindset is so important. How do you know what's the right mindset? Like I said, start by knowing what normal is. Unless you're a cashier, strange people don't normally walk up and talk to you.

Then take the monkey out of it. If something abnormal is happening don't assess the situation by monkey standards. While it *could* be innocent monkey issues by looking for JAM and the five stages, you'll see when it isn't innocent. Nor is what is going on what it appears to be. See if this was innocent, he wouldn't be leaking intent and trying to set up attack positioning . . .

The ability to articulate this intentional social trigger and deception is a counter for the Doubting Thomas response of, "Well, it looked innocent to me." Yes, of course it looked innocent. That's the *point!* Looking innocent is part of the intentional deception to set up the attack. But look what happened next …

The second tactical advantage criminals have is most people don't know what being set up for an asocial attack looks like. To explain what I mean I want to go back to the violence is a road analogy. Asocial violence is the *other* road of violence. Social violence is the main highway, and many know it. Changing it slightly, it would look like 1, 2, 3, 4, 5, 6, 7, 8, 9, 10 . . . The numbers are a normal social script.

Most people don't know what the alternate asocial route looks like. Not knowing that, they don't recognize the unique danger signs of being set up. If anything they might interpret what they're seeing as something that looks like 1, 2, 3, 5, 4, 6, 8, 7, 9, 8, *10, 10, 11, 12* . . . Wrong and out of sequence, but not dangerous. It's all still numbers, though.

You know the five stages and JAM. Remember that these are conditions that form a *unique* combination. While the elements are themselves not uncommon, the *combination* appears nowhere else except when you are about to be attacked. These key points will be embedded in whatever floor show put on by the criminal, but they *will* be there. If you know what to look for they will be out of place and very recognizable. Here's a visual of the idea: 1, 2, 3, A, 4, 5, 6, B, 7, 8, 9, C, 10, 11, 12 . . .

Steps A, B, and C are what the criminal needs to rob or attack you (first three of five stages). By embedding them in what should be a normal social process, he can develop what he needs to attack without scaring you off or—worse for him—you mentally shifting gears into resource protection mode. While the asocial road initially looks social—and by this I mean it often doesn't even look like violence at all—there are some very specific signs and intentionally distorted mile markers.

First, the set-up for this kind of violence is relatively slow. Yet, the attack is blindingly fast. Think of those nature shows where a fish is swimming by a rock and all of sudden a camouflaged fish lunges out of a crevice. Same idea. Yes, the attack *is* fast. But the predator developing that camouflage, finding the crack, and embedding itself took time. And because of the time spent in set up, *it's going to be effective.*

Second, forget all the bullshit and tacti-kool, quick draw, fantasy operator camps and blazing-kung-fu-mastery-when-ambushed training. If you are lulled into a monkey script and then bushwhacked, your chances of successfully resisting are slim to none. This is why it is critical to be able to spot the slow build up of greater danger.

But here's where it gets difficult to explain. It's hurrying slowly. Do you remember me talking about how someone speeding through the lower levels of social violence is something to articulate when use of force is required? Going back to the idea of embedding the set-up inside a social script, I originally showed this: 1, 2, 3, A, 4, 5, 6, B, 7, 8, 9, C, 10, 11, 12. I wrote it out that way so it's easy to see.

But now I'm going to mix in the false markers of the asocial road and speed things up:

123A456B789C10D.

Now, I'm going to speed it up even more: 12A56B78CD. Confusing isn't it? Well that's the plan. See, a common strategy for the predator is to act out a social script *very* fast. This is like speeding through low miles. It creates confusion and hides what he's doing.

Except if you know that when something happens too fast something is wrong, it's easier to spot the anomalies. In which case it looks like this: 12A56B789 . . . *Oh hell no!* We are *not* getting to C much less D.

Putting this into a functional example: As I've mentioned in the five stages and JAM, one of the most common mugger tricks is to politely ask about something as a distraction while closing in to attack range/positioning. When you see a polite request combined with him moving in *too close*, the social scripts take a back seat. His developing what he needs to attack becomes the main point. For the moment let's call coming too close B. (A means something is slightly off about his body language.)

When you shift out of the monkey, someone closing when they have no reason starts looking like this:

$$12A_{56}B_{78}\ldots$$

When you see that it is appropriate to say, "Don't you take another step, mister. If you do, it'll be the last C you ever see."

The trick to that strategy is to mean it. This isn't social. Yes, you're communicating, but what you're communicating is that you're both operating under asocial conditions. If this ball starts rolling, it's going to be a two way shooting range.

Remember I said fake scripts are easy to spot when you know what to look for? There it is. But also notice the dwindling importance of social numbers as asocial letters present themselves. Let's go deeper into this. Again, I re-stress that in order to recognize when something isn't normal, you first have to know what *is* normal.

Here's a nuts-and-bolts example. Depending on the circumstances, we normally allow between three to ten feet between strangers. In theory, we try to give each other as much room as possible. But in practice this distance is kind of like a rubber band, it stretches and contracts. It changes if we're in a line, a crowded elevator, bus, or other confined space. For example, standing in line, three feet; passing someone in a parking lot, ten is normal. And we subconsciously know the rules for the environment we're in.

A common interview technique for a robber or attacker is to start out by asking you for something. This is no big deal by itself. Strangers do approach us and ask—if not all the time, then enough that it's not uncommon. But if you stop and think about it, there are all kinds of rules and expected behavior. For someone to get information from you, they have *no* reason to approach closer than seven feet. Given certain circumstances, it can be ten to twenty (say, for instance, in a dark parking lot at night). We *know* not to approach strangers too closely when we are asking for information. Why? Because we are asking a favor, we don't want to make the person uncomfortable and uncooperative. That's normal and how a legitimate script works.

Conversely, to physically transfer something to someone we need to be within *six* feet.

Get your graffiti kit out on that one. I'm not talking mugging, yet. I'm still talking about normal legitimate scripts. Depending on how well we know the person or the size of the item determines proximity. Think how close you are when you hand money to a cashier or when a waitress hands you your meal. That is the range for transferring items between strangers. Now think about taking a shower with your spouse or significant other and handing over the shampoo. Much closer.

A complete stranger—who is asking you for directions—does *not* need to move into item transfer much less shower range. But this is the range a resource predator *needs* to move into in order to control your options. Moving into range is an integral part of ABC, so he can commit D. So while a stranger asking you for something is reason to mentally shift gears, his moving into transfer—much less shower—range should kick you into overdrive. Now his *hurrying slowly* becomes important. It isn't that he's running at you, per se. He's rushing through the social scripts and moving in way too close, too *soon*. Sorry, pal, but I gotta know you a whole lot better before I let you into shower range. You certainly don't need to be close enough to wash my back for me to tell you where Fifth Street is.

Back in the day when smoking was the norm, asking for a light was a common strategy for a mugger to use to move into attack range. If you still smoke be aware of this. Carrying a disposable pack of matches you can toss to someone is a good way to take away their excuse to close. (It's also a great cover for your other hand moving into proximity of your weapon.)

As an example of the more things change, the more they remain the same—a new strategy is for the criminal to pretend to text while he walks up on you. It's not that he's coming straight at you, he's looking at his phone. His approach and violation of the social norms of distance appear to be from distraction. But if you watch closely, you will see him looking up and targeting you as he adjusts his course to intercept you (silent, closing). Where a lot of people fall into monkey mode is they root to the spot and try to communicate. Thereby letting him approach.

Restating, unless you're in very specialized circumstances—like a crowded elevator or rush hour public transport—strangers have *no* business getting close to you. So someone trying to do that is a signal that something is off. How far off? . . . well . . . that depends. Oddly enough, the same goes for someone trying to get too close even in areas where crowding *is* common. For example, a common silent interview technique is to stand too close to someone in an otherwise empty elevator or while waiting for one. The criminal is looking to see how you'll react by doing a silent interview and closing.

Let me give you another example of accelerated social scripts as a sign there's something off. Although not necessarily related to crime, it is not uncommon with nonviolent crime strategies. You meet someone who wants to become your BFF (best friend forever) in a very short time. By this I mean, yeah, you like that person, but it all happens just a little too fast.

Odd thing is such a person often has all kinds of stories of people they know, but somehow those people aren't around to confirm this. Or confirm or deny the stories the person tells. There's especially nobody around to warn you about that person's dark side.

Keep such a person at arm's length. Friendships take years to grow and mature. People who screw other people over *don't* have long-term friends. They try to accelerate the friendship script so they can get close enough to screw over their new friends, too. While this is a more general warning about toxic people, con men and grifters use this strategy.[206] I also highly recommend Albert Bernstein's *Emotional Vampires: Dealing with People Who Drain You Dry* for more professional knowledge put into useful layman's terms.[207] I recommend you read this book for its detailed break down of common troublemaker tactics.

Criminals often use social acceleration to create surprise and confusion in people who don't recognize the significance of the asocial highway signs. Things are happening too fast for the monkey to figure out what's wrong. At the same time, they can't come in too fast or they'll spook their prey into running. So keep an eye out for speeding slowly. It's hard to describe, but once you start looking, you can see it. (You can get a small taste of it watching salesmen.)

Things kick into action stations when and if you've set a boundary using social scripts (e.g., "That's close enough. What can I do for you?")

206   Robert Ringer wrote a business book, *Winning Through Intimidation* (1973) where he identified three types of people who will screw you in business. 1) The guy who plans to take all he can and tells you. 2) The guy who plans to screw you and tells you he's not. 3) The guy who didn't mean to screw you, but something happened and he had no choice. It's been my experience they all have a core tactic in common. They set up the ability to cheat you way before it happens. Generally, this is by removing the safety checks common in business (often by saying they're unnecessary or too expensive). These are legitimate business men stacking the deck their way. Grifters and hustlers do pretty much the same thing, convincing you that you don't need normal safety protocols or you have to hurry lest the deal falls through (e.g., come up with a lot of cash right now). Again, that rush through and breaking of normal protocol patterns is something you need to watch out for.

207   Berstein does the personality disorder section of the *DSM IV* (*Diagnostic and Statistical Manual of Mental Disorders*, Fourth Edition) with the added benefit of showing you how to set boundaries with these types of people.

and he keeps coming *at* you. On your one to ten JAM scale that's an automatic plus-four, and it is time to start preparing for an attack. The monkey gets kicked out of the driver's seat and the lizard takes over. Your lizard has no problem committing resource protection violence (and your body language will reflect that). Again, you need to know what normal social behavior is so you can recognize asocial predation. When you tell a normal person to stop, they will stop and look at you in confusion. Or they step wide of you with a "what the hell is the matter with you" look on their faces. Or they hang back and become verbally abusive until they walk wide of you or you withdraw. If instead of that, you get a narrowing of the eyes and him accelerating. That's a problem, like he's developing a JAM to ten predicament.

Again it is not uncommon for someone to call you a jerk as they are walking wide and passing you. (Keen observation there, Sherlock.) But going back to hunting humans using social scripts, someone trying some variation of the 'why are you being so unfriendly' query while *still* closing is *not* kosher. He's still closing the distance and while guilt-tripping you he's developing attack range and positioning.

The third tactical advantage a resource predator has over most people is their monkeys' insecurities and doubts especially when he isn't overtly doing anything to trigger the other parts of their brains. Parts that don't like what they see and *could* come up with effective responses to the developing danger, but are being told, "Hush, this is just a guy who is _____ (fill in the blank)" by your monkey. That's why you need to be able to *recognize* the ABC road signs. Once you know how to spot them, they are as obvious and as easy to read as the real ones. If that mile marker reads B . . . we ain't going down this road no more. When the monkey says, "Hush," another part can step up and say, "No monkey, you shut up. It looks social, but something isn't right here." Until the situation actually can be determined, the monkey *doesn't* get to drive.

In resource predation, you can do this because you have stable data that the exact situation *isn't* what is being presented. Remember I mentioned intentional deception can be used to handle Doubting Thomas? Well, that starts with you. I tell people, "The Five Stages of Violent Crime are an external checklist you can use to overcome internal doubt. It's useful for shutting up the voice that whispers in your mind's ear, 'What if I'm wrong?' (This is another source of freezing, waiting too late before reacting, and reacting ineffectively.) That checklist is of known behavior, JAM, and what it looks like when someone is setting you up."

As a kind of playbook to help you, imagine me handing my monkey a checklist and saying, "Check 'em off as I call 'em." The monkey has the pen. "Intent? Check. Weapon check? Check. Witness check? Check.

Commencing interview? Check . . . ." The more boxes that get checked, the closer I am to flipping my werewolf switch. He's not going to be the only one at nine on the JAM scale.

At the same time, the part of me that has accepted that resource protection violence might become necessary is actively taking steps to keep him from developing ABC. If he tries to move into attack position, my lizard has no problem stepping out of that spot. He needs B to attack safely? *He's not going to get it.*

The biggest thing I'm doing is trying to fail the interview, often by using the monkey's scripts back against him. He tries to move too close? I move away and set a verbal, "That's close enough, now what do you want?" boundary. He can't come closer without:

a) Blowing the pretense of social normalcy

b) Tipping his hand

Those aren't particularly good ideas when there's a werewolf waiting for him to act. A werewolf who knows what he is, the game he's playing, and most of all has 'othered' him right back. A werewolf that's smiling at him and saying, "What do you say we pretend this isn't what it is so we both can walk out of it alive?"

Also as an aside, I'm a big fan of calmly taking away social control of the situation from the criminal. In doing so, you're being just as monkey fake as he is and—if he's smart—he'll figure out pretty damn quick that you're playing the same game he is. You're pretending everything is all nice and social when you're ready to shoot him in the face. (I will tell you, some of these clowns take a few seconds to catch on. So you might have to wrangle the situation for a bit while keeping him from developing his attack range.)

The fourth tactical advantage the resource predator has is what most people think they know about the way violence happens. The highway of social violence has totally different priorities and standards than what you need on the asocial road. Like I said, "You will not see the same signs. That *doesn't* mean the situation isn't *dangerous.* In fact, the actual physical danger is much higher."

For example, thinking someone has to be emotional in order to attack is a common element in social violence. Anger is the most common emotion believed to be an indicator. But extreme fear is another emotion that we associate with violence. We look for these as a sign of potential aggression. While anger *is* a legitimate monkey danger signal, it is *not* a common asocial indicator of aggression. But it's what most people know to look for. So if they don't see it . . . ? Why, there must not be any danger of course.

Presentation of false social scripts and lack of emotional danger signs confuse the victim's monkey. Not only do they see a seemingly innocent script, but there is no anger. It doesn't even look close to violence and danger. Like I said, it's amazing how many muggings start with the words, "Excuse me." He's being polite. Dangerous criminals aren't polite. So he must not be a dangerous criminal. At least that's what we tell ourselves before something happens. It's not that people don't know something is wrong with the situation, they just *don't* know what. The most obvious stimuli they are getting say that this is a social script. Often the prey becomes functionally blind to the developing danger because the monkey won't let the person acknowledge or see the subtle signs . . . because there aren't any big and overt signs, signals so big that an ordinary monkey can't dismiss, rationalize, or blow them off.

Gavin DeBecker made his fortune calling this *The Gift of Fear*. While I have serious issues with DeBecker's proposed solutions, his assessment of tactics used by bad guys is a worthwhile read. It's an excellent layman's introduction to predatory tactics that are well known to professionals. But more importantly, it's a good break down of how we fool ourselves into ignoring danger. Right now let me give you the short form. It is a saying to give yourself permission to keep from walking into the lion's jaws and also a way to keep from freezing as the lion strolls up to you while pretending to be something else. It's a simple little sentence: I don't know what's *wrong*, but I know something isn't *right*.

(Get your graffiti and tattoo kits out. That's a motto worth remembering.)

Ordinarily the monkey needs good reasons before it relinquishes control of your behavior and thoughts. It has to have a solid, justifiable reason before it will allow another part of the brain to take over. Just knowing something isn't right is normally not a good enough reason. Damn it, you're a smart, intelligent, competent, and assured person! You're not going to fall for any such foolishness. Because what would people think if you were rude . . . or showed you were scared . . . or . . .

Excuse me, but does anyone else see the monkey hijacking the human to justify doing what the monkey deems important? Here's the problem with that: By the time the monkey is convinced there's a good reason to relinquish control, it's too *late*. You're looking down the barrel of a gun. Allowing that you don't know what's wrong, but you know something isn't right gives you permission to shift gears. To pause in what you're doing, to pay attention to what is happening in front of you, and most importantly to take steps to keep a trap from being developed. But more than that, it starts you looking for what is *wrong* with the situation.

First, that changes the timing of the whole situation—up to and including while I'm trying to figure this out, I either have my hand on my weapon or am giving myself permission to prepare for trouble. Second, "I don't know what's wrong, but . . ." is the kind of scrutiny a predator *does not* want. It takes away his element of surprise and increases the danger to him. Third, it helps you identify—and later articulate—what was wrong with the situation. Instead of your monkey getting in the way of you acting, it's participating in your defense by looking for and articulating what it's good at seeing. If everything turns out kosher—fine and dandy. You step back when someone tries to get too close, tell him that's close enough, and the worst that happens is you get a weird look. No problem, no foul. Now he knows where Fifth Street is and everybody is happy. Today is a good day.

But there is another kind of 'nothing happened.' Turning your attention on something until you know what it is—in and of itself—is a big deterrent. If you are subtly but actively jamming his attempts to develop ABC—and at the same time preparing for resource protection violence— he's going to abort the mission. The odds of his breaking off are even greater if you shift gears and quietly take control of the situation without being a confrontational jerk. This isn't a monkey howling that it's a tiger. It's one form of asocial violence looking at another—while both pretend what's going on is socially innocent. (Oh, did I forget to mention you can play this game, too?) I've mentioned setting a verbal boundary ("that's close enough") and then asking him what he wants. I like this strategy for several reasons.

First, it disrupts his plans. It shows you're willing to step up, all the while pretending everything is sweetness and light. Except instead of his controlling the questioning, you're now asking *him*. Second, it's a chance for him to reassess the situation—the whole werewolf looking directly at him . . . Third, it's articulable. You set a verbal boundary and in a non-confrontational manner asked him what he wanted. If he continues to close the distance into attack range (or becomes aggressive before doing so) that is both jeopardy and developing means. Fourth, it's a safety issue. If he goes for his weapon right then and there, you have time and space to move and act, if he charges, same thing. Fifth, it gives him a face-saving exit. He can abort what he's doing, come up with some BS line and simply walk away.

Oh, by the way, remember I mentioned you're just an ATM to him? Here's a news flash, it's equally impersonal with you! Yeah, he just tried to interview you for a robbery. You failed the interview. When he walks away, it's over. *No* hard feelings. No reason to get excited. No need to beat your chest and yell profanities after him. It's all part of life in the big city.

I'm going to use a story by Kathy Jackson, author of *The Cornered Cat*, to exemplify the things I have been saying. Well, except for the part about asking, "Can I help you?" to throw him off his game. But what she did aborted the process:

——

Close Encounter of the Criminal Kind

Here's an example of how awareness and willingness to act can work together in real life. Several years ago, circumstances forced me to the grocery store, alone, in the middle of the night. Late night isn't my preferred time to hit the store, but we'd had some car trouble, and my husband had been out of town with our only working vehicle for over a week. He arrived home very late and was leaving again early the next morning, and I needed to get supplies before he left again. So it was past midnight when I walked out of the store pushing a full cart of groceries.

As I left the store, I noticed how beautiful the evening was with bright stars overhead and a refreshing breeze coming off the field next to the store. I heard the sound of traffic moving past on the freeway, and the laughter of one of the clerks as she joked with one of her co-workers. Because I was paying attention, I also noticed that two men followed me out of the store.

The men weren't particularly scary-looking. They were young adults, dressed in the casual way young guys dress: Jeans, hooded sweat shirts, tennis shoes. Nothing unusual. What was unusual was the way they split up when they left the building. One of them darted around the side of the building farthest from me, while the other sauntered slowly along the storefront as I walked to my car.

Because of their somewhat unusual movement pattern, my attention focused on these young men as a possible source of danger. In this heightened state of alertness, I had spotted a specific concern and was prepared to act on that concern if need be. I debated going back into the store, but the sauntering man was between me and the entrance, so I judged it smarter to go straight to my car. As I did so, the sauntering man lit up a cigarette. Staying about fifty feet away from me, he paralleled my movement, slowly moving the same general direction I was moving. After a moment, the other man came from behind the corner and walked very briskly away from the building down the main row of cars, two or three aisles over from where my own car was parked. At this point, I thought perhaps the sauntering man was simply taking a smoke break, while the other man was headed to his own car in the main part of the lot.

Everything changed when I reached my own vehicle. As I unlocked my car and began rapidly throwing the groceries into the back seat, the sauntering man casually threw down his cigarette—the one he had just lit. At the same time, the man who had walked out into the lot abruptly changed direction and began moving very rapidly toward my car. The sauntering man also turned and began slowly moving straight toward me. Picture these men closing two sides of a triangle, approaching me from opposite directions at an angle. They were moving different speeds, but would arrive at my vehicle around the same time.

Still in the same state of alertness—willing to act, aware of a specific danger—I slammed the back door of the car and kept the grocery cart in front of me as a physical barrier. I stood up straight and looked directly at the sauntering man, then at the other man who was rapidly closing the distance between us. That was all I did: Stand up straight and look directly at each of these men. As I did so, I was acutely aware of the concealed handgun I wear on my belt. Although I made no movement toward my firearm and did not put my hand on it, as I looked at the men I was thinking about what I might need to do next if my suspicions were confirmed. I had mentally chosen a "line in the sand," an imaginary spot between us that would trigger my decision to draw if they did not stop when I told them to stay away from me. But I kept my hands clear, and I didn't say anything. I just looked at them.

The sauntering man met my eyes. He saw how I stood, the expression on my face, and how I had positioned myself. Then he looked over at his companion, jerked his head with a no movement, and turned abruptly away. The other man nodded, and also turned away. Just like that, it was over.

The two men walked back to the store together without a backward glance. I got in my car and drove away. A mile later, I had to pull over because my hands were shaking, but that passed quickly enough and I drove home without any other excitement.

When I got home, I told the story to my husband. I was still shaken up and a little confused about what had just happened, and couldn't figure out why they'd backed off. "After all," I told him, "all I did was *look* at them."

Husband asked, "Well, okay, but what were you thinking when you looked at them?"

"Backstops."

———

In case you missed the reference, Jackson's answer applies to the solid cement block construction of the store behind one man and the empty parking lot behind the other. Important considerations when you're thinking about sending bullets at problems. (Remember, every bullet comes with a little lawyer attached.)

I also want remind you of the Lawrence Kane quote: *The difference between an amateur and a professional is to the amateur, the event is the big deal. To the pro, it's the before and after.* By thinking of backstops, her nonverbal leakage wasn't monkey. It was someone in resource protection mode. More than that, we're talking thinking along pro lines here not as the muggers had hoped a freaked-out monkey. But that's not why I used this story. I did so for five reasons.

First, remember when I said the willingness to use violence usually means you won't have to? While she didn't exactly turn into a werewolf, someone thinking about backstops as a response to your asocial behavior is not going to have a problem shooting you. That kind of leaked out—not because she's some kind of uber bad, tough chick, but because it's where her head was. That is what convinced the professional criminals to abort.

The second reason goes back to the purposes of fake social scripts, specifically they are *litmus tests*—if something goes wrong with the process they allow criminals to safely withdraw under the cover of social scripts (face-saving exits). The same 'nobody here but us chickens' approach they used while trying to set things up also served as a 'there's no need to shoot us, we're just going on our way.' By pretending that they were innocent people doing something else, they used the same cover to safely withdraw. The image of innocence worked to help them *set up* the attack. It also worked to cover their escape when their set-up failed. They were relying on Jackson to follow the social rules about not shooting people unless there was a good reason. In that regard, they were relying on her socially conscious monkey not to shoot them as they got the hell out of there.

The third reason is articulation. Officially, nothing happened in that story. Yet Jackson did a good job ticking off the elements of the situation that showed something was indeed happening. Still, a Doubting Thomas could argue it's all made up and nothing really was going on. Thomas can—and will—insist it was all in her head. The sad thing is that Ol' Tommy would have been mugged that night. But he (or she) *doesn't* believe that. Doubting Thomas only believes in things that fit in his (or her) agenda. In some cases, Thomas will never change his mind no matter what the evidence. He is so convinced he knew what was really happening in a situation, he will preach it with the conviction of a fundamentalist pastor. The good news is Jackson's situation didn't progress, so Tommy's opinion doesn't mean much.

But let's say that things had progressed to where she had to use the backstop. All of a sudden, Doubting Thomas is a lot more problematic. The biggest and most dangerous Doubting Thomas is the *prosecutor*. His 'nothing really was happening' attitude is tied into his certainty that you just went berserk and started shooting. The logical fallacy of personal incredulity[208] is a common strategy to get you arrested or convicted. It can be presented as a pulpit-thumping-gospel-preaching revival meeting act. Or the act can be from a position of a calm, intelligent professional, who knows how things really work. He will contend that you're making things up to avoid punishment for your bad (even criminal) behavior. In any variation, it's an *act*, but a very convincing one. Either version is based on the false belief that confidence equals truth. The holy-roller prosecutor pretends he knows what happened in the situation (despite not being there) and denounces you for lying. Or you can find the knowledgeable professional, who knows how violence really works, and states with firm conviction that you either didn't see what you testified you saw or you overreacted. When someone tries to tell you "that wasn't happening," (or sell that to the jury) *don't* try to disprove a negative. Instead, acknowledge the social scripts and add how criminals abuse them. Yes, the reason it looks as if nothing happened is because the criminal works at *making* it look that way.

One of the really cool things about the road of violence analogy—especially when it comes to asocial violence—is the idea of off ramps. The attacker has the ability to abort the process. Nothing happens because the guy saw something he didn't like and got off the highway. *Yay* for not having to do paperwork! On one hand, this is what gives Doubting Thomas his legs. Nothing happened. But the reason for that was the douche took an off ramp.

Flipping this over, let's say you end up explaining yourself to some unhappy people. Those off ramps still apply. Yes, I know he was pretending nothing was happening. But if nothing was happening, then he would have done *that* when I did *this*. He would have done this, when I did that. He did neither, he kept on coming.

Remember: 12A56B8C!

Thomas can doubt all he wants, but given this behavior, it is reasonable to believe D was being initiated.

The fourth, reason I wanted to relate this story concerns knowing when to stop. Remember that weird rambling thing I did about commitment? About stopping or not acting when you see commitment fade? This story? Primo example. Because she was looking, she saw not just the commitment fade, but the communication break off. And yes, surprise, surprise, criminals working together *do* a lot of nonverbal communication with each other. If you're looking for it, it's easy to see.

---

208   Personal incredulity is a logical fallacy where because you don't know something, understand something, or know how it works, you make it out to be false. Investigators and prosecutors do this all the time (e.g., "I find it hard to believe that . . ."). Don't fall for this. Personal incredulity is a logical fallacy, not a question.

Get the spray paint and tattoo kit out again. You have to be looking as *hard* for 'no go' signals as you are for 'go' signals. In time, seeing the signs of commitment is as easy as seeing the turn signal of a cop interrogating you. When you see them stand down, you *stand down.* Even better, do what she did and get the hell out of there.

The fifth reason I told you this story was to help you reframe winning. As in, if the dude(s) walks away as the outcome of the criminal interview, it's time to do a happy dance. Well, okay, dance when you get home after not having to kill someone.

I'm going to have to take what I consider to be a screwed up side trip here. You have no idea how often I—and any instructor who teaches tactical avoidance and the legal aspects of self-defense—am hit with, "Are you telling us to be wimps?" And, "Are you telling us to just roll over and give up?"

There apparently are too many people who are bound and determined to use their self-defense training on a bad guy. Unless they get to go in a flurry of martial arts badassery or a blazing shoot-out in the streets, they just don't chalk it up as a win. Not true.

Getting home to tell your spouse about the crime that *didn't* happen while you were getting groceries *is* a win. You aren't rushing to an extreme to use your training. Your training is first and foremost about developing the skills you need to have a chance in case things go that far. It *doesn't* mean you will be able to function in the extreme, but it increases your chances.

I also mentioned that only half of the people who get involved in violence 'win.' Knowing there's only a chance of success makes getting off the road before it escalates to a physical level the real win. A win of dancing around chanting, "Oh yeah, oh yeah, I didn't have to do paperwork. Oh yeah!" What training also can be a means to develop is the attribute to stay calm when you find yourself on the highway. Staying composed is critical in order to successfully use the off ramps. So in and of itself, training is useful—if you use it this way.

CHAPTER 19

Now that we know they're dangerous, they're not so fucking dangerous.

—Joel Rosenberg
Emile and the Dutchman

Asocial Violence: Process Predator

The process predator. The monster under the bed. The bogeyman in the closet. The movie psychopath. The serial killer lurking in the shadows. The serial rapist preying on your daughters. The guy who gets off on hurting people. The terror people in self-defense *train* to handle.

And most wouldn't know one if he bit them on their collective butts. Hell, arguably you have seen them and never known it. You might have sat next to one in a restaurant. You might have had one deliver a pizza to your home. You might have worked with one. Here's the thing about monsters, they aren't monsters until they act out. They don't wear signs or hand out event programs telling you who their next victim will be and when. And they're always in human form. But most of all, they're actually pretty rare especially when it comes to the extreme cases.

Having said that, there are environments where they tend to be more concentrated—prisons, forensic mental hospitals, juvenile detention centers, and the shadier parts of town. The latter not because poverty breeds them as much as they're often so messed up they find it impossible to function in the nicer parts of town. Still others are so specialized in their predation that they can fake it and function in normal society. You will *never* see them in their monster stage, unless:

a) You fit their target profile;

b) They can set up the circumstances.

Lacking those? No. This behavior and aspect of their personality simply *doesn't* manifest around you or others. In fact, when you hear about them you may actively deny it could be the person you know. I know of a powerful political player who had had the serial killer Ted Bundy attend several political dinners in his home. When Bundy was arrested, this person's response was a flat-out, "He didn't do it." This person refused to believe a nice, promising, politically active, young law student could be a serial killer. The basis of this opinion is that the player had never seen that aspect of his personality.[209]

Someone once said that we all have three lives: Public, personal, and secret. Ordinarily that translates into what you do at work and with friends, things you do in the privacy of your home, and the kind of porn you're into. Very few people see your private, much less secret, life. When I say privacy of your home, those with prurient interests immediately jump to thoughts of sex, but mostly what we do in privacy is watch TV, go to the bathroom, and raid the refrigerator while we wear fuzzy bunny slippers. To further torpedo the excitement, most people's secret lives are . . . well . . . pretty vanilla. Gee, two people screwing, good for you. Some people do engage in some kinky stuff in their secret lives. But, hey, as long as it's between consenting adults, whatever gets you through the night . . .

With monsters, however, their secret lives are nightmares. Horrendous dreams they want to visit on a select few. But like the time you spend whacking off, that amount of secret time makes up a *very* small portion of a monster's overall activities. I told you all this to show you exactly how little danger these big bogeymen (of our imaginations) actually represent. Do they exist? Yes. If you live a normal lifestyle and aren't doing stupid stuff are you likely to run into them? Not only no, but hell no. You usually you have to go well out of your way to run into monsters.

Sticking with this idea, if you're like twenty-seven-year-old Mia Zapata (lead singer of the Seattle band, *The Gits*) and decide to walk home alone at 2 a.m. from a bar while wearing head phones in a bad part of town— those actions increase your chances. I use Zapata as an example for three reasons. First, because she is the classic idealized victim— scooped up, kidnapped, tortured, raped, and murdered by a complete stranger.

Second, was she specifically the target? Probably not. The man convicted of her killing had an arrest record of violence against women, including rape, and other violent crimes. Evidence suggests she was in the wrong place at the wrong time, was the right size, and was sending the right body language messages. It was like the swirling chaos of a shark attack while swimming in the ocean at night. What happened to Zapata is what happens when:

a) You're the right kind of prey when a particular predator is in the area;

b) The predator is in the mood;

c) It's safe for it to attack.

---

[209]   That's an extreme case of a common human dynamic. We often judge people by the actions we see them display, failing to realize we don't see the rest of their behavior. The classic example is the middle manager who caters to the upper bosses and then turns around and is a tyrant to those under him or her. Big Boss never sees this aspect of the sycophant's behavior.

Had she exhibited the same behavior tens, if not hundreds, of times before? Probably. She'd just never had done it with those three conditions in place. She died when they came together.

The third reason I used Zapata as an example is because I can pretty well guarantee she'd both self-certified herself as capable of being able to take care of herself and was probably in the hermit crab mindset.[210] While you *don't* have to be at uber-tactical-battle-readiness not having the correct mindset in certain circumstances is an enticement to catastrophe. Like . . . oh, say . . . wearing head phones while walking alone through the night in the urban jungle—or to update things, walking and texting in the same environment.

But mostly, her murder was a result of her refusal to be armed and yet insisting on walking alone at 2 a.m. in a rotten part of town. You don't have to go armed, but if you chose not to do yourself a favor and be asleep in bed at 2 a.m. It's not that the night is dangerous, but some of the things in it *are*. That is a subtle but important point. It's *not* the environment that is dangerous, it's the menaces in that environment . . .

Let's add the chapter quote to that. That idea kept me alive on more occasions than I like to count. You *can* move safely through environments where danger exists—*if* you *know* what danger looks like. By that, I don't mean assume a person's appearance will always indicate his potential conduct, but know what dangerous behavior looks like (jeopardy). Know how predators operate and what they need to be successful. Most of all be willing to change your mindset and behavior—not just in the presence of danger—but when it's a block away and trying to walk up to you. The farther out you spot peril trying to get close to you, the *more* nonviolent options you have. As I often tell people: "It's hard to get raped, robbed, murdered, or beaten if you're not there."

The hermit crab mindset is the biggest impediment to the ability to spot a predator approaching you. Too many people—especially in these days of portable electronics—slide off into their own private Idahos when they're in situations where the predators are prone to lurk. They're so fixated on what they're doing that they don't pay attention to what is happening. This can be a fatal mistake.

Odds are good the man who beat, raped, and strangled Mia Zapata spotted her long before she saw him. Why? Because she wasn't paying

---

210   Hermit Crab: Bringing their attitudes, behavior, and expectations into dangerously different circumstances. What differentiates the Hermit Crab mentality from the Disneyland State of Mind is fun, excitement, and the chance to misbehave. Both assume safety. Both assume that whatever the person's subjective standards may be, they apply anywhere they go. While people with the Disneyland mindset will actively do things that are dangerous, wrong, and often illegal, usually the Hermit Crab is less aggressive. A Disney bedazzled person will go slumming to a biker or dive bar, get drunk, high, misbehave, and become quarrelsome when he's told to knock it off. A Hermit Crab will think it's her right to walk home in safety—and that right will keep her safe . . .

attention to what was in the night with her. Somehow, he got close enough to rape and kill her. If the reports of her wearing headphones are correct, it probably wasn't that difficult. It's almost certain she died not because the nights are dangerous, but because she assumed safety in an environment where predators are known to hunt. Her assumption of safety impeded her ability to act when she was approached by the predator that killed her.

"Now that we *know* they're dangerous, they're not so fucking dangerous." Thank you, Joel Rosenberg. I know of no line that better sums up handling process predators. Once you can recognize them (the signs are subtle, but learnable[211]) *and* you give yourself permission to stop what you're doing and pay attention to what's happening, the danger these people pose plummets like a paralyzed buzzard.

What really makes *these* people dangerous is:
a) People don't recognize what they are;
b) Those people's not just hesitation, but often outright refusal to use the necessary force against them when the predator moves.

I'm not saying Mia Zapata shouldn't have been walking alone at 2 a.m. You can do that. But you *don't* walk through certain parts of town at that time without carrying a gun or knife and having the commitment to use them. It was her insistence on high-risk behavior—while maintaining her comfort zone of *not* carrying something to defend herself—that killed her, as much as her murderer. That's harsh, but there is nobody who is more concerned about your personal safety than you. If you think your safety is someone else's responsibility then the results won't be pleasant if you ever find yourself in a situation.

But far more important than having a weapon is paying attention. I recently read a study by Rossomo and Hammerschlag that compared the hunting strategies of great white sharks and serial killers. Both lurk at a distance, watch their prey, hunt strategically, and target specific prey. Then they close the distance and attack unexpectedly. Where serial killers differ from sharks is that while they can do surprise positioning, *most* of the time they talk themselves into places where they can be alone with their victims. So framing this in terms you already know, they've already picked their victims by virtue of prolonged and silent interviews. Then they usually conduct what would be a regular interview, except they've already decided to attack. So that behavior is more to get the person into isolation—that is the set-up for the attack.

It's often said that Jeffrey Dahmer lured his victims into an isolated area. Realistically, he used the hook-up culture of the gay scene to get his

---

211   Again, I'll tell you to get Desmond Morris's *Manwatching* (1977). But I'll also suggest you look into the work on 'micro-expressions' of Paul Ekman. Although mostly based on lie detection, Ekman's work tells you of good ways to spot predators. When you start looking at their micro-expressions, predators 'leak' more than a spaghetti strainer.

victims into privacy where he could drug and kill them. Ted Bundy often wore a fake cast or sling and asked his victims for help. They voluntarily stepped into attack range. One reason prostitutes are commonly the target of serial killers is because they will willingly go off alone with strange men for money. Another not uncommon tactic for serial killers is to break into the homes of their victims and use the isolation there to commit their murders.

I'll throw this one out with a warning—if you mention it publicly, you will be attacked and condemned for blaming the victim. The trend in binge drinking among college students has been a bonanza for serial rapists. Forget slipping women ruffies and dragging them off to your lair. Why do all that work when the offer of free booze will convince the victims to walk into your room and deliberately incapacitate themselves? All the rapist needs to do is keep on pouring. What's the difference between this and plain old drunken sex? Welcome to why it's so hard to get rape convictions on these actual predators. Unfortunately, those changes in the law—supposedly to make it easier to convict the serial rapist who uses this tactic—make it easier to get a rape conviction for alcohol-driven sex that one party regrets the next morning.[212]

Another way you can increase your chances of running into an extreme process predator, however, is to be employed in certain jobs. I'm not just talking about being a stripper or a prison guard, I'm talking about working as a night cashier at a gas station or convenience store or as a bartender. But once again, extreme process predation—although pumped by the media—is *incredibly* rare. Your chances of being killed in a car accident in a single year are higher than the probability of your being attacked by a serial killer or rapist during your entire life.[213]

Before we move onto what's more common about the way process predators operate, I'd like to take a side trip that's related to that line

212   Yes, sex between two drunken people can be prosecuted as rape in some states. There are serious unexpected consequences of laws, lobbies, rape or domestic violence education campaigns, and demand for enforcement of these new standards. Discussion of this in depth is beyond the scope of this book, but four points are: A) If these laws were enforced equally, our legal system would collapse due to sheer volume. B) It will cost the accused at least $50,000 to defend him- or herself. C) Not only is any man you know at risk, but odds are good you've met the new and improved criteria for arrest for rape and domestic violence—probably several times this year. D) Low hanging fruit. (While conviction rates are the highest ever, in many ways real monsters are safer from arrest and conviction than they've ever been. Why spend the time and money to get a monster when you can get seven felony pleas and convictions for the same time and money?)

213   This statistic holds despite alarmists' estimated numbers, which are specifically enhanced for funding purposes. I once did a calculation of the estimated number of sexual assaults released by a Denver rape crisis group and realized that, according to their guesstimate, half of the female population of Denver was being raped *every* year. I think someone might have noticed that . . .

about process predators breaking into homes. A big brouhaha among those in the shooting world these days is home invasion robberies. Here's something you need to know—unofficially—the most common reason for home invasions is drugs. Not what's-in-your-medicine-cabinet medications, but drug dealing and money. Talking to a number of cops who have investigated these, the consensus is usually drugs have a lot to do with which homes are targeted. This makes most home invasions pretty straightforward resource violence.

So why the unofficial comment? When the cops ask, the drug dealer denies. "Oh great," you might say, "I don't deal drugs, so I'm safe." Yeah, fine, but what's your teenager up to? That's another big source of the cops' cynicism when it comes to investigating these kinds of crimes. The kid's denial isn't really convincing, but the cops can't prove anything. And, oh yeah, for the record conservative estimates are about 10 percent of the U.S. gross domestic product is made through illegal activities—so drugs may be a lot closer to home than you think.

The next most common target for home invasion robberies are ethnic communities that deal in cash, store the money in their homes, and don't trust banks. This is old country thinking, and merchants are prime targets. After that, you start getting into big ticket purchases and resulting home robberies. Although, garage doors left open often are a clear invitation. Then there is the randomly selected, let's invade a home, and see what's in it type of thinking. Do they happen to random citizens? Yes, but there are things that increase or decrease your risks. Combination video camera and door bell units are cheap. Cheaper still are peepholes. Both are easy to install. The hardest part is developing the habit of using them before opening the door when someone comes knocking — especially at odd hours.

But what about a night intruder? I will tell you something, most burglaries take place during *the day*—when people are at work. That time period is far safer for the burglar and significantly lesser charges are levied because the crime is charged as theft *not* robbery. There's also less chance of getting caught, no need to be quiet in an empty house, yada, yada, yada. Therefore, a night intruder in your home is a seriously uncool situation. While it might be about gaining resources, it's already taken a hinky turn from how things are normally done.

But that *doesn't* give you carte blanche to open fire. Even in states with a castle doctrine (laws allowing you to defend yourself in your home) there still needs to be JAM. Contrary to what critics of castle doctrines and stand your ground laws say, there are still standards and limitations about using force. Yes, because of the greater danger of home intruders they are lower, but they still exist. For example, you can't lure someone into your home and kill them nor can you shoot them in the back as they turn and try to run.[214]

Still, someone in your house at night? Let's say you're starting out with a pre-existing six on the JAM scale, so pay close attention to anything he does to add or subtract. His turning and running like hell is always good sign. (Let him go.) Other behavior, not so much. The privacy of your home is what makes it an automatic six on jeopardy.

I keep on coming back to privacy. I do so for two reasons. One, realize that while a lot of social violence will be public, most process predation occurs in privacy or isolation. And the privacy of your own home is perfect for *really* bad things to happen to you. (It's also makes for less clean-up for him as compared to doing something to you in his home or van.)

Two, a fair number of process predators are involved in other crimes. Monsters don't step out fully formed, they take time to develop and grow. That's where the other crimes become important. They often start to take chances in those crimes—likelihoods where they can run into people and bad things ~cough cough~ 'just happen.' The obvious example is instead robbing houses during the day, a budding monster starts breaking in at night—when someone's likely to be home. (Deniable malice anyone?)

That's why a nighttime intruder inside your home gets an automatic plus six. It *might* be a simple snatch-and-run burglar, it might be a full blown monster, or it could be a budding monster. It could just be a drunk in the wrong house (it happens). Or it could be your kid sneaking back into the house. That's why you need to use JAM *before* you pull the trigger or swing the samurai sword.[215] Cockroaches run when the lights are flipped on (dwindling JAM). Predators try to stall and move into attack position or flat out attack (increasing JAM). Drunks stand stupidly (reduced to five) but what they do next increases or decreases the danger. Starting with an automatic six when it comes to home intruders will help you keep from making mistakes—in either direction. By that, I mean either pulling the trigger when you don't need to or not being ready to pull it when you need to.

I started talking about serial killers first thing in this chapter to get them out of the way. When you talk about process predation, that's where

---

214   There also are limitations about attached and stand-alone garages (outlying buildings). Look into your state laws and take a course.

215   Back when I was involved in high-risk lifestyles, my girlfriends and I developed nonsensical sounds or words. Two examples were woof and geef. We would use these unique sounds to identify ourselves coming through the door and locate each other in crowds. It also served as a defusing sound for me. Given my past, I would come out of a dead sleep with a weapon in my hand. That silly sound was a safety protocol we developed to avoid accidents.

a lot of people's minds automatically go. The problem with starting at that extreme is most people don't really work their way back. So now it's back to understanding the less dangerous, but far more numerous manifestations of process predation. There're big, medium, and small process predators. Their size dictates their target selection and whether the victim will be alive afterward.

There is something critical to understand about process predation. It's the difference between this and other kinds of violence. Other types have goals that are achieved through violence—but mostly by the threat of violence. If those goals are achieved before violence occurs, physical aggression is averted. With process predation, *violence is the goal.*

Putting it into lies to a child mode for a second, the person gets off on the violence. When I say that people automatically assume I'm talking about a sadist. Yes, that is one type—someone who takes pleasure from and gets a rush out of inflicting pain on others.

But there are other forms, as well. There's the type that gets off on the power and control over another person. It is like a high for them. As I have heard it put, there is no other time they feel so alive. With some, it is self-southing. Their anger, frustration, and spleen build up and up until they explode in an orgasmic blast of violence. Is this a one-time spree shooter who kills himself, a repetitive domestic abuser, or what I call a 'rage-oholic?' (That's someone who uses violence like an alcoholic does booze—whether in a massive binge or as a constant and endless supply of conflict and aggression.) These people soothe their internal distress through physical aggression.

There's a special kind of loose-cannon-on-deck that Andrew Vachss calls "the lifestyle violent." In the extremes, these are utter monsters with absolutely no empathy for others. They will kill and torture without hesitation, but will have a total emotional melt down over the wrong done to them if someone breaks their radio.[216] And yes, killing you over slight insults and perceived wrongs make perfect sense to the lifestyle violent. Lifestyle violents are the sort of people who will shoot you or beat you to death over a perceived insult. With the extreme ones, when they go off nothing short of death or unconsciousness will stop them—but more than that, they *aren't* specialized. They're not rapists. They aren't serial killers. They aren't abusers. They're monsters.

Any of those heinous acts are just one of the many services they offer. Rape? That's a whim de jour. Aggravated assault? He was miffed. Murdering people during a robbery? He just wanted to make sure he had time before the cops were called. Smashing a baby's head against

216   "Who is the Serious, Violent Habitual Offender?" Andrew Vachss, *New Designs*, 1983, http://www.vachss.com/av_dispatches/lifestyle.html

the wall? The kid annoyed him by crying. And those are the warm fuzzy ones, there's far, far worse out there. Monsters so bad my editor took out some explicit examples I know about.

With the less extreme process predators, you can get them to back off without having to kill them, but you'd better spend the next few months looking over your shoulder and checking shadows. If you see him coming out of the shadows be ready to stop him with extreme prejudice. (Remember surprise positioning? He ain't there by accident.) All that stuff I talked about being out of balance in the *Vendetta* chapter? It applies here in spades.

When it comes to process predators our minds may run out to serial killers, rampage killers, and homicidal monsters, but *most* process predation is *not* lethal. Dead is no fun. I mean after all, if you kill someone you can't beat them again, continue to torture them, or savor how you destroyed this person's life. An abuser can keep on abusing for years. A bully can bully for years. A serial rapist enjoys the trauma he's inflicted. Understanding this will help you understand the second point.

That's most process predation is committed by someone the victim *knows*—especially when it comes to long-term abuse and violence. People who are specifically targeted by specialized predators are often groomed for the crime. A domestic abuser doesn't go out and beat *other* people's spouses. The abuser targets his/her spouse and kids, people whom the abuser has conditioned to take it. A pedophile isn't a danger to adults or to most children. The pedophile's victims are specifically chosen and groomed over time to ensure his/her success. Male serial rapists don't just grab women off the streets, they target specific women they've identified as people not likely to report the crime (much less come back and shoot their dicks off). Except for the lifestyle violent ones, these predators are *very* specific about whom they target with their violence.

But there's another reason for that. Truth be told, usually they really aren't that good at physical violence, which is another reason they're so selective about *whom* they target. Usually, they rely on the unexpectedness of their attack, the high intensity of it, and their target's inability to effectively resist. Jeffrey Dahmer would drug his victims, yet he was beaten to death in prison by one guy. Ted Bundy would get women to help him, pull a tire iron, and smash their skulls from behind. He allegedly was gang raped in prison. A majority of the victims of serial killers are physically smaller people (e.g., women, children, and invalids). Female serial killers usually rely on weapons, poisons or unplugging technology.

So recapping and to put process predators into perspective: They are real; they don't look like monsters. They often act normally until they reveal that secret aspect of themselves. The higher level ones are often so specialized they aren't much of a threat to the average person. (It's when you fit their target profile that you're in trouble.) They set up and time their attacks to increase their success. They usually hide their intent under social behavior. Most of their success comes from surprising and overwhelming their victims, not necessarily physical prowess.

But now I want to talk about the not so highly refined ones, the lifestyle violent ones—the ones who often mix their resource predation with their process predation and their process predation with social violence. Miller and I tend to disagree over the interpretation I'm about to give you. Let's start with the fact social and asocial are his models. I see his point and I don't disagree with it. His correctional background allowed him to closely study process predators. In fact, study them like bugs.

While I too have a correctional background, I have more street time with these guys and dealing with them outside of jail. You could call it dealing with them in their natural habitats. So what you're getting is basically two zoologists disagreeing about taxonomy over observed details.

Miller talks about stone cold process predators who know what they are. And yes, I agree these monsters exist. So too, however, do larvae. In case you slept through biology, that caterpillar, grub, maggot, and wiggler hasn't made the full transition into a moth, beetle, fly, or mosquito. I call them larvae because there are many undeveloped predators, who are floundering around between social, resource, and process violence. Yes, they get off on the violence and the pain they cause, but they're mixing it with other kinds of violence. They're so messed up, they usually think they're only doing one thing. While many will cross the line into flat out process predation, many will stay permanently in the larval stage.

This is why I say it's so important to understand the different types of violence in their 'pure' form. They're primary colors. [217] Like looking at one color knowing primary colors, once you know social, asocial, resource, and process, you can look at a situation and tell the major element in the mix. Mixed situations are *real* common among larvae. Their behavior is always an ugly and excessive hybrid of types of violence. Most will never cross the line where they take a life, but they still can do a lot of damage. This can be the robber who instead of following the robbery script insists on pistol whipping the victim. The store robber who jumps the counter and beats the clerk into unconsciousness before emptying the register. The rapist who beats the woman to a bloody

217   Three primary colors, magenta (red) yellow, and cyan (blue). Mix blue and yellow and you get green. More yellow gives you a lighter green, more blue you get a deeper green.

pulp before raping her (although one study I read reported that with a majority of women injured by rapists the injury or murder occurred after the rape). The robber who flies into a rage and hospitalizes an old man for disrespecting him by having only five dollars when he robs him. It can also be the guy who sees nothing wrong with putting you into a coma by stomping on your head after you've 'disrespected' him. At the same time, he's a touchy bastard who is always finding himself insulted. It's the guy in wolf pack that runs through a crowd, attacking strangers because of their race and who isn't there for social bonding. It's the parent who beats a child for some small infraction or breaks the child's arm while disciplining him or her. It's the guys who go to the gay part of town to harass "fags." They're not there for robbery or for religious reasons, but simply because they claim to hate homosexuals. In the exchange of insults, things escalate into a beating. Or it could be the store robber who herds everyone into the back room then opens fire.

The 'reason' for violence can be anything, but two things are consistent:
1) The extreme—and unnecessary—degree of violence
2) They don't follow the scripts of the kind of violence it's *supposed* to be

What's a robbery script? Close under false pretense, threaten, get what you want, leave. Pretty simple. Pretty straightforward. What's a typical fight script? By now you can describe it. With that in mind, let's move on to what most people are afraid of about process predators, their unpredictability. ~coughcoughbullshitcough~

Remember I said violence comes with instructions on how to avoid it? Well when the goal *is* violence, instructions how to avoid it are *lies*. Usually:
a) To make you more vulnerable to greater violence
b) To work himself up to that violence
c) To see if you'll fall for it

And yes, while resource predation doesn't require extreme emotions for extreme violence, many process predators *do use emotions* to work themselves up to attack. A warning sign (and articulable behavior) is the extreme escalation and speed of a negative emotion. In resource it's slowly hurrying until the attack. Often with this kind it's like a drag race. Everything seems normal until that green light and then incredible acceleration of dangerous emotions.

While this is an important element of the attack itself, it's also confusing. Which is a big part of why it's so successful. It's confusing because it often looks like another type of violence. The differences are:
1) The extremes it goes to
2) How fast they work themselves up to it
3) The off ramps for other types of violence don't work

An example is the guy who gets worked up over you 'disrespecting' him, but won't accept a sincere apology. Again, acceleration through social scripts *is a bad sign*. So too are closed off ramps. And this brings us to how to tell if what you are dealing with is process violence hiding under the guise of another type.

As an aside, the behavior I'm about to tell you about could be something other than process predation. But as I often say, *If it looks like a duck, quacks like a duck, floats like a duck, than it's not a peacock. No matter what anybody tries to tell you.* Seriously. It may *not* be a duck. But whatever it is, we're somewhere in the genus anseriform. And for your safety, that's close enough to do the prep work to kick things into resource protection mode.

Remember how many times I've said to see abnormal you need to know what normal is? I've spent so much time talking about different social scripts in order to help you recognize the following danger signals. While these elements can manifest in many different ways, I'm going to frame them in terms of a robbery going sideways. As you know there's a predictable robbery script. As in, you are in serious danger when the robber:
1) Breaks script;
2) Adds or stacks conditions;
3) Reduces your ability to resist;
4) Seeks to take you to a secondary location;
5) Gives instructions to avoid violence that are humiliating when carried out;
6) Doesn't stop.

When I say 'breaks script' we can start with the most obvious, excessive violence. Again, criminals know the higher the level of force they actually use (not just threaten but use) will increase the penalties and the intensity of the search for them. That's why the threat is used more than physical violence. If someone starts the dance *with* violence don't wait around to find out his intentions.

We're going to talk about the big wet dream of many concealed carry permit holders (or whatever they call people who legally carry concealed weapons in your area). That is being in a store when a robbery happens. Straight up, if a robbery is going according to script, there is very little reason for you to go all O.K. Corral. I'm not saying don't be ready. But if the script is being followed and you and yours aren't in immediate danger, you don't lose any cool points for not drawing fire toward your loved ones. (Yeah, that's the problem with shoot-outs, they work both ways. Unless you're busy being a meat shield, any bullet that misses you is likely to hit someone you're with.[218])

---

218   Drawing fire away from your loved ones is another reason to learn how to move and shoot. Even better is everyone practicing getting the hell out of the area when bullets are flying.

But if someone comes into a convenience store and the first thing he does is pistol whip the clerk, that person has already broken the script. First by the pistol whipping because—as any criminal who isn't high or just wanting to be violent *knows*—employees of chain stores, markets, and banks are instructed *not* to resist robbers. So there is no *need* for this brutal action to achieve resource goals. Second, robbery is already a felony. If someone dies during the commission of a (violent) felony the criminal is automatically facing a murder one charge in most states.[219] Being filmed cracking someone's head open just to show he's serious is a good way to go to prison for the rest of his life. And in states with the death penalty that may not be that long. He's got to be awfully high or stupid to do it. Third, he's taking extra chances by hitting the business when the clerk isn't alone. It doesn't take a rocket scientist to figure out that when the robber is alone, it's safer and easier to hit a business when there's no one else there except the clerk. It's far more stupid and he's more likely to lose control of the situation if more people are in the store. Sorry wannabe gunslingers, odds are better he's going to rob the place *after* you leave.

At the same time, a guy by himself hitting a place with customers? Not real good odds. And that's something you need to seriously stop and think about. Multiple robbers are not uncommon when it comes to stealing from places with people. This includes covert numbers. So if you happen to be in a place that does get hit by a seemingly lone robber, you might want to consider checking to see if he has silent back up before you go all Wyatt Earp. As long as he's not about to shoot someone, you might want to seriously think about it before acting.

That's ordinarily. If he comes in shooting or pistol whipping people, the kid gloves come off. But fer cryin' out loud, *cut across* to draw fire away from your loved ones before you open fire.

Here's another common way things go off script. That is when out of the clear blue, the guy starts to personalize it. The most obvious would be when during a robbery he looks at you quietly and says, "What did you say to me?" Or he starts getting upset about you looking at him. This is *never* a good sign, and it may be the only warning you get that things are going to take a seriously dangerous turn for the worse. Conversely, I do have to warn you: Standing with your hand on your weapon (or weapon drawn, but held down and out of sight) might just be the reason he notices you. Remember leaks? Still another way of going off script and personalization is when the guy starts getting cranky about you not having enough money. This is the guy who beats up an elderly person for only having five dollars and forcing him to go rob someone else.

---

219   It doesn't matter if it's the get-away car driver. If someone dies during a violent felony, everyone involved gets a murder charge.

There's no guaranteed answer about which way things are going to go. But that's why you'll need to be able to articulate the details of the situation to the cops.

Coming out of the robbery model for a second, I've told you that violence comes with instructions on how to avoid it (off ramps). If someone tells you to leave and you do (if you can keep your mouth shut and not have to get that last dig in as you're leaving) odds *are* good the person(s) will let you go. There's the contract, you take it, and leave quietly. End of story. If you try to leave, however, and they start closely following, they're breaking the script.

Now a couple of fast points. First, something I just alluded to. Don't be a douche about leaving. Don't try to walk away flipping them off, threatening them, or talking trash . . . just *leave*. What will happen isn't resource predation, it's violence over a *betrayal*. If you've do these things, then *you* have broken the script, deal, or contract, *not them*.

The number two danger signal that process predation is in the air is if the guy starts adding on or stacking conditions. Again sticking with a robbery on the way to going wrong, it's now not just about giving him your money . . . but your watch . . . your jewelry . . . your car keys . . .

You don't want a predator with an endless list of demands. They tend to get cranky when you can't meet them. Often that's why they're stacking them, they *want* you to

"What if he follows me?" That is the number one question I get when I tell people to accept the deal and make a good faith effort to withdraw. There are three problems with this question.

One is most of them come from the monkey that is looking for an excuse *not* to leave. The monkey telling you he'll follow is a reason not to even bother to try. Recognize this fear of being followed for the monkey trap it is.

Two, most of the people asking that question are also the very ones who would have to yell that parting shot about his ancestry to soothe their egos. (Once again, that damned monkey . . .) As I said, talking trash will provoke him into following because *you* broke the deal he offered. And violence over betrayal is the nastiest of all.

Three if he follows you, he's given you articulable evidence and facts that you tried to withdraw—and it *did not* work! When the DA (district attorney) tries to undermine your self-defense plea by asking why you didn't try to leave, you can honestly answer that you did. "It started there, and I said I was leaving. I withdrew, and he followed me to here." As sure as night follows day, the DA will hit you with, "Why'd you stop?" Leaving out a "well, dipstick . . ." precursor to your response, the answer is: "Because trying to withdraw from the situation *wasn't* working!" "Why did you turn around?" "Because I didn't want to get hit from behind, and he was moving into attack range." Where I'm from, his following you kicks it into resource protection. You ain't fighting him. Your goal is to end it.

Four sub-points about this. Range is the issue in all of them.

A) It's not uncommon after you've been told to leave a rough place for the locals to give you a head start for the door and then follow you out. They'll stop outside the door to watch and make sure you don't get a weapon from your car and try to return. Someone backing up and shooting them is a real life problem in rough neighborhoods. So their watching makes sense. But as long as they hang back at the door, it's *not* your problem.

B) **Never** allow yourself to be escorted out of an area by the locals. I'm *not* talking about a bouncer or property owner. Nor am I talking about people hanging back far out of attack range, but still keeping you in view. I'm talking about a pack that walks *with* you as though they are your escorts. (Or close enough that you could be one of their numbers.) This is a silent interview to see if you know how much danger you're in. If you try to pretend it's normal, that's a green light to attack. People who allow this often try to fight one person when the attack starts, but are hopelessly outnumbered.

C) Expect some huffing, puffing, chest beating, and threatening verbiage if you decide to leave. This is not a violation of the script, it's *part* of it. Threats like, "Don't come back or we'll kick your ass" are fine and dandy . . . as long as he's *not* trying to close to attack range. Or you're dumb enough to stop, turn around, come back, and get up in his face again. If you do the last, then you've flushed your claim of self-defense down the toilet.

D) Back away calmly. Communicate to the guy that you're leaving and proceed to match your actions to your words. Do not turn your back on him until you are well out of attack range. All of this sends the message that it's not your first rodeo as does your not reacting to his chest pounding and threats.

D-1) This is a little more advanced, which is why it's a sub-point. On occasion, you'll have to walk some retard through the process of letting you leave. That is to say as you're backing away, he might decide to not just to throw trash talk at you, but to move forward. Not start to and then stop (see point C) but keep on coming. This sort of situation requires a deft hand because:

a) You need to remind him you and he had a deal

b) A deal that's in *his* best interest to honor

c) Convince him to stop without provoking him

d) Be ready to flash into resource protection violence if this doesn't work

When retardo tries to follow too soon or too close, I've had success by stopping my withdrawal for a second, *leaning* forward, and snarling, "I said I was leaving!" When he stops, I straighten up, and continue to withdraw. This is *not* a bluff, this is *not* posturing. It's letting him see a flash of the werewolf. A werewolf that—if everyone keeps to the deal—is happy to leave so nobody has to go to the hospital tonight.

fail. That's their excuse to go off. A store clerk doesn't have the safe combo. While the demand for the cash in the register is within reason, ordering the clerk to open the safe or drop box isn't going to end well because it's now crossed over to kidnapping. Those are charges someone, who isn't drugged out of his mind or high on the power of violence, isn't going to want to risk. But when process predation is the goal, that doesn't matter.

Often these guys get more and more aggressive when their escalating demands aren't met or they think they aren't being met fast enough. Unfortunately, this often is not an act. They're working their way up to excessive aggression. Often in the larval phase, these guys still need an excuse to do what they want to do—hurt someone.

Danger sign number three— reducing your ability to resist.

Here's a green light for you to tear someone's throat out with your teeth. He tells you to handcuff yourself or tells you he's going to tie you up. Noooo . . . I don't think so. Being told to get down on your knees is not going to happen. Adding to the list, you're not getting into a car trunk, either. Categorically, nothing good ever comes from these kinds of demands. Someone telling you to do this has just called down the apocalypse on his head. This is not a

fight; it's not even a beating. It's a throat-crushing, disemboweling, shoot him kind of violence. You do *not* allow yourself to be rendered helpless.

I'd like to share a predatorial strategy Teja Van Wicklen from Devi Protective Offense explained to Miller and me. This is a trick that reduces your ability to resist by getting your cooperation from your hope of not being hurt—again. Teja talks about women who are unexpectedly hit by a man harder than they've ever been hit in their lives. (News flash: This is how hard men hit each other when they're mad. And yes, the first time you are hit this hard, it is a shocking and often overwhelming degree of force.) Then the predator kneels down and apologizes for having to hit her. He doesn't want to do it again, and if she just cooperates he won't have to hit her again …

Now, instead of reaching up and popping his eyeball out of its socket, the woman sees a glimmer of hope. A monkey's way out. A social way out. A way not to feel that horrible pain and shock again. She tells herself he doesn't want to hurt her. If she cooperates, she won't be hurt. She can manipulate and control the situation using social scripts. And on top of everything else, he's really sorry he had to do it. Yeah, that's a lie. He's using that hope to reduce her ability to effectively resist. How powerful is this? I'd like to quote Garry Smith from the Academy of Self-Defence. (He's in the England, they spell defense funny.) "Hope like this keeps concentration camps and torture cells quiet." Reduced capability to resist? Not good. Not good at all. (And yeah that also applies to you being plied with alcohol.)

This brings us to the fourth green light where you give yourself permission to disembowel someone—secondary locations.

Different sources have different numbers on how bad being taken to a second location can be. The more conservative sources say about 95 percent; most say about 97 percent. The real alarmists say 100 percent such brutality as rape, torture, and murder will result from allowing yourself to be moved to another location. In case you missed it when there's only a 5 percent difference between the most conservative and the most alarmist sources, it's safe to say allowing yourself to be moved to a secondary location is a *big* no-no. Starting with the fact that it is kidnapping. You can blend three and four to figure out that someone telling you to get into the trunk of a car isn't going to end well, either.

Quick observation here: If the guy breaks the script by going violent, it's time to go to town right there. Adding conditions, reducing ability, and moving you to a secondary location . . . those are pretty much go signs, but you don't have to act immediately. You have a little more time to figure out when action will give you the best chances. But here's a hint, the window for acting gets smaller. You cannot let him develop that kind of control over you. And when you do act, it's resource protection.

The fifth sign that you're going to have to punch someone in the throat is if the instructions on how to avoid violence are humiliating.

News flash here: Generally, instructions on how to avoid violence are actually pretty reasonable—*if* you can put your ego in your pocket. They're also pretty simple—shut up, leave, stop doing that, gimme, and other such directives. When I say humiliating, I'm not talking about you having too fragile an ego. It's not a case of "I'll be shamed and everyone will think I'm a wimp if I back down" humiliated. That's the monkey making things up to stay in charge of your actions. The monkey is trying to make it seem humiliating so it can stick around and tell the guy to go do unnatural acts to himself.

When I say humiliating, I'm talking you should never have to conduct fellatio in order not to get beaten. You should never have to lick piss off the floor to keep from getting jumped. Getting down on your hands and knees and barking like a dog also is off the to-do list. Someone demanding you beg and whimper, the same. Yeah, there's a chance you won't be attacked if you comply, but the odds are good you'll *still* be attacked even after you comply.

Demanding that you give everyone in the room a blow job is just the warm up. The sadistic pleasure and power the person gets from humiliating you is often foreplay to the beating or killing. When you get these kinds of instructions, it's time to start the engine for resource protection. When they start creating JAM, it's time to slam it into gear and go. Will you survive? Can't tell you. But if you don't, you ain't going alone.

Again, where most people screw up with this kind of situation is they try to fight instead of flashing into resource protection violence. When I say that, too many people think, "Ooooh time for my uber-cool combatives and martial arts." No, I'm *not* talking about MMA (mixed martial arts) and dressed-up sports fighting. I'm talking about empty handed popping out eyeballs, biting off noses, elbows to the throat, and driving skulls into concrete—especially if you're dealing with multiples. Or yes, weapons.

Ordinarily it would be hell to convince your attorney that intense violence was self-defense. I'm going to strongly recommend, however, a particular strategy to counter that problem. And that is you were engaging to *open* an escape route. The carnage wasn't to win. It was to blow open hole so you could haul ass out of there, especially when facing numbers.

Is there a chance they'll follow you? Yes. Welcome to violence. If you wanted guarantees, shop at chain stores, fill in the warrantee cards and buy service plans. Guarantees *don't* happen with violence. While there is a chance they'll pursue if you go four-wheeled get me the hell out of here (what I call "Fluffy the Cat"[220]) odds are the pursuit won't be very heartfelt. If you maul a few of theirs to get out (especially if it's their heavy hitter) there's a good chance they won't want to catch you. Would you want to catch that bobcat?

The sixth type is when things have already gone to hell in a hand basket—and the person *doesn't* stop.

This behavior isn't exclusive to process predators, but it's common to them. These are the people who will not just knock you over, but will continue kicking and stomping you. It could be a violent lifestyle offender or an enraged drunk past knowing when to stop. It could be a person with a mental condition, who is having an episode. It could be an out-of-control teen or an OOK. Or it could be Joe Pesci's character in *Casino*.

It doesn't matter. What matters is the person keeps up a berserk attack after you've tried to break contact. If you try to surrender, they increase their degree of violence. I'm not talking about getting in an extra lick or two to teach you a lesson, I'm saying they go psycho when you try to stop. Okay, now it's really gone off script—as in you're going to the hospital if you don't do something. Here is where you damned well better not have participated in the creation and escalation of the situation because you gotta injure him to incapacitation or kill him before he does the same to you. This isn't losing a fight, this is you being in immediate threat of death or grievous bodily injury because of what he's doing.

Remember the shod human foot is a lethal force instrument when applied to someone down on the ground. Being surrounded by four guys kicking and stomping you when you're down—same thing but times four. Being strangled. Someone jack hammering your head against the concrete. Someone who's cut you with a knife coming at you again. The level of violence I'm talking about here isn't anything monkey. I'm talking about an animal in survival mode. You gotta go in to incapacitate him. If you were a cop or part of a five-man cell extraction team, you'd be able to stop him without hurting him, and more importantly could do so without injury to yourself. I tell you this because it's time to embrace the suck.

If this not-stopping-berserk happens, you're dealing with damage control. The damage you're trying to limit is to you. There's a damned

---

220   One of the worst maulings I ever had in my life was, when after a hard day at work, I was relaxing in a hot bath and smoking a cigar. Then the cat slipped and fell into the tub. She. Ripped. The. Crap. Out. Of. Me. That cat, while using me for traction, wounded me more than I have ever been damaged in any knife attack I've faced. And all she was doing was climbing over me to get out. That is the kind of damage a person dedicated to climbing over someone to escape can and will cause. If you gotta climb over someone to escape, you give it your all. There's a reason cornered animals are dangerous—when they come out of that corner hell's coming with them.

good chance the best you're going to get out of this is waking up in the hospital and facing charges. This is still better than the alternative, which is not waking up at all or being crippled for the rest of your life. And if you lose the ability to resist, those possibilities *are* on the table.

About ten years ago, I was in the room when someone asked an emergency room doctor what the odds of survival would be for someone with a single gunshot wound. The doctor asked, "If he gets to me within two hours?" The questioner allowed that. The doc said, "About 80 percent." Triage has come a long way since then. So your odds of surviving a single gun shot or knife wound are good. Hell, you even have a good chance of making it if your head gets bounced off the concrete once. What you're *not* likely to survive is someone standing over you and emptying a clip into you. Or slamming you against the wall and stabbing you fifteen or twenty times. The same with being on the ground with someone repeatedly stomping your head into the concrete.

In case you missed it, this is miles beyond losing a fight. That is where a lot of people blow it when it comes to self-defense. They are losing a fight, so they flip out. They think being whupped has become a life-and-death situation and pull a weapon. Incredibly bad plan. Doing that will put them into prison because that's *not* self-defense, they still could have turned and run.

But if you are getting savaged, when you truly can't run, then that's the *only* plan. You need to do something desperate before you can't accomplish anything except curl up and bleed. For example, someone's stomping you while you're down. You roll into his legs, grab on, and keep rolling. The harder and faster you roll, the greater the chance—when he goes over backward—he's going crack his skull open, and you'll face manslaughter charges.

Why do you think this book is so damned long? You only do this kind of thing when your life actually is in danger. Not when your monkey is screaming that you'll die if you lose this fight. You *will* face felony charges if you have to take out a process predator. Like I said in the introduction, pick your poison. While this book is an antidote, the ride is still going to be a bitch . . .

I'm going to take a side trip for my next point—because I guarantee it's going to make a lot of people uncomfortable. I am different from most self-defense instructors. Starting with the fact my litmus test for bad is very different than most people's. When someone comes to me with a tale about a horrible and terrible event, my first question is, "Did the person live?" If the answer is yes, then my response is, "Good that means we can work with it." This sets certain folks squealing about what a horrible, insensitive person I am. They squeal how inconsiderate of the victim's trauma and suffering I am. Because they're so outraged, they don't hear my next question. That's the one when the answer is no. That is: "How many parts was the body found in?"

Dying can be real fast and impulsive or it can a take a long and torturous time. Like stuff my editor refused to let me put into this book. That's the level of bad I routinely dealt with. It's not that I have no compassion for those who lived, but I know just how far *bad* can go. I've seen enough and dealt with enough monsters to know bad extends far beyond most people's horizons.

The reason I told you that is to show you the need for reference points on a spectrum of bad. Not emotional monkey-brained wailing and gnashing of teeth or academic and intellectual curiosity, but practical standards and baselines to measure circumstances against. You need to know that there's bad, there's *bad* and then there's ***bad!***

Why? You cannot accurately assess where a situation is on the spectrum if you don't have stable data. And a huge stable data point is your ability to take a punch. Huh? Where'd that come from? Work with me for a bit.

Not knowing you can take a punch is the flat tire of most people's ability to make good use of force decisions. For the record, I am especially addressing people who carry a gun for self-defense. Regardless of your level of self-defense, you cannot intellectually or emotionally work around this gaping hole in your knowledge and understanding. Without it, you will *not* be able to accurately assess the danger to your person and act reasonably. (Yeah, remember that pesky legal term?)

Until you:

1) Develop the ability to take a hit without having an emotional melt down

2) Have firsthand experience that you can be struck, and it won't 'destroy' you

3) Don't get all trauma-drama-esque and 'triggered' over having been hit in your past

4) Get over your fear of being struck

You:

a) Have no baseline to accurately assess danger

b) Are likely to freak out and emotionally overreact when confronted

c) More likely to get furious and overreact to the insult of being struck rather than the actual danger

d) Will attempt to negotiate and de-escalate from a position of fear

e) Will attempt to deal with the situation from a position of overconfidence

f) Will be reacting to past events instead of what is happening *now*

Take the numbers from that list and imagine someone who hasn't developed those traits. Now mix and match by attaching the various letters to that number. Pretty much any of those combinations have a serious potential to go bad. In what, I might add, are some rather predictable ways—predictable as to whether your name is written on either the victim or the offender line of the police report.

This is why I tell people who want to learn self-defense that they're have to learn to take a punch. (Hell, sign up for boxing lessons for six months.) This is critical for instilling something that has been lost to most people's consciousness. And that is: You got hit—*so what?* A big part of boxing is learning that you can take a hit and keep going. Yeah, it hurts. Again, so what? Having stable data that you can take pain and keep going gives you confidence and an understanding that there is no way to intellectualize your way around it.

Our *fear* of getting hit is more debilitating *than* getting hit. You can take a hit. It's not the end of the world; it's not going to traumatize your psyche for the rest of your life (unless you go out of your way to define yourself by it). After you get the hang of it, you discover an amazing fact, you can get hit and *still* function. And by function, I mean *still* think. Your brain doesn't shut down because someone punched you. You can still mentally process—and most importantly assess—the danger and react with appropriate force. Remember something I said earlier? You are *not* adrenaline's bitch!

Why is this important? Well, let's look at what happens without it. Heading back to social violence you get a two-fer. First, so you don't make the mistake of getting hit and—when distance is created—closing the distance to fight, while thinking it's self-defense. Second, you could freak out and pull a weapon when you *shouldn't*. Coming back to resource and process aggression another option is you'll be so stunned with the level of force that's coming at you, you'll freeze. In pure process predation, you'll be incapable of sucking up the pain to stop further injury. You'll just give up—and get mauled or die.

Now the bad news, the same freeze and freak out goes double when you're attacked with social violence. So how does this tie back to a process predator attack or a berserk? Because like my dead-or-alive question, your ability to handle being punched is a stable data point on the spectrum of how bad things are—or are *going* get. How bad things are. Let's say someone hauls off and hits you, and you think, "Is that your best shot?" If that's the case, you *know*—given the current circumstances—a high level-of-force response is *not* justified. You don't get to go all kung-fu fists of fury on the guy. You can't pull out your knife and initiate the weed whacker of death on him. Nor can you pull your gun and go all Wyatt Earp on him.

Conversely, if you try to withdraw and the guy comes at you like a methed-out berserker, that's *far beyond* a normal punch. Therefore, a higher level of force is necessary. But you know that *because* you have stable data about a run-of-the-mill punch. You now know on which side of the bad spectrum this situation is located. Depending on other circumstances, it may be that nothing short of lethal force will give you any chance of survival. So get that scaling-a-punch out of the way now because you don't have time in an actual situation.

Another benefit is helping you recognize that strike was a slap. A slap that was designed to be more insulting than damaging. Going postal over a slap is going to sling you out of the SD square. That's something else that comes from having the ability to take a punch, you lose the knee-jerk reaction of feeling you *must* respond.

The only exception to this is if you are so infirm, old, or crippled that you physically cannot take a punch without injury (remember injury means a trip to the emergency room). If that's the case, what we're talking about is a change in the danger posed to you from *any* physical assault. (Here's a news flash, people, just being female doesn't automatically put you on this cannot be hit list. There has to be significant disparity of force or attempted rape before you can legally unleash lethal force). But your degree of physical infirmity is something you need to discuss with your attorney. That's because while it allows for a use of more effective force in order to protect

I've talked about a process predator coming at you really hard so you can understand that this level of violence and danger is much higher than that of social violence. Well, I should say most social violence. I'm going to remind you about something I said earlier in this chapter: That was about the person who doesn't stop. This behavior isn't exclusive to process predators, but it's common to them. These are the people who will not just knock you over, but will continue kicking and stomping you.

There are certain types of social violence that come at you as hard as a process predator. They pose just as much danger to the target. Basically, there are five—very unique—conditions where you get this degree of brutal and injurious violence. Yet these are not asocial circumstances. These are:

1) Violence between heavy hitters
2) Group monkey dance
3) OOKs
4) Outsider in the wrong place (especially misbehaving)
5) Betrayal

Violence between heavy hitters—Take the methodical set-up of resource predation, the negotiation between countries trying to avoid war, and two wolverines deciding to kill each other. If you don't know what to look for, everything is going to be really tense, but there won't be much movement—until it explodes. Then someone is going to the hospital or morgue.

Group monkey dance—Miller's definition of this is that it is fundamentally social in nature because it's a group activity. It's a bunch of people committing extreme violence on an outsider to prove their loyalty and that they belong to the group. So, yeah, it's a real social bonding moment for them, but potentially deadly if you're the outsider who has been 'othered.'

OOKs—Out-of-control monkeys. Once again we get into taxonomy. You have a status-seeking show of an insecure leader or alpha, hysterical amnesia, excited delirium, drunkenness, 'roid rage, and other similar factors. Much of the time, these come from the person screwing up social scripts. Other times, it's because he's flat out crazy, but what is setting him off is fundamentally social. Straight up, I don't really care why this sunnabitch has blown a gasket. What I care about is he's coming at me with excessive force for the situation, and I can't rely on him controlling of himself before he seriously injures me. Sorry, Pum'kin, you just called down resource protection.

Outsider in the wrong place and being a jerk—In case you haven't caught on yet, a) every place has it's own rules and b) every place is someone else's territory. Something that those in the hermit crab mindset don't consider and those in the Disneyland state of mind *ignore* is the fact they are a guests in someone else's house. You are a visitor, act like it. Do not make a mess on someone else's table.

Some of the worst beatings I have ever seen have resulted from someone who insisted on his or her right to be somewhere and his or her right to be a complete jerk. You're not a tribe member, and you're starting things? In many places—especially where people who behave like this tend to act out—the worst that happens is the owner or manager calling the police. In other places, you're lucky if they'll call an ambulance to come pick you up. Believe me, this can be a real problem when they drag your broken and unconscious body out and throw you into a snow bank. Some places your body will end up in a landfill or in a shallow grave out in the boonies. Oh, yeah, in some places the absolute last thing you'll ever do is defend yourself. (I once had an entire bar stand up against me.) You do not mess with certain tribes.

While this sounds scary, it is actually good news. That's because getting into such a situation usually requires you to be young, stupid, obnoxious, and have a sense of entitlement so big you gotta turn sideways to get through the door. If you don't, you're usually safe.

Betrayal—This is another one of those situations you really have to work at to call down on your head. But if you're the kind of person who cheats people, there's only one thing I can say . . . Can I have your flat screen?

yourself, the same strict standards about lethal force apply—especially about you participating in the creation and escalation of the situation. (Oops, there's that crossing out of the SD square thing again.)

A previous sentence ended with ". . . how bad things are—or are going to be." That last tag is important in two significant ways. One is with the experience of being hit, you also have a tendency to assess people's ability to punch. Yeah, that six-foot-four biker with the words pain and kill tattooed across his scarred knuckles probably won't hesitate to bust someone's jaw. Refraining from attacking him verbally or acting antagonistically probably are good ideas. It's amazing how much you have no problem walking away from when you have stable data about getting punched. Like, "Yeah, I could do this, but it's not worth it." And while we're at it, "Shut up, monkey. We're going to solve this another way." Your ability to size up his capabilities and knowing your limits removes any and all stigma about calling for back up. "Hey, monkey, read to me what's tattooed on his knuckles while I call for help." Or a tactical withdrawal: "Nope, I'm pretty sure I don't want to get hit by these guys, I think I'll take their invitation to leave."

Two, your ability to take a hit has a strong influence on your ability to de-escalate a situation. A longtime friend of mine, Richard Foss, once observed: "Negotiation without the ability to back it up is just begging." If you're *afraid* of being hit, you aren't negotiating for a nonviolent outcome, much less de-escalating. You're pleading. Usually what you're doing is placating. That might work with different types of violence, but if there's process predation in the mix, not so much.

I've told you the willingness to do violence to protect yourself usually keeps you from having to actually carry it out. Stable data about your ability to take a punch is the other side of that coin. It allows you to calmly understand and accept that it's going to hurt—if it comes to a physical altercation. Yet pain is a factor— not cause for an overwhelming freak out.

You need both aspects for de-escalation, as well as deterrence. Just being willing to be violent isn't enough (in fact that's a bad guy tactic). Nor am I saying you have to become someone's punching bag until they tire of hitting you. Basically, someone who calmly accepts the fact that pain is going to be the cost of not letting you act out is *not* someone you want to be go up against because if such a person isn't afraid of pain, they're not afraid of serving it up either.

When it comes to being attacked by a process predator the level of force is often so intense if you don't stop it immediately, you won't have a chance to do it later. This is why it's important to:

a)   Have stable data points about force
b)   Not reduce your ability to resist due to your use of alcohol, drugs, or both

When these bastards come at you, you need to be able to get your game on. And you won't be able to do that if you don't know how far past a regular attack they've gone.

In closing this chapter, I'd like to add two things. One is something I've noticed in certain process predators. In other types of violence, you get distinctive actions—things like the witness check, the weapon pat, the monkey dance, and other such actions. There's something these guys often do—especially rapists—that's a unique part of their interview. That's the pre-assault touch.

It's not an attack, per se, but more a test to see how the person will react. Will she or he do anything about it? Will that person set boundaries? Will that person pretend it didn't happen? Will that person not pay attention? Or will that person make it very clear that touching is not acceptable? All of these reactions communicate important information to the predator. If you're getting funky vibes off someone do yourself a favor and *don't* let them touch you. While you're at it don't let yourself be moved into isolation with such a person, even if that's a private room at a party or the person offers you a ride. Again, remember what I said about the fact most process predators know their victims.

The second point about process predators. They often hunt where people have fun. Scenes involving booze, drugs, sex, and good times are common hunting grounds. Not only are the boundaries already being pushed, but as I said before the predator doesn't really have to work too hard. Often people willingly go off with them into isolation while seeking a good time.

This brings us to an important attribute for you to develop. There is a scene from the movie *Dusk Till Dawn* (1996). The kidnapped family and their kidnappers are at a club where George Clooney's character is having a great time. He looks over his brother's shoulder and sees trouble approaching. His statement is, "Richie get back on the clock." His brother (Quinton Tarantino) immediately morphs from a person having a good time to a more serious personality and simply asks, "How many?"

Violence ensues.

I have partied with some extremely dangerous and competent people. One of the things that makes them dangerous is their ability to shift from having a good time to getting back on the clock. They are truly relaxed, having fun, and enjoying themselves—yet when something troublesome enters the environment, they set good times aside and 'punch in.' No hesitation. No outrage. No anger. They're simply on the clock again. If something happens, they immediately take care of business—because they're on the clock. If the trouble evaporates without incident, they clock out and go right back to enjoying themselves and having fun. Again, no attitude, outrage, or resentment.

I told you this to give you a contrast with how many people who are deeply involved in having fun *can't* come out of it in time to save themselves. I'm not even talking about getting on the clock, I'm talking about not slowing down and turning around when things start going down the wrong road. In fact, what they often do is hit the gas pedal.

For the record, in the following example, I am not talking about a process predator, a serial rapist. Let's start with an underage college girl sneaking into a frat party with a fake ID. She's pounding shots and Jager bombs to get to a BAC (blood alcohol content) of .25 in less than an hour. What could possibly go wrong—especially when a cute guy invites her up to his room to do Jell-O shots? As far as she's concerned, she's exercising her right to have fun.[221] Your classic Disneyland state of mind.

But let's look at the other side of this same page. Frat Rat is also in the Disneyland state of mind. He's working a buzz, too. In his little pickled Neanderthal brain[222] her agreeing to go up to his room with him means ...

With both parties deeply entrenched in Disneyland, things start to go wrong. "Wait! No! I'm here to drink your booze and do your drugs, not

---

221   The actual phrasing from a university's rape crisis center about this exact scenario.

222   Modern neuroscience has found the human brain isn't fully developed until the mid to late twenties. If you think about it, this makes a lot of sense when applied to young people's behavior.

have sex with you!" And that's when people get angry, outraged, and aggressive. This includes becoming physically violent when someone interferes with their fun or they're frustrated that things don't go their way—and that is *not* exclusively a male trait, either.

This *isn't* getting on the clock, it's usually displaying aggressive, stupid, and self-righteous behavior. Worse is when they both get violent—that's going to be a wreck. And when things get worse is when that wreck is intentional. That's when it is a process predator (e.g., serial rapist). In those circumstances, a drunken, angry monkey is hopelessly outgunned—especially a smaller female one. That is if she didn't binge drink herself into a black out and incapacitation.

Now you know why process predators hunt in these environments. It's a lot easier. And yes, this is how a number of sexual predators hunt. Include some specialized victim selection tactics and these monsters are really hard to catch and prosecute. (That's where you run into prosecutors going after low hanging fruit instead to boost their numbers.) These monsters are real, but *not as common* as and way more specialized than you're told. But with both the drunken frat rat or the serial rapist, if you can't get back on the clock, you're in deep trouble.

Changing tracks, years ago I was talking to someone about the problems of teaching people about personal safety. I was trying to describe the problem I had communicating to people about the need to have the right state of mind. The person looked at me and said, "So you're trying to tell them how to think?" My immediate response was *no!* What a horrible thing to say. (This incidentally is why I resisted becoming a teacher for so long.)

Over the years, I have come to revisit this idea. But not in the same way I interpreted it the first time. That is, I didn't know the difference in *how* and *what* to think. How is a way to process. *What* is controlling the data people are allowed to know and telling them *only* the acceptable conclusions. The last is what set me to twitching. I interpreted it in the sense of brain washing and "this is what you *have* to believe, say, and do."

After a few decades, I have come to recognize the importance of being able to process, to think a certain way in specific circumstances. It is indeed a learned skill, specifically when it comes to getting on the clock about functioning in a violent environment. But here's what I missed the first time: You don't have to be there *all* the time. It isn't permanent. You can think a certain way for a short time and then shift back to how you normally think.

Years ago, I realized we not only wear different hats, but we're actually *different* people when we wear them. Our behavior changes depending on whom we deal with. So, too, does our thinking when we're fulfilling these roles. In the same way—your thought process is different when you're doing math, driving, having sex, or simply relaxing. And you have a different mindset when you're at work or school.

I'm not making this up. Magnetic resonance imaging (MRI) technology has advanced to the point we can actually witness the different parts of the brain activating when given different stimuli. Ordinarily, when we feel threatened or emotional, the 'monkey parts' of the brain kick in. But that doesn't have to be. *We have choices.*

I've spent more than four hundred pages conditioning you so can now find your personal way to control that and to help you take conscious control of this mental shifting of the gears. When it comes to violence, you now have a better chance of *getting on the clock*, instead of turning into a freaked-out and emotional monkey—a monkey that will probably get you sent to prison for 'defending yourself.' It's important to know the difference between defending yourself and defending your monkey.

Will you be able to do it?

I can't tell you. That depends on you and your other training. And how much effort you are willing to put into *not* monkey sliding. But I've been helping you build a bridge across the gorge. We're three quarters of the way across. The last bit is up to you. I can only give you the tools so you can punch that clock and git 'r done when you need to—whether it is drunken Uncle Albert taking a swing at you, a mugger, or a monster coming at you.

CONCLUSION

"Your enemy is never a villain in his own eyes.
Keep this in mind; it may offer a way to make him your friend.
If not, you can kill him without hate — and quickly."
—**Robert A Heinlein**

Afterword

If this book could be summed in seven simple points they would be
1) Violence attracts violence.
2) Violence has consequences.
3) Don't be stupid about your violence (starting with denying when you're being violent).
4) Recognize what you're dealing with.
5) Do your best to avoid unnecessary violence.
6) Do not be too _____ (fill in the blank) to apologize, be polite or walk away.
7) When you must act, do so—but be able to explain why it was necessary, what the level of danger was and why the level of response was appropriate.

I thought about putting those seven right up front, but decided not to. They have a new depth and meaning for you now. Starting with, you're no longer going to look at them and say, "Well no duh!" Then skip past to the tacti-cool stuff. You now understand why they aren't simple and how easy it is to mess them up. More than that, what the consequences are for messing up.

This has been the hardest book I have ever written. Mostly because of the incredible amount of misinformation people adamantly cling to about violence—usually without having actually dealt with what they're *certain* they know so much about.

I recently ran into a few folks who were convinced the most dangerous people were the ones who had nothing to lose. They maintained these were the *most* dangerous and crazed fighters. This ignores the fact that humans when they've lost everything including hope usually sit there stunned. Sometimes to the point of just lying down and dying, but mostly they eventually get up and start moving again. Complete and total loss doesn't often turn people into berserks; zombies are more common.

On the other hand, someone who has lost something very important (or it is threatened) can indeed go wild. But that's not everything. That's a specific someone or something in combination with something else. Can these people be hard to handle? Oh yeah, especially if they target you for that loss or threat. (Oh, while we're at it, don't mistake cornered for lost everything either.) But what makes such folks hard to deal with is when *you* put the restriction on yourself about your priorities and staying inside your comfort zone. (E.g., "I don't want to kill someone, so I'll only learn empty hand;" *or* "I don't want to learn empty hand, so I'll carry a gun.") Those people are dangerous because of your choices and the *limitations* you put on yourself. That's not the same as the most dangerous. Realistically, people who aren't afraid to die can be easily accommodated—usually because their tactics tend to suck. The down side is their behavior makes it necessary to at least injure them, often more. And that means paper work.

Add to this the world is populated with people who are willing use violence—up to *you* dying—to achieve their goals. Thing is, this willingness is usually one-sided. They're okay with you dying, but they don't want to die themselves. The majority of such folks change their minds when they realize violence is *not* the one-way street they were planning on. While this can range from complete amateurs to professionals, fortunately the scale is loaded toward the amateur side. This means a lot of things can be de-escalated and deterred by simply being willing to make it a two-way street and offering an alternative. On the other hand, when pros decide to act it can be a real hassle. Speaking as a violence professional, it's the guy who doesn't mind dying to achieve his goal who you're going to have to put in some overtime to stop— especially if that goal is to take you out.

Kinda undermines 'got nothing to lose is the most dangerous' cliché doesn't it?

Another idea that seems to fly over people's heads is that someone having different priorities is *not* the same thing as nothing to lose. The threat of jail time scares most middle-class people. It serves as a silent influence on their behavior. One they don't even think about consciously anymore, it just guides their actions. For example, while you boldly drive 10 mph over the limit (in the absence of a cop), you don't drive 100 mph over. The fear of jail, penalty, or death is there subconsciously influencing your driving behavior.

The mistake many people make about violence and self-defense is assuming their same priorities dictate the behavior of others. Someone whose pride and status is more important than spending time in jail won't hesitate to assault you over you disrespecting him. In the same vein, if a busted nose is the cost of avenging his honor so be it. Understanding this—and not pushing people to the point where attacking you seems the best way to maintain their priorities or achieve their goals—has been a big part of what this book is about.

Clint Overland (one of my proof readers and fact checkers) observed that every other book he'd ever read on this subject presupposed readers had existing knowledge. "But this book didn't." The challenge of writing this book has been to start from the ground and build up. It's getting past what people think they know about crime, violence and the legal system. You'll never look at these subjects the same way again.

Two things I did put in the beginning are:
1) The greatest danger to you isn't the other guy, it's what *you think* you know.
2) Knowing what to do is not enough—what will kill you is all the stuff you *don't* know not to do.

Those should make a whole lot more sense now, along with those seven simple points. But where your perspective really has changed is with the quote that started this conclusion. Way too many people skip over the middle part and think the end is the solution. It's not. Your actual safety is mostly based in the middle part of the quote. And if not friend then plug in '. . . *it may offer a way to find a working, peaceful compromise.*'

If nothing else, this book has shown you what a can of worms physical violence opens.

Still, if you have to, you have to. But make sure you *have to* before you jump to the end of the quote—or anywhere near it.

Changing tracks, I tell instructors, "You're not teaching self-defense. You're training people to operate within the parameters of self-defense. That's a subtle, but important distinction." Conceptually, self-defense is easy. It's scaling your actions to remain inside the legal standards of self-defense, while at the same time ensuring your physical safety.

Being able to do that on the fly . . . not so easy especially if you bring not just your baggage, but a freight train of misconceptions, half-truths, fantasies, marketing, and flat out bullshit about the subject. It's also really hard to do if you're busy being self-offensive.

This book has been about all those things that make self-defense so easy to screw up. At the beginning of this book, I said there are no you-just-do-this answers. Now you know why. Everything about self-defense is scale, spectrum, shading, interaction between different factors, possibilities, and probabilities. Functioning effectively in a self-defense situation is *not* learning a set of facts and data. It's *not* knowing a list of do this, that, and the other thing. Most of all, it's *not* just physical action, what fighting style you know, or what's the best caliber for self-defense.

It's having information and processing it in a certain way in specific circumstances and different contexts. That's why I liken it to being on the clock. When you're at work, you think a different way, you have skills, knowledge, and the ability to assess circumstances and come up with answers that work within certain parameters. Same here. It's more than just a paradigm shift, although that too is important. When I talk about getting back on the clock as a necessary mindset, what I basically mean is that *you* take control of the situation—both internally and externally. Not your monkey, *you*. You don't leave the decision-making to an angry, scared monkey.

Another reason why making this shift is so important is you won't know the dynamics of a situation until you're in the middle of it. You have to scale your actions to stay inside the SD square. What's that going to be? I can't tell you. Hence, the doing it on the fly comment. Now you know why, there's no fixed just do this answer. You have to come up with an appropriate and effective answer.

Showing you what you need to do that is part of what this book has been about. But what this book has mostly been about is helping you to be able to shift your thinking. A shift you have to be able to make so you can do the job at hand. That shift allows you to calmly assess what the problem is and how to best solve it. And the shift will often get you out of trouble if you just make it. A shift that if—god forbid—things still happen in the aftermath, you'll be able to justify and defend your actions.

What you've read here is seriously going to influence how you look at your training and who you listen to about self-defense—starting with an eye toward, "Will I be able to justify that to the cops or the jury?"

Much of what is taught *as* self-defense deliberately panders to your monkey and its fears and beliefs. That would be fine except much of so-called self-defense training is actually teaching either fighting or murder. *And the instructors don't even know it.* But the monkey loves being told it's right, and it will pay for such lessons. So that kind of training has dominated the market. More than that, it makes all kinds of sense —in the training hall, classroom or shooting range.

But outside those that kind of teaching either fails or catapults you out of the SD square. When it comes to being in the situation, you *have* to be able to drop what your monkey believes and deal with what's in *front* of you. Not just to stay inside the SD square and successfully deal with the aftermath, but to survive by not trying to meet asocial violence with a social violence response.

I'm going to give you what a friend calls the "best bit of advice I ever got." That is: You're smart so if you don't understand something it's not because you're incapable, it's because you're missing information. You need to start asking questions to fill in that missing information instead of making assumptions about what fills in the gap.

Along those lines, I want you to start asking questions about information you might be missing or are not being taught. By definition, a blind spot isn't just a place you can't see, you don't know that you can't see it. This book has been about showing you the common blind spots in what is being taught as self-defense. Things your instructor couldn't tell you . . .

More than that, I don't want you to take *anything* I've said in this book on blind faith. I want you to go and check it out. Check it from other sources—especially those working in that field. Talk to cops, talk to lawyers, talk to psychologists, talk to bouncers. If you don't have access to those people, go to the library and read books in those fields. Take a use-of-force class. Attend lectures. Find what professionals say about how their fields apply to self-defense. *Don't* get all your information from self-defense instructors. It's not the instructor who is going to suffer if he or she is wrong, *it's you.*

A lot of what I was doing with this book was getting you to question what your monkey believes. But instead of replacing it with another set of beliefs, hopefully I've motivated you to adjust it with additional useful and reliable information. This is why I say read this book at least twice. My goal wasn't to get you to abandon what you already know, but to look at self-defense in a different light. So you could see where it works and works *well*—and where it's not so applicable.

There's a lot of information in this book your monkey didn't want you to know. But the most dangerous bit of information contained in this book is simple: You are *not* your monkey nor are you your monkey's minion. How is that dangerous? Well to you it isn't. Your monkey works for you, *not you for it.* Yet, we all have been doing what the monkey has been telling us for so long, it's not just become an unconscious habit, but it's who we think we are. The danger is to your monkey's control over your internal life. This would otherwise make this a self-help book—except for one thing. When it comes to self-defense *not* having your monkey on a leash *is* the greatest danger to you, your freedom, and your finances. An out-of-control monkey or a monkey slide *will* cost you. (As Adam Weitzel, the attorney I mentioned earlier, says, "Take an oil drum, stuff it full of twenties (dollars) and roll it into my office because that's what it's going to cost you.") Our legal system is really good at nailing people for their monkey violence. It's hard enough to stay out of prison for defending yourself, it's much harder when your monkey slipped the leash and was attacking.

Another advantage of keeping the monkey on a leash is it will keep you out of unnecessary conflicts, much less physical violence. The information in this book works for all kinds of situations other than just physical. Life actually gets easier when you don't have to constantly clean up the monkey messes. So don't hesitate to use it in your daily life.

Now having given you that, I'd like to close with one final idea. I've talked about the mindset. I've talked about doing the math. Most of all, I've hit you with massive amounts of information. But while it can be complex, it's really *not* that complicated. The fundamentals of violence and self-defense are pretty simple. Complexity arises from mixing and matching and how fundamental things combine. Which ones? In what proportions? How do they influence each other—and the whole?

This is why the analogies of a map telling you what part of town you're in, roads, mile markers, and landmarks are so useful. Instead of one giant, overwhelming whole, they help localize things. "I'm here. Here are the factors. Here are the options. This is what I have to plan for." Once you get the hang of it, it's *not* that complicated. On some subconscious level, you already knew most of what's in this book. You can't be human without experiencing conflict and violence. All I've done was to show you how to consciously recognize them and the different ways they can combine. It's important that you be able to consciously do the math because I'm not going to be there when something happens. The accuracy of your assessment, the appropriateness and effectiveness of your response, and your ability to articulate will affect you for the *rest of your life.* Helping you do that well is what this book is about.

But most importantly, this book has been to help you move beyond just self-defense and upgrade into the art of personal safety. That's a place where you don't have to be paranoid. Staying safe doesn't have to negatively affect your life. In fact, it should improve the quality of life because you can relax. You know what trouble looks like; you don't have to worry about it jumping out of the bushes. But better still, you can spot it coming when it's far enough away that you have lots more options.

I wish you well. More than that, I offer you a hope only the bloodied fully understand: *May you never need this information.*

Marc

Oh yeah, don't forget to reread this monstrosity in a few months. What can I say? You knew the job was dangerous when you took it.

Nonfiction books by Marc MacYoung

Cheap Shots, Ambushes and Other Lessons
Knives, Knife Fighting and Other Hassles
Pool Cues, Beer Bottles and Baseball Bats
Fists, Wits and a Wicked Right
Violence, Blunders and Fractured Jaws
Street E&E
Floor Fighting
A Professional Guide to Ending Violence Quickly
Safe in the City
Taking It to the Streets
Becoming a Complete Martial Artist
Secrets of Effective Offense
Camp Fire Tales From Hell
Writing Violence #1: Getting Shot
Writing Violence #2: Getting Stabbed
Writing Violence #3: Adrenaline
In the Name of Self-Defense

Fiction (as M.D. MacYoung)

Outright Kill

Video/DVD

Safe in the Street/Street Safe
Surviving a Street Knife Attack
Winning a Street Knife Fight
Threat Display: Pre-Attack Indicators (ACLDN)
Barroom Brawling

If you ever get a chance to have a sit down with Marc MacYoung, over cigars and scotch, don't pass it up. He's smart, insightful and will make you think. One of the funniest small furry men in existence. He grew up poor, mostly in Southern California, and made his living in various legal, illegal and quasi-legal ways. He's buried friends over the years. He's written books about the reality of violence (you're holding one in your hands right now) and was one of the first to write a book saying that maybe, just maybe, self-defense and martial arts aren't quite the same thing. He's also irreverent. Although his street name was Animal and he gained his original fame for violence, that wasn't what he was best at. He talked situations down and kept them from going physical.

Decades away from street life, he makes his living as a writer, teacher and expert witness from his home in a small town worlds away from the streets of L.A.

CPSIA information can be obtained at www.ICGtesting.com
Printed in the USA
LVOW10s1016210714

395306LV00015B/241/P